Fodor's

EUROPE'S GREAT CITIES

5TH EDITION

Where to Stay and Eat
for All Budgets

Must-See Sights
and Local Secrets

Ratings You Can Trust

Excerpted from *Fodor's Europe*

Fodor's Travel Publications New York, Toronto, London, Sydney, Auckland
www.fodors.com

FODOR'S EUROPE'S GREAT CITIES

Editors: Paul Eisenberg, Tom Holton

Editorial Production: Ira-Neil Dittersdorf

Editorial Contributors: Robert Andrews, Nuha Ansari, John Babb, Catherine Belonogoff, Carissa Bluestone, Graham Bolger, Muriel Bolger, Ryan Bradley, Stephen Brewer, Jacqueline Brown, Linda Cabasin, Susan Carroll, Jeffrey Carson, Naomi Coleman, Coral Davenport, Bonnie Dodson, Giovanna Dunmall, Elaine Eliah, Robert Fisher, Jane Foster, Sarah Fraser, James Gracie, Katrin Gygax, Valerie Hamilton, Louise Hart, Simon Hewitt, Lee Hogan, Julius Honnor, Alannah Hopkin, Anto Howard, Kate Hughes, Satu Hummasti, Raymond Johnston, Nicola Keegan, Laura Kidder, Christina Knight, Matt Lombardi, Taryn Luciani, Eduardo Luzuriaga, Jennifer McDermott, Diane Mehta, Tom Mercer, Olivia Mollet, Christopher Mooney, Karin Palmquist, Anneliese Paull, Jennifer Paull, Patricia Rucidlo, George Semler, Jonette Stabbert, Douglas Stallings, Melia Tatakis, Mei-Yin Teo, Amanda Theunissen, Mark Walters, Alex Wijeratna, Megan Williams, Kay Winzenried

Maps: David Lindroth, *cartographer;* Rebecca Baer and Robert Blake, *map editors*

Design: Fabrizio La Rocca, *creative director;* Guido Caroti, *art director;* Melanie Marin, *senior picture editor*

Production/Manufacturing: Robert B. Shields

Cover Photo (Old Town Square, Prague): Tibor Bognar/Corbis

COPYRIGHT

Fifth Edition

ISBN 1-4000-1308-9

ISSN 1074-1216

SPECIAL SALES

Fodor's Travel Publications are available at special discounts for bulk purchases for sales promotions or premiums. Special editions, including personalized covers, excerpts of existing guides, and corporate imprints, can be created in large quantities for special needs. For more information, contact your local bookseller or write to Special Markets, Fodor's Travel Publications, 1745 Broadway, New York, New York 10019. Inquiries from Canada should be directed to your local Canadian bookseller or sent to Random House of Canada, Ltd., Marketing Department, 2775 Matheson Boulevard East, Mississauga, Ontario L4W 4P7. Inquiries from the United Kingdom should be sent to Fodor's Travel Publications, 20 Vauxhall Bridge Road, London SW1V 2SA, England.

AN IMPORTANT TIP & AN INVITATION

Although all prices, opening times, and other details in this book are based on information supplied to us at press time, changes occur all the time in the travel world, and Fodor's cannot accept responsibility for facts that become outdated or for inadvertent errors or omissions. So **always confirm information when it matters,** especially if you're making a detour to visit a specific place. Your experiences—positive and negative—matter to us. If we have missed or misstated something, **please write to us.** We follow up on all suggestions. Contact the Europe's Great Cities editors at editors@fodors.com or c/o Fodor's at 1745 Broadway, New York, New York 10019.

PRINTED IN THE UNITED STATES OF AMERICA

10 9 8 7 6 5 4 3 2 1

DESTINATION EUROPE

A trip takes you out of yourself. Concerns of life at home completely disappear, driven away by more immediate thoughts—about, say, what marvels will beguile the next day, or where you'll have dinner. That's where Fodor's comes in. We make sure that you know all your options, so that you don't miss something that's around the next bend just because you didn't know it was there. Because the best memories of your trip might well have nothing to do with what you came to Europe to see, we guide you to sights large and small all over the continent. You might set out to see every art museum in your path, but back at home you find yourself unable to forget that boisterous bistro or quirky boutique you chanced upon on your way back from the gallery. With Fodor's at your side, serendipitous discoveries are never far away. Bon voyage!

Karen Cure

Karen Cure, Editorial Director

CONTENTS

Italic entries are maps.

About This Book F6
Europe F8–F9
Smart Travel Tips *F10*

1 Amsterdam 1

Amsterdam 4–5

2 Athens 21

Athens (Athina) 24–25

3 Barcelona 44

Barcelona 46–47

4 Berlin 64

Berlin 66–67

5 Brussels 81

Brussels (Bruxelles) 82–83

6 Budapest 97

Budapest 100–101

7 Copenhagen 116

Copenhagen (København) 118–119

8 Dublin 132

Dublin 134–135

9 Florence 152

Florence (Firenze) 154–155

10 London 169

London 172–173

11 Madrid 205

Madrid 208–209

12 Paris 222

Paris 226–227

Paris Métro 230–231

13 Prague 252

Prague (Praha) 254–255

14 Rome 269

Rome (Roma) 272–273

15 Venice 290

Venice (Venezia) 292–293

16 Vienna 305

Vienna (Wien) 308–309

17 Zurich 326

Zürich 328

Index 337

ABOUT THIS BOOK

	There's no doubt that the best source for travel advice is a like-minded friend who's just been where you're headed. But with or without that friend, you'll have a better trip with a Fodor's guide in hand. Once you've learned to find your way around its pages, you'll be in great shape to find your way around your destination.
SELECTION	Our goal is to cover the best properties, sights, and activities in their category, as well as the most interesting communities to visit. We make a point of including local food-lovers' hot spots as well as neighborhood options, and we avoid all that's touristy unless it's really worth your time. You can go on the assumption that everything you read about in this book is recommended wholeheartedly by our writers and editors. It goes without saying that no property mentioned in the book has paid to be included.
RATINGS	Orange stars ★ denote sights and properties that our editors and writers consider the very best in the area covered by the entire book. These, the best of the best, denote Fodor's Choice. Black stars ★ highlight the sights and properties we deem Highly Recommended, the don't-miss sights within any region. In cities, sights pinpointed with numbered map bullets ❶ in the margins tend to be more important than those without bullets.
BUDGET WELL	Hotel and restaurant price categories from ¢ to $$$$ or £ to £££££ are defined in the opening pages of each chapter—expect to find a balanced selection for every budget. For attractions, we always give standard adult admission fees; reductions are usually available for children, students, and senior citizens. Look in Discounts & Deals in Smart Travel Tips for information on destination-wide ticket schemes. Want to pay with plastic? AE, D, DC, MC, V following restaurant and hotel listings indicate whether American Express, Discover, Diners Club, MasterCard, or Visa are accepted.
BASIC INFO	Smart Travel Tips lists travel essentials for the entire area covered by the book; city- and region-specific basics end each chapter. To find the best way to get around, see the transportation section; see individual modes of travel ("Car Travel," "Train Travel") for details. We assume you'll check Web sites or call for particulars.
ON THE MAPS	Maps throughout the book show you what's where and help you find your way around. Black and orange numbered bullets ❶❶ in the text correlate to bullets on maps.
FIND IT FAST	Chapters are in alphabetical order by country. Each covers the country's essential information from A to Z, exploring, dining, lodging, nightlife and the arts, shopping, and side trips in cities and regions. Sites in major cities accompanied by maps are arranged alphabetically. Within regional sections, all restaurants and lodgings are grouped with the town. The Essentials list that ends all city or regional sections covers getting there and getting around. It also provides helpful contacts and resources.
DON'T FORGET	Restaurants are open for lunch and dinner daily unless we state otherwise; we mention dress only when there's a specific requirement and reservations only when they're essential or not accepted—

it's always best to book ahead. **Hotels** have private baths, phone, TVs, and air-conditioning and operate on the European Plan (a.k.a. EP, meaning without meals). We always list facilities but not whether you'll be charged extra to use them, so when pricing accommodations, find out what's included.

SYMBOLS

Many Listings

- ★ Fodor's Choice
- ★ Highly recommended
- ✉ Physical address
- ✣ Directions
- 📫 Mailing address
- ☎ Telephone
- 📠 Fax
- 🌐 On the Web
- ✉ E-mail
- 🎟 Admission fee
- ⏲ Open/closed times
- ⚑ Start of walk/itinerary
- M Metro stations
- S S-Bahn station
- U U-Bahn station (Berlin, Vienna), Underground Tube station (London)
- 💳 Credit cards

Outdoors

- ⛳ Golf
- ⛺ Camping

Hotels & Restaurants

- 🏨 Hotel
- 🛏 Number of rooms
- 👍 Facilities
- 🍽 Meal plans
- ✕ Restaurant
- ✍ Reservations
- 👔 Dress code
- 🚬 Smoking
- 🍷 BYOB
- ✕🏨 Hotel with restaurant that warrants a visit

Other

- ☺ Family-friendly
- 🛈 Contact information
- ⇨ See also
- ✉ Branch address
- ☞ Take note

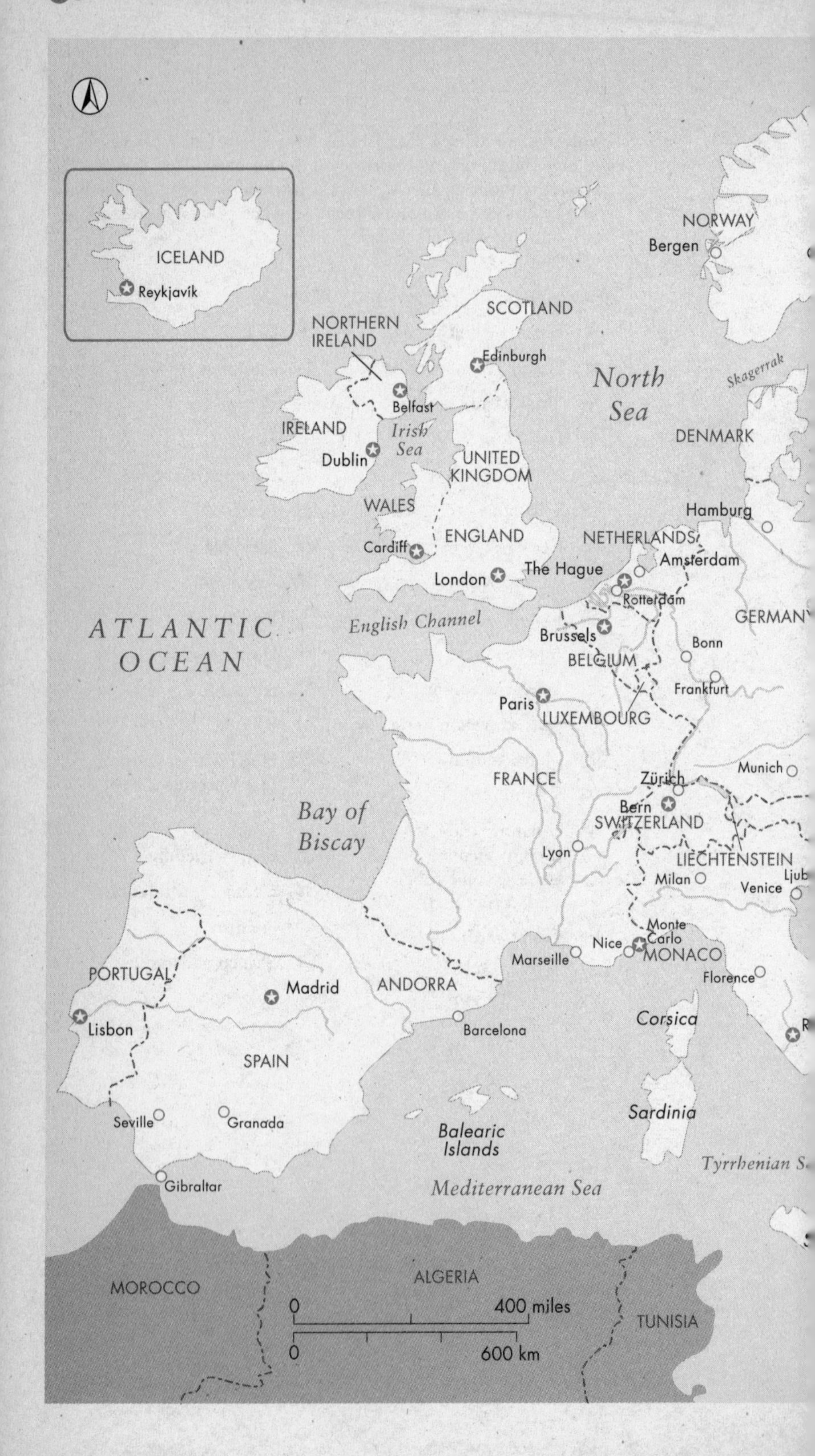
ICELAND
Reykjavík
NORWAY
Bergen
SCOTLAND
NORTHERN IRELAND
Edinburgh
North Sea
Skagerrak
Belfast
IRELAND
Irish Sea
DENMARK
Dublin
UNITED KINGDOM
WALES
Hamburg
ENGLAND
NETHERLANDS
Cardiff
Amsterdam
London
The Hague
Rotterdam
GERMANY
ATLANTIC OCEAN
English Channel
Brussels
Bonn
BELGIUM
Frankfurt
Paris
LUXEMBOURG
Munich
FRANCE
Zürich
Bern
Bay of Biscay
SWITZERLAND
LIECHTENSTEIN
Lyon
Milan
Venice
Monte Carlo
Nice
MONACO
Marseille
Florence
PORTUGAL
Madrid
ANDORRA
Lisbon
Barcelona
Corsica
SPAIN
Sardinia
Seville
Granada
Balearic Islands
Gibraltar
Mediterranean Sea
MOROCCO
ALGERIA
0
400 miles
0
600 km
TUNISIA

Europe
FINLAND
Gulf of Bothnia
Oslo
SWEDEN
Helsinki
Gulf of Finland
St. Petersburg
Tallinn
Stockholm
ESTONIA
Kattegat
Göteborg
Riga
LATVIA
Moscow
Copenhagen
LITHUANIA
Kaunas
Baltic Sea
RUSSIA
Vilnius
RUSSIA
Kaliningrad
Minsk
Berlin
POLAND
BELARUS
Warsaw
ANY
Kraków
Kiev
Prague
CZECH REPUBLIC
UKRAINE
SLOVAKIA
Vienna
Bratislava
Salzburg
AUSTRIA
Budapest
MOLDOVA
HUNGARY
Chişinău
SLOVENIA
Zagreb
Ljubljana
ROMANIA
CROATIA
Novi Sad
Bucharest
BOSNIA AND HERZEGOVINA
Belgrade
SERBIA
Black Sea
Sarajevo
YUGOSLAVIA
Adriatic Sea
MONTENEGRO
KOSOVO
BULGARIA
Rome
Priština
Sofia
Podgorica
Skopje
ITALY
MACEDONIA
Istanbul
Tirane
Naples
ALBANIA
Ankara
TURKEY
n Sea
GREECE
Aegean Sea
Ionian Sea
Athens
Sicily
CYPRUS
MALTA
Crete
Mediterranean Sea

SMART TRAVEL TIPS

Air Travel
Airports
Bike Travel
Boat & Ferry Travel
Bus Travel
Cameras & Photography
Car Rental
Car Travel
The Channel Tunnel
Children in Europe
Consumer Protection
Cruise Travel
Customs & Duties
Dining
Disabilities & Accessibility
Discounts & Deals
Electricity
Gay & Lesbian Travel
Insurance
Language
Lodging
Money Matters
Packing
Passports & Visas
Safety
Senior-Citizen Travel
Students in Europe
Taxes
Telephones
Time
Tours & Packages
Train Travel
Travel Agencies
Visitor Information
Web Sites
When to Go

Finding out about your destination before you leave home means you won't squander time organizing everyday minutiae once you've arrived. You'll be more streetwise when you hit the ground as well, better prepared to explore the aspects of Europe that drew you here in the first place. The organizations in this section can provide information to supplement this guide; contact them for up-to-the-minute details, and consult the A to Z sections at the start of each chapter for facts on the various topics as they relate to each country. Happy landings!

AIR TRAVEL

Before booking, **compare different modes of transportation.** Many city pairs are so close together that flying hardly makes sense. For instance, it may take just half an hour to fly between London and Paris, but you must factor in time spent getting to and from the airports, plus check-in time. A three-hour train ride from city center to city center seems a better alternative. It makes sense to **save air travel for longer distances**—say, between London and Rome, Paris and Vienna, Brussels and Stockholm—and do your local traveling from these hubs.

If you're flying so-called **national carriers,** full-fare tickets often remain the only kind available for one-way trips and restriction-free round-trips, and they are prohibitively expensive for most leisure travelers. On most European flights, your choice is between Business Class (which is what you get when paying full fare) and Economy (coach). Some flights are all Economy. First Class has ceased to exist in Europe. The most reasonable fares have long been nonrefundable and nontransferable round-trips (APEX fares), which require a Saturday night at the destination. But the near-monopoly that used to be enjoyed by these airlines is crumbling, and they have had to start offering less restrictive fares. Check before you fly.

Some national carriers reward transatlantic passengers with fixed-price flight coupons (priced at $100–$120) to destinations from their respective hubs and/or domestic or area air passes. These must be bought before leaving home. If you're young, **ask about youth standby fares,** which are available on a number of domestic and some international services.

Over the last few years, a substantial number of local airlines have been created to provide feeder services to major hubs and services between secondary city pairs. Do not, however, expect rock-bottom prices. **Seek advice from local branches of international travel agencies** like American Express or Carlson/Wagonlit.

Low-cost no-frills airlines base their fares on one-way travel, and a return ticket is simply twice the price. Advertised fares are always preceded by the word "from." To get the lowest fare, book two weeks ahead of time; it also helps to be flexible about your date of travel. In general, you have to book directly by calling the airline, credit card in hand. Some also accept reservations by fax. Reservation via Internet is available with companies such as the SABRE-powered Travelocity (🌐 www.travelocity.com) and Microsoft's Expedia (🌐 www.expedia.com). You can make secure payments via the Net and hunt the cheapest flight deals, as well as reserve hotels. You get a reservation number and pick up your boarding pass at the airport. Note that some flights use relatively distant secondary airports.

ARRIVALS

Passport control has become a perfunctory affair within most of the European Union (EU). The nine signatories to the Schengen Agreement (Austria, Belgium, France, Germany, Italy, Luxembourg, the Netherlands, Portugal, and Spain) have abolished passport controls for travelers between countries in that area, but individual countries can temporarily suspend it.

The most notable exception is Great Britain; when a number of flights from the United States arrive at Heathrow or Gatwick close together in the morning, **be prepared for a longish wait** (though rarely as long as Europeans have to wait at JFK in New York).

The Green Channel/Red Channel customs system in operation at most Western European airports and other borders is basically an honor system. If you have nothing to declare, walk through the Green Channel, where there are only spot luggage checks; if in doubt, go through the Red Channel. If you fly between two EU-member countries, go through the new **Blue Channel,** where there are no customs officers except the one who glances at baggage labels to make sure only people off EU flights get through. On average, you need to **count on at least half an hour from deplaning to getting out of the airport.**

BOOKING

When you book, **look for nonstop flights** and **remember that "direct" flights stop at least once.** Try to avoid connecting flights, which require a change of plane. Two airlines may operate a connecting flight jointly, so ask whether your airline operates every segment of the trip; you may find that the carrier you prefer flies you only part of the way. To find more booking tips and to check prices and make online flight reservations, log on to www.fodors.com.

CARRIERS

U.S. Airlines **American** ☎ 800/433-7300 in U.S.; 0845/778-9789 in U.K. 🌐 www.aa.com. **Continental** ☎ 800/525-0280 in U.S.; 0800/776-464 in U.K. 🌐 www.continental.com. **Delta** ☎ 800/221-1212 in U.S., 0800/414-767 in U.K. 🌐 www.delta.com. **Northwest** ☎ 800/225-2525 in U.S.; c/o alliance partner KLM, call 0990/750-9000 in U.K. 🌐 www.klm.com. **United** ☎ 800/538-2929 in U.S.; 0845/844-4777 in U.K. 🌐 www.ual.com. **US Airways** ☎ 800/428-4322 in U.S.; 0800/783-5556 in U.K. 🌐 www.usairways.com.

European Airlines Austria: **Austrian Airlines** ☎ 800/843-0002 in U.S.; 0845/601-0948 in U.K. 🌐 www.aua.com. Belgium: **Sabena Belgian World Airlines** ☎ 800/955-2000 in U.S.; 020/7494-2629 in U.K. 🌐 www.brussels-airlines.com. The Czech Republic and Slovakia: **Czech Airlines** (CSA) ☎ 212/765-6022 in U.S.; 0870/444-3747 in U.K. 🌐 www.csa.cz. Denmark: **Scandinavian Airlines** (SAS) ☎ 800/221-2350 in U.S.; 0870/6072-7727 in U.K. 🌐 www.scandinavian.net. Finland: **Finnair** ☎ 800/950-5000 in U.S., 0207/514-2429 in U.K. 🌐 www.finnair.com. France: **Air France** ☎ 800/237-2747 in U.S.; 0845/084-5111 in U.K. 🌐 www.airfrance.com. Germany: **LTU International Airways** ☎ 800/888-0200 in U.S. 🌐 www.ltu.com. **Lufthansa** ☎ 800/645-3880 in U.S.; 0845/7737-747 in U.K. 🌐 www.lufthansa.com. Great Britain: **British Airways** ☎ 800/247-9297 in U.S.; 0845/773-3377 in U.K. 🌐 www.ba.com. **Virgin Atlantic** ☎ 800/862-8621 in U.S.; 0129/345-0150 in U.K. 🌐 www.virgin-atlantic.com. Greece: **Olympic Airways** ☎ 800/223-1226 in U.S.; 0870/606-0460 in U.K. 🌐 www.olympic-airways.gr. Hungary: **Malév Hungarian Airlines** ☎ 212/757-6446; 800/223-6884 outside NY in U.S. 🌐 www.malev.hu. Iceland: **Icelandair** ☎ 800/223-5500 in U.S.; 020/7874-1000 in U.K. 🌐 www.icelandair.com. Ireland: **Aer Lingus** ☎ 888/474-7424 or 800/223-6537 in U.S.; 0845/

084-4444 in U.K. www.aerlingus.com. Italy: **Alitalia** 800/223-5730 in U.S.; 020/8745-8200 in U.K. www.alitalia.it. The Netherlands: **KLM Royal Dutch Airlines** 800/447-4747 in U.S.; 0870/507-4074 in U.K. www.klm.com. Norway: **SAS** 800/221-2350 in U.S.; 0845/600-7767 in U.K. www.scandinavian.net. Poland: **LOT Polish Airlines** 800/223-0593 in U.S.; 0845/601-0949 in U.K. www.lot.com. Portugal: **TAP Air Portugal** 800/221-7370 in U.S.; 0807/457273 in U.K. www.tap-airportugal.pt. Romania: **Tarom Romanian Air Transport** 212/560-0840 in U.S.; 020/7224-3693 in U.K. www.tarom.ro. Spain: **Iberia Airlines** 800/772-4642 in U.S.; 0845/601-2854 in U.K. www.iberia.es. Sweden: **SAS** 800/221-2350 in U.S.; 0845/600-7767 in U.K. www.scandinavian.net. Turkey: **THY Turkish Airlines** 212/339-9662 in U.S.; 0845/601-0956 in U.K. www.turkishairlines.com.

From Australia **Qantas Airways** 13-13-13 in Australia; 0845/774-7767 in U.K. www.qantas.com.

From Canada **Air Canada** 888/247-2262 www.aircanada.com. **Air Transat** 877/872-6728 www.airtransat.com.

From Ireland **Aer Lingus** 081/836-5000 in Ireland; 0845/084-4444 in U.K. www.aerlingus.com.

From New Zealand **Air New Zealand** 09/9357-3000 or 0800/028-4149 in New Zealand; 020/8741-2299 in U.K. www.airnewzealand.com.

From the U.K. **British Airways** Box 5619, Sudbury, Suffolk, CO10 2PG 0845/773-3377 www.ba.com. **British Midland** 0870/607-0555 www.flybmi.com. **EasyJet** 0870/600-0000 www.easyjet.com. **KLM U.K.** 0870/507-4074 www.klm.com. **Ryanair** 0871/246-0000 www.ryanair.com. **Virgin Express** 020/7744-0004 www.virgin-express.com.

No-Frills Carrier Reservations Within Europe Belgium: **Virgin Express** 020/744-0004 in U.K. www.virgin-express.com from Brussels to Milan, Rome, Nice, Madrid, Barcelona, Copenhagen, and London (Gatwick, Heathrow, Stansted); from Rome to Barcelona and Madrid; from London (Stansted) to Berlin and Shannon. Ireland: **Ryanair** 0818/303030 in Ireland; 0871/246-0000 in U.K. www.ryanair.com from Dublin to 12 U.K. destinations, to Paris (Beauvais) and Brussels (Charleroi); from London (Stansted, Luton, and Gatwick) to Dublin; from London (Stansted) to four other Irish destinations, five French destinations, four Scandinavian destinations, six Italian destinations, and Frankfurt. United Kingdom: **Buzz** 0870/240-7070 www.buzzaway.com from London (Stansted) to Bordeaux, Düsseldorf, Berlin, Frankfurt, Hamburg, Helsinki, Jerez (Spain), Lyon, Marseilles, Milan, Paris, and Vienna. **EasyJet** 0870/600-0000 www.easyjet.com from London (Luton) and Liverpool to Amsterdam, Barcelona, Belfast, Geneva, Madrid, Malaga, Nice; from London (Luton) to Athens, Palma de Mallorca, Zurich, and four Scottish destinations; from Geneva to Amsterdam, Barcelona, Liverpool, London (Luton, Gatwick, and Stansted), and Nice.

CHECK-IN & BOARDING

Always **ask your carrier about its check-in policy.** Plan to arrive at the airport about two hours before your scheduled departure time for domestic flights and 2½ to 3 hours before international flights. You may need to arrive earlier if you're flying from one of the busier airports or during peak air-traffic times.To avoid delays at airport-security checkpoints, try not to wear any metal. Jewelry, belt and other buckles, steel-toe shoes, barrettes, and underwire bras are among the items that can set off detectors.

Assuming that not everyone with a ticket will show up, airlines routinely overbook planes. When everyone does, airlines ask for volunteers to give up their seats. In return, these volunteers usually get a several-hundred-dollar flight voucher, which can be used toward the purchase of another ticket, and are rebooked on the next flight out. If there are not enough volunteers, the airline must choose who will be denied boarding. The first to get bumped are passengers who checked in late and those flying on discounted tickets, so **get to the gate and check in as early as possible,** especially during peak periods.

Always **bring a government-issued photo ID to the airport;** even when it's not required, a passport is best.

CUTTING COSTS

The least expensive airfares to Europe are priced for round-trip travel and must usually be purchased in advance. Airlines generally allow you to change your return date for a fee; most low-fare tickets, however, are nonrefundable. It's smart to **call a number of airlines and check the Internet;** when you are quoted a good price, **book it on the spot**—the same fare may not be available the next day, or even the next hour. Always **check different routings** and look into using alternate airports. Also, price off-peak flights, which may be significantly less expensive than others. Travel agents, especially low-fare specialists (⇨ Discounts & Deals), are helpful.

Consolidators are another good source. They buy tickets for scheduled flights at reduced rates from the airlines, then sell them at prices that beat the best fare available directly from the airlines. Sometimes you can even get your money back if you need to return the ticket. Carefully read the fine print detailing penalties for changes and cancellations, purchase the ticket with a credit card, and **confirm your consolidator reservation with the airline.**

When you **fly as a courier,** you trade your checked-luggage space for a ticket deeply subsidized by a courier service. There are restrictions on when you can book and how long you can stay. Some courier companies list with membership organizations, such as the Air Courier Association and the International Association of Air Travel Couriers; these require you to become a member before you can book a flight.

Many airlines, singly or in collaboration, offer discount air passes that allow foreigners to travel economically in a particular country or region. Ask your airline about purchasing discount passes for intra-European flights before you leave home to save significantly on travel between European cities. If you're going to be covering a lot of ground, consider Europebyair.com, which sells intra-European flights to more than 150 cities for $99 per segment. They also offer unlimited flight passes good for 15 or 21 days.

Information about passes often can be found on most airlines' international Web pages, which tend to be aimed at travelers from outside the carrier's home country. Enter the name of the pass into a search engine, or search for "pass" within the carrier's Web site.

Consolidators **AirlineConsolidator.com** ☎ 888/468-5385 🌐 www.airlineconsolidator.com; for international tickets. **Best Fares** ☎ 800/576-8255 or 800/576-1600 🌐 www.bestfares.com; $59.90 annual membership. **Cheap Tickets** ☎ 800/377-1000 or 888/922-8849 🌐 www.cheaptickets.com. **Expedia** ☎ 800/397-3342 or 404/728-8787 🌐 www.expedia.com. **Hotwire** ☎ 866/468-9473 or 920/330-9418 🌐 www.hotwire.com. **Now Voyager Travel** ✉ 45 W. 21st St., 5th fl., New York, NY 10010 ☎ 212/459-1616 📠 212/243-2711 🌐 www.nowvoyagertravel.com. **Onetravel.com** 🌐 www.onetravel.com. **Orbitz** ☎ 888/656-4546 🌐 www.orbitz.com. **Priceline.com** 🌐 www.priceline.com. **Travelocity** ☎ 888/709-5983; 877/282-2925 in Canada; 0870/876-3876 in U.K. 🌐 www.travelocity.com.

Courier Resources **Air Courier Association/Cheaptrips.com** ☎ 800/282-1202 🌐 www.aircourier.org or www.cheaptrips.com. **International Association of Air Travel Couriers** ☎ 308/632-3273 🌐 www.courier.org.

Discount Passes **FlightPass** EuropebyAir, ☎ 888/387-2479 🌐 www.europebyair.com. **SAS Air Passes** Scandinavian Airlines, ☎ 800/221-2350; 0845/6072-7727 in U.K.; 1300/727707 in Australia 🌐 www.scandinavian.net.

ENJOYING THE FLIGHT

State your seat preference when purchasing your ticket, and then repeat it when you confirm and when you check in. For more legroom, you can request one of the few emergency-aisle seats at check-in, if you are capable of lifting at least 50 pounds—a Federal Aviation Administration requirement of passengers in these seats. Seats behind a bulkhead also offer more legroom, but they don't have underseat storage. Don't sit in the row in front of the emergency aisle or in front of a bulkhead, where seats may not recline.

Ask the airline whether a snack or meal is served on the flight. If you have dietary concerns, **request special meals when booking.** These can be vegetarian, low-cholesterol, or kosher, for example. It's a good idea to pack some healthful snacks and a small (plastic) bottle of water in your carry-on bag. On long flights, try to maintain a normal routine, to help fight jet lag. At night, **get some sleep.** By day, **eat light meals, drink water** (not alcohol), and **move around the cabin** to stretch your legs. For additional jet-lag tips consult *Fodor's FYI: Travel Fit & Healthy* (available at bookstores everywhere).

Smoking policies vary from carrier to carrier. Many airlines prohibit smoking on all of their flights; others allow smoking only on certain routes or certain departures. Ask your carrier about its policy.

FLYING TIMES

Flights from New York to London take about 6½ hours, to Paris 7½ hours, to Frankfurt 7½ hours, and to Rome 8½ hours. From Sydney to London, flights take about 23 hours via Bangkok, to Paris 22¾ hours via Singapore, to Frankfurt 22 hours via Singapore, and to Rome 25 hours via Bangkok.

HOW TO COMPLAIN

If your baggage goes astray or your flight goes awry, complain right away. Most carriers require that you **file a claim immediately.** The Aviation Consumer Protection Division of the Department of Transportation publishes *Fly-Rights,* which discusses airlines and consumer issues and is available on-line.

Airline Complaints **Aviation Consumer Protection Division** ✉ U.S. Department of Transportation, C-75, Room 4107, 400 7th St. NW, Washington, DC 20590 ☎ 202/366-2220 🌐 www.dot.gov/airconsumer. **Federal Aviation Administration Consumer Hotline** ✉ for inquiries: FAA, 800 Independence Ave. SW, Room 810, Washington, DC 20591 ☎ 800/322-7873 🌐 www.faa.gov.

RECONFIRMING

Check the status of your flight before you leave for the airport. You can do this on your carrier's Web site, by linking to a flight-status checker (many Web booking services offer these), or by calling your carrier or travel agent. Always confirm international flights at least 72 hours ahead of the scheduled departure time.

AIRPORTS

See Essentials *in* city sections of country chapters.

DUTY-FREE SHOPPING

Duty-free shopping was eliminated for travelers between EU countries as of July 1, 1999. However, duty-free shopping still applies in non-EU countries, and tax-free shopping is available for tourists returning to non-EU countries from the EU. If you're looking for good deals associated with duty-free airport shopping, **check out liquor and beauty products,** although prices vary considerably. The amount of liquor you may buy is restricted, generally to two bottles.

Some airport concourses, notably in Amsterdam, Copenhagen, and Shannon, have practically been transformed into shopping malls, selling everything from electronics and chocolates to fashion and furs. These are tax-free rather than duty-free shops; if this is your last stop before leaving the EU, there's no value-added-tax (V.A.T.) and you can **avoid the tax-refund rigmarole** (⇨ Taxes).

BIKE TRAVEL

BIKES IN FLIGHT

Most airlines accommodate bikes as luggage, provided they are dismantled and boxed; check with individual airlines about packing requirements. Some airlines sell bike boxes, which are often free at bike shops, for about $15 (bike bags can be considerably more expensive). International travelers often can substitute a bike for a piece of checked luggage at no charge; otherwise, the cost is about $100. U.S. and Canadian airlines charge $40–$80 each way.

BOAT & FERRY TRAVEL

Ferry routes for passengers and vehicles link the countries surrounding the North Sea, the Irish Sea, and the Baltic Sea; Italy with Greece; and Spain, France, Italy, and Greece with their respective islands in the Mediterranean. Longer ferry routes—between, for instance, Britain and Spain or Scandinavia—can help you **reduce the amount of driving and often save time.** A number of modern ships offer improved comfort and entertainment ranging from one-armed bandits to gourmet dining.

FARES & SCHEDULES

See individual country chapters, or contact operators for specific information on fares and schedules.

Boat & Ferry Information Ferry operators between the British Isles and the Continent include **Brittany Ferries** ✉ Millbay Docks, Plymouth PL1 3EW ☎ 0870/3665-3333 🌐 www.brittanyferries.com, from Plymouth to Roscoff (Brittany) and Santander (Spain), from Poole to Cherbourg, and from Portsmouth to Caen and St. Malo. **DFDS Seaways** ✉ Scandinavia House, Parkeston Quay, Harwich, Essex CO12 4QG ☎ 0870/533-3000; 800/533-3755 in U.S. 🌐 www.dfdsseaways.com, from Harwich to Esbjerg (Denmark), Hamburg, and Gothenburg and from Newcastle-upon-Tyne to IJmuiden, 20 mi west of Amsterdam and (summer season) to Gothenburg and Hamburg. **Fjord Line** ✉ International Ferry Terminal, Royal Quays, North Shields NE29 6EE ☎ 0191/296-1313 🌐 www.fjordline.co.uk, from Newcastle to Bergen/Stavanger/Haugesund (Norway). **Hoverspeed** ✉ International Hoverport, Marine Parade, Dover, Kent CT17 9TG ☎ 0870/240-8070 🌐 www.hoverspeed.com, Dover-Calais, Dover-Oostende, Folkestone-Boulogne, and Newhaven-Dieppe. **Irish Ferries** ✉ Corn Exchange Building, Ground fl., Bunswick St., Liverpool L2 7TP ☎ 8705/171717 🌐 www.irishferries.ie, Holyhead-Dublin and

Pembroke-Rosslare; also Rosslare (Ireland; reservations 1890/313131) to Cherbourg, and Roscoff. **P&O European Ferries** ✉ Peninsular House, Wharf Rd., Portsmouth, PO2 8TA ☎ 0870/242-4999 or 0870/520-2020 🌐 ww1.poferries.com sails Portsmouth to Cherbourg, Le Havre, and Bilbao (Spain), and Cairnyarn (Scotland)-Larne (Belfast). **P&O North Sea Ferries** ✉ King George Dock, Hedon Rd., Hull HU9 5QA ☎ 0870/242-4999 🌐 ww1.poferries.com, from Hull to Rotterdam and Zeebrugge. **P&O Stena Line** ✉ Channel House, Channel View Rd., Dover, Kent CT17 9TJ ☎ 0870/242-4999 🌐 ww1.poferries.com, Dover-Calais. **SeaFrance** ✉ Eastern Docks, Dover, Kent CT16 1JA ☎ 0870/571-1711 🌐 www.seafrance.co.uk, Dover-Calais. **Stena Line** ✉ Charter House, Park St., Ashford, Kent TN24 8EX ☎ 0870/574-7474 or 0870/570-7070 🌐 www.stenaline.co.uk, Harwich-Hook of Holland, Holyhead-Dun Laoghaire (Dublin), Fishguard-Rosslare, and Stranraer (Scotland)-Belfast. **Swansea Cork Ferries** ✉ Harbour Office, Kings Dock, Swansea SA1 1SF ☎ 01792/456-116 🌐 www.swansea-cork.ie, Swansea-Cork (mid-Mar.-early Nov.).

BUS TRAVEL

International bus travel is rapidly expanding in Europe, thanks to changing EU rules and the Channel Tunnel, but it still has some way to go before it achieves the status of a natural choice, except in Britain and Sweden. In other northern European countries, bus services exist mostly to supplement railroads.

Within several southern European countries—including Portugal, Greece, parts of Spain, and Turkey—the bus has supplanted the train as the main means of public transportation, and is often quicker and more comfortable, with more frequent service, than the antiquated national rolling stock. Be prepared to discover that the bus is more expensive. Competition among lines is keen, so **ask about air-conditioning and reclining seats before you book.**

Eurolines comprises 30 motor-coach operators of international scheduled services, all no-smoking. They also transport passengers within each country. The 30-nation network serves more than 500 destinations with services ranging from twice weekly to five times daily. Eurolines has its own coach stations in Paris (28 av. du Général de Gaulle at Bagnelot; métro: Gallieni), Brussels (80 rue du Progrès, next to the Gare du Nord), and Amsterdam (adjacent to the Amstel Railway Station). In other cities, coaches depart from railway stations or municipal bus terminals.

From the U.K., Eurolines links London with 400 destinations on the European Continent and Ireland, from Stockholm to Rome, from Dublin to Bucharest. All are via Calais, using either ferry services or Le Shuttle/Eurotunnel under the English Channel. Buses leave from Victoria Coach Station (adjoining the railway station). Services link up with the National Express network covering the U.K.

National or regional tourist offices have information about bus services. For reservations on major lines before you go, **contact your travel agent at home.**

CUTTING COSTS

The **Busabout** service can take you to more than 85 cities in Europe with two options: the consecutive pass or the flexipass. If you're planning a whirlwind European tour on a small budget, two weeks of consecutive travel will run you $359; three weeks $479; and one month $589. For a more leisurely pace, the flexipass gives you 12 nonconsecutive traveling days in a two-month period for $579 or up to 20 days of nonconsecutive travel in a four-month period for $839. There are also links to Budapest ($49 supplement), Athens (a Greek Island Pass takes you to five islands for an $89 supplement), and Morocco ($59 supplement). There's an on-board guide who provides local information and, with notice, can book campsites, bungalows, budget hotels, or hostels.

The **Eurolines Pass** allows unlimited travel between 31 European cities on scheduled bus services. A 30-day summer pass costs $369 ($299 for those under 26 or over 60); a 60-day pass costs $429 ($329). Passes can be purchased from Eurolines offices and travel agents in Europe and from the companies listed below.

Discount Passes In the U.S.: Eurolines Passes can be purchased from **Destination Europe Resources** (DER) ✉ 9501 W. Devon Ave., Rosemont, IL 60018 ☎ 800/782-2424 🌐 www.der.com and from most Hostelling International and all STA offices (⇨ Students in Europe).

Bus Information **Busabout (U.K.) Ltd.** ✉ Victoria Bus Station, 258 Vauxhall Bridge Rd., London, SW1V 1BS ☎ 020/7950-1661 📠 020/7950-1662 🌐 www.busabout.com. **Eurolines (U.K.)** ✉ 4 Cardiff Rd., Luton LU1 1PP ☎ 0990/143219 📠 01582/400-694 🌐 www.eurolines.com. For brochures, timetables, and sales agents in the U.S. and Canada, contact the **Eurolines Pass Organization** ✉ Keizersgracht 317, 1016 EE Amsterdam, The Netherlands ☎ 020/625-3010 📠 020/420-6904.

CAMERAS & PHOTOGRAPHY

The *Kodak Guide to Shooting Great Travel Pictures* (available at bookstores everywhere) is loaded with tips.

Photo Help **Kodak Information Center** ☎ 800/242-2424 🌐 www.kodak.com.

EQUIPMENT PRECAUTIONS

Don't pack film and equipment in checked luggage, where it is much more susceptible to damage. X-ray machines used to view checked luggage are extremely powerful and therefore are likely to ruin your film. Try to **ask for hand inspection of film,** which becomes clouded after repeated exposure to airport X-ray machines, and **keep videotapes and computer disks away from metal detectors.** Always **keep film, tape, and computer disks out of the sun.** Carry an extra supply of batteries, and **be prepared to turn on your camera, camcorder, or laptop** to prove to airport security personnel that the device is real.

CAR RENTAL

The great attraction of renting is obviously that you become independent of public transport. Cost-wise, you should **consider renting a car only if you are with at least one other person;** single travelers pay a tremendous premium. Car rental costs vary from country to country; rates in Scandinavia and Eastern Europe are particularly high. If you're visiting a number of countries with varying rates, it makes sense to **rent a vehicle in the cheapest country.** For instance, if you plan to visit Normandy, the same company that rents you a car for a weekly rate of $246 in Paris will rent you one for $159 in Brussels, adding a few hours to your trip but at a 35% savings.

Picking up a car at an airport is convenient but often costs extra (up to 10%), as rental companies pass along the fees charged to them by airports.

Sample rates: London, $39 a day and $136 a week for an economy car with air-conditioning, a manual transmission, and unlimited mileage; Paris, $60 a day and $196 a week; Madrid, $37 a day and $132 a week; Rome, $49 a day and $167 a week; Frankfurt, $18 a day and $91 a week. These figures do not include tax on car rentals, which ranges from 15% to 21%.

Major Agencies **Alamo** ☎ 800/522-9696 🌐 www.alamo.com. **Avis** ☎ 800/331-1084; 800/879-2847 in Canada; 0870/606-0100 in U.K.; 02/9353-9000 in Australia; 09/526-2847 in New Zealand 🌐 www.avis.com. **Budget** ☎ 800/527-0700; 0870/156-5656 in U.K. 🌐 www.budget.com. **Dollar** ☎ 800/800-6000; 0124/622-0111 in U.K., where it's affiliated with Sixt; 02/9223-1444 in Australia 🌐 www.dollar.com. **Hertz** ☎ 800/654-3001; 800/263-0600 in Canada; 0870/844-8844 in U.K.; 02/9669-2444 in Australia; 09/256-8690 in New Zealand 🌐 www.hertz.com. **National Car Rental** ☎ 800/227-7368; 0870/600-6666 in U.K. 🌐 www.nationalcar.com.

CUTTING COSTS

For a good deal, **book through a travel agent who will shop around.** If you think you'll need a car in Europe but are unsure about when or where, ask your travel agent to check out Kemwel's CarPass. This gives the benefit of prepaid vouchers with the flexibility of last-minute bookings in Europe. Unused vouchers are refunded. Do **look into wholesalers,** companies that do not own fleets but rent in bulk from those that do and often offer better rates than traditional car-rental operations. Prices are best during off-peak periods. Rentals booked through wholesalers often must be paid for before you leave home.

Short-term leasing can save money if you need a rental for more than 17 days. Kemwel and Europe by Car are among the wholesalers offering such deals.

Also consider renting a diesel car, as it's more fuel efficient, the fuel is cheaper, and the rates can be less expensive as well.

Wholesalers **Auto Europe** ☎ 207/842-2000 or 800/223-5555 📠 207/842-2222 🌐 www.autoeurope.com. **Europe by Car** ☎ 212/581-3040 or 800/223-1516 📠 212/246-1458 🌐 www.europebycar.com. **Destination Europe Resources** (DER) ✉ 9501 W. Devon Ave., Rosemont, IL 60018 ☎ 800/782-2424 🌐 www.der.com. **Kemwel** ☎ 800/678-0678 📠 207/842-2124 🌐 www.kemwel.com.

INSURANCE

When driving a rented car you are generally responsible for any damage to or loss of the vehicle. Collision policies that car-rental companies sell for European rentals typically do not cover stolen vehicles. Before you rent—and purchase collision or theft coverage—see what coverage you already have under the terms of your personal auto-insurance policy and credit cards.

In Italy, when driving a rented car, you are generally responsible for any damage to or loss of the vehicle. Collision policies that car-rental companies sell for European rentals typically don't cover stolen vehicles. Indeed, all car-rental agencies operating in Italy require that you buy a theft-protection policy. Before you rent—and purchase collision coverage—see what coverage you already have under the terms of your personal auto-insurance policy and credit cards.

SURCHARGES

Before you pick up a car in one city and leave it in another, **ask about drop-off charges or one-way service fees,** which can be substantial. Note, too, that some rental agencies charge extra if you return the car before the time specified in your contract. To avoid a hefty refueling fee, **fill the tank just before you turn in the car,** but be aware that gas stations near the rental outlet may overcharge. It's almost never a deal to buy the tank of gas that's in the car when you rent it; the understanding is that you'll return it empty, but some fuel usually remains.

CAR TRAVEL

Your driver's license may not be recognized outside your home country. International driving permits (IDPs) are available from the American and Canadian automobile associations and, in the United Kingdom, from the Automobile Association and Royal Automobile Club. These international permits, valid only in conjunction with your regular driver's license, are universally recognized; having one may save you a problem with local authorities.

Unless you're in a rush to get to your next destination, you'll find it rewarding to **avoid the freeways and use alternative routes.**

Motorway tolls can easily add $25 a day to your costs in driving through France, and there are toll roads throughout southern Europe, as well as charges for many tunnels. When crossing borders into Switzerland, you'll be charged approximately €27.50 (about $30) for a *vignette* that entitles you to use Swiss freeways for 14 months; in Austria, a vignette begins at about €31 and you can choose its duration. To get a handle on toll costs, consult the national tourist office or car-rental firm before you travel.

If you are driving a rented car, **be sure to carry the necessary papers provided by the rental company.** For U.K. citizens, if the vehicle is your own, you will need proof of ownership, a certificate of roadworthiness (known as a Ministry of Transport, or MOT, road vehicle certificate), up-to-date vehicle registration or tax certificate, and a Green Card proof of insurance, available from your insurance company (fees vary depending on destination and length of stay).

Border controls have been abolished within the EU (except in the U.K., Ireland, Scandinavia, and Greece). The border posts are still standing, but drivers whiz through them without slowing down. Truck traffic is generally routed to separate checkpoints.

Drivers traveling between Great Britain and the Continent can now **consider using the Eurotunnel,** the train carrying cars, buses, motorbikes, and trucks, plus their passengers, through the Channel Tunnel between Folkestone and Calais in 35 minutes. The shuttle trains operate continuously—three to four trains per hour—and reservations are not needed, but to avoid queueing, tickets can be bought in advance from travel agents or by credit card from **Eurotunnel** (☎ 03/2100–6100 in France; 0870/535–3535 in the U.K., www.eurotunnel.com). Prices vary according to length of stay on the Continent, as well as the season and time of travel. Prices given are for return fares, with the maximum rate applying in the peak July and August holiday period. A short break (less than five days) costs £83–£117, and a standard return costs £193–£227. Club Class gives you the right to priority queueing and entry to the Club Class lounge for a premium of 25%–35%. To calculate single fares simply divide by two. Note that you must make advance reservations to benefit from promotional fares and special offers. *See* The Channel Tunnel.

AUTO CLUBS

In Australia Australian Automobile Association ☎ 02/6247-7311 🌐 www.aaa.asn.au.

In Canada Canadian Automobile Association (CAA) ☎ 613/247-0117 for membership 🌐 www.caa.ca.

In New Zealand New Zealand Automobile Association ☎ 09/377-4660 🌐 www.nzaa.co.nz.

In the U.K. Automobile Association (AA) ☎ 0870/600-0371 🌐 www.theaa.com. Royal Automobile Club (RAC) ☎ 0800/015-4435 for membership; 0800/092-2222 for insurance 🌐 www.rac.co.uk.

In the U.S. American Automobile Association ☎ 800/763-9900 🌐 www.aaa.com.

EMERGENCY SERVICES

You must carry a reflecting red triangle (to be placed 30 meters behind your car in case of breakdown). A first-aid kit and fire extinguisher are strongly recommended.

GASOLINE

Be prepared: gasoline costs three to four times more than in the United States, due to heavy taxes. The better fuel economy of European cars offsets the higher price to some extent.

ROAD CONDITIONS

During peak vacation periods, main routes can be jammed with holiday traffic. In the United Kingdom, **try to avoid driving during any of the long bank-holiday (public holiday) weekends,** when motorways are invariably clogged. The tunnels carrying traffic between Italy and the countries to the north are often overburdened with truck traffic; cross the Alps on a weekend, if you can. In France, Greece, Spain, and Italy, huge numbers of people still take a fixed one-month vacation in August, so **avoid driving** during *le départ,* the first weekend in August, when vast numbers of drivers head south; or *le retour,* when they head back.

RULES OF THE ROAD

Establishing a speed limit for German motorways has proved a tougher nut than any government could crack. On the rest of the Continent, the limit is generally 120 kph (74 mph), but the cruising speed is mostly about 140 kph (about 87 mph). In the United Kingdom, the speed limit is 112 kph (70 mph), but there, too, passing at considerably higher speeds is not uncommon. In suburban and urban zones, the speed limit is much lower. For safe driving, **stay in the slower lane unless you want to pass, and make way for faster cars wanting to pass you.**

In the United Kingdom, the Republic of Ireland, Cyprus, and Gibraltar, cars drive on the left. In other European countries, traffic is on the right. If you're coming off the Eurotunnel's shuttle, or ferries from Britain or Ireland to the Continent (or vice versa), beware the transition. *See* individual country chapters for national speed limits and rules of the road.

THE CHANNEL TUNNEL

Short of flying, taking the "Chunnel" is the fastest way to cross the English Channel: 35 minutes from Folkestone to Calais, 60 minutes from motorway to motorway, or 3 hours from London's Waterloo Station to Paris's Gare du Nord.

Car Transport Eurotunnel ☎ 0870/535-3535 in U.K.; 070/223210 in Belgium; 03-21-00-61-00 in France 🌐 www.eurotunnel.com. French Motorail/Rail Europe ☎ 0870/241-5415 🌐 www.frenchmotorail.com.

Passenger Service Eurostar ☎ 1233/617575; 0870/518-6186 in U.K. 🌐 www.eurostar.co.uk. Rail Europe ☎ 800/942-4866 or 800/274-8724; 0870/584-8848 U.K. inquiries and credit-card bookings 🌐 www.raileurope.com.

CHILDREN IN EUROPE

If you are renting a car, don't forget to **arrange for a car seat** when you reserve. For general advice about traveling with children, consult *Fodor's FYI: Travel with Your Baby* (available in bookstores everywhere).

FLYING

If your children are two or older, **ask about children's airfares.** As a general rule, infants under two not occupying a seat fly at greatly reduced fares or even for free. But if you want to guarantee a seat for an infant, you have to pay full fare. Consider flying during off-peak days and times; most airlines will grant an infant a seat without a ticket if there are available seats. When booking, **confirm carry-on allowances** if you're traveling with infants. In general, for babies charged 10% to 50% of the adult fare you are allowed one carry-on bag and a collapsible stroller; if the flight is full, the stroller may have to be checked or you may be limited to less.

Experts agree that it's a good idea to use safety seats aloft for children weighing less than 40 pounds. Airlines set their own policies: if you use a safety seat, U.S. carriers usually require that the child be ticketed, even if he or she is young enough to ride free, because the seats must be strapped into regular seats. And even if you pay the full adult fare for the seat, it may be worth it, especially on longer trips. Do **check your airline's policy about using safety seats during takeoff and landing.** Safety seats are not allowed everywhere in the plane, so get your seat assignments as early as possible.

When reserving, **request children's meals or a freestanding bassinet** (not available at all airlines) if you need them. But note that bulkhead seats, where you must sit to use the bassinet, may lack an overhead bin or storage space on the floor.

LODGING

Most hotels in Europe allow children under a certain age to stay in their parents' room at no extra charge, but others charge for them as extra adults; be sure to **find out the cutoff age for children's discounts.**

SIGHTS & ATTRACTIONS

Places that are especially appealing to children are indicated by a rubber-duckie icon (🐤) in the margin.

CONSUMER PROTECTION

Whether you're shopping for gifts or purchasing travel services, **pay with a major credit card** whenever possible, so you can cancel payment or get reimbursed if there's a problem (and you can provide documentation). If you're doing business with a particular company for the first time, **contact your local Better Business Bureau and the attorney general's offices** in your state and (for U.S. businesses) the company's home state as well. Have any complaints been filed? Finally, if you're buying a package or tour, always **consider travel insurance** that includes default coverage (⇨ Insurance).

BBBs **Council of Better Business Bureaus** ✉ 4200 Wilson Blvd., Suite 800, Arlington, VA 22203 ☎ 703/276-0100 📠 703/525-8277 🌐 www.bbb.org.

CRUISE TRAVEL

Europe is a major cruise center, with eight seas (Adriatic, Aegean, Baltic, Black, Ionian, Mediterranean, North, and Tyrrhenian) and the Atlantic Ocean. From the majesty of Norway's fjords to the ruins of ancient Greece, the region has more than one could possibly hope to see on one cruise vacation. **Select your ship as carefully as you choose your itinerary.** Cruises sail in Europe from April through November.

To learn how to plan, choose, and book a cruise-ship voyage, consult *Fodor's FYI: Plan & Enjoy Your Cruise* (available in bookstores everywhere).

Cruise Lines **Abercrombie & Kent** ✉ 1520 Kensington Rd., Suite 212, Oak Brook, IL 60523 ☎ 630/954-2944 or 800/323-7308 🌐 www.abercrombiekent.com. **Celebrity Cruises** ✉ 1050 Caribbean Way, Miami, FL 33132 ☎ 305/539-6000 or 800/437-3111 🌐 www.celebritycruises.com. **Clipper Cruise Line** ✉ 11969 Westline Industrial Dr., St. Louis, MO 63146 ☎ 314/655-6700 or 800/325-0010 🌐 www.clippercruise.com. **Crystal Cruises** ✉ 2049 Century Park E, Suite 1400, Los Angeles, CA 90067 ☎ 800/446-6620 🌐 www.crystalcruises.com. **Cunard Line Limited** ✉ 6100 Blue Lagoon Dr., Suite 400, Miami, FL 33126 ☎ 800/728-6273 🌐 www.cunardline.com. **Holland America Line** ✉ 300 Elliott Ave. W, Seattle, WA 98119 ☎ 877/932-4259 🌐 www.hollandamerica.com. **Orient Lines** ✉ 1510 S.E. 17th St., Suite 400, Fort Lauderdale, FL 33316 ☎ 954/527-6660 or 800/333-7300 🌐 www.orientlines.com. **Princess Cruises** ✉ 24844 Avenue Rockefeller, Santa Clarita, CA 91355 ☎ 310/553-1770; 800/774-6237 for brochures 🌐 www.princess.com. **Radisson Seven Seas Cruises** ✉ 600 Corporate Dr., Suite 410, Fort Lauderdale, FL 33334 ☎ 877/505-5370 🌐 www.rscc.com. **Royal Caribbean International** ✉ 1080 Caribbean Way, Miami, FL 33132 ☎ 305/539-6000 or 800/398-9819 🌐 www.royalcaribbean.com. **Royal Olympic Cruises** ✉ 805 3rd Ave., 18th fl., New York, NY 10022 ☎ 212/397-6400; 800/872-6400 in U.S. and Canada 🌐 www.royalolympiccruises.com. **Silversea Cruises** ✉ 110 E. Broward Blvd., Fort Lauderdale, FL 33301 ☎ 954/522-4499 or 800/722-9955 🌐 www.silversea.com. **Special Expeditions** ✉ 720 5th Ave., New York, NY 10019 ☎ 212/765-7740 or 800/397-3348 🌐 www.specialexpeditions.com. **Windstar Cruises** ✉ 300 Elliott Ave. W, Seattle, WA 98119 ☎ 800/258-7245 🌐 www.windstarcruises.com.

CUSTOMS & DUTIES

When shopping abroad, **keep receipts** for all purchases. Upon reentering the country,

be ready to show customs officials what you've bought. Pack purchases together in an easily accessible place. If you think a duty is incorrect, appeal the assessment. If you object to the way your clearance was handled, note the inspector's badge number. In either case, first ask to see a supervisor. If the problem isn't resolved, write to the appropriate authorities, beginning with the port director at your point of entry.

IN AUSTRALIA

Australian residents who are 18 or older may bring home A$400 worth of souvenirs and gifts (including jewelry), 250 cigarettes or 250 grams of cigars or other tobacco products, and 1,125 ml of alcohol (including wine, beer, and spirits). Residents under 18 may bring back A$200 worth of goods. Members of the same family traveling together may pool their allowances. Prohibited items include meat products. Seeds, plants, and fruits need to be declared upon arrival.

Australian Customs Service Regional Director, Box 8, Sydney, NSW 2001 02/9213-2000 or 1300/363263; 02/9364-7222 or 1800/803006 quarantine-inquiry line 02/9213-4043 www.customs.gov.au.

IN CANADA

Canadian residents who have been out of Canada for at least seven days may bring in C$750 worth of goods duty-free. If you've been away fewer than seven days but more than 48 hours, the duty-free allowance drops to C$200. If your trip lasts 24 to 48 hours, the allowance is C$50. You may not pool allowances with family members. Goods claimed under the C$750 exemption may follow you by mail; those claimed under the lesser exemptions must accompany you. Alcohol and tobacco products may be included in the seven-day and 48-hour exemptions but not in the 24-hour exemption. If you meet the age requirements of the province or territory through which you reenter Canada, you may bring in, duty-free, 1.5 liters of wine *or* 1.14 liters (40 imperial ounces) of liquor *or* 24 12-ounce cans or bottles of beer or ale. Also, if you meet the local age requirement for tobacco products, you may bring in, duty-free, 200 cigarettes and 50 cigars. Check ahead of time with the Canada Customs and Revenue Agency or the Department of Agriculture for policies regarding meat products, seeds, plants, and fruits.

You may send an unlimited number of gifts (only one gift per recipient, however) worth up to C$60 each duty-free to Canada. Label the package UNSOLICITED GIFT—VALUE UNDER $60. Alcohol and tobacco are excluded.

Canada Customs and Revenue Agency 2265 St. Laurent Blvd., Ottawa, Ontario K1G 4K3 800/461-9999, 204/983-3500, or 506/636-5064 www.ccra.gc.ca.

IN NEW ZEALAND

All homeward-bound residents may bring back NZ$700 worth of souvenirs and gifts; passengers may not pool their allowances, and children can claim only the concession on goods intended for their own use. For those 17 or older, the duty-free allowance also includes 4.5 liters of wine or beer; one 1,125-ml bottle of spirits; and either 200 cigarettes, 250 grams of tobacco, 50 cigars, *or* a combination of the three up to 250 grams. Meat products, seeds, plants, and fruits must be declared upon arrival to the Agricultural Services Department.

New Zealand Customs Head office: The Customhouse, 17–21 Whitmore St., Box 2218, Wellington 09/300-5399 or 0800/428-786 www.customs.govt.nz.

IN THE U.K.

If you are a U.K. resident and your journey was wholly within the European Union, you probably won't have to pass through customs when you return to the United Kingdom. If you plan to bring back large quantities of alcohol or tobacco, check EU limits beforehand. In most cases, if you bring back more than 200 cigars, 3,200 cigarettes, 10 liters of spirits, 110 liters of beer, and/or 90 liters of wine, you have to declare the goods upon return.

HM Customs and Excise Portcullis House, 21 Cowbridge Rd. E, Cardiff CF11 9SS 0845/010-9000 or 0208/929-0152; 0208/929-6731 or 0208/910-3602 complaints www.hmce.gov.uk.

IN THE U.S.

U.S. residents who have been out of the country for at least 48 hours may bring home, for personal use, $800 worth of foreign goods duty-free, as long as they haven't used the $800 allowance or any part of it in the past 30 days. This exemption may include 1 liter of alcohol (for travelers 21 and older), 200 cigarettes, and 100 non-Cuban cigars. Family members from the same household who are traveling together may pool their $800 personal exemptions. For fewer than 48 hours, the duty-free allowance drops to $200, which may include 50 cigarettes, 10 non-Cuban cigars, and 150 ml of alcohol (or 150 ml of perfume containing alcohol). The $200 allowance cannot be combined with other individuals' exemptions, and if you exceed it, the full value of all the goods will be taxed. Antiques, which the U.S. Bureau of Customs and Border Protection defines as objects more than 100 years old, enter duty-free, as do original works of art done entirely by hand, including paintings, drawings, and sculptures. This doesn't apply to folk art or handicrafts, which are in general dutiable.

You may also send packages home duty-free, with a limit of one parcel per addressee per day (except alcohol or tobacco products or perfume worth more than $5). You can mail up to $200 worth of goods for personal use; label the package PERSONAL USE and attach a list of its contents and their retail value. If the package contains your used personal belongings, mark it AMERICAN GOODS RETURNED to avoid paying duties. You may send up to $100 worth of goods as a gift; mark the package UNSOLICITED GIFT. Mailed items do not affect your duty-free allowance on your return.

To avoid paying duty on foreign-made high-ticket items you already own and will take on your trip, register them with Customs before you leave the country. Consider filing a Certificate of Registration for laptops, cameras, watches, and other digital devices identified with serial numbers or other permanent markings; you can keep the certificate for other trips. Otherwise, bring a sales receipt or insurance form to show that you owned the item before you left the United States.

U.S. Bureau of Customs and Border Protection For inquiries and equipment registration, 1300 Pennsylvania Ave. NW, Washington, DC 20229 www.customs.gov 202/354–1000 For complaints, Customer Satisfaction Unit, 1300 Pennsylvania Ave. NW, Room 5.5D, Washington, DC 20229.

IN EUROPE

Since the EU's 1992 agreement on a unified European market, the same customs regulations apply to all 15 member states (Austria, Belgium, Denmark, Finland, France, Germany, Great Britain, Greece, Ireland, Italy, Luxembourg, the Netherlands, Portugal, Spain, and Sweden). If you arrive from another EU country, you do not have to pass through customs.

Duty-free allowances for visitors from outside the EU are the same whatever your nationality (but you have to be over 17): 200 cigarettes or 50 cigars or 100 cigarillos or 250 grams of pipe tobacco; 1 liter of spirits or 2 liters of fortified or sparkling wine or liqueurs; 2 liters of still table wine; 60 milliliters of perfume; 250 milliliters of toilet water (note: 1 U.S. quart equals 0.946 liters); plus $200 worth of other goods, including gifts and souvenirs. Unless otherwise noted in individual country chapters, there are no restrictions on the import or export of currency. These limits remained in force after June 30, 1999, when duty-free shopping for travel within the EU was abolished.

See individual country chapters on non-EU countries for information on their import limits.

DINING

See discussions of dining in individual country chapters. The restaurants we list are the cream of the crop in each price category.

Reservations are always a good idea: we mention them only when they're essential or not accepted. We mention dress only when men are required to wear a jacket or a jacket and tie.

CUTTING COSTS

To save money on meals, consider eating at restaurants and cafeterias in department stores; the food and selection are surprisingly good. The stores also often have deli counters with local specialties and basics, so you can load up and nibble on the go or head out to the park for a picnic.

Many universities have cafeterias, usually called *mensas,* subsidized by the government and open to the public. Don't expect a grand buffet, but you'll find several choices daily accommodating most appetites.

Street vendors are popular throughout Europe, with stands reading *donor-kebab* or some variation thereof. These stands pop up on the street, in small take-out windows in buildings, even vans. The food is cheap, hot, and usually very good; food might range from pizza and french fries to lamb kebabs and falafel.

When in Spain, savor local flavors without going over-budget by ordering *tapas*, small appetizer-size plates of meats, vegetables, or cheeses. At many bars, a serving comes free when you order a drink.

As you walk around, the cost of buying sodas and juices throughout the day will certainly add up. Consider buying bottled water and iced tea mix, for instance, to create your own brew, and reuse the bottles with tap water (destination permitting) to save even more.

DISABILITIES & ACCESSIBILITY

Getting around in many European cities and towns can be difficult if you're using a wheelchair, as cobblestone-paved streets and sidewalks are common in older, historic districts. Generally, newer facilities (including museums, transportation, hotels) provide easier access for people with disabilities.

LODGING

Contact a support organization at home to see whether they have publications with lists of approved accommodations. The U.S.–based Society for the Advancement of Travel for the Handicapped (SATH) is dedicated to promoting access for travelers with disabilities. The British nonprofit Holiday Care Service produces an annual guide, *The Holiday Care Service Guide to Accessible Accommodation and Travel*, which lists more than 1,000 establishments inspected for access by Holiday Care in association with the National Tourist Boards. It has sections on accessible transportation, identifies accessible tourist attractions, and suggests sample itineraries.

Support Organizations **Holiday Care Service** ✉ 7th fl., Sunley House, 4 Bedford Pk., Croydon, Surrey, CR0 2AP ☎ 0845/124-9971 📠 0845/124-9922 🌐 www.holidaycare.org.uk. **The Society for the Advancement of Travel for the Handicapped** (SATH) ✉ 347 5th Ave., Suite 610, New York, NY 10016 ☎ 212/447-7284 📠 212/725-8253 🌐 www.sath.org.

RESERVATIONS

When discussing accessibility with an operator or reservations agent, **ask hard questions.** Are there any stairs, inside *or* out? Are there grab bars next to the toilet *and* in the shower/tub? How wide is the doorway to the room? To the bathroom? For the most extensive facilities meeting the latest legal specifications, **opt for newer accommodations.** If you reserve through a toll-free number, consider also calling the hotel's local number to confirm the information from the central reservations office. Get confirmation in writing when you can.

Complaints **Aviation Consumer Protection Division** (⇨ Air Travel) for airline-related problems. **Departmental Office of Civil Rights** ✉ For general inquiries, U.S. Department of Transportation, S-30, 400 7th St. SW, Room 10215, Washington, DC 20590 ☎ 202/366-4648 📠 202/366-9371 🌐 www.dot.gov/ost/docr/index.htm. **Disability Rights Section** ✉ NYAV, U.S. Department of Justice, Civil Rights Division, 950 Pennsylvania Ave. NW, Washington, DC 20530 ☎ ADA information line 202/514-0301; 800/514-0301; 202/514-0383 TTY; 800/514-0383 TTY 🌐 www.ada.gov. **U.S. Department of Transportation Hotline** ☎ For disability-related air-travel problems, 800/778-4838; 800/455-9880 TTY.

TRAVEL AGENCIES

In the United States, the Americans with Disabilities Act requires that travel firms serve the needs of all travelers. Some agencies specialize in working with people with disabilities.

Travelers with Mobility Problems **CareVacations** ✉ No. 5, 5110-50 Ave., Leduc, Alberta T9E 6V4, Canada ☎ 780/986-6404 or 877/478-7827 📠 780/986-8332 🌐 www.carevacations.com, for group tours and cruise vacations. **Flying Wheels Travel** ✉ 143 W. Bridge St., Box 382, Owatonna, MN 55060 ☎ 507/451-5005 or 800/535-6790 📠 507/451-1685 🌐 www.flyingwheelstravel.com. **Melwood** ✉ 5606 Dower House Rd., Upper Marlboro, MD 20772 ☎ 301/599-8000 📠 301/599-0180 🌐 www.melwood.com.

Travelers with Developmental Disabilities **New Directions** ✉ 5276 Hollister Ave., Suite 207, Santa Barbara, CA 93111 ☎ 805/967-2841 or 888/967-2841 📠 805/964-7344 🌐 www.newdirectionstravel.com. **Sprout** ✉ 893 Amsterdam Ave., New York, NY 10025 ☎ 212/222-9575 or 888/222-9575 📠 212/222-9768 🌐 www.gosprout.org.

DISCOUNTS & DEALS

Be a smart shopper and **compare all your options** before making decisions. A plane ticket bought with a promotional coupon from travel clubs, coupon books, and direct-mail offers or purchased on the Internet may not be cheaper than the least expensive fare from a discount ticket agency. And always keep in mind that what you get is just as important as what you save.

If you're looking to plan your trip around some free activities, try to be in town for a festival or other seasonal event that could yield street performances, concerts, and other goings-on. Year-round, check bulletin boards in tourist offices and churches for free concert announcements.

Many countries throughout Europe offer museum passes that can save you money and sometimes time if the pass enables you to circumvent long lines. In Paris, the *Cart Musees et Monuments* pass, available at major museums or métro stops, permits entry—usually without waiting in line—to 70 museums in greater Paris for €15 per day; you can buy a one-, three-, or five-day pass. In Berlin, one- or three-day *Tageskarte* or *Drei-Tage-Karte* passes, on sale at any of the state-owned museums, are good for all 20 museums run by the Staatliche Museen zu Berlin and cost €6 and €8, respectively. In Munich, you can buy a €15 day pass for all state-owned museums at any of the affiliated museums, or at a tourist office. The *Paseo del Arte* pass (€7.66) in Madrid gets you into the three most popular museums in the city—the Museo del Prado, the Centro de Arte Reina Sofia, and the Musee Thyssen-Bornemisza—and is available at any one of them.

There are also often free admission days at the state-owned museums in many countries, sometimes once a week but usually once a month, and often on Sunday. Inquire at tourist offices and museums when you visit for more information. There are usually student discounts at museums with proof of your student status; there are also discounts for teachers if you can present your dated union card.

Outlet malls have only recently become popular in Europe, and the leading provider of them is McArthur Glen (🌐 www.mcarthurglen.com). There are currently 12 locations: Ashford, Swindon, York, Mansfield, Cheshire Oaks, and Bridgend in England; Livingston, Scotland; Roermond, Holland; Roubaix and Troyes in France; Serravalle, Italy; and Parndorf, Austria. And if you're eager to get those gifts home and they happen to be paper products, save postage by mailing them through the media mail category; it does take longer than first-class but can be about a third of the price.

DISCOUNT RESERVATIONS

To save money, **look into discount reservations services** with Web sites and toll-free numbers, which use their buying power to get a better price on hotels, airline tickets (⇨ Air Travel), even car rentals. When booking a room, always **call the hotel's local toll-free number** (if one is available) rather than the central reservations number—you'll often get a better price. Always ask about special packages or corporate rates.

When shopping for the best deal on hotels and car rentals, **look for guaranteed exchange rates,** which protect you against a falling dollar. With your rate locked in, you won't pay more, even if the price goes up in the local currency.

Airline Tickets **Air 4 Less** ☎ 800/AIR4LESS; low-fare specialist.

Hotel Rooms **Accommodations Express** ☎ 800/444-7666 or 800/277-1064 🌐 www.accommodationsexpress.com. **Hotel Reservations Network** ☎ 800/964-6835 🌐 www.hotels.com. **Hotels.com** ☎ 800/246-8357 or 214/369-1246 🌐 www.hotels.com. **International Marketing & Travel Concepts** ☎ 800/790-4682 🌐 www.imtc-travel.com. **Steigenberger Reservation Service** ☎ 800/223-5652 🌐 www.srs-worldhotels.com. **Travel Interlink** ☎ 800/888-5898 🌐 www.travelinterlink.com. **Turbotrip.com** ☎ 800/473-7829 🌐 www.turbotrip.com.

PACKAGE DEALS

Don't confuse packages and guided tours. When you buy a package, you travel on your own, just as though you had planned the trip yourself. Fly/drive packages, which combine airfare and car rental, are often a good deal. In cities, ask the local visitor's bureau about hotel packages that include tickets to major museum exhibits or other special events. If you **buy a rail/drive pass,** you may save on train tickets and car rentals. All Eurailpass holders get a discount on Eurostar fares through the

Channel Tunnel and often receive reduced rates for buses, hotels, ferries, and car rentals. A German Rail Pass is also good for travel aboard some KD German Rhine Line steamers and on certain ferries to Finland, Denmark, and Sweden (if the pass includes those countries). Discounts are available on some Deutsche Touring/ Europabus routes. Greek Flexipass Rail 'n Fly includes two flight vouchers for selected air-travel routes within Greece and free or reduced fares on some ferries.

ELECTRICITY

To use electric-powered equipment purchased in the United States or Canada, **bring a converter and adapter.**

If your appliances are dual-voltage, you'll need only an adapter. Don't use 110-volt outlets marked FOR SHAVERS ONLY for high-wattage appliances such as blow-dryers. Most laptops operate equally well on 110 and 220 volts and so require only an adapter.

GAY & LESBIAN TRAVEL

Although big cities like Amsterdam, London, and Paris have a visible and happening gay scene (the newly elected mayor of Paris is openly gay), most of Europe has a view of homosexuality similar to that found away from big cities in the United States.

Gay- & Lesbian-Friendly Travel Agencies **Different Roads Travel** ✉ 8383 Wilshire Blvd., Suite 520, Beverly Hills, CA 90211 ☎ 323/651-5557 or 800/429-8747 (Ext. 14 for both) 📠 323/651-3678 ✉ lgernert@tzell.com. **Kennedy Travel** ✉ 130 W. 42nd St., Suite 401, New York, NY 10036 ☎ 212/840-8659 or 800/237-7433 📠 212/730-2269 🌐 www.kennedytravel.com. **Now, Voyager** ✉ 4406 18th St., San Francisco, CA 94114 ☎ 415/626-1169 or 800/255-6951 📠 415/626-8626 🌐 www.nowvoyager.com. **Skylink Travel and Tour** ✉ 1455 N. Dutton Ave., Suite A, Santa Rosa, CA 95401 ☎ 707/546-9888 or 800/225-5759 📠 707/636-0951; serving lesbian travelers.

INSURANCE

The most useful travel-insurance plan is a comprehensive policy that includes coverage for trip cancellation and interruption, default, trip delay, and medical expenses (with a waiver for preexisting conditions).

Without insurance you'll lose all or most of your money if you cancel your trip, regardless of the reason. Default insurance covers you if your tour operator, airline, or cruise line goes out of business. Trip-delay covers expenses that arise because of bad weather or mechanical delays. Study the fine print when comparing policies.

If you're traveling internationally, a key component of travel insurance is coverage for medical bills incurred if you get sick on the road. Such expenses aren't generally covered by Medicare or private policies. U.K. residents can buy a travel-insurance policy valid for most vacations taken during the year in which it's purchased (but check preexisting-condition coverage). British and Australian citizens need extra medical coverage when traveling overseas.

Always **buy travel policies directly from the insurance company;** if you buy them from a cruise line, airline, or tour operator that goes out of business, you probably won't be covered for the agency or operator's default, a major risk. Before making any purchase, **review your existing health and home-owner's policies** to find what they cover away from home.

Travel Insurers In the U.S.: **Access America** ✉ 6600 W. Broad St., Richmond, VA 23230 ☎ 800/284-8300 📠 804/673-1491 or 800/346-9265 🌐 www.accessamerica.com. **Travel Guard International** ✉ 1145 Clark St., Stevens Point, WI 54481 ☎ 715/345-0505 or 800/826-1300 📠 800/955-8785 🌐 www.travelguard.com.

In the U.K.: **Association of British Insurers** ✉ 51 Gresham St., London EC2V 7HQ ☎ 020/7600-3333 📠 020/7696-8999 🌐 www.abi.org.uk. In Canada: **RBC Insurance** ✉ 6880 Financial Dr., Mississauga, Ontario L5N 7Y5 ☎ 800/565-3129 📠 905/813-4704 🌐 www.rbcinsurance.com. In Australia: **Insurance Council of Australia** ✉ Insurance Enquiries and Complaints, Level 3, 56 Pitt St., Sydney, NSW 2000 ☎ 1300/363683 or 02/9251-4456 📠 02/9251-4453 🌐 www.iecltd.com.au. In New Zealand: **Insurance Council of New Zealand** ✉ Level 7, 111-115 Customhouse Quay, Box 474, Wellington ☎ 04/472-5230 📠 04/473-3011 🌐 www.icnz.org.nz.

LANGUAGE

A phrase book and language-tape set can help get you started. *Fodor's French for Travelers, Fodor's German for Travelers, Fodor's Italian for Travelers*, and *Fodor's Spanish for Travelers* (available at bookstores everywhere) are excellent.

LODGING

For discussions of accommodations in Europe, *see* the Lodging sections *in* individual country chapters.The lodgings we list are the cream of the crop in each price category. When pricing accommodations, always ask what facilities are included and what costs extra.

CUTTING COSTS

When booking a room, always **call the hotel's local toll-free number** (if one is available) rather than the central reservations number—you'll often get a better price. Always ask about special packages or corporate rates.

When looking for inexpensive lodging, consider asking local tourist offices about university dorms or religious housing. When schools are on break, many rent dorm rooms or convert other buildings into housing to bring in revenue. The spaces are comparable to hostel accommodations. For information on university housing in the U.K. contact Venuemasters. Religious housing is another alternative; convents and monasteries often allow guests as long as they are respectful of their rules. Such rules can include a curfew, no drinking, or single-sex guests only. This housing is popular in Spain and Italy—in fact, many paradors in Spain were once monasteries or convents. For information on lodging in Italy contact Italia SIXTINA. For more on lodging in Spain contact the Spanish Tourist Board, *see* Visitor Information.

There is also an accommodations network for teachers called Educators B&B Travel Network that helps find lodging with host teachers worldwide for $32 a night for a membership fee of $36 per year.

Another option are campgrounds, especially in southern Europe during the summer. You can bring your own tent or find sites with cabins or RVs for rent, some stocked with utensils and other amenities. The grounds can be extensive, including souvenir shops, food stores, pools, and gyms, and can offer multiple forms of entertainment. The rates are based on the season, the accommodations, and the number of people, but are almost uniformly inexpensive. The best resource for campground information is the European Federation of Campingsite Organization.

When traveling long distances by rail, consider reserving a bunk on a night train, not only to help pass the time more quickly but to save on lodging expenses; it isn't much more than a regular ticket.

European Federation of Campingsite Organization ✉ EFCO Secretariat, 6 Pullman Ct., Great Western Rd., Gloucester, England GL1 3ND ☎ 01452/526911 🌐 www.campingeurope.com. **Italia SIXTINA** ✉ Siege Social: R.R.B., 15 rue de pas Perdus, B.P. 8338-95804, Cergy Saint Christophe Cedex France ☎ 01/3425-4444 📠 01/3425-4445 🌐 www.sixtina.com. **Venuemasters** ✉ The Workstation, Paternoster Row, Sheffield, England S1 2BX ☎ 011/4449-3090 🌐 www.venuemasters.com.

APARTMENT & VILLA RENTALS

If you want a home base that's roomy enough for a family and comes with cooking facilities, **consider a furnished rental.** These can save you money, especially if you're traveling with a group. Home-exchange directories sometimes list rentals as well as exchanges.

International Agents **At Home Abroad** ✉ 405 E. 56th St., Suite 6H, New York, NY 10022 ☎ 212/421-9165 📠 212/752-1591 🌐 www.athomeabroadinc.com. **Drawbridge to Europe** ✉ 98 Granite St., Ashland, OR 97520 ☎ 541/482-7778 or 888/268-1148 📠 541/482-7779 🌐 www.drawbridgetoeurope.com. **Hideaways International** ✉ 767 Islington St., Portsmouth, NH 03802 ☎ 603/430-4433 or 800/843-4433 📠 603/430-4444 🌐 www.hideaways.com; membership $129. **Hometours International** ✉ 1108 Scottie La., Knoxville, TN 37919 ☎ 865/690-8484 or 866/367-4668 🌐 http://thor.he.net/~hometour. **Interhome** ✉ 1990 N.E. 163rd St., Suite 110, North Miami Beach, FL 33162 ☎ 305/940-2299 or 800/882-6864 📠 305/940-2911 🌐 www.interhome.us. **Vacation Home Rentals Worldwide** ✉ 235 Kensington Ave., Norwood, NJ 07648 ☎ 201/767-9393 or 800/633-3284 📠 201/767-5510 🌐 www.vhrww.com. **Villanet** ✉ 1251 N.W. 116th St., Seattle, WA 98177 ☎ 206/417-3444 or 800/964-1891 📠 206/417-1832 🌐 www.rentavilla.com. **Villas and Apartments Abroad** ✉ 370 Lexington Ave., Suite 1401, New York, NY 10017 ☎ 212/897-5045 or 800/433-3020 📠 212/897-5039 🌐 www.ideal-villas.com. **Villas International** ✉ 4340 Redwood Hwy., Suite D309, San Rafael, CA 94903 ☎ 415/499-9490 or 800/221-2260 📠 415/499-9491 🌐 www.villasintl.com.

HOME EXCHANGES

If you would like to exchange your home for someone else's, **join a home-exchange organization,** which will send you its updated listings of available exchanges for a year and will include your own listing in at least one of them. It's up to you to make specific arrangements. There is also a Web site that hosts a home exchange but is completely free, called GlobalFreeloaders; after signing up as a host for a six-month period you are given access to a database with more than 3,000 people in more than 100 countries who will host you for free in turn.

Exchange Clubs **Educators B&B Travel Network** Box 5279, Eugene, OR 97405 ☎ 800/956-4822; 0800/895891 from the U.K. 541/686-5818 www.edubabnet.com. **GlobalFreeloaders** www.globalfreeloaders.com. **HomeLink International** Box 47747, Tampa, FL 33647 ☎ 813/975-9825 or 800/638-3841 813/910-8144 www.homelink.org; $110 yearly for a listing, on-line access, and catalog; $40 without catalog. **Intervac U.S.** ✉ 30 Corte San Fernando, Tiburon, CA 94920 ☎ 800/756-4663 415/435-7440 www.intervacus.com; $105 yearly for a listing, on-line access, and a catalog; $50 without catalog.

HOSTELS

No matter what your age, you can **save on lodging costs by staying at hostels.** In some 4,500 locations in more than 70 countries around the world, Hostelling International (HI), the umbrella group for a number of national youth-hostel associations, offers single-sex, dorm-style beds and, at many hostels, rooms for couples and family accommodations. Membership in any HI national hostel association, open to travelers of all ages, allows you to stay in HI-affiliated hostels at member rates; one-year membership is about $28 for adults (C$35 for a two-year minimum membership in Canada, £13.50 in the U.K., A$52 in Australia, and NZ$40 in New Zealand); hostels charge about $10–$30 per night. Members have priority if the hostel is full; they're also eligible for discounts around the world, even on rail and bus travel in some countries.

Organizations **Hostelling International–USA** ✉ 8401 Colesville Rd., Suite 600, Silver Spring, MD 20910 ☎ 301/495-1240 301/495-6697 www.hiayh.org. **Hostelling International–Canada** ✉ 400-205 Catherine St., Ottawa, Ontario K2P 1C3 ☎ 613/237-7884 or 800/663-5777 613/237-7868 www.hihostels.ca. **YHA England and Wales** ✉ Trevelyan House, Dimple Rd., Matlock, Derbyshire DE4 3YH, U.K. ☎ 0870/870-8808 0870/770-6127 www.yha.org.uk. **YHA Australia** ✉ 422 Kent St., Sydney, NSW 2001 ☎ 02/9261-1111 02/9261-1969 www.yha.com.au. **YHA New Zealand** ✉ Level 3, 193 Cashel St., Box 436, Christchurch ☎ 03/379-9970 or 0800/278-299 03/365-4476 www.yha.org.nz.

HOTELS

All hotels listed have private baths unless otherwise noted.

RESERVING A ROOM

See individual country chapters for details on last-minute reservation services.

Toll-Free Numbers **Best Western** ☎ 800/528-1234 www.bestwestern.com. **Choice** ☎ 800/424-6423 www.choicehotels.com. **Clarion** ☎ 800/424-6423 www.choicehotels.com. **Comfort Inn** ☎ 800/424-6423 www.choicehotels.com. **Days Inn** ☎ 800/325-2525 www.daysinn.com. **Forte** ☎ 800/225-5843 www.roccofortehotels.com. **Four Seasons** ☎ 800/332-3442 www.fourseasons.com. **Hilton** ☎ 800/445-8667 www.hilton.com. **Holiday Inn** ☎ 800/465-4329 www.sixcontinentshotels.com. **Howard Johnson** ☎ 800/446-4656 www.hojo.com. **Hyatt Hotels & Resorts** ☎ 800/233-1234 www.hyatt.com. **Inter-Continental** ☎ 800/327-0200 www.intercontinental.com. **Marriott** ☎ 800/228-9290 www.marriott.com. **Le Meridien** ☎ 800/543-4300 www.lemeridien-hotels.com. **Nikko Hotels International** ☎ 800/645-5687 www.nikkohotels.com. **Quality Inn** ☎ 800/424-6423 www.choicehotels.com. **Radisson** ☎ 800/333-3333 www.radisson.com. **Ramada** ☎ 800/228-2828; 800/854-7854 international reservations www.ramada.com or www.ramadahotels.com. **Renaissance Hotels & Resorts** ☎ 800/468-3571 www.renaissancehotels.com. **Ritz-Carlton** ☎ 800/241-3333 www.ritzcarlton.com. **Sheraton** ☎ 800/325-3535 www.starwood.com/sheraton. **Westin Hotels & Resorts** ☎ 800/228-3000 www.starwood.com/westin.

MONEY MATTERS

Admission prices throughout this guide are included for attractions that charge more than $10 or the equivalent. Prices throughout this guide are given for adults. Substantially reduced fees are almost always available for children, students, and senior citizens. For information on taxes, *see* Taxes.

ATMS

ATMs are ubiquitous throughout Europe; you can draw local currency from an ATM in most airports as soon as you deplane.

CREDIT CARDS

Throughout this guide, the following abbreviations are used: **AE,** American Express; **DC,** Diners Club; **MC,** MasterCard; and **V,** Visa.

CURRENCY

On January 1, 2002, the new single European Union (EU) currency, the (€), finally became the official currency of the 11 countries participating in the European Monetary Union: Austria, Belgium, Finland, France, Germany, Ireland, Italy, Luxembourg, the Netherlands, Portugal, and Spain. Denmark, Great Britain, Greece, and Sweden, although a part of the EU, are not yet part of the monetary union, and therefore will retain the use of their local currencies, though some will accept euros while giving you local currency as change.

The euro makes life for the European traveler much, much easier. Gone are the days when a day trip to Belgium from France meant changing money into yet another currency and paying additional commissions. To make things even easier for travelers from the United States, the euro was created as a direct competitor with the U.S. dollar, which means that their values are quite similar. At press time, one euro was equal to US$1.15; 1.56 Canadian dollars, 1.73 Australian dollars, 1.97 New Zealand dollars, and .70 pounds sterling.

In the euro system there are eight coins: 1 and 2 euros, plus 1, 2, 5, 10, 20, and 50 centimes, or cents, of the euro. All coins have one side that has the value of the euro on it and the other side with one member country's unique national symbol. There are seven colorful notes: 5, 10, 20, 50, 100, 200, and 500 euros. Notes have the principal architectural styles from antiquity onward on one side and the map and the flag of Europe on the other and are the same for all countries.

CURRENCY EXCHANGE

For the most favorable rates, **change money through banks.** Although ATM transaction fees may be higher abroad than at home, ATM rates are excellent because they're based on wholesale rates offered only by major banks. You won't do as well at exchange booths in airports or rail and bus stations, in hotels, in restaurants, or in stores. To avoid lines at airport exchange booths, **get a bit of local currency before you leave home.**

Exchange Services **International Currency Express** ✉ 427 N. Camden Dr., Suite F, Beverly Hills, CA 90210 ☎ 888/278-6628 orders 📠 310/278-6410 🌐 www.foreignmoney.com. **Thomas Cook Currency Services** ☎ 800/287-7362 orders and retail locations 🌐 www.us.thomascook.com.

TRAVELER'S CHECKS

Do you need traveler's checks? It depends on where you're headed. If you're going to rural areas and small towns, go with cash; traveler's checks are best used in cities. Lost or stolen checks can usually be replaced within 24 hours. To ensure a speedy refund, buy your own traveler's checks—don't let someone else pay for them: irregularities like this can cause delays. The person who bought the checks should make the call to request a refund.

PACKING

You should **pack more for the season than for any particular dress code.** In general, northern and central Europe have cold, snowy winters, and the Mediterranean countries have mild winters, though parts of southern Europe can be bitterly cold, too. In the Mediterranean resorts **bring a warm jacket for mornings and evenings,** even in summer. The mountains usually are warm on summer days, but the weather is unpredictable, and the nights are generally cool.

For European cities, **pack as you would for an American city:** formal outfits for first-class restaurants and nightclubs, casual clothes elsewhere. Jeans are perfectly acceptable for sightseeing and informal dining. Sturdy walking shoes are appropriate for the cobblestone streets and gravel paths that fill many of the parks and surround some of the historic buildings. For visits to churches, cathedrals, and mosques, **avoid shorts and revealing outfits.** In Italy, women cover their shoulders and arms (a shawl will do). Women, however, no longer need to cover their heads in Roman Catholic churches. In Greece many monasteries bar women wearing pants; long skirts are often provided at the entrance as a cover-up for both women wearing pants and men dressed in shorts. In Turkey, women must have a head covering; a long-sleeve shirt and a long skirt or slacks are required.

To discourage purse snatchers and pickpockets, **take a handbag with long straps** that you can sling across your body, bandolier-style, and with a zippered compartment for money.

If you stay in budget hotels, **take your own soap.**

In your carry-on luggage, **pack an extra pair of eyeglasses or contact lenses and enough of any medication** you take to last a few days longer than the entire trip. You may also ask your doctor to write a spare prescription using the drug's generic name, as brand names may vary from country to country. In luggage to be checked, **never pack prescription drugs, valuables, or undeveloped film.** And don't forget to carry with you the addresses of offices that handle refunds of lost traveler's checks. Check *Fodor's How to Pack* (available at on-line retailers and bookstores everywhere) for more tips.

To avoid customs and security delays, carry medications in their original packaging. Don't pack any sharp objects in your carry-on luggage, including knives of any size or material, scissors, and corkscrews, or anything else that might arouse suspicion.

To avoid having your checked luggage chosen for hand inspection, don't cram bags full. The U.S. Transportation Security Administration suggests packing shoes on top and placing personal items you don't want touched in clear plastic bags.

CHECKING LUGGAGE

You're allowed to carry aboard one bag and one personal article, such as a purse or a laptop computer. Make sure what you carry on fits under your seat or in the overhead bin. Get to the gate early, so you can board as soon as possible, before the overhead bins fill up.

Baggage allowances vary by carrier, destination, and ticket class. On international flights, you're usually allowed to check two bags weighing up to 70 pounds (32 kilograms) each, although a few airlines allow checked bags of up to 88 pounds (40 kilograms) in first class. Some international carriers don't allow more than 66 pounds (30 kilograms) per bag in business class and 44 pounds (20 kilograms) in economy. On domestic flights, the limit may be 50 pounds (23 kilograms) per bag. Most airlines won't accept bags that weigh more than 100 pounds (45 kilograms) on domestic or international flights. Check baggage restrictions with your carrier before you pack.

Airline liability for baggage is limited to $2,500 per person on flights within the United States. On international flights it amounts to $9.07 per pound or $20 per kilogram for checked baggage (roughly $640 per 70-pound bag) and $400 per passenger for unchecked baggage. You can buy additional coverage at check-in for about $10 per $1,000 of coverage, but it often excludes a rather extensive list of items, shown on your airline ticket.

Before departure, **itemize your bags' contents** and their worth, and label the bags with your name, address, and phone number. (If you use your home address, cover it so potential thieves can't see it readily.) Include a label inside each bag and **pack a copy of your itinerary.** At check-in, **make sure each bag is correctly tagged** with the destination airport's three-letter code. Because some checked bags will be opened for hand inspection, the U.S. Transportation Security Administration recommends that you leave luggage unlocked or use the plastic locks offered at check-in. TSA screeners place an inspection notice inside searched bags, which are resealed with a special lock.

If your bag has been searched and contents are missing or damaged, file a claim with the TSA Consumer Response Center as soon as possible. If your bags arrive damaged or fail to arrive at all, file a written report with the airline before leaving the airport.

Complaints **U.S. Transportation Security Administration Consumer Response Center** ☎ 866/289-9673 www.tsa.gov.

PASSPORTS & VISAS

When traveling internationally, **carry your passport** even if you don't need one (it's always the best form of ID), and **make two photocopies of the data page** (one for someone at home and another for you, carried separately from your passport). If you lose your passport, promptly call the nearest embassy or consulate and the local police.

U.S. passport applications for children under age 14 require consent from both parents or legal guardians; both parents must appear together to sign the application. If only one parent appears, he or she must submit a written statement from the other parent authorizing passport issuance for the child. A parent with sole authority must present evidence of it when applying; acceptable documentation includes the child's certified birth certificate listing only the applying parent, a court order specifically permitting this parent's travel with the child, or a death certificate for the non-applying parent. Application forms and instructions are available on the Web site of the U.S. State Department's Bureau of Consular Affairs (www.travel.state.gov).

ENTERING EUROPE

Citizens of the United States, Canada, United Kingdom, Ireland, Australia, and New Zealand need passports for travel in Europe. Visas may also be required for visits to or through Turkey, Poland, Estonia, Latvia, Romania, Hungary, and the Czech and Slovak Republics even for short stays or train trips, and in some cases must be obtained before you'll be allowed to enter. Check with the nearest consulate of the country you'll be visiting for visa requirements and any other applicable information.

PASSPORT OFFICES

The best time to apply for a passport or to renew is in fall and winter. Before any trip, check your passport's expiration date, and, if necessary, renew it as soon as possible.

Australian Citizens **Passports Australia** 131-232 www.passports.gov.au.

Canadian Citizens **Passport Office** To mail in applications: 200 Promenade du Portage, Hull, Québec J8X 4B7 819/994-3500 or 800/567-6868 www.ppt.gc.ca.

New Zealand Citizens **New Zealand Passports Office** 0800/22-5050 or 04/474-8100 www.passports.govt.nz.

U.K. Citizens **U.K. Passport Service** 0870/521-0410 www.passport.gov.uk.

U.S. Citizens **National Passport Information Center** 900/225-5674; 900/225-7778 TTY (calls are 55¢ per minute for automated service or $1.50 per minute for operator service); 888/362-8668; 888/498-3648 TTY (calls are $5.50 each) www.travel.state.gov.

SAFETY

Europe, and Great Britain in particular, has been plagued in recent years by what has now become an agricultural crisis. The first cases of bovine spongiform encephalopathy (BSE), commonly known as "mad cow disease," surfaced in Great Britain in the mid-1980s. BSE is a fatal degenerative disease contracted by cattle. When contaminated beef is eaten by humans, it can result in Creutzfeldt-Jakob Disease (CJD), an extremely rare brain-wasting illness fatal to humans.

Europe reacted swiftly to the threat, placing a ban on all beef exported from Great Britain for a short period and immediately banning all use of feed prepared with animal by-products. People are still wary, but at press time the risk of contracting the disease was considered extremely remote. The Centers for Disease Control and Prevention (www.cdc.gov) reported "The current risk for infection with the BSE agent among travelers to Europe is extremely small, if it exists at all." But, as always, stay informed.

In summer 2001, Great Britain, and to a much lesser extent France and the Netherlands, was affected by yet another crisis, foot-and-mouth disease. Foot-and-mouth disease affects animals almost exclusively; human cases are extremely rare, and the United Kingdom Ministry of Agriculture, Fisheries, and Food considers it harmless to humans. Nevertheless, it had a catastrophic effect on the British economy due to the fact that all animals suspected of being infected must be slaughtered immediately.

To limit the spread of foot-and-mouth disease, some hiking routes and coastal footpaths were closed, especially in north and southwestern England, and certain festivities were canceled. Some rural tourist attractions were also closed due to the crisis, though many have since reopened. Expect stringent border controls, with an enforced ban on carrying English dairy and farm products out of the territory, and you might have to disinfect your luggage and shoes before leaving the country. The British Tourist Authority Web site (www.travelbritain.org) will have the latest information on any safety issues, so check before you go.

WOMEN IN EUROPE

If you carry a purse, choose one with a zipper and a thick strap that you can drape across your body; adjust the length so that the purse sits in front of you at or above hip level. (Don't wear a money belt or a waist pack.) Store only enough money in the purse to cover casual spending. Distribute the rest of your cash and any valuables between deep front pockets, inside jacket or vest pockets, and a concealed money pouch.

SENIOR-CITIZEN TRAVEL

Radisson SAS Hotels in Europe offer discounts of 25% or more to senior citizens, subject to availability. You need a confirmed reservation.

To qualify for age-related discounts, **mention your senior-citizen status up front** when booking hotel reservations (not when checking out) and before you're seated in restaurants (not when paying the bill). Be sure to have identification on hand. When renting a car, ask about promotional car-rental discounts, which can be cheaper than senior-citizen rates. Train and bus passes are sometimes discounted for senior citizens as well.

Educational Programs **Elderhostel** ✉ 11 Ave. de Lafayette, Boston, MA 02111-1746 ☎ 877/426-8056; 978/323-4141 international callers; 877/426-2167 TTY 📠 877/426-2166 🌐 www.elderhostel.org. **Interhostel** ✉ University of New Hampshire, 6 Garrison Ave., Durham, NH 03824 ☎ 603/862-1147 or 800/733-9753 📠 603/862-1113 🌐 www.learn.unh.edu.

STUDENTS IN EUROPE

Students in Europe are entitled to a wide range of discounts on admission and transportation. An **International Student Identity Card,** issued by Council Travel (⇨ IDs & Services), will help you to procure these discounts. The globally recognized ISIC card is issued by local student travel organizations that are members of the International Student Travel Confederation, best found by consulting their Web site (🌐 www.istc.org).

Many U.S. colleges and universities have study-abroad programs or can connect you with one, and numerous institutions of higher learning in Europe accept foreign students for a semester or year's study. Check with your college administration or contact the CIEE for contacts and brochures.

If you're between 18 and 26, the Ibis hotel chain will let you have a room for $50 or less, provided you show up after 9 PM and they have a room free. You'll be asked for your student ID. Your chances are best on weekends. There are more than 400 Ibis hotels in Europe, most of them in France.

IDs & Services **STA Travel** ✉ 10 Downing St., New York, NY 10014 ☎ 212/627-3111 or 800/777-0112 📠 212/627-3387 🌐 www.sta.com. **Travel Cuts** ✉ 187 College St., Toronto, Ontario M5T 1P7, Canada ☎ 416/979-2406; 800/592-2887; 866/246-9762 in Canada 📠 416/979-8167 🌐 www.travelcuts.com.

TAXES

VALUE-ADDED TAX

Information about national tax-refund programs is given in the A to Z section at the beginning of each country chapter. When making a purchase, **ask for a V.A.T. refund form** and find out whether the merchant gives refunds—not all stores do, nor are they required to. Have the form stamped like any customs form by customs officials when you leave the country or, if you're visiting several European Union countries, when you leave the EU. Be ready to show customs officials what you've bought (pack purchases together, in your carry-on luggage); budget extra time for this. After you're through passport control, take the form to a refund-service counter for an on-the-spot refund, or mail it back to the store or a refund service after you arrive home.

A refund service can save you some hassle, for a fee. Global Refund is a Europe-wide service with 190,000 affiliated stores and more than 700 refund counters—located at every major airport and border crossing. Its refund form is called a Tax Free Check. The service issues refunds in the form of cash, check, or credit-card adjustment, minus a processing fee. If you don't have time to wait at the refund counter, you can mail in the form instead.

V.A.T. Refunds **Global Refund** ✉ 99 Main St., Suite 307, Nyack, NY 10960 ☎ 800/566-9828 📠 845/348-1549 🌐 www.globalrefund.com.

TELEPHONES

Telephone systems in Europe are in flux; expect new area codes and extra digits in numbers. Keep in mind that some countries now rely on phone cards; it's a good idea to buy one. Country codes appear in the A to Z section at the beginning of each country chapter. Cellular telephone companies unfortunately opted for different standards in the United States and Europe, so only the most sophisticated models with dual or triple band possibilities will function on both sides of the Atlantic. Functionality of both cell phones and pagers will also depend on the kind of subscription you have with your cell-phone company.

LONG-DISTANCE SERVICES

AT&T, MCI, and Sprint access codes make calling long distance relatively convenient, but you may find the local access number blocked in many hotel rooms. First ask the hotel operator to connect you. If the hotel operator balks, ask for an international operator, or dial the international operator yourself. One way to improve your odds of getting connected to your long-distance carrier is to travel with more than one company's calling card (a hotel may block Sprint, for example, but not MCI). If all else fails, call from a pay phone.

TIME

Most of continental Europe ticks at Central European Time (CET), one hour ahead of Greenwich Mean Time (GMT), which prevails in Great Britain, Ireland, Iceland, Portugal, and Madeira. Eastern European countries, including the Baltic States (Estonia, Latvia, and Lithuania), Romania, Bulgaria, Greece, and Turkey are two hours ahead of GMT. In most of mainland Europe clocks are turned back one hour during the night of the last Saturday/Sunday in March and put forward one hour on the last Saturday/Sunday night in October.

Europe uses the 24-hour (or "military") clock for everything from airplane departures to opening arias. After noon continue counting forward: 13:00 is 1 PM, 14:00 is 2 PM, etc.

TOURS & PACKAGES

Because everything is prearranged on a prepackaged tour or independent vacation, you spend less time planning—and often get it all at a good price.

BOOKING WITH AN AGENT

Travel agents are excellent resources. But it's a good idea to collect brochures from several agencies, as some agents' suggestions may be influenced by relationships with tour and package firms that reward them for volume sales. If you have a special interest, **find an agent with expertise in that area**; the American Society of Travel Agents (ASTA; ⇨ Travel Agencies) has a database of specialists worldwide.

Make sure your travel agent knows the accommodations and other services of the place being recommended. Ask about the hotel's location, room size, beds, and whether it has a pool, room service, or programs for children, if you care about these. Has your agent been there in person or sent others whom you can contact?

Do some homework on your own, too: local tourism boards can provide information about lesser-known and small-niche operators, some of which may sell only direct.

BUYER BEWARE

Each year consumers are stranded or lose their money when tour operators—even large ones with excellent reputations—go out of business. So **check out the operator.** Ask several travel agents about its reputation, and try to **book with a company that has a consumer-protection program.** (Look for information in the company's brochure.) In the United States, members of the National Tour Association and the United States Tour Operators Association are required to set aside funds to cover payments and travel arrangements in the event that the company defaults. It's also a good idea to choose a company that participates in the American Society of Travel Agents' Tour Operator Program; ASTA will act as mediator in any disputes between you and your tour operator.

Remember that the more your package or tour includes, the better you can predict the ultimate cost of your vacation. Make sure you know exactly what is covered, and **beware of hidden costs.** Are taxes, tips, and transfers included? Entertainment and excursions? These can add up.

Tour-Operator Recommendations **American Society of Travel Agents** (⇨ Travel Agencies). **National Tour Association** (NTA) ✉ 546 E. Main St., Lexington, KY 40508 ☎ 859/226-4444 or 800/682-8886 🖷 859/226-4404 🌐 www.ntaonline.com. **United States Tour Operators Association** (USTOA) ✉ 275 Madison Ave., Suite 2014, New York, NY 10016 ☎ 212/599-6599 or 800/468-7862 🖷 212/599-6744 🌐 www.ustoa.com.

TRAIN TRAVEL

Some national high-speed train systems have begun to link up to form the nucleus of a pan-European system. On a long journey, you still have to change trains a couple of times, for the national railways are jealously guarding their prerogatives. Deregulation, so far achieved only in Britain and the Netherlands, is vigorously pushed by the European Commission. French TGV (Trains à Grande Vitesse), which serve most major cities in France, have been extended to Geneva, Lausanne, Bern, Zürich, Turin, and Milan. They connect with the latest generation of Italy's tilting Pendolino trains, also called Eurostar Italia. Italy's service extends beyond the country's borders with a service from Turin to Lyon and, in a joint venture with the Swiss Railways, from Milan to Geneva and Zürich. Express Thalys trains operate from Brussels to Paris on high-speed tracks and from Brussels to Amsterdam and Cologne on conventional track. Germany's equally fast ICE trains connect Hamburg and points in between with Basel, and Mannheim with Munich.

High-speed trains travel at speeds of up to 190 mph on dedicated track and more than 150 mph on old track, covering the distance from Paris to Marseille in just over four hours, Hamburg to Munich in less than six. They have made both expensive sleeper compartments and budget *couchettes* (seats that convert into bunks) all but obsolete. Their other attraction is the comfort of a super-smooth ride. The flip side is the reservations requirement; rather than just hopping on the next train, you need to **reserve in advance or allow enough time to make a reservation at the station.**

The **Orient Express,** a glamorous re-creation of a sumptuous past, takes two days to cover the distance from London to Venice, and if you want to know the price, you can't afford it. The Swiss Railways operate special services that allow you to enjoy superb scenery and railway buffs to admire the equally superb railroad technology. The **Panoramic Express** takes 3 hours to travel from Montreux via Gstaad to Interlaken; the **Glacier Express** (7½ hours) runs from Zermatt to St. Moritz and also offers en route gourmet dining as befits these famous resorts; and the **Bernina Express,** the most spectacular, runs from Chur over the 7,400-foot Bernina Pass (where you can turn around; each leg takes 2½ hours), or you can continue to Tirano in Italy (four hours, with connections to Lugano and Milan). Holders of a Swisspass can travel on all three, but reservations are needed. For additional information on rail services and special fares, contact the national tourist office of the country (⇨ Visitor Information).

CLASSES

Virtually all European systems, including the high-speed ones, operate a two-class system. First class costs substantially more and is usually a luxury rather than a necessity. Some of the poorer European countries retain a third class, but avoid it unless you're an adventure-minded budget traveler.

CUTTING COSTS

To save money, **look into rail passes.** But be aware that if you don't plan to cover many miles you may come out ahead by buying individual tickets.

Before you invest in a discount pass, compare the cost against the point-to-point fares on your actual itinerary. EurailPasses provide unlimited first-class rail travel for the duration of the pass in 17 European countries: Austria, Belgium, Denmark, Finland, France, Germany, Greece, Hungary, the Irish Republic, Italy, Luxembourg, the Netherlands, Norway, Portugal, Spain, Sweden, and Switzerland (but not the United Kingdom). If you plan to rack up miles, get a standard pass. These are available for 15 days ($588, £380), 21 days ($762, £492), one month ($946, £610), two months ($1,338, £863), and three months ($1,654, £1,067). Note that you will have to pay a supplement for certain high-speed trains—half the fare on Eurostar.

In addition to standard EurailPasses, check out special rail-pass plans. Among these are the Eurail Youthpass (in second class for those under 26, from $414 [£267] to $1,160 [£748]), the Eurail Saverpass (which gives a discount for two to five people traveling together; a minimum of two people; from $498 [£321] to $1,408 [£908] per person), and the Eurail Flexipass (which allows 10 or 15 travel days within a two-month period, $694 [£448] and $914 [£590], respectively). This is also available at a youth rate. If you're going to travel in just one part of Europe, look into a regional pass, such as the East Europe Pass.

If your plans call for only limited train travel, consider Eurail Selectpass, which costs less money than a EurailPass and is available in first class only. It has a number of conditions. You can travel through three, four, or five countries, depending on the pass, but they must all be adjoining. You also get from 5 to 15 travel days during a two-month time period, which can be used consecutively or nonconsecutively. The other side of the coin is that a Europass costs a couple of hundred dollars less than the least expensive EurailPass. A Eurail Selectpass ranges in price from \$356 (£230) to \$794 (£512), a Eurail Selectpass Youth from \$379 (£245) to \$437 (£282). Also, if you are traveling with a total of two or more people you can buy the Eurail Select Saver pass, which ranges from \$460 (£297) to \$530 (£342).

It used to be the rule that non-Europeans had to **purchase Eurail passes before leaving** for Europe. This remains the recommended option, but you can now buy a pass in person within six months of your arrival in Europe from Rail Europe (⇨ Train Information) in London. Also remember that you need to **book seats ahead even if you are using a rail pass**; seat reservations are required on the cross-channel Eurostar service and European high-speed trains, and are a good idea on other trains that may be crowded—particularly around Easter and at the beginning and end of European vacation periods. You will also need to purchase sleeper or couchette (sleeping berth) reservations separately.

European nationals and others who have resided in Europe for at least six months qualify for the **InterRail Pass.** It used to be exclusively for young people but can now also be purchased, at a premium, by older travelers. This entitles you to unlimited second-class travel within up to eight zones you have preselected. One zone for 22 days, for instance, costs £149 for travelers under 26 (£219 for over 26); all zones for one month, £265 (£319). InterRail Passes can be bought only in Europe at main railway stations, or in the United Kingdom from Rail Europe in London (⇨ Train Information).

FROM THE U.K.

Sleek, high-speed Eurostar trains use the Channel Tunnel to link London (Waterloo) with Paris (Gare du Nord) in three hours and with Brussels (Gare du Midi) in 2 hours, 40 minutes. When the British build their high-speed rail link to London (St. Pancras), another half hour will be shaved off travel time. There are a minimum of 14 daily services to Paris and 10 to Brussels.

Many of the trains stop at Ashford (Kent), and all at the Lille-Europe station in northern France, where you can change to French TGV trains to Brittany, southwest France, Lyon, the Alps, and the Riviera, eliminating the need to transfer between stations in Paris.

Passengers headed for Germany and the Netherlands can buy through tickets via Brussels to Cologne (5½ hours) and Amsterdam (5 hours, 45 minutes). Eurostar does not accept EurailPasses but allows discounts of 40%–50% to passholders. Check for special prices and deals before you book. Or, if money is no object, you can choose the Premium First Class (to Paris only), complete with limo delivery and pick-up at the stations, improved catering, and greater comfort.

Conventional boat trains from London are timed to dovetail with ferry departures at Channel ports. The ferries connect with onward trains at the main French, Belgian, Dutch, and Irish ports. Be sure to ask when making your reservation which London railway station to use.

INDIVIDUAL COUNTRY PASSES

Single-country passes are issued by most national railways, and the majority are sold by Rail Europe (⇨ Train Information *and* individual country chapters). Almost all countries have national passes or passes that include a couple of other countries; the France N'Italy pass, for example, can save you money if you plan to travel by rail often. Also ask about discount passes before buying your tickets, as many countries have weekend rates, and some offer lower rates if you're traveling in groups.

FARES & SCHEDULES

A good rail timetable is indispensable if you're doing extensive rail traveling. The Thomas Cook Timetables are updated monthly. There's also an annual summer edition (limited to Britain, France, and the Benelux).

Train Information CIT Tours Corp. ✉ 15 W. 44th St., 10th fl., New York, NY 10036 ☎ 800/248-7245 for rail; 800/248-8687 for tours and hotels ✉ rail@cit-rail.com for rail; tour@cittours.com for tours and hotels, 🌐 www.cit-tours.com. **DER Travel Services** (⇨ Discount Passes, Eurolines, *in* Bus Travel). **Eurostar** ☎ 800/356-6711; 202/659-2973 in U.S.; 0345/303030 in U.K.; 0123/361-7575 to the U.K. from other countries 🌐 www.eurostar.com. **Rail Europe** ✉ 226-230 Westchester Ave., White Plains, NY 10604 ☎ 877/257-2887 📠 800/432-1329 ✉ info@raileurope.com 🌐 www.raileurope.com ✉ 2087 Dundas E, Suite 105, Mississauga, Ontario L4X 1M2 Canada ☎ 800/361-7245 ✉ 179 Piccadilly, and Victoria Station, London W1V 8BA U.K. ☎ 0990/848-848 in U.K.; 020/7647-4900 to the U.K. from other countries. **Venice Simplon-Orient Express** ✉ Sea Containers House, 20 Upper Ground, London SE1 9PF ☎ 800/524-2420 in U.S.; 020/7805-5100 in U.K.; 0870/161-5060 brochures 🌐 www.orient-express.com.

TRAVEL AGENCIES

A good travel agent puts your needs first. Look for an agency that has been in business at least five years, emphasizes customer service, and has someone on staff who specializes in your destination. In addition, **make sure the agency belongs to a professional trade organization.** The American Society of Travel Agents (ASTA)—the largest and most influential in the field with more than 20,000 members in some 140 countries—maintains and enforces a strict code of ethics and will step in to help mediate any agent-client disputes involving ASTA members if necessary. ASTA (whose motto is "Without a travel agent, you're on your own") also maintains a Web site that includes a directory of agents. (If a travel agency is also acting as your tour operator, *see* Buyer Beware *in* Tours & Packages.)

Local Agent Referrals **American Society of Travel Agents** (ASTA) ✉ 1101 King St., Suite 200, Alexandria, VA 22314 ☎ 703/739-2782; 800/965-2782 24-hr hot line 📠 703/739-3268 🌐 www.astanet.com. **Association of British Travel Agents** ✉ 68-71 Newman St., London W1T 3AH ☎ 020/7637-2444 📠 020/7637-0713 🌐 www.abtanet.com. **Association of Canadian Travel Agents** ✉ 130 Albert St., Suite 1705, Ottawa, Ontario K1P 5G4 ☎ 613/237-3657 📠 613/237-7052 🌐 www.acta.ca. **Australian Federation of Travel Agents** ✉ Level 3, 309 Pitt St., Sydney, NSW 2000 ☎ 02/9264-3299 📠 02/9264-1085 🌐 www.afta.com.au. **Travel Agents' Association of New Zealand** ✉ Level 5, Tourism and Travel House, 79 Boulcott St., Box 1888, Wellington 6001 ☎ 04/499-0104 📠 04/499-0786 🌐 www.taanz.org.nz.

VISITOR INFORMATION

Learn more about foreign destinations by checking government-issued travel advisories and country information. For a broader picture, consider information from more than one country.

Austrian National Tourist Office **U.S.** ✉ 500 5th Ave, #800, New York, NY 10110 ☎ 212/944-6880 📠 212/730-4568 🌐 www.austria-tourism.at. **Canada** ✉ 2 Bloor St. E, Suite 3330, Toronto, Ontario M4W 1A8 ☎ 416/967-3381 📠 416/967-4101. **U.K.** ✉ 14 Cork St., London, W1X 1PF ☎ 020/7629-0461 📠 020/7499-6038. **Australia and New Zealand** ✉ 36 Carrington St., 1st fl., Sydney, NSW 2000 ☎ 02/9299-3621 📠 02/9299-3808. **Ireland** ✉ Merrion Center, Nutley La., Dublin 4 ☎ 01/283-0488 📠 01/283-0531.

Belgian National Tourist Office **U.S.** ✉ 780 3rd Ave., Suite 1501, New York, NY 10017 ☎ 212/758-8130 📠 212/355-7675 🌐 www.visitbelgium.com. **Canada** ✉ Box 760, Station NDG, Montréal, Québec H4A 3S2 ☎ 514/484-3594 📠 514/489-8965. **U.K.** ✉ 29 Princess St., London W1R 7RG ☎ 0891/887799 📠 0171/629-0454.

British Tourist Authority **U.S.** ✉ 551 5th Ave., Suite 701, New York, NY 10176 ☎ 212/986-2200 or 800/462-2748 📠 212/986-1188; 818/441-8265 24-hour fax information line 🌐 www.visitbritain.com ✉ walk-in service only, 625 N. Michigan Ave., Suite 1510, Chicago, IL 60611. **Canada** ✉ 5915 Airport Rd., Suite 120, Mississauga, Ontario L4V 1T1 ☎ 905/405-1720 or 888/847-4885 📠 905/405-1835. **U.K.** ✉ Britain Visitors Centre, 1 Regent St., London SW1Y 4XT ☎ 020/7808-3864; 0891/600-109 for 24-hour brochure line, costs 60p per minute ✉ Thames Tower, Black's Rd., London, W6 9EL ☎ No phone. **Australia** ✉ Level 16, Gateway, 1 Macquarie Pl., Sydney, NSW 2000 ☎ 02/9377-4400 📠 02/9377-4499. **New Zealand** ✉ Level 17, NZI House, 151 Queen St., Auckland 1 ☎ 09/303-1446 📠 09/377-6965. **Ireland** ✉ 18-19 College Green, Dublin 2 ☎ 01/670-8000 📠 01/670-8244.

Bulgaria **U.S. and Canada** Balkan Tourist USA, authorized agent, ✉ 20 E. 46th St., Suite 1003, New York, NY 10017 ☎ 212/338-6838 or 800/822-1106 📠 212/822-5910. **U.K.** Balkan Tourist U.K., ✉ 111 Bartholomew Rd., London NW2 BJ ☎ 0500/245165 for 24-hour brochure line ✉ Balkan Holidays, 19 Conduit St., Sofia House, London W1S 2BH ☎ 020/7491-4499 📠 020/7543-5577.

Cyprus Tourist Office **U.S. and Canada** ✉ 13 E. 40th St., New York, NY 10016 ☎ 212/683-5280 📠 212/683-5282 🌐 www.cyprustourism.org. **U.K.**

✉ 17 Hanover St., London W1R 0H8 ☎ 020/7569-8800 📠 020/7499-4935 ✉ Turkish Republic of Northern Cyprus Tourist Office, 29 Bedford Sq., London WC1B 3EG ☎ 020/7631-1920 📠 020/7631-1948.

Czech Center **U.S. and Canada** ✉ 1109 Madison Ave., New York, NY 10028 ☎ 212/288-0830 📠 212/288-0971 🌐 www.czechcenter.com. **Canada** Czech Tourist Authority, ✉ c/o Czech Airlines, 401 Bay St., Suite 1510, Toronto, Ontario M5H 2Y4 ☎ 416/363-9928 📠 416/363-0239. **U.K.** ✉ 26-30 Kensington Palace Gardens, London W8 4QY ☎ 020/7243-1115 📠 020/7727-9654 ✉ Czech and Slovak Tourist Centre, 16 Frognal Parade, Finchley Rd., London NW3 5HG ☎ 020/7794-3263 📠 020/7794-3265.

Danish Tourist Board **U.S. and Canada** ✉ 655 3rd Ave., 18th fl., New York, NY 10017 ☎ 212/885-9700 📠 212/885-9726 🌐 www.dt.dk. **U.K.** ✉ 55 Sloane St., London SW1X 9SY ☎ 020/7259-5959; 0900/160-0109 for 24-hour brochure line, costs 60p per minute 📠 020/7259-5955.

Estonian Tourist Office **U.S.** Consulate, ✉ 600 3rd Ave., 26th fl., New York, NY 10016 ☎ 212/883-0636 📠 212/883-0648 🌐 www.tourism.ee. **Canada** Consulate, ✉ 958 Broadview Ave., Suite 202, Toronto, Ontario M4K 2R6 ☎ 416/461-0764 📠 416/461-0353. **U.K.** Embassy, ✉ 16 Hyde Park Gate, London, SW7 5DG ☎ 020/7589-3428 📠 020/7589-3430. **Australia** Consulate, ✉ 86 Louisa Rd., Birchgrove, NSW 2041 ☎ 02/9810-7468 📠 02/9818-1779.

Finnish Tourist Board **U.S. and Canada** ✉ 655 3rd Ave., 18th fl., New York, NY 10017 ☎ 212/885-9700 📠 212/885-9710 🌐 www.mek.fi. **U.K.** ✉ 66 Haymarket, London SW1Y 4RF ☎ 020/7930-5871 📠 020/7321-0696. **Australia** ✉ c/o Finnesse Communications, Level 4, 81 York St., Sydney, NSW 2000 ☎ 02/9290-1980 📠 02/9290-1981.

French Government Tourist Office **U.S.** ✉ 444 Madison Ave., 16th fl., New York, NY 10022 ☎ 212/838-7800 📠 212/838-7855 🌐 www.francetourism.com ✉ 676 N. Michigan Ave., Suite 3360 Chicago, IL 60611 ☎ 312/751-7800 ✉ 9454 Wilshire Blvd., Suite 715, Beverly Hills, CA 90212 ☎ 310/271-6665 📠 310/276-2835. **Canada** ✉ 1981 Ave. McGill College, Suite 490, Montréal, Québec H3A 2W9 ☎ 514/288-4264 📠 514/845-4868. **U.K.** ✉ 178 Piccadilly, London W1J 9AL ☎ 068/244123, 60p per minute 📠 020/7493-6594. **Australia** ✉ 10 Suffolk St., Sydney, NSW 2000 ☎ 02/9231-5244 📠 02/9221-8682. **Ireland** ✉ 10 Suffolk St., Dublin 1 ☎ 01/679-0813 📠 01/874-7324.

German National Tourist Office **U.S.** ✉ 122 E. 42nd St., 52nd fl., New York, NY 10168 ☎ 212/661-7200 📠 212/661-7174 🌐 www.deutschland-tourismus.de ✉ Box 59594, Chicago, IL 60659 ☎ 773/539-6303 📠 773/539-6378. **Canada** ✉ Box 65162, Toronto, Ontario M4K 3Z2 ☎ 416/968-1570 📠 416/968-1986. **U.K.** ✉ Box 2695, London W1A 3TN ☎ 020/7317-0908; 0891/600-100 for brochures, 50p per minute 📠 020/7495-6129. **Australia** ✉ GPO Box 1461, Sydney, NSW 2001 ☎ 02/8296-0488 📠 02/8296-0487.

Gibraltar Information Bureau **U.S. and Canada** ✉ 1155 15th St. NW, Washington, DC 20005 ☎ 202/452-1108 📠 202/452-1109 🌐 www.gibraltar.gi. **U.K.** Gibraltar Tourist Board, ✉ Arundel Great Court, 179 The Strand, London WC2R 1EH ☎ 020/7836-0777 📠 020/7240-6612.

Greek National Tourist Organization **U.S.** ✉ 645 5th Ave., New York, NY 10022 ☎ 212/421-5777 📠 212/826-6940 🌐 www.gnto.gr. **Canada** ✉ 91 Scollard St., 2nd fl., Toronto, Ontario M5R IG4 ☎ 416/968-2220 📠 416/968-6533. **U.K.** ✉ 4 Conduit St., London W1R 0DJ ☎ 020/7734-5997 📠 020/7287-1369. **Australia** ✉ 51-57 Pitt St., Sydney, NSW 2000 ☎ 02/9241-1663 📠 02/9235-2174.

Hungarian National Tourist Office **U.S. and Canada** ✉ 150 E. 58th St., 33rd fl., New York, NY 10155 ☎ 212/355-0240 📠 212/207-4103 🌐 www.hungarytourism.hu. **U.K.** ✉ Embassy of the Republic of Hungary, Commercial Section, 35B Eaton Pl., London SW1X 8BY ☎ 020/7235-2664 📠 020/7235-8630.

Iceland Tourist Board **U.S. and Canada** ✉ Scandinavia Tourism Inc., 655 3rd Ave., New York, NY 10017 ☎ 212/885-9700 📠 212/885-9710 🌐 www.goscandinavia.com. **U.K.** ✉ 1 Eaton Terr., London SW1W 8EY ☎ 0170/590-1100; 020/7874-1000 for IcelandAir.

Irish Tourist Board **U.S.** ✉ 345 Park Ave., New York, NY 10154 ☎ 212/418-0800 or 800/223-6470 📠 212/371-9052 🌐 www.ireland.travel.ie. **Canada** ✉ 2 Bloor St. E, Suite 1501, Toronto, Ontario M4W 3E2 ☎ 800/223-6470. **U.K.** ✉ Ireland Desk, British Visitor Centre 1 Regent St., London SW1Y 4XT ☎ 020/7493-3201 📠 020/7493-9065. **Australia** ✉ 36 Carrington St., 5th fl., Sydney, NSW 2000 ☎ 02/9299-6177 📠 02/9299-6323. **Ireland** ✉ Bishops Square, Redmonds Hill, Dublin 2 ☎ 01/476-3400.

Italian Government Travel Office (ENIT) **U.S.** ✉ 630 5th Ave., Suite 1565, New York, NY 10111 ☎ 212/245-4822 📠 212/586-9249 🌐 www.italiantourism.com ✉ 500 N. Michigan Ave., Suite 2240, Chicago, IL 60611 ☎ 312/644-0996 📠 312/644-3019 ✉ 12400 Wilshire Blvd., Suite 550, Los Angeles, CA 90025 ☎ 310/820-1898 📠 310/820-6357. **Canada** ✉ 175 Bloor St. E, Suite 907 South Tower, Toronto, Ontario H4W 3R8 ☎ 416/925-4882 📠 416/925-4799. **U.K.** ✉ Italian State Tourist Board, 1 Princess St., London W1B 2AY ☎ 020/7399-3562. **Australia** ✉ c/o Italian Chamber of Commerce, Level 26, 44 Market St., Sydney, NSW 2000 ☎ 02/9262-1666 📠 02/9262-1677.

Lithuanian Tourist Board **U.S.** Lithuanian Tourist Information Center, ✉ 40-24 235th St., Douglaston, NY 11363 ☎ 718/423-6161 📠 718/423-3979 www.tourism.lt. **Canada** Embassy, ✉ 130 Albert St., Suite 204, Ottawa, Ontario K1P 5G4 ☎ 613/567-5458 📠 613/567-5315. **U.K.** Embassy, ✉ 84 Gloucester Pl., London W1U 6AU ☎ 020/7486-6401 📠 020/7468-6403.

Luxembourg National Tourist Office U.S. and Canada ✉ 17 Beekman Pl., New York, NY 10022 ☎ 212/935-8888 📠 212/935-5896 www.ont.lu. **U.K.** ✉ 122 Regent St., London W1B 5SA ☎ 020/7434-2800 📠 020/7734-1205.

Monaco Government Tourist Office & Convention Bureau U.S. and Canada ✉ 565 5th Ave., New York, NY 10017 ☎ 212/286-3330 📠 212/286-9890 www.monaco-tourism.com. **U.K.** ✉ The Chambers, Chelsea Harbour, London SW10 0XF ☎ 020/7352-9962 or 0500/006-114 📠 020/7352-2103.

Netherlands Board of Tourism U.S. ✉ 225 N. Michigan Ave., Suite 1854, Chicago, IL 60601 ☎ 312/819-1500 or 888/464-6552 📠 312/819-1740 www.holland.com. **Canada** ✉ Adelaide St. E, Box 1078, Toronto, Ontario M5C 2K5 ☎ 888/464-6552 in English; 888/729-7227 in French 📠 416/363-1470. **U.K.** ✉ Box 523, London SW1E 6NT ☎ 020/7539-7950; 0906/871-7777 for 24-hour brochure line, costs 60p per minute 📠 020/7828-7941.

Norwegian Tourist Board U.S. and Canada ✉ 655 3rd Ave., Suite 1810, New York, NY 10017 ☎ 212/885-9700 📠 212/885-9710 www.goscandinavia.com. **U.K.** ✉ Charles House, 5 Lower Regent St., London SW1Y 4LR ☎ 020/7839-6255 📠 020/7839-6014.

Polish National Tourist Office U.S. and Canada ✉ 275 Madison Ave., Suite 1711, New York, NY 10016 ☎ 212/338-9412 📠 212/338-9283 www.polandtour.org. **U.K.** ✉ Remo House, 1st fl., 310-312 Regent St., London W1R 5AJ ☎ 020/7580-8811 📠 020/7580-8866.

Portuguese National Tourist Office U.S. ✉ 590 5th Ave., 3rd fl., New York, NY 10036 ☎ 212/354-4610 📠 212/575-4737 www.portugal.org. **Canada** ✉ 60 Bloor St. W, Suite 1005, Toronto, Ontario M4W 3B8 ☎ 416/921-7376 📠 416/921-1353. **Ireland** ✉ 54 Dawson St., Dublin 2 ☎ 01/670-9133 📠 01/670-9141. **U.K.** ✉ 2nd fl., 22-25A Sackville St., London W1S 3LY ☎ 020/7494-5720; 0900/160-0370 24-hour brochure line, costs 65p per minute 📠 020/7494-1868.

Romanian National Tourist Office U.S. and Canada ✉ 14 E. 38th St., 12th fl., New York, NY 10016 ☎ 212/545-8484 📠 212/251-0429. **U.K.** ✉ 22 New Cavendish St., London W1M 74T ☎ 020/7224-3692 📠 020/7935-6435.

Slovak Tourist Office U.S. and Canada Embassy, ✉ 3523 International Ct., NW, Washington, DC 20008 ☎ 202/237-1054 📠 202/237-6438 www.sacr.sk. **U.K.** Czech and Slovak Tourist Center, ✉ 16 Frognal Parade, Finchley Rd., London NW3 5HG ☎ 020/7794-3263 📠 020/7794-3265.

Slovenian Tourist Office U.S. ✉ 345 E. 12th St., New York, NY 10003 ☎ 212/358-9686 📠 212/358-9025 www.slovenia-tourism.si. **U.K.** ✉ New Barn Farm, Tadlow, Royston, Herts 5G8 0EP ☎ 0870/225-5305 📠 0176/763-1166.

Tourist Office of Spain U.S. ✉ 666 5th Ave., 35th fl., New York, NY 10103 ☎ 212/265-8822 📠 212/265-8864 www.okspain.org ✉ 845 N. Michigan Ave., Suite 915 E, Chicago, IL 60611 ☎ 312/642-1992 📠 312/642-9817 ✉ 8383 Wilshire Blvd., Suite 956, Los Angeles, CA 90211 ☎ 323/658-7188 📠 323/658-1061 ✉ 1221 Brickell Ave., Suite 1850, Miami, FL 33131 ☎ 305/358-1992 📠 305/358-8223. **Canada** ✉ 2 Bloor St. W, Suite 3402, Toronto, Ontario M4W 3E2 ☎ 416/961-3131 📠 416/961-1992. **U.K.** ✉ 22-23 Manchester Sq., London W1M 5AP ☎ 020/7486-8077; 0891/669920 24-hour brochure line, costs 60p per minute 📠 020/7486-8034.

Swedish Travel & Tourism Council U.S. and Canada Box 4649, Grand Central Station, New York, NY 10163-4649 ☎ 212/885-9700 📠 212/885-9764. **U.K.** ✉ 11 Montagu Pl., London W1H 2AL ☎ 0147/657-8811 24-hour brochure line 📠 020/7724-5872.

Switzerland Tourism U.S. ✉ 608 5th Ave., New York, NY 10020 ☎ 877/794-8037 📠 212/262-6116 www.switzerlandtourism.ch ✉ 501 Santa Monica Blvd., Suite 607, Santa Monica, CA 90401 ☎ 310/260-2421 📠 310/260-2923. **Canada** ✉ 926 The East Mall, Etobicoke (Toronto), Ontario M9B 6KI ☎ International toll-free 800/1002-0030 📠 416/695-2774. **U.K.** ✉ Swiss Centre, 1 New Coventry St., London W1V 8EE ☎ 020/7734-1921 📠 020/7851-1720. **Australia** ✉ Swissair Building, 33 Pitt St., Level 8, Sydney, NSW 2000 ☎ 02/9231-3744 📠 02/9251-6531.

Turkish Tourist Office U.S. ✉ 821 UN Plaza, New York, NY 10017 ☎ 212/687-2194 📠 212/599-7568 www.turkey.org ✉ 2525 Massachusetts Ave. NW, Washington, DC 20008 ☎ 202/429-9844 📠 202/429-5649. **Canada** ✉ 360 Albert St., Suite 801, Ottawa, Ontario K1R 7X7 ☎ 613/612-6800 📠 613/319-7446. **U.K.** ✉ Egyptian House, 170-173 Piccadilly, London W1V 9DD ☎ 020/7355-4207; 0900/188-7755, 24-hour brochure line, costs 65p per minute 📠 020/7491-0773.

U.S. Government Advisories U.S. Department of State ✉ Public Communication Division, PA/PL Room 2206, U.S. Department of State, 2201 C St. NW, Washington, DC 20520 ☎ 202/647-5225 for interactive hot line http://travel.state.gov; enclose a self-addressed, stamped, business-size envelope.

WEB SITES

Do check out the World Wide Web when planning your trip. You'll find everything from weather forecasts to virtual tours of famous cities. Be sure to **visit Fodors.com**

(🌐 www.fodors.com), a complete travel-planning site. You can research prices and book plane tickets, hotel rooms, rental cars, vacation packages, and more. In addition, you can post your pressing questions in the Travel Talk section. Other planning tools include a currency converter and weather reports, and there are loads of links to travel resources.

Also check out the European Travel Commission's site, 🌐 www.visiteurope.com.

WHEN TO GO

For information about travel seasons and for the average daily maximum and minimum temperatures of the major European cities, *see* the A to Z section *in* each country chapter.

Forecasts **Weather Channel Connection** ☎ 900/932-8437, 95¢ per minute from a Touch-Tone phone 🌐 www.weather.com.

AMSTERDAM

1

Amsterdam has as many facets as a 40-carat diamond polished by one of the city's gem cutters: a font for artistic geniuses such as Rembrandt and van Gogh; a cornucopia bursting with parrot tulips; and a social scene that takes in cozy bars, brown cafés, and outdoor markets. While impressive gabled houses bear witness to the golden age of the 17th century, their upside-down reflections in the city's canal waters below symbolize the contradictions within broader Dutch society. With a mere 730,000 friendly souls and with almost everything a scant 10-minute bike ride away, Amsterdam is actually more of a village—albeit a largish global one—that packs the cultural wallop of a megalopolis.

EXPLORING AMSTERDAM

The old heart of the city consists of canals, with narrow streets radiating out like the spokes of a wheel. The hub of this wheel and the most convenient point to begin sightseeing is Centraal Station (Central Station). Across the street, in the same building as the Old Dutch Coffee House, is a tourist information office. The Rokin, once an open canal, is the main route from Central Station via the Dam to the Muntplein. Amsterdam's key points of interest can be covered within two or three days, including visits to one or two of the important museums and galleries. Small and densely packed, the city center is divided into districts that are easily covered on foot.

Around the Dam

The Dam (Dam Square) is the official center of town. It traces its roots to the 12th century, when wanderers from central Europe floated their canoes down the Amstel River and stopped to build a dam. Soon this muddy mound became the focal point of the small city of Amstelledamme and the location of the local weigh house. From these inauspicious beginnings, by the 17th century Amsterdam had developed into one of the richest and most powerful cities in the world.

Numbers in the margin correspond to points of interest on the Amsterdam map.

14 **Anne Frankhuis** (Anne Frank House). Immortalized by the poignant diary kept by the young Jewish girl from 1942 to 1944, when she and her family hid here from the German occupying forces, this canal-side house also has an educational exhibition and documents about the Holocaust and civil liberty. Consider visiting during summer evenings to avoid the crowds. ✉ *Prinsengracht 267* ☎ *020/556–7100* 🌐 *www.annefrank.nl* ⊙ *Apr. and June–Aug., daily 9–9; May, daily 9–7; Sept.–Mar., daily 9–7* ⊙ *Closed Yom Kippur.*

Fodor's Choice ★

10 **Beurs van Berlage** (Berlage's Stock Exchange). This impressive building, completed in 1903, was designed by Hendrik Petrus Berlage, whose aesthetic principles were to guide modernism. The sculpture and rich decoration of the plain brick interior are among modernism's embryonic masterpieces. It now houses two concert halls, a large exhibition space, and its own museum, which offers the chance to climb the 138-foot-high tower for its superb views. ✉ *Damrak 277* ☎ *020/530–4141* 🌐 *www.beursvanberlage.nl* ⊙ *Museum Tues.–Sun. 11–5.*

1 **Centraal Station** (Central Station). The flamboyant redbrick and stone portal was designed by P. J. H. Cuijpers and built in 1884–89. Cuijpers's other significant contribution to Amsterdam's architectural heritage is the Rijksmuseum. ✉ *Stationsplein.*

11 **Dam** (Dam Square). This is the broadest square in the old section of the town. Fishermen used to come here to sell their catch. Today it is a busy crossroads, circled with shops and bisected by traffic; it is also a popular spot for outdoor performers. At one side of the square stands a simple monument to Dutch victims of World War II. Eleven urns contain soil from the 11 provinces of the Netherlands, and a 12th contains soil from the former Dutch East Indies, now Indonesia. ✉ *Junction of Rokin, Damrak, Moses en Aaronstraat, and Paleisstraat.*

6 **De Waag** (The Weigh House). Dating from 1488, when it was built as a city gate, this turreted, redbrick monument dominates the Nieuwmarkt (New Market) in the oldest part of Amsterdam. It became a weigh house and was once the headquarters for ancient professional guilds. The magnificently restored **Theatrum Anatomicum,** up the winding stairs, was added in 1691 and set the scene for Rembrandt's painting the *Anatomy Lesson of Dr. Tulp*. The upper floors are now home to the media lab of the Society for Old and New Media, which hosts occasional conferences and exhibitions. Downstairs is a grand café and restaurant. ✉ *Nieuwmarkt 4* ☎ *020/557–9898* 🌐 *www.waag.org.*

13 **Het Koninklijk Paleis te Amsterdam** (Royal Palace in Amsterdam). The vast, well-proportioned classical structure dominating the Dam was completed in 1655. It is built on 13,659 pilings sunk into the marshy soil. The great pediment sculptures are an allegorical representation of Amsterdam surrounded by Neptune and mythological sea creatures. Filled with opulent 18th- and early 19th-century furnishings, it is the official royal residence but is used only on high state occasions. ✉ *Dam* ☎ *020/624–8698* 🌐 *www.koninklijkhuis.nl* ⊙ *July and Aug., daily 12:30–5; May, June, Sept., and Oct., irregular Tues.–Thurs. 1–4. Call for detailed annual schedule. Closed for state events.*

9 **Museum Amstelkring.** The facade carries the inscription "*Ons Lieve Heer Op Solder*" ("Our Lord in the Attic"). In 1578 Amsterdam embraced Protestantism and outlawed the church of Rome. The municipal authorities were so tolerant that secret Catholic chapels were allowed to exist; at one time there were 62 in Amsterdam alone. One such chapel

was established in these three buildings—one canal-side house with two adjoining houses in the alley—built around 1661. Services were held in the attics regularly until 1888, the year the St. Nicolaaskerk was consecrated for Catholic worship. Of interest are the baroque altar with its revolving tabernacle, the swinging pulpit that can be stowed out of sight, and the upstairs gallery with its displays of religious artifacts. The authentic 17th-century merchant's living quarters are extremely rare. ✉ *Oudezijds Voorburgwal 40* ☎ *020/624–6604* 🌐 *www.museumamstelkring.nl* ⏲ *Mon.–Sat. 10–5, Sun. and holidays 1–5.*

5 **Nederlands Scheepvaartmuseum** (Netherlands Maritime Museum). This former naval warehouse maintains a collection of restored vessels and a replica of a three-masted trading ship from 1749. The museum explains the history of Dutch shipping, from dugout canoes right through to modern container ships, with maps, paintings, and models. ✉ *Kattenburgerplein 1* ☎ *020/523–2222* 🌐 *www.scheepvaartmuseum.nl* ⏲ *Mid-June–mid-Sept., daily 10–5; mid-Sept.–mid-June* ⏲ *Closed Mon.*

3 **NEMO Science & Technology Center.** Renzo Piano, architect of the Centre Pompidou in Paris, designed this interactive museum. Hands-on exhibits cover topics from elementary physics to the latest technological gadgets. The rooftop terrace offers a panoramic view across the city. ✉ *Oosterdok 2* ☎ *0900/919–1100, €0.35 per min* 🌐 *www.e-nemo.nl* ⏲ *Tues.–Sun. 10–5.*

12 **Nieuwe Kerk** (New Church). This huge Gothic structure was gradually expanded until 1540, when it reached its present size. Gutted by fire in 1645, it was reconstructed in an imposing Renaissance style, as interpreted by strict Calvinists. The superb oak pulpit, the 14th-century nave, the stained-glass windows, and the great organ are all noteworthy. As befits the Netherlands' national church, it is the site of all coronations and the 2001 royal wedding between Prince Willem Alexander and Princess Maxima. In democratic Dutch spirit, the church is also used as a meeting place, has a lively café, and hosts temporary exhibitions and concerts. ✉ *Dam* ☎ *020/638–6909* 🌐 *www.nieuwekerk.nl* ⏲ *Mon.–Wed. and Fri.–Sun. 10–6; Thurs. 10–10.*

8 **Oude Kerk** (Old Church). The city's oldest house of worship dates from the early 14th century, but it was badly damaged by iconoclasts after the Reformation. The church still retains its original bell tower and a few remarkable stained-glass windows. Rembrandt's wife, Saskia, is buried here. ✉ *Oudekerksplein 23* ☎ *020/625–8284* 🌐 *www.oudekerk.nl* ⏲ *Mon.–Sat. 11–5, Sun. 1–5.*

7 **Rosse Buurt** (Red-Light District). This area is defined by two of the city's oldest canals. In the windows at canal level, women in sheer lingerie slouch, stare, or do their nails. The area can be shocking, but is generally safe, although midnight walks down dark side streets are not advised. If you do explore the area, watch for purse snatchers and pickpockets. ✉ *Bordered by Oudezijds Voorburgwal and Oudezijds Achterburgwal.*

4 **Scheepvaartshuis** (Shipping Offices). Designed by J. M. der Mey and the Van Gendt brothers in the early 1910s, this office building is the earliest example of the Amsterdam School's unique building style. The fantastical facade is richly decorated in brick and stone, with lead and zinc roofing pouring from on high. ✉ *Prins Hendrikkade 108–119.*

2 **Schreierstoren.** This lookout tower was erected on the harbor in 1486 as the endpoint of the city wall. The term *schreiren* suggests the Dutch word for "wailing," and hence the folklore arose that this Weeping Tower was where women came to cry when their sailor husbands left for sea. The word *schreier* actually comes from the Old Dutch word for "sharp

Amsterdam
Westerstraat
Prinsenstr.
Herenstr.
Tuinstraat
Egelantiers
straat
gracht
Egelantiers
Nieuwe Lelie straat
Prinsengracht
Keizersgracht
Leliegracht
Herengracht
Singel
Spuistr.
Frederik Hendrikstraat
Van Oldenb. Straat
Nassau Kade
Singelgracht
Marnix Kade
Lijnbaansgracht
Hugo de Grootstr.
Bloem
gracht
Bloemstraat
Westermarkt
Raadhuisstraat
Damrak
Dam
Rozengracht
Rozenstraat
Laurierstraat
Lauriers
gracht
Reestraat
Hartenstraat
De Clercqstraat
Nassau
Marnix Straat
Lijnbaans
Singel gracht
Kade
Elandsstraat
Elandsgracht
Berenstraat
Wolvenstraat
Nieuwe zijds Voorburg wal
Kalverstraat
Rokin
Nes
Da Costastraat
Da Costa
gracht
Kinkerstraat
Runstraat
Huidenstraat
Spui
Looiersgracht
gracht
J. van Lennepstraat
J. van Lennep Kanaal
Singel
Reguliersdwarsstraat
Leidse
Lange
Leidsestraat
Leidsedwarsstraat
Kerkstraat
Heren
Keizersgracht
Vijzelstraat
Constantijn Huygensstraat
Helmersstraat
Overtoom
Stadhouderskade
Nieuwe Spiegelstr.
Vondelstraat
Lijnbaans
Wetering
dwarstr.
Prinsengracht
Noorderstr.
gracht
Singel
Weteringschans
Nieuwe Looiersstr.
Vijzelgracht
Vossiusstraat
Hobbemastr.
Pieter Cornelisz Hooftstraat
Honthorststr.
Jan Luykenstraat
Vondelpark
Van Baerle Str.
Paulus Potterstr.
Museumplein
Vermeerstraat
Hobbema Kade
Boeren - Wetering
Ruysdael Kade
Halsstr.
F. Bol Straat
Wetering Pl.
Weteringschans
Van Eeghenstraat
Willemspark Weg
J. Van Campen str.
Nicolaas Witsen
Stadhoude

Around the Dam

Anne Frankhuis 14
Beurs van Berlage 10
Centraal Station 1
Dam .11
De Waag 6
Het Koninklijk Paleis te Amsterdam 13
Museum Amstelkring 9
Nederlands Scheepvaartmuseum 5
NEMO Science & Technology Center 3
Nieuwe Kerk 12
Oude Kerk 8
Rosse Buurt 7
Scheepvaartshuis 4
Schreierstoren 2
Westerkerk 15

South of the Dam

Amsterdam Historisch Museum 16
Begijnhof 17
Bloemenmarkt 21
Gouden Bocht 19
Munttoren 20
Museum Willet-Holthuysen 22
Spui 18

Jewish Amsterdam

Jodenbreestraat 23
Joods Historisch Museum 27
Muiderstraat 25
Museum het Rembrandthuis . .24
Muziektheater/ Stadhuis 28
Portugese Israelitische Synagoge 26

Museum Quarter

Concertgebouw 32
Leidseplein 34
Rijksmuseum 29
Stedelijk Museum 31
Van Gogh Museum 30
Vondelpark 33

The Jordaan

Jordaan 35

corner"—the building's rounded harbor face forms a sharp corner with its straight street face. A tablet marks the point from which Henrik (aka Henry) Hudson set sail on the *Half Moon* on April 4, 1609, on a voyage that eventually took him to what is now New York and the river that bears his name. ✉ *Prins Hendrikkade 94–95.*

⓯ **Westerkerk** (West Church). The church's 279-foot tower is the city's highest; it also has an outstanding carillon. Rembrandt and his son Titus are buried in the church, which was completed as early as 1631. In summer you can climb to the top of the tower for a fine view over the city. ✉ *Prinsengracht 281 (corner of Westermarkt)* ☎ *020/624–7766* ⏲ *Church: Apr.–Sept., weekdays 11–3; July and Aug., weekdays 11–3, Sat. 11–3. Tower: June–Sept., daily 10–5. Closed during private services.*

SOUTH OF THE DAM

From the south of Dam Square to Museumplein lies the artistic heart of Amsterdam, with its wealth of museums and fine architecture. The Golden Bend, the grandest stretch of canal in town, has some of the finest mansions built by Amsterdam's prosperous merchants.

⓰ **Amsterdam Historisch Museum** (Amsterdam Historical Museum). The museum traces the city's history from its origins as a fishing village, through the 17th-century golden age of material and artistic wealth, to the decline of the trading empire during the 18th century. In the courtyard off Kalverstraat, a striking Renaissance gate guards a series of tranquil inner courtyards. In medieval times, this area was an island devoted to piety. Today the bordering canals are filled in. ✉ *Kalverstraat 92* ☎ *020/523–1822* 🌐 *www.ahm.nl* ⏲ *Weekdays 10–5, weekends 11–5.*

★ ⓱ **Begijnhof** (Beguine Court). This enclosed square of almshouses, founded in 1346, is a surprising oasis of peace just a stone's throw from the city's hectic center. The Beguines were women who led a form of convent life, often taking the vow of chastity. The last Beguine died in 1974, and her house, No. 26, has been preserved as she left it. Dating from the 15th century, No. 34 is the oldest house and the only one to retain its wooden Gothic facade. A small passageway and courtyard link the Begijnhof to the Amsterdam Historisch Museum. The small **Engelse Kerk** (English Church) across from here at No. 48 dates from 1400. This church was given to Amsterdam's English and Scottish Presbyterians early in the 17th century. On the church wall and in the chancel are tributes to the Pilgrim Fathers, who sailed from Delftshaven (in Rotterdam) to the New World in 1620. Opposite the church is another of the city's secret Catholic chapels, whose exterior looks as though it were two adjoining houses, built in 1671. At press time, the future of public access to the Begijnhof was unclear; please contact VVV Amsterdam for updated information. ✉ *Enter at Begijnhof 29* ☎ *020/623–3565* 🌐 *www.begijnhofamsterdam.nl* ⏲ *Daily 9–11[am]; contact VVV Amsterdam for access information.*

㉑ **Bloemenmarkt** (Flower Market). Here floating stalls carry a bright array of freshly cut flowers and foliage, as well as an enviable variety of bulbs and plants. ✉ *Along Singel Canal, from Muntplein to Koningsplein* ⏲ *Mon.–Sat. (occasionally Sun.) 8:30–6.*

★ ⓳ **Gouden Bocht** (Golden Bend). The Herengracht (Gentlemen's Canal) is the city's most prestigious canal. The stretch of the canal from Leidsestraat to Vijzelstraat is named for the sumptuous patrician houses that line it. Seventeenth-century merchants moved here from the Amstel River to escape the by-products of their wealth: noisy warehouses, unpleasant brewery smells, and the risk of fire in the sugar refineries. The houses display the full range of Amsterdam architectural detailing, from gables in a variety of shapes to elaborate Louis XIV–style cornices and frescoed ceilings. They are best seen from the east side of the canal. ✉ *Herengracht, Leidsestraat to Vijzelstraat.*

⓴ **Munttoren** (Mint Tower). Built in 1620 at this busy crossroads, the graceful tower that was later added to this former royal mint has a clock and bells that still seem to mirror the golden age. There are frequent carillon recitals. ✉ *Muntplein.*

㉒ **Museum Willet-Holthuysen.** Built in 1690, the elegant residence was bequeathed to the city of Amsterdam on condition that it be retained as a museum. It provides a peek into the lives of the city's well-heeled merchants. ✉ *Herengracht 605* ☎ *020/523–1822* 🌐 *www.willetholthuysen.nl* ⏲ *Weekdays 10–5, weekends 11–5.*

⓲ **Spui** (Sluice). In the heart of the university area, the lively square was a center for revolutionary student rallies in 1968. Now you'll find bookstores and bars, including cozy brown cafés. ✉ *Junction of Nieuwezijds Voorburgwal, Spuistraat, and Singel Canal.*

Jewish Amsterdam

The original settlers in the Jodenbuurt (old Jewish Amsterdam) were wealthy Sephardic Jews from Spain and Portugal, later followed by poorer Ashkenazic refugees from Germany and Poland. At the beginning of the 20th century this was a thriving community of Jewish diamond polishers, dyers, and merchants.

㉓ **Jodenbreestraat.** During World War II this street marked the southwestern border of the *Joodse wijk* (Jewish neighborhood), then a Nazi-controlled ghetto surrounded by barbed wire. The character of the area was largely destroyed by construction of both the Metro and the Muziektheater/Stadhuis complex. However, you can still find a flavor of times past by wandering around the quaint and peaceful canals and streets. ✉ *Jodenbreestraat, between the Rechtboomsloot and the Oude Schans.*

㉗ **Joods Historisch Museum** (Jewish Historical Museum). This complex of four synagogues, the oldest dating from 1671, opened in 1987 as a unique museum. The succession of synagogues was gradually constructed to accommodate Amsterdam's growing community of Jews, many of whom had fled from oppression and prejudice elsewhere. Before the war, there were about 120,000 Jews here, but only 20,000 of them survived the Nazis and the war. Founded by American and Dutch Jews, the museum displays religious treasures in a clear cultural and historical context. Because the synagogues lost most of their treasures in the war, their architecture and history are more compelling than the exhibits. ✉ *Nieuwe Amstelstraat 1* ☎ *020/626–9945* 🌐 *www.jhm.nl* ⏲ *Daily 11–5* ⏲ *Closed Yom Kippur.*

㉕ **Muiderstraat.** This pedestrian area east of Waterlooplein retains much of the neighborhood's historic charm. Notice the gateways decorated with pelicans, symbolizing great love; according to legend, the pelican will feed her starving young with her own blood. ✉ *Muiderstraat/Waterlooplein.*

★ ㉔ **Museum het Rembrandthuis** (Rembrandt's House). From 1639 to 1658, Rembrandt lived at Jodenbreestraat 4. For more than 20 years he used the ground floor as living quarters; the sunny upper floor was his studio. The museum has a superb collection of his etchings as well as work by his contemporaries. The modern wing next door houses a multimedia auditorium, two exhibition spaces, and a shop. ✉ *Jodenbreestraat 4–6* ☎ *020/520–0400* 🌐 *www.rembrandthuis.nl* ⏲ *Mon.–Sat. 10–5, Sun. 1–5.*

㉘ **Muziektheater/Stadhuis** (Music Theater/Town Hall complex). Amsterdammers come to the Town Hall section of the building by day to obtain driver's licenses, pick up welfare payments, and get married. They return by night to the rounded, marble-clad facade overlooking the Amstel River to see opera and ballet performed by the Netherlands' national companies. You can wander into the Town Hall for a look at some interesting sculptures and other displays. A guided tour of the Muziektheater takes you around the dressing rooms, dance studios, backstage, and even to the wig department. ✉ *Amstel 3/Waterlooplein 22* ☎ *020/551–8117; 020/551–8103 tour information* 🌐 *www.muziektheater.nl* ⏲ *Guided tours Sat. at 3.*

★ ㉖ **Portugese Israelitische Synagoge** (Portuguese Israelite Synagogue). As one of Amsterdam's five neighboring synagogues, this was part of the largest Jewish religious complex in Europe. The beautiful, austere interior of the 17th-century building is still intact, even if the building itself is marooned on a traffic island. ✉ *Mr. Visserplein 3* ☎ *020/624–5351* 🌐 *www.esnoga.com* ⏲ *Apr.–Oct., Sun.–Fri. 10–4; Nov.–Mar., Sun.–Thurs. 10–4, Fri. 10–3* ⏲ *Closed Jewish holidays.*

The Museum Quarter

Amsterdam's wealth of art—from Golden Age painters, through van Gogh, up to the present day—is concentrated on the area around the grassy Museumplein, which also serves as the transition point between the central canal area and the modern residential sections of the city. The nearby Leidsplein is dotted with cafés and discos and attracts young visitors to the city.

㉜ **Concertgebouw** (Concert Hall). The sounds of the country's foremost orchestra resonate in this imposing, classical building. The smaller of the two auditoriums is used for chamber music and solo recitals. The main hall hosts world-class concerts. ✉ *Concertgebouwplein 2–6* ☎ *020/671–8345* 🌐 *www.concertgebouw.nl.*

㉞ **Leidseplein.** This square is the pulsing heart of the city's nightlife. In summer you can enjoy the entertainment of street performers on the many café terraces. ✉ *Junction of Leidsestraat, Marnixstraat, and Weteringschans.*

㉙ **Rijksmuseum** (State Museum). This, the most important Dutch museum, was founded in 1808, but the current, rather lavish building dates from 1885 and was designed by the architect of Central Station, P. J. H. Cuijpers. The museum's fame rests on its unrivaled collection of Dutch 16th- and 17th-century masters. Rembrandt's masterpiece, the *Night Watch,* concealed during World War II in a cave in Maastricht, was misnamed because of its dull layers of varnish; in reality it depicts the Civil Guard in daylight. Also worth searching out are Frans Hals's family portraits, Jan Steen's drunken scenes, Van Ruysdael's romantic but menacing landscapes, and Vermeer's glimpses of everyday life bathed in his limpid light. A complete renovation and restructuring of the Rijksmuseum will close much of it until 2008. However, the museum's most famous works will still be on view in the Philips Wing. ✉ *Stadhouderskade 42* ☎ *020/674–7047* 🌐 *www.rijksmuseum.nl* ⏲ *Daily 10–5; only the Philips Wing open during renovations.*

Fodor'sChoice ★

㉛ **Stedelijk Museum** (Museum of Modern Art). Renovations are planned for 2004 and beyond, which will likely close the museum. When it is open, the Stedelijk has a stimulating collection of modern art and ever-changing displays of the works of contemporary artists, including Cézanne, Chagall, Kandinsky, and Mondrian. ✉ *Paulus Potterstraat 13* ☎ *020/573–2911* 🌐 *www.stedelijk.nl* ⏲ *Closed for renovations until further notice.*

★ 30 **Van Gogh Museum.** This museum contains the world's largest collection of the artist's works—200 paintings and nearly 500 drawings—as well as works by some 50 of his contemporaries. The main building was designed by Gerrit Rietvelt and completed in 1972. A wing, designed by Japanese architect Kisho Kurokawa, was added later to exhibit van Gogh's prints and accommodate temporary exhibitions, which focus on art from the late 19th and early 20th centuries. ✉ *Paulus Potterstraat 7* ☎ *020/570–5252* 🌐 *www.vangoghmuseum.nl* ⏲ *Daily 10–6.*

33 **Vondelpark.** Amsterdam's central park is an elongated rectangle of paths, lakes, and pleasant, shady greenery. A monument honors the 17th-century epic poet Joost van den Vondel, after whom the park is named. There are special children's areas with paddling pools and sandboxes. From June through August, the park hosts free outdoor concerts and plays Wednesday–Sunday. ✉ *Stadhouderskade* 🌐 *www.openluchttheater.nl.*

The Jordaan

35 **Jordaan.** In this old part of Amsterdam the canals and side streets are named for trees, flowers, and plants. When it was the French quarter of the city, the area was known as *le jardin* (the garden), a name that over the years has become Jordaan. The best time to explore the district is in the evening or on a Sunday morning. The Jordaan has attracted many artists and is something of a bohemian quarter, where run-down buildings are being converted into restaurants, antiques shops, boutiques, and galleries. ✉ *Bordered by Prinsengracht, Lijnbaansgracht, Brouwersgracht, and Elandsgracht.*

WHERE TO EAT

Health-conscious Amsterdammers prefer set menus and early dinners. For traditionalists the NEDERLANDS DIS soup tureen sign is a promise of regional recipes and seasonal ingredients. For a superbly luxurious culinary experience try the restaurant at Blake's Hotel, which is one of the city's best.

WHAT IT COSTS In euros

	$$$$	$$$	$$	$
AT DINNER	over €36	€25–€36	€14–€24	under €14

Prices are per person for a main course.

$$$–$$$$ ✕ **Dynasty.** Surrounded by luxurious Oriental furniture and murals, you can savor dishes from Thailand, Malaysia, and China. Main-course delicacies include mixed seafood in banana leaves and succulent duck and lobster on a bed of watercress. In one of the city's most active nightlife areas, it can get very busy, but service is always impeccable. ✉ *Reguliersdwarsstraat 30* ☎ *020/626–8400* 💳 *AE, DC, MC, V* ⏲ *Closed Tues. No lunch.*

★ $$$–$$$$ ✕ **Excelsior.** The restaurant at the Hôtel de l'Europe offers a varied menu of French cuisine based on local ingredients. There are no fewer than 15 splendid set menus. Service is discreet and impeccable, and the view over the Amstel River, to the Muntplein on one side and the

Muziektheater on the other, is the best in Amsterdam. ✉ *Hôtel de l'Europe, Nieuwe Doelenstraat 2–8* ☎ *020/531–1705* *Reservations essential* *Jacket required* *AE, DC, MC, V* *No lunch weekends.*

★ $$$–$$$$ ✕ **La Rive.** The light French cuisine, with an awe-inspiring "truffle menu" of dishes prepared with exotic (and expensive) ingredients, can be tailored to meet your every whim. Epicureans should inquire about the "chef's table": with a group of six you can sit at a table alongside the open kitchen and watch chefs prepare and describe each of your courses. At this world-class restaurant, you can also enjoy the city's most elegant view of the river Amstel. ✉ *Amstel Inter-Continental Hotel, Professor Tulpplein 1* ☎ *020/622–6060* *Jacket and tie* *AE, DC, MC, V.*

$$$–$$$$ ✕ **Oesterbar.** The "Oyster Bar" specializes in seafood—grilled, baked, or fried. The upstairs dining room is more formal than the downstairs bistro, but prices don't vary. The sole is prepared in four different ways, or you can try local specialties such as halibut and eel; oysters are a stimulating, if pricey, appetizer. ✉ *Leidseplein 10* ☎ *020/623–2988* *AE, DC, MC, V.*

★ $$$ ✕ **De Silveren Spiegel.** In an alarmingly crooked 17th-century house, you can have an outstanding meal while you enjoy the personal attention of the owner at one of just a small cluster of tables. Local ingredients such as Texel lamb and wild rabbit are cooked with subtlety and flair. ✉ *Kattengat 4–6* ☎ *020/624–6589* *AE, MC, V* *Closed Sun.*

$$–$$$ ✕ **Blauw aan de Wal.** At the end of a cul-de-sac, the hidden courtyard and flowering garden forms an oasis of peace in the busy red-light district. The French/Italian courses and legendary warm chocolate tart make this an "in" spot with foodies. The ground floor is a completely no-smoking area—a rarity in Amsterdam. ✉ *O.Z. Achterburgwal 99* ☎ *020/330–2257* *Reservations essential* *AE, MC, V* *Closed Sun.*

$$–$$$ ✕ **D' Theeboom.** Just behind the Dam, the ground floor of this historic canal-side warehouse has been converted into a stylish, formal restaurant. The seasonal menu might include a delicious parcel of vegetables flavored with a selection of mushrooms, followed by carefully prepared red mullet with a saffron sauce. ✉ *Singel 210* ☎ *020/623–8420* *AE, DC, MC, V* *No lunch.*

★ $$–$$$ ✕ **Long Pura.** Lonny Gerungan's family have been cooks on Bali for generations—even preparing banquets for visiting Dutch royals. His plush restaurant in Amsterdam, draped in silky fabrics, serves the finest authentic Indonesian cuisine. Even the simplest rijsttafel is a feast of more than 15 delicately spiced dishes. ✉ *Rozengracht 46–48* ☎ *020/623–8950* *Reservations essential* *AE, DC, MC, V.*

$$–$$$ ✕ **Segugio.** Finely prepared meals served in this stylish and spacious interior include unusual risottos, white truffles, seafood, and game. The restaurant's name means "research," and the staff pride themselves on seeking out hard-to-find regional Italian ingredients. ✉ *Utrechtsestraat 96* ☎ *020/330–1503* *AE, MC, V* *Closed Sun.*

$$ ✕ **In de Waag.** The lofty, beamed interior below the Theatrum Anatomicum has been converted into a grand café and restaurant. The reading table harbors computer terminals for Internet enthusiasts. Dinnertime brings a seasonal selection of hearty cuisine to be savored by candlelight. ✉ *Nieuwmarkt 4* ☎ *020/422–7772* *AE, DC, MC, V.*

★ $$ ✕ **L'Indochine.** This is one of the city's first ventures into Vietnamese cuisine, and the chef's skillful preparation of the freshest ingredients, some specially imported, has been an immediate success. Sample the healthful, mint-flavored spring rolls or the meatier seared prawn and beef skewers to start, followed by lightly fried fish with vegetables in a subtly spiced sauce. ✉ *Beulingstraat 9* ☎ *020/627–5755* *Reservations essential* *AE, DC, MC, V* *Closed Mon. No lunch.*

★ $$ ✕ **Pier 10.** This former shipping office is on a pier behind Centraal Station. The candlelighted interior and unusual view—be certain to book a table in the "glass room" overlooking the river—makes this a popular spot for romantic dining. The food is international, with a French influence. Dinner splits into two distinct shifts, so lingering is not an option. ✉ *De Ruyterkade, pier 10* ☎ *020/624–8276* *Reservations essential* ▭ *AE, DC, MC, V.*

$$ Fodor'sChoice ★ ✕ **Puyck.** Owner/chef Jacob Preyde's new restaurant is a sensation on the Amsterdam scene. His French-Asian-Caribbean fusion dishes are prepared with exotic herbs and spices. Even top wines are affordable, due to a fixed cork charge. Attractive paintings, oak flooring, and an open kitchen enhance the experience. ✉ *Ceintuurbaan 147* ☎ *020/676–7677* ▭ *MC, V* ⊙ *Closed Sun. and Mon. No lunch.*

$–$$ ✕ **De Knijp.** Dutch food and French bistro fare are served here in a traditional Dutch environment. The mezzanine level is especially cozy. Alongside tamer dishes, there are seasonal specialties including wild boar, ham with red cabbage, and fillet of hare. After-midnight dinner draws concert goers and performers from the neighboring Concertgebouw. ✉ *Van Baerlestraat 134* ☎ *020/671–4248* *Reservations not accepted* ▭ *AE, DC, MC, V.*

$–$$ ✕ **Rose's Cantina.** Rose's fills a sad Tex-Mex void in the Amsterdam dining market, but connoisseurs should prepare themselves to deem the food merely "sufficient." In addition to heaps of food, this place has buckets of lethal margaritas and a noise level that careens up the decibel scale. ✉ *Reguliersdwarsstraat 38* ☎ *020/625–9797* *Reservations essential on weekends* ▭ *AE, DC, MC, V.*

$–$$ ✕ **Walem.** At this popular, all-day grand café, elegant breakfast and brunch options are served on chic *ciabatta* (a crispy, white Italian bread). At dinnertime the chefs prepare up-to-the-minute fusion cooking with a French influence—and affix a higher price tag. ✉ *Keizersgracht 449* ☎ *020/625–3544* ▭ *AE, MC, V.*

$ ✕ **Het Gasthuys.** In this bustling restaurant you'll be served handsome portions of traditional Dutch home cooking—choice cuts of meat with excellent fries and piles of mixed salad. Sit at the bar or take a table high up in the rafters at the back. In summer the enchanting terrace on the canal side opens. ✉ *Grimburgwal 7* ☎ *020/624–8230* ▭ *No credit cards.*

$ ✕ **Song Kwae.** The traditional offerings in Amsterdam's Chinatown, based around the Nieuwmarkt and Zeedijk, have now been complemented by a surge of Thai restaurants, and this buzzing joint offers speedy service and quality food for a budget price. Alongside the traditional red and green Thai curries and the stir-fry options, there are specialties such as green papaya salad with crab. ✉ *Kloveniersburgwal 14* ☎ *020/624–2568* ▭ *AE, DC, MC, V.*

WHERE TO STAY

WHAT IT COSTS In euros				
	$$$$	**$$$**	**$$**	**$**
FOR 2 PEOPLE	over €350	€180–€350	€105–€180	under €105

Prices are for two people sharing a double room in high season.

$$$$ Fodor'sChoice ★ **Amstel Inter-Continental.** Amsterdam's grande dame first opened in 1867. The spacious rooms have Oriental rugs, brocade upholstery, Delft lamps, and a color scheme inspired by the warm, earthy tones of Makkum pottery. The Amstel is frequented by many of the nation's top businesspeople and sometimes hosts members of the royal family.

✉ Professor Tulpplein 1, 1018 GX ☎ 020/622–6060 📠 020/622–5808 🌐 www.intercontinental.com 55 rooms, 24 suites Restaurant, pool AE, DC, MC, V.

$$$$ **Blake's.** British designer Anouska Hempel's luxury hotel continues to be an "in" spot. The beautifully appointed interior has an Oriental influence, and the entire hotel and courtyard offer serenity in a bustling city. The restaurant is one of Amsterdam's best, with a Thai/French fusion kitchen. *✉ Keijzersgracht 384, 1016 GB ☎ 020/530–2010 📠 020/530–2030 🌐 www.slh.com 22 rooms, 19 suites Restaurant AE, DC, MC, V.*

★ **$$$$** **Grand Amsterdam.** Parts of this elegant building, which used to serve as Amsterdam's city hall, date from the 16th century, but most of it belongs to the early 20th, when the country's best artists and architects were commissioned to create a building the city could be proud of. Features include a mural by Karel Appel, Jugendstil stained-glass windows, Gobelin tapestries, and palatially luxurious reception areas and rooms. The kitchen of the brasserie-style restaurant, Café Roux, is supervised by the incomparable Albert Roux. *✉ Oudezijds Voorburgwal 197, 1012 EX ☎ 020/555–3111 📠 020/555–3222 🌐 www.thegrand.nl 160 rooms, 6 suites, 16 apartments Restaurant, pool AE, DC, MC, V.*

★ **$$$$** **Hôtel de l'Europe.** Behind the stately facade of this late-19th-century building is a full complement of modern facilities, as befits a hotel often ranked among the world's best. Large, bright rooms overlooking the Amstel are done in pastel colors; others have warm, rich colors and antiques. In addition to its world-renowned Excelsior restaurant, the hotel houses a sophisticated fitness center. *✉ Nieuwe Doelenstraat 2–8, 1012 CP ☎ 020/531–1777 📠 020/531–1778 🌐 www.leurope.nl 80 rooms, 20 suites 2 restaurants, pool AE, DC, MC, V.*

★ **$$$$** **Pulitzer.** The Pulitzer is one of Europe's most ambitious hotel restorations, using the structures of a block of 25 17th- and 18th-century merchants' houses. The refined interior is marked by a modern art gallery and lovingly restored brickwork and oak beams. No two of the split-level rooms are alike, and many have antique furnishings to match period architectural features. *✉ Prinsengracht 315–331, 1016 GZ ☎ 020/523–5235 📠 020/627–6753 🌐 www.luxurycollection.com 224 rooms, 6 suites Restaurant AE, DC, MC, V.*

$$–$$$$ **NH Grand Hotel Krasnapolsky.** This fine hotel is enhanced by the Winter Garden restaurant, which dates from 1818. The large-scale expansion into neighboring buildings has provided space for extensive conference and business facilities and an amazing selection of additional restaurants. The cosmopolitan atmosphere carries through all the well-equipped rooms, with styles ranging from Victorian to art deco. *✉ Dam 9, 1012 JS ☎ 020/554–9111 📠 020/622–8607 🌐 www.krasnapolsky.nl 431 rooms, 7 suites, 36 apartments 7 restaurants AE, DC, MC, V.*

$$$ **Ambassade.** With its beautiful canal-side location, its Louis XV–style decoration, and its Oriental rugs, the Ambassade seems more like a stately home than a hotel. Breakfast is served in an elegant room overlooking the canal. For other meals, the neighborhood has a good choice of restaurants. *✉ Herengracht 341, 1016 AZ ☎ 020/555–0222 📠 020/555–0277 🌐 www.ambassade-hotel.nl 51 rooms, 7 suites, 1 apartment AE, DC, MC, V.*

$$–$$$ **Canal House Hotel.** The Irish owners of this canal-side hotel have opted for antiques rather than TVs as furnishings, producing a real sense of stepping back in time. Spacious rooms overlook the canal or the atmospheric garden. A hearty Dutch breakfast served in the breakfast room is included in the price. Children under age 12 are not permitted. *✉ Keizersgracht 148, 1015 CX ☎ 020/622–5182 📠 020/624–1317 🌐 www.canalhouse.nl 26 rooms AE, DC, MC, V.*

$$–$$$ **Seven Bridges Hotel.** Named for the view from its front steps, this small canal-house hotel has rooms decorated with individual flair. Oriental rugs warm wooden floors, and there are comfy antique armchairs and marble washstands. The Rembrandtsplein is nearby. For a stunning view, request a canal-side room, but make sure to reserve weeks in advance. One of the pleasures here is breakfast in bed. ✉ *Reguliersgracht 31, 1017 LK* ☎ *020/623–1329* *8 rooms* *AE, DC, MC, V.*

★ **$$** **Agora.** The cheerful bustle of the nearby Singel flower market carries over to this small hotel in an 18th-century house. Rooms are light and spacious, and some are decorated with vintage furniture; the best overlook the canal and the university. The Agora has a considerate staff, and the neighborhood is relaxed. Book well in advance. ✉ *Singel 462, 1017 AW* ☎ *020/627–2200* *020/627–2202* *www.hotelagora.nl* *15 rooms, 13 with bath or shower* *AE, DC, MC, V.*

$$ **Hotel de Filosoof.** On a quiet street near Vondelpark, the hotel attracts artists, thinkers, and people looking for something a little unusual. Each room is decorated in a different philosophical or cultural motif—such as an Aristotle room and a Goethe room adorned with texts from *Faust.* A large Dutch breakfast is included in the price. ✉ *Anna van den Vondelstraat 6, 1054 GZ* ☎ *020/683–3013* *020/685–3750* *www.hotelfilosoof.nl* *38 rooms* *AE, MC, V.*

$$ **Hotel Washington.** On a peaceful street, the hotel is just a few blocks from the Museum District and the Concertgebouw. Many of the world's top musicians find it the ideal place to reside when performing in Amsterdam. Period furniture and attentive service lend this small establishment a homey feel. All except the cheaper upper-floor rooms have bath or shower and toilet. ✉ *Frans van Mierisstraat 10, 1071 RS* ☎ *020/679–6754* *020/673–4435* *21 rooms, 19 with bath or shower* *AE, DC, MC, V.*

$ **Amstel Botel.** The floating hotel moored near Central Station is an appropriate place to stay in watery Amsterdam. The rooms are small and basic, but the large windows offer fine views across the water to the city. Make sure you don't get a room on the land side of the vessel, or you'll end up staring at a postal sorting office. ✉ *Oosterdokskade 2–4, 1011 AE* ☎ *020/626–4247* *020/639–1952* *www.amstelbotel.com* *175 rooms* *AE, DC, MC, V.*

$ **Hotel Acro.** This friendly tourist hotel is on a quiet street within easy walking distance to the main museums and the Vondelpark. The light blue rooms are clean and pleasant. ✉ *Jan Luykenstraat 44, 1071 CR* ☎ *020/662–5538* *020/675–0811* *www.acro-hotel.nl* *65 rooms* *AE, DC, MC, V.*

NIGHTLIFE & THE ARTS

The Arts

The arts flourish in cosmopolitan Amsterdam. The best source of information about performances is the monthly English-language *Day by Day in Amsterdam,* published by the VVV tourist office, where you can also secure tickets for the more popular events. *De Uitkrant* is available in Dutch and covers practically every event. You can also find the latest information and make personal or phone bookings for a small charge at the **Amsterdam Uitburo** (✉ Stadsschouwburg, Leidseplein 26 ☎ 0900/0191, €0.40 per min www.uitlijn.nl Daily 9–9).

Film

The greatest concentration of movie theaters is around Leidseplein and near Muntplein. Most foreign films are subtitled rather than dubbed.

Conveniently located close to Leidseplein, **City 1–7** (✉ Kleine Gartmanplantsoen 13–25 ☎ 0900/1458, €0.35 per min for recorded info) has seven screens. **Pathe de Munt** (✉ Vijselstraat 15 ☎ 0900/1458, €0.35 per min for recorded info) is the largest multiplex cinema in Amsterdam, with 13 screens.

Music

The **Concertgebouw** (✉ Concertgebouwplein 2–6 ☎ 020/671–8345) is the home of one of Europe's finest orchestras. A smaller hall in the same building hosts chamber music, recitals, and even jam sessions. Ticket prices for international orchestras are high, but most concerts are good value, and Wednesday lunchtime concerts at 12:30 are free. The **Muziekgebouw** (✉ Piet Heinkade 1 ☎ 020/668–1805 🌐 www.muziekgebouw.nl) is opening to the public in mid-2004. The huge structure is intended to serve as a venue for all types of music; it also contains a documentation center, rehearsal spaces, and rooms for classes and workshops. A spectacular glass facade overlooks IJ river.

Opera & Ballet

The Dutch national ballet and opera companies perform in the **Muziektheater** (✉ Waterlooplein 22 ☎ 020/625–5455 🌐 www.hetmuziektheater.nl). Guest companies from other countries perform here during the Holland Festival in June. The country's smaller regional dance and opera companies usually include performances at the **Stadsschouwburg** (City Municipal Theater; ✉ Leidseplein 26 ☎ 020/624–2311 🌐 www.stadsschouwburgamsterdam.nl) in their schedules.

Theater

Boom Chicago (✉ Leidseplein Theater, Leidseplein 12 ☎ 020/423–0101 🌐 www.boomchicago.nl) offers improvised comedy with a local touch. For experimental theater, contemporary dance, and colorful cabaret in Dutch, catch the shows at **Felix Meritis** (✉ Keizersgracht 324 ☎ 020/623–1311 🌐 www.felix.meritis.nl).

Nightlife

Amsterdam has a wide variety of dance clubs, bars, and exotic shows. The more respectable—and expensive—after-dark activities are in and around Leidseplein and Rembrandtsplein; fleshier productions are on Oudezijds Achterburgwal and Thorbeckeplein. Most bars are open Sunday to Thursday to 1 AM and later on weekends; clubs stay open until 4 AM or later and at least 5 AM on weekends. On weeknights very few clubs charge admission, though the livelier ones sometimes ask for a "club membership" fee of €15 or more. Watch out around the red-light district, where street touts will offer tempting specials for louche clubs with floor shows—the experience may turn out to cost more than you bargained for.

Cafés & Bars

Amsterdam, and particularly the Jordaan, is renowned for its brown cafés. There are also grand cafés, with spacious interiors, snappy table service, and well-stocked reading tables. Two other variants of Amsterdam's buzzing bar scene are the *proeflokalen* (tasting houses) and *brouwerijen* (breweries). The Dutch have a relaxed tolerance of soft drugs like marijuana and hashish, which can be encountered in "coffee shops" with the green leaves of the marijuana plant showing in the window.

Among more fashionable cafés is **Café Nielsen** (✉ Berenstraat 19 ☎ 020/330–6006), serving delicious, healthful lunches. Everything here is fresh and organic, with plenty of vegetarian and vegan dishes. The beamed interior of **De Admiraal Proeflokaal en Bar Spijshuis** (✉ Herengracht 319 ☎ 020/625–4334) is an intimate setting in which to enjoy the Jenevers and unique liqueurs. **De Gijs** (✉ Lindegracht 249 ☎ 020/638–0740) is an atmospheric brown café. **De Jaren** (✉ Nieuwe Doelenstraat 20 ☎ 020/625–5771), a spacious grand café with a canal-side terrace, attracts young businesspeople, arts and media workers, and other trendy types. At the **Rooie Nelis** (✉ Laurierstraat 101 ☎ 020/624–4167), you can spend a rainy afternoon chatting with friendly strangers over homemade meatballs and a beer or apple tart and coffee. **Tweede Kamer** (✉ Heisteeg 6, just off the Spui ☎ 020/422–2236), named after the Dutch parliament's lower house, offers chess and backgammon in a convivial, civilized atmosphere permeated with the smoke of hemp.

Casino

Holland Casino (✉ Max Euweplein 62 ☎ 020/521–1111), just off Leidseplein, has blackjack, roulette, and slot machines in elegant, canal-side surrounds. You'll need your passport to get in, and although you don't have to wear a tie, sneakers will not get you past the door; the minimum age is 18.

Dance Clubs

Dance clubs tend to fill up after midnight. The cavernous **Escape** (✉ Rembrandtsplein 11–15 ☎ 020/622–1111) has taken on a much hipper mantle. The **iT** (✉ Amstelstraat 24 ☎ 020/489–7285) has gay nights on Saturday; it's primarily straight on Friday—but could never be accused of being straitlaced. **Seymour Likely Lounge** (✉ Nieuwezijds Voorburgwal 161 ☎ 020/420–5663) has a lively, trendy crowd hopping to the latest music.

Gay & Lesbian Nightlife

Amsterdam has a vibrant gay and lesbian community. **Spijker** (✉ Kerkstraat 4 ☎ 020/620–5919) is a popular late-night bar with a sociable pool table and pinball machine. **Café Rouge** (✉ Amstel 60 ☎ 020/420–9881) has traditional Dutch oompapa music and frivolity. The **Amstel Taverne** (✉ Amstel 54 ☎ 020/623–4254) is the oldest existing gay bar in Amsterdam and is an early-evening venue. The trendy set prevails at bars along the Reguliersdwarsstraat. A mixed blend of nationalities and ages meets early in the evening at **April** (✉ Reguliersdwarsstraat 37 ☎ 020/625–9572). The **You II** (✉ Amstel 178 ☎ 020/421–0900) is an all-women disco open Thursday to Sunday. The lesbian community meets at the **Saarein II** (✉ Elandsstraat 119 ☎ 020/623–4901), a traditional bar in the Jordaan.

The **Gay & Lesbian Switchboard** (☎ 020/623–6565) has friendly operators who provide up-to-the-minute information on events in the city, as well as general advice for gay or lesbian visitors. The **COC** (✉ Rozenstraat 14 ☎ 020/626–3087), the Dutch lesbian and gay organization, operates a coffee shop and hosts a popular Saturday night women-only disco.

Jazz Clubs

The **Bimhuis** (✉ Oude Schans 73–77 ☎ 020/623–3373) offers the best jazz and improvised music in town. The adjoining BIM café has a magical view across the Oude Schans canal.

Rock Clubs

Melkweg (✉ Lijnbaansgracht 234 ☎ 020/531–8181) is a major rock and pop venue with a large auditorium; it also has a gallery, theater, cinema, and café. The **Paradiso** (✉ Weteringschans 6–8 ☎ 020/626–4521 🌐 www.paradiso.nl), converted from a church, is a vibrant venue for rock, New Age, and even contemporary classical music.

SHOPPING

Department Stores

De Bijenkorf (✉ Dam 1), the city's number one department store, is excellent for contemporary fashions and furnishings. **Maison Bonneterie** (✉ Rokin 140) is gracious, genteel, and understated. The well-stocked departments of **Vroom & Dreesmann** (✉ Kalverstraat 203) carry all manner of goods.

Gift Ideas

Diamonds

Since the 17th century, "Amsterdam cut" has been synonymous with perfection in the quality of diamonds. At the diamond-cutting houses, the craftsmen explain how a diamond's value depends on the four *c*'s—carat, cut, clarity, and color—before encouraging you to buy. There is a cluster of diamond houses on the Rokin. **Amsterdam Diamond Centre** (✉ Rokin 1–5 ☎ 020/624–5787) is the largest institution on the Rokin and offers free tours. You can take a free guided factory tour at **Gassan Diamonds** (✉ Nieuwe Uilenburgerstraat 173–175 ☎ 020/622–5333).

Porcelain

The Dutch have been producing Delft, Makkum, and other fine porcelain for centuries. **Hogendoorn & Kaufman** (✉ Rokin 124 ☎ 020/638–2736) sells pieces ranging from affordable, hand-painted, modern tiles to expensive Delft blue-and-white pitchers, as well as quality crystal.

Markets

The **Bloemenmarkt** (flower market) on the Singel canal near the Muntplein is world-famous for its bulbs, many certificated for export, and cut flowers. Amsterdam's lively **Waterlooplein flea market,** open Monday–Saturday 9–5, next to the Muziektheater, is the ideal spot to rummage for secondhand clothes, inexpensive antiques, and other curiosities. In summer, you'll find etchings, drawings, and watercolors at the Sunday **art markets** on Thorbeckeplein and the Spui. There are as many English-language books as Dutch ones for browsing at the **book market** on the Spui, every Friday 10–6. A small but choice **stamp market,** open Wednesday and Saturday 1–4, is held on the Nieuwezijds Voorburgwal. **Kunst & Antiekmarkt De Looier** (De Looier Art & Antiques Market; ✉ Elandsgracht 109 ☎ 020/624–9038 🌐 www.looier.nl) is a bustling, warrenlike indoor market, with myriad stalls selling everything from expensive antiques and art to kitschy bric-a-brac; it's open Saturday to Thursday 11–5.

Shopping Districts

Leidsestraat, Kalverstraat, Utrechtsestraat, and Nieuwendijk, Amsterdam's chief shopping districts, have largely been turned into **pedestrian-only areas,** but watch out for trams and bikes nevertheless. The imposing **Kalvertoren shopping mall** (✉ Kalverstraat near Munt) has a rooftop restaurant with magnificent views of the city. **Magna Plaza shopping center** (✉ Nieuwezijds Voorburgwal 182), built inside the glorious turn-of-the-last-century post office behind the Royal Palace at the Dam, is *the* place for A-to-Z shopping in the huge variety of stores. The **Spiegelkwartier** (✉ Nieuwe Spiegelstraat and Spiegelgracht), just a stone's throw from the Rijksmuseum, is Amsterdam's antiques center, with galleries for wealthy collectors as well as old curiosity shops. **P. C. Hooftstraat,** and

www.PrivateGuidesInEurope.com

also Van Baerlestraat and Beethovenstraat, are the homes of haute couture and other fine goods. **Rokin** is hectic with traffic and houses a cluster of boutiques and renowned antiques shops selling 18th- and 19th-century furniture, antique jewelry, art deco lamps, and statuettes. The **Jordaan** to the west of the main ring of old canals, and the quaint streets crisscrossing these canals, is filled with trendy small boutiques and unusual crafts shops. The tax-free shopping center at **Schiphol Airport** is often lauded as the world's best.

AMSTERDAM A TO Z

AIRPORTS & TRANSFERS

Most international flights arrive at Amsterdam's Schiphol Airport. Immigration and customs formalities on arrival are relaxed, with no forms to be completed.

TRANSFERS The best link is the direct rail line to the central train station, where you can get a taxi or tram to your hotel. The train runs every 10 to 15 minutes throughout the day and takes about a half hour. Make sure you buy a ticket before boarding, or ruthless conductors will impose a fine. Second-class single fare is €3.10. Taxis from the airport to central hotels cost about €35.

BIKE TRAVEL

Rental bikes are widely available for around €6.50 per day with a €50 deposit and proof of identity. Several rental companies are close to the central train station; ask at tourist offices for details. Lock your bike to something immovable whenever you park it. Also, check with the rental company to see what your liability is under their insurance terms. MacBike has various rental points around the center.

MacBike ✉ Mr. Visserplein 2 ☎ 020/620-0985 ✉ Marnixstraat 220 ☎ 020/626-6964 ✉ Stationsplein 12 ☎ 020/624-8391.

BOAT & FERRY TRAVEL

A day pass for the Canalbus costs €15 and provides unlimited travel on the canals with stops at major points of interest between the central train station to the Rijksmuseum. The Museum Boat (€13.25) stops near major museums. Water taxis are more expensive than land taxis: standard-size water taxis—for up to eight people—cost €75 for a half hour, and €60 per half hour thereafter. They offer different types of catering services and are a popular way to enjoy the city or celebrate special occasions.

Canalbus ✉ Nieuwe Weteringschans 24 ☎ 020/623-9886. **Museum Boat** ✉ Prinshendrikkade 26 ☎ 020/530-1090. **Water taxis** ☎ 020/535-6363 🌐 www.water-taxi.nl.

CAR TRAVEL

The city's concentric ring of canals, one-way systems, hordes of cyclists, and lack of parking facilities make driving here unappealing. It's best to put your car in one of the parking lots on the edge of the old center and abandon it for the rest of your stay.

CONSULATES

United Kingdom ✉ Koningslaan 44 ☎ 020/676-4343.
United States ✉ Museumplein 19 ☎ 020/575-5309.

EMERGENCIES

The Central Medical Service supplies names and opening hours of pharmacists and dentists, as well as doctors, outside normal surgery hours.

Doctors & Dentists **Central Medical Service** ☎ 020/592-3434.
Emergency Services **Ambulance, Fire, Police, and Rescue** ☎ 112.

ENGLISH-LANGUAGE MEDIA

Bookstores **American Book Center** ✉ Kalverstraat 185 ☎ 020/625-5537. **Athenaeum Boekhandel** ✉ Spui 14 ☎ 020/622-6248. **English Bookshop** ✉ Lauriergracht 71 ☎ 020/626-4230. **Waterstone's** ✉ Kalverstraat 152 ☎ 020/638-3821.

TAXIS

Taxis are expensive: a 5-km (3-mi) ride costs around €12. Taxis are not usually hailed on the street but are picked up at stands near stations and other key points, where you will see a yellow column. You can order a taxi by dialing Taxi Centrale. Always check that the meter is set to "tariff 1" for daytime fares; "tariff 2" is for evening.

Taxi Centrale ☎ 020/677-7777.

TOURS

BICYCLE TOURS From April through October, guided bike tours are an excellent way to discover Amsterdam. There are also supervised tours to the idyllic countryside and quaint villages just north of the city. The three-hour city tour costs €17, and the six-hour countryside tour costs €22.50, arranged by Yellow Bike Guided Tours.

Yellow Bike Guided Tours ✉ Nieuwezijds Kolk 29 ☎ 020/620-6940 🌐 www.yellowbike.nl.

BOAT TOURS The most enjoyable way to get to know Amsterdam is on a boat trip along the canals. Departures are frequent from points opposite Central Station, along the Damrak, and along the Rokin and Stadhouderskade (near the Rijksmuseum). For a tour lasting about an hour, the cost is around €8.50, but the student guides expect a small tip for their multilingual commentary. A candlelight dinner cruise costs upward of €24. Trips can be booked through the tourist office.

The Museum Boat combines a scenic view of the city with seven stops near 20 museums. Tickets, good for the day and including discounted entry to museums, are €13.25. At Canal-Bike, a pedal boat for four costs €28 per hour.

Canal-Bike ✉ corner of Leidsestraat and Keizersgracht ✉ Leidsekade ✉ Stadhouderskade opposite Rijksmuseum ✉ Prinsengracht opposite Westerkerk ☎ 020/623-9886 🌐 www.canal.nl. **Museum Boat** ✉ Prinshendrikkade 26 ☎ 020/530-1090.

BUS TOURS Guided bus tours provide an excellent introduction to Amsterdam. Bus-and-boat tours with Canalbus include the inevitable trip to a diamond factory. Costing €30, a comprehensive, 2½-hour tour can be booked through Key Tours.

Key Tours ✉ Dam 19 ☎ 020/623-5051. **Canalbus** ✉ Weteringschans 24 ☎ 020/623-9886 🌐 www.canal.nl.

WALKING TOURS Amsterdam is a compact city of narrow streets and canals, ideal for exploring on foot. The tourist office issues seven excellent guides in English that detail self-guided walking tours around the center.

TRAIN TRAVEL

The city has excellent rail connections with the rest of Europe. Central Station is in the center of town.

Central Station ✉ Stationsplein ☎ 0900/9296 international service information, €0.35 per min and sometimes a long wait.

TRANSPORTATION AROUND AMSTERDAM

A zonal fare system is used for the public transportation system, which includes metro, tram, and bus. Tickets (starting at €1.60) are available from automated dispensers on the metro or from the drivers on trams and buses; or buy a money-saving strippenkaart. Even simpler is the dagkaart, which covers all city routes for €5.50. These discount tickets can be obtained from the main GVB ticket office (open weekdays 7 AM–9 PM and weekends 8 AM–9 PM), in front of Central Station, and from many newsstands, along with route maps of the public transportation system.

TRAVEL AGENCIES

American Express ✉ Damrak 66 ☎ 020/504-8787. **Holland International** ✉ Damrak 90 ☎ 020/555-0808. **Key Tours** ✉ Dam 19 ☎ 020/623-5051.

VISITOR INFORMATION

VVV Amsterdam Tourist Office has offices at Schiphol Airport, at Stationsplein 10, in front of Central Station in the Old Dutch Coffee House, as well as one in the station itself. The information number, listed below, costs €0.55 per minute, and the electronic queue has a long wait.

VVV Amsterdam Tourist Office ✉ Schiphol Airport ✉ Stationsplein 10, in front of Central Station in the Old Dutch Coffee House ✉ Spoor 2 (Platform 2) inside the station ☎ 0900/400-4040 🌐 www.amsterdamtourist.nl.

The Netherlands Basics

To research prices, get advice from other travelers, and book travel arrangements, visit www.fodors.com.

BUSINESS HOURS

BANKS & OFFICES Banks are open weekdays 9–4. Some banks are closed Monday mornings. GWK Border Exchange Offices at major railway stations are generally open Monday–Saturday 8–8, Sunday 10–4. GWK offices at border checkpoints are generally open 8–8 and at Schiphol Airport 7 AM–10 PM.

MUSEUMS & SIGHTS Museums in Amsterdam are open daily. Elsewhere they close on Monday, but there are exceptions, so check with local tourist offices. In rural areas, some museums close or operate shorter hours in winter. Usual hours are 10–5.

SHOPS Shops are open weekdays and Saturday 8:30 or 9 to 5:30 or 6, but outside the cities some close for lunch; many shops don't open until 1 PM on Monday. In major cities there is usually late-night shopping until 9 PM on Thursday or Friday. Sunday opening, from noon to 5, varies from city to city.

CUSTOMS & DUTIES

For details on imports and duty-free limits, *see* Customs & Duties *in* Smart Travel Tips.

EMBASSIES

All embassies are in the Hague.

Australia ✉ Carnegielaan 4 ☎ 070/310-8200.
Canada ✉ Sophialaan 7 ☎ 070/311-1600.
Ireland ✉ Dr. Kuyperstraat 9 ☎ 070/363-0993.
New Zealand ✉ Carnegielaan 10 ☎ 070/346-9324.
South Africa ✉ Wassenaarseweg 40 ☎ 070/392-4501.
United Kingdom ✉ Lange Voorhout 10 ☎ 070/427-0427.
United States ✉ Lange Voorhout 102 ☎ 070/310-9209.

HOLIDAYS

New Year's Day; Easter; Queen's Day (April 30); Ascension (mid-May); Pentecost/Whitsunday and Whitmonday (late May); Christmas; and Boxing Day (day after Christmas).

LANGUAGE

Dutch is a difficult language for foreigners, but the Dutch are fine linguists, so almost everyone speaks at least some English, especially in larger cities and tourist centers.

MONEY MATTERS

The Netherlands is prosperous, with a high standard of living, so overall costs are similar to those in other northern European countries. Prices for hotels and services in major cities are 10%–20% higher than those in rural areas. Amsterdam and the Hague are the most expensive. Hotel and restaurant service charges and the 6% value-added tax (V. A.T.) are usually included in the prices quoted. Some sample prices include half bottle of wine, €11; glass of beer, €1.50; cup of coffee, €2; ham and cheese sandwich, €2.25; 2-km (1-mi) taxi ride, €6.50.

CURRENCY The Netherlands is one of 12 nations that have adopted the euro, the European Union currency, written as euro or simply €.

At press time (summer 2003), the exchange rate for the euro was €0.89 to the U.S. dollar, €0.64 to the Canadian dollar, €1.40 to the pound sterling, €0.56 to the Australian dollar, €0.50 to the New Zealand dollar, and €0.12 to the South African rand.

VALUE-ADDED TAX (V.A.T.) Stores carrying the TAX FREE SHOPPING sign guarantee that you can get a V.A.T. (value-added tax, called BTW in Holland) refund by means of a Global Refund check, which you request from the salesperson. Stores without this sign may be willing to privately arrange to help you receive the refund, but this is an unwieldy procedure and not likely to happen. Purchases of goods in one store on one day amounting to €136 or more qualify for a V.A.T. refund of 19%, less a service charge. After the refund check has been validated by customs at the airport, you can submit it when you leave the Netherlands or exit the European Union, or by mail, and the refund will be credited to your credit card within five weeks. This arrangement is valid only if you export the goods within three months after date of purchase.

TELEPHONES

COUNTRY & AREA CODES The country code for the Netherlands is 31. When dialing a number in the Netherlands from outside the country, drop the initial 0 from the local area code.

INTERNATIONAL CALLS Direct-dial international calls can be made from any phone booth. To reach an AT&T, MCI (called WorldPhone in the Netherlands), or Sprint operator, dial one of the access codes below.

Access Codes **AT&T** ☎ 0800/022-9111. **MCI** ☎ 0800/022-9122. **Sprint** ☎ 0800/022-9119.

LOCAL CALLS All towns and cities have area codes that are used only when you are calling from outside the area. All public phone booths require phone cards, which may be purchased from post offices, railway stations, and newsdealers in €5 and €10 amounts. Most operators speak English. Dial 0900–8418 for international assistance (€1.15 per minute).

ATHENS

2

Athens is the point to which all roads lead in Greece and from which many tours take off if for no reason other than that the greatest sight of "the glory that was Greece" is here: the Parthenon and other legendary buildings of the Acropolis. But this perpetual shrine of Western civilization, set high on a rocky bluff, dominates and overlooks a 21st-century boomtown. In 1834, when it became the capital of modern Greece, Athens had a population of fewer than 10,000. Now it houses more than a third of the entire Greek population—around 4.6 million. A modern concrete city has engulfed the old village and spreads for 388 square km (244 square mi), covering all the surrounding plain from the sea to the encircling mountains. Athens has long had problems with air pollution, traffic congestion, and inefficient bureaucracy, but preparations for the 2004 summer Olympic Games have brought sweeping changes: improved infrastructure, expanded and more environmentally friendly public transportation, and much-needed renovations to many sights and museums. The modern city's sprawling concrete has failed to overwhelm the astonishing reminders of the legendary classical metropolis. The vibrant mix of ancient and new, and East and West, continues to make Athens one of the most exciting cities in Europe.

EXPLORING ATHENS

The central district of modern Athens is small, stretching from the Acropolis to Mt. Lycabettus, with its small white church on top. The layout is simple: three parallel streets (Stadiou, Panepistimiou, and Akademias) link two main squares (Syntagma and Omonia). Try to wander off this beaten tourist track: seeing the Athenian butchers in the central market near Monastiraki sleeping on their cold marble slabs during the heat of the afternoon siesta may give you more of a feel for the city than looking at hundreds of fallen pillars. In summer, closing times often depend on each site's available personnel, but throughout the year, arrive at least 45 minutes before the official closing time to ensure that you can buy a ticket. Flash photography is forbidden in museums.

Numbers in the margin correspond to points of interest on the Athens map.

7 **Agios Eleftherios** (St. Eleftherios). What's fascinating about the city's former cathedral is that the walls of this 12th-century Byzantine church incorporate reliefs—fanciful figures and zodiac signs—from buildings that date back to the classical period. The church is also known as Little Mitropolis and Panagia Gorgoepikoos (Virgin Who Answers Prayers Quickly), based on its 13th-century icon, said to perform miracles. ✉ *Pl. Mitropolis* ☎ *No phone* 🌐 *www.culture.gr* ⏲ *Daily 8–1; hrs depend on services.*

1 **Akropolis** (Acropolis). Even in its bleached and silent state, the Parthenon—the great temple that crowns the Acropolis, the tablelike hill that represented the "upper city" of ancient Athens—has the power to stir the heart as few other ancient relics can. Whether bathed in the sunlight of the south, or sublimely swathed in moonglow, it endures as a vital monument of ageless intellect. Well, not completely ageless. The Athenians built this complex during the 5th century BC to honor the goddess Athena, patron of the city. The first ruins you'll see are the **Propylaia,** the monumental gateway that led worshipers from the temporal world into the spiritual world of the sanctuary; now only the columns of Pentelic marble and a fragment of stone ceiling remain. Above, to the right, stands the graceful **Naos Athenas Nikis,** or **Apterou Nikis** (Wingless Victory). The temple was mistakenly called the latter because common tradition often confused Athena with the winged goddess Nike. The elegant and architecturally complex **Erechtheion,** most sacred of the shrines of the Acropolis (later turned into a harem by the Turks), has dull, heavy copies of the caryatids (draped maidens) supporting the roof. The **Acropolis Museum** houses five of the six originals, their faces much damaged by acid rain. The sixth is in the British Museum in London.

Fodor's Choice ★

The **Parthenonas** (Parthenon) dominates the Acropolis and indeed the Athens skyline. Designed by Ictinus, with Pheidias as master sculptor, it was completed in 438 BC and is the most architecturally sophisticated temple of that period. Even with hordes of people wandering around the ruins, it still inspires wonder. The architectural decorations were originally painted vivid red and blue, and the roof was of marble tiles. Time and neglect have given the marble pillars their golden-white shine, and the beauty of the building is all the more stark and striking. The British Museum in London houses the largest remaining part of the original 532-foot frieze (the Elgin Marbles), but Greece has long campaigned for its return. The building has 17 fluted columns along each side and eight at the ends; these were cleverly made to lean slightly inward and to bulge, counterbalancing the natural optical distortion. The Parthenon was made into a brothel by the Romans, a church by the Christians, and a mosque by the Turks. The Turks also stored gunpowder in the Propylaia. When the Propylaia was hit by a Venetian bombardment in 1687, 28 columns of the Parthenon were blown out and a fire raged for two days, leaving the temple in its present condition. Piece by piece, the entire Parthenon complex is now undergoing conservation, as part of an ambitious rescue plan launched with international support in 1983 by Greek architects; the completion date is around 2010. An elevator being added to the north side of the Acropolis for the summer 2004 Olympics should help people with mobility concerns. ✉ *Top of Dionyssiou Areopagitou* ☎ *210/321–4172 or 210/321–0219* *www.culture.gr €12 includes admission to the Theatro Dionyssou, Archaia Agora, Olimbion, Roman Agora, and Kerameikos Apr.–Dec., daily 8–sunset; Jan.–Mar., daily 8:30–2:30.*

4 **Archaia Agora** (Ancient Agora). Now a sprawling confusion of stones, slabs, and foundations, this was the civic center and focal point of community life in ancient Athens, where Socrates met with his students while merchants haggled over the price of olive oil. It is dominated by the best-preserved Doric temple in Greece, the **Hephaisteion,** built during the 5th century BC. Nearby, the Stoa Attalou (Stoa of Attalos II), reconstructed in the mid-1950s by the American School of Classical Studies in Athens, houses the **Museo tis Agoras** (Museum of Agora Excavations). The museum focuses on everyday life in ancient Athens, its objects ranging from a child's terra-cotta chamber pot to the shards (*ostraka,* from which the word "ostracism" is derived) used in secret ballots to recommend the banishment of Themistocles and other powerful citizens. *Three entrances: from Monastiraki, on Adrianou; from Thission, on Apostolos Pavlou; from the Acropolis, on descent along Ag. Apostoli 210/321–0185 www.culture.gr Mar.–Dec., daily 8–5; Jan. and Feb., daily 8–3.*

3 **Areios Pagos** (Areopagus). From this rocky outcrop, ancient Athens's supreme court, you can view the Propylaia, the Agora, and the modern city. Legend claims it was here that Orestes was tried for the murder of his mother, and much later St. Paul delivered his Sermon to the Unknown God. It was so moving that a senator named Dionysius converted to Christianity and became the first bishop of Athens. *Opposite Acropolis entrance Daily 24 hrs.*

★ 19 **Benaki Museum.** Established in 1926 by an illustrious Athenian family, this museum was one of the first to place emphasis on Greece's later heritage at a time when many archaeologists were destroying Byzantine artifacts to access ancient objects. The collection (more than 20,000 items are on display in 36 rooms—and that's only a sample of the holdings) moves chronologically from the ground floor upward, from prehistory to the formation of the modern Greek state. You might see anything from a 5,000-year-old gold bowl to Lord Byron's pistols. Other parts of the collection—Islamic art, Chinese porcelain—will be displayed in branches throughout the city sometime after 2004. *Koumbari 1, Kolonaki 210/367–1000 www.benaki.gr Mon., Wed., Fri., and Sat. 9–5, Thurs. 9 AM–midnight, Sun. 9–3.*

20 **Ethniko Archaiologiko Museo** (National Archaeological Museum). The city's most important museum contains artistic highlights from every period of ancient Greek civilization, from Neolithic to Roman times. Among the collection of antiquities are the sensational archaeological finds of Heinrich Schliemann in 1874 at Mycenae; 16th-century BC frescoes from the Akrotiri ruins on Santorini; and the 6½-foot-tall bronze sculpture *Poseidon,* an original work circa 470 BC that was found in the sea off Cape Artemision. The museum will close periodically through 2006 as it undergoes major expansion. *28 Oktovriou (Patission) 44, 10-min walk north of Pl. Omonia 210/821–7717 www.culture.gr Apr.–Oct., Mon. 12:30–7, Tues.–Fri. 8–7, weekends and holidays 8:30–3; Nov.–Mar., Mon. 11–5, Tues.–Fri. 8–5, weekends and holidays 8:30–3.*

Fodor'sChoice ★

16 **Goulandri Museo Kikladikis ke Ellinikis Archaias Technis** (Goulandris Museum of Cycladic and Greek Ancient Art). This outstanding collection spans 5,000 years and includes 350 objects from the Cycladic civilization (3000–2000 BC), with many of the marble figurines that fascinated such artists as Picasso and Modigliani. *Neofitou Douka 4 or Irodotou 1 210/722–8321 through 210/722–8323 www.cycladic.gr Mon. and Wed.–Sat. 10–4.*

Fodor'sChoice ★

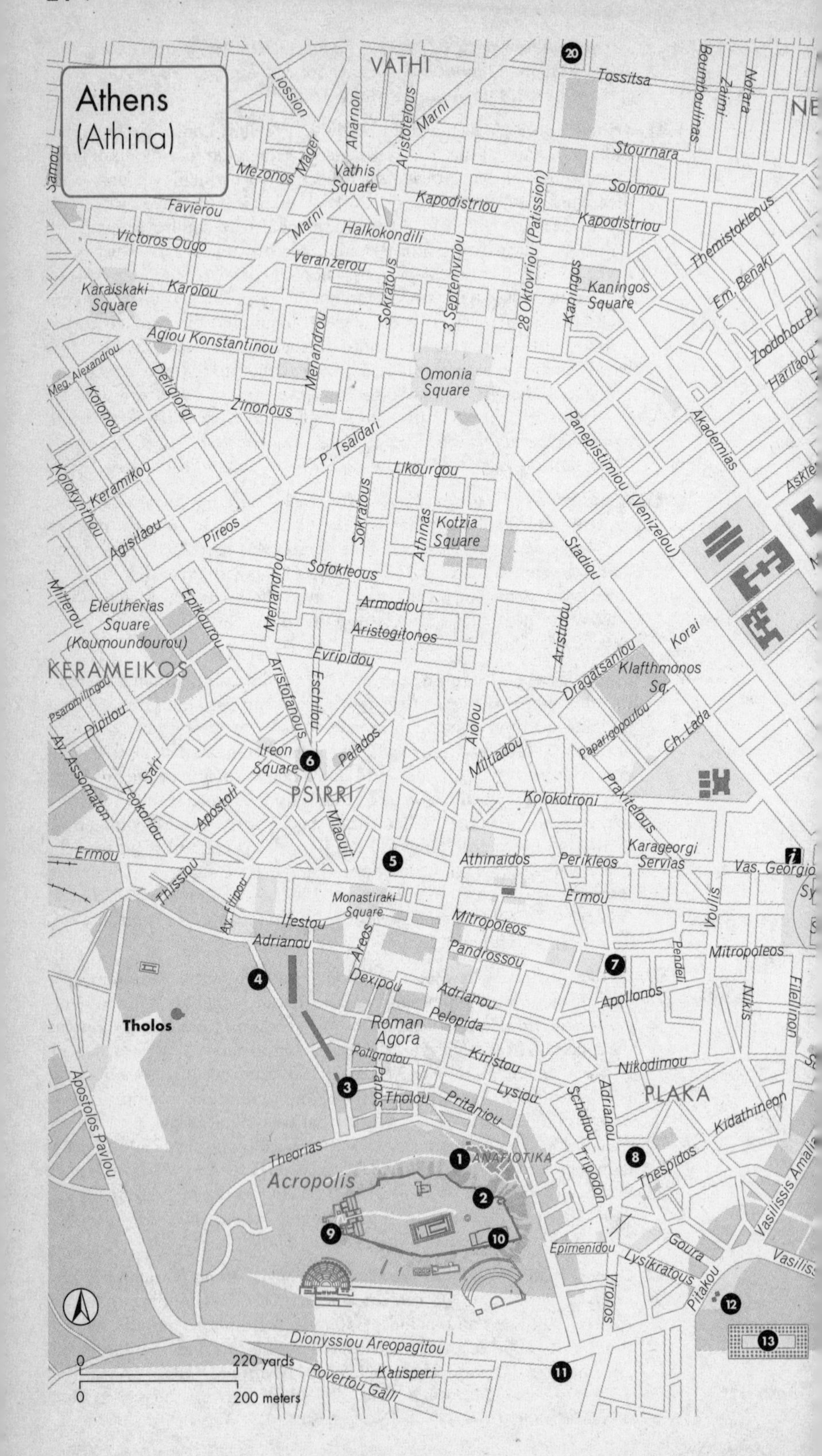
Athens
(Athina)
VATHI
Tossitsa
Liossion
Aharnon
Aristotelous
Marni
Boumboulinas
Zaimi
Notara
Stournara
Samou
Mezonos
Mager
Vathis Square
Solomou
Kapodistriou
28 Oktovriou (Patission)
Favierou
Kapodistriou
Themistokleous
Victoros Ougo
Marni
Halkokondili
Veranzerou
Sokratous
3 Septemvriou
Kaningos
Kaningos Square
Em. Benaki
Karaiskaki Square
Karolou
Zoodohou Pi
Agiou Konstantinou
Menandrou
Omonia Square
Harilaou
Meg. Alexandrou
Kotonou
Deligiorgi
Zinonous
Panepistimiou (Venizelou)
Akademias
P. Tsaldari
Likourgou
Kolokynthou
Keramikou
Sokratous
Athinas
Kotzia Square
Askle
Agisilaou
Pireos
Stadiou
Sofokleous
Menandrou
Mitterou
Eleutherias Square
(Koumoundourou)
Epikourou
Armodiou
Aristogitonos
Aristidou
Korai
KERAMEIKOS
Evripidou
Aristofanous
Eschilou
Dragatsaniou
Klafthmonos Sq.
Psaromilingou
Dipilou
Paparigopoulou
Ch. Lada
Ay. Assomaton
Sari
Ireon Square
Palados
Aiolou
Miltiadou
Leokoriou
Apostoli
PSIRRI
Kolokotroni
Praxitelous
Miaouli
Ermou
Thissiou
Athinaidos
Perikleos
Karageorgi Servias
Vas. Georgio
Ay. Filipou
Monastiraki Square
Ermou
Voulis
Ifestou
Mitropoleos
Adrianou
Areos
Pandrossou
Pendeli
Mitropoleos
Dexipou
Adrianou
Apollonos
Nikis
Filellinon
Tholos
Roman Agora
Pelopida
Polignotou
Kiristou
Nikodimou
Apostolos Pavlou
Panos
Tholou
Lysiou
Scholiou
Adrianou
PLAKA
Pritaniou
Kidathineon
Theorias
ANAFIOTIKA
Tripodon
Thespidos
Acropolis
Vasilissis Amalia
Epimenidou
Lysikratous
Goura
Vasiliss
Vironos
Pitakou
Dionyssiou Areopagitou
0
220 yards
Kalisperi
Rovertou Galli
0
200 meters

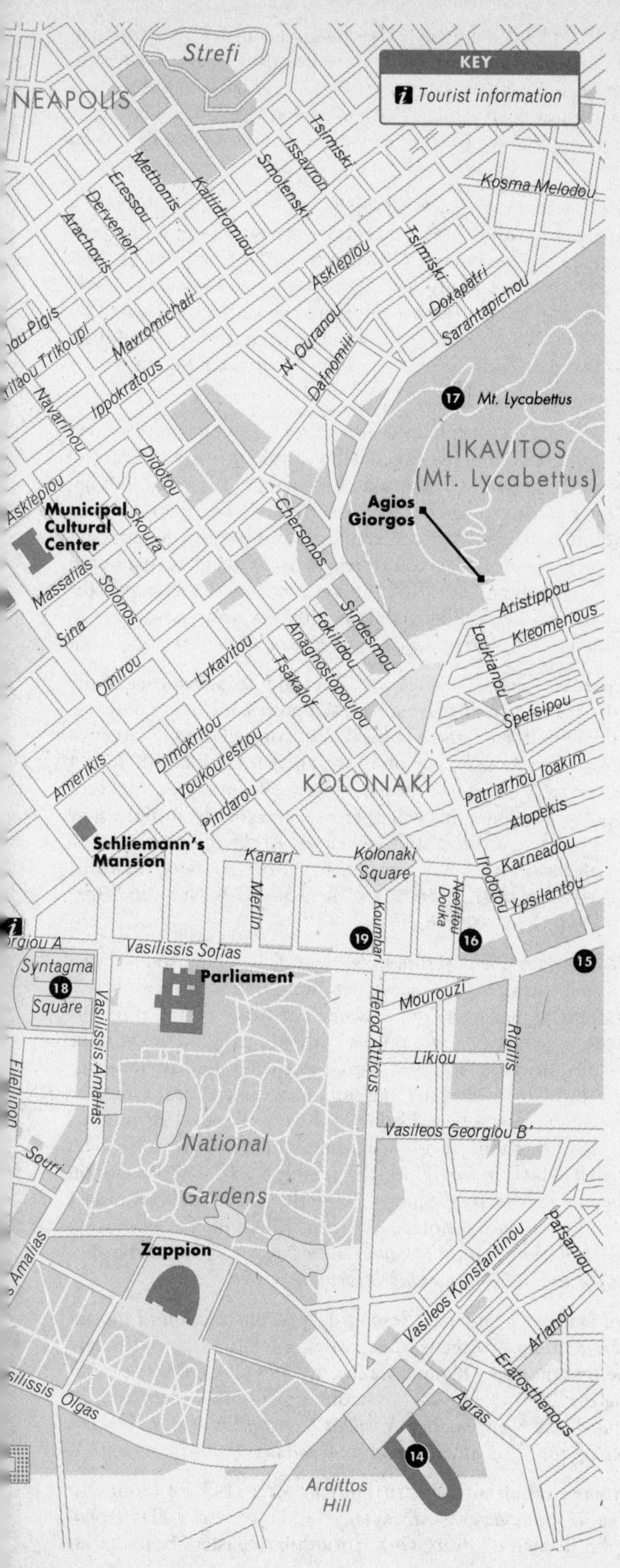

Agios Eleftherios **7**
Akropolis **1**
Archaia Agora **4**
Areios Pagos **3**
Benaki Museum **19**
Ethniko Archaiologiko Museo **20**
Goulandri Museo Kikladikis ke Ellinikis Archaias Technis **16**
Irodion **9**
Likavitos **17**
Monastiraki **5**
Museo Akropoleos **2**
Neos Museo Akropolos **11**
Panathinaiko Stadio **14**
Pili tou Adrianou **12**
Plaka **8**
Psirri **6**
Stiles Olymbiou Dios **13**
Syntagma **18**
Theatro Dionyssou **10**
Vizantino Museo **15**

❾ **Irodion** (Odeon of Herod Atticus). Hauntingly beautiful, this 2nd-century AD theater was built Greek-style into the hillside but with typical Roman archways in its three-story stage building and barrel-vaulted entrances. The theater hosts Athens Festival performances from late June through September. ✉ *Dionyssiou Areopagitou, across from Propylaia* ☎ *210/323–2771* ⏲ *Open only to audiences during performances.*

★ ⓱ **Likavitos** (Mt. Lycabettus). Athens's highest hill borders Kolonaki, a residential quarter worth a visit if you enjoy window-shopping and people-watching. A steep **funicular** (✉ Ploutarchou 1 at Aristippou ☎ 210/722–7065 ⏲ Nov.–Apr., daily 9:15 AM–11:45 PM; May–Oct., daily 9:15 AM–12:45 AM; every 10 min) climbs to the summit, crowned by whitewashed Agios Giorgios chapel. The view from the top—pollution permitting—is the finest in Athens. ✉ *Base: 15-min walk northeast of Syntagma.*

❺ **Monastiraki.** The old Turkish bazaar area takes its name from Panayia Pantanassa Church, commonly called Monastiraki (Little Monastery). Near the church stands the Tzistarakis Mosque (1759), exemplifying the East-West paradox that characterizes Athens. The district's real draw is the Sunday flea market, centered on tiny Abyssinia Square and running along Ifestou and Kynetou streets, where Greeks bargain with wildly gesturing hands and dramatic facial expressions. Everything's for sale, from gramophone needles to old matchboxes, from nose rings to cool white linens. ✉ *South of junction of Ermou and Athinas.*

★ ❷ **Museo Akropoleos** (Acropolis Museum). Tucked into one corner of the Acropolis, this institution displays superb sculptures, including the caryatids from the Erechtheion and a collection of colored *korai* (statues of women dedicated to Athena, patron of the ancient city). In 2004, part of the collection will move to the Neo Museo Akropoleos, at the foot of the Acropolis. The museums will operate concurrently until the new museum is completed, around 2006, when the Acropolis Museum will close. ✉ *Southeastern corner of Acropolis* ☎ *210/323–6665* 🌐 *www.culture.gr* ⏲ *Mid-Apr.–Oct., Mon. 11–6, Tues.–Sun. 8–6; Nov.–mid-Apr., Mon. 10:30–2:30, Tues.–Sun. 8:30–3.*

⓫ **Neo Museo Akropoleos** (New Acropolis Museum). This new, state-of-the-art museum will showcase the marvelous Acropolis sculptures. It will also send a political message: Greece wants Great Britain to return the Elgin Marbles, which once stood on the Parthenon and are now in the British Museum. Britain maintains that Greece cannot adequately display the marbles; Greece says the museum answers that criticism. The museum's centerpiece will be a display of the marbles in their original order, with gaps left to indicate the sculptures still in Britain, and a glass ceiling through which you will see the temple itself. The Parthenon room is scheduled to open in summer 2004, the rest of the museum by 2006, when it will replace the older Acropolis Museum. ✉ *Dionyssiou Areopagitou and Makriyianni* 🌐 *www.culture.gr* ☞ *Contact Acropolis Museum for updates on opening information.*

⓮ **Panathinaiko Stadio** (Panathenaic Stadium). A reconstruction of the ancient Roman stadium in Athens, this gleaming-white marble structure built for the first modern Olympic Games in 1896 seats 50,000 spectators. During the 2004 Olympics, the stadium will host archery and the marathon finish. ✉ *Near junction Vasileos Konstantinou and Vasilissis Olgas* ☎ *No phone* 🌐 *www.culture.gr* ⏲ *Weekdays 8:30–1 and 3:30–7.*

⓬ **Pili tou Adrianou** (Hadrian's Arch). Built in AD 131–32 by Emperor Hadrian to show where classical Athens ended and his new city, Hadriaopolis, began, the Roman archway with Corinthian pilasters bears an inscription on the side facing the Acropolis that reads THIS IS ATHENS, THE ANCIENT CITY OF THESEUS. The side facing the Temple of Olympian Zeus proclaims THIS IS THE CITY OF HADRIAN AND NOT OF THESEUS. ✉ *Junction Vasilissis Amalias and Dionyssiou Areopagitou* 🌐 *www.culture.gr.*

★ 8 **Plaka.** Stretching east from the Agora, the Plaka, almost all that's left of 19th-century Athens, is a lovely quarter of neoclassical houses, medieval churches, and many intriguing smaller sights tucked among the winding walkways. The **Museo Ellinikis Laikis Technis** (Greek Folk Art Museum; ✉ Kidathineon 17 ☎ 210/322–9031 ⏲ Tues.–Sun. 10–2) has a rich collection of embroideries, carvings, and jewelry from as long ago as 1650. The **Roman Agora** (✉ Pelopidas and Aiolou ☎ 210/324–5220 🌐 www.culture.gr ⏲ Tues.–Sun. 8:30–3), founded by Julius Caesar and Augustus, replaced the Archaia Agora in the 1st century AD. Its highlight is the octagonal Aerides (Tower of the Winds), a 1st-century BC water clock. A visit to the delightful **Museo Ellinikon Laikon Musikon Organon** (Museum of Greek Popular Musical Instruments; ✉ Diogenous 1–3 ☎ 210/325–0198 ⏲ Tues. and Thurs.–Sun. 10–2, Wed. noon–6), around the corner from the Roman Agora, is a crash course in the development of Greek music, with three floors of instruments and headphones so you can listen to all kinds of recorded sounds, from goatskin bagpipes to the Cretan lyra (a string instrument). The **Mnimeio Lysikratous** (Monument of Lysikrates; ✉ Herefondos and Lysikratous) is one of the few surviving tripods on which stood the award for the producer of the best play in the Dionyssia festival. Above Plaka, at the northeastern base of the Acropolis, is **Anafiotika,** the closest thing you'll find to a village in Athens. Take time to wander among its whitewashed, bougainvillea-framed houses and tiny churches.

6 **Psirri.** During the day, little in this former industrial district indicates that at night this quarter becomes a whirl of clubs and restaurants, dotted with dramatically lighted churches and lively squares. Whether you want to dance on tabletops to live Greek music, sing along with a soulful accordion player, listen to salsa in a Cuban club, or just watch the hoi polloi go by as you snack on trendy or traditional mezedes, this is the place. ✉ *Off Ermou, centered on Iroon and Ag. Anargiron Sqs.*

13 **Stiles Olymbiou Dios** (Temple of Olympian Zeus). Begun during the 6th century BC, this temple, also known as the Olymbion, was larger than all other temples in Greece when it was finally completed 700 years later. It was destroyed during the invasion of the Goths in the 4th century; only a few towering, sun-bleached columns remain. ✉ *Vasilissis Olgas 1* ☎ *210/922–6330* 🌐 *www.culture.gr* ⏲ *Daily 8–5.*

18 **Syntagma** (Constitution Square). At the top of the square stands the **Vouli** (Parliament), formerly the royal palace, completed in 1838 for the new monarchy. From the Parliament you can watch the changing of the Evzone honor guard at the **Mnimeio Agnostou Stratiotou** (Tomb of the Unknown Soldier), with its text from Pericles's funeral oration and a bas-relief of a dying soldier modeled after a sculpture on the Temple of Aphaia in Aegina. The most elaborate ceremony takes place on Sunday, when the sturdy young guards don their *foustanellas* (kilts) with 400 pleats, one for each year of the Ottoman occupation. The procession usually arrives in front of Parliament at 11:15 AM. Pop into the gleaming **Stathmo Syntagma** (Syntagma metro station: at upper end of the square) to take a look at artifacts from the subway excavations and a vast cross section of earth behind glass. The cross section shows finds in chronological layers, including a skeleton in its ancient grave, traces of the 4th-century BC road to Mesogeia, and a Turkish cistern. On the southern side of Syntagma is the lush **Ethnikos Kipos** (National Gar-

den), its dense foliage, gazebos, and trellised walkways providing a quick escape from the center's bustle. For young visitors, there are two playgrounds, a miniature zoo, duck pond, and refreshments at the stone cottage café. ✉ *Corner of Vasilissis Sofias and Vasilissis Amalias.*

⑩ **Theatro Dionyssou** (Theater of Dionysus). In this theater dating from about 330 BC, the ancient dramas and comedies were performed in conjunction with bacchanalian feasts. The throne in the center was reserved for the priest of Dionysus: it is adorned with regal lions' paws, and reliefs of satyrs and griffins decorate the back. ✉ *Dionyssiou Areopagitou, opposite Mitsaion* ☎ *210/322–4625* 🌐 *www.culture.gr* ⏲ *Apr.–Dec., daily 8–6; Jan.–Mar., daily 8:30–2:30.*

⑮ **Vizantino Museo** (Byzantine Museum). This museum, part of which occupies an 1848 mansion, has a unique collection of icons, mosaics, and tapestries. Sculptural fragments provide an excellent introduction to Byzantine architecture. The museum will be closed periodically through 2006 to accommodate extensive renovations. When it finally reopens, much of the collection will be displayed for the first time, including some magnificent illuminated manuscripts. You will also be able to explore the on-site archaeological dig of Aristotle's Lyceum. ✉ *Vasilissis Sofias 22* ☎ *210/723–2178* 🌐 *www.culture.gr* ⏲ *Tues.–Sun. 8:30–3.*

WHERE TO EAT

Search for places with at least a half dozen tables occupied by Athenians—they're discerning customers.

WHAT IT COSTS In euros

	$$$$	$$$	$$	$
AT DINNER	over €21	€16–€21	€10–€15	under €10

Prices are per person for a main course or, for restaurants that serve only mezedes, two mezedes.

$$$$ ✕ **Boschetto.** The restaurant near the Hilton pampers diners with its park setting, expert maître d', and creative nouvelle Italian food. The specialty here is fresh pasta, such as the shrimp cannelloni or green gnocchi with Gorgonzola sauce. Entrées may include sea bass with a potato crust or grilled wild buffalo steak with a sauce of coffee, figs, and Mavrodaphne wine. The tables tend to be close together; reserve near the window or in the courtyard during the summer. ✉ *Alsos Evangelismos* ☎ *210/721–0893 or 210/722–7324* ✍ *Reservations essential* 💳 *AE, V* ⏲ *Closed Sun. and 2 wks in Aug. No lunch Oct.–Apr.*

$$$$ ✕ **Spondi.** The ambience here is as cool and contemporary as the cuisine. Savor the artichoke terrine with duck confit or black ravioli with honeyed leek and shrimp. Interesting entrées may include a lamb tail so tender it falls from the bone, with couscous, raisins, and cumin; and chicken with foie gras, truffles, and asparagus in porcini sauce. In good weather, you can sit in the bougainvillea-draped courtyard. ✉ *Pirronos 5, Pangrati* ☎ *210/756–4021 or 210/752–0658* ✍ *Reservations essential* 💳 *AE, DC, MC, V* ⏲ *No lunch.*

$$$$ ✕ **Vardis.** A meal at this French restaurant is worth the trip to the northern suburb of Kifissia. The clientele may be a little sedate, but the food dazzles. The chef is committed to the classics and to quality ingredients—he brings in sweetwater crayfish from Orhomenos and tracks down rare large shrimp from Thassos island. Especially good are the caramelized lamb cutlets with morel and porcini mushrooms, and salt-crusted duck filled with foie gras and served with a sherry sauce. ✉ *Diligianni 66,* *in Pentelikon Hotel, Kefalari, Kifissia* ☎ *210/623–0650 through 210/623–0656* ✍ *Reservations essential* ▭ *AE, DC, MC, V* ⊙ *Closed Sun. and Aug. No lunch.*

$$$–$$$$ Fodor's Choice ★ ✕ **Aristera-Dexia.** Chef Chrisanthos Karalomengos's forte is fusion—artful combinations such as a tower of *haloumi* (Cypriot cheese) and feta croquettes in a melon-mirin-chili sauce, or the Greek version of sushi, raw squid on a puree of eggplant with anchovies and trout roe. The restaurant is strikingly designed, with two large partitions dividing the large room (hence the name, which means "Left-Right") and a glass runway that let you peek into the city's best wine cellar. You should take a taxi to this gritty neighborhood on the edge of the newly trendy Gazi cultural district. ✉ *Andronikou 3, Rouf* ☎ *210/342–2380* ✍ *Reservations essential* ▭ *AE, MC, V* ⊙ *Closed Sun. and Aug. No lunch.*

$$$–$$$$ Fodor's Choice ★ ✕ **To Varoulko.** Chef Lefteris Lazarou is constantly trying to outdo himself, with magnificent results. You can sample such appetizers as crab salad studded with mango and grapes, with bits of leek to cut the sweetness; or fresh mullet roe laced with honey and accompanied by cinnamony cauliflower puree. This restaurant is famous for monkfish, but the many other seafood dishes include cockles steamed in Limnos sweet wine, and lobster with wild rice, celery, and champagne sauce. ✉ *Deligeorgi 14, Piraeus* ☎ *210/411–2043 or 210/422–1283* ✍ *Reservations essential* ▭ *AE, DC, MC, V* ⊙ *Closed Sun. and Aug. No lunch.*

$$$ ✕ **Daphne's.** It may be a little ostentatious to display a laminated catalog of celebrity diners at the entrance, but Daphne's does have reason to boast. Athenians as well as luminaries from Hillary Clinton to Luciano Pavarotti have long cherished the restaurant's authentic but sophisticated take on regional Greek classics. Try the tender rabbit stewed in sweet Mavrodaphne wine, shrimp dressed in crunchy almond flakes, or pork braised with quince. In summer, diners can move from the frescoed 1830s mansion to a flower-filled courtyard. ✉ *Lysikratous 4, Plaka* ☎ *210/322–7971* ✍ *Reservations essential* ▭ *AE, MC, V.*

$$–$$$ ✕ **Azul.** The space may be a bit cramped, but the Mediterranean food is superb. Start with salmon and trout in pastry with champagne sauce. The spaghetti *à la nona* (godmother's) with chamomile, Gorgonzola, and bacon is an unparalleled combination. Other memorable dishes are beef fillet with raisins and cedar needles, and chicken prepared with lemon leaves. In summer, Azul sets up tables outside. ✉ *Haritos 43, Kolonaki* ☎ *210/725–3817* ✍ *Reservations essential* ▭ *AE, DC, MC, V* ⊙ *Closed last 2 wks in Aug. and Sun. Oct.–Apr. No lunch.*

$$–$$$ ✕ **Mamacas.** This was the first in a wave of "modern" tavernas now springing up all over Athens, and it helped transform the former industrial district of Gazi into one of the hippest parts of town. The cool pastel linen interior is a refreshing visual counterpart to the surrounding warehouses. Amid all this modernity, the hearty, vibrant flavors of traditional taverna food remain, although they have been tweaked with contemporary sensibility in dishes such as pork with prunes, black-eyed pea salad, and cuttlefish with spinach. ✉ *Persofonis 41, Gazi* ☎ *210/346–4984* ▭ *MC, V* ⊙ *Closed Mon.*

$$–$$$ ✕ **Tade Efi Anna.** This stylish restaurant near the end of the Ermou pedestrian zone serves regional Greek cuisine with a modern touch. The space itself is trendy, with funky lighting fixtures, loud music, and an ultracool clientele. Try the *pita Kaisarias* (the spicy, cured meat called *pastourmas* with tomato and kasseri cheese in crisp phyllo), or *melitzanes amigdalou* (sliced eggplant layered with tomatoes and cheese with a thick topping of crushed almonds). ✉ *Ermou 72, Monastiraki* ☎ *210/321–3652* ▭ *V* ⊙ *Closed Mon.*

$$ ✕ **Kollias.** Friendly owner Tassos Kollias creates his own dishes, from the humble to the aristocratic: sea urchin salad or lobster with lemon,

balsamic vinegar, and a shot of honey. He's known for bringing in the best-quality catch, whether mullet from Messolonghi or oysters culled by Kalymnos sponge divers, and his prices are usually 25% lower than most fish tavernas. Call for directions—even locals get lost trying to find this obscure street in the working-class quarter of Piraeus. ✉ *Stratigou Plastira 3, near junction of Dramas and Kalokairinou, Tabouria* ☎ *210/461–9150 or 210/462–9620* *Reservations essential* *AE, DC, MC, V* *No lunch Mon.–Sat., no dinner Sun.*

$–$$ Fodor'sChoice ★ ✕ **Vlassis.** Relying on recipes from Thrace, Roumeli, Thessaly, and the islands, the chefs whip up Greek home cooking in generous portions. Musts are the peppery cheese dip called *tirokafteri,* pastitsio (made here with bits of lamb liver), *lahanodolmades* (cabbage leaves stuffed with minced meat), goat with oil and oregano, and octopus *stifado* (stew), tender and sweet with lots of onions. ✉ *Paster 8, Platia Mavili (near American embassy)* ☎ *210/646–3060* *Reservations essential* *No credit cards* *Closed Aug.–mid-Sept. No dinner Sun.*

$ ✕ **Margaro.** Near Piraeus, next to the Naval Academy, this popular, no-nonsense fish taverna serves just four items, along with excellent barrel wine: fried crayfish, fried red mullet, fried *marida* (a small white fish), and huge Greek salads. If this place is crowded, you may be asked to go into the kitchen and prepare your own salad. Tables on the terrace have a view of the port. Try to arrive between 6 and 8 PM, before Greeks eat dinner. ✉ *Hatzikyriakou 126, Piraeus* ☎ *210/451–4226* *Reservations not accepted* *No credit cards* *Closed 15 days at Greek Easter. No dinner Sun.*

★ $ ✕ **O Platanos.** One of Plaka's oldest yet least touristy tavernas occupies a picturesque courtyard. The waiters are fast and the place is packed with Greeks. Don't miss the oven-baked potatoes, savory lamb fricassee, green beans in olive oil, and exceptionally cheap but delicious barrel retsina. ✉ *Diogenous 4, Plaka* ☎ *210/322–0666* *No credit cards* *Closed Sun.*

$ ✕ **Sigalas–Bairaktaris.** Run by the same family for more than a century, this is one of the best places to eat in Monastiraki. After admiring the painted wine barrels and black-and-white stills of Greek film stars, go to the window case to view the day's magirefta—beef *kokkinisto* (stew with red sauce), spicy meat patties seasoned with clove—or sample the gyro platter. Appetizers include tiny cheese pies with sesame seeds and fried zucchini with a garlicky dip. ✉ *Pl. Monastiraki 2, Monastiraki* ☎ *210/321–3036* *AE, MC, V.*

WHERE TO STAY

It's always advisable to reserve a room. Hotels are clustered around the center of town and along the seacoast. Modern hotels are more likely to be air-conditioned and to have double-glazed windows; the center of Athens can be so noisy that it's hard to sleep. In the year before the summer 2004 Olympics, prices have risen considerably, and they may double for the games themselves (and decline, to some degree, after the event). One benefit of the Olympics has been stylish renovations of existing hotels and the building of some new ones, including boutique hotels.

WHAT IT COSTS In euros

	$$$$	$$$	$$	$
FOR 2 PEOPLE	over €250	€175–€250	€100–€175	under €100

Prices are for a standard double room during high season, including taxes.

$$$$ Fodor's Choice ★ **Andromeda Athens Hotel.** On a quiet street near the U.S. Embassy and the city's concert hall, this small luxury hotel caters to business travelers, but all guests relish the meticulous service and sumptuous furnishings. During 2003, each room was renovated and refurnished according to a different theme, such as art deco, Asian, and African. All rooms have business essentials, as well as wide-screen TVs and DVD players. A new spa and fitness center are also being built. The hotel operates a property across the street with a security system and 12 stylish executive suites (one- and two-room apartments). ✉ *Timoleondos Vassou 22, Pl. Mavili, 11521* ☎ *210/641–5000* 📠 *210/646–6361* 🌐 *www.andromedaathens.gr* *21 rooms, 8 suites, 1 penthouse* *Restaurant* 💳 *AE, DC, MC, V* 🍽 *BP.*

$$$$ **Athens Hilton.** A two-year, head-to-toe renovation completed in 2003 gave this hotel a new look that reflects the trend sweeping most of Athens's high-end properties as they prepare to face the world for the summer 2004 Olympics: all is modern, clean-lined, and uncluttered. The once-traditional lobby is a vast expanse of white marble with sleek benches. Rooms are fitted out in light wood, brushed metal, etched glass, and crisp white duvets. Facilities include an executive check-in lounge and huge conference rooms, along with a spa and the biggest pool in Athens. ✉ *Vasilissis Sofias 46, 11528* ☎ *210/728–1000, 210/728–1100 reservations* 📠 *210/333–0160* 🌐 *www.athens.hilton.com* *498 rooms, 19 suites* *4 restaurants, pool, wading pool* 💳 *AE, DC, MC, V.*

★ **$$$$** **Divani Apollon Palace.** For those who need a break from city bustle, this seaside resort is the perfect solution. Casual but sophisticated, it has excellent service and sparkling facilities. Spend an hour on the tennis court, dip into the Aegean across the street, or take the hotel shuttle to Glyfada for some serious shopping (the van continues on to downtown Athens). The airy, white-and-yellow rooms all have balconies with a sea view. Best, though, are the hotel's gleaming public spaces, the outdoor pool with hydromassage, and the Pelagos Bar with its leather sofas. ✉ *Ag. Nikolaou 10 and Iliou, Vouliagmeni, 16671* ☎ *210/891–1100* 📠 *210/965–8010* 🌐 *www.divaniapollon.gr* *286 rooms, 7 suites* *2 restaurants, 2 pools (1 indoor), wading pool* 💳 *AE, DC, MC, V* 🍽 *BP.*

★ **$$$$** **Grande Bretagne.** Built in 1842, the G. B. is an Athens landmark, with a guest list of more than 150 years' worth of royals, rock stars, and heads of state testifying to its colorful history. A 2003 renovation recaptured the hotel's original grandeur, restoring antiques, oil paintings, and sumptuous hand-carved details, and adding a spa, pools, and every possible modern convenience, including rooms with fax machines, photocopiers, DVD players, and Bose stereos. The only complaint is that many rooms, albeit luxuriously fitted out, are rather small. ✉ *Vasileos Georgiou A' 1, Pl. Syntagma, 10564* ☎ *01/333–0000; 01/331–5555 through 01/331–5559 reservations* 📠 *01/322–8034; 01/322–2261; 01/333–0910 reservations* 🌐 *www.grandebretagne.gr* *290 rooms, 37 suites* *3 restaurants, 2 pools* 💳 *AE, DC, MC, V.*

$$$$ **Kefalari Suites.** A turn-of-the-20th-century building among the neoclassical mansions and tree-lined boulevards of the suburb of Kifissia contains imaginative theme suites with names such as Malmaison and Jaipur. The suites include kitchenettes with utensils, a modem connection, and verandas or balconies; the sundeck has a whirlpool tub. A deluxe Continental breakfast (cheese, cold cuts, cereal, yogurt, cake) is included in the room rate. ✉ *Pentelis 1 and Kolokotroni, Kifissia, 14562* ☎ *210/623–3333* 📠 *210/623–3330* 🌐 *www.kefalarisuites.gr* *13 suites* 💳 *AE, DC, MC, V* 🍽 *CP.*

$$$$ **N. J. V. Athens Plaza.** The fresh, spacious rooms at this hotel right in the center of Syntagma Square are equipped with top-of-the-line amenities, including large marble bathrooms with phone extensions. Double-glazed windows and air-conditioning keep rooms peaceful and quiet. The suites on the eighth and ninth floors have breathtaking Acropolis views, and interiors decked out with designer furnishings. ✉ *Vasileos Georgiou A' 2, Pl. Syntagma, 10564* ☎ *210/335–2400* 📠 *210/323–5856* 🌐 *www.grecotel.gr* *182 rooms, 15 suites* *Restaurant* *AE, DC, MC, V.*

$$$ **Electra Palace.** Long the nicest hotel in Plaka, the Electra Palace has cozy rooms, a roof garden with a pool and whirlpool tub, stunning Acropolis views, and barbecues in summer; the sumptuous buffet breakfasts are among the best in the city. A head-to-toe renovation in 2003 has added an indoor pool, gym, and sauna, and rooms are being completely redecorated with new furniture. The owners are also expanding into the building next door, which they expect will add about 50 new rooms sometime in 2004. ✉ *Nikodimou 18, Plaka, 10557* ☎ *210/337–0000* 📠 *210/324–1875* *106 rooms, 5 suites* *Restaurant, 2 pools (1 indoor), bar* *AE, DC, MC, V* *BP.*

$$ **Acropolis View Hotel.** Major sights are just a stone's throw away from this hotel tucked into a quiet neighborhood below the Acropolis. About half of the agreeable rooms with balconies have Parthenon views. There is a roof garden, and staff members in the homey lobby are efficient. ✉ *Webster 10, Acropolis, 11742* ☎ *210/921–7303, 210/921–7304, or 210/921–7305* 📠 *210/923–0705* 🌐 *www.acropolisview.gr* *32 rooms* *DC, MC, V* *BP.*

$$ **Art Gallery Pension.** On a side street not far from the Acropolis, this friendly, handsome house has an old-fashioned look, with family paintings on the muted white walls, comfortable beds, hardwood floors, and ceiling fans. Many rooms have balconies with views of Filopappou or the Acropolis. ✉ *Erecthiou 5, Koukaki, 11742* ☎ *210/923–8376 or 210/923–1933* 📠 *210/923–3025* *ecotec@otenet.gr* *21 rooms, 2 suites* *No credit cards* *Closed Nov.–Feb.*

$$ **Athens Cypria Hotel.** A cool oasis in the city center, this hotel is a few minutes from Syntagma Square, offering a reasonably priced alternative for those who want convenience and comfort. Enter the vaguely art deco lobby from the quiet street to find simple guest rooms, done in shades of blue and furnished with basic amenities. Some of the upper floors open out onto a balcony; those on the sixth floor have Acropolis views. ✉ *Diomias 5, Syntagma, 10557* ☎ *210/323–8034 through 210/323–8038* 📠 *210/324–8792* *71 rooms* *Bar* *AE, V* *BP.*

$$ **Hotel Achilleas.** This modern, family-owned hotel just a few minutes from Syntagma has spacious, pleasant rooms with minibars, safes, and air-conditioning, unusual features in this category. Breakfast is served in an interior courtyard filled with jungly plants and marble-top blue tables. ✉ *Lekka 21, Syntagma, 10562* ☎ *210/322–5826, 210/322–8531, or 210/323–3197* 📠 *210/322–2412* 🌐 *www.tourhotel.gr/achilleas* *36 rooms* *AE, DC, MC, V* *CP.*

$$ **Plaka Hotel.** Close to the ancient sights and the Monastiraki Square metro, this hotel has a roof garden overlooking the Plaka district's rooftops to the Parthenon. Double-glazed windows cut down the noise; the highest floors are the quietest. All rooms have TV and are simply furnished; those in back from the fifth floor up have the best Acropolis views. ✉ *Kapnikareas 7 and Mitropoleos, Plaka, 10556* ☎ *210/322–2096 through 210/322–2098* 📠 *210/322–2412* 🌐 *www.plakahotel.gr* *67 rooms* *AE, DC, MC, V* *CP.*

$–$$ **Acropolis House.** The artists and academics who frequent this pension in a 19th-century Plaka residence appreciate its large rooms, original frescoes, and genteel owners. Most rooms have private bathrooms; about 10 have their bath immediately outside in the hallway. Rooms with air-conditioning cost extra. ✉ *Kodrou 6–8, Plaka, 10558* ☎ *210/322–2344 or 210/322–6241* 🖷 *210/324–4143* *20 rooms* ▭ *V* *CP.*

$ **Cecil Hotel.** A gracefully restored 1920s mansion between Monastiraki and the Central Market holds this friendly hotel with polished wood floors, spacious, high-ceilinged rooms, and cozy furnishings. All rooms have air-conditioning, and a roof garden is planned for summer 2004. ✉ *Athinas 39, Monastiraki, 10554* ☎ *210/321–7079* 🖷 *210/321–8005* 🌐 *www.cecil-hotel.com* *39 rooms* ▭ *MC, V* *CP.*

2

NIGHTLIFE & THE ARTS

The English-language newspapers *Athens News* and *Kathemerini* (inserted in the *International Herald Tribune*) list current performances, gallery openings, and films. The magazines *Odyssey* and *Inside Out,* distributed at some hotels and available at English-language bookstores and kiosks, carry extensive information on culture and entertainment in the capital.

The Arts

The **Athens Festival** (box office ✉ Panepistimiou 39 ☎ 210/928–2900 🌐 www.greekfestival.gr) runs from late June through September with concerts, opera, ballet, folk dancing, and drama. Performances are in various locations, including the theater of Herod Atticus below the Acropolis and Mt. Lycabettus. Tickets range in price from €20 to €120 and are available two weeks before the performance.

Technopolis (✉ Pireos 100, Gazi ☎ 210/346–0981), a stunningly converted foundry in a former industrial neighborhood now filled with chic galleries and restaurants, is a multipurpose arts and performance venue for everything from photography exhibits to indie music concerts.

Concerts

Greek and international orchestras perform September through June at the **Megaron Athens Concert Hall** (✉ Vasilissis Sofias and Kokkali ☎ 210/728–2333 through 210/728–2337 🖷 210/728–2300 🌐 www.megaron.gr). Prices range from €18 to €90. Inexpensive and often free classical concerts are held November through May at the **Philippos Nakas Conservatory** (✉ Ippokratous 41 ☎ 210/363–4000 🖷 210/360–2827). Tickets cost €10 to €20.

Dance

The acclaimed **Dora Stratou Troupe** (✉ Theater, Filopappou Hill ☎ 210/324–4395 troupe's offices 🖷 210/324–6921 🌐 www.grdance.org) performs authentic Greek and Cypriot folk dances. Tickets cost €13 and are available outside the theater. Performances are from the end of May to the end of September, Tuesday–Saturday at 9:30 PM and Sunday at 8:30.

Film

Almost all Athens cinemas now show foreign films; for listings, consult the *Athens News* and the *Kathemerini* insert in the *International Herald Tribune.* Tickets run about €7 to €10. In summer, films are shown in open-air cinemas.

Nightlife

Athens has an active nightlife; most bars and clubs stay open until at least 3 AM. Drinks are rather steep (about €6–€10) but generous. Often there is a surcharge on weekends at the most popular clubs, which also have bouncers. Few clubs take credit cards for drinks. In summer most major downtown clubs move to the seaside, and some open up in new winter spaces each season. Ask your hotel for recommendations and check ahead for summer closings. For a uniquely Greek evening, visit a club featuring *rembetika* music, a type of blues, or the popular *bouzoukia* (clubs with live bouzouki music). In the larger bouzouki venues, there is usually a per-person minimum or an overpriced, second-rate prix-fixe menu; a bottle of whiskey costs about €120.

Bars & Clubs

Bedlam (✉ Zappio Gardens, Syntagma ☎ 210/336–9340), in lush Zappio Gardens, with tables placed among trees hung with crystals, is a glamorous escape from the city within the city. **Central** (✉ Pl. Kolonaki 14, Kolonaki ☎ 210/724–5938), open day and night, is the place to see all of Athens's beautiful people enjoying cocktails and sushi in the cool, creamy interior. **Exo** (✉ Markou Mousourou 1, Mets ☎ 210/923–5818), a downtown summer favorite, attracts a trendy, mixed-age crowd with its roof garden and spectacular Acropolis views. **Folie** (✉ Eslin 4, Ambelokipi ☎ 210/646–9852) has a congenial crowd of all ages dancing to reggae, Latin, funk, and ethnic music. **Island** (✉ Limanakia Vouliagmenis, Varkiza ☎ 210/965–3563), the summer incarnation of Central, is dreamily decked out in gauzy linens; it overlooks the Aegean. **Mommy** (✉ Delfon 4, Kolonaki ☎ 210/361–9682), a funky bar-restaurant popular with lifestyle magazine writers, has pop-art sofas, Chinese finger food, and frequent theme nights. **Plus Soda** (✉ Ermou 161, Thissio ☎ 210/345–6187), the dance temple of Athens, hires Europe's top DJs; it moves to a different spot each summer.

Bouzoukia

Apollon (✉ Syngrou 259, Nea Smyrni ☎ 210/942–7580 through 210/942–7583) is one of Athens's most popular venues, showcasing singers such as dueling divas Anna Vissi and Kaiti Garbi. It's closed Monday and Tuesday. **Rex** (✉ Panepistimiou 48, Syntagma ☎ 210/381–4591) is an over-the-top laser-light show and plate-smashing extravaganza, with performances by top pop and bouzouki stars.

Rembetika Clubs

Rembetika, the blues sung by refugees from Asia Minor who came to Greece in the 1920s, still enthralls Greeks. At **Mnissikleous** (✉ Mnissikleous 22 and Lyceiou, Plaka ☎ 210/322–5558 or 210/322–5337), the authentic music of popular *rembetis* Bobis Goles draws audience participation. **Stoa ton Athanaton** (✉ Sofocleous 19 and Stoa Athanaton in the Central Market arcade, Omonia ☎ 210/321–4362), open day and night, is the city's premier *rembetatiko*.

Rock, Jazz & Blues

House of Art (✉ Santouri 4 and Sarri, Psirri ☎ 210/321–7678) hosts small groups in a laid-back setting. **Half Note Jazz Club** (✉ Trivonianou 17, Mets ☎ 210/921–3310 or 210/923–2460) is the premier venue for international jazz and blues bands. **Parafono** (✉ Asklipiou 130, Exarchia ☎ 210/644–6512), a cozy hole-in-the-wall, has good jazz and reggae. **Rodon** (✉ Marni 24, Pl. Vathis ☎ 210/524–7427), an informal venue, showcases big names in popular music; in summer, they usually appear at the outdoor Lycabettus amphitheater. The **Rockwave Festival** (Ticket House box office ✉ Panepistimiou 42 in arcade, Syntagma ☎ 210/360–8366) takes place over three days in mid-July, usually somewhere on the Athens coast. Downtown record stores have details.

SHOPPING

Antiques

Pandrossou Street in Monastiraki is especially rich in shops selling small antiques and icons. Keep in mind that fakes are common and that you must have government permission to export objects from the classic, Hellenistic, Roman, or Byzantine periods. **Martinos** (✉ Pandrossou 50 ☎ 210/321–2414) attracts serious collectors looking for items such as ancient statuettes, pottery fragments, wooden dowry chests, and antique Venetian glass. **Motakis** (✉ Pl. Abyssinia 3, in basement ☎ 210/321–9005) sells antiques and other beautiful old objects. **Nasiotis** (✉ Ifestou 24, Monastiraki ☎ 210/321–2369) has interesting finds in a basement stacked with engravings, old magazines, and books, including first editions.

Flea Markets

The **Sunday-morning flea market** (✉ Pandrossou and Ifestou, Monastiraki) sells everything from secondhand guitars to Russian caviar. However little your treasured find costs, you should haggle. **Ifestou,** in Monastiraki, is the place to go weekdays for inexpensive copper wine jugs, candlesticks, and cookware.

Gift Ideas

Better tourist shops sell copies of traditional Greek jewelry; silver filigree; Skyrian pottery; onyx ashtrays and dishes; woven bags; attractive rugs, including shaggy woolen flokatis; worry beads in amber or silver; and blue-and-white amulets to ward off the *mati* (evil eye). Reasonably priced natural sponges from Kalymnos also make good gifts. **Goutis** (✉ Dimokritou 40, Kolonaki ☎ 210/361–3557) displays an eclectic assortment of costumes, embroidery, and old, handcrafted silver items. **Ilias Kokkonis** (✉ Stoa Arsakeiou 8, Omonia, enter from Panepistimiou or Stadiou ☎ 210/322–1189 or 210/322–6355) stocks any flag you've hankered after—large or small, from any country. **Mati** (✉ Voukourestiou 20, Syntagma ☎ 210/362–6238) has finely designed amulets to battle the evil eye, as well as a collection of monastery lamps and candlesticks. **Mazarakis** (✉ Voulis 31–33, Syntagma ☎ 210/323–9428) sells a large selection of flokatis and will ship.

Baba (✉ Ifestou 30, Monastiraki ☎ 210/321–9994), a hole-in-the-wall shop, sells backgammon boards and pieces in all sizes and designs. Greeks spend hours heatedly playing the game, known as *tavli.* **Loumidis** (✉ Aiolou 106, Syntagma ☎ 210/321–1540), the oldest remaining coffee roaster in Greece, is a good place to buy some freshly ground Greek coffee and the special coffeepot called *briki.*

Handicrafts

The **Kentro Ellinikis Paradosis** (Center of Hellenic Tradition; ✉ Mitropoleos 59, Monastiraki ☎ 210/321–3023) is an outlet for quality handicrafts. The **Organismos Ethnikos Pronoias** (National Welfare Organization; ✉ Ipatias 6, and Apollonos, Plaka ☎ 210/321–8272) displays work by Greek craftspeople—stunning handwoven carpets, flat-weave kilims, hand-embroidered tablecloths, and flokatis.

At **Amorgos** (✉ Kodrou 3, Plaka ☎ 210/324–3836) the owners make wooden furniture using motifs from regional Greek designs. They also sell needlework, handwoven fabrics, hanging ceiling lamps, shadow puppets, and other decorative accessories. The Greek cooperative **EOMMEX** (✉ Mitropoleos 9, Syntagma ☎ 210/323–0408) operates a showroom with folk and designer rugs made by more than 30 weavers around the country.

Jewelry

Prices for gold and silver are much lower in Greece than in many Western countries, and jewelry is of high quality. Many shops in Plaka carry original-design pieces available at a good price if you bargain hard enough. For more expensive items, the Voukourestiou pedestrian mall off Syntagma Square has a number of the city's leading jewelry shops. **Byzantino** (✉ Adrianou 120, Plaka ☎ 210/324–6605) carries great values in gold, including pieces designed by the owners. **Fanourakis** (✉ Patriarchou Ioakeim 23, Kolonaki ☎ 210/721–1762 ✉ Evangelistrias 2, Mitropoleos ☎ 210/324–6642 ✉ Panagitsas 6, Kifissia, ☎ 210/623–2334) produces some of the most original work in gold. Contemporary Athenian artists use gold like a fabric—creasing, scoring, and fluting it. The **Goulandris Cycladic Museum** (✉ Neofitou Douka 4, Kolonaki ☎ 210/724–9706) carries modern versions of ancient jewelry designs. **LALAoUNIS** (✉ Panepistimiou 6, Syntagma ☎ 210/361–1371) showcases pieces by Ilias Lalaounis, who takes his ideas from nature, science, and ancient Greek pieces. **Xanthopoulos** (✉ Voukourestiou 4, Syntagma ☎ 210/322–6856) displays diamond necklaces, magnificently large gems, and the finest pearls; you can also order custom-made jewelry.

Music

Metropolis (✉ Panepistimiou 54 ☎ 210/380–8549) is part of an excellent Greek chain; this branch sells only Greek music and stocks a wide selection.

ATHENS A TO Z

AIRPORTS & TRANSFERS

Athens International Airport S.A., Eleftherios Venizelos (ATH), an efficient facility opened in 2001, lies about 27 km (17 mi) southeast of Athens, in Spata, and is accessible via the city ring road, Attiki Odos.

Eleftherios Venizelos International Airport ✉ Spata-Elefsina Hwy., also called Attiki Othos, Spata ☎ 210/353-0000 flight information; 210/353-0445 visitor information; 210/353-0515 Lost and Found 🌐 www.aia.gr.

TRANSFERS Express buses (⇨ Bus Travel Within Athens) run between the airport and Syntagma Square, Ethnikis Aminas metro, and Piraeus. All run 24 hours and depart at 20-minute intervals. Bus E94 leaves from Ethniki Aminas metro station. Bus E95 leaves from Syntagma Square, stopping at the Hilton and the American Embassy. Bus E96 leaves from Karaiskaki Square in Piraeus, stopping at Platia Glyfada and Voula Beach. At the airport, all three buses depart from the area in front of the arrivals terminal. Tickets cost €2.90 and can be purchased from kiosks at the bus stops or on the bus. Hang on to your ticket—it acts as a travel pass and can be used on any form of public transport in Athens for 24 hours after you validate it. The trip to or from the airport takes 40 to 90 minutes, depending on traffic. All airport express buses have baggage storage areas and air-conditioning. The express buses are generally the best deal for getting into Athens. If you must take a cab, be aware that fares can top €20, especially if you have a lot of heavy baggage. An express train linking to the metro is expected to be finished by summer 2004.

BOAT & FERRY TRAVEL

Most ships serving the Greek islands dock at Piraeus (port authority), 10 km (6 mi) from the center. Boat schedules are published in *Kathemerini,* sold with the *International Herald Tribune,* and you can also call a daily Greek recording for departure times. From the main harbor you can take the nearby metro right into Omonia Square (€0.60) or Syntagma Square (change at Omonia; take the line going to Ethniki Aminas, €0.70) The trip takes 25–30 minutes. A taxi takes longer because of traffic and costs around €8. Because the driver may wait until he fills the taxi with several passengers headed in the same direction, it's faster to walk to the main street and hail a cab there. If you arrive by hydrofoil in the smaller port of Zea Marina, take Bus 905 or Trolley 20 to the Piraeus metro. At Rafina Port, which serves some of the closer Cyclades and Evia, taxis are hard to find. KTEL buses, which stop slightly uphill from port, leave every 30 minutes from about 5:30 AM until 9:30 PM and cost €1.55.

Departure times ☎ 143. **KTEL** ☎ 210/821-0872 🌐 www.ktel.org. **Piraeus** ☎ 210/422-6000 through 210/422-6004. **Rafina Port** ☎ 22940/22300.

BUS TRAVEL TO & FROM ATHENS

Greek buses serving parts of northern Greece, including Thessaloniki, and the Peloponnese (Corinth, Olympia, Nafplion, Epidauros, Mycenae) arrive at Terminal A in Athens. Those traveling from Evia, most of Thrace, and central Greece, including Delphi, pull in to Terminal B; call terminals for information. From Terminal A, take Bus 051 to Omonia Square; from Terminal B, take Bus 24 downtown. To get to the stations, catch Bus 051 at Zinonos and Menandrou off Omonia Square for Terminal A and Bus 024 on Amalias Avenue in front of the National Gardens for Terminal B. International buses drop their passengers off on the street, usually in the Omonia or Syntagma Square area or at Stathmos Peloponnisos.

Most buses to the east Attica coast, including those for Sounion (€3.70 for inland route and €4.10 on coastal road) and Marathon (€2.40), leave from the KTEL terminal, which is in Platia Aigyptiou on the corner of Mavromateon and Alexandras near Pedion Areos park.

KTEL terminal ✉ Pl. Aigyptiou ☎ 210/821-3203 for information on bus to Sounion; 210/821-0872 for information on bus to Marathon 🌐 www.ktel.org. **Terminal A** ✉ Kifissou 100 ☎ 210/512-4910. **Terminal B** ✉ Liossion 260 ☎ 210/831-7096 Delphi; 210/831-7173 Livadia (Ossios Loukas via Distomo); 210/831-1431 Trikala (Meteora).

BUS TRAVEL WITHIN ATHENS

EOT can provide bus information, as can the Organization for Public Transportation. The office itself is open weekdays 7:30–3. The fare on buses and trolleys is €0.45–€0.75; monthly passes are sold at the beginning of each month for €17.50 (bus and trolley). Purchase tickets at curbside kiosks or from booths at terminals. Booths also provide booklets with maps of bus routes (in Greek). Validate your ticket in the orange machines when you board to avoid a €30 fine. Buses run from the center to all suburbs and nearby beaches from 5 AM until about midnight. For suburbs north of Kifissia, change at Kifissia's main square, Platia Platanou.

Organization for Public Transportation ✉ Metsovou 15 ☎ 185 from 7:30-3 and 7 PM–9 PM 🌐 www.oasa.gr.

CAR TRAVEL

You enter Athens by the Ethniki Odos (or National Road, as the main highways going north and south are known) and then follow signs for the center. Routes from Athens to the National Road are marked with signs in English; they usually name Lamia for the north and Corinth or Patras for the southwest.

CONSULATES

New Zealand ✉ Kifissias 268, Halandri ☎ 210/687-4700 or 210/687-4701.

EMERGENCIES

You can call an ambulance in the event of an emergency, but taxis are often faster. Most hotels will call a doctor or dentist for you; you can also contact your embassy for referrals to both. Not all hospitals are open nightly; ask your hotel to check for you, or call for a Greek listing. The *Athens News* often lists available emergency hospitals, as do most Greek newspapers. Many pharmacies in the center have someone who speaks English. For late-night pharmacies, call the information line, or check the *Athens News*. For auto accidents, call the city police.

Emergency Services **Ambulance** ☎ 166. **City Police** ☎ 100. **Coast Guard** ☎ 108. **Fire** ☎ 199. **Hospital line** ☎ 106. **Tourist police** ✉ Dimitrakopoulou 77, Koukaki ☎ 171.

24-hour Pharmacies **Late-night Pharmacy Information Line** ☎ 107 information in Greek.

ENGLISH-LANGUAGE MEDIA

Bookstores **Booknest** ✉ Folia tou Bibliou, Panepistimiou 25-29, Syntagma ☎ 210/322-9560. **Compendium** ✉ Nikis 28, upstairs, Syntagma ☎ 210/322-1248. **Eleftheroudakis** ✉ Nikis 4, Syntagma ☎ 210/322-9388 ✉ Panepistimiou 17 ☎ 210/331-4180. **Pantelides** ✉ Amerikis 11, Syntagma ☎ 210/362-3673.

THE OLYMPICS

The 2004 Olympics will take place in Athens from August 13 to August 29. A year before the games, the city was a gigantic construction site preparing to welcome millions of people eager to watch discus throwing in the shadow of the Parthenon or to cheer runners as they follow the original route from Marathon. Those who attend will see a city with a new airport, a new metro and tram, new highways, and many renovated hotels. By mid-2003, about 80 percent of the city's hotel rooms were already booked, and businesses from luxury hotels to souvlaki joints have indicated that they plan to raise rates—perhaps to double them or more—during the games. Visit the Athens 2004 Web site for information on every aspect of the Athens Games, and the main Olympic Web site for general information about the Olympics and links to each country's official Olympic travel agencies.

Athens 2004 🌐 www.athens2004.com. **Olympic Movement** 🌐 www.olympic.org.

LODGING

By summer 2003, prices were skyrocketing for the decreasing number of rooms available for the Olympics. Two official Greek agencies, Alpha Filoxenia and Elliniki Filoxenia, will handle the rental of furnished homes and apartments; rates will be €30–€300 per person per day. Greek officials have also arranged for cruise ships to dock in Piraeus during the Olympics, so that people can stay in cabins. People can also stay on nearby islands such as Aegina and Hydra and take the hydrofoil to Athens. The simplest way to book accommodations—even unconventional ones—is through your country's official Olympic travel agent.

Apartment & Home Rentals **Alpha Filoxenia 2004** ✉ Panepistimiou 43, Athens ☎ 210/327-7400. **Elliniki Filoxenia** ✉ Artemidos 3, Athens ☎ 210/684-9222.

PARALYMPIC GAMES

From September 17 through September 28, 2004, Athens will host the Paralympic Games, which are designed for athletes with physical disabilities. Paralympic events will take place in Olympic venues; these will be accessible for athletes and spectators with disabilities. The Athens 2004 and International Paralympic Committee Web sites have further information.

International Paralympic Committee 🌐 www.paralympic.org.

TICKETS The first round of Olympic ticket applications concluded in June 2003, and the balance of tickets went on sale in October 2003. Although tickets to opening and closing ceremonies and finals are expected to sell out quickly, last-minute tickets to other events will likely be available in 2004. To purchase tickets, buyers must contact their country's official Olympic ticket agencies (⇨ Travel Agencies). Other brokers may have tickets, but they will be far more expensive. During the games, any remaining tickets will be on sale in Athens. Ticket prices average around €35, though prime seats for finals and ceremonies cost between €300 and €950.

TRANSPORTATION All Olympic ticket holders are entitled to free public transportation to and from events. Shuttle buses will take you from hubs in Athens to venues outside the city. The Athens 2004 Web site will have details.

TRAVEL AGENCIES Each country has its own official Olympic travel agencies, which sell packages including tickets, accommodations, meals, transportation, and other services during and before or after the Olympics. To contact your country's official Olympic travel agencies, log on to the main Olympic Web site. From the pull-down menu, select "National Olympic Committees." Select your country and follow the links.

Official U.S. Travel Agencies **Cartan Tours** ☎ 800/360–2004 🌐 www.cartan.com. **CoSport** ☎ 877/457–4647 🌐 www.cosport.com.

VENUES Of the 32 Olympic venues in and around Athens, many will be temporary. The most important venue will be the Athens Olympic Sports Complex, a multi-stadium venue that will host the opening and closing ceremonies, tennis, gymnastics, swimming, diving, water polo, cycling, and the basketball finals. Architect Santiago Calatrava has designed the building and an adjoining park. After the Olympics, the complex will host cultural and sporting events. Another major venue is the enormous Hellenikon Sports Complex, on the site of the city's old airport. It will host basketball, baseball, softball, fencing, handball, hockey, and the canoe slalom. In central Athens, the Panathinaiko Stadio, which was used for the first modern Olympic Games in 1896, will be the site of archery events and the marathon finish.

Venues **Athens Olympic Sports Complex** ✉ Kifissas, next to Igiea Hospital. **Hellenikon** ✉ Poseidonos, Agios Kosmas.

SUBWAY TRAVEL

The metro system's slow, gritty Line 1, which dates from the 19th century, runs from Piraeus to the northern suburb of Kifissia, with several downtown stops. At press time, all Line 1 stations were undergoing renovations. Lines 2 and 3 opened to great fanfare in 2000. They are safe and fast but cover limited territory, mostly downtown. Extensions will be under way until 2006 and will go through all the main suburbs. By 2004, there will be stops at the major Olympic venues as well as a new airport express extension. Maps of the metro, including planned extensions, are available in stations. The fare is €0.60 if you stay only on Line 1; otherwise, it's €0.70. A daily travel pass, valid for use on all forms of public transportation, is €2.90; it's good for 24 hours after you validate it. Trains run between 5:30 AM and 11:30 PM. There is no phone number for information about the system, so check the Web site, which has updates on planned extensions.

Metro Information 🌐 www.ametro.gr.

TAXIS

Although you can find an empty taxi, it's often faster to call out your destination to one carrying passengers; if the taxi is going in that direction, the driver will pick you up. Most drivers speak basic English. The meter starts at €0.73, and even if you join other passengers, you must add this amount to your final charge. The minimum fare is €1.50. The basic charge is €0.23 per kilometer (½ mi); this increases to €0.44 between midnight and 5 AM or if you go outside city limits. There are surcharges for holidays (€0.50), trips to and from the airport (€1.17), and rides to, but not from, the port, train stations, and bus terminals (€0.59). There is also a €0.29 charge for each suitcase over 10 kilograms (22 pounds), but drivers expect €0.29 for each bag they place in the trunk anyway. Waiting time is €7 per hour. Make sure drivers turn on the meter and use the high tariff ("Tarifa 2") only after midnight; if you encounter trouble, threaten to go to the police. Radio taxis charge an additional €1.17 for the pickup or €2 for a later appointment. Some fairly reliable services are Ermis, Hellas, Kosmos, and Parthenon.

Ermis ☎ 210/411-5200. **Hellas** ☎ 210/645-7000 or 210/801-4000. **Kosmos** ☎ 1300. **Parthenon** ☎ 210/532-3300.

TOURS

BOAT TOURS Cruises to the four most popular islands—Mykonos, Rhodes, Crete, and Santorini—usually operate from mid-March through October. Try Golden Star Cruises and Royal Olympia Cruises. Most also have downtown Athens representatives. All tour operators also offer a full-day cruise of the Saronic Gulf islands. The €75 cruise includes an on-board buffet lunch.

Golden Star Cruises ✉ Akti Miaouli 85, Piraeus ☎ 210/429-0650 through 210/429-0660 📠 210/420-0660 for reservations 🌐 www.goldenstarcruises.com. **Royal Olympia Cruises** ✉ Akti Miaouli 87 ☎ 210/429-0700 for reservations 📠 210/429-0636 for reservations 🌐 www.royalolympiacruises.com.

BUS TOURS All travel agents (⇨ Travel Agencies) offer the same bus tours of Athens, as well as a handful of one-day excursions out of the city. The four-hour Athens tour covers the city's major sights, including a guided tour of the Acropolis (€43). Full-day tours include excursions to Sounion (€29), Delphi and Mycenae. The Delphi and Mycenae trips cost €76 with lunch included; €66 without lunch. Evening tours of the monuments, including dinner and a floor show in Plaka, cost €47. Make reservations at your hotel or at any travel agency.

PRIVATE GUIDES All the major tourist agencies can provide English-speaking guides for personally organized tours, or call the Union of Official Guides. Hire only those licensed by EOT. A four-hour tour including the Acropolis and its museums costs about €120.

Union of Official Guides ✉ Apollonas 9A ☎ 210/322-9705 📠 210/323-9200.

TRAIN TRAVEL

Athens has two railway stations, side by side, not far from Omonia Square off Deligianni Street. International trains and those coming from north of Athens use Stathmos Larissis. Trains from the Peloponnese use the ornate Stathmos Peloponnisos. Line 2 of the metro has a stop at Larissa station. As the station phones are almost always busy, it's easier to get departure times from the main information phone service and call about seat availability or buy tickets at a railway office downtown, open Monday–Saturday 8–2.

Railway offices ✉ Sina 6 ☎ 210/529-8910 ✉ Filellinon 17 ☎ 210/323-6747 ✉ Karolou 1 ☎ 210/529-7006 or 210/529-7007. **Stathmos Larissis** ☎ 210/529-8837. **Stathmos Peloponnisos** ☎ 210/529-8735.

TRAM TRAVEL

A tram line running from central Athens to the southern seaside suburbs was under construction at press time, with a projected completion date of summer 2004. Plans call for the tram to run between Glyfada and Fix metro stations on the outskirts of central Athens, with possible extensions to Voula and Syntagma Square. Tram tickets will be available at kiosks.

TRANSPORTATION AROUND ATHENS

Many of the sights and most of the hotels, cafés, and restaurants are within a fairly small central area. It's easy to walk everywhere, though sidewalks are often obstructed by parked cars. You can buy a monthly pass covering the metro, buses, and trolleys for €35 at the beginning of each month. Validate your ticket by stamping it in the orange machines at the entrance to the platforms, or you will be fined. Further information is at www.oasa.gr.

TRAVEL AGENCIES

Local Agents **American Express** Ermou 2 210/324-4975 210/322-7893. **CHAT Tours** Stadiou 4 210/322-2886 210/323-5270 www.chatours.com. **Condor Travel** Stadiou 43 210/321-2453 or 210/321-6986 210/321-4296. **F-Zein** Syngrou 132, 5th fl. 210/921-6285 210/922-9995. **Key Tours** Kallirois 4 210/923-3166 210/923-2008 www.keytours.gr. **Travel Plan** Christou Lada 9 210/323-8801 through 210/323-8804 210/322-2152. **Trekking Hellas** Fillelinon 7, 3rd floor 210/331-0323 through 210/331-0326 210/323-4548 www.trekking.gr.

VISITOR INFORMATION

There is a visitor information office at Eleftherios Venizelos airport (⇨ Airports & Transfers).

EOT Tsochas 7, Ambelokipi 210/870-7000 Piraeus, EOT Building, 1st fl., Zea Marina 210/452-2591 or 210/452-2586 www.gnto.gr.

Greece Basics

To research prices, get advice from other travelers, and book travel arrangements, visit www.fodors.com.

BUSINESS HOURS

Office and shopping hours vary from season to season. Check with your hotel for up-to-the-minute information on opening and closing times.

BANKS & OFFICES Banks are open weekdays 8–2, except Friday, when they close at 1:30; they are closed weekends and public holidays. In Athens one branch of the National Bank of Greece has extended hours for foreign exchange only, Monday–Thursday 3:30–6:30, Friday 3–6:30, Saturday 9–3, Sunday 9–1. Even smaller towns have at least one bank with an ATM.

National Bank of Greece Karageorgi Servias 2, Syntagma, Athens 210/334-0011.

MUSEUMS & SIGHTS Museums and archaeological sites are open 8:30–3 off-season, or winter (November–mid-April). Depending on available personnel, sites usually stay open longer mid-April–October, sometimes as late as 7 PM in July and August. Many museums are closed one day a week, usually Monday. Archaeological sites and museums are closed January 1, March 25, Good Friday morning until noon, Easter Sunday, May 1, and December 25–26; for reduced visiting hours on other holidays, check the handout from EOT.

SHOPS Shops may stay open from 9 AM to 9 PM in summer, though most stores close Monday, Wednesday, and Saturday around 3 or 4 PM. On Tuesday, Thursday, and Friday, many shops take a break and close between 3 and 5 PM. In winter (November–mid-April) hours are slightly reduced, though this changes every year. Most establishments are closed Sunday. Supermarkets are open weekdays until about 8:30 PM, with reduced hours on Saturday. In tourist areas such as Athens's Plaka, souvenir shops stay open late.

CUSTOMS & DUTIES

For details on imports and duty-free limits, *see* Customs & Duties *in* Smart Travel Tips.

IN GREECE You may bring in only one each of such expensive portable items as camcorders and computers. You should register these with Greek customs upon arrival, to avoid any problems when taking them out of the country again. Foreign banknotes amounting to more than $2,500 must be declared for re-export, although there are no restrictions on traveler's checks; foreign visitors may export no more than €295.

EMBASSIES

New Zealand maintains a consular office in Athens (⇨ Athens Essentials).

Australia ✉ Soutsou 37 and Tsochas 24, Athens ☎ 210/645-0404 🌐 www.ausemb.gr.

Canada ✉ Gennadiou 4, Athens ☎ 210/727-3400 🌐 www.dfait-maeci.gc.ca.

Ireland ✉ Vasilissis Konstantinou 7, Athens ☎ 210/723-2771.

United Kingdom ✉ Ploutarchou 1, Athens ☎ 210/727-2600 🌐 www.britishembassy.gr.

United States ✉ Vasilissis Sofias 91, Athens ☎ 210/721-2951 through 210/721-2959 🌐 www.usembassy.gr.

HOLIDAYS

January 1; January 6 (Epiphany); Clean Monday and first day of Lent; March 25 (Independence Day); Good Friday; Greek Easter Sunday; Greek Easter Monday; May 1 (Labor Day); June 3 (Pentecost); August 15 (Assumption); October 28 (Ochi Day); December 25–26.

LANGUAGE

In Greece, the native language uses the 24-letter Greek alphabet. English is widely spoken in hotels and elsewhere, especially by young people, and even in out-of-the-way places someone is always happy to lend a helping word. In this guide names are given in the Roman alphabet according to the Greek pronunciation.

MONEY MATTERS

On the whole, Greece offers good value compared with many other European countries. One exception is lodging in Athens, which has become very expensive because of the summer 2004 Olympics. Here are some sample prices: cup of coffee, €2.50–€3.80; bottle of beer, €2.10–€3; soft drink, €1.80; grilled cheese sandwich, €2.50; 1-km (½-mi) taxi ride, around €1.50. Admission to most museums and archaeological sites is free on Sunday from November through March.

CURRENCY The Greek monetary unit is the euro (€). Bills are in the denominations of 5, 10, 20, 50, 100, 200, and 500 euros; coins in 1, 2, 5, 10, 20, and 50 euro cents, and 1 and 2 euros. At press time, the exchange rate was about Australian $1.73, British £0.70, Canadian $1.58, New Zealand $1.95, South African R8.65 (rands), and U.S. $1.12 to the euro. Daily exchange rates are prominently displayed in banks.

SHOPPING

Prices in large stores are fixed. Bargaining may take place in small, owner-managed souvenir and handicrafts shops and in antiques shops. In flea markets bargaining is expected. You are required to have an export permit (not normally given if the piece is of any value) for antiques and Byzantine icons, but reproductions can be bought fairly cheaply, although even these require a certificate saying they are copies.

TAXES

VALUE-ADDED TAX (V.A.T.) Value-added tax, 4% for books and about 18% (13% on the Aegean Islands) for almost everything else, called FPA (pronounced fee-pee-ah) by Greeks, is included in the cost of most consumer goods and services, except groceries. If you are a citizen from a non-EU country, you may get a V.A.T. refund on products worth €118 or more (including V.A.T.) bought in Greece from licensed stores, which usually display the Tax-Free Shopping sticker. Ask the shop to complete a refund form called a Tax-Free Check, which Greek customs will stamp after viewing the item to make sure you are exporting it. Send the refund form back to the shop for repayment by check or credit card.

TELEPHONES

COUNTRY & AREA CODES The country code for Greece is 30. For Athens, or dialing within Athens, the area code is 210, and this must be added before local as well as long-distance calls. Whether you are dialing Greece from outside the country or making local or regional calls within Greece, you must dial the full 10-digit number, including the area code (which may be three, four, or five numbers).

DIRECTORY & OPERATOR ASSISTANCE For directory information, dial 131; many of the operators speak English. Many places are listed under the owner's name, not the official name, so you must know the name of the establishment's owner, even if it is a taverna or shop. For operator-assisted calls and international directory information in English, dial 161.

INTERNATIONAL CALLS Phone cards worth €3, €6, €12, or €24 can be purchased at kiosks, convenience stores, or the local OTE (Hellenic Telecommunications Organization) office, and are the easiest way to make calls from anywhere in Greece. Kiosks frequently have metered phones for long-distance calls, but their location is often on a bustling street corner. For more privacy, go to the local OTE office. There is a three-minute minimum charge for operator-assisted station-to-station and person-to-person connections. Numbers for major companies with long-distance operator assistance are listed below.

Access Codes AT&T ☎ **00/800-1311. Worldphone (MCI)** ☎ **00/800-1211. Sprint** ☎ **00/800-1411.**

LOCAL CALLS Many kiosks have pay telephones for local calls only. You pay the kiosk owner €0.10 per call after you've finished, unless it was a lengthy call, in which case you pay for the number of units you racked up. It's easier to buy a phone card from an OTE office, kiosks, or convenience shops and use it at card phones. The price drops about 50% for long-distance calls daily 10 PM–8 AM; for local calls, Sundays 10 PM–8 AM.

BARCELONA

As the capital of Catalunya (Catalonia), 2,000-year-old Barcelona commanded a vast Mediterranean empire when Madrid was still a dusty Moorish outpost on the Spanish steppe. Relegated to second-city status only after Madrid was chosen as site of the royal court in 1561, Barcelona more than rivals Madrid for architecture, culture, commerce, and nightlife. Industrious, creative, and playful in even parts, the citizens of this thriving metropolis are proud to have and use their own language: street names, museum exhibits, newspapers, radio programs, and movies are all in Catalan. An important milestone here was the city's long-awaited opportunity to host the Olympic Games in summer 1992, an event of singular importance in Barcelona's modernization. Ring roads, highways, a renovated port and beaches, and the creation of an entire neighborhood in what used to be the run-down industrial district of Poble Nou were among Barcelona's main 1992 achievements. Preparations for the 2004 Forum de les Cultures have gone even further in creating an entire new city, Diagonal Mar, on the city's eastern Mediterranean waterfront. The Gothic Quarter's narrow alleys, the elegance and distinction of the moderniste (a Spanish and mainly Catalan version of art nouveau) Eixample, and the many fruits of Gaudí's whimsical imagination make Barcelona's two millenniums of art and architecture a world center for design.

EXPLORING BARCELONA

It should take you two full days of sightseeing to complete the following tour. The first part covers the Gothic Quarter, the Picasso Museum, and Las Ramblas. The second part takes you to Passeig de Gràcia and the church of the Sagrada Família; and the third, to Montjuïc.

The Barri Gòtic (Gothic Quarter) & Las Ramblas

Numbers in the margin correspond to points of interest on the Barcelona map.

★ ❶ **Catedral de la Seu** (Cathedral). Citizens of Barcelona gather on Sunday morning to dance the *sardana,* a symbol of Catalan identity, on Plaça de la Seu, in front of the cathedral. The elaborate Gothic structure was built between 1298 and 1450, though the spire and Gothic facade were not added until 1892. Inside, highlights are the beautifully carved **choir stalls**; Santa Eulàlia's tomb in the crypt; the battle-scarred crucifix from Don Juan's galley in the naval battle of Lepanto, in the **Capella de Lepanto** (Lepanto Chapel); and the cloisters. ✉ *Plaça de la Seu* ☎ *93/315–2213* ⏲ *Daily 7:45–1:30 and 4–7:45.*

⓬ **Gran Teatre del Liceu.** Barcelona's famous opera house was gutted by fire in 1994 but, phoenixlike, reopened five years later, a modern replica of its original self. Built between 1845 and 1847, the Liceu was famed as one of the world's most beautiful opera houses, with ornamental gilt and plush red-velvet fittings. Anna Pavlova danced here in 1930, and Maria Callas sang here in 1959. The restored building has recovered much of its original charm with a state-of-the-art technical infrastructure as well. The downstairs Espai Liceu provides the city with daily cultural and commercial interaction with its opera house: a cafeteria; a shop specializing in opera-related gifts, books, and recordings; a circular concert hall that can accommodate 50; and a *Mediateca* (music library) with recordings and films of past opera productions. ✉ *La Rambla 51–59* ☎ *93/485–9900* 🌐 *www.liceubarcelona.com* ⏲ *Daily at 10 AM.*

❾ **Monument a Colom** (Columbus Monument). You can ride an elevator to the top for a commanding view of the city and port. Columbus faces out to sea, pointing, ironically, east toward Naples. Nearby you can board the cable car to cross the harbor to Barceloneta or catch it in the other direction up Montjuïc. ✉ *Portal de la Pau s/n* ☎ *93/302–5224* ⏲ *Weekdays 10–1:30 and 3–6:30, weekends 10–6:30.*

⓯ **Museu d'Art Contemporani de Barcelona** (MACBA; Barcelona Museum of Contemporary Art). Designed by American Richard Meier, the contemporary-art museum is an important addition to Barcelona's treasury of art and architecture. In the once rough-and-tumble Raval district, it and the neighboring **Centre de Cultura Contemporànea** (CCCB; Center for Contemporary Culture) have reclaimed important buildings and spaces as part of the city's renewal of its historic quarters and traditional neighborhoods. ✉ *Plaça dels Àngels* ☎ *93/412–0810* ⏲ *Weekdays 11–7, Sat. 10–8, Sun. 10–3.*

❷ **Museu Frederic Marès.** Here you can browse for hours among the miscellany assembled by sculptor-collector Frederic Marès, including everything from polychrome wood crucifixes to hat pins, pipes, and walking sticks. ✉ *Plaça Sant Iu 5* ☎ *93/310–5800* ⏲ *Tues.–Wed. and Fri.–Sat. 10–7, Thurs. 10–5, Sun. 10–3.*

❿ **Museu Marítim** (Maritime Museum). Housed in the 13th-century Drassanes Reiales (Royal Shipyards), this museum is packed with ships, figureheads, and nautical paraphernalia. You can pore over early navigation charts, including a map by Amerigo Vespucci and the 1439 chart of Gabriel de Valseca, the oldest chart in Europe. ✉ *Plaça Portal de la Pau 1* ☎ *93/342–9920* ⏲ *Daily 10–7.*

★ ❺ **Museu Picasso.** Two 15th-century palaces provide a striking setting for these collections of Picasso's early art, donated by Picasso's secretary

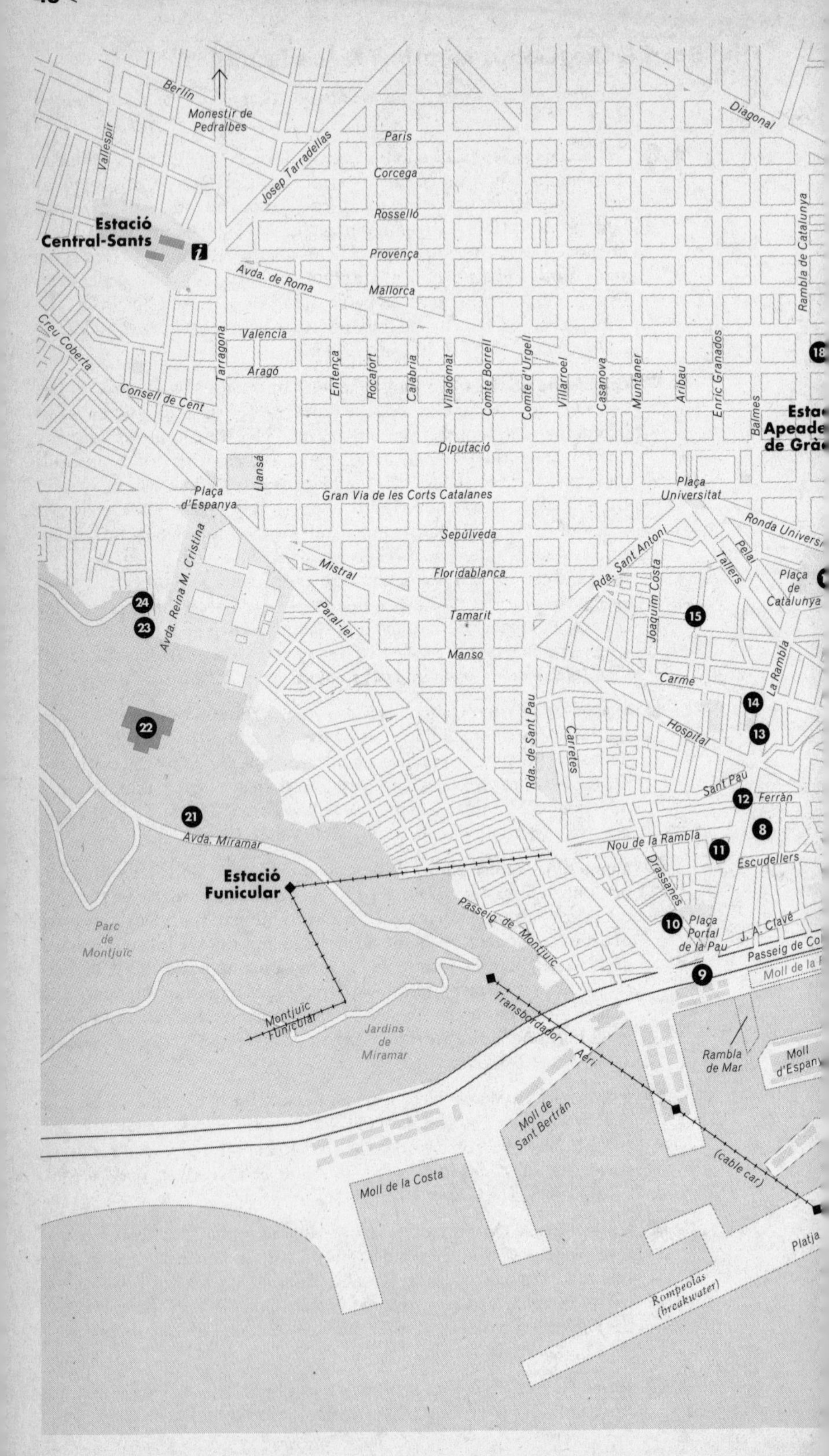
Berlin
Monestir de Pedralbes
Vallespir
Josep Tarradellas
Paris
Corcega
Rosselló
Provença
Mallorca
Diagonal
Rambla de Catalunya
Estació Central-Sants
Avda. de Roma
Creu Coberta
Valencia
Aragó
Tarragona
Consell de Cent
Entença
Rocafort
Calabria
Viladomat
Comte Borrell
Comte d'Urgell
Villarroel
Casanova
Muntaner
Aribau
Enric Granados
Balmes
Diputació
Llansá
Plaça d'Espanya
Gran Via de les Corts Catalanes
Plaça Universitat
Ronda Universi
Sepúlveda
Avda. Reina M. Cristina
Mistral
Floridablanca
Rda. Sant Antoni
Tallers
Pelai
Plaça de Catalunya
Paral-lel
Tamarit
Joaquim Costa
Manso
Carme
La Rambla
Hospital
Rda. de Sant Pau
Carretes
Sant Pau
Ferràn
Avda. Miramar
Nou de la Rambla
Escudellers
Drassanes
Estació Funicular
Passeig de Montjuïc
Plaça Portal de la Pau
J. A. Clavé
Passeig de Co
Moll de la
Parc de Montjuïc
Montjuïc Funicular
Jardins de Miramar
Transbordador Aeri
(cable car)
Rambla de Mar
Moll d'Espany
Moll de Sant Bertrán
Moll de la Costa
Rompeolas (breakwater)
Platja

The Barri Gòtic (Gothic Quarter) & Las Ramblas

Catedral de la Seu 1
Gran Teatre del Liceu 12
Monument a Colom 9
Museu d'Art Contemporani de Barcelona 15
Museu Frederic Marès 2
Museu Marítim 10
Museu Picasso 5
Palau de la Música Catalana ... 4
Palau de la Virreina 14
Palau Güell 11
Plaça de Catalunya 16
Plaça del Rei 3
Plaça Reial 8
Plaça Sant Jaume 7
Rambla St. Josep 13
Santa Maria del Mar 6

Eixample

Casa Milà 19
Casa Montaner i Simó–Fundació–Tàpies 18
Mançana de la Discòrdia 17
Temple Expiatori de la Sagrada Família 20

Montjuïc

Caixaforum 24
Fundació Miró 21
Mies van der Rohe Pavilion ... 23
Museu Nacional d'Art de Catalunya 22

and then by the artist himself. The works range from childhood sketches to exhibition posters done in Paris shortly before the artist's death. In rare abundance are the Rose Period and Blue Period paintings and the variations on Velázquez's *Las Meninas.* ✉ *Carrer Montcada 15–19* ☎ *93/319–6310* ⏲ *Tues.–Sat. 10–8, Sun. 10–3.*

★ ❹ **Palau de la Música Catalana** (Catalan Music Palace). This flamboyant tour de force designed by Domènech i Muntaner in 1908 is the flagship of Barcelona's moderniste architecture. Wagnerian cavalry explodes from the right side of the stage while flowery maidens languish on the left; an inverted stained-glass cupola overhead seems to offer the manna of music straight from heaven, and even the stage is dominated by the busts of muselike art nouveau instrumentalists. *Box office* ✉ *Sant Francesc de Paula 2 (off Via Laietana, around a corner from the hall itself)* ☎ *93/295–7200* ⏲ *English-language tours daily at 10:30, 2, and 3.*

⓮ **Palau de la Virreina.** Built by a onetime Spanish viceroy to Peru in 1778, this building is now a major exhibition center. Check to see what's showing while you're in town. ✉ *Rambla de les Flors 99* ☎ *93/301–7775* ⏲ *Mon. 4:30–9, Tues.–Sat. 10–2 and 4:30–9, Sun. 10–2.*

★ ⓫ **Palau Güell.** Gaudí built this mansion between 1886 and 1890 for his patron, Count Eusebi de Güell. Gaudí's artful creation of light in the dark Raval neighborhood is one of the highlights in this key visit along the Ruta Modernista. The playful rooftop will remind you of the later Gaudí of Parc Güell. ✉ *Nou de la Rambla 3–5* ☎ *93/317–3974* ⏲ *Weekdays 10–2 and 4–7:30.*

⓰ **Plaça de Catalunya.** This intersection, interesting mainly for its various sculptures and statues, is the transport hub of the modern city. Café Zurich, at the top of Las Ramblas, is Barcelona's most popular meeting point. ✉ *Top of Las Ramblas.*

❸ **Plaça del Rei.** Several historic buildings surround what is widely considered the most beautiful square in the Gothic Quarter. Following Columbus's first voyage to America, the Catholic Monarchs received him in the **Saló de Tinell,** a magnificent banquet hall built in 1362. Other ancient buildings around the square are the **Palau del Lloctinent** (Lieutenant's Palace); the 14th-century **Capella de Santa Àata** (Chapel of St. Agatha), built right into the Roman city wall; and the **Palau Padellàs** (Padellàs Palace), which houses the **Museu d'Història de la Ciutat** (City History Museum). ✉ *Palau Padellàs, Carrer del Veguer 2* ☎ *93/315–1111* ⏲ *Tues.–Sat. 10–2 and 4–8, Sun. 10–2.*

❽ **Plaça Reial.** An elegant and symmetrical 19th-century arcaded square, Plaça Reial is bordered by elegant ocher facades with balconies overlooking the wrought-iron Fountain of the Three Graces and the lampposts designed by Gaudí in 1879. The place is most colorful on Sunday morning, when crowds gather to sell and trade stamps and coins; at night it's a center of downtown nightlife. **Bar Glaciar,** on the uphill corner toward Las Ramblas, is a booming beer station for young internationals. The **Taxidermist,** across the way, is the square's only good restaurant, and **Tarantos** and **Jamboree** are top venues for jazz, flamenco, and rock. ✉ *C. Colom, off Las Ramblas.*

❼ **Plaça Sant Jaume.** This impressive square in the heart of the Gothic Quarter, originally the Roman Forum 2000 years ago, was built in the 1840s, but the two imposing buildings facing each other across it are much older. The 15th-century **ajuntament** (city hall) has an impressive black-and-gold mural (1928) by Josep María Sert (who also painted the murals in New York's Waldorf-Astoria) and the famous **Saló de Cent,** the first European parliament, from which the Council of One Hundred ruled the city from 1372 to 1714. To visit the interior, check with the protocol office. The **Palau de la Generalitat,** seat of the Autonomous Catalonian Government, is a 15th-century palace open to the public on special days or by arrangement. ✉ *Junction of C. de Ferràn and C. Jaume I.*

⓭ **Rambla St. Josep.** This stretch of the Rambla is one of the most fascinating. The colorful paving stones on the Plaça de la Boquería were designed by Joan Miró. Glance up at the swirling moderniste dragon on the **Casa Bruno Quadras** and the art nouveau street lamps; then take a look inside the **Boquería market** and the **Antiga Casa Figueras,** a vintage art nouveau pastry shop on the corner of Petxina, with a splendid mosaic facade. ✉ *Between Plaça de la Boquería and Rambla de les Flors.*

★ ❻ **Santa Maria del Mar** (St. Mary of the Sea). Simply the best example of Mediterranean Gothic architecture, this church is widely considered Barcelona's loveliest. It was built between 1329 and 1383 in fulfillment of a vow made a century earlier by James I to build a church for the Virgin of the Sailors. The structure's simple beauty is enhanced by a colorful rose window and slender soaring columns. ✉ *Plaça Santa Maria* ⏲ *Weekdays 9–1:30 and 4:30–8.*

Eixample

Above the Plaça de Catalunya you enter modern (post-1860) Barcelona and an elegant area known as the Eixample (literally, "widening"), built in the late 19th century as part of the city's expansion scheme. Much of the building here was done at the height of the moderniste movement, a Spanish and mainly Catalan version of art nouveau, whose leading exponents were the architects Lluís Domènech i Montaner, Josep Puig i Cadafalch, and Antoni Gaudí. The main thoroughfares are the Rambla de Catalunya and the Passeig de Gràcia, both lined with some of the city's most elegant shops and cafés. Moderniste houses are among Barcelona's drawing cards.

★ ⓳ **Casa Milà.** This Gaudí house is known as **La Pedrera** (stone quarry). Its remarkable curving stone facade, with ornamental balconies, ripples its way around the corner of the block. In the attic of La Pedrera is the superb **Espai Gaudí,** Barcelona's only museum dedicated exclusively to the architect's work. ✉ *Passeig de Gràcia 92* ☎ *93/484–5995* ⏲ *Casa Milà: daily 10–8; guided tours weekdays at 6 PM, weekends at 11 AM; Espai Gaudí and rooftop: July–Sept., also open 9 PM–midnight with bar and live music.*

⓲ **Casa Montaner i Simó–Fundació Tàpies.** This former publishing house exhibits the work of preeminent contemporary Catalan painter Antoni Tàpies, as well as temporary exhibits. On top of the building is a tangle of metal entitled *Núvol i Cadira* (*Cloud and Chair*). ✉ *Carrer d'Aragó 255* ☎ *93/487–0315* ⏲ *Tues.–Sun. 10–8.*

⓱ **Mançana de la Discòrdia** (Block of Discord). The name is a pun on the Spanish word *manzana,* which means both "block" and "apple." The houses here are quite fantastic: the floral **Casa Lleó Morera** (No. 35) is by Domènech i Montaner, the pseudo-Flemish **Casa Amatller** (No. 41) is by Puig i Cadafalch, and No. 43 is Gaudí's **Casa Batlló.** ✉ *Passeig de Gràcia, between Consell de Cent and Aragó.*

★ ⓴ **Temple Expiatori de la Sagrada Família** (Expiatory Church of the Holy Family). Barcelona's most eccentric landmark was designed by Gaudí, though only one tower was standing upon his death in 1926. Gaudí's intent was to evangelize with stone, to create an entire history of Christianity on the building's facade. The angular figures on the southwestern Passion Facade by sculptor Joseph Maria Subirach are a stark contrast to Gaudí's Nativity Facade on the opposite lateral facade. Don't miss the museum, with Gaudí's scale models, or the elevator to the top of one of the towers for a magnificent view of the city. Gaudí is buried in the crypt. ✉ *Plaça de la Sagrada Familia* ☎ *93/207–3031* ⏲ *Nov.–Mar. and Sept.–Oct., daily 9–6; Apr.–Aug., daily 9–8.*

Montjuïc

The hill of Montjuïc is thought to have been named for the Jewish cemetery once located here. Montjuïc has a fortress, delightful gardens, a model Spanish village, an illuminated fountain, the Mies van der Rohe Pavilion, Caixaforum, and a cluster of museums. The 1992 Olympics were held in the Olympic stadium here.

❷❹ **Caixaforum** (Casaramona). Built as a factory in 1911 by architect Josep Puig i Cadafalch, this redbrick art nouveau fortress was opened in early 2002 as a center for art exhibits, concerts, lectures, and other cultural events. The restoration is a paradigmatic example of the fusion of modern design and traditional architecture. ✉ *Av. Marquès de Comillas 6–8* ☎ *93/476–8600* ⏲ *Tues.–Sun. 10–8.*

★ ❷❶ **Fundació Miró** (Miró Foundation). A gift from the artist Joan Miró to his native city, this is one of Barcelona's most exciting galleries, with much of its exhibition space devoted to Miró's droll, colorful works. ✉ *Avda. Miramar 71* ☎ *93/329–1908* ⏲ *Tues.–Wed., Fri., and Sat. 10–7, Thurs. 10–9:30, Sun. 10–2:30.*

❷❸ **Mies van der Rohe Pavilion.** The reconstructed Mies van der Rohe Pavilion—the German contribution to the 1929 Universal Exhibition, reassembled between 1983 and 1986—is a stunning "less is more" study in interlocking planes of white marble, green onyx, and glass: Barcelona's aesthetic antonym for the moderniste Palau de la Música. ✉ *Av. Marquès de Comillas s/n* ☎ *93/423–4016* ⏲ *Daily 10–8.*

★ ❷❷ **Museu Nacional d'Art de Catalunya** (National Museum of Catalan Art). In the **Palau Nacional** atop a long flight of steps up from the Plaça Espanya, this collection of Romanesque and Gothic art treasures, medieval frescoes, and altarpieces—most from small churches and chapels in the Pyrenees—is simply staggering. The museum's last renovation was directed by architect Gae Aulenti, who also remodeled the Musée d'Orsay, in Paris. ✉ *Mirador del Palau 6* ☎ *93/423–7199* ⏲ *Tues., Wed., Fri., and Sat. 10–7, Thurs. 10–9, Sun. 10–2:30.*

Elsewhere in Barcelona

Barceloneta. Take a stroll around what was once the fishermen's quarter, built in 1755. Hike out to the end of the *rompeolas* (breakwater), extending 4 km (2½ mi) southeast into the Mediterranean, for a panoramic view of the city and a few breaths of fresh air. The modernized port has one of Europe's best aquariums; the Maremagnum shopping center; an IMAX wide-format cinema; the World Trade Center business development; and numerous bars and restaurants. The 1992 Olympic Village, now a hot tapas and nightlife spot, is up the beach to the north and is easily identifiable by the enormous, gold, Frank Gehry–designed fish sculpture next to the Hotel Arts. ✉ *East of Estació de França and Ciutadella Park.*

Gràcia. This small, once-independent village within the city is a warren of narrow streets whose names change at every corner. Tiny shops sell everything from old-fashioned tin lanterns to feather dusters. Gaudí's first house, at Carrer de les Carolines 24–26; Plaça Rius i Taulet, with its clock tower; and the Llibertat and Revolució markets are key sights. ✉ *Around C. Gran de Gràcia above Diagonal.*

Monestir de Pedralbes. This is one of Barcelona's best visits, a onetime Clarist convent with a triple-tier cloister and now home of the Thyssen-Bornemisza collection of early paintings. ✉ *Baixada Monestir 9* ☎ *93/203–9282* ⏲ *Tues.–Sun. 10–2.*

★ **Parc Güell.** This park in the upper part of town above Gràcia is Gaudí's magical attempt at creating a garden city. ✉ *C. D'Olot s/n* ⏲ *May–Aug., daily 10–9; Sept.–Apr., daily 10–7.*

Port Vell. The Old Port now includes an extension of the Rambla, the **Rambla de Mar,** which crosses the inner harbor from just below the Columbus Monument. This boardwalk connects the Rambla with the **Moll d'Espanya,** which in turn comprises a shopping mall, restaurants, an aquarium, a cinema, and two yacht clubs. A walk around Port Vell leads past the marina to Passeig Joan de Borbó, both lined with restaurants and their outdoor tables. From here you can go south out to sea along the *rompeolas,* a 3-km (2-mi) excursion, or north (left) down the San Sebastián beach to the Passeig Marítim, which leads to the **Port Olímpic.** The **Golondrinas** boats tour the harbor and up the coast past the Olympic Port.

Sarrià. Originally an outlying hamlet overlooking the city, Sarrià retains a distinctive village charm. ✉ *North of the western end of the Diagonal (best reached by the Sarrià train from Plaça Catalunya to the Reina Elisenda stop).*

WHERE TO EAT

Spanish restaurants are officially classified from five forks down to one fork, with most places earning two or three forks. Prices are for one dinner entrée. Sales tax (IVA) is usually included in the menu price; check the menu for *IVA incluído* or *IVA no incluído.* When it's not included, an additional 7% will be added to your bill. Most restaurants have a prix-fixe menu called a *menú del día,* generally available only at lunch. *Menús* are usually the cheapest way to eat; à la carte dining is more expensive. Service charges are generally included in your bill, though leaving 5%–10% extra is customary.

WHAT IT COSTS In Euros

	$$$$	$$$	$$	$
AT DINNER	over €25	€18–€25	€12–€18	under €12

Prices are per person for a main course.

★ $$$$ ✕ **Can Gaig.** This exquisite Barcelona favorite is famous for superb design *and* cuisine. Market-fresh ingredients and experimental cooking are based on ancient recipes from Catalan home cooking, and the menu balances seafood and upland specialties, game, and domestic raw materials. Try the *perdiz asada con jamón ibérico* (roast partridge with Iberian ham). ✉ *Passeig de Maragall 402* ☎ *93/429–1017* 📠 *93/429–7002* ✍ *Reservations essential* 💳 *AE, DC, MC, V* ⏲ *Closed Mon., Holy Week, and Aug.*

★ $$$$ ✕ **Comerç 24.** Artist, aesthete, and chef Carles Abellan playfully reinterprets traditional Catalan favorites at this minimalist treasure. Try the *arròs a banda* (paella without the morsels), *tortilla de patatas* (potato omelet), and, for dessert, a postmodern version of the traditional after-school snack of chocolate, olive oil, salt, and bread. The menu is far out, but always hits the mark. ✉ *Carrer Comerç 24* ☎ *93/319–2102* ✍ *Reservations essential* ▭ *AE, DC, MC, V* ⊙ *Closed Sun.*

$$$$ ✕ **Jean Luc Figueras.** Every restaurant Figueras has touched has shot straight to the top. This one, installed in an elegant Gràcia town house that was once couturier Cristóbal Balenciaga's studio, may be the best of all. The taster's menu is an extra $20 or so, but it's the best choice. ✉ *C. Santa Teresa 10* ☎ *93/415–2877* ✍ *Reservations essential* ▭ *AE, DC, MC, V* ⊙ *Closed Sun. No lunch Sat.*

★ $$$$ ✕ **Tram-Tram.** At the end of the old tram line above the village of Sarrià, Isidre Soler and his stunning wife, Reyes, have put together one of Barcelona's finest culinary offerings. Try the taster's menu and you might score cod medallions or venison filet mignons. Reservations are a good idea, but Reyes can almost always invent a table. ✉ *Major de Sarrià 121* ☎ *93/204–8518* ▭ *AE, DC, MC, V* ⊙ *Closed Sun. and late Dec.–early Jan. No lunch Sat.*

★ $$$–$$$$ ✕ **Botafumeiro.** Barcelona's most exciting Galician spot is open continuously from 1 PM to 1 AM and always filled with ecstatic people in mid-feeding frenzy. The main attraction is the *mariscos Botafumeiro,* a succession of myriad plates of shellfish. Try the half rations at the bar, such as *pulpo a feira* (squid on potato) or *jamón bellota de Guijuelo* (acorn-fed ham from a town near Salamanca). ✉ *Gran de Gràcia 81* ☎ *93/218–4230* ▭ *AE, DC, MC, V.*

★ $$$–$$$$ ✕ **Can Majó.** On the beach in Barceloneta is one of Barcelona's premier seafood restaurants. House specialties include *caldero de bogavante* (a cross between paella and lobster bouillabaisse) and *suquet* (fish stewed in its own juices), but whatever you choose will be excellent. In summer, the terrace overlooking the Mediterranean is the closest you can come to beachside dining. ✉ *Almirall Aixada 23* ☎ *93/221–5455* ▭ *AE, DC, MC, V* ⊙ *Closed Sun. and Mon.*

$$$–$$$$ ✕ **Casa Calvet.** This art nouveau space in Antoni Gaudí's 1898–1900 Casa Calvet is Barcelona's only opportunity to break bread in one of the great modernist's creations. The dining room is a graceful and spectacular design display, and the cuisine is light and Mediterranean with more contemporary than traditional fare. ✉ *Casp 48* ☎ *93/412–4012* ▭ *AE, DC, MC, V* ⊙ *Closed Sun. and Aug. 15–31.*

$$$–$$$$ ✕ **El Racó de Can Freixa.** This is one of Barcelona's hottest restaurants, with young chef Ramón Freixa taking the work of his father, José María, in new directions. The cuisine is innovative and yet traditionally Catalan; try one of the game specialties in season. One specialty is *peus de porc en escabetx de guatlle* (pig's feet with quail in a garlic-and-parsley gratin). ✉ *Sant Elíes 22* ☎ *93/209–7559* ✍ *Reservations essential* ▭ *AE, DC, MC, V.*

$$$–$$$$ ✕ **El Tragaluz.** *Tragaluz* means skylight—literally, "light-swallower"—an excellent choice if you're on a design high. The sliding roof opens to the stars, and the furnishings by Javier Mariscal (creator of 1992 Olympic mascot Cobi) reflect Barcelona's passion for playful design. The Mediterranean cuisine is light and innovative. ✉ *Passatge de la Concepció 5* ☎ *93/487–0196* ▭ *AE, DC, MC, V* ⊙ *Closed Jan. 5. No lunch Mon.*

$–$$ ✕ **Agut.** Simple, hearty Catalan fare awaits you in this unpretentious restaurant in the lower reaches of the Gothic Quarter. Founded in 1924, this place continues to be popular. There's plenty of wine to go with the traditional home cooking. ✉ *Gignàs 16* ☎ *93/315–1709* ▭ *AE, MC, V* ⊙ *Closed Mon. and July. No dinner Sun.*

$–$$ ✕ **El Convent.** Behind the Boqueria market, this traditional restaurant offers good value. Catalan home cooking, such as *faves a la catalana* (broad beans stewed with sausage), comes straight from the Boqueria. The intimate balconies and dining rooms have marble-top tables for 2 or 20. ✉ *Jerusalem 3* ☎ *93/317–1052* ▭ *AE, DC, MC, V.*

WHERE TO STAY

Hotels around Las Ramblas and in the Gothic Quarter have generous helpings of old-fashioned charm but are weaker on creature comforts; those in the Eixample are mostly '50s or '60s buildings, often more recently renovated; and the newest hotels are out along the Diagonal or beyond, with the exception of the Hotel Arts, in the Olympic Port. The Airport and Sants Station have hotel-reservation desks.

Hotel rates are generally quoted per room, not per person. Single occupancy of a double room costs 80% of the usual price. Breakfast is rarely included in the quoted room rate. The quality of rooms, particularly in older properties, can be uneven; always ask to see your room *before* you sign the acceptance slip. If you want a private bathroom in a less expensive hotel, state your preference for shower or bathtub; the latter usually costs more, though many hotels have both. All hotels and hostels are listed with their rates in the annual *Guía de Hoteles,* available from bookstores and kiosks or for perusal in local tourist offices.

WHAT IT COSTS In Euros

	$$$$	$$$	$$	$
HOTELS	over € 225	€150–€ 225	€80–€150	under €80

Prices are for two people in a standard double room in high season, excluding tax and breakfast.

$$$$ Fodor'sChoice ★ **Claris.** Widely considered Barcelona's best hotel, this wonderful place is a fascinating mélange of design and tradition. The rooms come in 60 different modern layouts, some with restored 18th-century English furniture and some with contemporary furnishings from Barcelona's endlessly playful legion of lamp and chair designers. Lavishly endowed with wood and marble, the hotel also has a Japanese water garden and a rooftop pool. The restaurant East 47 is stellar. ✉ *Carrer Pau Claris 150, 08009* ☎ *93/487–6262* 🖷 *93/215–7970* 🌐 *www.derbyhotels.es* *80 rooms, 40 suites* *2 restaurants, pool, bar* 💳 *AE, DC, MC, V.*

$$$$ Fodor'sChoice ★ **Condes de Barcelona.** Reserve well in advance—this is one of Barcelona's most popular hotels. The pentagonal lobby has a marble floor and the original columns and courtyard from the 1891 building. The newest rooms have hot tubs and terraces overlooking interior gardens. An affiliated fitness club nearby has golf, squash, and swimming. The restaurant, Thalassa, is excellent. ✉ *Passeig de Gràcia 75, 08008* ☎ *93/467–4780* 🖷 *93/467–4785* 🌐 *www.condesdebarcelona.com* *183 rooms* *Restaurant, pool, bar* 💳 *AE, DC, MC, V.*

$$$$ **Hotel Arts.** This luxurious Ritz-Carlton monolith overlooks Barcelona from the Olympic Port, providing views of the Mediterranean, the city, and the mountains behind. A short taxi ride from the center of the city, the hotel is virtually a world of its own, with three restaurants (one specializing in California cuisine), an outdoor pool, and the beach. ✉ *C. de la Marina 19–21, 08005* ☎ *93/221–1000* 🖷 *93/221–1070* 🌐 *www.harts.es* *397 rooms, 59 suites, 27 apartments* *3 restaurants, pool, bar* 💳 *AE, DC, MC, V.*

$$$$ Fodor'sChoice ★ **Majestic.** On Barcelona's most stylish boulevard, surrounded by fashion emporiums, you'll find this near-perfect place to stay. The building is part Eixample town house and part modern extension, but each room is stylishly decorated. The superb restaurant, Drolma, is a destination in itself. ✉ *Passeig de Gràcia 70, 08008* ☎ *93/488–1717* 🖷 *93/488–1880* 🌐 *www.hotelmajestic.es* *273 rooms, 30 suites* *2 restaurants, pool, bar* 💳 *AE, DC, MC, V.*

$$$$ **Princesa Sofía.** This modern high-rise has everything from shops to the 19th-floor Top City, with breathtaking views. The rooms, decorated in soft colors, are ultracomfortable. ✉ *Plaça Pius XII 4, at Av. Diagonal, 08028* ☎ *93/508–1000* 📠 *93/508–1001* 🌐 *www.interconti.com* *475 rooms, 25 suites* *3 restaurants, 2 pools (1 indoor), bar* 💳 *AE, DC, MC, V.*

★ **$$$$** **Rey Juan Carlos I–Conrad International.** Towering over the western end of Barcelona's Avinguda Diagonal, this luxury hotel is also an exciting commercial complex where you can even buy or rent a fur or limousine. The lush garden, which includes a pond with swans, has an Olympic-size swimming pool, and the green expanses of Barcelona's finest in-town country club, El Polo, are beyond. ✉ *Av. Diagonal 661–671, 08028* ☎ *93/364–4040* 📠 *93/364–4232* 🌐 *www.hrjuancarlos.com* *375 rooms, 37 suites* *2 restaurants (3 in summer), pool, 2 bars* 💳 *AE, DC, MC, V.*

★ **$$$$** **Ritz.** Founded in 1919 by Caesar Ritz, this grande dame of Barcelona hotels has been restored to the splendor of its earlier years. The imperial lobby is at once loose and elegant; guest rooms contain Regency furniture, and some have Roman baths and mosaics. Service is generally excellent. ✉ *Gran Via 668, 08010* ☎ *93/318–5200* 📠 *93/318–0148* 🌐 *www.ritzbcn.com* *122 rooms* *Restaurant, bar* 💳 *AE, DC, MC, V.*

$$$–$$$$ Fodor'sChoice ★ **Colón.** Charming and intimate, this Barcelona standby across from the cathedral overlooks weekend sardana dancing, Thursday antiques markets, and, of course, the floodlighted cathedral by night. Rooms are comfortable and tasteful. Rooms with views of the cathedral are better and more expensive. Considering its combination of comfort, style, and location it may be the best place to stay in Barcelona. ✉ *Av. Catedral 7 08002* ☎ *93/301–1404* 📠 *93/317–2915* 🌐 *www.hotelcolon.es* *147 rooms* *Restaurant, bar* 💳 *AE, DC, MC, V.*

$$ **Gran Vía.** This 19th-century town house is a moderniste enclave, with an original chapel, hall-of-mirrors breakfast room, ornate moderniste staircase, and belle epoque phone booths. Guest rooms have plain alcoved walls, bottle-green carpets, and Regency-style furniture; those overlooking Gran Via itself have better views but are quite noisy. ✉ *Gran Via 642, 08007* ☎ *93/318–1900* 📠 *93/318–9997* 🌐 *www.nnhotels.es* *53 rooms* 💳 *AE, DC, MC, V.*

$$ **San Agustí.** Just off the Rambla in the leafy square of the same name, this place has long been popular with musicians performing at the Liceu opera house. Rooms are small but pleasantly modern, with plenty of fresh wood and clean lines. There is a cafeteria here. ✉ *Pl. de San Agustín 3, 08001* ☎ *93/318–1658* 📠 *93/317–2928* 🌐 *www.hotelsa.com* *77 rooms* *Bar* 💳 *AE, DC, MC, V.*

$–$$ **Continental.** This modest hotel stands at the top of the Rambla, below Plaça de Catalunya. Space is tight, but rooms manage to accommodate large, firm beds. It's high enough over the Rambla to escape street noise, so ask for a room overlooking Barcelona's most emblematic street. This is a good place to read *Homage to Catalonia,* as George Orwell stayed here with his wife in 1937. ✉ *Rambla 138, 08002* ☎ *93/301–2570* 📠 *93/302–7360* 🌐 *www.hotelcontinental.com* *35 rooms* 💳 *AE, DC, MC, V.*

$ Fodor'sChoice ★ **Jardí.** Perched over the traffic-free and charming Plaça del Pi and Plaça Sant Josep Oriol, this chic budget hotel has rooms with views of the Gothic church of Santa Maria del Pi. All rooms have pine furniture and small bathrooms. With five floors and an elevator, this is not the Ritz, and it can be noisy in summer, but it's still a great value. ✉ *Pl. Sant Josep Oriol 1, 08002* ☎ *93/301–5900* 📠 *93/342–5733* 🌐 *www.hoteljardi.com* *40 rooms* 💳 *AE, DC, MC, V.*

NIGHTLIFE & THE ARTS

The Arts

To find out what's on, look in the daily papers or the weekly *Guía del Ocio. Actes a la Ciutat* is a weekly list of cultural events published by City Hall and available from its information office on Plaça Sant Jaume, or at the Palau de la Virreina. *El País* lists all events of interest on its *agenda* page.

3

Concerts

Musical events are held in some of Barcelona's finest early architecture, such as the medieval shipyards, **Drassanes,** the church of **Santa Maria del Mar,** or the **Monestir de Pedralbes.** The **Auditori de Barcelona** (✉ Carrer Lepant 150, near Plaça de les Glòries ☎ 93/247–9300) has a full program of classical music, with occasional jazz and pop thrown in. The **Liceu** (✉ La Rambla 51–59 ☎ 93/485–9913), Barcelona's opera house, is alive and thriving. The art nouveau **Palau de la Música** is not to be missed for the music and the venue itself. Sunday-morning concerts (11 AM) are a local tradition (✉ Sant Francesc de Paula 2 ☎ 93/295–7200).

Dance

El Mercat de les Flors (✉ Lleida 59 ☎ 93/426–1875), not far from Plaça d'Espanya, always has a rich program of modern dance and theater. **L'Espai de Dansa i Música de la Generalitat de Catalunya** (✉ Travessera de Gràcia 63 ☎ 93/414–3133), usually listed simply as L'Espai (The Space), is Barcelona's prime venue for ballet and contemporary dance. **Teatre Tivoli** (✉ Casp 8 ☎ 93/412–2063), just above Plaça de Catalunya, hosts major ballet and flamenco troupes.

Film

Many if not most Barcelona theaters show foreign movies in their original languages—indicated by "VO" (*versión original*). The Olympic Port's 15-screen **Icaria Yelmo** (✉ Salvador Espriu 61 ☎ 93/221–7585) shows everything in VO. **Renoir Les Corts** (✉ Eugeni d'Ors 12), near the Corte Inglés Diagonal, has four VO theaters. The Gràcia neighborhood's **Verdi** (✉ Verdi 32 ☎ 93/237–0516) is a standard VO cinema favorite. **Verdi Park** (✉ Torrijos 49 ☎ 93/238–7990) in the Gràcia neighborhood is a popular spot.

Theater

Most plays are in Catalan, but top Spanish productions also open in Barcelona. **El Mercat de les Flors** holds theater and dance performances. The **Teatre Lliure** (✉ Montseny 47, Gràcia ☎ 93/218–9251) has top theater, dance, and musical events. The **Teatre Nacional de Catalunya** (✉ Plaça de les Arts 1 ☎ 93/900–121133) covers everything from Shakespeare to ballet to avant-garde theater. **Teatre Poliorama** (✉ Rambla Estudios 115 ☎ 93/317–7599), on the upper Rambla, holds excellent theater performances. **Teatre Romea** (✉ Hospital 51 ☎ 93/317–7189) is a traditional haven for dramatic events. **Teatre Tívoli** (✉ Casp 10 ☎ 93/412–2063) stages flamenco, ballet, and plays.

Nightlife

Bars

Xampanyerías, or champagne bars serving sparkling Catalan *cava,* are a Barcelona specialty. **El Xampanyet** (✉ Montcada 22 ☎ 93/319–7003), near the Picasso Museum, serves cava, cider, and tapas. **La Cava del Palau** (✉ Verdaguer i Callis 10 ☎ 93/310–0938), near the Palau de la Música, has a wide selection of cavas, wines, and cocktails.

You'll find the **Passeig del Born,** near the Picasso Museum, is lined with cocktail bars. **Dry Martini** (✉ Aribau 162 ☎ 93/217–5072) has more than 80 different gins. **El Copetín** (✉ Passeig del Born 19 ☎ 93/317–7585) looks exciting and has good cocktails. **Miramelindo** (✉ Passeig del Born 15 ☎ 93/319–5376) offers a large selection of cocktails, and often has live jazz. Stylish **El Paraigua** (✉ Plaça Sant Miquel, behind City Hall ☎ 93/217–3028) serves cocktails, along with classical music.

Ambitiously named **La Vinya del Senyor** (Lord's Vineyard; ✉ Pl. de Santa Maria 5 ☎ 93/310–3379), across from Santa Maria del Mar, has a new wine list every fortnight. **Cal Pep** (✉ 8 Plaça de les Olles ☎ 93/319–6183), near Santa Maria del Mar, is a popular spot, with the best and freshest selection of tapas. **Sagardi** (✉ Argenteria 62 ☎ 93/319–9993), near Santa Maria del Mar, is one of many, uniformly good, Basque taverns. **El Irati** (✉ Cardenal Casañas 17 ☎ 93/302–3084), just off Plaća del Pi, is a good, if usually overcrowded, Basque bar. **Ciudad Condal** (✉ Rambla de Catalunya 24 ☎ 93/412–9414), at the intersection of Gran Via and Rambla Catalunya, has lots of appetizing morsels. **Cata 1.81** (✉ Valencia 181 ☎ 93/322–6818) is a wine taster's delight—with designer cuisine to match. **La Santa Maria** (✉ Comerç 17 ☎ 93/315–4536) serves postmodern morsels at bar and table.

Cabaret

Barcelona City Hall (✉ Rambla de Catalunya 2–4, access through New Canadian Store ☎ 93/317–2177) presents sophisticated cabaret in a beautiful music hall.

Cafés

The **Café de l'Opera** (✉ Rambla 74 ☎ 93/317–7585), across from the Liceu opera house, is a perennial hangout, open daily until 2 AM. **Café Zurich** (✉ Plaça de Catalunya 1 ☎ 93/302–4140), at the head of Las Ramblas, is Barcelona's number one rendezvous spot. **Carrer Petritxol** (from Portaferrissa to Plaça del Pi) is famous for its *chocolaterías* (serving hot chocolate, tea, coffee, and pastries) and tearooms. Picasso hung out at **Els Quatre Gats** (✉ Montsió 3 ☎ 93/302–4140), which is a great place to people-watch.

Discos & Nightclubs

A line forms at **Bikini** (✉ Deu i Mata 105, at Entença ☎ 93/322–0005) on festive Saturday nights. **Costa Breve** (✉ Aribau 230 ☎ 93/414–2778) welcomes all ages, even those over 35. **Danzatoria** (✉ Avda. Tibidabo 61 ☎ 93/211–6261), a fusion of Salsitas and Partycular, is a "multispace" with five venues. At **Luz de Gas** (✉ Muntaner 246 ☎ 93/209–7711), live guitar and soul shows are followed by dance music and wild abandon. **Oliver y Hardy** (✉ Diagonal 593, next to Barcelona Hilton ☎ 93/419–3181) is popular with over-35s. **Otto Zutz** (✉ Lincoln 15, below Via Augusta ☎ 93/238–0722) is a top spot. **Sala Razzmatazz** (✉ Almogavers 122 ☎ 93/320–8200) offers Friday and Saturday disco madness 'til dawn. Weeknight concerts include international stars such as Ani diFranco and Enya. **Torres de Avila** (✉ Marquès de Comillas 25 ☎ 93/424–9309), in Pueblo Espanyol, is wild and woolly until daylight on weekends. **Up and Down** (✉ Numancia 179 ☎ 93/280–2922), pronounced "pendow," is a lively classic for elegant carousers.

Flamenco

El Patio Andaluz (✉ Aribau 242 ☎ 93/209–3378) is a solid option but rather expensive. **Los Tarantos** (✉ Plaça Reial 17 ☎ 93/318–3067) is the most happening flamenco spot. **El Tablao del Carmen** (✉ Arcs 9, Poble Espanyol ☎ 93/325–6895) hosts touring troupes up on Montjüic.

Jazz Clubs

La Cova del Drac (✉ Vallmajor 33 ☎ 93/200–7032) is Barcelona's most traditional jazz venue. The Gothic Quarter's **Harlem Jazz Club** (✉ Comtessa Sobradiel 8 ☎ 93/310–0755) is small but sizzling. **Jamboree** (✉ Plaça Reial 17 ☎ 93/301–7564), downstairs from Los Tarantos, has regular jazz performances featuring top musicians from New York and all over the world.

SHOPPING

3

Elegant shopping districts are the Passeig de Gràcia, Rambla de Catalunya, and the Diagonal. For more affordable, old-fashioned, and typically Spanish-style shops, explore the area between the Rambla and Via Laietana, especially around Carrer de Ferràn. The area around Plaça del Pi from Boquería to Portaferrisa and Canuda is well stocked with youthful fashion stores and imaginative gift shops.

El Triangle mall in Plaça de Catalunya includes FNAC, Habitat, and the Sephora perfume emporium. **Les Glories** (✉ Avda. Diagonal 208, Plaça de les Glories ☎ 93/486–0639) is near the *encants,* Barcelona's flea market. **L'Illa** (✉ Diagonal 545, between Numancia and Entenza ☎ 93/444–0000) has everything from FNAC to Decathlon to Marks & Spencer. **Maremagnum** (✉ Moll d'Espanya s/n, Port Vell ☎ 93/225–8100) is well stocked with shops. **Carrer Tuset,** north of Diagonal between Aribau and Balmes, has many small boutiques.

Antiques

Carrer de la Palla and Banys Nous, in the Gothic Quarter, are lined with antiques shops. An **antiques market** is held every Thursday in front of the cathedral. The **Centre d'Antiquaris** (✉ Passeig de Gràcia 57 ☎ 93/215–4499) has some 75 antiques stores. **Gothsland** (✉ Consell de Cent 331 ☎ 93/488–1922) specializes in moderniste designs.

Boutiques

Fashionable boutiques line Passeig de Gràcia and Rambla de Catalunya. Others are on Gran Via between Balmes and Pau Claris, and on the Diagonal between Ganduxer and Passeig de Gràcia. **Adolfo Domínguez** (✉ Passeig de Gràcia 89, Valencia 245 ☎ 93/487–3687) is one of Spain's most popular clothing designers. **Joaquín Berao** (✉ Rosselló 277 ☎ 93/218–6187) is a top jewelry designer. **La Manual Alpargartera** (✉ Avinyó 7), just off Carrer Ferran, is a lovely shop specializing in handmade rope-soled sandals and espadrilles.

Loewe (✉ Passeig de Gràcia 35, Diagonal 570 ☎ 93/216–0400) is Spain's top leather store. Lovers of fine stationery will linger in the Gothic Quarter's **Papirum** (✉ Baixada de la Llibreteria 2), a tiny, medieval-tone shop with exquisite hand-printed papers, marbleized blank books, and writing implements. **Zapata** (✉ Buenos Aires 64, at Diagonal ☎ 93/430–4785) is a major jewelry dealer.

Department Stores

With four locations in Barcelona alone, **El Corte Inglés** (✉ Plaça de Catalunya 14 ☎ 93/302–1212 ✉ Porta de l'Angel 19–21 ☎ 93/306–3800 ✉ Avda. Francesc Macià 58 ☎ 93/419–2020 ✉ Diagonal 617, near María Cristina metro stop ☎ 93/419–2828) is Spain's great consumer emporium. Both Plaça de Catalunya's Mançana de Oro (aka El Triangle) and L'Illa have FNAC stores.

Food & Flea Markets

The **Boqueria Market** (✉ Las Ramblas between Carme and Hospital) is an exuberant cornucopia, a colorful display of both food and humanity; it's open every day except Sunday. **Els Encants** (✉ End of Dos de Maig, on the Plaça Glòries Catalanes), Barcelona's wild-and-woolly flea market, is held every Monday, Wednesday, Friday, and Saturday 8–7. **Sant Antoni Market** (✉ End of Ronda Sant Antoni) is an old-fashioned food and clothes market, best on Sunday when there's a **secondhand-book market** with old postcards, press cuttings, lithographs, and prints. There's a **stamp and coin market** (✉ Plaça Reial) on Sunday morning. An **artists' market** (✉ Placeta del Pi, off Las Ramblas and Boquería) sets up on Saturday morning.

Gifts

A number of stores and boutiques specialize in design items (jewelry, furnishings, knickknacks). **Xavier Roca i Coll** (✉ Sant Pere mes Baix 24, off Via Laietana ☎ 93/215–1052) specializes in silver models of Barcelona's buildings. **Art Escudellers** (✉ C. Escudellers 5, Barri Gòtic) has ceramics from all over Spain, with more than 140 different artisans represented and maps showing where the work is from. Don't miss the art gallery and wine, cheese, and ham tasting bar downstairs.

Bd (Barcelona Design; ✉ Mallorca 291293 ☎ 93/458–6909) sells reproduction furniture from many designers. **Dos i Una** (✉ Rosselló 275 ☎ 93/217–7032) is a good source for clever gifts. **Vinçon** (✉ Passeig de Gràcia 96 ☎ 93/215–6050) has a huge selection of stylish housewares.

BARCELONA A TO Z

AIRPORTS & TRANSFERS

All international and domestic flights arrive at El Prat de Llobregat airport, 14 km (8½ mi) south of Barcelona just off the main highway to Castelldefels and Sitges. For information on arrival and departure times, call the airport or Info-Iberia.

El Prat de Llobregat ☎ 93/478-5000 or 93/478-5032. **Info-Iberia** ☎ 93/412-5667.

TRANSFERS The airport-to-city train leaves every 30 minutes between 6:30 AM and 11 PM, costs €2.50, and reaches the Barcelona Central (Sants) Station in 15 minutes and Plaça de Catalunya, in the heart of the old city (at the head of Las Ramblas), in 20–25 minutes. From there a short taxi ride of €3–€6 will take you to most of central Barcelona's hotels. The Aerobus service connects the airport with Plaça de Catalunya every 15 minutes between 6:25 AM and 11 PM; the fare of €3 can be paid with all international credit cards. A taxi from the airport to your hotel, including airport and luggage surcharges, will cost about €20.

BOAT & FERRY TRAVEL

Golondrinas (harbor boats) make short trips from the Portal de la Pau, near the Columbus Monument. The fare is €4.50 for a 30-minute trip. Departures are Holy Week–September, daily 11–7; October–Holy Week, weekends and holidays only 11–5. It's closed December 16–January 2. A one-way ticket lets you off at the end of the breakwater for a 4-km (2½-mi) stroll, surrounded by the Mediterranean, back into Barceloneta.

Golondrinas ☎ 93/442-3106.

BUS TRAVEL TO & FROM BARCELONA

Barcelona's main bus station is Estació del Nord, east of the Arc de Triomf. The Estació Autobuses de Sants also dispatches long-distance buses—Julià runs buses to Zaragoza and Montserrat, and Alsina Graëlls runs to Lérida and Andorra. Buses also depart from the depots of Barcelona's various private bus companies. Rather than pound the pavement (or the telephone, usually futile because of overloaded lines) trying to sort out Barcelona's complex and confusing bus system, go through a travel agent, who can quickly book you the best bus passage to your destination.

Alsina Graëlls ✉ Ronda Universitat 4 ☎ 93/265-6866. **Estació Autobuses de Sants** ✉ C. Viriato, next to Sants Central train terminal ☎ 93/490-0202. **Estació del Norte** ✉ End of Avda. Vilanova ☎ 93/893-5312. **Julià** ✉ Ronda Universitat 5 ☎ 93/317-6454.

3

BUS TRAVEL WITHIN BARCELONA

City buses run from about 5:30 or 6 AM to 10:30 PM, though some stop earlier. There are also night buses to certain destinations. The flat fare is €1. Route plans are displayed at bus stops. For multiple journeys you can purchase a *tarjeta multiviatge,* good for 10 rides, at the transport kiosk on Plaça de Catalunya (€6).

CONSULATES

Australia ✉ Gran Via Carles III 98 ☎ 93/330-9496.
Canada ✉ Elisenda de Pinós ☎ 93/204-2700.
New Zealand ✉ Travessera de Gràcia 64 ☎ 93/209-0399.
United Kingdom ✉ Diagonal 477 ☎ 93/419-9044.
United States ✉ Passeig Reina Elisenda 23 ☎ 93/280-2227.

EMERGENCIES

The general emergency number in all EU nations (akin to 911 in the United States) is 112.

Doctors & Dentists **Medical emergencies** ☎ 061.
Emergency Services **Police** ☎ 091 National Police; 092 Municipal Police. **Tourist Attention** ✉ La Rambla 43 ☎ 93/317-7016 24-hr assistance for crime victims.
24-hour Pharmacies **Pharmacies** ☎ 010.

ENGLISH-LANGUAGE MEDIA

BOOKS

BCN Books is one of Barcelona's top spots for books in English. Come In is another good option for English books. El Corte Inglés sells English guidebooks and novels, but the selection is limited. For variety, try English Bookshop. The bookstore at the Palau de la Virreina has good books on art, design, and Barcelona.

Bookstores **BCN Books** ✉ Aragó 277 ☎ 93/487-3123. **Come In** ✉ Provença 203 ☎ 93/253-1204. **English Bookshop** ✉ Entençan 63 ☎ 93/425-4466.

SUBWAY TRAVEL

The metro is the fastest and easiest way to get around. You can pay a flat fare of €1 or buy a tarjeta multiviatge, good for 10 rides (€6). Maps of the system are available at main metro stations and branches of the Caixa savings bank.

TAXIS

Taxis are black and yellow. When available for hire, they show a LIBRE sign in the daytime and a green light at night. The meter starts at €3 (which lasts for six minutes), and there are supplements for luggage, night travel, Sunday and holidays, and rides from a station or to the airport. There are cab stands all over town, and you can also hail cabs on the street. To call a cab, try one of the numbers listed below, 24 hours a day.

24-hr Service ☎ 93/387-1000, 93/490-2222, or 93/357-7755.

TOURS

BUS TOURS

City sightseeing tours are run by Julià Tours. Pullmantur also has city sightseeing. Tours leave from the terminals listed below, though you may be able to arrange a pickup at your hotel. Both agencies offer the same tours at the same prices. A morning sightseeing tour visits the Gothic Quarter and Montjuïc; an afternoon tour concentrates on Gaudí and the Picasso Museum. You can visit Barcelona's Olympic sites from May through October.

Fees & Schedules **Julià Tours** ✉ Ronda Universitat 5 ☎ 93/317-6454. **Pullmantur** ✉ Gran Viá de les Corts Catalanes 635 ☎ 93/318-5195.

SINGLE-DAY TOURS Trips out of town are run by Julià Tours and Pullmantur. The principal attractions are a half-day tour to Montserrat to visit the monastery and shrine of the famous Black Virgin; a full-day trip to the Costa Brava resorts, including a boat cruise to the Medes Isles; and, from June through September, a full-day trip to Andorra for tax-free shopping. If you are not an EU citizen, bring your passport with you.

WALKING TOURS La Ruta del Modernisme (the Modernism Route), created by Barcelona's *ajuntament* (city hall), connects four key art nouveau sites: the Palau de la Música, the Fundació Tàpies, the Museu d'Art Modern (in Ciutadella), and the Museo de Zoologia (in Doménech i Muntaner's Castell dels Tres Dragons en la Ciutadella). Guided tours, some in English, are given at the Palau de la Música. Buy your tickets at Casa Amatller, open Monday through Saturday 10–7, Sunday 10–2. The price, €3, gets you 50% discounts at all nine locations.

The bookstore in the Palau de la Virreina rents cassettes whose walking tours follow footprints painted on sidewalks—different colors for different tours—through Barcelona's most interesting areas. The do-it-yourself method is to pick up the guides produced by the tourist office, *Discovering Romanesque Art* and *Discovering Modernist Art,* which have art itineraries for all of Catalonia. El Consorci Turisme de Barcelona (Barcelona Tourism Cortium) leads walking tours of the Gothic Quarter in English at 10 AM on Saturday. The tour costs €6 and includes a visit to the Town Hall.

Fees & Schedules **Casa Amatller** ✉ Passeig de Gràcia 41 ☎ 93/488-0139. **El Consorci Turisme de Barcelona** ✉ Plaça de Catalunya 17, lower level ☎ 906/301282. **Palau de la Virreina** ✉ La Rambla 99.

TRAIN TRAVEL

The Sants Central Station at Plaça Països Catalans is Barcelona's main train station, serving international and national destinations as well as suburban areas. The old and elegant Estació de França (Avda. Marquès de l'Argentera) now serves only certain points in Spain. Inquire at the tourist office to get current travel information and to find out which station you need. Many trains also stop at the Passeig de Gràcia underground station (at C. Aragó), which is closer to the Plaça de Catalunya and Rambla area than Sants. Tickets and information are available here, but luggage carts are not. You can also get information on fares and schedules from RENFE with their 24-hour hot line.

RENFE ☎ 902/240202.

TRAMS & CABLE CARS

The Montjuïc Funicular is a cog railroad that runs from the junction of Avenida Parallel and Nou de la Rambla to the Miramar Amusement Park on Montjuïc; it's open 10:45 AM–8 PM, except in summer (late June to mid-September), when it runs 11 AM–10 PM. A *teleferico* (cable car) runs from the amusement park up to Montjuïc Castle October–June 21, weekends 11–2:45 and 4–7:30; June 22–September, daily 11:30–9.

The Transbordador Aeri Harbor Cable Car runs from Miramar on Montjuïc to the Torre de Jaume I across the harbor on Barcelona *moll* (quay), and on to the Torre de Sant Sebastià at the end of Passeig Joan de Borbó in Barceloneta. You can board at either stage. Hours are October–June, weekdays noon–5:45, and weekends noon–6:15; and July–September, daily 11–8. A round-trip ticket costs €9 (one-way €7.50).

To reach Tibidabo summit, take either Bus 58 or the Ferrocarrils de la Generalitat train from Plaça de Catalunya to Avenida Tibidabo, then the *tramvía blau* (blue tram) to Peu del Funicular, and the *Tibidabo Funicular* from there to the Tibidabo Fairground. The funicular runs every half hour from 7:15 AM to 9:45 PM.

El Consorci Turisme de Barcelona ✉ Plaça de Catalunya 17, lower level ☎ 906/301282.

TRANSPORTATION AROUND BARCELONA

Modern Barcelona, the Eixample—above the Plaça de Catalunya—is built on a grid system; the Gothic Quarter, from the Plaça de Catalunya to the port, is a warren of narrow streets. Almost all sightseeing can be done on foot, but you may need to use taxis, the metro, or buses to link certain areas, depending on how much time you have. The **Bus Turistic** offers 27 stops at major tourist sights for €15. The two circuits (red for upper Barcelona, blue for the lower city) coincide (for transfers from one line to the other) at Plaça Catalunya, Avinguda Diagonal, and Passeig de Gràcia. The bus originates in Plaça Catalunya and runs from 9 AM to 8 PM.

Turisme de Barcelona sells the very worthwhile Barcelona Card, which costs €17 for 24 hours, €20 for 48 hours, €23 for 72 hours, and €27 for five days. Travelers get unlimited travel on all public transport as well as discounts at 27 museums, 10 restaurants, 14 leisure spots, 20 stores, and various other services including walking tours, the airport shuttle, the bus to Tibidabo, and the Tombbus between Barcelona's key shopping areas.

Turisme de Barcelona ☎ 93/368-9732 🌐 www.barcelonaturisme.com.

TRAVEL AGENCIES

Local Agents American Express ✉ Roselló 257, corner of Passeig de Gràcia ☎ 93/217-0070. **Bestours** ✉ Diputación 241 ☎ 93/487-8580. **Viajes Iberia** ✉ Rambla 130 ☎ 93/317-9320. **Wagons-Lits Cook** ✉ Passeig de Gràcia 8 ☎ 93/317-5500.

VISITOR INFORMATION

El Prat Airport and Centre d'Informació Turística have general information on Catalonia and Spain. The other offices listed below focus mostly on Barcelona. You can also get general information on the city by dialing 010.

Ajuntament ✉ Pl. Sant Jaume 1, Barri Gòtic. **Centre d'Informació Turistic de Barcelona** ✉ Plaça de Catalunya 17, lower level ☎ 906/301282 📠 93/304-3155. **Estació de Sants** ✉ Pl. Països Catalans s/n, Eixample ☎ 93/491-4431. **Centre d'Informació Turística** ✉ Palau Robert, Passeig de Gràcia 107, at Diagonal ☎ 93/238-4000. **El Prat Airport** ☎ 93/478-4704. **Palau de Congressos** during special events and conferences ✉ Avda. María Cristina ☎ 93/423-3101 Ext. 8356. **Palau de la Virreina** ✉ Rambla de les Flors 99 ☎ 93/301-7775.

Spain Basics

To research prices, get advice from other travelers, and book travel arrangements, visit www.fodors.com.

BUSINESS HOURS

Banks are open Monday–Saturday 8:30 or 9 until 2 from October through June; in summer they are closed on Saturday. Hours for museums and churches vary; most are open in the morning, but most museums close one day a week, often Monday. Stores are open weekdays from 9 or 10 until 1:30 or 2, then in the afternoon from around 5 to 8. Larger department stores and supermarkets do not close at midday. In some cities, especially in summer, stores close on Saturday afternoon.

HOLIDAYS

New Year's; Epiphany (January 6); Good Friday; Easter; May Day (May 1); St. James's Day (July 25); Assumption (August 15); National Day (October 12); All Saints' Day (November 1); Constitution (December 6); Immaculate Conception (December 8); Christmas. Local holidays vary from one Autonomous Community, or province, to another.

LANGUAGE

Spanish (called Castellano, or Castilian) is spoken and understood throughout Spain. However, the Basques speak Euskera; in Catalonia, you'll hear Catalan; and in Galicia, Gallego. If you don't speak Spanish, you should have little trouble finding people who speak English in major cities and coastal resorts, but you won't necessarily be able to count on the bus driver or the passerby on the street. Fortunately, Spanish is fairly easy to pick up, and your efforts to speak the local tongue will be graciously received.

MONEY MATTERS

The cost of living in Spain is on a par with that of most other European nations. However, currency fluctuations have increased the buying power of those visiting from North America and the United Kingdom. A cup of coffee costs between €.75 and €1; a glass of wine in a bar, €.60–€1; a sandwich, €2–€3; a local bus or subway ride, €.75–€1.20; a 2-km (1-mi) taxi ride, about €3.

CREDIT CARDS Most hotels, restaurants, and stores accept credit cards. Visa is the most widely accepted card, followed by MasterCard (also called EuroCard in Spain).

CURRENCY The euro is Spain's standard currency, and banks and ATMs dispense all money in euros. Euro notes come in denominations of 5, 10, 20, 50, 100, 200, and 500; coins are worth 1 cent of a euro, 2 cents, 5 cents, 10 cents, 20 cents, 50 cents, 1 euro, and 2 euros. At press time (summer 2003), the exchange rate was €.86 to the U.S. dollar, €.63 to the Canadian dollar, €1.40 to the pound sterling, €.56 to the Australian dollar, €.50 to the New Zealand dollar.

You may take any amount of foreign currency in bills or traveler's checks into Spain, as well as any amount of euros. When leaving Spain you may take out only €3,000 or the equivalent in foreign currency, unless you can prove you declared the excess at customs on entering the country.

CURRENCY EXCHANGE The word to look for is CAMBIO (exchange). Most Spanish banks take a 1½% commission, though some less scrupulous places charge more. Hotels offer rates lower than banks, but they rarely charge a commission, so you may well break even. Restaurants and stores generally do not accept payment in dollars or traveler's checks. If you have a credit card with a personal identification number, you'll have no trouble drawing cash from automated teller machines.

TAXES

VALUE-ADDED TAX (V.A.T.) Value-added tax, called IVA, is levied on most goods and services. It's 7% at hotels and restaurants and 16% on goods and car rentals.

A number of shops, particularly large stores and boutiques in holiday resorts, participate in Global Refund (formerly Europe Tax-Free Shopping), a V.A.T. refund service that makes getting your money back relatively hassle-free. On purchases of more than €90, you're entitled to a refund of the 16% tax (there is no refund for the 7% tax). Ask for the Global Refund form (called a Shopping Cheque) in participating stores. You show your passport and fill out the form; the vendor then mails you the refund, or you present your original receipt to the V.A.T. office at the airport when you leave Spain. (In both Madrid and Barcelona, the office is near the duty-free shops. Save time for this process, as lines can be long.) Customs signs the original and either refunds your money on the spot in cash, or sends it to their central office to process a credit-card refund. Credit-card refunds take a few weeks.

TELEPHONES

The country code for Spain is 34.

DIRECTORY & OPERATOR ASSISTANCE For the operator and directory information for any part of Spain, dial 1–1818. The international information and assistance operator is at 1–18–25 (some operators speak English). If you're in Madrid, dial 1008 to make collect calls to countries in Europe; 1005 for the rest of the world.

INTERNATIONAL CALLS You can call abroad from any pay phone marked TELÉFONO INTERNACIONAL. Some are coin-operated, but it is best to purchase a *tarjeta telefónica* (telephone card), available at most newsdealers and many shops. A few public phones also accept credit cards. Dial 00, then dial 1 for the United States, 0101 for Canada, or 44 for the United Kingdom, followed by the area code and number. For lengthy calls, go to the *telefónica,* a phone office found in all sizable towns: here an operator assigns you a private booth and collects payment at the end of the call. This is the cheapest and by far the easiest way to call overseas, and you can charge calls costing more than €3 to Visa or MasterCard. Private long-distance companies, such as AT&T, MCI, and Sprint, have special access numbers.

Access Codes **AT&T** ☎ **900/990011. MCI** ☎ **900/990014. Sprint** ☎ **900/990013.**

LOCAL CALLS Note that to call anywhere within Spain—even locally—you need to dial the area code first. All provincial codes begin with a 9.

PUBLIC PHONES Most pay phones have a digital readout, so you can see your money ticking away. You need at least €.20 for a local call, €.50 to call another province, and at least €.60 if you are calling a Spanish cell phone. Some pay phones take only phone cards, which can be purchased at any tobacco shop in various denominations.

BERLIN

Berlin is a city of striking modern architecture, masterworks of art and antiquity, provocative performances, raffish bars, sleek stores, canal-side cafés, and above all, history. A royal residence during the 15th century, Berlin came into its own under the rule of King Friedrich II (1712–86)—Frederick the Great—whose liberal reforms and artistic patronage led the city's development into a major cultural capital. In the 20th century Hitler and his supporters destroyed Berlin's reputation for tolerance and plunged it headlong into the war that led to its wholesale destruction, and to its eventual division by the infamous Wall in 1961. The Wall was breached in the Peaceful Revolution of 1989, and East and West are now relatively seamless. A large Turkish and European population make Berlin the most international city in Germany, and it is also the city with the most active arts and nightlife scene.

EXPLORING BERLIN

Berlin is laid out on an epic scale but its extensive subway, bus, and streetcar (tram) services make it easy to get around. You can rely on the timetables posted at subway stations and bus and streetcar stops (the latter two marked by signs bearing the letter "H"). Board the subway in the right direction by knowing the name of the end station you're heading toward.

Western Berlin

The western districts include Charlottenburg, Tiergarten, Kreuzberg, and Schöneberg, and the entire area is best known for the constant commerce on Kurfürstendamm. The boulevard of shops, art galleries, restaurants, and bars stretches 3 km (2 mi) through the downtown.

Numbers in the margin correspond to points of interest on the Berlin map.

★ ⓮ **Ägyptisches Museum** (Egyptian Museum). This small but outstanding museum is home to the portrait bust of Nefertiti known around the world.

The 3,300-year-old queen is the centerpiece of a fascinating collection of Egyptian antiquities that includes some of the finest-preserved mummies outside Cairo. ✉ *Schlosstr. 70* ☎ *030/3435–7311* 🌐 *www.smpk.de* 🕒 *Tues.–Sun. 10–6.*

⓱ **Bildungs- und Gedenkstätte Haus der Wannsee-Konferenz** (Wannsee Conference Memorial Site). On January 20, 1942, this lakeside Berlin villa hosted the conference at which Nazi leaders planned the systematic deportation and genocide of Europe's Jewish population. An exhibition documents the conference, and more extensively, the escalation of persecution against Jews, and the Holocaust itself. From the U-bahn Wannsee station take Bus 114. ✉ *Am Grossen Wannsee 56–58* ☎ *030/805–0010* 🌐 *www.ghwk.de* 🕒 *Mon.–Sun. 10–6.*

★ ❼ **Brandenburger Tor** (Brandenburg Gate). This is the sole remaining gate of 14 built by Carl Langhans in 1788–91, designed as a triumphal arch for King Frederick Wilhelm II. Troops paraded through the gate after successful campaigns—the last time in 1945, when victorious Red Army troops took Berlin. During Berlin's division, the gate was stranded in a no-man's-land, but it now serves as the center of festivities on Unification Day and New Year's Eve. In front of the gate is **Pariser Platz** (Paris Square), and to the south of it is Germany's national **Holocaust Mahnmal** (Holocaust Memorial). ✉ *Unter den Linden at Pariser Pl.*

⓲ **Dahlemer Museen** (Dahlem Museums). This unique complex of four museums includes the **Ethnologisches Museum** (Ethnographic Museum), famous for its artifacts from Africa, Asia, the South Seas, and the Americas. The other museums present early European cultures, ancient Indian culture, and East Asian art. ✉ *Lansstr. 8* ☎ *030/8301–438* 🌐 *www.smpk.de* 🕒 *Tues.–Fri. 10–6, weekends 11–6* Ⓤ *U-bahn 2 to Dahlem-Dorf.*

⓰ **Grunewald** (Green Forest). Together with its Wannsee lakes, this splendid forest is a popular retreat for Berliners, who come out in force, swimming, sailing their boats, tramping through the woods, and riding horseback. In winter a downhill ski run and ski jump operate on the modest slopes of Teufelsberg hill. Excursion steamers ply the Wannsee, the Havel River, and the Müggelsee. Ⓢ *S-bahn 1 to Nikolassee or Wannsee; S-Bahn 7 to Grunewald.*

㉙ **Hamburger Bahnhof, Museum für Gegenwart–Berlin** (Museum of Contemporary Art). The best place in Berlin to survey Western art after 1960 is in this light-filled remodeled 19th-century train station. You can see installations by German artists Joseph Beuys and Anselm Kiefer as well as paintings by Andy Warhol, Cy Twombly, Robert Rauschenberg, and Robert Morris. ✉ *Invalidenstr. 50–51* ☎ *030/397–83463* 🌐 *www.smpk.de* 🕒 *Tues.–Fri. 10–6, weekends 11–6.*

★ ⓫ **Haus am Checkpoint Charlie.** The seemingly homespun museum reviews events leading up to the Wall's construction and displays actual tools, equipment, records, and photographs documenting methods used by East Germans to cross over to the West. Come early to avoid the tour buses that stop here. ✉ *Friedrichstr. 43–45* ☎ *030/253–7250* 🌐 *www.mauermuseum.com* 🕒 *Daily 9 AM–10 PM.*

⓬ **Jüdisches Museum** (Jewish Museum). The history and culture of Germany's Jews from the Middle Ages through today is chronicled in this jagged building designed by architect Daniel Libeskind (who is also rebuilding the World Trade Center site in New York). Various physical "voids" represent the loss German society faces as a result of the Holocaust, and a portion of the exhibits document the Holocaust as well. You'll need at least three hours to do the museum justice. Go through

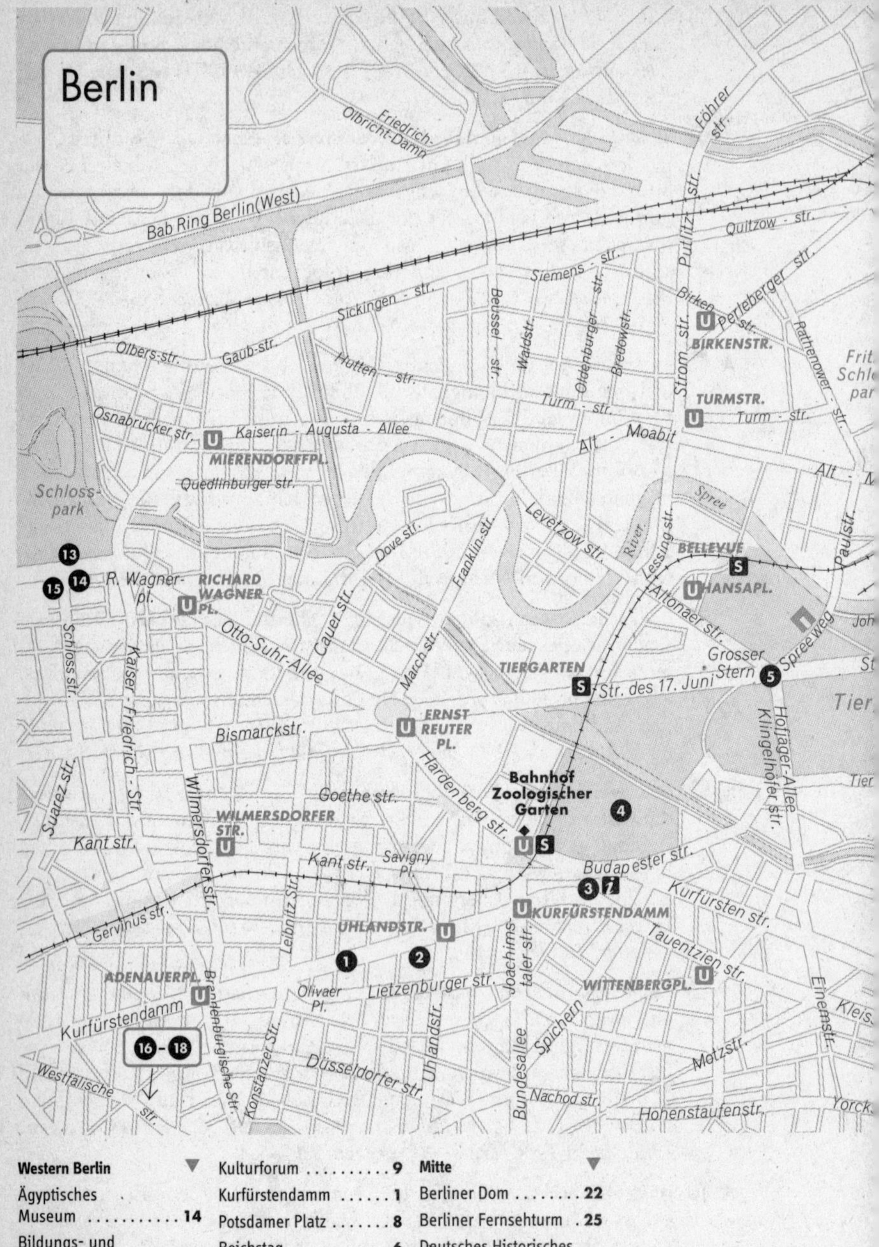

Western Berlin ▼

- Ägyptisches Museum 14
- Bildungs- und Gedenkstätte Haus der Wannsee-Konferenz .. 17
- Brandenburger Tor 7
- Dahlemer Museen 18
- Grunewald 16
- Hamburger Bahnhof 29
- Haus am Checkpoint Charlie 11
- Jüdisches Museum 12
- Kaiser-Wilhelm-Gedächtniskirche 3
- Kulturforum 9
- Kurfürstendamm 1
- Potsdamer Platz 8
- Reichstag 6
- Sammlung Berggruen 15
- Schloss Charlottenburg 13
- Siegessäule 5
- The Story of Berlin 2
- Topographie des Terrors 10
- Zoologischer Garten ... 4

Mitte ▼

- Berliner Dom 22
- Berliner Fernsehturm . 25
- Deutsches Historisches Museum 20
- Gedenkstätte Berliner Mauer 28
- Gendarmenmarkt..... 19
- Hackesche Höfe 26
- Museumsinsel 21
- Neue Synagoge 27
- Nikolaiviertel 23
- St. Marienkirche 24

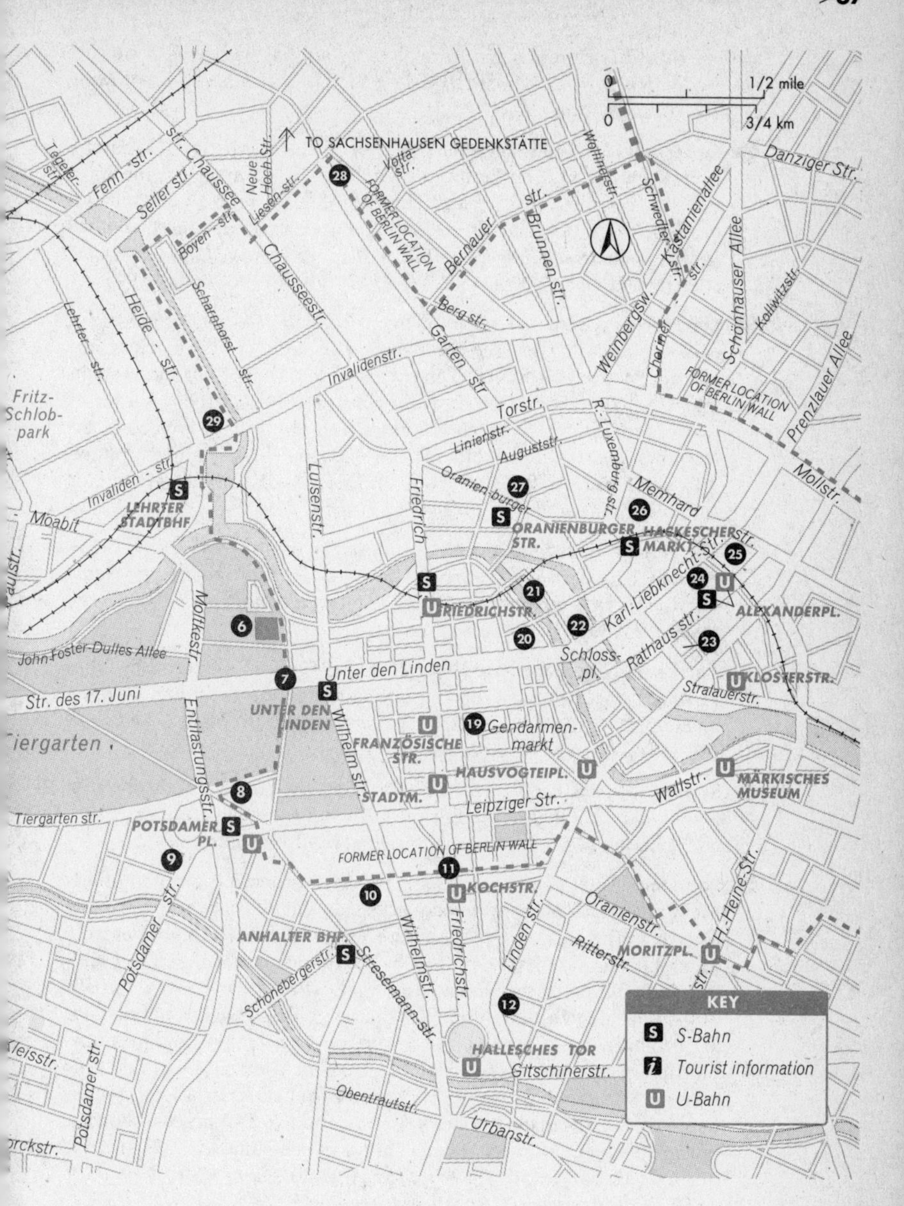

1/2 mile
3/4 km
TO SACHSENHAUSEN GEDENKSTÄTTE
FORMER LOCATION OF BERLIN WALL
LEHRTER STADTBHF.
ORANIENBURGER STR.
HACKESCHER MARKT
FRIEDRICHSTR.
ALEXANDERPL.
UNTER DEN LINDEN
FRANZÖSISCHE STR.
HAUSVOGTEIPL.
KLOSTERSTR.
MÄRKISCHES MUSEUM
STADTM.
POTSDAMER PL.
KOCHSTR.
ANHALTER BHF.
MORITZPL.
HALLESCHES TOR
Tiergarten
Fritz-Schlob-park
Moabit
Unter den Linden
Str. des 17. Juni
Leipziger Str.
Gendarmen-markt
Schloss-pl.
KEY
S-Bahn
Tourist information
U-Bahn

the third floor quickly if you're already familiar with Jewish culture. ✉ *Lindenstr. 9–14* ☎ *030/30878–5681* 🌐 *www.jmberlin.de* 🕓 *Mon. 10–10, Tues.–Sun. 10–8.*

★ ❸ **Kaiser-Wilhelm-Gedächtniskirche** (Kaiser Wilhelm Memorial Church). Long a symbol of West Berlin, this landmark is a dramatic reminder of the futile destructiveness of war. The shell of the tower is all that remains of the 19th-century church. Adjoining it are a modern church and bell tower. ✉ *Breitscheidpl.* ☎ *030/218–5023* 🌐 *www.gedaechtniskirche.com* 🕓 *Old Tower: Mon.–Sat. 10–4, Memorial Church: daily 9–7.*

★ ❾ **Kulturforum** (Cultural Forum). With its unique ensemble of museums, galleries, and libraries, the complex is a cultural jewel. The **Gemäldegalerie** (Painting Gallery) has an extensive selection of European paintings from the 13th through 18th centuries, among them works by Rembrandt, Dürer, Cranach the Elder, and Holbein, as well as of the Italian masters—Botticelli, Titian, Giotto, Lippi, and Raphael. ✉ *Matthäikirchpl. 8* ☎ *030/2660 or 030/266–2951* 🌐 *www.smpk.de* 🕓 *Tues., Wed., and Fri.–Sun. 10–6, Thurs. 10–10.*

The **Kunstgewerbemuseum** (Museum of Decorative Arts) exhibits European arts and crafts from the Middle Ages to the present. ✉ *Matthäikirchpl. 8* ☎ *030/266–2902* 🌐 *www.smpk.de* 🕓 *Tues.–Fri. 10–6, weekends 11–6.*

The **Neue Nationalgalerie** (New National Gallery), designed by Mies van der Rohe, exhibits 20th-century paintings and sculpture. ✉ *Potsdamer Str. 50* ☎ *030/266–2651* 🌐 *www.smpk.de* 🕓 *Tues., Wed., and Fri. 10–6, Thurs. 10–10, weekends 11–8.*

★ ❶ **Kurfürstendamm.** Ku'damm, as Berliners call the boulevard, throbs with activity day and night. The **Europa Center,** a shopping center, and Breitscheidplatz in front of it are a buzzing, central meeting point.

❽ **Potsdamer Platz.** Sony, Mercedes Benz, Asea Brown Boveri, and others maintain their company headquarters at this entirely reconstructed square, Europe's busiest plaza before World War II. The **Sony Center** is an architectural marvel designed by German-American architect Helmut Jahn. Within it, the **Filmmuseum Berlin** (✉ Potsdamer Str. 2 ☎ 030/300–9030 🌐 www.filmmuseum-berlin.de 🕓 Tues., Wed., and Fri.–Sun. 10–6, Thurs. 10–8) presents the history of moviemaking and memorabilia of German movie stars, including Marlene Dietrich. Also in the center is the Kaisersaal (Emperor's Hall), a café from the prewar Grand Hotel Esplanade. The **Potsdamer Platz Arkaden** houses 140 upscale shops, a musical theater, a variety stage, cafés, a movie complex, a 3D-IMAX cinema, and a casino. ✉ *Arkaden Alte Potsdamer Str. 7* ☎ *030/2559–2766 Arkaden* 🕓 *Arkaden: weekdays 9:30–8, Sat. 9:30–4.*

★ ❻ **Reichstag** (German Parliament). The monumental building served as Germany's seat of parliament from its completion in 1894 until 1933, when it was gutted by fire under suspicious circumstances. Remodeled under the direction of British architect Sir Norman Foster, the Reichstag is once again hosting the Deutscher Bundestag, Germany's federal parliament. You can get a stunning view of Berlin from underneath the glass cupola. Lines can be long, so it's best to visit very early or very late on a weekday. ✉ *Pl. der Republik 1* ☎ *030/2273–2152* 🌐 *www.bundestag.de* 🕓 *Daily 8 AM–midnight; last admission 11 PM.*

★ ⓯ **Sammlung Berggruen** (Berggruen Collection). This small museum focuses on modern art, with work from such artists as Van Gogh, Cézanne, Picasso, Giacometti, and Klee. ✉ *Schlossstr. 1* ☎ *030/3269–5815* 🌐 *www.smpk.de* 🕓 *Tues.–Sun. 10–6.*

★ 13 **Schloss Charlottenburg.** Built at the end of the 17th century by King Frederick I for his wife, Queen Sophie Charlotte, this grand palace and its magnificent gardens were progressively enlarged for later royal residents and now include museums. The baroque apartments can be seen on tours only. ✉ *Luisenpl.,* Ⓤ *U-bahn 7 subway line to Richard-Wagner-Pl. station; from station walk east along Otto-Suhr-Allee* ☎ *030/3209–1440* 🌐 *www.smpk.de* ⏲ *Altes Schloss: Tues.–Fri., 9–5, weekends 10–5; New Wing: Tues.–Fri. 10–6, weekends 11–6.*

5 **Siegessäule** (Victory Column). The memorial, erected in 1873, commemorates four Prussian military campaigns. It stands at the center of the 630-acre Tiergarten (Animal Park), the former hunting grounds of the Great Elector. Climb 285 steps to see the view from its 213-foot summit. ✉ *Am Grossen Stern* ☎ *030/391–2961* ⏲ *Nov.–Mar., daily 9:30–5; Apr.–Oct., daily 9:30–6 (last admission ½ hr before closing).*

2 **The Story of Berlin.** Eight hundred years of the city's history, from the first settlers to the fall of the Wall, is conveyed through hands-on exhibits, film footage, and multimedia devices in this unusual venue. An eerie relic is the 1974 nuclear shelter, which you can visit by tour. Museum placards are also in English. ✉ *Ku'damm Karree, Kurfürstendamm 207–208* ☎ *030/8872–0100* 🌐 *www.story-of-berlin.de* ⏲ *Daily 10–8 (last admission: 6).*

10 **Topographie des Terrors** (Topography of Terror). The buildings that once stood on these grounds housed the headquarters of the Gestapo, the secret security police, and other Nazi security organizations. After the war, the buildings were leveled. In 1987, the prison cellars, which are just behind a remaining stretch of the Wall, were excavated. The outdoor exhibit documents the structure of Nazi organizations, the atrocities they committed, and their victims. The free audio guide is a must. ✉ *Niederkirchnerstr. 8* ☎ *030/2548–6703* 🌐 *www.topographie.de* ⏲ *Oct.–Apr., daily 10–5; May–Sept., daily 10–8.*

★ 4 **Zoologischer Garten** (Zoological Gardens). Berlin's enchanting zoo has the world's largest variety of individual types of fauna, along with a fascinating aquarium. ✉ *Hardenbergpl. 8 and Budapester Str. 34* ☎ *030/254–010* 🌐 *www.zoo-berlin.de* 🎫 *Combined ticket €13* ⏲ *Zoo: Nov.–Mar., daily 9–5; Apr.–Sept., daily 9–6:30; Oct., daily 9–6; Aquarium: daily 9–6.*

Mitte

Most of the historic architecture of the prewar capital is in the Mitte district.

Numbers in the margin correspond to points of interest on the Berlin map.

22 **Berliner Dom** (Berlin Cathedral). The impressive 19th-century cathedral with its enormous green copper dome is one of the great ecclesiastical buildings in Germany. The relatively easy climb to the dome lookout is worth it. ✉ *Am Lustgarten* ☎ *030/2026–9136* ⏲ *Apr.–Sept., Mon.–Wed., Fri., and Sat., 9–8, Thurs. 9–10, Sun. noon–8; Oct.–Mar., Mon.–Sat. 9–7, Sun. noon–7; crypt closes 2 hrs earlier; dome open same hrs as church, weather permitting.*

25 **Berliner Fernsehturm** (Berlin TV Tower). At 1,198 feet high, eastern Berlin's TV tower is a proud 710 feet *taller* than western Berlin's. Within a disco-ball-like enclosure, the observation level affords the best view of Berlin; take a coffee break (but skip the food) in the revolving café. ✉ *Panoramastr. 1a* ☎ *030/242–3333* 🌐 *www.berlinerfernsehturm.de*

⏲ Nov.–Feb., daily 10 AM–midnight; Mar.–Oct., daily 9 AM–1 AM (last admission 1½ hrs before closing).

⑳ **Deutsches Historisches Museum** (German Historical Museum). This magnificent baroque building, constructed in 1695–1730, was once the Prussian Zeughaus (arsenal). It now houses Germany's national history museum. The modern glass wing by I. M. Pei opened in 2003. ✉ *Unter den Linden 2* ☎ *030/203–040* 🌐 *www.dhm.de* ⏲ *Daily 10–6.*

㉘ **Gedenkstätte Berliner Mauer** (Berlin Wall Memorial Site). A documentation center details the history of the Wall and the division of Germany. You can hear radio broadcasts from both the east and west reporting the building of the Wall, as well as eyewitness accounts. Part of the memorial is the Reconciliation Church, completed in 2000 to replace the church dynamited by the Communists in 1985. The church had been walled into the "death strip" and was seen as a hindrance to patrolling it. ✉ *Bernauer Str. 111* ☎ *030/464–1030* 🌐 *www.berliner-mauer-gedenkstaette.de* ⏲ *Wed.–Sun. 10–5.*

★ ⑲ **Gendarmenmarkt.** Anchoring this large square are the beautifully reconstructed 1818 **Schauspielhaus,** one of Berlin's main concert halls (now called the Konzerthaus), and the **Deutscher Dom and Französischer Dom** (German and French cathedrals). The **Deutscher Dom** (✉ Gendarmenmarkt 1 ☎ 030/2273–0431 ⏲ Sept.–May, Tues. 10–10, Wed.–Sun. 10–6; June–Aug., Tues. 10–10, Wed.–Sun. 10–7) holds an extensive exhibition on the emergence of the parliamentary system in Germany, sponsored by the German parliament. An English audio guide covers a portion of the exhibits.

㉖ **Hackesche Höfe** (Hackesche Warehouses). Built in 1905–07, the tiled Hackesche Höfe is the finest example of art nouveau industrial architecture in Berlin. Within eight connecting courtyards are several art galleries and pricey shops. Its restaurants and theaters are a nightlife hub. ✉ *Rosenthaler Str. 40–41* 🌐 *www.hackeschehoefe.de.*

㉑ **Museumsinsel** (Museum Island). This unique complex contains four world-class museums. The **Nationalgalerie** (National Gallery; ✉ Bodestr.) has 19th- and 20th-century paintings and sculptures, mostly by German artists, including Caspar David Friedrich. The **Altes Museum** (Old Museum; ✉ Am Lustgarten), a red marble, neoclassical building, was designed by Schinkel and in 1830, was the first building ever purposefully erected as a museum. It is home to artworks from ancient Greece. Etruscan art is a highlight. The **Pergamonmuseum** (Pergamon Museum; ✉ Am Kupfergraben) takes its name from its principal exhibit, the Pergamon Altar, a monumental Greek altar dating from 180 BC. The gateways of Miletus and Ishtar are the other architectural wonders. The museums are free the first Sunday of the month. ✉ *Museumsinsel (off Unter den Linden along the Spree Canal)* ☎ *030/209–5577 or 030/2090–5560* 🌐 *www.smpk.de* ⏲ *Pergamonmuseum: Fri.–Wed. 10–6, Thurs. 10–10; Alte Nationalgalerie and Altes Museum: Tues.–Sun. 10–6.*

Fodor'sChoice ★

㉗ **Neue Synagoge** (New Synagogue). A stunning, gilded cupola marks this landmark. The faintly Middle Eastern–looking building was completed in 1866, when its 3,200 seats made it the largest synagogue in Europe. It was destroyed on November 9, 1938 (*Kristallnacht*—Night of the Broken Glass), when Nazis vandalized, looted, and burned synagogues and Jewish shops across Germany. The exhibit on the history of the building and its congregants includes fragments of the original architecture and furnishings. ✉ *Oranienburger Str. 28–30* ☎ *030/882–8316* 🌐 *www.cjudaicum.de* ⏲ *Oct.–Apr., Sun.–Thurs. 10–6, Fri. 10–2; May–Sept., Sun.*

and Tues.–Thurs. 10–6, Mon. 10–8, Fri. 10–5. Tours Wed. at 4, Sun. at 2, 4. Cupola open Apr.–late Sept.

23 **Nikolaiviertel** (Nikolai Quarter). Berlin's oldest quarter is filled with shops, cafés, and restaurants. Nikolaikirchplatz has Berlin's oldest building, the **St. Nikolaikirche** (St. Nicholas's Church), dating from 1230. At Breite Strasse 35 is the **Ribbeckhaus**, the city's only surviving Renaissance structure, dating from 1624. ✉ *Nikolaikirchpl.* ☎ *030/240–020* 🌐 *www.stadtmuseum.de* ⏲ *Tues.–Sun. 10–6.*

24 **St. Marienkirche** (Church of St. Mary). This medieval church, one of the finest in Berlin, is worth a visit for its late-Gothic fresco *Der Totentanz* (*Dance of Death*). The cross on top of the church tower was an everlasting annoyance to Communist rulers, as its golden metal was always mirrored in the windows of the Fernsehturm TV tower, the pride of socialist construction genius. ✉ *Karl-Liebknecht-Str. 8* ☎ *030/242–4467* ⏲ *Mon.–Thurs. 10–4, weekends noon–4; tour Mon. and Tues. at 1, Sun. at 11:45.*

WHERE TO EAT

Typical Berliner meals include *Eisbein mit Sauerkraut* (knuckle of pork with sauerkraut), *Spanferkel* (suckling pig), Turkish *Döner kebab* (grilled lamb or chicken served with salad in a flat-bread pocket), and *Currywurst* (chubby and spicy frankfurters sold at wurst stands).

WHAT IT COSTS In Euros

	$$$$	$$$	$$	$
AT DINNER	over €26	€20–€25	€15–€20	under €15

Prices are per person for a main course.

★ $$$$ ✕ **First Floor.** Chef Matthias Buchholz's traditional German fare has earned him high honors. The menu changes according to the season and his moods, but most of the menu items are interpretations of German dishes such as *Müritzlammrücken in Olivenkruste mit Bohnenmelange* (Müritz lamb back in olive crust, served with green beans). The four-course menu costs €66.50. ✉ *Hotel Palace, Budapester Str. 42* ☎ *030/2502–1020* ✍ *Reservations essential* 💳 *AE, DC, MC, V* ⏲ *No lunch Sat.*

★ $$$$ ✕ **VAU.** The German fish and game dishes prepared by Chef Kolja Kleeberg have earned him endless praise and awards. Daring combinations include *Ente mit gezupftem Rotkohl, Quitten und Maronen* (duck with red cabbage, quinces, and sweet chestnuts) and *Steinbutt mit Kalbbries auf Rotweinschalotten* (turbot with veal sweetbread on shallots in red wine). A four-course menu runs €75; a six-course, €100. VAU's cool interior is all style and modern art. ✉ *Jägerstr. 54/55* ☎ *030/202–9730* ✍ *Reservations essential* 💳 *AE, DC, MC, V* ⏲ *Closed Sun.*

★ $$$ ✕ **Borchardt.** The menu changes daily at this fashionable meeting place where columns, red plush benches, and an art nouveau mosaic create the impression of a 1920s salon. Entrées lean to French preparations. ✉ *Französische Str. 47* ☎ *030/2038–7110* ✍ *Reservations essential* 💳 *AE, MC, V.*

$$–$$$ ✕ **Paris Bar.** This late-night Charlottenburg restaurant attracts a polyglot clientele of film stars, artists, and executives. The cuisine is creative but medium-quality French. ✉ *Kantstr. 152* ☎ *030/313–8052* 💳 *AE.*

$–$$$ ✕ **Schwarzenraben.** Berlin's successful frequent this stylish restaurant that epitomizes the rise of the New East. Though there are open spaces at the front and back, many of the tables are uncomfortably squeezed together along a long, narrow stretch. The environment is unfortunately a bit noisy. The menu, written in German and Italian, has a large selection of appetizers and presents new Italian recipes such as risotto with quail breast and leg, port wine, and goat cheese. ✉ *Neue Schönhauser Str. 13* ☎ *030/2839–1698* *Reservations essential* ▭ *AE, MC, V.*

$–$$ ✕ **Hackescher Hof.** At one of the most "in" places in Mitte, the food is a mixture of German cooking and international cuisine such as Argentinian beef, grilled tuna with arugula pesto, and Wiener schnitzel. Menus are available in English and a reasonably priced breakfast is served until 1 PM during the week and 3 PM on weekends. Dinner reservations are advised. ✉ *Rosenthaler Str. 40/41* ☎ *030/2835–293* ▭ *AE, MC, V.*

$–$$ ✕ **Reinhard's.** Berliners of all stripes meet here in the Nikolai Quarter to enjoy the carefully prepared entrées and to sample spirits from the amply stocked bar. *Adlon* (honey-glazed breast of duck) is one of the house specialties. Reinhard's has a smaller, more elegant restaurant on the Ku'damm. ✉ *Poststr. 28* ☎ *030/242–5295* ✉ *Kurfürstendamm 190* ☎ *030/881–1621* *Reservations essential* ▭ *AE, DC, MC, V.*

$ ✕ **Café Oren.** This popular nonkosher Jewish eatery is next to the Neue Synagoge. Its vegetarian and Middle Eastern dishes round out the menu. The restaurant buzzes with loud chatter all evening, and the atmosphere and service are friendly. The small backyard is a wonderful spot to enjoy a cool summer evening or a warm autumn afternoon. ✉ *Oranienburger Str. 28* ☎ *030/282–8228* ▭ *AE, DC, MC, V.*

★ **$** ✕ **Grossbeerenkeller.** The cellar restaurant, with its massive, dark-oak furniture and decorative antlers, is one of the most original dining spots in town. Owner and bartender Ingeborg Zinn-Baier presents such dishes as *Sülze vom Schweinekopf mit Bratkartoffeln und Remoulade* (diced pork with home fries and herb sauce). Her fried potatoes are famous. ✉ *Grossbeerenstr. 90* ☎ *030/251–3064* ▭ *No credit cards* ⊗ *Closed Sun.*

$ ✕ **Zur Letzten Instanz.** Established in 1621, Berlin's oldest restaurant combines the charming atmosphere of old-world Berlin with a limited (but tasty) choice of dishes. The emphasis here is on beer, both in the recipes and in the mug. Service can be erratic, though engagingly friendly. Chancellor Schroder treated French President Chirac to a meal here in 2003. ✉ *Waisenstr. 14–16* ☎ *030/242–5528* ▭ *AE, DC, MC, V.*

WHERE TO STAY

Make reservations well in advance. Prices for rooms can fluctuate wildly based on season and day of the week.

WHAT IT COSTS In Euros				
	$$$$	$$$	$$	$
HOTELS	over €200	€150–€200	€75–€150	under €75

Hotel prices are for two people in a standard double room in high season.

$$$$ **Kempinski Hotel Bristol Berlin.** This grand hotel in the heart of the city has the best of Berlin's shopping at its doorstep. All rooms and suites are luxuriously decorated and equipped, with marble bathrooms, cable TV, and English-style furnishings. Kids under 12 stay free if they share their parents' room. ✉ *Kurfürstendamm 27, D-10719* ☎ *030/884–340* *030/883–6075* 🌐 *www.kempinskiberlin.de* *301 rooms, 52 suites* *2 restaurants, pool, bar* ▭ *AE, DC, MC, V.*

★ **$$$$** **Four Seasons Hotel Berlin.** Smooth and up-to-date services, such as cell phone rentals, complement turn-of-the-20th-century luxury here. Thick carpets, heavy crystal chandeliers, and a romantic restaurant with an open fireplace make for a sophisticated and serene atmosphere. ✉ *Char-*

lottenstr. 49, D-10117 ☎ *030/20338* 📠 *030/2033–6119* 🌐 *www.fourseasons.com* 162 *rooms, 42 suites* *Restaurant, bar* *AE, DC, MC, V.*

★ $$$$ **Grand Hyatt Berlin.** Europe's first Grand Hyatt is *the* address for those attending the Berlinale film festival in February. Stylish guests feel at home with a minimalist, Feng Shui–approved design that combines Japanese and Bauhaus elements. A special attraction of the first-class hotel is the top-floor spa and swimming pool, which has a great view of Berlin's skyline. ✉ *Marlene-Dietrich-Pl. 2, D-10785* ☎ *030/2553–1234* 📠 *030/2553–1235* 🌐 *www.berlin.grand.hyatt.com* *325 rooms, 17 suites* *Restaurant, pool, bar* *AE, DC, MC, V.*

★ $$$$ **Hotel Adlon Berlin.** This elegant hotel next to Pariser Platz lives up to its almost mythical predecessor, the old Hotel Adlon, which, until its destruction during World War II, was considered Europe's premier resort. The city's priciest hotel has impeccable service. Guest rooms are furnished in '20s style with dark-wood trimmings and bathrooms in black marble. ✉ *Unter den Linden 77, D-10117* ☎ *030/22610* 📠 *030/2261–2222* 🌐 *www.hotel-adlon.de* *255 rooms, 82 suites* *3 restaurants, pool, bar* *AE, DC, MC, V.*

$$$–$$$$ Fodor's Choice ★ **Swissôtel Berlin.** This ultramodern hotel excels with its reputable Swiss hospitality— from accompanying guests to their floor after check-in, to equipping each room with an iron, umbrella, and Lavazza espresso machine that preheats the cups. The biggest advantage is the location at the corner of Ku'damm and Joachimsthaler Strasse. All rooms have soundproof windows, and the nightly view of the bright city lights is fantastic. ✉ *Augsburger Str. 44 (corner of Joachimsthaler Strasse), D–10789* ☎ *030/220–100* 📠 *030/2201–02222* 🌐 *www.swissotel.com* *316 rooms, 31 suites* *Restaurant, bar* *AE, DC, MC, V.*

$$–$$$ **Riehmers Hofgarten.** Surrounded by the bars and restaurants of the colorful Kreuzberg district, this hotel has fast connections to the center of town. The small rooms may be too spartan for many travelers, but they are modern, quiet, and functional. The Riehmers's true appeal comes from its location in an impressive, late-19th-century apartment house. ✉ *Yorckstr. 83, D-10965* ☎ *030/7809–8800* 📠 *030/7809–8808* 🌐 *www.riehmers-hofgarten.de* *22 rooms* *Bar* *AE, MC, V.*

★ $$ **Charlottenburger Hof.** A creative flair, a convenient location across from an S-bahn station, and room computers with free Internet access make this low-key hotel a great value for no-fuss travelers. The variety of rooms can suit friends, couples, or families. Kurfürstendamm is a 10-minute walk, and the bus to and from Tegel Airport stops a block away. ✉ *Stuttgarter Pl. 14, D-10627* ☎ *030/329–070* 📠 *030/323–3723* 🌐 *www.charlottenburger-hof.de* *46 rooms* *Restaurant* *AE, MC, V.*

$$ **Hotel Astoria.** You'll be well attended to in this small, privately owned and run hotel. Each room in the simple 1898 building is different, so when making a reservation, say whether you'd like a bathtub or shower. Ask about weekend specials or package deals for longer stays. The location is good for exploring the Ku'damm area, and the side street makes for a wonderful stroll. An unusual perk is free use of the Internet terminal in the lobby. ✉ *Fasanenstr. 2, D-10623* ☎ *030/312–4067* 📠 *030/312–5027* 🌐 *www.hotelastoria.de* *31 rooms, 1 suite* *AE, DC, MC, V.*

$$ **Hotel-Pension Dittberner.** The Dittberner, close to Olivaer Platz and Kurfürstendamm, is a family-run hotel in a turn-of-the-20th-century house. Some of the furniture is worn, but the warm atmosphere and the breakfast buffet more than make up for it. ✉ *Wielandstr. 26, D-10707* ☎ *030/884–6950* 📠 *030/885–4046* *21 rooms, 1 suite* *No credit cards.*

$–$$ **Hotel am Scheunenviertel.** This simply furnished but well-kept small hotel offers personal service and a good breakfast buffet. The biggest advantage is its location near the nightlife and cultural hot spots of the old Jewish neighborhood around the Neue Synagogue. The drawback is that it can be noisy. ✉ *Oranienburger Str. 38, D-10117* ☎ *030/282–2125* 📠 *030/282–1115* 🌐 *www.hotelas.com* *18 rooms with shower* 💳 *AE, DC, MC, V.*

$ **Mitte's Backpacker Hostel.** Accommodations are simple but creative in this orange-painted hostel, and service goes the extra mile with cheap bike rentals, free city maps, ticket services, and ride-sharing arrangements. The location is convenient for both sightseeing and nightlife, but in the evenings you can also opt to stay in for happy hour or a film. ✉ *Chauseestr. 102, D-10115* ☎ *030/2839–0965* 📠 *030/2839–0935* 🌐 *www.backpacker.de* *8 double rooms, 4 with bath* *Bar* 💳 *AE, MC, V.*

NIGHTLIFE & THE ARTS

The Arts

The quality of opera and classical concerts in Berlin is high. If your hotel can't book a seat for you, you can go to one of several ticket agencies. **Hekticket offices** (✉ Karl-Liebknecht-Str. 12, off Alexanderpl., ☎ 030/2431–2431 ✉ at Zoo-Palast, Hardenbergstr. 29a ☎ 030/230–9930) offers discounted and last-minute tickets. **Showtime Konzert- und Theaterkassen** (✉ KaDeWe, Tauentzienstr. 21 ☎ 030/217–7754 ✉ Wertheim, Kurfürstendamm 181 ☎ 030/882–2500) has offices within the major department stores. Details about what's going on in Berlin can be found in *Berlin–Kalender,* published by Berlin's Tourism Board; the *Ex-Berliner,* a monthly English-language newspaper; and the listings magazines *tip* and *zitty,* which appear every two weeks.

Concerts

The Berliner Philharmonisches Orchester, one of the world's best, resides at the **Philharmonie mit Kammermusiksaal** (✉ Herbert-von-Karajan-Str. 1 ☎ 030/2548–8132 or 030/2548–8301). The **Konzerthaus Berlin** (✉ Gendarmenmarkt ☎ 030/2030–92101 or 030/2030–92102) is a prime venue for classical music concerts.

Opera & Ballet

The **Deutsche Oper** (✉ Bismarckstr. 34–37 ☎ 030/343–8401), by the U-bahn stop of the same name, is home to both opera and ballet. The grand **Staatsoper Unter den Linden** (✉ Unter den Linden 7 ☎ 030/2035–4555) is Berlin's main opera house, led by Maestro Daniel Barenboim. **Komische Oper** (✉ Behrenstr. 55–57 ☎ 030/4799–7400) presents opera and dance performances. On the day of the performance, discount tickets are sold at the box office on Unter den Linden 41.

Variety Shows

The music programs in the art nouveau tent of **Bar jeder Vernuft** (✉ Schaperstr. 24 ☎ 030/8831–582) are intimate and intellectually entertaining. The **Chamäleon Varieté** (✉ Rosenthaler Str. 40/41 ☎ 030/2827–118) puts on hilarious shows that even non-German-speakers can appreciate. The world's largest revue is at the **Friedrichstadtpalast** (✉ Friedrichstr. 107 ☎ 030/2326–2326), a glossy showcase famous for its female dancers. The classy **Wintergarten Varieté** (✉ Potsdamer Str. 96 ☎ 030/2500–8888) pays romantic homage to the '20s.

Nightlife

Nightlife in Berlin is no halfhearted affair. The centers of the nocturnal scene are around Savignyplatz in Charlottenburg; the side streets of Winterfeldplatz and Nollenplatz in Schöneberg; Oranienstrasse and Wienerstrasse in Kreuzberg; Kollwitzplatz in the Prenzlauer Berg district; and Oranienburger Strasse, Rosenthaler Platz, and Hackesche Höfe in Mitte.

Bars & Dance Clubs

A Berlin classic, **Bar am Lützowplatz** (✉ Am Lützowpl. 7 ☎ 030/262–6807) has the longest bar counter and best-made cocktails in town. The decor and the energetic gay crowd at **Hafen** (✉ Motzstr. 18, ☎ 030/211–4118) in Schöneberg make it ceaselessly popular and a favorite singles mixer. At 4 AM people move next door to Tom's Bar, open until 6 AM. A gay and hetero crowd mingles within the kitschy carpeted walls of rowdy **Kumpelnest 3000** (✉ Lützowstr. 23 ☎ 030/261–6918). The historic **Leydicke** (✉ Mansteinstr. 4 ☎ 030/216–2973) is a must for out-of-towners. The proprietors operate their own distillery and have a superb selection of sweet wines and liqueurs.

Club nights at the docked boat ***Hoppetosse*** (✉ Eichenstr. 4 ☎ 030/4171–5437) most often feature reggae and Dancehall. It's a bit out of the way in Treptow, but you get a fantastic Spree Canal view from either the lower level dance floor or the top deck. The fashionable club **90 Grad** (✉ Dennewitzstr. 37 ☎ 030/2300–5954) plays hip-hop, house, and some techno. Women go right in, but men usually have to wait outside until they get picked by the doorman. The Prenzlauer Berg beer garden **Prater** (✉ Kastanienallee 7–9 ☎ 030/448–5688) has a year-round space to accommodate bands and crowds on its dance floors. It's near the Eberswalder U-2 subway station.

SHOPPING

The most popular shopping area in western Berlin is the Kurfürstendamm and its side streets, especially between Breitscheidplatz and Olivaer Platz. Large retail and department stores border Tauentzienstrasse, which starts where Ku'damm ends at Breitscheidplatz. The Mitte district's poshest wares are found along historic Friedrichstrasse, whose Friedrichstadtpassagen make up a mall-like shopping and business complex. New designer labels and trendier clothes are found in the storefronts of Mitte's Scheunenviertel, near the Hackescher Markt S-bahn station.

Antiques

Not far from Wittenbergplatz, several streets are good for antiquing, including Eisenacher Strasse, Fuggerstrasse, Keithstrasse, Kalckreuthstrasse, Motzstrasse, and Nollendorfstrasse. On weekends from 10 to 5, the lively **Berliner Trödelmarkt und Kunstmarkt** (Berlin Flea- and Art Market; ✉ Strasse des 17. Juni) swings into action. The flea-market stands are nearer the Tiergarten S-bahn station; the handicrafts begin past the Charlottenburg gates.

Department Stores

Galeries Lafayette (✉ Französische Str. 23 ☎ 030/209–480), off Friedrichstrasse, carries almost exclusively French products, including designer clothes, perfume, and produce. The small but most luxurious **Department Store Quartier 206** (✉ Friedrichstr. 71 ☎ 030/2094–6240) offers primarily French designer clothes, perfumes, and home accessories. **Galleria Kaufhof** (✉ Alexanderpl. 9 ☎ 030/247–430) is the main department store in Mitte, on Alexanderplatz. One of Berlin's classiest department stores is the **Kaufhaus des Westens** (KaDeWe; ✉ Tauentzienstr. 21 ☎ 030/21210); the food department occupies the whole sixth floor.

Gift & Souvenir Ideas

All the books, posters, and souvenirs focus on the city at **Berlin Story** (✉ Unter den Linden 10 ☎ 030/2045–3842), which is open even on Sunday. Fine porcelain is sold at the **Königliche Porzellan Manufaktur** (Royal Prussian Porcelain Factory, or KPM; ✉ KPM's store, Kurfürstendamm 27 ☎ 030/886–7210 ✉ Unter den Linden 35 ☎ 030/206–4150 ✉ factory salesroom, Wegelystr. 1 ☎ 030/390–090). In the homey setting of **Wohnart Berlin** (✉ Uhlandstr. 179–180 ☎ 030/882–5252) you can imagine how the stylish European furnishings, lamps, housewares, or stationery items might suit your own pad.

BERLIN A TO Z

AIRPORTS & TRANSFERS

Tegel Airport is 7 km (4 mi) from downtown. Tempelhof, even closer to downtown, is used for commuter plane traffic. Schönefeld Airport is about 24 km (15 mi) from downtown; it is used primarily for charter flights to Asia and southern and eastern Europe. You can reach all three airports by calling the central service phone number.

Central Service ☎ 0180/500–0186 🌐 www.berlin-airport.de.

TRANSFERS The express X9 airport bus runs at 10-minute intervals between Tegel and Bahnhof Zoologischer Garten (Zoo Station). From here you can connect to bus, train, or subway. The trip takes 25 minutes; the fare is €3.10. Alternatively, you can take Bus 128 to Kurt Schumacher Platz or Bus 109 to Jakob Kaiser Platz and change to the subway, where your bus ticket is also valid. Expect to pay about €14 for a taxi from Tegel to the western downtown area. If you rent a car at the airport, follow the signs for the Stadtautobahn into Berlin. The Halensee exit leads to Kurfürstendamm.

Tempelhof is linked directly to the city center by the U-6 subway line. From Schönefeld a shuttle bus leaves every 10–15 minutes for the nearby S-bahn station. Bus 171 also leaves every 20 minutes for the Rudow subway station. A taxi ride from the Schönefeld Airport takes about 40 minutes and will cost around €28. By car, follow the signs for Stadtzentrum Berlin.

BUS TRAVEL TO & FROM BERLIN

BerlinLinien Bus is the only intra-Germany company serving Berlin. Make reservations through ZOB-Reisebüro, or buy your ticket at their office at the central bus terminal, the Omnibusbahnhof. Only EC credit cards and cash are accepted.

ZOB-Reisebüro ✉ Zentrale Omnibusbahnhof, Masurenallee 4–6 at Messedamm ☎ 030/301–0380 for reservations 🌐 www.berlinlinienbus.de.

CAR RENTAL

Avis ✉ Tegel Airport ☎ 030/4101–3148 ✉ Tempelhof Airport ☎ 030/6951–2340 ✉ Budapester Str. 43, at Europa Center ☎ 030/230–9370. **Europcar** ✉ Tegel Airport, ☎ 030/417–8520 ✉ Kurfürstenstr. 101–104 ☎ 030/235–0640 ✉ Zentrale Omnibushahnhof, Messedamm 8 ☎ 030/306–9590. **Hertz** ✉ Tegel Airport ☎ 030/4170–4674 ✉ Budapester Str. 39 ☎ 030/261–1053. **Sixt** ✉ Tegel Airport ☎ 030/4101–2886 ✉ Nürnberger Str. 65 ☎ 030/212–9880 ✉ Kaiserdamm 40 ☎ 030/411–7087.

CAR TRAVEL

The eight roads linking the western part of Germany with Berlin have been incorporated into the countrywide autobahn network, but be prepared for traffic jams, particularly on weekends. Follow signs for BERLIN–ZENTRUM to reach downtown.

EMBASSIES

See Germany Basics.

EMERGENCIES

Pharmacies in Berlin offer late-night service on a rotating basis. Every pharmacy displays a notice indicating the location of the nearest shop with evening hours.

Doctors & Dentists **Dentist emergency assistance** ☎ 030/8900-4333.

Emergency Services **Ambulance** ☎ 030/112. **Emergency poison assistance** ☎ 030/19240. **Pharmaceutical emergencies** ☎ 01189. **Police** ☎ 030/110.

Hospitals **Charite** ✉ Schumannstr. 20-21, Mitte ☎ 030/28020.

Hot Lines **American Hotline** ☎ 0177/814-1510 for all English-speakers. **International Emergency Hotline** ☎ 030/3100-3222 or 030/3100-3243.

ENGLISH-LANGUAGE MEDIA

The monthly *Ex-Berliner* (€2) has feature articles plus event listings.

Bookstores **Dussmann Kulturkaufhaus** ✉ Friedrichstr. 90 ☎ 030/2025-2410. **Hugendubel** ✉ Tauentzienstr. 13 ☎ 030/214-060. **Marga Schoeller Bücherstube** ✉ Knesebeckstr. 33 ☎ 030/881-1112.

TAXIS

The base rate is €2.50, after which prices vary according to a complex tariff system. Figure on paying around €8 for a ride the length of the Ku'damm. If you've hailed a cab on the street and are taking a short ride of less than 2 km (1 mi), ask the driver as soon as you start off for a special fare (€3) called *Kurzstreckentarif*. You can also get cabs at taxi stands or order one by calling. U-bahn employees will call a taxi for passengers after 8 PM, and bars will often call for you late at night as well.

Taxis ☎ 030/210-101, 030/210-202, 030/443-322, or 030/261-026.

TOURS

BOAT TOURS Tours of downtown Berlin's Spree and Landwehr canals give you up-close and unusual views of landmarks—bring plenty of film. Tours usually depart twice a day from several bridges and piers, such as Schlossbrücke in Charlottenburg, Hansabrücke in Tiergarten, Kottbusser Brücke in Kreuzberg, Potsdamer Brücke, and Haus der Kulturen der Welt in Tiergarten. Drinks, snacks, and wursts are available during the narrated trips.

A tour of the Havel Lakes (which include Tegeler See and Wannsee) is the thing to do in summer. Trips begin at the Schlossbrücke Charlottenburg or at the Greenwich Promenade in Tegel (U-bahn station Tegel).

Fees & Schedules **Reederei Bruno Winkler** ☎ 030/349-9595. **Reederei Riedel** ☎ 030/693-4646 inner Berlin tours only. **Stern- und Kreisschiffahrt** ☎ 030/536-3600.

BUS TOURS Four companies jointly offer city tours on yellow double-decker City Circle buses, which run every 15 or 30 minutes, depending on the season. The full circuit runs two hours as does the audio guide. For €18 you can jump on and off at the 14 stops. The bus driver sells tickets. During the warmer months, the last circuit leaves at 4 PM from the corner of Rankestrasse and Kurfürrstendamm. Most companies have tours to Potsdam. Severin & Kühn also runs all-day tours to Dresden.

Fees & Schedules **Berliner Bären Stadtrundfahrten** ☎ 030/3519-5270 🌐 www.sightseeing.de. **Berolina Berlin-Service** ☎ 030/8856-8030 🌐 www.berolina-berlin.com. **Severin & Kühn** ☎ 030/880-4190 🌐 www.severin-kuehn-berlin.de. **Stadtrundfahrtbüro Berlin** ☎ 030/2612-001 🌐 www.stadtrundfahrtbuero-berlin.de.

WALKING TOURS A walking tour is one of the best ways to familiarize yourself with Berlin's history and sights, and several companies offer native English-speakers and thematic tours from which to choose. Tours usually meet at major subway stations or hostels.

Fees & Schedules **Berlin Walks** ☎ 030/301–9194 🌐 www.berlinwalks.com. **Insider Tours** ☎ 030/692–3149 🌐 www.insidertour.com. **Brewer's Best of Berlin** ☎ 030/9700–2906 🌐 www.brewersberlin.com. **StattReisen** ☎ 030/455–3028 🌐 www.stattreisen.berlin.de.

TRAIN TRAVEL

Most trains to and from Berlin pass through Bahnhof Zoo. Trains from the east usually stop first at Ostbahnhof station.

TRANSPORTATION AROUND BERLIN

The city has an excellent public transportation system: a combination of U-bahn and S-bahn lines, buses, and streetcars. For €2.20, you can buy a ticket that covers travel on the entire downtown system (fare zones A and B) for two hours. Buy a *Kurzstreckentarif* for a short trip; it allows you to ride six bus stops or three U-bahn or S-bahn stops for €1.20. The Day Card, for €5.60, is valid until 3 AM of the day of validation.

If you're caught without a validated ticket, the fine is €40. Tickets are available from vending machines at U-bahn and S-bahn stations or from bus drivers. The Berlin Tourist Office sells a Welcome Card (€19) that grants three days of free transportation and 25%–50% discounts at museums and theaters.

Berliner Verkehrsbetriebe (BVG; Berlin Public Transportation) ☎ 030/19449 🌐 www.bvg.de.

TRAVEL AGENCIES

Euroaide specifically serves English-speakers.

Euroaide ✉ Hardenbergpl., inside the Zoologischer Garten train station 🌐 www.euraide.com. **Reiseland American Express Reisebüro** ✉ Wittenbergerpl., Bayreuther Str. 37 ☎ 030/214–9830 🌐 www.reiseland-american-express.de ✉ Friedrichstr. 172 ☎ 030/238–4102.

VISITOR INFORMATION

The main information office of Berlin Tourismus Marketing is in the Europa Center on Breitscheidplatz; it's open 10–7 Monday–Saturday, 10–6 on Sunday. The other two branches are at the Brandenburger Tor and at the base of the Fernsehnturm (TV tower) at Alexanderplatz and are open daily 10–6. The tourist information centers have longer hours April–October. If you want materials sent to you, write to Berlin Tourismus Marketing GmbH.

The Staatliche Museen zu Berlin (state museums) sells a €6 Tageskarte and a €10 Dreitageskarte good for one- and three-day admission to all of its museums. Admission to the state museums is free on the first Sunday of the month. A free audio guide is included at all state museums.

Berlin Tourismus Marketing GmbH ✉ Am Karlsbad 11, D-10785 Berlin ☎ 49/700/8623–7546 for all calls from outside Germany; 030/250–025 for hotel, restaurant, ticket reservations; 0190/016–316 €.45 per minute, for general information 📠 030/2500–2424 🌐 www.berlin-tourist-information.de. **Staatliche Museen zu Berlin** ☎ 030/266–2951 operator; 030/2090–5555 recorded information 🌐 www.smpk.de.

Germany Basics

To research prices, get advice from other travelers, and book travel arrangements, visit www.fodors.com.

BUSINESS HOURS

Banks are usually open weekdays from 8:30 or 9 to 3 or 4 (5 or 6 on Thursday). Some close from 12:30 to 1:30. Branches at airports and main train stations open as early as 6:30 AM and close as late as 10:30 PM.

Museums are generally open Tuesday through Sunday 10–5. Many stay open late one night a week. Stores are allowed to be open until 8 PM on Saturday, though some shops opt to close earlier. Shops at major train stations have the latest closing hours, and are the only ones open on Sunday.

EMBASSIES

Australia ✉ Wallstr. 76-79 D-10179 Berlin ☎ 030/880-0880 📠 030/8800-88210 🌐 www.australian-embassy.de.

Canada ✉ Friedrichstr. 95, 12th floor, D-10117 Berlin ☎ 030/203-120 📠 030/203-12121 🌐 www.canada.de.

Ireland ✉ Friedrichstr. 200, D-10117 Berlin ☎ 030/220-720 📠 030/220-72299 🌐 www.botschaft-irland.de.

New Zealand ✉ Friedrichstr. 60, D-10117 Berlin ☎ 030/206-2110 📠 030/206-21114 🌐 www.nzembassy.com.

South Africa ✉ Friedrichstr. 60, D-10117 Berlin ☎ 030/220-730 📠 030/2207-3202 🌐 www.suedafrika.org.

United Kingdom ✉ Wilhelmstr. 70-71, D-10117 Berlin ☎ 030/204-570 🌐 www.britischebotschaft.de.

United States ✉ Neustädtische Kirchstr. 4-5, D-10117 Berlin ☎ 030/832-9233 📠 030/8305-1215 🌐 www.us-botschaft.de.

HOLIDAYS

January 1; January 6 (Epiphany—Bavaria, Baden-Württemberg, and Saxony-Anhalt only); Good Friday; Easter Monday; May 1 (Worker's Day); Ascension, Pentecost Monday, in May; May 30 (Corpus Christi—south Germany only); August 15 (Assumption Day—Bavaria and Saarland only); October 3 (German Unity Day); November 1 (All Saints' Day—Baden Württemberg, Bavaria, North Rhine Westphalia, Rheinland-Pfalz, and Saarland only); December 24–26.

LANGUAGE

Among Germany's many dialects, probably the most difficult to comprehend is Bavaria's. Virtually everyone can also speak *Hochdeutsch*, the German equivalent of Oxford English. Many people under age 40 speak some English.

MONEY MATTERS

The most expensive cities are Berlin, Frankfurt, Hamburg, and Munich. Costs are somewhat lower in eastern Germany, but businesses that cater specifically to visitors are increasingly charging western German rates. Some sample prices include cup of coffee €1.80; mug of beer in a beer hall, €3; soft drink, €1.80; ham sandwich, €2.80; 3-km (2-mi) taxi ride, €6.

CREDIT CARDS All major U.S. credit cards are accepted in Germany. German ATMs accept four-digit personal identification numbers.

American Express (☎ 069/97970). **Diners Club** (☎ 01805/336–696). **MasterCard** (☎ 0800/819–1040). **Visa** (☎ 0800/814–9100).

CURRENCY Germany shares a common currency, the euro (€), with 11 other countries: Austria, Belgium, Finland, France, Greece, Ireland, Italy, Luxembourg, the Netherlands, Portugal, and Spain. The euro is divided into 100 cents. There are bills of 5, 10, 20, 50, 100, and 500 euros and coins of €1 and €2, and 1, 2, 5, 10, 20, and 50 cents.

At press time (summer 2003), the exchange rate for the euro was €0.89 to the U.S. dollar, €0.62 to the Canadian dollar, €1.40 to the pound sterling, €0.56 to the Australian dollar, €0.50 to the New Zealand dollar, and €0.12 to the South African rand.

TELEPHONES

COUNTRY & AREA CODES Germany's country code is 49. When calling Germany from outside the country, drop the initial 0 in the regional code. Numbers that begin 0180 cost an average of €0.12 per minute; those that begin 0190 can cost €1.85 per minute and more.

LONG DISTANCE & INTERNATIONAL CALLS Calls can be made from just about any telephone booth, most of which are card operated. It costs only €0.13 per minute to call the United States, day or night. If you expect to do a lot of calling, international or local, purchase a telephone card. Collect calls to the United States can be made by dialing 0180/200–1033 (this is also the number to call if you have problems dialing out). For information in English dial 11837 for numbers within Germany, and 11834 for numbers elsewhere. But first look for the number in the phone book or on the Web (www.teleauskunft.de), because directory assistance costs at least €0.50, more if the call lasts more than 30 seconds.

Access Codes **AT&T** 0800-888-012. **MCI WorldCom** 0130-0012. **Sprint** 0800-888-013.

LOCAL CALLS A local call from a telephone booth costs €.10 per minute. Drop the local area code.

BRUSSELS

5

Brussels has become synonymous with the EU, but although diplomats, politicians, lobbyists, and journalists have flocked to the city, it's far from becoming gray and faceless. Brussels's strength is its diversity. A bilingual city where French- and Dutch-speaking communities are too often divided, Brussels is home to all the cultures of Europe—east and west—as well as Americans, Canadians, Congolese, Rwandans, Vietnamese, Turks, and Moroccans. Art nouveau flourished in Brussels as nowhere else, and its spirit lives on in gloriously individualistic town houses. Away from the winding alleys of the city center, parks and squares are plentiful, and the Bois de la Cambre, at the end of avenue Louise, leads straight into a forest as large as the city itself.

EXPLORING BRUSSELS

Give yourself at least two days to explore the many riches of Brussels, devoting one day to the lower town (whose cobblestones call for comfortable walking shoes) and the other to the great museums and uptown shopping streets.

Around the Grand'Place

The Grand'Place, whose gilded splendor makes it one of Europe's most impressive squares, serves as an anchor for an area where the ghosts of the past mingle with a lively contemporary scene. Narrow, cobbled streets radiate off the square, with a rich offering of cafés, restaurants, and souvenir shops.

Numbers in the margin correspond to points of interest on the Brussels map.

9 **Cathédrale des Sts-Michel-et-Gudule.** The names of the archangel and an obscure 7th-century local saint have been joined for the cathedral of Brussels. Begun in 1226, it combines architectural styles from the Romanesque to full-blown Gothic. The chief treasures are the stained-glass windows inspired by the drawings of Bernard Van Orley, an early-16th-century court painter. The ornately carved pulpit (1699) depicts Adam

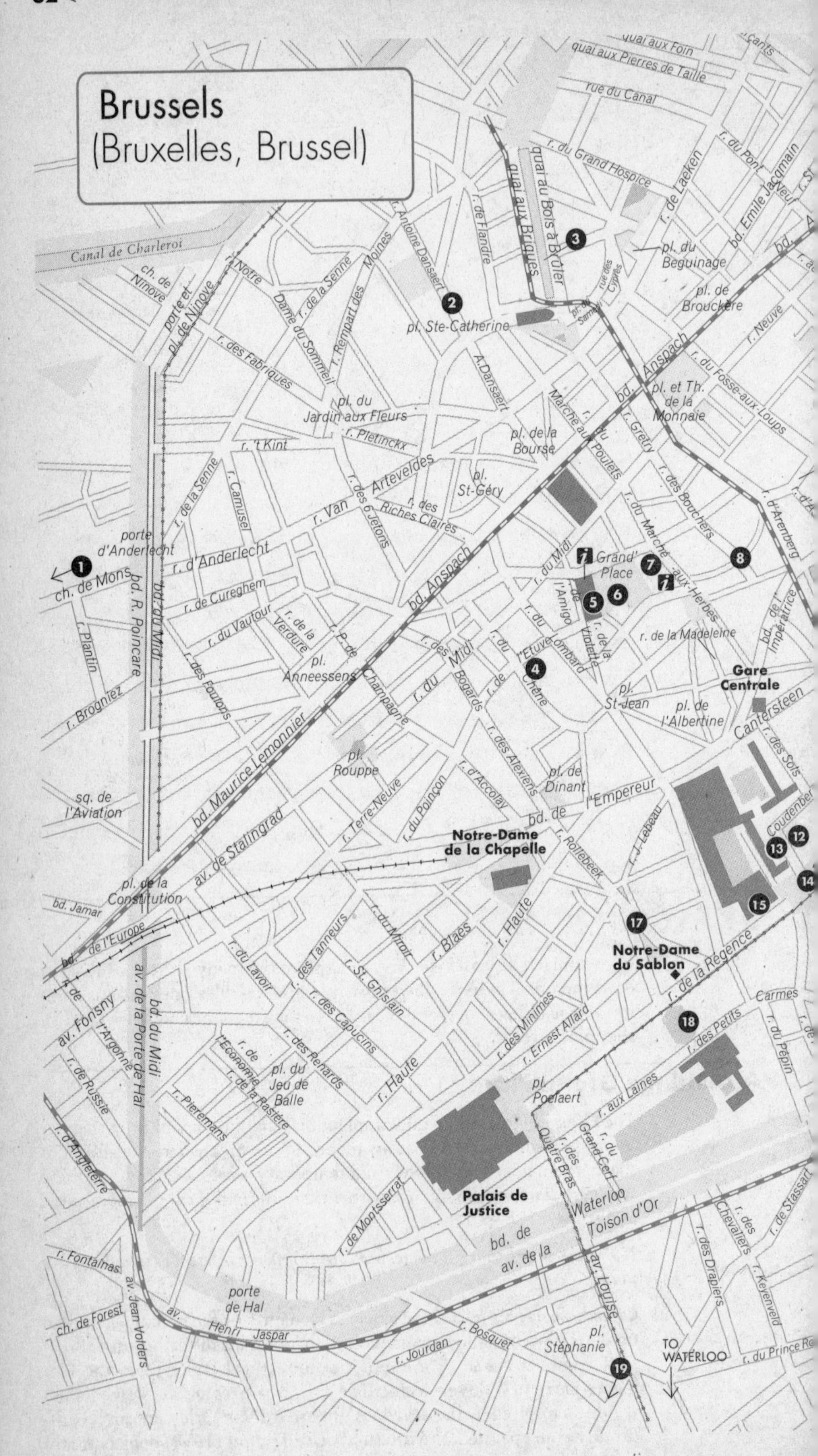
Brussels
(Bruxelles, Brussel)
quai aux Foin
quai aux Pierres de Taille
rue du Canal
r. du Grand Hospice
quai au Bois à Brûler
quai aux Briques
r. de Laeken
r. du Pont Neuf
bd. Emile Jacqmain
pl. du Beguinage
rue des Cyprès
pl. de Brouckère
Canal de Charleroi
ch. de Ninove
porte et pl. de Ninove
r. Notre Dame du Sommeil
r. de la Senne
r. Rempart des Moines
r. Antoine Dansaert
r. de Flandre
pl. Ste-Catherine
r. Neuve
r. du Fosse-aux-Loups
bd. Anspach
pl. et Th. de la Monnaie
r. des Fabriques
pl. du Jardin aux Fleurs
r. Pletinckx
A. Dansaert
Marché aux Poulets
r. du Grétry
pl. de la Bourse
r. 't Kint
r. de la Senne
r. Camusel
r. Van Artevelde
r. des 6 Jetons
r. des Riches Claires
pl. St-Géry
r. des Bouchers
r. d'Arenberg
porte d'Anderlecht
r. d'Anderlecht
ch. de Mons
r. du Midi
Grand' Place
r. du Marché aux Herbes
r. de Cureghem
bd. R. Poincare
bd. du Midi
r. du Vautour
r. de la Verdure
r. de l'Amigo
r. de la Violette
r. de la Madeleine
bd. de l'Impératrice
r. Plantin
r. des Foulons
pl. Anneessens
r. P. de Champagne
r. des Bogards
r. de l'Etuve
r. Lombard
r. du Chêne
Gare Centrale
pl. St-Jean
pl. de l'Albertine
r. Brogniez
bd. Anspach
r. du Midi
Cantersteen
r. des Sols
pl. Rouppe
r. des Alexiens
pl. de Dinant
bd. Maurice Lemonnier
r. d'Accolay
bd. de l'Empereur
sq. de l'Aviation
r. Terre-Neuve
r. du Poinçon
r. J. Lebeau
Coudenberg
Notre-Dame de la Chapelle
av. de Stalingrad
r. Rollebeek
pl. de la Constitution
bd. Jamar
r. du Miroir
r. Haute
bd. de l'Europe
r. du Lavoir
r. des Tanneurs
r. Blaes
Notre-Dame du Sablon
r. de la Régence
r. St. Ghislain
r. des Capucins
r. des Minimes
Carmes
r. de Fonsny
av. Fonsny
r. de l'Argonne
av. de la Porte de Hal
bd. du Midi
r. de l'Economie
r. de la Rasière
r. des Renards
pl. du Jeu de Balle
r. Haute
r. Ernest Allard
r. des Petits
r. du Pépin
r. de Russie
r. Pieremans
pl. Poelaert
r. aux Laines
r. d'Angleterre
r. des Quatre Bras
r. du Grand Cerf
Palais de Justice
bd. de Waterloo
av. de la Toison d'Or
r. de Montserrat
r. des Chevaliers
r. de Stassart
r. Fontainas
r. des Drapiers
r. Keyenveld
av. Louise
ch. de Forest
av. Jean Volders
porte de Hal
av. Henri Jaspar
r. Bosquet
r. Jourdan
pl. Stéphanie
TO WATERLOO
r. du Prince Ro
1
2
3
4
5
6
7
8
12
13
14
15
17
18
19

Around the Grand'Place

Cathédrale des Sts.-Michel-et-Gudule 9
Centre Belge de la Bande Dessinée 10
Galeries St-Hubert 8
Grand'Place 6
Hôtel de Ville 5
Maison du Roi 7
Manneken-Pis 4
Rue Anoine Dansaert 2
Vismet 3

Around the Place Royale

Grand Sablon 17
Musée d'Art Ancien 15
Musée d'Art Moderne 13
Musée Instrumental 12
Palais Royal 16
Petit Sablon 18
Place Royale 14

Elsewhere in Brussels

European Union Institutions 21
Koninklijke Museum voor Midden-Afrika/Musée Royale de l'Afrique Centrale 20
Maison d'Erasme 1
Mini-Europe 11
Musée Horta 19

and Eve being expelled from the Garden of Eden. ✉ *Parvis Ste-Gudule* ☎ *02/217–8345* ⏲ *Daily 7:30–6.*

★ ⑩ **Centre Belge de la Bande Dessinée** (Belgian Comic Strip Center). This museum celebrates the comic strip, focusing on such famous Belgian graphic artists as Hergé, Tintin's creator; Morris, the progenitor of Lucky Luke; and many others. The former draper's wholesale warehouse was designed in 1903 by art nouveau pioneer Victor Horta (1861–1947). A library, a bookstore, and an airy brasserie are also here. ✉ *Rue des Sables 20* ☎ *02/219–1980* 🌐 *www.brusselsbdtour.com/cbbd.htm* ⏲ *Tues.–Sun. 10–6.*

❽ **Galeries St-Hubert.** The oldest covered shopping arcade in western Europe—and still one of its most elegant—was constructed in 1847 and is filled with shops, restaurants, and theaters. Diffused daylight penetrates the gallery from the glazed vaults, and neoclassical gods and heroes look down from their sculpted niches. The gallery is traversed by **rue des Bouchers,** which forms the main restaurant area. Caveat: the more lavish the display of food outside, the poorer the cuisine inside. ✉ *Between rue du Marché-aux-Herbes and rue d'Arenberg.*

❻ **Grand'Place.** The ornate baroque guild houses here, with their burnished facades, were completed in 1695, just three years after a French bombardment destroyed everything but the Town Hall. The houses are topped by gilded statues of saints and heroes and the market square is Europe's most sumptuous. On summer nights, music and colored light flood the entire area. Shops, restaurants, and taverns occupy most ground floors. The Maison des Brasseurs houses the **Brewery Museum** (✉ Grand'Place 10 ☎ 02/511–4987). During Ommegang (first Tuesday and Thursday in July), a magnificent pageant reenacts Emperor Charles V's reception in the city. ✉ *Rue au Beurre, rue du Chair et du Pain, rue des Harengs, rue de la Colline, rue de l'Étuve, rue de la Tête d'Or.*

Fodor'sChoice ★

❺ **Hôtel de Ville** (Town Hall). Dominating the Grand'Place, the Town Hall is around 300 years older than the guild houses that line the square. The slender central tower is topped by a statue of the archangel Michael crushing the devil under his feet. The halls are embellished with some of the finest examples of local tapestries from the 16th, 17th, and 18th centuries. ✉ *Grand'Place* ☎ *02/279–2340* ⏲ *English-speaking tours Tues. 11:30 and 3:15, Wed. 3:15, Sun. 12:15. No individual visits.*

❼ **Maison du Roi** (King's House). Despite the name, no king ever lived in this neo-Gothic–style palace facing the Town Hall. It contains the **Musée de la Ville de Bruxelles** (City Museum), whose collections include Gothic sculptures, porcelain, silverware, lace, and paintings such as Brueghel's *The Wedding Procession.* Don't miss the extravagant collection of some 600 costumes for the Manneken-Pis. ✉ *Grand'Place* ☎ *02/279–4350* ⏲ *Tues.–Fri. 10–5, weekends 10–1.*

❹ **Manneken-Pis.** The first mention of the "little man" dates from 1377, but the present version, a small bronze statue of a chubby little boy peeing, was made by Jérôme Duquesnoy in 1619. The statue is in fact a copy; the original was kidnapped by 18th-century French soldiers. ✉ *Corner rue de l'Étuve and rue du Chêne, 3 blocks southwest of Grand'Place.*

❷ **Rue Antoine Dansaert.** This is the flagship street of Brussels's fashionable quarter, which extends south to the place St-Géry. Boutiques sell Belgian-designed men's and women's fashions along with other designer names. Slick restaurants, trendy bars, jazz clubs, and cozy cafés rub shoulders with avant-garde galleries and stylish furniture shops. ✉ *Between rue Van Artevelde at Grand'Place and Porte de Flandre.*

❸ **Vismet** (Fish Market). The canals around which this lively quay district sprang up have been filled in, but many pricey seafood restaurants popular with residents remain. When the weather is good, tables and chairs fill the wide promenade where cargoes of fish were once unloaded. ✉ *Quai au Bois-à-Brûler and quai aux Briques.*

Around the Place Royale

The neoclassical place Royale is home of Brussels's art museums. The rather austere Palais Royal (Royal Palace) anchors the northern end of the square.

★ ⓱ **Grand Sablon.** A well-to-do, sophisticated square, it's alive with cafés, restaurants, art galleries, and antiques shops, as well as an antiques market on weekends. At the upper end of the square stands the church of **Notre-Dame du Sablon,** built in flamboyant Gothic style in 1304 by the crossbowmen who used to train here. The stained-glass windows are illuminated from within at night. Downhill from the Grand Sablon stands the 12th-century church of **Notre-Dame de la Chapelle** (✉ pl. de la Chapelle). Its Gothic exterior and surprising baroque belfry have been splendidly restored. This was the parish church of Pieter Brueghel the Elder (1520–69); he is buried here in a marble tomb.

⓯ **Musée d'Art Ancien** (Fine Arts Museum). The collection of old masters focuses on Flemish and Dutch paintings from the 15th to the 19th century, including Rubens, Hieronymus Bosch, Memling, Van Dyck, and many others. The Brueghel Room has one of the world's finest collections of Pieter the Elder's works, including *The Fall of Icarus.* An underground passage links the museum with the adjacent Museum of Modern Art. ✉ *Rue de la Régence 3* ☎ *02/508–3211* 🌐 *www.fine-arts-museum.be* ⏲ *Tues.–Sun. 10–5.*

★ ⓭ **Musée d'Art Moderne** (Museum of Modern Art). Housed in an exciting feat of modern architecture, the museum descends eight floors into the ground around a central light well. Its strength lies in the quality of Belgian modern art: not only Magritte's luminous fantasies, Delvaux's nudes in surrealist settings, and James Ensor's hallucinatory carnival scenes but also the works of artists such as Léon Spilliaert, Constant Permeke, Leo Brusselmans, and Rik Wouters from the first half of the century; the post-war COBRA group, including Pierre Alechinsky and Henri Michaux; and on to contemporary works. ✉ *Pl. Royale 1–2* ☎ *02/508–3211* 🌐 *www.fine-arts-museum.be* ⏲ *Tues.–Sun. 10–5.*

★ ⓬ **Musée Instrumental** (Musical Instruments Museum). Seven thousand instruments, from the Bronze Age to today, make up this extraordinary collection in a glass-and-steel art nouveau masterpiece designed by Paul Saintenoy (1862–1952) for the Old England department store in 1899. Audio headsets let you listen to the instruments as you look at them. The saxophone family is well represented, as befits the country of its inventor, Adolphe Sax (1814–94). Enjoy views over the city from the sixth-floor tearoom and restaurant. ✉ *Rue Montagne-de-la-Cour 2* ☎ *02/545–0130* 🌐 *www.mim.fgov.be* ⏲ *Tues., Wed., Fri. 9:30–5, Thurs. 9:30–8, weekends 10–5. Concerts Thurs. at 8.*

⓰ **Palais Royal** (Royal Palace). The palace facing the Royal Park was rebuilt in 1904 to suit the expansive tastes of Leopold II (1835–1909). The king's architect, Alphonse Balat, achieved his masterpiece with the monumental stairway and the Throne Hall. The Belgian royal family uses this address only on state occasions. When the Belgian flag is flying, you'll know that the king is in Brussels. ✉ *Pl. des Palais* ☎ *02/551–2020* ⏲ *July 22–early Sept., Tues.–Sun. 10–4.*

18 **Petit Sablon.** Statues of the counts of Egmont and Horne, who were executed by the Spanish in 1568, hold pride of place here. The tranquil square is surrounded by a magnificent wrought-iron fence, topped by 48 small statues representing Brussels's medieval guilds. ✉ *Rue de la Régence.*

14 **Place Royale.** This white, symmetrical square is neoclassical Vienna transposed to Brussels. From here you have a superb view over the lower town. Excavations have revealed the *Aula Magna* (Great Hall), where the Flanders-born king of Spain and Holy Roman emperor Charles V (1500–58) was crowned. In the center of the square stands the equestrian statue of Godefroid de Bouillon (1060–1100), leader of the First Crusade and ruler of Jerusalem. ✉ *Jct. rue de la Régence, rue Royale, rue de Namur, and rue Montagne-de-la-Cour.*

Elsewhere in Brussels

21 **European Union Institutions.** The various offices of the European Commission are centered on Rond Point Schuman. The rounded glass summit of the **European Parliament building** (✉ Rue Wiertz 43) looms behind the Gare de Luxembourg. ✉ *Rond Point Schuman, rue de la Loi, rue Archimède, bd. Charlemagne, rue Wiertz* Ⓜ *Schuman.*

20 **Koninklijke Museum voor Midden Afrika/Musée Royale de l'Afrique Centrale** (Africa Museum). King Leopold II (1835–1909) was sole owner of the Congo (later Zaire, and now the Republic of Congo)—a colonial adventure that brought great wealth to the exploiters and untold misery to the exploited. He built a museum outside Brussels to house some 250,000 objects emanating from his domain. The museum has since become a leading research center for African studies. ✉ *Leuvensesteenweg 13, Tervuren* ☎ *02/769–5211* 🌐 *www.africamuseum.be* ⏲ *Tues.–Fri. 10–5, weekends 10–6* Ⓜ *Tram 44 from place Montgomery.*

★ **1** **Maison d'Erasme** (Erasmus House). In the middle of a nondescript neighborhood in Anderlecht, western Brussels, this remarkable redbrick 16th-century house was home to the great humanist Erasmus in 1521. Every detail is authentic, with period furniture, paintings by Holbein and Bosch, prints by Dürer, and first editions of Erasmus's works, including *In Praise of Folly.* ✉ *Rue du Chapître 31* ☎ *02/521–1383* ⏲ *Mon., Wed., Thurs., and weekends 10–noon and 2–5* Ⓜ *St-Guidon.*

11 **Mini-Europe.** At the foot of the landmark **Atomium,** this popular attraction in a 5-acre park is a collection of 300 models (on a 1:25 scale) of buildings from the 15 EU countries. ✉ *Brupark* ☎ *02/478–0550* 🎫 *€11.50* ⏲ *Oct.–Mar., daily 10–5; Apr.–June, daily 9:30–5; July and Aug., daily 9:30–8, July 17–Aug. 18 open until 11 on Fri., Sat., and Sun.; Sept., daily 9:30–5* Ⓜ *Heysel.*

★ **19** **Musée Horta** (Horta Museum). Victor Horta, the Belgian master of art nouveau, designed this building for himself and lived and worked here until 1919. From cellar to attic, every detail of the house displays the exuberant curves of the art nouveau style. Horta's aim was to put nature and light back into daily life, and here his floral motifs give a sense of opulence and spaciousness where in fact space is very limited. ✉ *Rue Américaine 25* ☎ *02/543–0490* ⏲ *Tues.–Sat. 2–5:30* Ⓜ *Tram 91 or 92 from pl. Louise.*

WHERE TO EAT

Brussels is one of the great dining cities in the world. Three thousand–odd restaurants are supplemented by a multitude of fast-food establishments and snack bars, and most cafés also offer *petite restauration* (light meals).

Lip-smackingly tasty *frites* (french fries) with dollops of mayonnaise can be found at mobile friteries. Fixed-price menus, especially in top-dollar restaurants, sometimes cost only half of what you would pay dining à la carte, and the quality of your meal is likely to be just as good. There's less smoking than in the past, but no-smoking areas are rare.

WHAT IT COSTS In Euros

	$$$$	$$$	$$	$
AT DINNER	over €30	€22–€30	€12–€22	under €12

Prices are per person for main course and include a 21% value-added tax. Belgian restaurants include a 16% service charge on all bills.

$$$$ Fodor's Choice ★ **Comme Chez Soi.** Master chef Pierre Wynants runs Brussels's most celebrated restaurant, and the array of toques and stars he has earned is well deserved. Fillet of sole with a white wine mousseline and shrimp is always on the menu, but the perfectionist owner-chef is constantly creating new masterpieces. The set menus can take a little of the sting out of the bill. The stunning art nouveau restaurant is small, so reserve well ahead; you may have to wait up to six weeks for a table. Don't be put off by the scruffy neighborhood. *Pl. Rouppe 23* *02/512–2921* *Reservations essential* *Jacket and tie* *AE, DC, MC, V* *Closed Sun. and Mon., July, and Dec. 25–Jan. 1. No lunch Sat.*

★ $$$–$$$$ **La Truffe Noire.** Luigi Ciciriello's "Black Truffle" is a spacious eatery with cuisine that draws on classic Italian and modern French cooking. Carpaccio, prepared at the table, comes with strips of truffle and Parmesan, and main courses include pigéon de Vendé with truffles and steamed John Dory with truffles and leeks. *Bd. de la Cambre 12* *02/640–4422* *Reservations essential* *Jacket and tie* *AE, DC, MC, V* *Closed Sun., Mon. lunch, and last 3 weeks in Aug.*

★ $$–$$$$ **Sea Grill.** Gigantic etched-glass murals convey the cool of the Arctic fjords that provide inspiration and ingredients for one of Belgium's best seafood restaurants. Chef Yves Mattagne's gift for applying meat preparations to fish is showcased in dishes like noisettes of tuna Rossini, and house classics include whole sea bass baked in salt and Brittany lobster pressed at your table. *Radisson SAS, rue du Fossé-aux-Loups 47* *02/227–3120* *Jacket and tie* *AE, DC, MC, V* *Closed Sun. and 4 wks in July and Aug. No lunch Sat.*

$–$$$$ **Au Vieux St-Martin.** Belgian specialties dominate the menu here, and portions are generous. The restaurant claims to have invented the now ubiquitous *filet américain* (the well-seasoned Belgian version of steak tartare). The walls are hung with bright contemporary paintings, and picture windows face the pleasant square. *Pl. du Grand Sablon 38* *02/512–6476* *AE, MC, V.*

★ $$$ **L'Ogenblik.** With green-shaded lamps over marble-top tables, sawdust on the floor, and ample servings, l'Ogenblik is a true bistro. The long and imaginative menu changes frequently but generally includes millefeuille with lobster and salmon, and saddle of lamb. The kitchen stays open until midnight, making it a favorite for artists and actors. *Galerie des Princes 1* *02/511–6151* *AE, DC, MC, V* *Closed Sun.*

$–$$$ **Aux Armes de Bruxelles.** One of the few restaurants to escape the "tourist trap" label on this hectic street, the child-friendly Aux Armes has three rooms with a lively atmosphere and cheerful service. It offers the classics of Belgian cooking—tomatoes stuffed with crevettes, waterzooi mussels steamed in white wine, and, of course, frites. *Rue des Bouchers 13* *02/511–5550* *AE, DC, MC, V* *Closed Mon. and mid-June–mid-July.*

$–$$$ ✕ **Chez Léon.** Critics deride it as McMoules-frites, but this century-old eatery is enormously popular, with franchises across Belgium and even in Paris and Japan. The secret is heaping plates of steaming mussels, specialties such as anguilles au vert, free children's meals to those under 12, and great fries. It's loud, brightly lit, and has a charm all its own. ✉ *Rue des Bouchers 18* ☎ *02/511–1415* ▭ *AE, DC, MC, V.*

$$ ✕ **Au Stekerlapatte.** In the shadow of the monstrous Palais de Justice, this bustling Marolles bistro is packed nightly with diners craving liberal portions of Belgian specialties. Try black pudding with caramelized apples, sauerkraut, beef fried with shallots, grilled pig's trotters, or spareribs. ✉ *Rue des Prêtres 4* ☎ *02/512–8681* ▭ *MC, V* ⊙ *Closed Sun. and Mon. July and Aug. No lunch.*

$–$$ ✕ **Chez Patrick.** This old-timer next to the Grand'Place has been dishing up good, honest Belgian food for nearly 70 years, in an unpretentious, old-fashioned setting with waitresses in black and white, and specials chalked up on the mirrors. Expect large, tasty portions of shrimp croquettes, salmon and endives cooked with beer, and chicken with *kriek* (cherry-flavored beer) and cherries. ✉ *Rue des Chapeliers 6* ☎ *02/511–9815* ▭ *AE, DC, MC, V.* ⊙ *Closed Mon.*

$–$$ ✕ **Kasbah.** An Aladdin's den of stained-glass lamps and dark, sumptuous decor, this is one of the best of the capital's many North African restaurants. Steaming portions of couscous and *tajines* (Moroccan casseroles with fish or meat, usually involving fruit, vegetables, and spices) are served in this lively restaurant. ✉ *Rue Antoine Dansaert 20* ☎ *02/502–4026* ▭ *AE, MC, V.*

★ **$–$$** ✕ **Les Salons de Wittamer.** The elegant upstairs rooms at Brussels's best-known patisserie house a stylish breakfast and lunch restaurant, where meals are topped off with a celebrated pastry or ice-cream concoction. ✉ *Pl. du Grand Sablon 12–13* ☎ *02/512–3742* ▭ *AE, DC, MC, V* ⊙ *Closed Mon.*

$–$$ ✕ **'t Kelderkerke.** This busy restaurant serves honest-to-goodness Belgian food in a 17th-century vaulted cellar on the Grand'Place. Try *stoemp et saucisses* (tasty mashed potatoes and sausages) if you aren't tempted by the excellent mussels. Open 'til 2 AM, this is a great place for a late-night feast. ✉ *Grand'Place 15* ☎ *02/513–7344* ✍ *Reservations not accepted* ▭ *AE, DC, MC, V.*

★ **$–$$** ✕ **Taverne Falstaff.** This huge tavern with an art nouveau interior fills up for lunch and keeps going until the wee hours. Students to pensioners consume onion soup, filet mignon, salads, and other brasserie fare. On the heated terrace, a favorite meeting point for groups, the surliness of the waiters is legendary. ✉ *Rue Henri Maus 17–21* ☎ *02/511–8987* ▭ *AE, DC, MC, V.*

$ ✕ **Le Pain Quotidien.** These bakeries–cum–snack bars have spread like wildfire all over Brussels (and even to New York and Los Angeles) with the same formula: copious salads, hearty homemade soups, and delicious open sandwiches on farm-style bread, served at a communal table from 7:30 AM to 7 PM. ✉ *Rue des Sablons 11* ☎ *02/513–5154* ✉ *Rue Antoine Dansaert 16* ☎ *02/502–2361* ✍ *Reservations not accepted* ▭ *No credit cards.*

WHERE TO STAY

The main hotel districts are around the Grand'Place, the place de Brouckère, and in the avenue Louise shopping area. If you have a problem finding accommodations, go to the TIB tourist office in the Hôtel de Ville at the Grand'Place or telephone Belgian Tourist Reservations for their free service. Weekend and summer discounts, often of 50% or more, are available in almost all hotels. Most new hotels have set aside rooms or floors for nonsmokers and offer a limited number of rooms equipped for people with disabilities.

WHAT IT COSTS In Euros				
	$$$$	$$$	$$	$
FOR 2 PEOPLE	over €223	€161–€223	€87–€161	under €87

Prices are for a standard double room, excluding a 16% service charge and a 14.9% room tax. The tax is slightly lower at suburban hotels.

5

★ $$$$ **Amigo.** Although it was built in the 1950s, this family-owned hotel off the Grand'Place has the charm of an earlier age. Each room has its own look with silk, velvet, and brocades, and most have marble bathrooms. Check for special offers when booking. Ask for a quiet room, away from the main tourist trail. ✉ *Rue de l'Amigo 1–3, 1000* ☎ *02/547–4747* 🖷 *02/513–5277* 🌐 *www.hotelamigo.com* *185 rooms, 7 suites* *Restaurant* 💳 *AE, DC, MC, V.*

$$$$ **Brussels Hilton.** The 27-story Hilton was one of the capital's first high-rises, dating from the 1960s, and remains a distinctive landmark with great views of the inner town. Corner rooms are the most desirable; there are four floors of executive rooms and superb business facilities. The second-floor Maison du Boeuf restaurant is much appreciated by Brussels gourmets. The hotel is in the luxury avenue de la Toison d'Or and boulevard de Waterloo shopping area, overlooking the tiny Parc d'Egmont. ✉ *Bd. de Waterloo 38, 1000* ☎ *02/504–1111* 🖷 *02/504–2111* *430 rooms, 39 suites* *2 restaurants* 💳 *AE, DC, MC, V.*

$$$$ **Conrad International.** Opened by the Hilton group in 1993, the Conrad combines the European grand hotel tradition with American tastes and amenities, and has become *the* place to stay for visiting dignitaries. Rooms are spacious, with three telephones, bathrobes, and in-room check-out. Breakfast is included. The Maison de Maître restaurant maintains the same high standard, and the large bar is pleasantly clublike. ✉ *Av. Louise 71, 1050* ☎ *02/542–4242* 🖷 *02/542–4200* 🌐 *www.hilton.com* *269 rooms, 20 suites* *2 restaurants* 💳 *AE, DC, MC, V.*

$$$$ **Manos Stéphanie.** This former town house has a marble lobby, Louis XV furniture, and elegant rooms. Service is friendly, breakfast is included, and children under 12 stay free. ✉ *Chaussée de Charleroi 28, 1060* ☎ *02/539–0250* 🖷 *02/537–5729* 🌐 *www.manoshotel.com* *55 rooms, 7 suites* *Bar* 💳 *AE, DC, MC, V.*

★ $$$$ **Le Méridien.** Conveniently located opposite the Gare Centrale, Le Méridien's marble and gilt-edged lobby recalls palatial Parisian hotels, and the restaurant sets out brightly colored Limoges china. Rooms, in dark blue or green, come with three telephones, large desks, and data ports. ✉ *Carrefour de l'Europe 3, 1000* ☎ *02/548–4211* 🖷 *02/548–4080* 🌐 *www.meridien.be* *224 rooms, 17 suites* *Restaurant* 💳 *AE, DC, MC, V.*

$$$$ **Le Metropole.** Built in 1895, this belle epoque masterpiece is the last trace of elegance in what was once one of Brussels's most charming squares. The lobby has a high coffered ceiling, chandeliers, and Oriental rugs, and the staircase and original elevator are as stunning as they were when Sarah Bernhardt stayed here. The theme extends to the restaurant and the café, which opens onto a heated terrace. It is planning extensive renovations in 2004. Rooms are decorated in art deco style and breakfast is included. ✉ *Pl. de Brouckère 31, 1000* ☎ *02/217–2300* 🖷 *02/218–0220* 🌐 *www.metropole.be* *400 rooms, 10 suites* *2 restaurants* 💳 *AE, DC, MC, V.*

$$$$ **Radisson SAS.** This excellent hotel has guest rooms decorated with great panache in four different styles: Scandinavian, Asian, Italian, and art deco. A portion of the 12th-century city wall forms part of the atrium. Children under 17 stay free. ✉ *Rue du Fossé-aux-Loups 47, 1000* ☎ *02/219–2828* 📠 *02/219–6262* *263 rooms, 16 suites* *2 restaurants* 💳 *AE, DC, MC, V.*

$$$ **Le Dixseptième.** In this stylish 17th-century hotel, originally the residence of the Spanish ambassador, each room is named for a Belgian artist. Suites are up a splendid Louis XV staircase, and the standard rooms surround an interior courtyard. Whitewashed walls, bare floors, exposed beams, and colorful textiles are the style here. Some rooms have kitchenettes; suites have working fireplaces and fax machines. Breakfast is included. ✉ *Rue de la Madeleine 25, 1000, 1000* ☎ *02/517–1717* 📠 *02/502–6424* *24 rooms, 12 suites* 💳 *AE, DC, MC, V.*

$$ **Citadine.** This residential hotel accepts overnight guests; it's a good choice for families. The exterior is plain, but the location on the Vismet is plum. Rooms have pull-out twin beds; junior suites sleep four. All have kitchenettes. ✉ *Quai au Bois-à-Brûler 51, 1000* ☎ *02/221–1411* 📠 *02/221–1599* *169 rooms* 💳 *AE, DC, MC, V.*

$ **Bed & Brussels.** This upscale B&B accommodations service arranges stays with 100 host families in Brussels or surrounding areas, most of them with room to spare after children have flown the coop. Many rooms come with private bath, and breakfast with the hosts is included. ✉ *Rue Gustave Biot 2* ☎ *02/646–0737* 📠 *02/644–0114* 🌐 *www.bnb-brussels.be* 💳 *MC, V.*

$ **Matignon.** Only the belle epoque facade of this family-run hotel opposite the Bourse was preserved when the building was converted. The lobby is tiny to make room for the bustling café-brasserie. Rooms are small but have large beds (and large TVs), and the duplex suites are good value for families. It's noisy but very central. Breakfast is included. ✉ *Rue de la Bourse 10, 1000* ☎ *02/511–0888* 📠 *02/513–6927* *37 rooms, 9 suites* *Restaurant* 💳 *AE, DC, MC, V.*

★ $ **Welcome Hotel.** Owners Michel and Sophie Smeesters run this charming 15-room hotel, the smallest in Brussels. The rooms, with king- or queen-size beds, would be a credit to far more expensive establishments; it's essential to book well ahead. There's a lovely breakfast room, and Michel is also chef at the excellent seafood restaurant around the corner, La Truite d'Argent. ✉ *Rue du Peuplier 5, 1000* ☎ *02/219–9546* 📠 *02/217–1887* 🌐 *www.hotelwelcome.com* *15 rooms, 3 apartments for stays of at least one month* *Restaurant* 💳 *AE, DC, MC, V.*

NIGHTLIFE & THE ARTS

The Arts

The best way to find out what's going on in Brussels—and throughout the country—is to buy a copy of the English-language weekly the *Bulletin*. It's published every Thursday.

Film

Movies are mainly shown in their original language (indicated as v.o., or *version originale*). For unusual movies or screen classics, visit the **Musée du Cinéma** (Film Museum; ✉ rue Baron Horta 9 ☎ 02/507–8370), where three sound films and two silents with piano accompaniment are shown every evening. Those under 16 are not admitted.

Music

Free Sunday morning concerts take place at various churches, including the Cathédrale Sts-Michel-et-Gudule. Major symphony concerts and recitals are held at the **Palais des Beaux-Arts** (✉ rue Ravenstein 23 ☎ 02/507–8200). Chamber music is best enjoyed at the intimate **Conservatoire Royal de Musique** (✉ rue de la Régence 30 ☎ 02/511–0427). The **Église des Minimes** (✉ rue des Minimes 62) offers Sunday morning concerts. **Ancienne Belgique** (✉ bd. Anspach 110 ☎ 02/548–2424) hosts folk, rock, pop, funk, and jazz concerts.

Opera & Dance

The national opera company, based at the handsome **Théâtre Royal de la Monnaie** (✉ pl. de la Monnaie ☎ 070/233939), stages productions of international quality. Touring dance and opera companies often perform at **Cirque Royal** (✉ rue de l'Enseignement 81 ☎ 02/218–2015).

Theater

The **Théâtre Royal du Parc** (✉ rue de la Loi 3 ☎ 02/505–3030) stages productions of Molière and other French classics. Avant-garde theater is performed at **Théâtre Varia** (✉ rue du Sceptre 78 ☎ 02/640–8258). **Théâtre de Poche** (✉ Chemin du Gymnase 1a, in the Bois de la Cambre ☎ 02/649–1727) presents modern productions.

Nightlife

Bars

There's a café on virtually every corner in Brussels, and all of them serve beer from morning to late at night. A young crowd fills **Au Soleil** (✉ rue Marché au Charbon 86 ☎ 02/513–3430) in the fashionable place St-Gery part of town. The lively **Beursschouwburg-Café** (✉ rue Auguste Orts 22 ☎ 02/513–8290) attracts earnestly trendy young Flemish intellectuals. **Le Cirio** (✉ rue de la Bourse 18 ☎ 02/512–1395) is a seemingly time-warped café with 1900s-era advertisements and price lists on the mirror-lined walls. Another 1900s-style café-bar with a lost-in-time atmosphere is **À La Mort Subite** (✉ rue Montagne-aux-Herbes-Potagères 7 ☎ 02/513–1318). Hang out with the cool Flemish crowd in art nouveau masterpiece **De Ultieme Hallucinatie** (✉ rue Royale 316 ☎ 02/217–0614). On the Grand'Place, **Le Cerf** (✉ Grand'Place 20 ☎ 02/511–4791) is particularly pleasant, with atmosphere and furnishings out of the 17th century. Only a 10-minute stroll from the Grand'Place is **La Fleur en Papier Doré** (✉ rue des Aléxiens 53 ☎ 02/511–1659), a quaint tavern with a surrealist decor that appeals to an artsy crowd. **Rick's Café Américain** (✉ av. Louise 344 ☎ 02/648–1451) is a favorite with the American and British expat community. Brussels has a sizable number of "Irish" bars, but **James Joyce** (✉ rue Archimède 34 ☎ 02/230–9894) was the first in Brussels and is the most genuinely Gaelic.

Dance Clubs

Electronica fans prefer **Fuse** (✉ rue Blaes 208 ☎ 02/511–9789), a bunker-style techno haven with regular gay and lesbian nights. Cutting edge **Recyclart** (✉ rue des Ursulines 25 ☎ 02/502–5734) combines art exhibitions with eclectic beats in an old railway station while trains rattle overhead. **Le Mirano Continental** (✉ Chaussée de Louvain 38 ☎ 02/227–3970) remains the glitzy hangout of choice for the self-styled beautiful people.

Jazz

Most of Brussels's dozen or so jazz haunts present live music only on certain nights; check before you go. **New York Café Jazz Club** (✉ Chaussée de Charleroi 5 ☎ 02/534–8509) is an American restaurant by day and a modern jazz hangout on Friday and Saturday evenings. **Sounds Jazz Club** (✉ rue de la Tulipe 28 ☎ 02/512–9250), a big café, emphasizes jazz-rock, blues, and other modern trends. **Travers** (✉ rue Traversière 11 ☎ 02/218–4086), a café–cum–jazz club, is a cramped but outstanding showcase for the country's leading players.

SHOPPING

Gift Ideas

Belgium is where the *praline*—rich chocolate filled with flavored creams, liqueur, or nuts—was invented. Try Corné Toison d'Or, Godiva, Neuhaus, or the lower-priced Leonidas, available at shops throughout the city. **Wittamer** (✉ pl. du Grand Sablon 12 ☎ 02/512–3742) is an excellent patisserie with a sideline in superb chocolates. **Pierre Marcolini** (✉ pl. du Grand Sablon 39 ☎ 02/514–1206) is the boy wonder of the chocolate world. Exclusive handmade pralines can be bought at **Mary** (✉ rue Royale 73 ☎ 02/217–4500), official purveyor of chocolates to the Belgian court.

Many stores sell crystal tableware and ornaments, including **Art & Selection** (✉ rue du Marché-aux-Herbes 83 ☎ 02/511–8448) near the Grand'Place. Only the Val-St-Lambert mark guarantees handblown, hand-carved Belgian lead crystal.

When shopping for lace, ask whether it is genuine handmade Belgian or machine-made in East Asia. **Maison F. Rubbrecht** (✉ Grand'Place 23 ☎ 02/512–0218) sells authentic Belgian lace. For a choice of old and modern lace, try **Manufacture Belge de Dentelles** (✉ Galerie de la Reine 6–8 ☎ 02/511–4477).

Markets

On Saturday (9–6) and Sunday (9–2), the upper end of the Place du Grand Sablon becomes an open-air **antiques and book market** with more than 100 stalls. The **Vieux Marché** (✉ pl. du Jeu de Balle), open daily 7–2, is a flea market worth visiting in the working-class Marolles district. To make real finds, get here early.

Shopping Districts

The shops in the **Galeries St-Hubert** sell mostly luxury goods or gift items. The **rue Neuve** and the **City 2** mall are good for less expensive boutiques and department stores. Avant-garde clothes are sold in boutiques on **rue Antoine Dansaert,** near the Bourse.

Uptown, **avenue Louise,** with the arcades Galerie Louise and Espace Louise, counts a large number of boutiques selling expensive clothes and accessories. The **boulevard de Waterloo** is home to the same fashion names as Bond Street and Rodeo Drive. The **Grand Sablon** has more charm; this is the center for antiques and art galleries.

BRUSSELS A TO Z

AIRPORTS & TRANSFERS

Most international flights arrive at Brussels National Airport at Zaventem (sometimes called simply Zaventem), 15 km (9 mi) northeast of the city center. No-frills airline Ryanair runs flights to European destinations including London and Rome from Brussels South Airport in Charleroi, 55 km (34 mi) south of Brussels.

Brussels National Airport ☎ 0900–70000. **Brussels South Airport** ☎ 071/251211.

TRANSFERS Shuttle trains run between Zaventem and all three main railway stations in Brussels: Midi (South), Central (Central), and Nord (North). The Airport City Express runs every 20 minutes, from about 5:30 AM to midnight. The journey takes 23 minutes. A one-way second-class ticket costs €2.10. A taxi to the city center takes about a half hour and costs about

€30. The number 12 bus runs to and from the airport to the city center every 30 minutes. One-way tickets cost €3. A shuttle bus service runs between Brussels South Airport and the Gare du Midi. It leaves the station two and a half hours before each flight is due to depart. The hour-long journey costs €10 one-way.

BOAT & FERRY TRAVEL

Hoverspeed operates a Hovercraft catamaran service between Dover and Calais, carrying cars and foot passengers. Travel time is 35 minutes and there is a coach connection to Oostende. P&O North Sea Ferries operates an overnight ferry service between Hull and Zeebrugge.

Hoverspeed ☎ 44/870-5240241 in the U.K. 🌐 www.hoverspeed.co.uk. **P&O North Sea Ferries** ☎ 44/870-5202020 in the U.K.; 02/710-6444 in Belgium 🌐 www.ponsf.com.

BUS TRAVEL TO & FROM BRUSSELS

Eurolines operates up to three daily express services from and to Amsterdam, Berlin, Frankfurt, Paris, and London. The Eurolines Coach Station in Brussels adjoins the Gare du Nord.

Eurolines ✉ pl. de Brouckère 50 ☎ 02/217-0025 🌐 www.eurolines.be. **Eurolines Coach Station** ✉ rue du Progrès 80 ☎ 02/203-0707.

METRO, TRAM & BUS TRAVEL WITHIN BRUSSELS

The Métro (subway), trams (streetcars), and buses (STIB/MIVB) are parts of a unified system. A single ticket, valid for one hour's travel, costs €1.40. The best buy is a 10-trip ticket for €9.20 or a one-day card costing €3.70. Tickets are sold in metro stations and at newsstands. Single tickets can be purchased on the bus or tram.

CAR TRAVEL

If you use Le Shuttle under the English Channel or a ferry to Calais, note that the E40 (via Oostende and Brugge) connects with the French highway, cutting driving time from Calais to Brussels to less than two hours.

EMERGENCIES

Every pharmacy displays a list of pharmacies on duty outside normal hours.

Doctors & Dentists **Doctor/Pharmacy** ☎ 02/479-1818 for all-night and weekend services. **Dentist** ☎ 02/426-1026.

Emergency Services **Ambulance and Fire Brigade** ☎ 100. **Police** ☎ 101.

Hot Lines **Lost/Stolen Bank/Credit Cards** ☎ 070/344344. **24-Hour English-Speaking Info and Crisis Line** ☎ 02/648-4014.

Pharmacy **Pharmacy** ☎ 0900-10500 🌐 www.pharmacie.be.

ENGLISH-LANGUAGE MEDIA

Bookstores **The Reading Room** ✉ av. Georges Henri 503 ☎ 02/734-7917. **Sterling Books** ✉ rue du Fossé-aux-Loups 38 ☎ 02/223-6223. **Waterstone's** ✉ bd. Adolphe Max 71-75 ☎ 02/219-2708.

TOURS

BUS TOURS

Expertly guided half-day English-language coach tours are organized by ARAU, from March through November, including "Brussels 1900: Art Nouveau" (every Saturday) and "Brussels 1930: Art Deco" (every third Saturday). Tours (€15) begin in front of Hotel Métropole on place de Brouckère. Chatterbus tours (early June–September) include visits by minibus or on foot to the main sights. De Boeck Sightseeing Tours operates city tours with cassette commentary. It also has tours of Antwerp, the Ardennes, Brugge, Gent, Ieper, and Waterloo.

Fees & Schedules **ARAU** ✉ bd. Adolphe Max 55 ☎ 02/219-3345 information and reservations. **Chatterbus** ✉ rue des Thuyas 12 ☎ 02/673-1835. **De Boeck Sightseeing Tours** ✉ rue de la Colline 8, Grand'Place ☎ 02/513-7744.

PRIVATE GUIDES Qualified guides are available for individual tours from the TIB. Three hours costs €85 for up to 20 people.
Fees & Schedules TIB ☎ 02/513-8940.

WALKING TOURS Chatterbus organizes visits (early June–September) on foot or by minibus to the main sights and a walking tour with a visit to a bistro. Walking tours organized by the tourist office depart from the Brussels Tourist Office (TIB) in the Town Hall, May–September, Monday–Saturday.

TAXIS

Cabs don't cruise for fares; order one from Taxis Verts or go to a cab stand. The tip is included in the fare.
Taxi Companies Taxis Verts ☎ 02/349-4949.

TRAIN TRAVEL

Ten Eurostar passenger trains a day link Brussels's Gare du Midi with London's Waterloo station via the Channel Tunnel in two hours, 40 minutes. A one-way trip costs €310 in business class and from €224 in economy; rail pass holders qualify for 50% discounts. Reservations are required. Check-in is 20 minutes before departure.

All rail services between Brussels and Paris are on Thalys high-speed trains (1 hr, 25 mins). A one-way trip costs €102 ("Confort 1"), €64 ("Confort 2"). Reservations are required.
Eurostar ☎ 02/528-2828 www.eurostar.com. **Gares du Midi, Central, and Nord Brussels** ☎ 02/203-3640. **Thalys** ☎ 070/667788 information and reservations www.thalys.com.

TRAVEL AGENCIES

Local Agent Referrals **American Express** ✉ Houtweg 24, 1170 Brussels ☎ 02/245-2250. **Carlson Wagonlit Travel** ✉ bd. Clovis 53, 1040 Brussels ☎ 02/287-8811.

VISITOR INFORMATION

At Tourist Information Brussels you can buy a Tourist Passport (€7.50), a one-day public transport card that includes €50 worth of museum admissions and reductions.
Tourist Information Brussels (TIB) ✉ Hôtel de Ville, Grand'Place ☎ 02/513-8940 📠 02/513-8320 www.tib.be.

Belgium Basics

To research prices, get advice from other travelers, and book travel arrangements, visit www.fodors.com.

BUSINESS HOURS

Banks are usually open weekdays 9–4 or 4:30; some close for an hour at lunch. Currency exchange facilities (*bureaux de change* or *wisselkantoren*) are usually open evenings and weekends, but you'll get a better rate in banks. For instant cash, ATMs are nearly everywhere (but not at railway stations) and accept major credit cards. Museums are generally open 10–5 Tuesday through Sunday. Many museums will refuse to admit you after 4:15 or so. Large stores are open weekdays and Saturday from 9:30 or 10 to 6:30 or 7 and generally stay open an hour later on Friday. "Night" shops, for newspapers, tobacco, drinks, and limited grocery items, are open seven days a week from 6 PM until dawn.

CUSTOMS & DUTIES

For details on imports and duty-free limits for visitors from outside the EU, *see* Customs & Duties *in* Smart Travel Tips.

EMBASSIES

Australia ✉ Rue Guimard 6, 1040 Brussels ☎ 02/286-0500 🌐 www.austemb.be.

Canada ✉ Av. de Tervueren 2, 1040 Brussels ☎ 02/741-0611 🌐 www.ambassade-canada.be.

Ireland ✉ Ferdinand Verbiestlaan 38, 2650 Antwerp ☎ 03/289-0611.

New Zealand ✉ Sq. de Meeus 1, 7/F, 1000 Brussels ☎ 02/512-1040 🌐 www.nzembassy.com.

South Africa ✉ Rue de la Loi 26, 1000 Brussels ☎ 02/285-4400 🌐 www.ambassade.net/southafrica.

United Kingdom ✉ Rue d'Arlon 85, 1040 Brussels ☎ 02/287-6211 🌐 www.british-embassy.be.

United States ✉ Bd. du Régent 25-27, 1000 Brussels ☎ 02/508-2111 🌐 www.usembassy.be.

HOLIDAYS

January 1; Easter Monday; May 1 (Labor Day); Ascension; Pentecost or Whit Monday; July 21 (Belgian National Day); August 15 (Assumption); November 1 (All Saints' Day); November 11 (Armistice Day); December 25.

LANGUAGE

Language is a sensitive subject and exerts a strong influence on politics at the national and regional levels. There are three official languages in Belgium: French, spoken primarily in the south of the country (Wallonia); Flemish, spoken in the north (Flanders); and German, spoken in a small area near the German border. Brussels is bilingual, with both French and Flemish officially recognized, though the majority of residents are francophones. Many people speak English in Brussels and throughout Flanders; in Wallonia, English-speakers tend to be thin on the ground. Flemish and Belgian French both contain slight differences from the corresponding languages spoken in the neighboring countries to the north and south.

MONEY MATTERS

Costs in Brussels are roughly on a par with those in London and New York. All taxes and service charges (tips) are included in hotel and restaurant bills and taxi fares. Gasoline prices are steep, but highways are toll-free.

Cup of coffee in a café, €1.25–€1.50; glass of draft beer, €1.25–€1.75; glass of wine, about €2.97; single bus/metro/tram ride €1.24.

CURRENCY

In January 2002, Belgium, as one of the euro zone currency countries, introduced euro (€) notes and coins. Belgian francs have completely disappeared from circulation, and only the Banque Nationale will still exchange old franc notes. The euro comes in bills of 5, 10, 20, 50, 100, 200, and 500 and coins of 1, 2, 5, 10, 20, 50 cents, and 1 and 2 euros.

VALUE-ADDED TAX (V.A.T.)

V.A.T. in Belgium is between 6% on food and clothing and 33% on luxury items. Residents outside the European Union can qualify for a V.A.T. refund but must spend €125 or more in the same shop on the same day. You must also carry the goods out of the country personally within 30 days. After you have had the invoice stamped by customs at your last port of call in the EU, you mail it back to the store of purchase, and the V.A.T. amount will be credited to your credit card or bank account.

TELEPHONES

COUNTRY & AREA CODES

The country code for Belgium is 32. All calls within the country must include the regional telephone code. When dialing Belgium from outside the country, drop the first zero in the regional code.

INTERNATIONAL CALLS You can place direct calls from pay phones by using a telecard, sold at most tobacconists. For credit card and collect calls, dial AT&T, MCI Worldphone, or Sprint Global One. For English-language telephone assistance, dial 1405.

Access Codes **AT&T** ☎ 0800-10010. **MCI Worldphone** ☎ 0800-10012. **Sprint Global One** ☎ 0800-10014.

PUBLIC PHONES Pay phones work mostly with telecards, available at post offices, supermarkets, neighborhood shops, railway stations, and many newsstands. Cards are sold in denominations of €5 and €10. An average local call costs €0.50. Coin-operated phones (on the platforms of metro stations) take €1 and €2 coins. All telephone numbers must be preceded by their area code prefix, regardless of the location in Belgium from where the call is made.

BUDAPEST

6

Budapest, lying on both banks of the Danube, unites the hills of Buda and the wide boulevards of Pest. It was the site of a Roman outpost in the first century, and the modern city was not created until 1873, when the towns of Óbuda, Pest, and Buda were joined. The resulting capital is the cultural, political, intellectual, and commercial heart of the nation; for the 20% of the nation's population who live here, anywhere else is just "the country."

Much of the charm of a visit to Budapest consists of unexpected glimpses into shadowy courtyards and long vistas down sunlit cobbled streets. Although some 30,000 buildings were destroyed during World War II and in 1956, the past lingers on in the often crumbling architectural details of the antique structures that remain and in the memories and lifestyles of Budapest's citizens.

EXPLORING BUDAPEST

The principal sights of the city fall roughly into three areas, each of which can be comfortably covered on foot. The Budapest hills are best explored using public transportation. Many street names have been changed since 1989 to purge all reminders of the Communist regime—you can sometimes still see the old name, negated with a victorious red *x*, next to the new. By tradition, the district number—a Roman numeral designating one of Budapest's 22 districts—precedes each address. For the sake of clarity, in this book, the word "District" precedes the number. However, if you are addressing an envelope, remember that full postal addresses do not cite this Roman numeral, as the district is indicated by the zip code. Districts V, VI, and VII are in downtown Pest; District I includes Castle Hill, the main tourist district of Buda. The maps provided by tourist offices are not very detailed, so arm yourself with one from any of the bookshops in Váci utca or from a stationery shop or newsstand.

Getting around is easier if you learn a few basic terms: *utca* (abbreviated *u.*) and *út,* which mean "street" and "road" or "avenue," respectively; *tér* or *tere* (square); and *körút* (ring road).

Várhegy

Numbers in the margin correspond to points of interest on the Budapest map.

Most of Buda's main sights are on Várhegy (Castle Hill), a long, narrow plateau laced with cobblestone streets, clustered with beautifully preserved baroque, Gothic, and Renaissance houses and crowned by the stately Royal Palace. Painstaking reconstruction work has been in progress here since the area was nearly leveled during World War II.

❺ **Hadtörténeti Múzeum** (Museum of Military History). The collection here includes uniforms and regalia, many belonging to the Hungarian generals who took part in the abortive uprising against Austrian rule in 1848. Other exhibits trace the military history of Hungary from the original Magyar conquest in the 9th century up to the middle of the 20th century. English-language tours can be arranged in advance. ✉ *Tóth Árpád sétány 40* ☎ *1/356–9522* 🌐 *www.militaria.hu* ⏲ *Apr.–Sept., Tues.–Sun. 10–6; Oct.–Mar., Tues.–Sun. 10–4.*

★ ❸ **Halászbástya** (Fishermen's Bastion). This wondrous porch overlooking Pest and the Danube was built at the turn of the 20th century as a lookout tower to protect what was once a thriving fishing settlement. Its neo-Romanesque columns and arches frame views over the city and the river. ✉ *East of Szentháromság tér.*

★ ❶ **Királyi Palota** (Royal Palace, also known as Buda Castle). The Nazis made their final stand here and left it a blackened wasteland. Under the rubble, archaeologists discovered the medieval foundations of the palace of King Matthias Corvinus, who, in the 15th century, presided over one of the most splendid courts in Europe. The rebuilt palace is now a vast museum complex and cultural center.

The **Budapesti Történeti Múzeum** (Budapest History Museum), the southern block of the Royal Palace, displays a permanent exhibit of the city's history from Buda's liberation from the Turks in 1686 through the 1970s. The 19th- and 20th-century photos and videos of the castle, the Chain Bridge, and other Budapest monuments provide a helpful orientation to the city. Down in the cellars are the original medieval vaults of the palace, a palace chapel, and more royal relics. ✉ *Királyi Palota (Wing E), Szt. György tér 2* ☎ *1/375–7533* 🌐 *www.btm.hu* ⏲ *Mar.–mid-May and mid-Sept.–Oct., Wed.–Mon. 10–6; mid-May–mid-Sept., daily 10–6; Nov.–Feb., Wed.–Mon. 10–4.*

In the Royal Palace's northern wing, the **Ludwig Múzeum** (Ludwig Museum) houses a collection of more than 200 pieces of Hungarian and contemporary world art, including works by Picasso and Lichtenstein. ✉ *Királyi Palota (Wing A), Dísz tér 17* ☎ *1/375–7533* ⏲ *Tues.–Sun. 10–6.*

The central section of the Royal Palace houses the **Magyar Nemzeti Galéria** (Hungarian National Gallery), which exhibits a wide range of Hungarian fine art. Names to look for are Munkácsy, a 19th-century Romantic painter, and Csontváry, an early Surrealist admired by Picasso. Tours for up to five people with an English-speaking guide can be booked in advance. ✉ *Királyi Palota (entrance in Wing C), Dísz tér 17* ☎ *1/375–7533; 1/224–3700 Ext. 423 for tours* ⏲ *Mid-Mar.–Nov., Tues.–Sun. 10–6; Dec.–mid-Mar., Tues.–Sun. 10–4.*

❷ **Mátyás templom** (Matthias Church). This venerable church, with its distinctive roof of colored, diamond-pattern tiles and skeletal Gothic spire, dates from the 13th century. Built as a mosque by the Turks, it was destroyed and reconstructed during the 19th century, only to be bombed

Fodor's Choice ★

during World War II. Only the south porch survives from the original structure. The Habsburg emperors were crowned kings of Hungary here. High mass—in Latin—is held every Sunday at 10 AM with an orchestra and choir, and organ concerts are often held in the summer on Friday at 8 PM. Visitors are asked to remain at the back of the church during services (it's least intrusive to come after 9:30 AM weekdays and between 1 PM and 5 PM Sunday and holidays). ✉ *Szentháromság tér 2* ☎ *1/355–5657* ⏲ *Church daily 7 AM–8:30 PM. Treasury daily 9:30–5:30.*

❹ **Zenetörténeti Múzeum** (Museum of Music History). The handsome, 18th-century gray-stone palace that once belonged to the noble Erdődy family hosts intimate recitals of classical music and displays rare manuscripts and antique instruments. ✉ *Táncsics Mihály u. 7* ☎ *1/214–6770* ⏲ *Mid-Mar.–mid-Nov., Tues.–Fri. 10–5, weekends 10–6.*

The Heart of the City

Pest fans out from the Belváros (Inner City), which is bounded by the Kiskörút (Little Ring Road). The Nagykörút (Grand Ring Road) describes a wider semicircle from the Margaret Bridge to the Petőfi Bridge.

⓫ **Belvárosi plébánia templom** (Inner-City Parish Church). The oldest church in Pest dates from the 12th century. It incorporates a succession of Western architectural styles and preserves a Muslim prayer niche from the time when the Turks ruled the country. Liszt, who lived only a few yards away, often played the organ here. ✉ *Március 15 tér 2.*

★ **Korzó.** This elegant promenade runs south along the Pest side of the river, providing views of Castle Hill, the Chain Bridge, and Gellért Hill on the other side of the Danube. ✉ *from Eötvös tér to Március 15 tér.*

★ ⓱ **Magyar Állami Operaház** (Hungarian State Opera House). Flanked by a pair of marble sphinxes, this 19th-century neo-Renaissance treasure was the crowning achievement of architect Miklós Ybl. It has been restored to its original ornate glory—particularly inside. ✉ *Andrássy út 22* ☎ *1/331–2550* 🌐 *www.opera.hu* ☞ *Foreign-language tours (45 mins) daily at 3 and 4; meet at the Sphinx statue in front of opera house on right-hand side.*

⓬ **Magyar Nemzeti Múzeum** (Hungarian National Museum). The stern, classical edifice was built between 1837 and 1847. On its steps, on March 15, 1848, Petőfi Sándor recited his revolutionary poem, "Nemzeti Dal" ("National Song"), declaring "By the God of Magyar, / Do we swear, / Do we swear, chains no longer / Will we wear." This poem, along with the "12 Points," a formal list of political demands by young Hungarians, called upon the people to rise up against the Habsburgs. Celebrations of the national holiday—long banned by the Communist regime—are now held here (and throughout the city) every year on March 15. A host of royal relics can be seen in the domed Hall of Honor. The museum's epic Hungarian history exhibition includes displays chronicling the end of Communism and the much-celebrated exodus of the Russian troops. ✉ *Múzeum körút 14–16* ☎ *1/338–2122* 🌐 *www.hnm.hu* ⏲ *Mid-Mar.–mid-Oct., Tues.–Sun. 10–6; mid-Oct.–mid-Mar., Tues.–Sun. 10–5.*

❿ **Március 15 tér** (March 15 Square). This square is not particularly picturesque, but it commemorates the 1848 struggle for independence from the Habsburgs with a statue of the poet Petőfi Sándor, who died in a later uprising. On March 15, the national holiday commemorating the revolution, the square is packed with patriotic Hungarians. ✉ *end of Apácai Csere János u. just north of Erzsébet Bridge.*

Budapest
Margit-sziget (Margaret Is.)
Margit híd (Margaret Br.)
Danube
BUDA
PEST
West Station
South Station
Gellért Hill
Széchenyi lánchíd (Chain Br.)
Erzsébet híd (Elizabeth Br.)
Szabadság híd (Liberty Br.)
Kossuth Lajos tér
Szabadság tér
Roosevelt tér
Erzsébet tér
Vörösmarty tér
Deák tér
Ferenciek tere
Kálvin tér
Fővám tér
Szent Gellért tér
Döbrentei tér
Clark Ádám tér
Dísz tér
Nyugati tér
Lehel tér
Széll Kálmán tér
Várhegy
Vérmező
KEY
Tourist Information

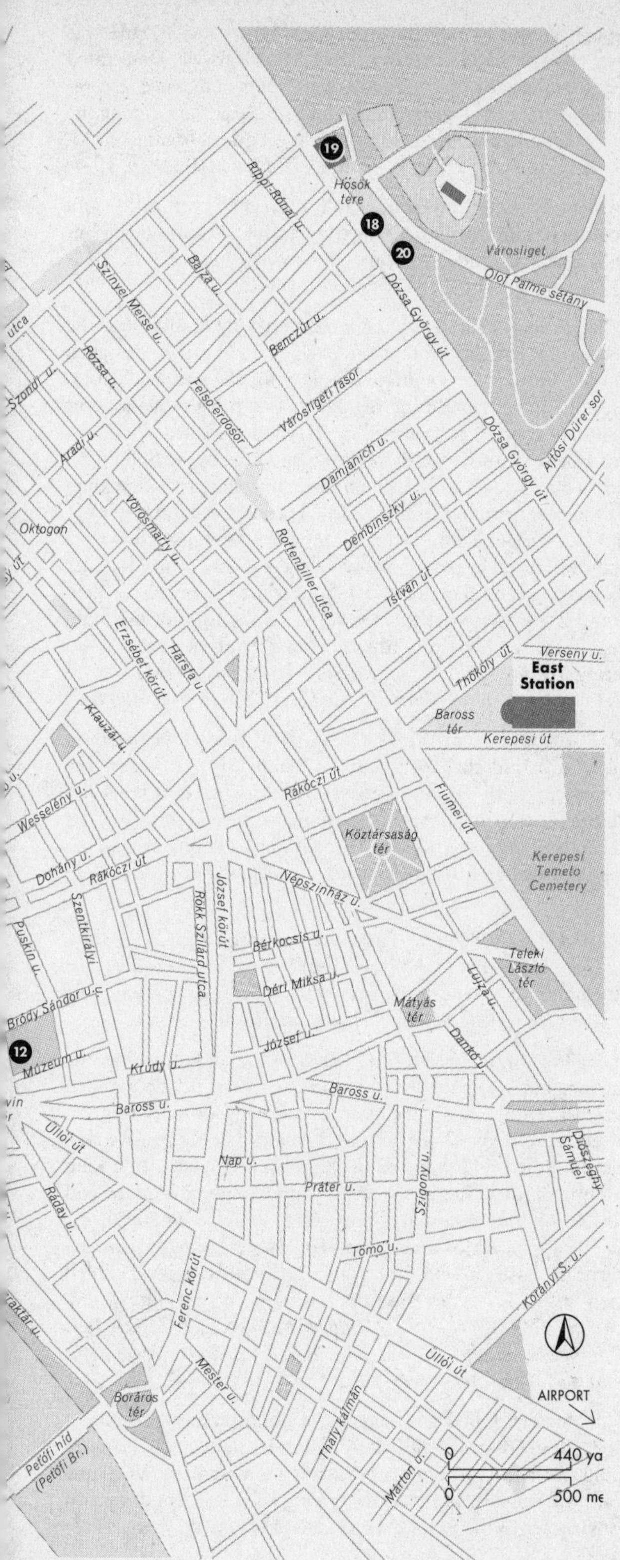

Várhegy

Hadtörténeti Múzeum 5
Halászbástya 3
Királyi Palota 1
Mátyás templom 2
Zenetörténeti Múzeum 4

The Heart of the City

Belvárosi plébánia templom 11
Magyar Állami Operaház 17
Magyar Nemzeti Múzeum 12
Március 15 tér 10
Nagy Zsinagóga 13
Néprajzi Múzeum 15
Országház 14
Roosevelt tér 6
Szent István Bazilika 16
Váci utca 9
Vigadó 8
Vörösmarty tér 7

Hő´sök Tere & Városliget

Hő´sök tere 18
Mű´csarnok 20
Szépmű´vészeti Múzeum 19

⓭ **Nagy Zsinagóga** (Great Synagogue). Europe's largest synagogue was built between 1844 and 1859 in a Byzantine-Moorish style. Desecrated by German and Hungarian Nazis, it underwent years of massive restorations in the post-Communist years. Liszt and Saint-Saëns are among the great musicians who once played the synagogue's grand organ. ✉ *Dohány u. 2–8* ☎ *1/342–1335* ⏲ *Mon.–Thurs. 10–5, Fri. 10–3, Sun. 10–1.*

Fodor's Choice ★

⓯ **Néprajzi Múzeum** (Museum of Ethnography). Elegant both inside and out, this museum has impressive, exhaustive exhibits—captioned in English—of folk costumes and traditions. ✉ *Kossuth Lajos tér 12* ☎ *1/473–2400* 🌐 *www.neprajz.hu* ⏲ *Tues.–Sun. 10–6.*

Fodor's Choice ★

⓮ **Országház** (Parliament). The riverfront's most striking landmark is the imposing neo-Gothic Parliament, now minus the red star on top, designed by Imre Steindl. Although it is still a workplace for the nation's legislators, the interior can be seen during regular guided tours that show off the gilded cathedral ceilings, frescoed walls, intricate glass windows, and majestic stairways (of which there are some 12 mi in the building!). The highlight is the nation's Holy Crown, made for Hungary's first king, Szent István (St. Stephen), in the year 1000. The crown, Hungary's national symbol, was relocated from the National Museum and now rests on a velvet pillow flanked by two sword-wielding uniformed guards under Parliament's soaring central cupola. One-hour tours in English are held daily at 10 and 2. Purchase tickets at Gate X, to the right of the main entrance steps. You are advised to arrive at least a half hour early, and you must bring a valid passport. ✉ *Kossuth Lajos tér* ☎ *1/441–4904 or 1/441–4415* 🌐 *www.mkogy.hu* ⏲ *Weekdays 8–6, Sat. 8–4, Sun. 8–2.*

❻ **Roosevelt tér** (Roosevelt Square). On this picturesque square opening onto the Danube you'll find the 19th-century neoclassical **Magyar Tudományos Akadémia** (Hungarian Academy of Sciences) and the 1907 **Gresham Palota** (Gresham Palace), a crumbling tribute to the age of art nouveau currently undergoing massive renovations and eventually to become a Four Seasons hotel. ✉ *at Pest end of Széchenyi lánchíd (Chain Bridge).*

★ **Széchenyi lánchíd** (Chain Bridge). The most beautiful of the Danube's eight bridges, the Széchenyi lánchíd was built twice: once in the 19th century and again after it was destroyed by the Nazis. ✉ *Spanning the Danube between Roosevelt tér and Clark Ádám tér in District I.*

⓰ **Szent István Bazilika** (St. Stephen's Basilica). Massive and imposing, the 19th-century basilica is one of the landmarks of Pest. It was planned early in the 19th century as a neoclassical building, but by the time it was completed more than 50 years later, it was decidedly neo-Renaissance. The mummified right hand of St. Stephen, Hungary's first king and patron saint, is preserved in the Szent Jobb Chapel; the guard will illuminate it for you for a minimal charge. A climb up to the cupola (or a lift on the elevator) affords a sweeping city view. An ongoing, massive cleaning of the basilica's exterior, which at this writing is scheduled to be finished in 2005, has restored the marble to a sparkling white. ✉ *Szt. István tér* ☎ *1/317–2859* ⏲ *Church Mon.–Sat. 7–7, Sun 1–7. Szt. Jobb Chapel Apr.–Sept., Mon.–Sat. 9–5; Oct.–Mar., Mon.–Sat. 10–4. Cupola mid-Apr.–Oct., daily 10–5.*

Fodor's Choice ★

❾ **Váci utca** (Váci Street). Lined with expensive boutiques and dozens of souvenir shops, this pedestrian-only thoroughfare is Budapest's most upscale shopping street and one of its most kitschy tourist areas. Váci utca stretches south of Kossuth Lajos utca, making the total length extend from Vörösmarty tér to the Szabadság Bridge. ✉ *from Vörösmarty tér to Fővám tér.*

8 **Vigadó** (Concert Hall). Designed in a striking romantic style by Frigyes Feszl and inaugurated in 1865 with Franz Liszt conducting his own *St. Elizabeth Oratorio,* the concert hall is a curious mixture of Byzantine, Moorish, Romanesque, and Hungarian motifs, punctuated by statues of dancing figures and sturdy pillars. Brahms, Debussy, and Casals are among the musicians who have graced its stage. Mahler's Symphony No. 1 and many works by Bartók were first performed here. You can go into the lobby on your own, but the hall is open only for concerts. ✉ *Vigadó tér 2* ☎ *1/318–9167 box office.*

7 **Vörösmarty tér** (Vörösmarty Square). In this handsome square in the heart of the Inner City, street musicians and sidewalk cafés combine to make one of the liveliest, albeit sometimes too touristy, atmospheres in Budapest. It's a great spot to sit and relax—but prepare to be approached by caricature artists and money changers. ✉ *at northern end of Váci u.*

Hosök Tere & Városliget

Heroes' Square is the gateway to Városliget (City Park): a square km (almost ½ square mi) of recreation, entertainment, nature, and culture.

18 **Hősök tere** (Heroes' Square). Budapest's grandest boulevard, Andrássy út, ends at this sweeping piazza flanked by the Szépművészeti Múzeum and the Műcsarnok. In the center stands the 120-foot bronze **Millenniumi Emlékmű** (Millennium Monument), begun in 1896 to commemorate the 1,000th anniversary of the Magyar Conquest. Statues of Árpád and six other founders of the Magyar nation occupy the base of the monument, while Hungary's greatest rulers and princes stand between the columns on either side. ✉ *Andrássy út at Dózsa György út.*

20 **Műcsarnok** (Palace of Exhibitions). This striking 1895 structure on Heroes' Square schedules exhibitions of contemporary Hungarian and international art and a rich series of films, plays, and concerts. ✉ *Dózsa György út 37* ☎ *1/363–2671* 🌐 *www.mucsarnok.hu* ⏲ *Tues.–Sun. 10–6.*

19 **Szépművészeti Múzeum** (Fine Arts Museum). An entire section of this Heroes' Square museum is devoted to Egyptian, Greek, and Roman artifacts, including many rare Greco-Roman ceramics. The institution's collection of Spanish paintings is among the best of its kind outside Spain. ✉ *Dózsa György út 41* ☎ *1/363–2675* 🌐 *www2.szepmuveszeti.hu* ⏲ *Tues.–Sun. 10–5:30.*

FodorśChoice ★

★ **Városliget** (City Park). Just behind Heroes' Square, this park harbors Budapest's zoo, the state circus, an amusement park, and the outdoor swimming pool of the Széchenyi mineral baths. Inside is **Vajdahunyad Vár** (Vajdahunyad Castle), an art historian's Disneyland, created for the millennial celebration in 1896 and incorporating architectural elements typical of various periods of Hungary's history all in one complex. ✉ *between Dózsa György út and Hungária körút, and Vágány u. and Ajtósi Dürer sor.*

Elsewhere in the City

Aquincum. The reconstructed remains of the capital of the Roman province of Pannonia, dating from the 1st century AD, lie in northern Budapest's Óbuda District. A varied selection of artifacts and mosaics has been unearthed, giving a tantalizing inkling of what life was like on the northern fringes of the Roman empire. The on-site **Aquincum Museum** displays the dig's most notable finds. ✉ *Szentendrei út 139* ☎ *1/250–1650* ⏲ *Apr. and Oct., Tues.–Sun. 10–5; May–Sept., Tues.–Sun. 10–6. Grounds open at 9.*

Jánoshegy (János Hill). A *libegő* (chairlift) will take you to the summit, the highest point in Budapest, where you can climb a lookout tower for the best view of the city. Take Bus 158 from Moszkva tér to the last stop, Zugligeti út. ✉ *Zugligeti út 97* ☎ *1/394–3764* ⏲ *Mid-May–mid-Sept., daily 9–6; mid-Sept.–mid-May (depending on weather), daily 9:30–4. Closed alternate Mon.*

Szobor Park (Statue Park). For a look at Budapest's too-recent Iron Curtain past, make the 30-minute drive out to this open-air exhibit cleverly nicknamed "Tons of Socialism." Forty-two Communist statues and memorials that once dominated the city have been exiled here since the political changes in 1989. You can wander among mammoth figures of Lenin and Marx while listening to songs from the Hungarian and Russian workers' movement blaring from loudspeakers. To get here by public transport, take the yellow bus (number 6) at Etele ter. ✉ *Balatoni út, corner of Szabadkai út* ☎📠 *1/424–7500* 🌐 *www.szoborpark.hu* ⏲ *Daily 10–dusk.*

WHERE TO EAT

Private restaurateurs are breathing excitement into the Budapest dining scene. You can choose from Chinese, Mexican, Italian, French, Indian, or various other cuisines—there are even vegetarian restaurants. Or you can stick to solid, traditional Hungarian fare. Be sure to check out the less expensive spots favored by locals. If you get a craving for sushi or tortellini, consult the restaurant listings in the *Budapest Sun, Where Budapest* magazine, and *Budapest in Your Pocket.*

WHAT IT COSTS In Hungarian Forints

	$$$$	$$$	$$	$
AT DINNER	over 3,500	2,500–3,500	1,500–2,500	under 1,500

Prices are per person for a main course.

$$$$ Fodor's Choice ★ ✕ **Gundel.** George Lang, Hungary's best-known restaurateur, showcases his country's cuisine at this turn-of-the-20th-century palazzo in City Park. Dark-wood paneling, rich navy blue–and–pink fabrics, and tables set with Zsolnay porcelain make the oversized dining room plush and handsome. Violinist György Lakatos, of the Lakatos Gypsy musician dynasty, strolls from table to table playing folk music. Waiters in black tie serve traditional favorites such as tender beef tournedos topped with goose liver and forest mushroom sauce or excellent fish specialties. The most affordable choice here is one of the tasting menus, a six-course affair with complementary wines. ✉ *Állatkerti út 2* ☎ *1/468–4040* ⚠ *Reservations essential* ▭ *AE, DC, MC, V.*

$$–$$$$ ✕ **Kacsa.** Hungarian and international dishes with a focus on duck are done with a light touch, with quiet chamber music in the background, in this small, celebrated restaurant just a few steps from the river. Try the crisp wild duck stuffed with plums, but be wary of the pricey wine list. ✉ *Fő u. 75* ☎ *1/201–9992* ⚠ *Reservations essential* ▭ *AE, DC, MC, V* ⏲ *No lunch weekends.*

$$–$$$$ ✕ **Múzeum.** Named for its location just steps from the National Museum, this elegant salon with mirrors, mosaics, and swift waiters serves authentic Hungarian cuisine with a lighter touch. The salads are fresh, the Hungarian wines are excellent, and the chef dares to be creative. ✉ *Múzeum körút 12* ☎ *1/267–0375 or 1/338-4221* ▭ *MC, V* ⏲ *Closed Sun.*

$$–$$$$ ✕ **Tom-George.** Well situated in the heart of downtown, Tom-George is Budapest's answer to urban chic. The spacious bar blends blond wood

and wicker, giving the interior a relaxed yet sophisticated feel. Minimalism at the table, though, belies exotic creativity in the kitchen, all with an Asian touch. House specialties include *nasi goreng* (Indonesian fried rice) and lamb with satay sauce. Sushi—perhaps Budapest's best—is glamorously prepared by the in-house sushi chef. ✉ *Október 6 utca 8* ☎ *1/266-3525* ✍ *Reservations essential* ▭ *AE, V.*

$$–$$$ Fodor's Choice ★ ✕ **Baraka.** The white stucco walls and airy balcony are offset by the gleam of varnished floorboards in this cozy and hospitable restaurant tucked away on Magyar utca. The friendly husband and wife owners are never too far away, and they will tell you the source of every ingredient on the menu. The ginger-seared tuna is recommended, as is the caprese salad with mint-basil dressing. Don't miss the unforgettable chocolate volcano for dessert. ✉ *Magyar u. 12–14* ☎ *1/483–1355* ✍ *Reservations essential* ▭ *AE, DC, MC, V* ⊗ *Closed Sun.*

$$–$$$ ✕ **Kisbuda Gyöngye.** This Budapest favorite, hidden away on a small street in Óbuda, is filled with mixed antique furniture, and its walls are covered with a patchwork of antique, carved wooden cupboard doors. Try the fresh trout smothered in cream sauce with mushrooms and capers. ✉ *Kenyeres u. 34* ☎ *1/368–6402 or 1/368–9246* ✍ *Reservations essential* ▭ *AE, DC, MC, V* ⊗ *Closed Sun.*

★ $$–$$$ ✕ **Vörös és Fehér.** This smart wine bar and restaurant opened by the Budapest Wine Society is the place to enjoy Hungary's excellent vintages. Tapas-style snacks, such as smoked venison ham or marinated salmon, are perfect alongside a glass of the local favorite. The stylish wood and wrought-iron interior are all contemporary bistro, and the big glass windows facing bustling Andrássy út make you feel like you're in the center of it all. After dinner, don't miss the chance to taste some *tokaji aszú*—the celebrated Hungarian dessert wine. ✉ *Andrássy út 41* ☎ *1/413–1545* ▭ *AE, MC, V.*

★ $–$$$ ✕ **Náncsi Néni.** "Aunt Nancy's" out-of-the-way restaurant is irresistibly cozy. The dining room feels like a country kitchen: chains of paprikas and garlic dangle from the low wooden ceiling, and shelves along the walls are crammed with jars of home-pickled vegetables. On the Hungarian menu (which means large portions), turkey dishes are given a creative flair, such as breast fillets stuffed with apples, peaches, mushrooms, cheese, and sour cream. Special touches include an outdoor garden in summer and free champagne for all couples in love. Reservations are recommended. ✉ *Ördögárok út 80* ☎ *1/397–2742* ▭ *MC, V.*

★ $–$$ ✕ **Café Kör.** Vaulted ceilings, low lighting, and wood floors with Oriental-style rugs render a warm and classy atmosphere. Service is excellent. The kitchen has won tremendous popularity for its lighter touch on Hungarian and Continental meat dishes and ample salads. The Kör appetizer platter, generously piled with pâtés, Brie, vegetables, goose liver, salmon, and more, is perfect for sharing. Avoid the tables by the bathroom doors and immediately at the entrance. ✉ *Sas u. 17* ☎ *1/311-0053* ✍ *Reservations essential* ▭ *No credit cards* ⊗ *Closed Sun.*

$ ✕ **Tüköry Söröző.** At this traditional Hungarian spot, carnivores can sample the beefsteak tartare, topped with a raw egg; many say it's the best in town. ✉ *Hold u. 15* ☎ *1/269–5027* ▭ *AE, MC, V* ⊗ *Closed weekends.*

WHERE TO STAY

Some 30 million tourists come to Hungary every year, and the boom has encouraged hotel building; nearly every major Western chain has a full-service hotel here. If you arrive in Budapest without a reservation, go to the 24-hour Tribus Hotel Service or to one of the tourist offices at any of the train stations or at the airport.

WHAT IT COSTS In euros				
	$$$$	$$$	$$	$
FOR 2 PEOPLE	over €250	€150–€250	€90–€150	under €90

Hotel prices are for a standard double room in high season.

$$$$ **Budapest Hilton.** Built in 1977 around a 13th-century monastery adjacent to the Matthias Church, this perfectly integrated architectural wonder overlooks the Danube from the best site on Castle Hill. Every ample room has a remarkable view. Service is of the highest caliber. *Hess András tér 1–3, H-1014 1/488–6600; 800/445–8667 in U.S. and Canada 1/488–6688 www.danubiusgroup.com 295 rooms, 27 suites 3 restaurants, 2 bars AE, DC, MC, V.*

★ $$$$ **Hotel Inter-Continental Budapest.** This modern, riverside hotel consistently wins applause for its superior business facilities, friendly service, and gorgeous views across the Danube to Castle Hill. Sixty percent of the rooms face the river (and are slightly more expensive than those that don't). The rooms are decorated in pleasant pastels and furnished in the Central European Biedermeier style. The bustling lobby café serves fresh pastries and sandwiches. *Apáczai Csere János u. 12–14, H-1368 1/327–6333; 800/327–0200 in U.S. 1/327–6357 www.intercontinental.com 382 rooms, 16 suites 2 restaurants, pool, bar AE, DC, MC, V.*

$$$$ **Kempinski Hotel Corvinus Budapest.** Afternoon chamber music sets the tone at this sleek luxury hotel. Rooms are spacious, with elegant contemporary decor accented by geometric blond-and-black Swedish inlaid woods. The large, sparkling bathrooms are among the best in Budapest. *Erzsébet tér 7–8, H-1051 1/429–3777; 800/426–3135 in U.S. and Canada 1/429–4777 www.kempinski-budapest.com 340 rooms, 29 suites 4 restaurants, pool, bar AE, DC, MC, V.*

★ $$$$ **Le Méridien Budapest.** From Persian carpets and heavy silk draperies in the hushed lobby to polished walnut surfaces and twinkling chandeliers in the guest rooms, refined old-world elegance is everywhere. In a 1913 historic landmark building in the heart of downtown Pest, this five-star hotel is well situated for business as well as sightseeing. Breakfast and afternoon high tea are served under the lobby's soaring stained-glass cupola. *Erzsébet tér 9–10, H-1051 1/429–5500; 800/225–5843 in U.S. and Canada 1/429–5555 www.lemeridien-hotels.com 192 rooms, 26 suites Restaurant, pool, bar AE, DC, MC, V.*

$$$ **art'otel.** Boutique hotels may not be anything new in the West, but art'otel has the distinction of being the only one in Budapest, and it is a tribute to its class. From the multimillion-dollar art collection on the walls to the carpet and water fountains, the interior is all the work of one man, American artist Donald Sultan. Encompassing one new building and four 18th-century baroque houses on the Buda riverfront, the hotel adroitly blends old and new. Some rooms also have splendid views of Fisherman's Bastion and the Matthias Church. *Bem rakpart 16–19, H-1011 1/487–9487 1/487–9488 156 rooms, 9 suites Restaurant AE, DC, MC, V.*

$$$ **Budapest Marriott.** At this sophisticated yet friendly hotel near downtown Pest, every detail sparkles, including the marble floors and dark-wood paneling in the lobby. Stunning vistas open from every guest room, the ballroom, and even the outstanding fitness room. Most rooms have a balcony. *Apáczai Csere János u. 4, H-1052 1/266–7000; 800/228–9290 in U.S. and Canada 1/266–5000 www.marriotthotels.com 351 rooms, 11 suites 3 restaurants AE, DC, MC, V.*

$$$ **Danubius Hotel Gellért.** Built between 1912 and 1918, Budapest's most
Fodor'sChoice ★ renowned art nouveau hotel was favored by Otto von Habsburg, son of the last emperor. The Gellért is undergoing an incremental overhaul, which is refurnishing rooms in the original Jugendstil style. It's a good idea to inquire about completed rooms when you reserve. Weekend rates can be more affordable. All guests have free access to the monumental and ornate thermal baths, the most stunning in Budapest. ✉ *Gellért tér 1, H-1111* ☎ *1/385–2200* 📠 *1/466–6631* 🌐 *www.danubiusgroup.com* *220 rooms, 14 suites* *2 restaurants, pool, bar* 💳 *AE, DC, MC, V.*

$$$ **Danubius Thermal Hotel Helia.** A sleek Scandinavian design and a less hectic location upriver from downtown make this spa hotel on the Danube a change of pace from its Pest peers. Rooms are reasonably spacious and furnished in the ubiquitous "Scandinavian" style popularized by IKEA. The spa facilities are the most spotlessly clean in Budapest, and an on-site medical clinic caters to English-speaking clients—including everything from electrotherapy to fitness tests. The staff is friendly and helpful, and most of the comfortable rooms have Danube views. All room rates include use of the thermal bath and free parking. ✉ *Kárpát u. 62–64, H-1133* ☎ *1/452–5800* 📠 *1/452–5801* 🌐 *www.danubiusgroup.com* *254 rooms, 8 suites* *Restaurant, pool, bar* 💳 *AE, DC, MC, V.*

$$ **Carlton Budapest.** Tucked into an alley at the foot of Castle Hill, this spotless, modern hotel is a short walk via the Chain Bridge from business and shopping districts. The reception area is simply furnished in white and pale-gray contemporary shades. Rooms on the upper floors offer majestic Danube views. About half the rooms have a shower only. A buffet breakfast is included in the room price. ✉ *Apor Péter u. 3, H-1011* ☎ *1/224–0999* 📠 *1/224–0990* 🌐 *www.carltonhotel.hu* *95 rooms* *Bar* 💳 *AE, DC, MC, V.*

$$ **Victoria.** The stately Parliament building is visible from every room of this intimate establishment right on the Danube. The absence of conventioneers is a plus, and the location—an easy walk from Castle Hill and downtown Pest—couldn't be better. Room rates include breakfast. ✉ *Bem rakpart 11, H-1011* ☎ *1/457–8080* 📠 *1/457–8088* 🌐 *www.victoria.hu* *27 rooms, 1 suite* *Bar* 💳 *AE, DC, MC, V.*

$ **Kulturinov.** One wing of a magnificent 1902 neo-baroque castle now houses basic budget accommodations. Rooms come with two or three beds and are clean and peaceful; breakfast is included in the rates. The neighborhood—one of Budapest's most famous squares in the luxurious castle district—is magical. ✉ *Szentháromság tér 6, H-1014* ☎ *1/355–0122* 📠 *1/375–1886* *16 rooms* 💳 *AE, DC, MC, V.*

$ **Molnár Panzió.** Fresh air, peace, and quiet reign at this immaculate
Fodor'sChoice ★ guest house high above Buda on Széchenyi Hill, 20 minutes from downtown Pest. Rooms in the octagonal main house are polyhedral, clean, and bright; most have distant views of Castle Hill and Gellért Hill, and some have balconies. Twelve rooms in a building next door are more private and have superior bathrooms. Service is friendly and professional, and the restaurant is first-rate. A Finnish sauna and garden setting add to the pension's appeal. ✉ *Fodor u. 143, H-1124* ☎ *1/395–1873 or 1/395–1874* ☎📠 *1/395–1872* 🌐 *www.hotel-molnar.hu* *23 rooms* *Restaurant* 💳 *AE, DC, MC, V.*

NIGHTLIFE & THE ARTS

The Arts

The English-language *Budapest Sun* has a weekly calendar of entertainment and cultural events. *Budapest in Your Pocket,* published six times a year, has a thorough list of entertainment venues. Both are available at most newsstands. Buy tickets at venue box offices, your hotel desk, many tourist offices, or ticket agencies. Arts festivals begin to fill the calendar in early spring. The season's first and biggest, the **Budapest Spring Festival** (early to mid-March), showcases Hungary's best opera, music, theater, fine arts, and dance, as well as visiting foreign artists. The weeklong **BudaFest** opera and ballet festival (mid-August) takes place at the Opera House. Information and tickets are available from ticket agencies. For music in Budapest, try the **National Philharmonic Ticket Office** (☒ Mérleg u. 10 ☎ 1/318–0281). For various cultural events in Budapest, contact the **Vigadó Ticket Office** (☒ Vörösmarty tér 1 ☎ 1/327–4322).

Concerts & Musicals

Several excellent orchestras, such as the Budapest Festival Orchestra, are based in Budapest. Concerts frequently include works by Hungarian composers Bartók, Kodály, and Liszt. **Liszt Ferenc Zeneakadémia** (Franz Liszt Academy of Music; ☒ Liszt Ferenc tér 8 ☎ 1/342–0179) is Budapest's premier classical concert venue; orchestra and chamber music performances take place in its splendid main hall. Operettas and Hungarian renditions of popular Broadway musicals are staged at the **Operett Színház** (Operetta Theater; ☒ Nagymező u. 17 ☎ 1/353–2172). Classical concerts are also held at the **Pesti Vigadó** (Pest Concert Hall; ☒ Vigadó tér 2 ☎ 1/327–4322). The **Régi Zeneakadémia** (Old Academy of Music; ☒ Vörösmarty u. 35 ☎ 1/322–9804) is a smaller venue for chamber music. The 1896 **Vígszínház** (Comedy Theater; ☒ Pannónia út 8 ☎ 1/329–2340) presents mostly musicals.

Opera & Dance

In additional to the main venues for folk dancing, there are regular participatory folk-dance evenings—with instructions for beginners—at district cultural centers; consult the entertainment listings of *Where Budapest* and the *Budapest Sun* for schedules and locations, or check with a hotel concierge. Budapest has two opera houses, both of which stage opera and ballet. The main opera house is the gorgeous neo-Renaissance **Magyar Állami Operaház** (Hungarian State Opera House; ☒ Andrássy út 22 ☎ 1/353–0170), which is also the city's main venue for classical ballet. The rather plain **Erkel Színház** (Erkel Theater; ☒ Köztársaság tér ☎ 1/333–0540) is the State Opera's homely little theater.

From May through September, displays of Hungarian folk dancing take place at the **Folklór Centrum** (Folklore Center; ☒ Fehérvári út 47 ☎ 1/203–3868). The Hungarian State Folk Ensemble performs regularly at the **Budai Vigadó** (☒ Corvin tér 8 ☎ 1/201–3766). The young **Trafó Kortárs Művészetek Háza** (Trafo House of Contemporary Arts; ☒ Liliom u. 41 ☎ 1/456–2044) has become the hub of Budapest's modern and avant-garde dance and music productions.

Nightlife

Budapest is a lively city by night. Establishments stay open well past midnight, and Western European–style bars and British-style pubs have sprung up all over the city. For quiet conversation, hotel bars are a good choice, but beware the inflated prices. Expect to pay cash for your night on the town. The city also has its share of seedy go-go clubs and "cabarets," some of which have been shut down for scandalously excessive billing and physical intimidation and assault. Avoid places where women lingering nearby "invite" you in, and never order without first seeing the price.

Bars

The most popular of Budapest's Irish pubs and a favorite expat watering hole is **Becketts** (✉ Bajcsy-Zsilinszky út 72 ☎ 1/311–1035), where Guinness flows amid polished-wood and brass decor. **Buena Vista** (✉ Liszt Ferenc tér 4–5 ☎ 1/344–6303) in the heart of the "tér"—Listz Ferenc tér—has cool jazz trios and classy bar snacks. **Café Pierrot** (✉ Fortuna u. 14 ☎ 1/375–6971) is an elegant café and piano bar on a small street on Castle Hill.

Casinos

Most casinos are open daily from 2 PM until 4 or 5 AM and offer gambling in hard currency—usually euros—only. You must be 18 to enter a casino in Hungary. The popular **Las Vegas Casino** (✉ Roosevelt tér 2 ☎ 1/317–6022) is centrally located in the Atrium Hyatt Hotel. In an 1879 building designed by the architect Miklós Ybl, who also designed the Hungarian State Opera House, the **Várkert Casino** (✉ Miklós Ybl tér 9 ☎ 1/202–4244) is the most attractive in the city.

Jazz & Dance Clubs

Established Hungarian headliners and young up-and-comers perform nightly at the **Jazz Garden** (✉ Veres Pálné u. 44/a ☎ 1/266–7364). Shows start at 9 PM; there is a 700-Ft. cover charge.

A welcoming, gay-friendly crowd flocks to late-night hot spot **Café Capella** (✉ Belgrád rakpart 23 ☎ 1/318–6231) for glittery drag shows (held nightly) and DJ'd club music. There's a 500-Ft. drink minimum every night, plus a cover charge (500 Ft. Wed., Thurs., and Sun., 1,000 Ft. Fri. and Sat.). **Club Seven** (✉ Akácfa 7 ☎ 1/478–9030) has more than one place to play, including an elegant cocktail bar separate from the main room, where an outgoing Hungarian crowd grooves to a mixture of live jazz, rock cover bands, and recorded dance music.

SHOPPING

You'll find plenty of expensive boutiques, folk art and souvenir shops, and classical record shops on or around **Váci utca,** Budapest's pedestrian-only promenade. Browsing among some of the smaller, less touristy, more typically Hungarian shops in Pest—on the **Kiskörút** (Small Ring Boulevard) and **Nagykörút** (Great Ring Boulevard)—may prove more interesting and less pricey. Artsy boutiques are springing up in the section of District V south of Ferenciek tére toward the Danube and around Kálvin tér. **Falk Miksa utca,** north of Parliament, is home to some of the city's best antiques stores. You'll also encounter Transylvanian women dressed in colorful folk costume standing on busy sidewalks selling their own handmade embroideries and ceramics at rock-bottom prices. Look for them at **Moszkva tér, Jászai Mari tér,** outside the **Kossuth tér Metro,** and around **Váci utca.**

For a Hungarian take on a most American concept, you can visit one of the many mega-malls springing up around the city. **Mammut** (✉ Lövőház u. 2–6 ☎ 1/345–8020) is in central Buda, and is open on Sunday. There's also a cinema there. The **West End** (✉ Váci út 1–3 ☎ 1/238–7777), behind Nyugati train station in downtown Pest, comes complete with a waterfall, a T.G.I. Friday's restaurant, and a multiplex cinema.

A good place for special gifts, **Holló Műhely** (✉ Vitkovics Mihály u. 12 ☎ 1/317–8103) sells the work of László Holló, a master wood craftsman who has resurrected traditional motifs and styles of earlier centuries. There are lovely hope chests, chairs, jewelry boxes, candlesticks, and more, all hand-carved and hand-painted with cheery folk motifs—a predominance of birds and flowers in reds, blues, and greens.

Stores specializing in Hungary's excellent wines have become a trend in Budapest. Among the best of them is the store run by the **Budapest Bortársaság** (Budapest Wine Society; ✉ Batthyány u. 59 ☎ 1/212-0262). The cellar shop, at the base of Castle Hill, always has an excellent selection of Hungary's finest wines, chosen by the wine society's discerning staff, who will happily help you with your purchases. Tastings are held Saturday afternoons from 2 to 5.

Markets

The magnificent, cavernous, three-story **Vásárcsarnok** (Central Market Hall; ✉ Vámház körút 1–3) teems with shoppers browsing among stalls packed with salamis, red paprika chains, and other enticements. Upstairs you can buy folk embroideries and souvenirs.

A good way to find bargains (and adventure) is to make an early-morning trip out to **Ecseri Piac** (✉ Nagykőrösi út), a vast, colorful, chaotic flea market on the outskirts of Budapest. Try to go Saturday morning, when the most vendors are out. To get there, take Bus 54 from Boráros tér. Foreigners are a favorite target for overcharging, so be tough when bargaining.

BUDAPEST A TO Z

AIR TRAVEL

The most convenient way to fly between Hungary and the United States is with Malév Hungarian Airlines' nonstop direct service between JFK International Airport in New York and Budapest's Ferihegy Airport—still the only such flight that exists. Several other airlines offer connecting service from North America, including Austrian Airlines (through Vienna), British Airways (through London), Czech Airlines (through Prague), and Lufthansa (through Frankfurt or Munich).

Austrian Airlines ☎ 1/296-0660. **British Airways** ☎ 1/411-5555. **ČSA** (Czech Airlines) ☎ 1/318-3175. **Lufthansa** ☎ 1/429-8011. **Malév** ☎ 1/235-3535 ticketing, 1/235-3888 flight information. **Swiss** ☎ 1/328-5000.

AIRPORTS & TRANSFERS

Ferihegy Repülőtér, Hungary's only commercial airport with regularly scheduled service, is 24 km (15 mi) southeast of downtown Budapest. All non-Hungarian airlines operate from Terminal 2B; those of Malév, from Terminal 2A. (The older part of the airport, Terminal 1, no longer serves commercial flights, so the main airport is now often referred to as Ferihegy 2 and the terminals simply as A and B.)

Ferihegy Repülőtér ☎ 1/296-9696, 1/296-8000 same-day arrival information, 1/296-7000 same-day departure information.

TRANSFERS Many hotels offer their guests car or minibus transportation to and from Ferihegy, but all of them charge for the service. You should arrange for a pickup in advance. If you're taking a taxi, allow anywhere between 25 minutes during nonpeak hours and at least an hour during rush hours (7 AM–9 AM from the airport, 4 PM–6 PM from the city).

Official airport taxis are queued at the exit and overseen by a taxi monitor; their rates are fixed according to the zone of your final destination. A taxi ride to the center of Budapest will cost around 4,500 Ft. Trips to the airport are about 3,500 Ft. from Pest, 4,000 Ft. from Buda. Avoid taxi drivers who approach you before you are out of the arrivals lounge.

Minibuses run every half hour from 5:30 AM to 9:30 PM from the Hotel Kempinski on Erzsébet tér (near the main bus station and the Deák tér metro hub) in downtown Budapest. It takes almost the same time as taxis but costs only 800 Ft.

The LRI Airport Shuttle provides convenient door-to-door service between the airport and any address in the city. To get to the airport, call to arrange a pickup; to get to the city, make arrangements at LRI's airport desk. Service to or from either terminal costs 1,800 Ft. per person; since it normally shuttles several people at once, remember to allow time for a few other pickups or drop-offs.

6

BIKE TRAVEL

On Margaret Island in Budapest, Bringóvár, across from the Thermal Hotel, rents four-wheeled pedaled contraptions called *Bringóhintós,* as well as traditional two-wheelers; mountain bikes cost about 850 Ft. per hour, 2,500 Ft. for 24 hours. One-speeders cost less.

Bringóvár ✉ Hajós Alfréd sétány 1 ☎ 1/212-0330.

BUS TRAVEL TO & FROM BUDAPEST

Most buses to Budapest from the western region of Hungary and from Vienna arrive at Népliget station. In general, buses to and from the eastern part of Hungary go from Népstadion.

Népliget bus station ✉ Üllői út. 131 ☎ 1/219-8080. **Népstadion bus station** ✉ Hungária Körút 46-48 ☎ 1/252-1896.

EMERGENCIES

Doctors & Dentists **R-Klinika** ☎ 1/325-9999 private English-speaking.

Emergency Services **Ambulance** ☎ 104, 1/200-0100 private English-speaking. **Police** ☎ 107.

24-hour Pharmacies **Gyógyszertár** ☎ 1/311-4439 in Pest; 1/355-4691 in Buda.

ENGLISH-LANGUAGE MEDIA

Bestsellers ✉ Október 6 u. 11 ☎ 1/312-1295. **Central European University Academic Bookshop** ✉ Nádor u. 9 ☎ 1/327-3096.

TAXIS

Taxis are plentiful and are a good value, but be careful to avoid the also plentiful rogue cabbies. For a hassle-free ride, avoid unmarked "freelance" taxis; stick with those affiliated with an established company. Rather than hailing a taxi in the street, your safest bet is to order one by phone; a car will arrive in about 5 to 10 minutes. The average initial charge for taxis ordered by phone is 300 Ft., to which is added about 200 Ft. per kilometer (½ mi) plus 50 Ft. per minute of waiting time. The best rates are offered by Citytaxi, where English is spoken by the dispatchers, and Főtaxi.

Citytaxi ☎ 1/211-1111. **Főtaxi** ☎ 1/222-2222.

TOURS

IBUSZ Travel and Cityrama organize a number of unusual tours, including horseback riding, bicycling, and angling, as well as visits to the National Gallery. These companies provide personal guides on request. Also check at your hotel's reception desk. Chosen Tours offers an excellent three-hour combination bus and walking tour, "Budapest Through Jewish Eyes," highlighting the sights and cultural life of the city's Jewish community.

Chosen Tours ☎ 1/355-2022). **Cityrama** ✉ Báthori u. 22 ☎ 1/302-4382 🌐 www.cityrama.hu. **IBUSZ Travel** ✉ Petőfi tér 3 ☎ 1/318-5707 🌐 www.ibusz.hu.

BOAT TOURS From April through October, boats leave from the quay at Vigadó tér on 1½-hour cruises between the railroad bridges north and south of the Árpád and Petőfi bridges, respectively. The trip, organized by MAHART Tours, runs only on weekends and holidays until late April, then once or twice a day, depending on the season; the trip costs around 1,000 Ft.

MAHART Tours ☎ 1/484-4013.

BUS TOURS Cityrama offers a three-hour city bus tour (about 6,000 Ft. per person). Year-round, IBUSZ Travel sponsors three-hour bus tours of the city that cost about 6,000 Ft; starting from Roosevelt tér (in front of the Hotel Inter-Continental), they take in parts of both Buda and Pest. Specify whether you prefer live or recorded commentary.

Cityrama ✉ Báthori u. 22 ☎ 1/302-4382. **IBUSZ Travel** ✉ Petőfi tér 3 ☎ 1/318-5707. 🌐 www.ibusz.hu.

SINGLE-DAY TOURS Excursions farther afield include daylong trips to the Puszta (Great Plain), the Danube Bend, the Eger wine region, and Lake Balaton. IBUSZ Travel offers trips to the Buda Hills and stays in many of Hungary's historic castles and mansions.

TRAIN TRAVEL

Call the MÁV Passenger Service for train information. Call one of the three main train stations in Budapest for information during off-hours (8 PM–6 AM): Déli, Keleti, and Nyugati. Trains for Vienna usually depart from Keleti station, those for Lake Balaton from Déli.

MÁV Passenger Service ✉ Andrássy út 35 ☎ 1/461-5500 international, 1/461-5400 domestic **Déli** ✉ Alkotás u. ☎ 1/375-6293. **Keleti** ✉ Rákóczi út ☎ 1/313-6835. **Nyugati** ✉ Nyugati tér ☎ 1/349-0115.

TRANSPORTATION AROUND BUDAPEST

The Budapest Transportation Authority (BKV) runs the public transportation system—the Metro (subway) with three lines, buses, streetcars, and trolleybuses—and it's cheap, efficient, and simple to use. Most of it closes down around 11:30 PM, but certain trams and buses run on a limited schedule all night. A *napijegy* (day ticket) costs about 925 Ft. (a *turista-jegy*, or three-day tourist ticket, costs around 1,825 Ft.) and allows unlimited travel on all services within the city limits. Metro stations or newsstands sell single-ride tickets for about 120 Ft. You can travel on all trams, buses, and on the subway with this ticket, but you can't change lines or direction.

Bus, streetcar, and trolleybus tickets must be validated onboard—watch how other passengers do it. Metro tickets are validated at station entrances. Plainclothes agents wearing red armbands spot-check frequently, often targeting tourists, and you can be fined 1,500 Ft. if you don't have a validated ticket.

TRAVEL AGENCIES

American Express ✉ Déak Ferenc u. 10 ☎ 1/235-4330. **Travel One** ✉ Nádor u. 23 ☎ 1/312-6666. **Vista Travel Center** ✉ Andrássy út 1 ☎ 1/269-6032; 1/269-6033 air tickets; 1/328-4030 train, bus, and boat tickets and youth and student travel 🌐 www.vista.hu.

VISITOR INFORMATION

Vista Visitor Center/Café has created a uniquely welcoming environment for visitors seeking information about Budapest and Hungary. You can linger over lunch in the popular café, browse through brochures, and get information about (and make bookings for) tours, events, accommodations, and more from the young, English-speaking staff. Computer terminals are rented by the hour for Internet surfing and e-mailing; storage lockers are also available, as are international telephone stations with good rates.

The monthly *Where Budapest* magazine and the *Budapest in Your Pocket* guide are good sources. The English-language weekly *Budapest Sun* covers news, business, and culture and includes entertainment listings.

The Tourism Office of Budapest has developed the Budapest Card, which entitles holders to unlimited travel on public transportation; free admission to many museums and sights; and discounts on various purchases, entertainment events, tours, meals, and services from participating businesses. The cost is 3,950 Ft. for two days, 4,950 Ft. for three days; one card is valid for an adult plus a child under 14. Budapest Cards are sold at main metro ticket windows, tourist information offices, and hotels. IBUSZ Travel is a tour company and travel agency that organizes and runs tours all over the country but also helps book accommodations. Tourinform is the national tourism agency, which dispenses advice and information but will also help you book accommodations and transportation. You'll find Tourinform offices everywhere, not just in Budapest.

IBUSZ Travel ✉ Ferenciek tere 10 ☎ 1/485-2762; 06/20-944-9091; 1/317-7767 tours and programs ✉ Vörösmarty tér 6 ☎ 1/317-0532. **Tourinform** ✉ Vörösmarty tér, at Vigadó u. ☎ 1/438-8080; 06/80-660-044 24-hr automated telephone service ✉ Sütő u. 2 ☎ 1/317-9800 🌐 www.hungarytourism.hu 🌐 www.tourinform.hu. **Tourism Office of Budapest** ✉ Liszt Ferenc tér 11 ☎ 1/322-4098 🖷 1/342-9390 ✉ Nyugati pályaudvar ☎ 1/302-8580 ✉ Szentháromság tér ☎ 1/488-0453. **Tribus Hotel Service** ✉ Apáczai Csere János u. 1 ☎ 1/318-5776 or 1/266-8042. **Vista Visitor Center/Café** ✉ Paulay Ede u. 7 ☎ 1/267-8603.

Hungary Basics

To research prices, get advice from other travelers, and book travel arrangements, visit www.fodors.com.

BUSINESS HOURS

BANKS & OFFICES Banks are generally open weekdays 8–2 or 3, often with a one-hour lunch break around noon; most close at 2 on Friday.

MUSEUMS & SIGHTS Museums are generally open 10–6 Tuesday–Sunday; many stop selling admission 30 minutes before closing. Note that some museums change their opening and closing times by an hour or so at the beginning and end of peak seasons based on visitor traffic; it's prudent to double-check hours. Many have free admission one day a week.

SHOPS Department stores are open weekdays 10–5 or 6, Saturday until 1. Grocery stores are generally open weekdays 7–6 or 7, Saturday until 1; "nonstops" or *éjjeli-nappali* (24-hour convenience stores) are (theoretically) open 24 hours.

CUSTOMS & DUTIES

Objects for personal use may be imported freely. If you are over 16, you may also bring in 250 cigarettes or 50 cigars or 250 grams of tobacco, plus 2 liters of wine, 1 liter of spirits, 5 liters of beer, and 0.25 liters of perfume. A customs charge is made on gifts valued in Hungary at more than 27,000 Ft.

Keep receipts of any purchases from Konsumtourist, Intertourist, or Képcsarnok Vállalat. A special permit is needed for works of art, antiques, or objects of museum value. You are entitled to a VAT refund on new goods (i.e., not works of art, antiques, or objects of museum value) valued at more than 50,000 Ft.

Hungarian Customs and Revenue Office ✉ Hungária körút 112–114, Budapest, ☎ 1/470-4121.

EMBASSIES

Australia ✉ Királyhágó tér 8-9, Budapest, 1126 ☎ 1/457-9777.
Canada ✉ Budakeszi út 32, Budapest, 1121 ☎ 1/392-3360.
United Kingdom ✉ Harmincad u. 6, Budapest, 1051 ☎ 1/266-2888.
United States ✉ Szabadság tér 12, Budapest, 1054 ☎ 1/475-4400.

HOLIDAYS

January 1; March 15 (Anniversary of 1848 Revolution); Easter and Easter Monday; May 1 (Labor Day); Pentecost and Pentecost Monday; August 20 (St. Stephen's and Constitution Day); October 23 (1956 Revolution Day); November 1 (All Saints' Day); December 25, 26.

LANGUAGE

Hungarian (Magyar) tends to look and sound intimidating to English-speakers. Generally, older people speak some German, and many younger people speak at least rudimentary English, which has become the most popular language to learn. It's a safe bet that anyone in the tourist trade will speak at least one of the two languages.

MONEY MATTERS

The Hungarian Forint (HUF) has held steady against most major currencies in the last few years, though the weakening of the U.S. dollar has made Hungary more expensive for Americans in recent years. Nevertheless, even with inflation and the 25% value-added tax (VAT) in the service industry, enjoyable vacations with all the trimmings remain less expensive than in nearby Western European cities such as Vienna.

ATMS

Hundreds of ATMs have appeared throughout the capital and in other major towns. Some accept Plus network bank cards and Visa credit cards, others Cirrus and MasterCard. You can withdraw forints only (automatically converted at the bank's official exchange rate) directly from your account; most levy a 1% or $3 service charge. Many cash-exchange machines, into which you feed paper currency for forints, have also sprung up.

CURRENCY

The unit of currency is the forint (Ft.). There are bills of 200, 500, 1,000, 2,000, 5,000, 10,000, and 20,000 forints and coins of 1, 2, 5, 10, 20, 50, and 100 forints. At this writing, the exchange rate was 243 Ft. to the European euro, 226 Ft. to the U.S. dollar, 149 Ft. to the Canadian dollar, 368 Ft. to the pound sterling, and 134 Ft. to the Australian dollar. Always change money at a bank or an official exchange office.

TRAVELER'S CHECKS

Eurocheque holders can cash personal checks in all banks and in most hotels. Many banks now also cash American Express and Visa traveler's checks. American Express has a full-service office in Budapest, and a smaller branch on Castle Hill—in the Sissi Restaurant, closed January–mid-March—offers only currency exchange. Hungary's first Citibank offers full services to account holders, including a 24-hour ATM.

American Express ✉ Deák Ferenc u. 10, Budapest ☎ 1/235-4330 travel service; 1/235-4349 cardmember services 📠 1/267-2028 ✉ Sissi Restaurant, Dísz tér 8 ☎ 1/224-0118. **Citibank** ✉ Vörösmarty tér 4, Budapest.

PASSPORTS & VISAS

U.S., British, and Canadian citizens must carry a valid passport.

TAXES

VALUE-ADDED TAX (V.A.T.)

You are entitled to a V.A.T. (ÁFA, in Hungarian) refund on new goods (i.e., not works of art, antiques, or objects of museum value) valued at more than 50,000 Ft. (V.A.T. inclusive). Cash refunds are given only in forints. If you made your purchases by credit card, you can file for a credit to your card or to your bank account (again in forints), but this process is slow at best. If you intend to apply for the credit, make sure you get customs to stamp the original purchase invoice before you leave the country. For more information, pick up a tax refund brochure from any tourist office or hotel, or contact a tax refund agency. IBUSZ Travel Agency can assist individuals with tax refunds.

IBUSZ Travel Agency ✉ Ferenciak tere 10, Budapest, ☎ 1/485-2700.

TELEPHONES

COUNTRY & AREA CODES The country code for Hungary is 36.

DIRECTORY & OPERATOR ASSISTANCE For operator-assisted calls within Hungary, dial 191. Dial 198 for directory assistance throughout the country. Operators are unlikely to speak English. A safer bet is to consult *The Phone Book,* an English-language Yellow Pages–style telephone directory that also has cultural and tourist information; it's free in most major hotels, at many restaurants, and at English-language bookstores.

INTERNATIONAL CALLS Direct calls to foreign countries can be made from Budapest and all major provincial towns by dialing "00" and waiting for the international dialing tone; on pay phones the initial charge is 60 Ft. Operator-assisted international calls can be made by dialing 190. To reach a long-distance operator, call AT&T, MCI, or Sprint.

AT&T ☎ 06-800-01111. **MCI** ☎ 06-800-01411. **Sprint** ☎ 06-800-01877.

LOCAL CALLS The cost of a three-minute local call is 20 Ft. Pay phones use 10, 20, 50, and 100 Ft. coins. Most towns in Hungary can be dialed direct—dial 06 and wait for the buzzing tone, then dial the local number. It is unnecessary to use the city code (1) when dialing within Budapest.

Hungary's telephone system continues to be modernized, so phone numbers are subject to change—usually without forewarning and sometimes several times. A recording in Hungarian and English may provide the new number. If you're having trouble getting through, ask your concierge to check the number.

PUBLIC PHONES Gray card-operated telephones are common in Budapest and the Balaton region. The cards—available at post offices, newsstands, and kiosks—come in units of 60 (800 Ft.) and 90 (1,800 Ft.) calls.

COPENHAGEN

After you arrive at Copenhagen Airport on the isle of Amager, the taxi ride into the city will not stun you with a dramatic skyline or a seething metropolis. Instead, you will be greeted by elegant spires, green copper roofs, and cobbled streets. Copenhagen is not divided like most other cities into single-purpose districts, but is instead a rich, multilayered capital where people work, play, shop, and live throughout its central core. Surrounded by water, be it sea or canal, and connected by bridges and drawbridges, it has a maritime atmosphere.

EXPLORING COPENHAGEN

Copenhagen is a lively northern capital with about 1 million inhabitants. It's a city meant for walking; as you stroll through the cobbled streets and squares, you'll find that Copenhagen combines the excitement and variety of big-city life with a small-town atmosphere. If there's such a thing as a cozy metropolis, this is it.

The original city is built upon two main islands, Slotsholmen and Christianshavn, connected by drawbridges. The ancient heart of the city is intersected by two heavily peopled pedestrian streets—part of the five such streets known collectively as Strøget—and around them curls a maze of cobbled streets packed with tiny boutiques, cafés, and restaurants, all best explored on foot.

Numbers in the margin correspond to points of interest on the Copenhagen map.

⓮ **Amalienborg** (Amalia's Castle). During the fall and winter, when members of the royal family return to their principal residence, the Changing of the Guard is publicly announced each day at noon with the Royal Guard and band marching through the city. Amalienborg's other big attraction is the second division of the Royal Collection (the first is at Rosenborg), housed inside the **Amalienborg Museum.** The collection includes the study of King Christian IX (1818–1906) and the drawing room of his wife, Queen Louise. **Amalienhaven** (Amalia's Gardens) includes modern sculptures and manicured flower beds. ✉ *Amalienborg Pl., DK 1257* ☎ *33/12–08–08* ⊙ *May–Oct., daily 11–4; Nov.–Apr., Tues.–Sun. 11–4.*

8 **Børsen** (Stock Exchange). This edifice is believed to be the oldest such structure still in use, though it functions only on special occasions. It was built by the 16th-century monarch King Christian IV, a scholar, warrior, and the architect of much of the city. With its steep roofs, tiny windows, and gables, the building is one of Copenhagen's treasures. ✉ *Christiansborg Slotspl.* ⏲ *Not open to public.*

23 **Botanisk Have** (Botanical Garden). Copenhagen's 25-acre botanical garden, with a spectacular Palm House containing tropical and subtropical plants, upstages the palatial gardens of **Rosenborg Slot** (Rosenborg Castle). Also on the grounds are an observatory, a geological museum, and individual houses for cacti, orchids, and carnivorous plants. ✉ *Gothersg. 128* ☎ *35/32–22–40* 🌐 *www.botanic-garden.ku.dk* ⏲ *Grounds May–Sept., daily 8:30–6; Oct.–Apr., Tues.–Sun. 8:30–4. Palm House daily 10–3. Cactus House Wed., weekends, and holidays 1–3. Orchid House Wed., weekends, and holidays 2–3. Carnivorous Plants House daily 10–3.*

28 **Carlsberg Bryggeri** (Carlsberg Brewery). Granite elephants guard the entrance to the first Carlsberg brewery, opened in 1847; inside you can visit the draft-horse stalls and **Carlsberg Visitors' Centre,** and taste the local product. ✉ *Gl. Carlsbergvej 11* ☎ *33/27–13–14* 🌐 *www.carlsberg.dk* ⏲ *Tues.–Sun. 10–4; groups book in advance* ⏲ *Closed holidays and Dec. 23–31.*

10 **Christiania.** In the 1970s, a group of locals founded Christiania as a free town, independent from Denmark. They wanted to live in a community based on peace and freedom—an idea that's been variously challenged or tolerated by the Danish authorities through the years. The colony still exists, however, and Christiania has developed into a district for cultural tourism. With guided tours, cafés, restaurants, craftsmen's workshops, and music venues, it stays lively night and day. Be aware though, that Christiania has some seedy areas, where drug dealers are known to operate. ✉ *Prinsesseg.–Bådmandsst.* ☎ *32/57–96–70 guided tours* 🌐 *www.christiania.org.*

5 **Christiansborg Slot** (Christiansborg Castle). This massive gray complex, containing the Folketinget (Parliament House) and the Royal Reception Chambers, is situated on the site of the city's first fortress, which was erected in 1167 by Bishop Absalon. As a result of two disastrous fires in 1794 and 1884 that caused massive damage to the original structure, the present construction represents three architectural styles: the main building, finished in 1928, is in the new baroque style; the church shows the new classical architecture of the 19th century; and the riding ground is an example of grand 18th-century baroque. Also worth a visit are the remains of Bishop Absalon's fortress from 1167, which were excavated beneath the castle. ✉ *Christiansborg, Christiansborg Plads, DK 1218* ☎ *33/92–64–94 Christiansborg ruins; 33/37–55–00 Folketinget; 33/92–64–94 Royal Reception Chambers* 🌐 *www.ses.dk* ⏲ *Christiansborg ruins: May–Sept., daily 9:30–3:30; Oct.–Apr., Tues., Thurs., and weekends 9:30–3:30. Folketinget: guided tours Sun. 10–4. Royal Reception Chambers: May–Sept., daily 11–3; guided tours in English.*

18 **Den Lille Havfrue** (The Little Mermaid). This statue was erected in 1913 to commemorate Hans Christian Andersen's lovelorn creation. **Langelinie,** the spit of land you follow to reach the famed nymph, is thronged with promenading Danes and tourists—many of whom are themselves more absorbing to watch than the somewhat overrated sculpture. ✉ *Langelinie promenade.*

16 **Frihedsmuseet** (Liberty Museum). Evocative displays commemorate the heroic World War II Danish resistance movement, which saved 7,000

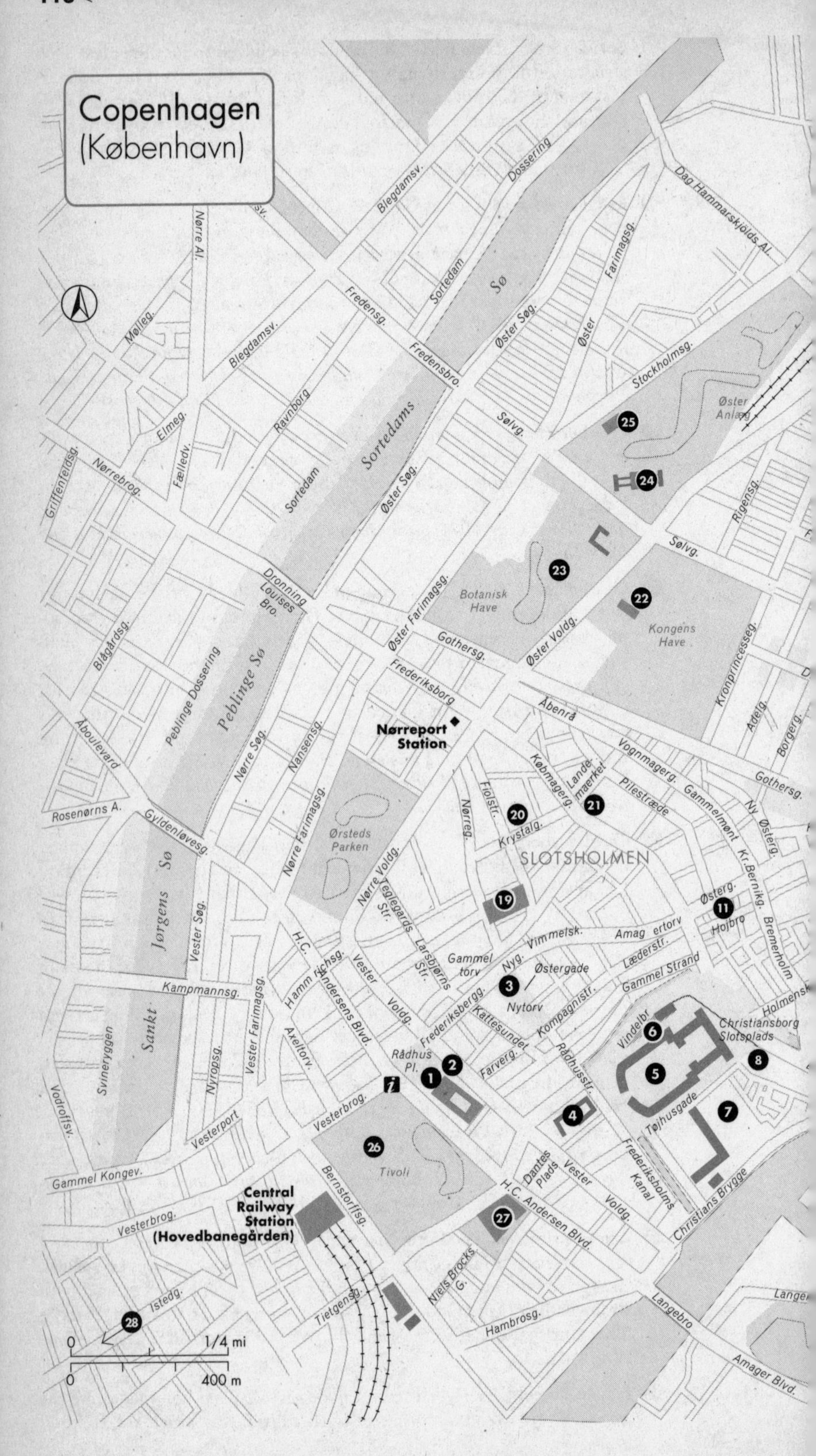
Copenhagen
(København)
Nørreport Station
Central Railway Station (Hovedbanegården)
Botanisk Have
Kongens Have
Østre Anlæg
Ørsteds Parken
Tivoli
SLOTSHOLMEN
Christiansborg Slotsplads
Sortedams
Peblinge Sø
Sankt Jørgens Sø
Sø
Dronning Louises Bro.
Gammel torv
Nytorv
Rådhus Pl.
Dantes Plads
Frederiksholms Kanal
Christians Brygge
Langebro
Amager Blvd.
H.C. Andersens Blvd.
Vesterbrog.
Gammel Kongev.
Istedg.
Tietgensg.
Hambrosg.
Niels Brocks G.
Bernstorffsg.
Nørrebrog.
Blegdamsv.
Fredensg.
Fredensbro.
Øster Søg.
Nørre Søg.
Vester Søg.
Østergade
Amagertorv
Gothersg.
Frederiksborg
Købmagerg.
Vimmelsk.
Kampmannsg.
0 1/4 mi
0 400 m

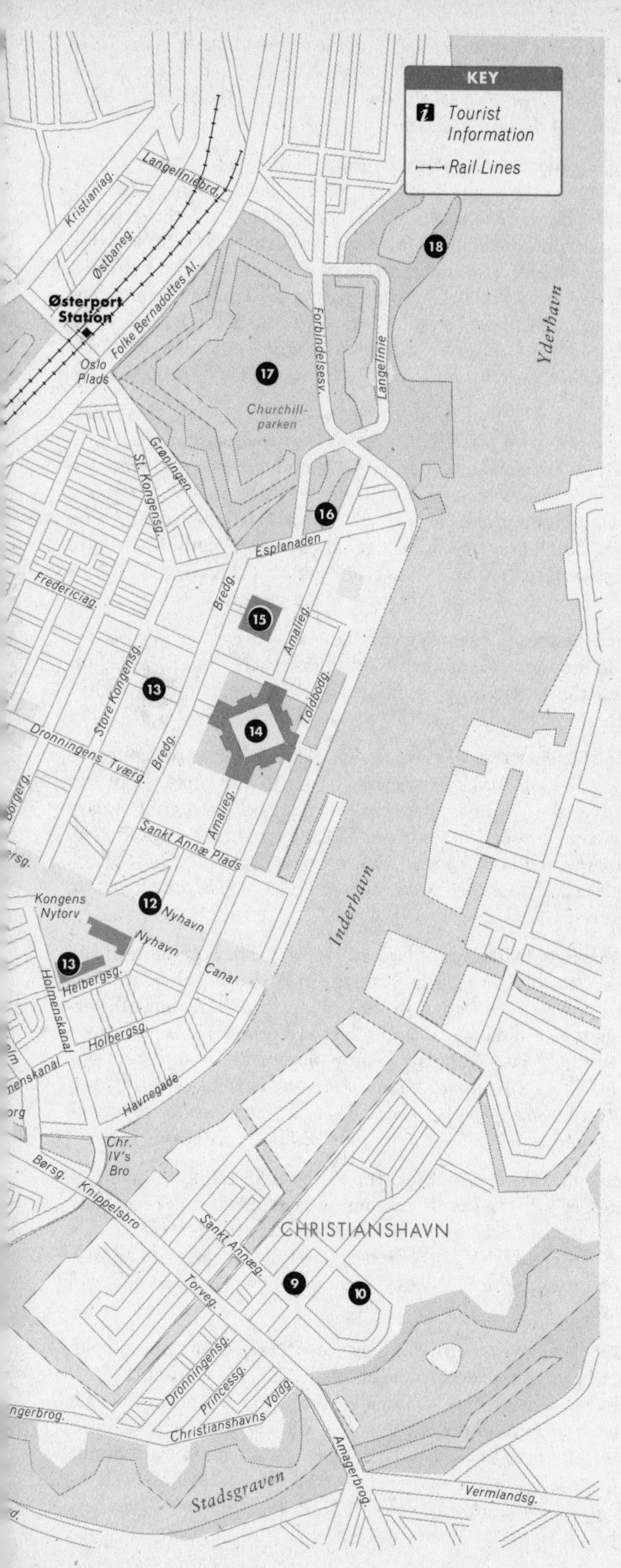

Amalienborg 14
Børsen 8
Botanisk Have 23
Carlsberg Bryggeri 28
Christiania 10
Christiansborg Slot 5
Den Lille Havfrue 18
Frihedsmuseet 16
Hirschsprungske Samling 25
Kastellet 17
Københavns Synagoge 20
Kongelige Bibliotek 7
Kunstindustrimuseet 15
Lurblæserne 2
Marmorkirken 13
Nationalmuseet 4
Nikolaj Kirken 11
Ny Carlsberg Glyptotek 27
Nyhavn 12
Rådhus Pladsen 1
Rosenborg Slot 22
Rundetårn 21
Statens Museum for Kunst 24
Strøget 3
Thorvaldsen Museum 6
Tivoli 26
Vor Frelsers Kirken 9
Vor Frue Kirken 19

Jews from the Nazis by hiding them and then smuggling them across to Sweden. ✉ *Churchillparken* ☎ *33/13–77–14* 🌐 *www.natmus.dk* ⏲ *May–Sept. 15, Tues.–Sat. 10–4, Sun. and holidays 10–5; Sept. 16–Apr. 30, Tues.–Sat. 11–3, Sun. and holidays 11–4.*

25 **Den Hirschsprungske Samling** (Hirschsprung Collection). This cozy museum focuses on works from Denmark's golden age of painting. The mid-19th-century school of Naturalism was pioneered by C. W. Eckersberg, whose pictures contain a remarkable wealth of detail and technical skill combined with limpid, cool, luminescent color. Other prominent painters of the movement included Christian Købke and Julius Exner. The Hirschsprungske also hosts a collection of paintings by the late-19th-century artists of the Danish Skagen school. ✉ *Stockholmsg. 20* ☎ *35/42–03–36* 🌐 *www.hirschsprung.dk* ⏲ *Thurs.–Mon. 11–4, Wed. 11–9.*

17 **Kastellet** (Citadel). Once surrounded by two rings of moats, this building was the city's main fortress during the 17th century, but, in a grim reversal during World War II, the Germans used it as one of their headquarters during their occupation of Denmark. The lovely green area around it, **Churchillparken,** cut throughout with walking paths, is a favorite among the Danes, who flock here on sunny weekends. If you have time, walk past the spired **St. Alban's,** an Anglican church at the park's entrance. ✉ *Churchillparken* ⏲ *Grounds daily 6 AM–sunset.*

20 **Københavns Synagoge** (Copenhagen Synagogue). This synagogue was designed by contemporary architect Gustav Friedrich Hetsch, who borrowed from the Doric and Egyptian styles in creating the arklike structure. ✉ *Krystalg. 12* ☎ *33/12–88–86* ⏲ *Daily services 4:15.*

7 **Det Kongelige Bibliotek** (Royal Library). This library houses the country's largest collection of books, newspapers, and manuscripts. Look for early records of the Viking journeys to America and Greenland. A dark marble annex next door, known as the Black Diamond, houses the **National Museum of Photography.** ✉ *Søren Kierkegaards Pl. 1* ☎ *33/47–47–47* 🌐 *www.kb.dk* ⏲ *Library, weekdays 10–5; Black Diamond, Mon.–Sat. 10–5.*

15 **Kunstindustrimuseet** (Museum of Decorative Art). The highlights of this museum's collection are a large assortment of European and Asian handicrafts, as well as ceramics, silver, and tapestries. The quiet library full of design tomes and magazines doubles as a primer for Danish functionalism with its Le Klint paper lamp shades and wooden desks. ✉ *Bredg. 68* ☎ *33/18–56–56* 🌐 *www.kunstindustrimuseet.dk* ⏲ *Special exhibits Tues.–Fri. 10–4, weekends and holidays noon–4; permanent exhibition Tues.–Fri. 1–4, weekends and holidays noon–4.*

2 **Lurblæserne** (Lur Blower Column). Topped by two Vikings blowing an ancient trumpet called a *lur,* this column was erected in 1914 and displays a good deal of artistic license: the lur dates from 1500 BC—the Bronze Age—whereas the Vikings lived a mere 1,000 years ago. The monument is a starting point for sightseeing tours of the city. ✉ *East side of Rådhus Pl.*

13 **Marmorkirken** (Marble Church). The ponderous Frederikskirke, commonly called Marmorkirken, is a baroque church that was begun in 1749 in costly Norwegian marble. It was finally completed and consecrated in 1894. Perched around the exterior are 16 statues of various religious leaders from Moses to Luther, and below them stand sculptures of outstanding Danish ministers and bishops. ✉ *Frederiksgade 4* ☎ *33/15–01–44* 🌐 *www.marmorkirken.dk* ⏲ *Mon. and Tues. and Thurs. and Fri. 10–5, Wed. 10–6, weekends noon–5.*

4 **Nationalmuseet** (National Museum). The extensive collections of this museum chronicle the cultural history of Denmark right up to modern times and include relics such as original Viking runic stones. Also on display are Egyptian, Greek, and Roman antiquities. The children's museum is an excellent place for kids to learn history and, although the original relics are secured behind glass, there are plenty of curiosities for kids to play with, including period clothing to dress up in and an old-world school to explore. ✉ *Ny Vesterg. 10* ☎ *33/13–44–11* 🌐 *www.natmus.dk* ⏲ *Tues.–Sun. 10–5.*

11 **Nikolaj Kirken** (St. Nicholas Church). In Østergade, the easternmost of the streets that make up Strøget, you cannot miss the green spire of this building. The present structure was built in the 20th century; the previous one, dating from the 13th century, was destroyed by fire in 1728. Today the building is no longer a church but an art gallery and exhibition center. ✉ *Nikolaj Pl. 10* ☎ *33/93–16–26* 🌐 *www.nikolaj-ccac.dk* ⏲ *Daily noon–5.*

★ 27 **Ny Carlsberg Glyptotek** (New Carlsberg Sculpture Museum). An elaborate neoclassical building houses one of Europe's greatest collections of Greek and Roman antiquities and sculpture. A modern wing displays an impressive pre-impressionist collection, including works from the Barbizon school; impressionist paintings, with works by Monet, Sisley, and Pissarro; and a post-impressionist section, with 50 Gauguin paintings plus 12 of his rare sculptures. ✉ *Dantes Pl. 7* ☎ *33/41–81–41* 🌐 *www.glyptoteket.dk* ⏲ *Tues.–Sun. 10–4.*

★ 12 **Nyhavn** (New Harbor). You can relax with a beer in one of the most gentrified parts of the city. Previously popular with sailors, the area's restaurants and cafés now outnumber tattoo shops. The name refers to both the street and the canal leading southeast out of Kongens Nytorv. The area still gets rowdy on long, hot summer nights, with Danes reveling against the backdrop of a fleet of old-time sailing ships and well-preserved 18th-century buildings. Hans Christian Andersen lived at numbers 18 and 20. ✉ *East of Kongens Nytorv.*

1 **Rådhus Pladsen** (City Hall Square). This hub of Copenhagen's commercial district is the best place to start a stroll. The Renaissance-style building dominating it is the **Rådhuset** (City Hall), completed in 1905. A statue of Copenhagen's 12th-century founder, Bishop Absalon, sits atop the main entrance. Inside, you can see the first World Clock, an astrological timepiece invented and built by Jens Olsen and set in motion in 1955. You can take a guided tour partway up the 350-foot tower for a panoramic view. ✉ *Square in Strøget at eastern end of Vesterbrog. and western end of Frederiksbergg.* ☎ *33/66–33–66* ⏲ *Rådhus weekdays 8–5; Tower tours Oct.–May, Mon.–Sat. at noon; June–Sept., weekdays 10, noon, and 2, Sat. at noon.*

22 **Rosenborg Slot** (Rosenborg Castle). This Renaissance palace—built by jack-of-all-trades Christian IV—houses the Crown Jewels, as well as a collection of costumes and royal memorabilia. Don't miss Christian IV's pearl-studded saddle. ✉ *Øster Voldg. 4A* ☎ *33/15–32–86* ⏲ *Nov.–Apr., Tues.–Sun. 11–2; May and Sept., daily 10–4; June–Aug., daily 10–5; Oct., daily 11–3.*

21 **Rundetårn** (Round Tower). It is said that Peter the Great of Russia drove a horse and carriage up the 600 feet of the inner staircase of this round tower, built as an observatory in 1642 by Christian IV. It's a formidable climb, but the view is worth it. At the base of the tower is the university church, Trinitas; halfway up you can take a break in the tower's art

gallery. ✉ *Købmagerg. 52A* ☎ *33/73–03–73* 🌐 *www.rundetaarn.dk* ⏲ *Tower: Sept.–May, Mon.–Sat. 10–5, Sun. noon–5; June–Aug.; Mon.–Sat. 10–8, Sun. noon–8.*

24 **Statens Museum for Kunst** (National Art Gallery). The original 100-year-old building and a new, modern structure house works of Danish art from the golden age (early 19th century) to the present, as well as paintings by Rubens, Dürer, the impressionists, and other European masters. The space also includes a children's museum, an amphitheater, a documentation center and study room, a bookstore, and a restaurant. ✉ *Sølvg. 48–50* ☎ *33/74–84–94* 🌐 *www.smk.dk* ⏲ *Tues.–Sun. 10–5, Wed. 10–8.*

3 **Strøget.** Beginning at City Hall, Frederiksberggade is the first of five pedestrian streets making up Strøget, Copenhagen's shopping district and promenade area. Stroll past the cafés and trendy boutiques to the twin squares of **Gammeltorv** and **Nytorv.** The bustling sidewalks have the festive aura of a street fair. Marking the end of Strøget is a square known as **Kongens Nytorv** (King's New Market), where you'll find **Det Kongelige Teater** (The Royal Theater).

6 **Thorvaldsens Museum.** The 19th-century Danish sculptor Bertel Thorvaldsen, whose tomb stands in the center of the museum, was greatly influenced by the statues and reliefs of classical antiquity. In addition to his own works, the collection includes drawings and paintings by others that illustrate the influence of Italy on the artists of Denmark's golden age. ✉ *Bertel Thorvaldsen Pl. 2* ☎ *33/32–15–32* 🌐 *www.thorvaldsensmuseum.dk* ⏲ *Tues.–Sun. 10–5.*

26 Fodor's Choice ★ **Tivoli.** Each year from May to September, about 4 million people pass through the gates of this unique little amusement park. More sophisticated than a typical fun fair, Tivoli has pantomime theater on an open-air stage, elegant restaurants, and frequent classical, jazz, and rock concerts. Try to see Tivoli at least once by night when the trees, Chinese pagoda, and main fountain are brilliantly illuminated. In the month leading up to Christmas, a festive Christmas market is held at Tivoli. ✉ *Vesterbrog. 3* ☎ *33/15–10–01* 🌐 *www.tivoli.dk* 🎫 *DKr45 plus DKr10 per attraction ticket (each attraction requires from 1 to 5 tickets)* ⏲ *Mid-Apr.–mid-Sept., Sun.–Tues. 11–11, Wed. and Thurs. 11–midnight, Fri. and Sat. 11–1* AM*; mid-Nov.–Dec. 23, Sun.–Wed. 11–9, Fri. and Sat. 11–10.*

9 **Vor Frelsers Kirke** (Our Savior's Church). Legend has it that the staircase climbing up the exterior of the fantastic golden spire on this 1696 baroque structure was built spiraling in the wrong direction. The architect, upon reaching the top of his creation, realized what he had done and decided to jump to his death because of it. ✉ *Skt. Annæg. 29* ☎ *32/57–27–98* 🌐 *www.vorfrelserskirke.dk* ⏲ *Apr.–Aug., daily 11–4:30; Sept.–Mar., daily 11–3:30* ⏲ *Tower closed Nov.–Mar., and in inclement weather.*

19 **Vor Frue Kirke** (Church of Our Lady). This has been Copenhagen's cathedral since 1924, but the site itself has been a place of worship since the 13th century, when Bishop Absalon built a chapel here. The spare, neoclassical facade is a 19th-century innovation repairing damage suffered during Nelson's bombing of the city in 1801. If the church is open, you can see Thorvaldsen's marble sculptures of Christ and the Apostles. ✉ *Nørregade 8* ☎ *33/37–65–40* 🌐 *www.koebenhavnsdomkirke.dk* ⏲ *Daily 8–5.*

WHERE TO EAT

Food is one of the great pleasures in Copenhagen, and traditional Danish cuisine can span the entire spectrum of prices. You can order a light lunch of smørrebrød, snack from a store *kolde bord*, or dine on lobster, Limfjord oysters, and shrimp. You can also dig into fast food Danish-style in the form of *pølser* (hot dogs) sold from wagons on the street. Team this with pastries from one of the numerous bakeries (the shops displaying an upside-down gold pretzel), and you've got yourself a meal on the go. Many restaurants close from Christmas to the New Year.

WHAT IT COSTS In Danish Krone

	$$$$	$$$	$$	$
PER PERSON	over 200	150–200	100–150	under 100

Prices are per person for a main course.

★ $$$$ ✕ **Kommandanten.** The 300-year-old building houses Scandinavia's most celebrated restaurant. The ever varying, set-course menu follows whatever is freshest at the market, including sliced breast of guinea fowl with quail eggs or wild duck with confit. Expect adventurous French cooking of the highest caliber and impeccable service to match. If possible, book before your trip—this epicurean favorite seats only 50. ✉ *Ny Adelgade 7* ☎ *33/12–09–90* 🌐 *www.kommandanten.dk* 💳 *AE, DC, MC, V* ⏲ *Closed Sun. and holidays.*

$$$$ Fodor's Choice ★ ✕ **Kong Hans Kælder.** In this hushed cloister with medieval vaulted ceilings you'll find one of the city's outstanding restaurants. The menu is classic French, with a focus on the creative use of local ingredients, including mushrooms brought by bicycle from nearby forests. You haven't tasted salmon like this before, prepped for 36 hours in the restaurant's own cold smoker. Save room for the outstanding selection of cheeses, many homemade. ✉ *Vingårdstr. 6* ☎ *33/11–68–68* 🌐 *www.konghans.dk* 💳 *AE, DC, MC, V* ⏲ *Closed Mon. No lunch.*

$$$$ ✕ **Krogs.** Gilded mirrors, high ceilings, and 19th-century paintings make up a study in old-fashioned opulence, as does the menu here, with its grilled lobster, poached fish in Parmesan bouillon, and the locally famous bouillabaisse. Krogs's excellent reputation is reflected in its high prices. ✉ *Gammel Strand 38* ☎ *33/15–89–15* 🌐 *www.krogs.dk* ✍ *Reservations essential* 💳 *AE, DC, MC, V* ⏲ *Closed Sun.*

$$$ ✕ **El Mesón.** Ceiling-hung pottery, knowledgeable waiters, and a top-notch menu make this Copenhagen's best Spanish restaurant. Choose carefully for a moderately priced meal, which might include beef spiced with spearmint, lamb with honey sauce, or paella. ✉ *Hauser Pl. 12* ☎ *33/11–91–31* 💳 *AE, DC, MC, V* ⏲ *Closed Sun. No lunch.*

$$$ ✕ **Els.** Said to be a favorite of the queen, Els is a piece of Danish history, largely unchanged since it first catered to the theater crowd in 1853. The flip side of the restaurant's proud past is an occasionally supercilious attitude toward foreigners, but a touch of stiffness seems in keeping with the 19th-century tiles, Renaissance-style painted muses, and the antique samovar at the bar. The fine French cooking has a focus on fish and wild game and fowl. ✉ *Store Strandstr. 3* ☎ *33/14–13–41* 🌐 *www.restaurant-els.dk* ✍ *Reservations essential* 💳 *AE, DC, MC, V.*

$$$ Fodor's Choice ★ ✕ **Ida Davidsen.** Five generations old, this world-renowned lunch spot has become synonymous with smørrebrød. Choose from these creative open-face sandwiches, piled high with such ingredients as pâté, bacon, and steak tartare, or even kangaroo, or try smoked duck served with a

beet salad and potatoes. ✉ *St. Kongensg. 70* ☎ *33/91–36–55* 🌐 *www.idadavidsen.dk* ✍ *Reservations essential* 💳 *AE, DC, MC, V* ⊙ *Closed weekends and July. No dinner.*

$$$ ✕ **Le Sommelier.** Classic French country cooking is served here with a dazzling selection of wines by the glass. The steamed mussels are popular, as is homemade foie gras, and pigeon breast with mushrooms and glazed beets. Take a break from worrying about secondhand smoke and give in to the elegant surroundings. You can select from 30 brands of cigarettes to go with any of 12 varieties of coffee. ✉ *Bredg. 63–65* ☎ *33/11–45–15* 🌐 *www.lesommelier.dk* 💳 *AE, DC, MC, V.*

★ **$$$** ✕ **Reinwalds.** The chairs here are exceptionally comfortable, and there's enough space between tables to afford diners some privacy. And that's just the start. The food is French, and artfully presented; the three- to five-course menu changes monthly, according to what's in season. The waiters are attentive and will help you navigate the menu. ✉ *Farveg. 15* ☎ *33/91–82–80* 🌐 *www.reinwalds.dk* 💳 *AE, MC, DC, V* ⊙ *Closed Sun.*

$$$ ✕ **Schiøtt's.** Seasonal freshness as well as the cook's mood will each have bearing on the menu selection for this Copenhagen favorite. A cozy cellar restaurant offering superb creative fare in the Provençal style, this is an elegant experience for a very fair price. The walk along Christianshavn Canal on a warm summer night can only add pleasure to the overall experience. ✉ *Overgaden neden vandet 17* ☎ *32/54–54–08* 🌐 *www.schioetts.dk* 💳 *AE, DC, MC, V* ⊙ *Closed Sun.*

$–$$ ✕ **Riz Raz.** An inexpensive all-you-can-eat buffet is the draw of this Middle Eastern restaurant. Health-conscious patrons fill up on lentils, bean salads, and falafel. Standouts on the menu are the grilled dishes, both meat and fish. On a corner just off Strøget, behind the church of Vor Frue Kirke, this restaurant packs in the young and old, families and singles, every night. Reservations are essential on weekends. ✉ *Kompagnistr. 20* ☎ *33/15–05–75* ✉ *Store Kannikestr. 19* ☎ *33/32–33–45* 🌐 *www.rizraz.dk* 💳 *DC, MC, V.*

$ ✕ **Atlas Bar.** This health-food basement café serves excellent meals to a steady stream of students and hipsters. The food is mostly East Asian–influenced such as the tasty Manila Chicken. Atlas also has a large number of vegetarian dishes. ✉ *Larsbjørnsstr. 18* ☎ *33/15–03–52* 💳 *DC, MC, V* ⊙ *Closed Sun.*

$ ✕ **Molevitten.** This spacious café-restaurant-club combo serves Malaysian and other Asian-inspired dishes. A house favorite is *Laksasuppe,* a Malaysian salmon soup. Molevitten is spread over three floors and caters to brunch, lunch, and dinner crowds. After dinner on weekend evenings, the sound is turned up and it turns into a dance club. ✉ *Nørrebrog. 13* ☎ *35/39–49–00* 🌐 *www.molevitten.com* 💳 *MC, V.*

WHERE TO STAY

Copenhagen is well served by its hotels, which are mostly comfortable and well run. Most but not all Danish hotels include breakfast in the room rate. Summertime reservations are a good idea, but if you should arrive without one, try the hotel booking service at the Danish Tourist Board. They can also give you a "same-day, last-minute price," which is about DKr500 for a double hotel room. This service will also locate rooms in private homes, with rates starting at about DKr300 for a double. Also try the **Ungdoms Information lodging service** (✉ Rådhusstr. 13 ☎ 33/73–06–50 🌐 www.ui.dk) for listings of budget lodgings, or their youth information center "Use It" (🌐 www.useit.dk).

WHAT IT COSTS In Danish Krone				
	$$$$	$$$	$$	$
FOR 2 PEOPLE	over 1,700	1,400–1,700	900–1,400	under 900

Hotel prices are for a standard double room in high season.

$$$$ **Radisson SAS Scandinavia.** Strategically located on the principal route between the airport and the city center, this is one of northern Europe's largest hotels and Copenhagen's token skyscraper. A spacious lobby with cool, recessed lighting and streamlined furniture leads into the city's first and only casino. Though somewhat institutional in design, the guest rooms are large, with every modern convenience. A visit to the 25th-floor restaurant, The Dining Room (DKr200–DKr350), is a delightful experience both for its food and its view. Breakfast is not included in the rates. *Amager Blvd. 70, DK 2300 KBH S 33/96–50–00 33/96–55–00 www.radissonsas.com 542 rooms, 43 suites 4 restaurants, indoor pool AE, DC, MC, V.*

★ $$$$ **D'Angleterre.** The grande dame of Copenhagen hotels has undergone major changes but still retains its period charm. The rooms are done in pinks and blues, with overstuffed chairs and antique escritoires and armoires. Bathrooms sparkle with brass, mahogany, and marble. If you are a light sleeper, choose a back room; there is some noise from the nearby bars, and from early-morning delivery trucks. *Kongens Nytorv 34, DK 1021 KBH K 33/12–00–95 33/12–11–18 www.remmen.dk/hda.htm 118 rooms, 19 suites Restaurant, indoor pool AE, DC, MC, V.*

$$$ **Clarion Neptun.** A central Copenhagen hotel that's been in business for nearly 150 years, the Neptun shows no signs of flagging. Rooms are decorated with blond wood. Though charming, this hotel can become very busy with tour groups. Moreover, because it's an old building, room sizes vary greatly, and so does the noise from the street. *Skt. Annæ Pl. 18–20, DK 1250 KBH K 33/96–20–00 33/96–20–66 133 rooms Restaurant, bar AE, DC, MC, V.*

$$$ **71 Nyhavn.** In a 200-year-old warehouse overlooking the old ships of Nyhavn, this quiet hotel is a good choice for those seeking privacy. The maritime interiors have been preserved with their original plaster walls and exposed brick. Rooms are tiny but cozy, with warm woollen spreads, dark woods, soft leather furniture, and exposed timbers. *Nyhavn 71, DK 1051 KBH K 33/43–62–00 33/43–62–01 www.71nyhavnhotelcopenhagen.dk 150 rooms, 3 suites Restaurant, bar AE, DC, MC, V.*

$$$ **Phoenix Copenhagen.** This luxury hotel has crystal chandeliers and gilt touches everywhere. It's popular for business trips and with cruise passengers. Suites and executive-class rooms have Biedermeier-style furniture and 18-karat-gold-plated bathroom fixtures. Standard rooms are small, about 9 by 15 feet. If you're a light sleeper, ask for a room above the second floor to avoid street noise. *Bredg. 37, DK 1260 KBH K 33/95–95–00 33/33–98–33 www.phoenixcopenhagen.dk 206 rooms, 7 suites Restaurant, bar AE, DC, MC, V.*

$$–$$$ **Ascot.** A charming old building downtown, this family-owned hotel has classical columns at the entrance, and an excellent breakfast buffet. Rooms are colorful and cozy; bathrooms are on the small side. A few rooms have kitchenettes. *Studiestr. 61, DK 1554 KBH K 33/12–60–00 33/14–60–40 www.ascothotel.dk 161 rooms, 4 suites Bar AE, DC, V.*

$$–$$$ **Copenhagen Admiral.** Overlooking old Copenhagen and Amalienborg, the monolithic Admiral, with its massive stone walls and rows of

tiny windows, was once a grain warehouse. It now has minimalist, airy rooms with jutting beams and modern prints. ✉ *Toldbodg. 24–28, DK 1253 KBH K* ☎ *33/74–14–14* 📠 *33/74–14–16* 🌐 *www.admiralhotel.dk* *314 rooms, 52 suites* *Restaurant, bar* 💳 *AE, DC, V.*

$–$$ **Missionhotellet Nebo.** This budget hotel is comfortable and well maintained, with a friendly staff. The dormlike guest rooms are furnished with industrial carpeting, polished pine furniture, and soft duvet covers. Baths, showers, and toilets are clustered at the center of each hallway. There is a breakfast restaurant downstairs. ✉ *Istedg. 6, DK 1650 KBH V* ☎ *33/21–12–17* 📠 *33/23–47–74* 🌐 *www.nebo.dk* *88 rooms, 40 with bath; 9 suites* 💳 *AE, DC, MC, V.*

$ **Cab-Inn Scandinavia.** Winter business travelers, budget-minded summer backpackers, and cost-conscious families converge on Copenhagen's answer to Japanese-style hotel minirooms. The shiplike "cabins" are brightly decorated with standard furnishings, including a small, wall-hung desk with chair. The breakfast buffet will set you back DKr50. Those wanting a little more comfort should request a Commodore Class room for an extra DKr100. ✉ *Vodroffsvej 55, DK 1900 FR C* ☎ *35/36–11–11* 📠 *35/36–11–14* 🌐 *www.cabinn.dk* *201 rooms with shower* *Bar* 💳 *AE, DC, MC, V.*

$ **Ibis Copenhagen Triton.** Despite seedy surroundings, this streamlined hotel attracts a cosmopolitan clientele thanks to a central location in Vesterbro. The large rooms, in blond wood and warm tones, have state-of-the-art fixtures. The buffet breakfast included in the price is exceptionally generous, and the staff is friendly. There are also family rooms, each with a separate bedroom and fold-out couch. ✉ *Helgolandsg. 7–11, DK 1653 KBH K* ☎ *33/31–32–66* 📠 *33/31–69–70* 🌐 *www.ibishotel.dk* *123 rooms* *Bar* 💳 *AE, DC, MC, V.*

NIGHTLIFE & THE ARTS

The English-language ***Copenhagen This Week*** (🌐 www.ctw.dk) prints information about musical and theatrical happenings, as well as special events and exhibitions. The Web site **www.aok.dk** is a good resource for finding nightlife, bars, and cafés around Copenhagen—it also has similar information about other Danish cities. Concert and festival information is available from the **Dansk Musik Information Center** (DMIC; ✉ Gråbrødre Torv 16 ☎ 33/11–20–66 🌐 www.mic.dk).

Copenhagen's main theater and concert season runs from September through May, and tickets can be obtained either directly from theaters and concert halls or from ticket agencies; ask your hotel concierge for advice. **Billetnet** (☎ 70/15–65–65 🌐 www.billetnet.dk), a box-office service available at all large post offices, has tickets for most major events. Keep in mind that same-day purchases at the box office at **Tivoli** (✉ Vesterbrogade 3 ☎ 33/15–10–12 ⏲ weekdays 11–5) are half price if you pick them up after noon.

The Arts

Classical Music

The **Tivoli Concert Hall** (✉ Tietensg. 20 ☎ 33/15–10–12) has more than 150 concerts each summer. There are performances by a host of Danish and foreign soloists, conductors, and orchestras.

Theater

Det Kongelige Teater (The Royal Theater) (✉ Kongens Nytorv ☎ 33/69–69–33 🌐 www.kgl-teater.dk) is the place to go for ballet or opera. If you're in search of experimental opera, then **Den Anden Opera** (✉ Kronprinsensg. 7 ☎ 33/32–38–30 🌐 www.denandenopera.dk) is worth a visit.

London Toast Theatre (✉Kochsvej 18 ☎33/22–86–86 🌐www.londontoast.dk) hosts English-language theater. Modern dance is popular in Copenhagen, and **Dansescenen** (✉ Øster Fælled Torv 34 ☎ 34/35–83–00 🌐 www.dansescenen.dk) is a good place to see it. **Kanonhallen** (✉ Øster Fælled Torv 37 ☎ 70/15–65–65 🌐 www.kanonhallen.net) showcases up-and-coming modern dancers. **Nyt Dansk Danseteater** (✉ Guldbergsg. 29A ☎ 35/39–87–87 🌐 www.nddt.dk) is very active in promoting Scandinavian modern dance.

Nightlife

Many of the city's restaurants, cafés, bars, and clubs stay open after midnight, some as late as 5 AM. Copenhagen is famous for jazz, but you'll find nightspots catering to musical tastes ranging from hip-hop to ballroom music. In the inner city, most discos open at 11 PM, have a cover charge (about DKr50), and charge steep prices for drinks.

Jazz

The upscale **Copenhagen Jazz House** (✉ Niels Hemmingsensg. 10 ☎ 33/15–26–00 🌐 www.jazzhouse.dk) draws major international names and the cream of Danish jazz. Jam sessions often take place spontaneously. It's a dimly lit, smoky place, but with ample room on two floors. **La Fontaine** (✉ Kompagnistr. 11 ☎ 33/11–60–98) is Copenhagen's quintessential jazz dive, with sagging curtains, impenetrable smoke, and crusty lounge lizards. It is a must for jazz lovers.

Live Music

Copenhagen has a fine selection of music clubs where you can hear excellent local talent, as well as smaller or up-and-coming international acts. **Loppen** in Christiania (✉ Bådsmandsstræde 43 ☎ 32/57–84–22 🌐 www.loppen.dk) is a medium-size concert venue where you can catch some of the bigger names in Danish music, as well as budding international artists.**Vega** (✉ Enghavevej 40 ☎ 32/25–70–11 🌐 www.vega.dk) hosts established pop, rock, urban, and jazz artists and is a great spot for catching the next big act. It also has a dance club and bar where the action continues into the wee hours. **Rust** (✉ Guldbergsg. 8 ☎ 35/24–52–00 🌐 www.rust.dk) and **Stengade 30** (✉ Stengade 18 [address does not match name of club] ☎ 35/36–09–38 🌐 www.stengade30.dk) are smaller clubs, mainly featuring rock, pop, and urban acts. They double as bars that remain open through the night.

Nightclubs & Dancing

A younger crowd gets down on the floor at the fashionable **Park Café** (✉ Østerbrog. 79 ☎ 35/42–62–48 🌐 www.parkcafe.dk). Mellower folks come for brunch when the place transforms back into a café. **Rosie McGee's** (✉ Vesterbrog. 2A ☎ 33/32–19–42 🌐 www.rosiemcgee.dk) is a very popular Irish-style pub (but with Mexican food) that has dancing. **Sabor Latino** (✉ Vester Voldg. 85 ☎ 26/16–46–96 🌐 www.saborlatino.dk) is a United Nations of disco, with an international crowd dancing to salsa and other Latin beats. Among the most enduring clubs is **Woodstock** (✉ Vesterg. 12 ☎ 33/11–20–71), where a mixed crowd grooves to 1960s classics.

SHOPPING

Strøget's pedestrian streets are synonymous with shopping.

Specialty Shops

Just off Østergade is **Pistolstræde,** a typical old courtyard filled with intriguing boutiques. Farther down the street toward the City Hall Square is a compound that includes several important stores: **Georg Jensen**

(✉ Amagertorv 4 ☎ 33/11–40–80 🌐 www.georgjensen.com), one of the world's finest silversmiths, gleams with silver patterns and jewelry. Don't miss the **Georg Jensen Museum** (✉ Amagertorv 6 ☎ 33/14–02–29), which showcases glass and silver creations ranging from tiny, twisted-glass shot glasses to an $85,000 silver fish dish. **Royal Copenhagen Porcelain** (✉ Amagertorv 6 ☎ 33/13–71–81 🌐 www.royalcopenhagen.com) carries both old and modern china, plus porcelain patterns and figurines.

Along Strøget, at furrier **Birger Christensen** (✉ Østerg. 38 ☎ 33/11–55–55 🌐 www.birger-christensen.com), you can peruse designer clothes and chic furs. **Illum** (✉ Østerg. 52 ☎ 33/14–40–02) is a department store that has a fine basement grocery and eating arcade. Don't confuse Illum with **Illums Bolighus** (✉ Amagertorv 10 ☎ 33/14–19–41), where designer furnishings, porcelain, quality clothing, and gifts are displayed in near-gallery surroundings. **Magasin** (✉ Kongens Nytorv 13 ☎ 33/11–44–33 🌐 www.magasin.dk), one of the largest department stores in Scandinavia, offers all kinds of clothing and gifts, as well as an excellent grocery department.

COPENHAGEN A TO Z

AIRPORTS & TRANSFERS

The main airport for both international and domestic flights is Kastrup International Airport, 10 km (6 mi) southeast of town.

TRANSFERS Trains from the airport's subterranean train station take 12 minutes to zip into Copenhagen's main station. Buy a ticket upstairs in the airport train station (DKr22,50); three trains an hour go into Copenhagen, and a fourth travels farther to Roskilde. Bus service to the city is frequent, but not as convenient. Bus 250S takes you to Rådhus Pladsen, the city-hall square. A taxi ride takes 15 minutes and costs about DKr170, though slightly more after 4 PM and weekends.

BIKE TRAVEL

It is estimated that more than half the 5.5 million Danish population rides bicycles regularly. Bike rental costs DKr75–DKr200 a day, though weekly rates are available, with a deposit of DKr500–DKr1,000. Contact Københavns Cykler or Østerport Cykler, both stores that belong to the Rent a Bike company.

Bike Rental **Københavns Cykler** ✉ Central Station, Reventlowsg. 11 ☎ 33/33–86–13 🌐 www.rentabike.dk. **Østerport Cykler** ✉ Oslo Plads 9 ☎ 33/33–85–13 🌐 www.rentabike.dk.

BUS & METRO TRAVEL WITHIN COPENHAGEN

Buses, suburban trains, and metro trains all operate on the same ticket system, which divides Copenhagen into three zones. Tickets are validated on both a time and a distance basis: on a basic ticket, which costs DKr15, you can travel anywhere within a single zone for an hour. You can purchase a discounted *klip kort* (clip card), equivalent to 10 basic tickets, for DKr95. Buses and suburban trains run from 5 AM (6 AM on Sunday) to 12:30 AM daily with a reduced network of buses continuing through the night. The Metro runs from 5 AM to 1 AM weekdays, and all night on weekends.

Buses and suburban trains ☎ 36/13–14–15 buses; 70/13–14–15 S-trains (wait for the Danish message to end and an operator will answer) 🌐 www.ht.dk; www.rejseplan.dk. **Metro** ☎ 70/15–16–15 🌐 www.m.dk.

CAR TRAVEL

Copenhagen is a city for walkers, not drivers. To maintain the charm of its pedestrian streets, the city has a complicated one-way road system and it's difficult to park. Leave your car in the garage: attractions are relatively close together, and public transportation is excellent.

EMERGENCIES

For emergency dental service you should go directly to the Tandlægevagt (Emergency Dental Clinic). It's open weekdays from 8 AM to 9:30 PM; weekends and holidays from 10 AM to noon. Expect to pay cash. Fees for the Doctor Emergency Service are also payable in cash only. The hours for this service are 4 PM to 8 AM, but house calls are made after 10 PM. You will need to make an appointment by phone. Note that nighttime visits include a DKr350 surcharge. Casualty Wards (Skadestuen) are open 24 hours.

Doctors & Dentists **Casualty Wards** ✉ Italiensvej 1, DK 2300 Amager area ☎ 32/34-35-00 ✉ Niels Andersens Vej 65, DK 2900 Hellerup ☎ 39/77-37-64 or 39/77-39-77 🌐 www.laegevagten.dk. **Doctor Emergency Service** ☎ 70/13-00-41 or 44/53-44-00. **Emergency Dental Clinic** ✉ Tandlægevagt: Oslo Plads 14, DK 2100.

Emergency Services **Auto Rescue/Falck** ☎ 70/10-20-30 🌐 www.falck.dk. **Police, fire, ambulance** ☎ 112.

24-hour Pharmacies **Steno Apotek** ✉ Vesterbrog. 6C ☎ 33/14-82-66. **Sønderbro Apotek** ✉ Amagerbrog. 158, Amager area ☎ 32/58-01-40 🌐 www.apoteket.dk.

ENGLISH-LANGUAGE MEDIA

The Copenhagen Post is a weekly newspaper covering Danish news in English. You can pick it up for DKr15 at some bookstores and information kiosks, the tourist office, and a few hotels. It has a helpful "In & Out" section with reviews and listings of entertainment events taking place in town.

Bookstores **Arnold Busck** ✉ Købmagerg. 49 ☎ 33/73-35-00 🌐 www.arnoldbusck.dk. **Boghallen** ✉ Rådhus Pl. 37 ☎ 33/47-25-60 🌐 www.boghallen.dk. **Copenhagen Post** 🌐 www.cphpost.dk.

TAXIS

The computer-metered Mercedeses and Volvos are not cheap. The base charge is DKr22, plus DKr10–DKr13 per kilometer (½ mi). A cab is available when it displays the green sign FRI (free); you can either hail a cab (though this can be difficult outside the center), pick one up at a taxi stand, or call the number listed below. Surcharges apply if you order a cab by night or if you are out of town.

Taxa 4x35 ☎ 35/35-35-35 🌐 www.35353535.dk.

TOURS

The Danish Tourist Board can recommend multilingual private guides for individual needs; travel agents have details on hiring a limousine and guide. The tourist board also has full details relating to excursions outside the city, including visits to castles (such as Hamlet's castle) and the Viking Ship Museum; they can also supply maps and brochures, and recommend walking tours.

BOAT TOURS Viewing Copenhagen from the canals is a must in the summer months. The relaxing hour-long tours give a great impression of the city; they're run by DFDS Canal Tours and depart from Nyhavn and Gammel Strand. If the weather is nice, go for a *Nettobåd* (Netto boat) tour, which departs from Holmens Church. It lasts an hour and is cheaper than Canal Tours, whose only advantage is a cover to shield against the rain (or sun). Boat tours are available April through mid-October and run every half hour from 10 to 5.

Fees & Schedules **DFDS Canal Tours** ☎ 32/64-04-31 🌐 www.canal-tours.dk. **Nettobåd** ☎ 32/54-41-02 🌐 www.netto-baadene.dk.

BUS TOURS Several bus tours leave from the Lur Blowers Column in Rådhus Pladsen 57, late March–September.

Fees & Schedules **Copenhagen Excursions** 32/54-06-06 www.cex.dk. **Open Top Tours** 32/66-00-00 www.sightseeing.dk.

TRAIN TRAVEL

Copenhagen's clean and convenient central station, Hovedbanegården, is the hub of the country's train network. Intercity express trains leave hourly, from 6 AM to 10 PM, for principal towns in Fyn and Jylland. To find out more, contact DSB.

DSB Information 70/13-14-15 www.dsb.dk. **Hovedbanegården,** south of Vesterbrog 33/14-17-01 www.hovedbanen.dk.

TRANSPORTATION AROUND COPENHAGEN

The Copenhagen Card offers unlimited travel on buses, and metro and suburban trains (S-trains) as well as admission to some 60 museums and sights throughout both metropolitan Copenhagen and Malmö, Sweden. They're valid for a limited time, though, and therefore worthwhile only if you're planning a nonstop, intense sightseeing tour. You can buy the card, which costs about DKr225 (24 hours), DKr375 (48 hours), or DKr500 (72 hours)—half price for children ages 5 to 11—at bus/train stations, tourist offices, and hotels or from travel agents.

TRAVEL AGENCIES

Carlson Wagonlit Travel Vester Farimagsg. 7, 2nd fl. 33/63-78-78 www.cwt.dk. **DSB Rejsebureau** Central Station 70/13-14-18 www.dsb.dk. **Spies** Rådhuspl. 45-47 70/10-42-00 www.spies.dk.

Denmark Basics

To research prices, get advice from other travelers, and book travel arrangements, visit www.fodors.com.

BUSINESS HOURS

BANKS & OFFICES Banks in Copenhagen are open weekdays 9:30–4. Some branches have extended hours on Thursday until 6. Several bureaux de change, including those at Copenhagen's central station and airport, stay open until 10 PM. Outside Copenhagen, banking hours vary.

MUSEUMS & SIGHTS Museums are generally open Tuesday to Saturday from 10–3 or 11–4. Opening hours in winter are usually shorter, and some museums close entirely for the season, especially on the smaller islands. Check local papers or ask at tourist offices.

SHOPS Small shops and boutiques are open for business weekdays 10–5:30, and most stay open on Friday until 7. On Saturday, doors close at 1 or 2, though larger department stores remain open until 5. On the first Saturday of every month, most shops stay open until 4. Call ahead to verify weekend opening hours for specific stores. Grocery stores in the Nørreport neighborhood are open until 11 PM or even longer. The same goes for many kiosks in the big towns.

EMBASSIES

All embassies are in Copenhagen.

Canada Kristen Bernikowsg. 1, DK 1105 KBH K 33/48-32-00 www.canada.dk.

Ireland Østbanegade 21, DK 2100 KBH, Ø 35/42-32-33 35/43-18-58.

South Africa Gammel Vartov Vej 8, DK 2900 Hellerup 39/18-01-55 www.southafrica.dk.

United Kingdom Kastelsvej 36-40, DK 2100 KBH Ø 35/44-52-00 www.britishembassy.dk.

United States Dag Hammarskjölds Allé 24, DK 2100 KBH Ø 35/55-31-44 www.usembassy.dk.

HOLIDAYS

January 1; Easter (Thursday–Monday); Common Prayer (May); Ascension (40 days after Easter); June 5 (Constitution Day; shops close at noon); Whitsun/Pentecost (Sunday and Monday; 10 days after Ascension); December 24–26.

LANGUAGE

Danish is a difficult tongue for foreigners—except those from Norway and Sweden—to understand, let alone speak. Danes are good linguists, however, and almost everyone, except perhaps elderly people in rural areas, speaks English well in addition to a third language, usually French or German.

MONEY MATTERS

Denmark's economy is stable, and inflation remains reasonably low. The standard of living is high, but so is the cost, especially for such luxury items as alcohol and cigarettes. The steepest prices are found in Copenhagen, and the least expensive areas are Fyn and Jylland. Some sample prices: cup of coffee, DKr15–DKr25; bottle of beer, DKr20–DKr30; soda, DKr20-DKr25; ham sandwich, DKr20–DKr40; 1½-km (1-mi) taxi ride, DKr50.

CURRENCY The monetary unit in Denmark is the krone (kr., DKr, or DKK), which is divided into 100 øre. Denmark has not adopted the euro, but the Danish krone is firmly bound to it. Exchange rates are typically about DKr7.5 to 1€. At press time (summer 2003), the krone stood at DKr8.20 to the U.S. dollar, DKr5.27 to the Canadian dollar, DKr11.71 to the pound sterling, DKr4.50 to the Australian dollar, DKr3.49 to the New Zealand dollar, and DKr1.05 to the South African rand. Most credit cards are accepted in Denmark, though it is wise to inquire about American Express and Diners Club beforehand. Traveler's checks can be cashed in banks as well as in many hotels, restaurants, and shops.

TAXES

VALUE-ADDED TAX (V.A.T.) Non-EU citizens can save 20% (less a handling fee) off the purchase price if they shop in one of the hundreds of stores throughout Denmark displaying the TAX FREE SHOPPING sign. The purchased merchandise must be valued at more than DKr300. The taxes will be refunded after submitting the application with customs authorities at their final destination before leaving the EU.

TELEPHONES

COUNTRY & AREA CODES The country code for Denmark is 45.

DIRECTORY & OPERATOR ASSISTANCE Dial 118 to speak with an operator for local assistance. Most operators are fluent in English. For an international operator, dial 113.

INTERNATIONAL CALLS Dial 00, then the country code, area code, and the desired number. You can reach AT&T, MCI, and Sprint by dialing one of the access codes.
Access Codes AT&T ☎ 800/10010. **MCI WorldCom** ☎ 800/10022. **Sprint** ☎ 800/10877.

LOCAL CALLS Pay phones take DKr1, DKr2, DKr5, DKr10, and DKr20 coins. Area codes must be used even when calling a local number, which means dialing all eight digits for numbers anywhere within the country. Calling cards, which are sold at Danish State Railways stations, post offices, and some kiosks, are increasingly necessary as pay phones that accept coins become a thing of the past.

DUBLIN

Europe's most intimate capital has changed forever—the soul of the Republic of Ireland has experienced the nation's most dramatic period of transformation since the Georgian era. For the last decade, Dublin has ridden the back of its "Celtic Tiger" economy, and massive construction cranes hover over both shiny new hotels and old Georgian houses. Irish culture became hot: patriot Michael Collins became a Hollywood box-office star, Frank McCourt's *Angela's Ashes* conquered best-seller lists in the United States and was made into a movie, and *Riverdance* became a worldwide old-Irish mass jig. Because of these and other attractions, travelers are coming to Dublin in ever-greater numbers, so don't be surprised if you stop to consult your map in Temple Bar—the city's most happening neighborhood—and are swept away by the ceaseless flow of bustling crowds. Dublin has become a colossally entertaining, engaging city—all the more astonishing considering its gentle size. The quiet pubs and little empty backstreets might be harder to find now that Dublin has been "discovered," but a bit of effort and research can still unearth the old "Dear Dirty Dumpling," a city that Joyce was so fond of.

EXPLORING DUBLIN

Originally a Viking settlement, Dublin sits on the banks of the River Liffey, which divides the city north and south. The liveliest round-the-clock spots, including Temple Bar and Grafton Street, are on the south side, although several construction projects on the north side have helped to reinvigorate these areas. The majority of the city's most notable buildings date from the 18th century—the Georgian era—and, although many of its finer Georgian buildings disappeared in the redevelopment of the '70s, enough remain to recall the elegant Dublin of centuries past. Dublin is small as capital cities go, with a compact downtown area, and the best way to soak in the full flavor of the city is on foot. Literary Dublin can still be recaptured by following the footsteps of Leopold Bloom's progress, as described in James Joyce's *Ulysses*. Trinity College, alma mater of Oliver Goldsmith, Jonathan Swift, and Samuel Beckett, among others, is a green, Georgian oasis, alive with students.

South of the Liffey

South of the Liffey are graceful squares and fashionable terraces from Dublin's elegant heyday, and, interspersed with some of the city's leading sights, this area is perfect for an introductory city tour. You might begin at O'Connell Bridge—as Dublin has no central focal point, most natives regard it as the city's Piccadilly Circus or Times Square—then head south down Westmoreland Street to Parliament House. Continue on to Trinity College—the Book of Kells, Ireland's greatest artistic treasure, is on view here—then eastward to Merrion Square and the National Gallery; south to St. Stephen's Green and Fitzwilliam Square; west to Dublin's two beautiful cathedrals, Christ Church and St. Patrick's; and end with dinner in a Temple Bar restaurant overlooking the Liffey.

Numbers in the margin correspond to points of interest on the Dublin map.

2 **Bank of Ireland.** With a grand facade of marble columns, the Bank of Ireland is one of Dublin's most striking buildings. Across the street from the front entrance to Trinity College, the Georgian structure was once the home of the Irish Parliament. Built in 1729, it was bought by the Bank of Ireland in 1803. Hurricane-shape rosettes adorn the coffered ceiling in the pastel-hued, colonnaded, clerestoried main banking hall, once the Court of Requests, where citizens' petitions were heard. Just down the hall is the original House of Lords, with tapestries, an oak-paneled nave, and a 1,233-piece Waterford glass chandelier; ask a guard to show you in. Visitors are welcome during normal banking hours; a brief guided tour is given every Tuesday at 10:30, 11:30, and 1:45. ✉ *2 College Green* ☎ *01/677–6801* ⏲ *Mon.–Wed. and Fri. 10–4, Thurs. 10–5; Arts Center Tues.–Fri. 10–4, Sat. 2–5, Sun. 10–1.*

17 **Christ Church Cathedral.** You'd never know from the outside that the first Christianized Danish king built a wooden church at this site in 1038; thanks to the extensive 19th-century renovation of its stonework and trim, the cathedral looks more Victorian than Anglo-Norman. Stone construction was begun in 1172 by Strongbow, a Norman baron and conqueror of Dublin for the English crown. The vast, sturdy **crypt,** with its 12th- and 13th-century vaults, is Dublin's oldest surviving structure and the building's most notable feature. At 6 PM on Wednesday and Thursday you can enjoy a choral evensong. ✉ *Christ Church Pl. and Winetavern St.* ☎ *01/677–8099* ⏲ *Weekdays 9:45–5, weekends 10–5.*

16 **City Hall.** Facing the Liffey from the top of Parliament Street, this grand Georgian municipal building (1769–79), once the Royal Exchange, was designed by Thomas Cooley. It has a central rotunda encircled by 12 columns, a fine mosaic floor, and 12 frescoes depicting Dublin legends and ancient Irish historical scenes. The building now holds an exhibition tracing the evolution of Ireland's 1,000-year-old capital. ✉ *Dame St.* ☎ *01/672–2204* 🌐 *www.dublincorp.ie* ⏲ *Mon.–Sat. 10–5:15, Sun. 2–5.*

15 **Dublin Castle.** The film *Michael Collins* captures this structure's near-indomitable status in the city. Just off Dame Street behind City Hall, the grounds of the castle encompass a number of buildings, including the **Record Tower,** a remnant of the original 13th-century Norman castle that was the seat of English power in Ireland for almost 7½ centuries,

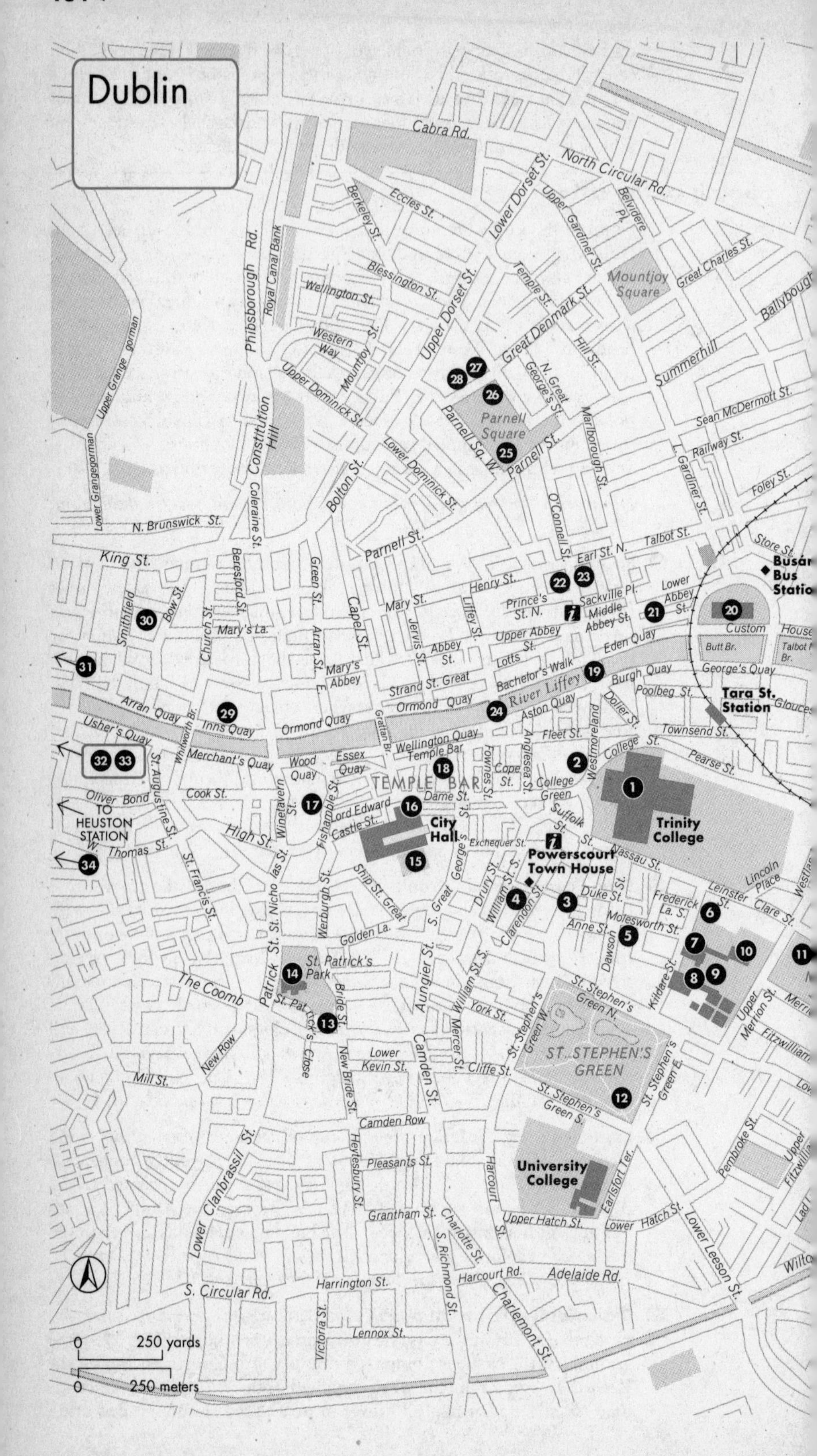
Dublin
Cabra Rd.
North Circular Rd.
Eccles St.
Berkeley St.
Lower Dorset St.
Upper Gardiner St.
Belvidere Pl.
Phibsborough Rd.
Royal Canal Bank
Blessington St.
Wellington St.
Temple St.
Mountjoy Square
Great Charles St.
Ballybough
Upper Dorset St.
Great Denmark St.
Hill St.
Western Way
Mountjoy St.
Upper Grange gorman
Upper Dominick St.
Parnell Square
N. Great George's St.
Summerhill
Sean McDermott St.
Constitution Hill
Parnell Sq. W.
Parnell St.
Marlborough St.
Railway St.
Lower Grangegorman
Lower Dominick St.
Bolton St.
L. Gardiner St.
Foley St.
N. Brunswick St.
Coleraine St.
O'Connell St.
Parnell St.
Talbot St.
Store St.
King St.
Beresford St.
Green St.
Earl St. N.
Busár Bus Station
Henry St.
Lower Abbey St.
Smithfield
Bow St.
Church St.
Mary's La.
Capel St.
Mary St.
Liffey St.
Prince's St. N.
Sackville Pl.
Middle Abbey St.
Custom House
Arran St. E.
Jervis St.
Abbey St.
Upper Abbey St.
Lotts
Eden Quay
Butt Br.
Talbot Br.
Mary's Abbey
Strand St. Great
Bachelor's Walk
River Liffey
Burgh Quay
George's Quay
Arran Quay
Whitworth Br.
Ormond Quay
Aston Quay
Poolbeg St.
Tara St. Station
Usher's Quay
Inns Quay
Ormond Quay
Grattan Br.
Wellington Quay
Fleet St.
Doller St.
Townsend St.
Merchant's Quay
Essex Quay
Temple Bar
Fownes St.
Anglesea St.
Westmoreland
College St.
Pearse St.
St. Augustine St.
Wood Quay
TEMPLE BAR
Cope St.
College Green
Oliver Bond
TO HEUSTON STATION
Cook St.
Winetavern St.
Fishamble St.
Lord Edward
Dame St.
Suffolk St.
Trinity College
High St.
Castle St.
City Hall
Exchequer St.
Powerscourt Town House
Nassau St.
Lincoln Place
W. Thomas St.
St. Nicholas St.
Ship St. Great
George's St.
Drury St.
William St. S.
Clarendon St.
Duke St.
Dawson St.
Frederick La. S.
Leinster St.
Clare St.
Westland
St. Francis St.
Werburgh St.
Golden La.
S. Great
Anne St.
Molesworth St.
Kildare St.
St. Patrick's Park
Aungier St.
William St. S.
St. Stephen's Green N.
Upper Merrion St.
Merrion
The Coomb
Patrick St.
St. Patrick's Close
Bride St.
York St.
St. Stephen's Green W.
Fitzwilliam
New Row
Lower Kevin St.
Camden St.
Mercer St.
Cliffe St.
ST. STEPHEN'S GREEN
St. Stephen's Green E.
Mill St.
New Bride St.
St. Stephen's Green S.
Camden Row
Lower Clanbrassil St.
Heytesbury St.
Pleasants St.
Pembroke St.
Upper Fitzwilliam
University College
Harcourt St.
Earlsfort Ter.
Grantham St.
Charlotte St.
Upper Hatch St.
Lower Hatch St.
Lower Leeson St.
S. Richmond St.
Harcourt Rd.
Adelaide Rd.
S. Circular Rd.
Harrington St.
Charlemont St.
Victoria St.
Lennox St.
0 250 yards
0 250 meters

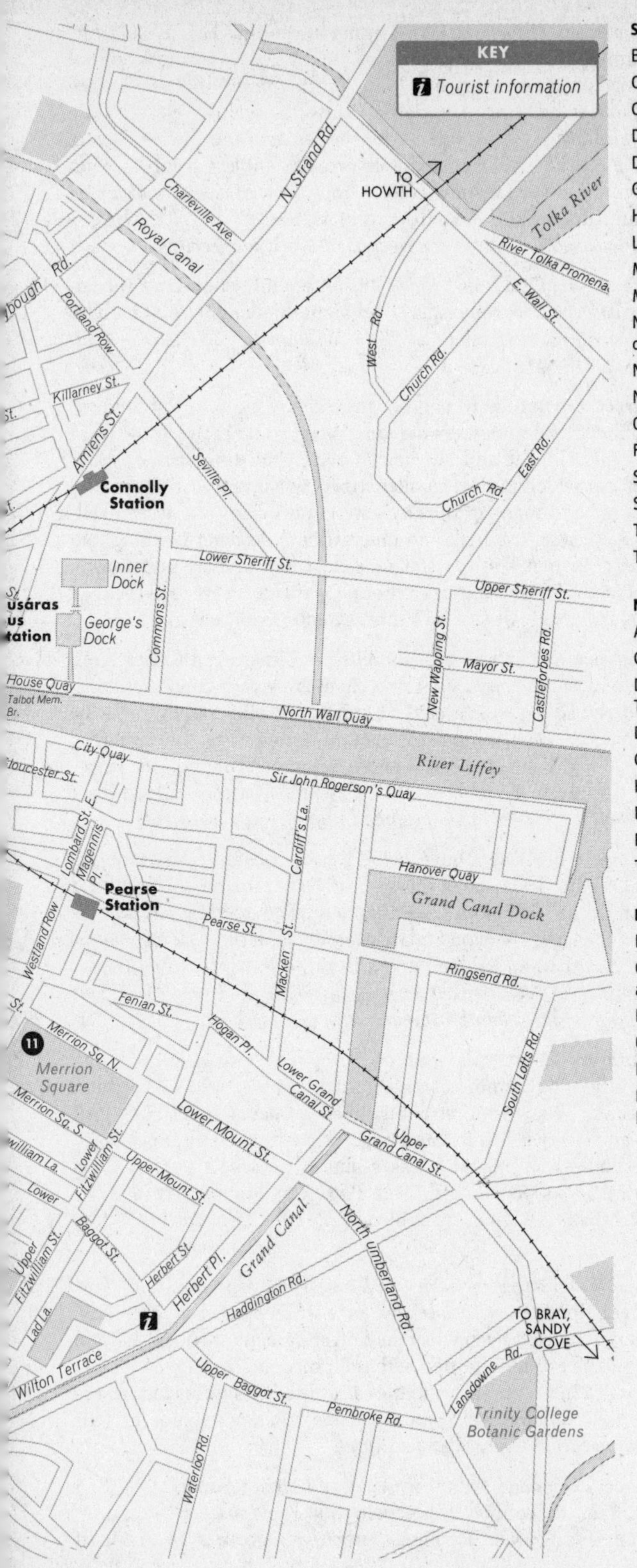

South of the Liffey

Bank of Ireland 2
Christ Church Cathedral 17
City Hall 16
Dublin Castle 15
Dublin Civic Museum 4
Grafton Street 3
Heraldic Museum 6
Leinster House 9
Marsh's Library 13
Merrion Square 11
National Gallery of Ireland 10
National Library 7
National Museum 8
O'Connell Bridge 19
Royal Irish Academy 5
St. Patrick's Cathedral 14
St. Stephen's Green 12
Temple Bar 18
Trinity College 1

North of the Liffey

Abbey Theatre 21
Custom House 20
Dublin City Gallery The Hugh Lane 28
Dublin Writers Museum 27
General Post Office 22
Ha'penny Bridge 24
Parnell Square 26
Rotunda Hospital 25
The Spire 23

Dublin West

Four Courts 29
Guinness Brewery and Storehouse 34
Kilmainham Gaol 33
Old Jameson Distillery 30
Phoenix Park 31
Royal Hospital Kilmainham 32

as well as various 18th- and 19th-century additions. The lavishly furnished **state apartments** are now used to entertain visiting heads of state. Guided tours run every half hour, but the rooms are closed when in official use, so call first. The **Castle Vaults** now hold an elegant little patisserie and bistro. The castle is also the home of the **Chester Beatty Library.** Among the library's exhibits are clay tablets from Babylon dating from 2700 BC, Japanese color wood-block prints, Chinese jade books, and Turkish and Persian paintings. ✉ *Castle St.* ☎ *01/677–7129* 🌐 *www.dublincastle.ie* ⏲ *Weekdays 10–5, weekends 2–5.*

❹ **Dublin Civic Museum.** Built in 1765–71 as an assembly house for the Society of Artists, the museum displays drawings, models, maps of Dublin, and other civic memorabilia. ✉ *58 S. William St.* ☎ *01/679–4260* ⏲ *Tues.–Sat. 10–6, Sun. 11–2.*

★ ❸ **Grafton Street.** Open only to pedestrians, brick-lined Grafton Street is one of Dublin's vital spines: it's the most direct route between the front door of Trinity College and Stephen's Green; the city's premier shopping street, off which radiate smaller streets housing stylish shops and pubs; and home to many of the city's street musicians and flower sellers. Browse through the Irish and international designer clothing and housewares at **Brown Thomas,** Ireland's most elegant department store. The **Powerscourt Town House** is a shopping arcade installed in the covered courtyard of one of Dublin's most famous Georgian mansions.

❻ **Heraldic Museum.** If you're a Fitzgibbon from Limerick, a Cullen from Waterford, or a McSweeney from Cork, chances are your family designed, begged, borrowed, or stole a coat of arms somewhere along the way. The Heraldic Museum has hundreds of family crests, flags, coins, stamps, and silver, all highlighting the uses and development of heraldry in Ireland. ✉ *2 Kildare St.* ☎ *01/661–4877* ⏲ *Mon.–Wed. 10–8:30, Thurs. and Fri. 10–4:30, Sat. 10–12:30; guided tours by appointment.*

❾ **Leinster House.** When it was built in 1745 it was the largest private residence in Dublin. Today it is the seat of Dáil Éireann (pronounced "Dawl Erin"), the Irish House of Parliament. The building has two facades: the one facing Merrion Square is designed in the style of a country house; the other, on Kildare Street, is in the style of a town house. ✉ *Kildare St.* ☎ *01/618–3000* 🌐 *www.irlgov.ie* ⏲ *Tours Mon. and Fri. by appointment (when Parliament is not in session).*

⓭ **Marsh's Library.** A short walk west from Stephen's Green and accessed through a tiny but charming cottage garden lies a gem of old Dublin: the city's—and Ireland's—first public library, opened in 1701 to "All Graduates and Gentlemen." Its interior has been left practically unchanged since it was built—it still contains "cages" into which scholars who wanted to peruse rare books were locked. ✉ *St. Patrick's Close* ☎ *01/454–3511* 🌐 *www.kst.dit.ie* ⏲ *Mon. and Wed.–Fri. 10–12:45 and 2–5, Sat. 10:30–12:45.*

★ ⓫ **Merrion Square.** Created between 1762 and 1764, this tranquil Georgian square is lined on three sides by some of Dublin's best-preserved Georgian town houses. Even when the flower gardens are not in bloom, the vibrant green grounds, dotted with sculpture and threaded with meandering paths, are worth a walk. **No. 1,** at the northwest corner, was the home of Sir William and Sperenza Wilde, Oscar's parents. ✉ *East end of Nassau St.* ⏲ *Daily sunrise–sunset.*

★ ❿ **National Gallery of Ireland.** On the west side of Merrion Square, this 1854 building contains the country's finest collection of old masters—treasures include Vermeer's *Woman Writing a Letter* (twice stolen from Sir Alfred

Beit and now safe at last), Gainsborough's *Cottage Girl,* and Caravaggio's *The Arrest of Christ.* The gallery's restaurant is one of the city's best spots for an inexpensive, top-rate lunch. The new Millennium Wing, a standout of postmodern architecture in Dublin, also houses part of the permanent collection, and stages major international traveling shows. Free guided tours are available on Saturday at 3 PM and on Sunday at 2:15, 3, and 4. ✉ *Merrion Sq. W* ☎ *01/661–5133* 🌐 *www.nationalgallery.ie* 🕓 *Mon.–Wed., Fri., and Sat. 10–5:30, Thurs. 10–8:30, Sun. 2–5.*

❼ **National Library.** The collections here include first editions of every major Irish writer. Temporary exhibits are held in the entrance hall, off the colonnaded rotunda. The main reading room, opened in 1890, has a dramatic dome ceiling. The library also offers a free genealogical consultancy service that advises you on how to trace your Irish ancestors. ✉ *Kildare St.* ☎ *01/661–8811* 🌐 *www.nli.ie* 🕓 *Mon.–Wed. 10–9, Thurs. and Fri. 10–5, Sat. 10–1.*

❽ **National Museum.** On the other side of Leinster House from the National Library, the museum is most famous for its spectacular collection of Irish artifacts from 7000 BC to the present, including the Tara Brooch, the Ardagh Chalice, the Cross of Cong, and a fabled hoard of Celtic gold jewelry. Upstairs, Viking Age Ireland is a permanent exhibit on the Norsemen, featuring a full-size Viking skeleton, swords, leather works recovered in Dublin and surrounding areas, and a replica of a small Viking boat. ✉ *Kildare St.* ☎ *01/660–1117* 🌐 *www.museum.ie* 🕓 *Tues.–Sat. 10–5, Sun. 2–5.*

⓳ **O'Connell Bridge.** Strange but true: the main bridge spanning the Liffey is wider than it is long. The north side of the bridge is dominated by an elaborate memorial to Daniel O'Connell, "The Liberator," erected as a tribute to the great 19th-century orator's achievement in securing Catholic Emancipation in 1829. Today **O'Connell Street,** one of the widest in Europe, is less a street to loiter in than to pass through on your way to elsewhere. **Henry Street,** to the left just beyond the General Post Office, is, like a downscale Grafton Street, a busy pedestrian thoroughfare where you'll find throngs of Dubliners out doing their shopping. A few steps down Henry Street off to the right is the colorful **Moore Street Market,** where street vendors recall their most famous ancestor, Molly Malone, by singing their wares—mainly flowers and fruit—in the traditional Dublin style.

❺ **Royal Irish Academy.** The country's leading learned society houses important manuscripts in its 18th-century library. Just below the academy is the **Mansion House,** the official residence of the Lord Mayor of Dublin. Its Round Room, the site of the first assembly of Dáil Éireann in January 1919, is now used mainly for exhibitions. ✉ *19 Dawson St.* ☎ *01/676–2570* 🌐 *www.ria.ie* 🕓 *Weekdays 9:30–5.*

⓮ **St. Patrick's Cathedral.** Legend has it that St. Patrick baptized many converts at a well on the site of the cathedral in the 5th century. The building dates from 1190 and is mainly early English Gothic in style. At 305 feet, it is the longest church in the country. In the 17th century Oliver Cromwell, dour ruler of England and no friend of the Irish, had his troops stable their horses in the cathedral. It wasn't until the 19th century that restoration work to repair the damage was begun. St. Patrick's is the national cathedral of the Anglican Church in Ireland and has had many illustrious deans. The most famous was Jonathan Swift, author of *Gulliver's Travels,* who held office from 1713 to 1745. Swift's tomb is in the south aisle. Memorials to many other celebrated figures from Ireland's past line the walls. "Living Stones" is the cathedral's permanent exhibition celebrating St. Patrick's place in the life of the city. Matins (9:45 AM) and evensong (5:35 PM) are still sung on most days, a real treat for the music lover. ✉ *Patrick St.* ☎ *01/453–9472* 🌐 *www.stpatrickscathedral.ie* ⏲ *May and Sept.–Oct., weekdays 9–6, Sat. 9–5, Sun. 10–11 and 12:30–3; June–Aug., weekdays 9–6, Sat. 9–4, Sun. 9:30–3 and 4:15–5:15; Nov.–Apr., weekdays 9–6, Sat. 9–4, Sun. 10–11 and 12:45–3.*

⓬ **St. Stephen's Green.** Dubliners call it simply Stephen's Green; green it is—strikingly so, year-round (you can even spot a palm tree or two). Among the park's many statues are a memorial to Yeats and another to Joyce by Henry Moore. The north side is dominated by the magnificent **Shelbourne Méridien Hotel.** A drink in one of its two bars, or afternoon tea in the elegant Lord Mayor's Room is the most financially painless way to soak in the old-fashioned luxury.

★ ⓲ **Temple Bar.** Dublin's hippest neighborhood—bordered by Dame Street to the south, the Liffey to the north, Fishamble Street to the west, and Westmoreland Street to the east—is the city's version of the Latin Quarter, the playing ground of "young Dublin." Representative of the improved fortunes of the area, with its narrow, winding pedestrian-only cobblestone streets, is the **Clarence** (✉ 6–8 Wellington Quay ☎ 01/670–9000), a favorite old Dublin hotel now owned by Bono and the Edge of U2. The area is chock-full of small hip stores, art galleries, and inexpensive restaurants and pubs. The **Irish Film Centre** (✉ 6 Eustace St. ☎ 01/679–5744) is emblematic of the area's vibrant mix of high and alternative culture.

FodorsChoice ★

❶ **Trinity College.** Ireland's oldest and most famous college is the heart of college-town Dublin. Trinity College, Dublin (officially titled Dublin University but familiarly known as Trinity), was founded by Elizabeth I in 1592 and offered a free education to Catholics—providing they accepted the Protestant faith. As a legacy of this condition, until 1966 Catholics who wished to study at Trinity had to obtain a dispensation from their bishop or face excommunication. Today more than 70% of Trinity's students are Catholics, an indication of how far away those days seem now.

The pedimented, neoclassical Georgian facade, built between 1755 and 1759, consists of a magnificent portico with Corinthian columns. The design is repeated on the interior, so the view from outside the gates and from the quadrangle inside is the same. On the quad's lawn are statues of two of the university's illustrious alumni—statesman Edmund Burke and poet Oliver Goldsmith. Other famous students include the philosopher George Berkeley (who gave his name to the northern California city), Jonathan Swift, Thomas Moore, Oscar Wilde, John Millington Synge, Bram Stoker, Edward Carson, and Samuel Beckett. The 18th-century building on the left, just inside the entrance, is the **chapel.** There's an identical building opposite, the **Examination Hall.** The oldest buildings are the library in the far right-hand corner, completed in 1712, and a 1690 row of redbrick buildings known as the **Rubrics,** which contain student apartments.

Ireland's largest collection of books and manuscripts is housed in **Trinity College Library,** entered through the library shop. Its principal treasure is the Book of Kells, generally considered the most striking manuscript ever produced in the Anglo-Saxon world. Only a few pages from the 682-page, 9th-century gospel are displayed at a time, but an informative exhibit has reproductions of many of them. At peak hours you may have to wait in line to enter the library; it's less busy early in the day. Don't miss the grand and glorious Long Room, an impressive 213 feet long and

42 feet wide, which houses 200,000 volumes in its 21 alcoves. ☎ *01/677–2941* 🌐 *www.bookofkells.ie* ⏲ *Mon.–Sat. 9:30–4:45, Sun. noon–4:30.*

In the Thomas Davis Theatre in the Arts Building, **"Dublin Experience"** is an audiovisual presentation devoted to the history of the city over the last 1,000 years. ☎ *01/677–2941* ⏲ *Late May–Oct., daily 10–5; shows every hr on the hr.*

North of the Liffey

The Northside city center is a mix of densely thronged shopping streets and slightly run-down sections of once-genteel homes, which are now being bought up and renovated. There are some classic sights in the area, including gorgeous Georgian monuments—the Custom House, the General Post Office, Parnell Square, and Dublin City Gallery The Hugh Lane—and two landmarks of literary Dublin, the Dublin Writers Museum and the James Joyce Cultural Center, hub of Bloomsday celebrations. A good way to begin is by heading up O'Connell Street to Parnell Square and the heart of James Joyce Country.

21 **Abbey Theatre.** Ireland's national theater was founded by W. B. Yeats and Lady Gregory in 1904. Works by Yeats, Synge, O'Casey, Kavanagh, and Friel have premiered here. The original building was destroyed in a fire in 1951; the present, rather austere theater was built in 1966. It has some noteworthy portraits and mementos in the foyer. Seats are usually available for about €15; all tickets are €10 for Monday performances. ✉ *Lower Abbey St.* ☎ *01/878–7222* 🌐 *www.abbeytheatre.ie.*

20 **Custom House.** Extending 375 feet on the north side of the Liffey, this is the city's most spectacular Georgian building (1781–91), the work of James Gandon, an English architect. The central portico is linked by arcades to the pavilions at each end. A statue of Commerce tops the graceful copper dome; additional allegorical statues adorn the main facade. Republicans set the building on fire in 1921, but it was completely restored; it now houses government offices and a visitor center tracing the building's history and significance, and the life of Gandon. ✉ *Custom House Quay* ☎ *01/876–7660* ⏲ *Mid-Mar.–Oct., weekdays 10–12:30, weekends 2–5; Nov–mid-March., Wed.–Fri. 10–12:30, Sun. 2–5.*

★ 28 **Dublin City Gallery The Hugh Lane.** The imposing Palladian facade of this town house, once the home of the Earl of Charlemont, dominates the north side of Parnell Square. Sir Hugh Lane, a nephew of Lady Gregory (Yeats's patron), collected impressionist paintings and 19th-century Irish and Anglo-Irish works. Among them are canvases by Jack Yeats (W. B.'s brother) and Paul Henry. The late Francis Bacon's partner donated the entire contents of the artist's studio to the Hugh Lane Gallery, where it has been reconstructed. ✉ *Parnell Sq.* ☎ *01/874–1903* 🌐 *www.hughlane.ie* ⏲ *Tues.–Thurs. 9:30–6, Fri. and Sat. 9:30–5, Sun. 11–5.*

★ 27 **Dublin Writers Museum.** Two restored 18th-century town houses on the north side of Parnell Square, an area rich in literary associations, lodge one of Dublin's finest cultural sights. Rare manuscripts, diaries, posters, letters, limited and first editions, photographs, and other mementos commemorate the lives and works of the nation's greatest writers, including Joyce, Shaw, Wilde, Yeats, and Beckett. The bookshop and café make this an ideal place to spend a rainy afternoon. ✉ *18–19 Parnell Sq. N* ☎ *01/872–2077* 🌐 *www.visitdublin.com* ⏲ *June–Aug., Mon.–Sat. 10–6, Sun. 11–5; Sept.–May, Mon.–Sat. 10–5, Sun. 11–5.*

22 **General Post Office.** The GPO (1818), still a working post office, is one of the great civic buildings of Dublin's Georgian era, but its fame de-

rives from the role it played during the Easter Rising. Here, on Easter Monday, 1916, the Republican forces stormed the building and issued the Proclamation of the Irish Republic. After a week of shelling, the GPO lay in ruins; 13 rebels were ultimately executed. Most of the original building was destroyed; only the facade—you can still see the scars of bullets on its pillars—remained. ✉ *O'Connell St.* ☎ *01/872–8888* 🌐 *www.anpost.ie* ⏲ *Mon.–Sat. 8–8, Sun. 10:30–6:30.*

24 **Ha'penny Bridge.** This heavily trafficked footbridge crosses the Liffey at a prime spot: Temple Bar is on the south side, and the bridge provides the fastest route to the thriving Mary and Henry Street shopping areas to the north. Until early in this century, a half-penny toll was charged to cross it. Yeats was one among many Dubliners who found this too high a price to pay—more a matter of principle than of finance—and so made the detour via O'Connell Bridge.

26 **Parnell Square.** This is the Northside's most notable Georgian square and one of Dublin's oldest. Some of the brick-face town houses have larger windows than others—some fashionable hostesses liked passersby to be able to peer into the first-floor reception rooms and admire the distinguished guests.

25 **Rotunda Hospital.** Founded in 1745 as the first maternity hospital in Ireland or Britain, the Rotunda is now most worth a visit for its **chapel,** with elaborate plasterwork, appropriately honoring motherhood. The **Gate Theatre,** housed in an extension, attracts large crowds with its fine repertoire of classic Irish and European drama. ✉ *Parnell St.* ☎ *01/873–0700.*

★ 23 **The Spire.** Also known as the Monument of Light, The Spire was originally planned as part of the city's millennium celebrations. Ian Ritchie's spectacular 395-foot-high monument was finally erected at the beginning of 2003. Though christened "The Stiletto in the Ghetto" by some local wags, most agree the needlelike sculpture is the most exciting thing to happen to Dublin's skyline this century. The stainless steel structure is seven times taller than the nearby GPO. ✉ *O'Connell St.*

Dublin West

If you're not an enthusiastic walker, hop a bus or find a cab to take you to these sights in westernmost Dublin.

29 **Four Courts.** Today the seat of the High Court of Justice of Ireland, the Four Courts are James Gandon's second Dublin masterpiece, built between 1786 and 1802. The courts were destroyed during the Troubles of the 1920s and restored by 1932. Its distinctive copper-covered dome atop a colonnaded rotunda makes this one of Dublin's most recognizable buildings. You are allowed to listen in on court proceedings, which can often be interesting, educational, even scandalous. ✉ *Inns Quay* ☎ *01/872–5555* 🌐 *www.courts.ie* ⏲ *Daily 10:30–1 and 2:15–4.*

★ 34 **Guinness Brewery and Storehouse.** Founded by Arthur Guinness in 1759, Ireland's all-dominating brewery is on a 60-acre spread west of Christ Church Cathedral. It is the most popular tourist destination in town. The brewery itself is closed to the public, but the Storehouse is a spectacular tourist attraction with a high-tech exhibition about the brewing process of the "dark stuff." In a cast-iron and brick warehouse, it covers six floors built around a huge central glass atrium. But without doubt the star attraction is the top-floor **Gravity Bar,** with its 360°, floor-to-ceiling glass walls and a stunning view over the city. The funky new Guinness Shop on the ground floor is full of lifestyle merchandise. ✉ *St. James's Gate* ☎ *01/408–4800* 🌐 *www.guinness.com* 🎫 *€13.50* ⏲ *Apr.–Sept., Mon.–Sat. 9:30–7, Sun. 11–5; Oct.–Mar., daily 9:30–5.*

33 **Kilmainham Gaol.** This grim, forbidding structure was where leaders of the 1916 Easter Rising, including Pádrig Pearse and James Connolly, were held before being executed. A guided tour and a 30-minute audiovisual presentation relate a graphic account of Ireland's political history over the past 200 years from a Nationalist viewpoint. ✉ *Inchicore Rd.* ☎ *01/453–5984* 🌐 *www.heritageireland.ie* ⏲ *Apr.–Sept., daily 9:30–5; Oct.–Mar., Mon.–Sat. 9:30–4, Sun. 10–5.*

30 **Old Jameson Distillery.** The birthplace of one of Ireland's best whiskeys has been fully restored and offers a fascinating insight into the making of *uisce batha*, or "holy water." There is a 40-minute guided tour of the old distillery, a 20-minute audiovisual tour, and a complimentary tasting. ✉ *Bow St.* ☎ *01/807–2355* 🌐 *www.irish-whiskey-trail.com* ⏲ *Daily 9–6, tours every ½ hr.*

★ 31 **Phoenix Park.** Europe's largest public park encompasses 1,752 acres of verdant lawns, woods, lakes, playing fields, a zoo, a flower garden, and two residences—those of the president of Ireland and the ambassador for the United States. A 210-foot-tall obelisk, built in 1817, commemorates the Duke of Wellington's defeat of Napoléon. It is a runner's paradise, but Sunday is the best time to visit, when all kinds of games are likely to be in progress.

★ 32 **Royal Hospital Kilmainham.** A short ride by taxi or bus from the city center, this structure is regarded as the most important 17th-century building in Ireland. Completed in 1684 as a hospice for soldiers, it survived into the 1920s as a hospital. The ceiling of the Baroque chapel is extraordinary. It now houses the **Irish Museum of Modern Art,** which displays works by such non-Irish greats as Picasso and Miró but concentrates on the work of Irish artists. ✉ *Kilmainham La.* ☎ *01/612–9900* 🌐 *www.modernart.ie* ⏲ *Tues.–Sat. 10–5:30, Sun. noon–5:30; Royal Hospital tours every ½ hr; museum tours Wed. and Fri. at 2:30, Sat. at 11:30.*

WHERE TO EAT

Beyond the restaurants recommended here, the area between Grafton Street and South Great George's Street has many to offer, as does Temple Bar, just across Dame Street. It's also worth checking out suburban villages like Ranelagh, Blackrock, and Sandycove for good local restaurants.

WHAT IT COSTS In Euros

	$$$$	$$$	$$	$
AT DINNER	over €26	€18–€26	€12–€18	under €12

Prices are per person for a main course.

$$$$ ✕ **The Commons Restaurant.** This restaurant is in a large, elegant room with French windows in the basement of Newman House, where James Joyce was a student in the original premises of University College Dublin. The seasonal menu encompasses a light treatment of classic themes. ✉ *85–86 St. Stephen's Green* ☎ *01/478–0530* ▭ *AE, DC, MC, V* ⏲ *Closed weekends.*

$$$$ Fodor's Choice ★ ✕ **Patrick Guilbaud.** Everything is French here, including the eponymous owner, his chef, and the maître d'. Guillaume Le Brun's cooking is a fluent expression of modern French cuisine—not particularly flamboyant, but coolly professional. ✉ *Merrion Hotel, 21 Upper Merrion St.* ☎ *01/676–4192* ▭ *AE, DC, MC, V* ⏲ *Closed Sun. and Mon.*

★ $$$$ ✕ **Thornton's.** If you are passionate about food, this place is mandatory—owner Kevin Thornton has forged a reputation as one of the very best chefs in Ireland. The dining room is simply decorated—there's little to distract you from the exquisite food. ✉ *Fitzwilliam Hotel, St. Stephen's Green,* ☎ *01/454–9067* ✍ *Reservations essential* ▭ *AE, DC, MC, V* ⊗ *Closed Sun. and Mon.*

$$$–$$$$ ✕ **Chapter One.** In the vaulted, stone-walled basement of the Dublin Writers Museum, this is one of the most notable restaurants in Northside Dublin. Typical dishes include roast venison with mustard and herb lentils and roast beetroot. ✉ *18–19 Parnell Sq.* ☎ *01/873–2266* ▭ *AE, DC, MC, V* ⊗ *Closed Sun. and Mon. No lunch Sat.*

$$–$$$$ ✕ **Brownes Brasserie.** Huge mirrors reflect the light from crystal chandeliers onto jewel-colored walls and upholstery. The food is rich and heartwarming, with classics such as Irish smoked salmon and confit of duck with lentils. ✉ *22 St. Stephen's Green* ☎ *01/638–3939* ▭ *AE, DC, MC, V* ⊗ *No lunch Sat.*

$$–$$$ ✕ **Bruno's.** At this French–Mediterranean bistro on one of the busiest corners in Temple Bar, enjoy simple but stylish dishes: starters include feuilleté of crab meat and saffron sauce, and main dishes include roast scallops with Jerusalem artichoke purée and warm smoked bacon. ✉ *30 Essex St. E* ☎ *01/670–6767* ▭ *AE, DC, MC, V* ⊗ *Closed Sun.*

$$–$$$ ✕ **Caviston's.** The Cavistons have been dispensing recipes for years from their fish counter and delicatessen in Sandycove, just south of the ferry port of Dun Laoghaire, 30 minutes by taxi or DART train south of Dublin. The fish restaurant next door is a lively and intimate spot for lunch, but you should book in advance. ✉ *59 Glasthule Rd., Dun Laoghaire* ☎ *01/280–9120* ▭ *MC, V* ⊗ *Closed Sun., Mon., and late Dec.–early Jan. No dinner.*

$$–$$$ ✕ **Eden.** This popular brasserie-style restaurant overlooking one of Temple Bar's main squares turns out good contemporary cuisine, such as vegetarian buckwheat pancake filled with garlic, spinach, and cheddar, and duck leg confit with lentils. Try to go when there are open-air movies in the square. ✉ *Meeting House Sq.* ☎ *01/670–5372* ✍ *Reservations essential* ▭ *AE, MC, V.*

★ $$–$$$ ✕ **La Stampa.** One of the most dramatic dining rooms in Dublin, La Stampa has huge gilt mirrors and elaborate candelabra that are gloriously over the top. The menu changes frequently to reflect an eclectic, international style. For a main course you may get rack of organic lamb with braised beans, tomatoes, and rosemary jus, or roast scallops with artichoke mash and a tomato vinaigrette. ✉ *35 Dawson St.* ☎ *01/677–8611* ▭ *AE, DC, MC, V* ⊗ *No lunch.*

$$–$$$ ✕ **The Lord Edward.** Creaking floorboards and an old fireplace give the impression of being in someone's drawing room at this restaurant, one of the oldest in the city. Start with classic fish dishes such as prawn cocktail or smoked salmon, followed by fresh and simply cooked Dover sole, salmon, or lobster. ✉ *23 Christ Church Pl.* ☎ *01/454–2420* ▭ *AE, DC, MC, V* ⊗ *No lunch Sat. Closed Sun.*

$ ✕ **Milano.** In a well-designed dining room with lots of brio, choose from a tempting array of inventive, thin-crust pizzas. ✉ *38 Dawson St.* ☎ *01/670–7744* ✉ *19 Essex St. E* ☎ *01/670–3384* ✉ *38–39 Lower Ormond Quay* ☎ *01/872–0003* ✉ *IFSC, Clarion Quay* ☎ *01/611–9012* ▭ *AE, DC, MC, V.*

Pub Food

Most pubs serve food at lunchtime, some throughout the day. Food ranges from hearty soups and stews to chicken curries, smoked salmon salads, and sandwiches. Expect to pay €5.10–€7.60 for a main course. Larger pubs tend to take credit cards.

✕ **Davy Byrne's.** James Joyce immortalized Davy Byrne's in *Ulysses.* Nowadays it's more akin to a cocktail bar than a Dublin pub, but it's good for fresh and smoked salmon, salads, fresh oysters, and a hot daily special. ✉ *21 Duke St.* ☎ *01/671–1298.*

✕ **Old Stand.** Conveniently close to Grafton Street, the Old Stand serves grilled food, including steaks. ✉ *37 Exchequer St.* ☎ *01/677–7220.*

✕ **Porterhouse.** Ireland's first brew pub has an open kitchen and a dazzling selections of beers—from pale ales to dark stouts. ✉ *16–18 Parliament St.* ☎ *01/679–8847.*

✕ **Stag's Head.** The Stag's Head is a favorite of Trinity students and businesspeople, who come for one of the best pub lunches in the city. ✉ *1 Dame Ct.* ☎ *01/679–3701.*

✕ **Zanzibar.** This is a spectacular and cavernous bar that looks as though it might be more at home in downtown Marakesh. While away an afternoon on one of its wicker chairs. ✉ *34–35 Lower Ormond Quay* ☎ *01/878–7212.*

Cafés

Though Dublin has nowhere near as many cafés as pubs, it's easier than ever to find a good cup of coffee at most hours of the day or night.

✕ **Bewley's Coffee House.** The granddaddy of the capital's cafés, Bewley's has been supplying Dubliners with coffee and buns for more than a century. ✉ *78 Grafton St.* ✉ *12 Westmoreland St.* ☎ *01/677–6761 for both.*

✕ **Kaffe Moka.** One of Dublin's hottest haunts for the caffeine-addicted, this spot has three hyperstylish floors and a central location in the heart of the city center. ✉ *39 S. William St.* ☎ *01/679–8475.*

✕ **Thomas Read's.** By day it's a café, by night a pub. Its large windows overlooking a busy corner in Temple Bar make it a great spot for people-watching. ✉ *1 Parliament St.* ☎ *01/671–7283.*

WHERE TO STAY

On the lodging front Dublin is in the midst of a major hotel boom. For value, stay in a guest house or a B&B; both tend to be in suburban areas—generally a 10-minute bus ride from the center of the city. **Bord Fáilte** can usually help find you a place to stay if you don't have reservations.

WHAT IT COSTS In euros				
	$$$$	$$$	$$	$
HOTELS	over €200	€150–€200	€100–€150	under €100

Prices are for two people in a standard double room in high season.

$$$$ **Conrad Dublin International.** A subsidiary of Hilton Hotels, the Conrad is aimed at the international business executive. The seven-story red-brick and smoked-glass building is just off Stephen's Green. The spacious rooms are done in light brown and pastel greens. Alfie Byrne's, the main bar, attempts to re-create a traditional Irish pub. ✉ *Earlsfort Terr., Dublin 2* ☎ *01/676–5555* 📠 *01/676–5424* 🌐 *www.conrad-international.ie* *182 rooms, 9 suites* *2 restaurants, bar* 💳 *AE, DC, MC, V.*

$$$$ **Hibernian.** An early-20th-century Edwardian nurses' home was converted into this hotel, retaining the distinctive red-and-amber brick facade. Every room is a different shape, though all are done in light pastels

with deep-pile carpets. Public rooms are slightly small but are attractive in cheerful chintz and stripes. ✉ *Eastmoreland Pl., off Upper Baggot St., Dublin 4* ☎ *01/668–7666* 📠 *01/660–2655* 🌐 *hibernianhotel.com* ⇨ *40 rooms* ♨ *Restaurant, bar* ▭ *AE, DC, MC, V.*

$$$$ **Jurys and the Towers.** These adjacent seven-story hotels, a short cab ride from the center of town, are popular with businesspeople and vacationers. Both have more atmosphere than most comparable modern hotels, though the Towers has an edge over Jurys, which is older, larger, and less expensive. ✉ *Pemroke Rd., Ballsbridge, Dublin 4* ☎ *01/660–5000* 📠 *01/660–5540* 🌐 *www.jurys.com* ⇨ *Jurys: 300 rooms, 3 suites. The Towers: 100 rooms, 5 suites* ♨ *3 restaurants, pool* ▭ *AE, DC, MC, V.*

$$$$ Fodor's Choice ★ **Merrion.** Four exactingly restored Georgian town houses make up part of this luxurious hotel. The stately rooms have been richly appointed in classic Georgian style down to the last detail. Leading Dublin restaurateur Patrick Guilbaud's eponymous restaurant is here. ✉ *21 Upper Merrion St., Dublin 2* ☎ *01/603–0600* 📠 *01/603–0700* 🌐 *www.merrionhotel.com* ⇨ *127 rooms, 18 suites* ♨ *2 restaurants, 2 bars* ▭ *AE, DC, MC, V.*

★ $$$$ **Shelbourne Méridien Hotel.** Old-fashioned luxury prevails at this magnificent showplace, which has presided over Stephen's Green since 1824. Each room has its own fine, carefully selected furnishings. Those in front overlook the green; rooms in the back are quieter. The restaurant, 27 The Green, is one of the most elegant rooms in Dublin; Lord Mayor's Room, off the lobby, serves a lovely afternoon tea. ✉ *27 Stephen's Green, Dublin 2* ☎ *01/663–4500; 800/543–4300 in U.S.* 📠 *01/661–6006* 🌐 *www.shelbourne.ie* ⇨ *181 rooms, 9 suites* ♨ *2 restaurants, pool, 2 bars* ▭ *AE, DC, MC, V.*

$$$$ **Westbury.** This comfortable, modern hotel has a spacious main lobby furnished with antiques and large sofas, where you can have afternoon tea. Rooms are rather utilitarian; the suites, which combine European decor with Japanese prints and screens, are more inviting. The flowery Russell Room serves formal lunches and dinners. ✉ *Grafton St., Dublin 2* ☎ *01/679–1122* 📠 *01/679–7078* 🌐 *www.jurysdoyle.com* ⇨ *203 rooms, 8 suites* ♨ *2 restaurants, bar* ▭ *AE, DC, MC, V.*

$$$–$$$$ **Chief O'Neill's.** This modern hotel—named after a 19th-century Corkman who became chief of police in Chicago—has a huge lobby-bar area looking out onto a cobbled courtyard. Smallish, high-tech rooms all have chrome fixtures and minimalist furnishings. Top-floor suites have delightful rooftop gardens with views of the city on both sides of the Liffey. ✉ *Smithfield Village, Dublin 7* ☎ *01/817–3838* 📠 *01/817–3839* 🌐 *www.chiefoneills.com* ⇨ *70 rooms, 3 suites* ♨ *Restaurant, bar* ▭ *AE, DC, MC, V.*

★ $$$–$$$$ **Number 31.** Two strikingly renovated Georgian mews are connected via a small garden to the grand town house they once served; together they form a marvelous guest house a short walk from Stephen's Green. Owners Deirdre and Noel Comer offer gracious hospitality and made-to-order breakfasts. ✉ *31 Leeson Close, Dublin 2* ☎ *01/676–5011* 📠 *01/676–2929* 🌐 *www.number31.ie* ⇨ *18 rooms* ▭ *AE, MC, V.*

★ $$–$$$ **Ariel Guest House.** Dublin's leading guest house is in a tree-lined suburb, a 10-minute walk from Stephen's Green, and close to a DART stop. Rooms in the main house are lovingly filled with antiques; those at the back of the house are more spartan; all are immaculate. Owner Michael O'Brien is a helpful and gracious host. ✉ *52 Lansdowne Rd., Dublin 4* ☎ *01/668–5512* 📠 *01/668–5845* 🌐 *www.ariel-house.com* ⇨ *40 rooms* ♨ *Wine bar* ▭ *MC, V.*

$$–$$$ **Mount Herbert Hotel.** Close to the luxury hotels in the tree-lined inner suburb of Ballsbridge, a 10-minute DART ride from Dublin's center, the

Loughran family's sprawling accommodation is popular with budget-minded visitors. Rooms are small, but have all the necessary amenities. There's no bar on the premises, but there are plenty to choose from nearby. *✉ 7 Herbert Rd., Ballsbridge, Dublin 4 ☎ 01/668–4321 📠 01/660–7077 🌐 www.mountherberthotel.ie ⇒ 200 rooms ♨ Restaurant ▭ AE, DC, MC, V.*

$$–$$$ **Paramount.** This medium-size hotel at the heart of Temple Bar has kept its classy Victorian facade. The bedrooms are all dark woods and subtle colors, very 1930s. If you're fond of a tipple try the hotel's art deco Turks Head Bar and Chop House. *✉ Parliament St. and Essex Gate, Dublin 2 ☎ 01/417–9900 📠 01/417–9904 🌐 www.paramounthotel.ie ⇒ 70 rooms ♨ Restaurant, bar ▭ AE, DC, MC, V.*

$$ **Central Hotel.** Established in 1887, this grand, old-style redbrick hotel is in the heart of the city. Rooms are small but have high ceilings and tasteful furnishings. The Library Bar on the second floor is one of the best spots in the city for a quiet pint. *✉ 1–5 Exchequer St., Dublin 2 ☎ 01/679–7302 📠 01/679–7303 🌐 www.centralhotel.ie ⇒ 67 rooms, 3 suites ♨ Restaurant, 2 bars ▭ AE, DC, MC, V.*

$ **Avalon House.** Many young, independent travelers rate this cleverly restored, Victorian redbrick building the most appealing of Dublin's hostels. A five-minute walk from Grafton Street and 5–10 minutes from some of the city's best music venues, it has a mix of dormitories, rooms without bath, and rooms with bath. The Avalon Café serves food until 10 PM, but is open as a common room after hours. *✉ 55 Aungier St., Dublin 2 ☎ 01/475–0001 📠 01/475–0303 🌐 www.avalon-house.ie ⇒ 312 beds ♨ Restaurant, bar ▭ AE, MC, V.*

$ **Jurys Christchurch Inn.** Expect few frills at this functional budget hotel (part of an otherwise upscale hotel chain), where there's a fixed room rate for up to three adults or two adults and two children. The biggest plus: the pleasant location, facing Christ Church Cathedral and within walking distance of most city-center attractions. Rooms are in pastel colors. The bar serves a pub lunch, and the restaurant, breakfast and dinner. *✉ Christchurch Pl., Dublin 8 ☎ 01/454–0000 📠 01/454–0012 🌐 www.jurys.com ⇒ 182 rooms ♨ Restaurant, bar ▭ AE, DC, MC, V.*

NIGHTLIFE & THE ARTS

The weekly magazines *In Dublin* and the *Big Issue* (at newsstands) contain comprehensive details of upcoming events, including ticket availability. *The Event Guide* also lists events and is free at many pubs and cafés. In peak season, consult the free Bord Fáilte leaflet "Events of the Week."

Cabarets

The following all have cabaret shows, with dancing, music, and traditional Irish song; they are open only in peak season (roughly May–October; call to confirm): **Abbey Tavern** (✉ Howth, Co. Dublin ☎ 01/839–0307). **Burlington Hotel** (✉ Upper Leeson St. ☎ 01/660–5222). **Clontarf Castle** (✉ Castle Ave., Clontarf ☎ 01/833–2321). **Jurys Hotel** (✉ Pembroke Rd., Ballsbridge ☎ 01/660–5000).

Classical Music

The **National Concert Hall** (✉ Earlsfort Terr. ☎ 01/475–1666), just off Stephen's Green, is the place to hear the National Symphony Orchestra of Ireland and is Dublin's main theater for classical music of all kinds. **St. Stephen's Church** (✉ Merrion Sq. ☎ 01/288–0663) has a regular program of choral and orchestral events.

Nightclubs

The **POD** (✉ Harcourt St. ☎ 01/478–0166) is the city's hippest spot for twentysomethings. **Rí Ra** (✉ Dame Court ☎ 01/677–4835) means "uproar" in Irish, and on most nights the place does go a little wild; it's one of the best spots for no-frills, fun dancing in Dublin. **Sugar Club** (✉ Lower Lesson St. ☎ 01/678–7188) is a refreshing mix of cocktail bar, nightclub, and performance venue. The place is known for its smooth Latin sounds and plush surroundings.

Pubs

Check advertisements in evening papers for folk, ballad, Irish traditional, or jazz music performances. The pubs listed below generally have some form of musical entertainment. The **Brazen Head** (✉ 20 Lower Bridge St. ☎ 01/677–9549)—Dublin's oldest pub, dating from 1688—has music every night. **Chief O'Neill's** (✉ Smithfield Village ☎ 01/817–3838) has an open, airy bar-café. The **Cobblestone** (✉ N. King St. ☎ 01/872–1799) is a glorious house of ale in the best Dublin tradition. **Doheny & Nesbitt's** (✉ 5 Lower Baggot St. ☎ 01/676–2945) is frequented by local businesspeople, politicians, and legal eagles. In the **Horseshoe Bar** (✉ Shelbourne Méridien Hotel, St. Stephen's Green ☎ 01/676–6471) you can eavesdrop on Dublin's social elite. **Kehoe's** (✉ 9 S. Anne St. ☎ 01/677–8312) is popular with students, artists, and writers. Locals and tourists bask in the theatrical atmosphere of **Neary's** (✉ 1 Chatham St. ☎ 01/676–2807). **O'Donoghue's** (✉ 15 Merrion Row ☎ 01/661–4303) has some form of musical entertainment on most nights. The **Palace Bar** (✉ 21 Fleet St. ☎ 01/677–9290) is a journalists' haunt.

Theaters

Ireland has a rich theatrical tradition. The **Abbey Theatre** (✉ Marlborough St. ☎ 01/878–7222) is the home of Ireland's national theater company, its name forever associated with J. M. Synge, W. B. Yeats, and Sean O'Casey. The **Peacock Theatre** is the Abbey's more experimental small stage. The **Gaiety Theatre** (✉ S. King St. ☎ 01/677–1717) shows musical comedy, opera, drama, and revues. The **Gate Theatre** (✉ Cavendish Row, Parnell Sq. ☎ 01/874–4045) is an intimate spot for modern drama and plays by Irish writers. The **Olympia Theatre** (✉ Dame St. ☎ 01/677–7744) has comedy, vaudeville, and ballet performances. The **Project Arts Centre** (✉ 39 E. Essex St. ☎ 01/679–6622) is an established fringe theater.

SHOPPING

The rest of the country is well supplied with crafts shops, but Dublin is the place to seek out more specialized items—antiques, haute couture, designer ceramics, books and prints, silverware and jewelry, and designer hand-knit items.

Shopping Centers & Department Stores

The shops north of the river—many of them chain stores and lackluster department stores—tend to be less expensive and less design-conscious. The one exception is the **Jervis Shopping Center** (✉ Jervis St. at Mary St. ☎ 01/878–1323), a major shopping center with chain stores as well as smaller boutiques. **Arnotts** (✉ Henry St. ☎ 01/805–0400) is Dublin's largest department store and carries a good range of cut crystal. **Brown Thomas** (✉ Grafton St. ☎ 01/605–6666) is Dublin's most elegant department store. **St. Stephen's Green Center** (✉ St. Stephen's

Green ☎ 01/478–0888) contains 70 stores in a vast Moorish-style glass-roof building.

Shopping Districts

Grafton Street is the most sophisticated shopping area in Dublin's city center. **Francis Street** and **Dawson Street** are the places to browse for antiques. **Nassau Street** and **Dawson Street** are for books; the smaller side streets are good for jewelry, art galleries, and old prints. The pedestrianized **Temple Bar** area, with its young, offbeat crowd, has a number of small art galleries, specialty shops (music and books), and inexpensive, trendy clothing shops. The area is further enlivened by buskers (street musicians) and street artists.

Bookstores

Fred Hanna's (✉ 29 Nassau St. ☎ 01/677–1255) sells old and new books, with a good choice of books on travel and Ireland. **Hodges Figgis** (✉ 56–58 Dawson St. ☎ 01/677–4754) is Dublin's leading independent, with a café on the first floor. **Hughes & Hughes** (✉ St. Stephen's Green Centre ☎ 01/478–3060) has strong travel and Irish-interest sections. There is also a store at Dublin Airport. **Waterstone's** (✉ 7 Dawson St. ☎ 01/679–1415) is the Dublin branch of the renowned British chain.

Gift Items

Blarney Woollen Mills (✉ Nassau St. ☎ 01/671–0068) has a good selection of tweed, linen, and woolen sweaters. **Dublin Woolen Mills** (✉ Metal Bridge Corner, 41 Lower Ormond Quay ☎ 01/677–5014), at Ha'penny Bridge, sells hand-knit and other woolen sweaters at competitive prices. **Kevin & Howlin** (✉ Nassau St. ☎ 01/677–0257) carries tweeds for men. **Kilkenny Shop** (✉ Nassau St. ☎ 01/677–7066) is good for contemporary Irish-made ceramics, pottery, and silver jewelry. **McDowell** (✉ 3 Upper O'Connell St. ☎ 01/874–4961), in business for more than 100 years, is a popular jewelry shop. **Tierneys** (✉ St. Stephen's Green Centre ☎ 01/478–2873) carries a good selection of crystal, china, claddagh rings, pendants, and brooches.

Outdoor Markets

Bric-a-brac is sold at the **Liberty Market** on the north end of Meath Street, open on Friday and Saturday 10–6, Sunday noon–5:30. **Moore Street** (✉ Henry St.), a large mall behind the Ilac Center, is open from Monday to Saturday 9–6; stalls lining both sides of the street sell fruits and vegetables. The indoor **Mother Redcap's Market,** opposite Christ Church, is open Friday, Saturday, and Sunday 10–5; come here for antiques and other finds.

DUBLIN A TO Z

AIRPORTS & TRANSFERS

All flights arrive at Dublin Airport, 10 km (6 mi) north of town.
ℹ ☎ 01/814–1111.

TRANSFERS Express buses leave every 20 minutes from outside the Arrivals door for the central bus station in downtown Dublin. The ride takes about 30 minutes, depending on the traffic, and the fare is €5. If you have time, take a regular bus for €1.30. A taxi ride into town will cost from €17 to €19, depending on the location of your hotel; be sure to ask in advance if the cab has no meter.

BOAT & FERRY TRAVEL

Irish Ferries has a regular car and passenger service directly into Dublin port from Holyhead in Wales. Stena Sealink docks in Dublin port (3½-hour service to Holyhead) and in Dun Laoghaire (High Speed Service, known as HSS, which takes 99 minutes). Prices and departure times vary according to season, so call to confirm. In summer, reservations are strongly recommended. Dozens of taxis wait to take you into town from both ports, or you can take DART or a bus to the city center.

Irish Ferries ✉ Merrion Row ☎ 01/661-0511. **Stena Sealink** ✉ Ferryport, Dun Laoghaire ☎ 01/204-7777.

BUS TRAVEL TO & FROM DUBLIN

The central bus station is Busaras; some bus lines also terminate near O'Connell Bridge. Bus Éireann provides express and provincial service.

Busaras ✉ Store St. near the Custom House. **Bus Éireann** ☎ 01/836-6111.

BUS TRAVEL WITHIN DUBLIN

Dublin Bus provides city service, including transport to and from the airport. Most city buses originate in or pass through the area of O'Connell Street and O'Connell Bridge. If the destination board indicates AN LÁR, that means that the bus is going to the city center. Timetables (€3.20) are available from Dublin Bus; the minimum fare is €0.70.

Dublin Bus ✉ 59 Upper O'Connell St. ☎ 01/873-4222.

CAR TRAVEL

The main access route from the north is N1; from the west, N4; from the south and southwest, N7; from the east coast, N11. All routes have clearly marked signs indicating the center of the city: AN LÁR. The M50 motorway encircles the city from Dublin Airport in the north to Tallaght in the south.

The number of cars in Ireland has grown exponentially in the last few years, and nowhere has their impact been felt more than in Dublin, where the city's complicated one-way streets are often congested. Avoid driving a car in the city except to get into and out of it, and be sure to ask your hotel or guest house for clear directions when you leave.

EMERGENCIES

Doctors & Dentists **Dentist: Dublin Dental Hospital** ☎ 01/662-0766. **Doctor: Eastern Help Board** ☎ 01/679-0700.

Emergency Services **Ambulance** ☎ 999. **Police** ☎ 999.

Pharmacies **Hamilton Long** ☎ 01/874-8456.

TAXIS

Official licensed taxis, metered and designated by roof signs, do not cruise; they can be found beside the central bus station, at train stations, at O'-Connell Bridge, Stephen's Green, College Green, and near major hotels. The initial charge is €2.30, with an additional charge of about €2 per 2 km (1 mi) thereafter (make sure the meter is on). Hackney cabs, which also operate in the city, have neither roof signs nor meters and will sometimes respond to hotels' requests for a cab. Negotiate the fare before your journey begins.

TOURS

BUS TOURS

Bus Éireann runs day trips to all the major sights around the capital. Gray Line Tours organizes bus tours of Dublin and its major sights; they also have daylong tours into the surrounding countryside and longer tours elsewhere (the price for excursion tours includes accommodations, breakfast, and admission). Dublin Bus runs a continuous guided open-top bus tour (€12) that allows you to hop on and off the bus as often as you wish and visit some 15 sights along its route.

Bus Éireann 01/836-6111. **Dublin Bus** 01/873-0000. **Gray Line Tours** 01/670-8822.

SPECIAL INTEREST TOURS Elegant Ireland arranges tours for groups interested in architecture and the fine arts; these include visits with the owners of some of Ireland's stately homes and castles.

Elegant Ireland 01/475-1665.

WALKING TOURS The tourist office has leaflets giving information on a selection of walking tours, including "Literary Dublin," "Georgian Dublin," and "Pub Tours." Bord Fáilte has a "Tourist Trail" walk, which takes in the main sites of central Dublin and can be completed in about three hours, and a "Rock 'n Stroll" tour, which covers the city's major pop and rock music sites.

TRAIN TRAVEL

Irish Rail provides train service throughout the country. Dublin has three main stations. Connolly Station is the departure point for Belfast, the east coast, and the west. Heuston Station is the departure point for the south and southwest. Pearse Station is for Bray and connections via Dun Laoghaire to the Liverpool-Holyhead ferries.

An electric train commuter service, DART, serves the suburbs out to Howth, on the north side of the city, and to Bray, County Wicklow, on the south side. Fares are about the same as for buses. Street-direction signs to DART stations read STAISIUN/STATION.

Connolly Station At Amiens St. **Heuston Station** At Kingsbridge. **Irish Rail** 35 Lower Abbey St. 01/836-6222 information. **Pearse Station** On Westland Row.

TRAVEL AGENCIES

American Express 116 Grafton St. 01/677-2874. **Thomas Cook** 118 Grafton St. 01/677-1721.

VISITOR INFORMATION

In addition to the visitor information offices in the entrance hall of the headquarters of Bord Fáilte, Dublin Tourism has visitor information at the airport (Arrivals level), open daily 8 AM–10 PM; and at the Ferryport, Dun Laoghaire, open daily 10 AM–9 PM.

Ireland Basics

To research prices, get advice from other travelers, and book travel arrangements, visit www.fodors.com.

CUSTOMS & DUTIES

For details on imports and duty-free limits, *see* Customs & Duties *in* Smart Travel Tips.

EMBASSIES

Australia Fitzwilton House, Fitzwilton Terr., Dublin 2 01/676-1517.

Canada 65 St. Stephen's Green, Dublin 2 01/478-1988.

South Africa Alexandra House, 2nd fl., Earlsfort Terrace, Dublin 2 01/661-5553.

United Kingdom 31 Merrion Rd., Dublin 2 01/205-3700.

United States 42 Elgin Rd., Ballsbridge, Dublin 4 01/668-8777.

HOLIDAYS

January 1; March 17 (St. Patrick's Day); April 9 (Good Friday); April 12 (Easter Monday); May 5 (May Day); June 2 and August 2 (summer bank holidays); October 25 (October Holiday); and December 25–26 (Christmas and St. Stephen's Day).

LANGUAGE

Officially, Irish (Gaelic) is the first language of the Republic, but the everyday language of the vast majority of Irish people is English. The Gaeltacht (pronounced "*gale*-tocked")—areas in which Irish *is* the everyday language of most people—constitutes only 6% of the land, and all its inhabitants are, in any case, bilingual. Except for isolated parts of the northwest and Connemara, where many signs are not translated, most signs in the country are written in English, with an Irish translation. There is one important exception to this rule, with which you should familiarize yourself: FIR (pronounced "fear") and MNÁ (pronounced "muh-*naw*") translate, respectively, into "men" and "women."

MONEY MATTERS

Dublin is expensive—an unfortunate state of affairs that manifests itself most obviously in hotel rates and restaurant menus. You can generally keep costs lower if you visit Ireland on a package tour. Alternatively, consider staying in a guest house or a B&B; they provide an economical and atmospheric option. The rest of the country—with the exception of the better-known hotels and restaurants—is less expensive than Dublin. That the Irish themselves complain bitterly about the high cost of living is partly attributable to the rate of value-added tax (V. A.T.)—a stinging 21% on "luxury" goods and 13½% on hotel accommodations. A double room in a moderately priced Dublin hotel will cost about €114, with breakfast; the current rate for a country B&B is around €32 per person. Modest, small-town hotels generally charge around €50 per person.

Sample prices include cup of coffee, €1; pint of beer, €3; Coca-Cola, €1.20; a sandwich, €2.30; 2-km (1-mi) taxi ride, €5.10. Prices are about 10% higher in Dublin.

CURRENCY The Irish Republic is a member of the European Monetary Union (EMU) and the euro is legal tender. Euro notes come in denominations of €500, €200, €100, €50, €20, €10, and €5. The euro is divided into 100 cents and coins are available as €2 and €1, and 50, 20, 10, 5, 2, and 1 cent. Although the euro is the only legal tender in the Republic, U.S. dollars and British currency are often accepted in large hotels and shops licensed as "bureaux de change." Banks give the best rate of exchange. There is likely to be some variance in the rates of exchange between Ireland and the United Kingdom (which includes Northern Ireland). Change U.K. pounds at a bank when you get to Ireland (note that pound coins are not accepted). The rate of exchange at press time was €0.94 to the U.S. dollar, €0.61 to the Canadian dollar, €1.51 to the pound sterling, €0.55 to the Australian dollar, €0.52 to the New Zealand dollar, and €0.11 to the South African rand.

TAXES

VALUE-ADDED TAX (V.A.T.) Visitors from outside Europe can take advantage of the "cash-back" system on value-added tax (V.A.T.) in two ways. The first is by having your invoice receipt stamped by customs on departure and mailing it back to the store for V.A.T. refund. You must, however, verify at the time of purchase that the store operates by this system. The second and more popular option is to use one of the private cash-back companies, which charge a commission.

TELEPHONES

COUNTRY & AREA CODES The country code for the Republic of Ireland is 353; for Northern Ireland it's 44.

INTERNATIONAL CALLS In the Republic and Northern Ireland, calls to the United States and Canada can be made by dialing 001 followed by the area code. For calls to the United Kingdom, dial 0044 followed by the number, dropping the beginning zero. For long-distance operators, call one of the service providers below.

Access Codes **AT&T** ☎ 800/550-000. **MCI** ☎ 800/551-001. **Sprint** ☎ 800/552-001.

LOCAL CALLS Pay phones can be found in all post offices and most hotels and bars, as well as in street booths. Local calls cost €0.25 for three minutes, calls within Ireland cost about €1 for three minutes, and calls to Britain cost about €2.50 for three minutes. Telephone cards are available at post offices and most newsdealers. Prices range from €2.55 for 10 units to €10.15 for 50 units. Card-operated booths are as common as coin-operated booths. Rates go down by about a third after 6 PM and all day Saturday and Sunday.

FLORENCE

The birthplace of the Renaissance and one of Europe's preeminent treasures, Florence draws visitors from all over the world. Lining the narrow streets of the historic center are 15th-century palazzi whose plain and sober facades often give way to delightful courtyards. The classical dignity of the High Renaissance and the exuberant invention of the baroque are mostly absent in Florentine buildings; here, the typical exterior gives nothing away of the treasures contained within.

EXPLORING FLORENCE

Founded by Julius Caesar, according to legend, Florence was built in the familiar grid pattern common to all Roman colonies. Except for the major monuments, which are appropriately imposing, the buildings are low and unpretentious and the streets are narrow. At times Florence can be a nightmare of mass tourism. Plan, if you can, to visit the city in late fall, early spring, or even in winter to avoid the crowds.

Piazza del Duomo & Piazza della Signoria

The area between Piazza del Duomo and Piazza della Signoria constitutes the core of the centro storico. Piazza del Duomo has been the center of Florence's religious life for centuries; work began on the Duomo in 1296, and the structure that sprang from the site is testament to religious fervor and a wealthy populace. Via Calzaiuoli links this piazza to Piazza della Signoria, the center of Florentine government since the end of the 13th century. The piazza is lined with Renaissance sculpture (some originals, some copies). The Galleria degli Uffizi, next to Palazzo Vecchio, houses one of the most important collections of Renaissance paintings in the world.

Numbers in the margin correspond to points of interest on the Florence map.

★ 3 **Battistero** (Baptistery). In front of the Duomo is the octagonal baptistery, one of the city's oldest (modern excavations suggest its foundations date from the 4th to 5th and the 8th to 9th centuries) and most beloved buildings. The interior dome mosaics are famous but cannot outshine the building's renowned gilded bronze east doors (facing the Duomo), the work of Lorenzo Ghiberti (1378–1455). The ones you see at the Baptistery, however, are copies; the originals are preserved in the Museo dell'Opera del Duomo. ✉ *Piazza del Duomo* ☎ *055/2302885* 🌐 *www.operaduomo.firenze.it* ⏲ *Mon.–Sat. noon–7, Sun. 8:30–2.*

❷ **Campanile** (Bell tower). This early-14th-century bell tower, designed by Giotto (circa 1267–1337), is richly decorated with colored marble and sculpture reproductions; the originals are in the Museo dell'Opera del Duomo. The 414-step climb to the top is less strenuous than that to the cupola on the Duomo. ✉ *Piazza del Duomo* ☎ *055/2302885* 🌐 *www.operaduomo.firenze.it* ⏲ *Daily 8:30–7:30.*

★ ❶ **Duomo.** The Cattedrale di Santa Maria del Fiore is dominated by a cupola representing a landmark in the history of architecture. Work began on the cathedral in 1296 under the supervision of master sculptor and architect Arnolfo di Cambio, and its construction took 140 years to complete. Gothic architecture predominates; the facade was added in the 1870s but is based on Tuscan Gothic models. Inside, the church is cool and austere, a fine example of the architecture of the period. Take a good look at the frescoes of equestrian figures on the left wall of the nave: the one on the right is by Paolo Uccello (1397–1475), the one on the left by Andrea del Castagno (circa 1419–57). The dome frescoes by Vasari take second place to the dome itself, Brunelleschi's (1377–1446) greatest architectural and technical achievement. The dome was also the inspiration for the one Michelangelo designed for St. Peter's in Rome and even for the dome of the Capitol in Washington. You can visit early medieval and ancient Roman remains of previous constructions excavated under the cathedral. And you can climb to the top of the dome, 463 exhausting steps up between the two layers of the double dome for a fine view. ✉ *Piazza del Duomo* ☎ *055/2302885* 🌐 *www.operaduomo.firenze.it* ⏲ *Crypt: weekdays 10–5:40, Sat. 8:30–5:40, first Sat. of the month 8:30–4. Cupola: weekdays 8:30–7, Sat. 8:30–5:40, first Sat. of the month 8:30–4. Duomo: weekdays 10–5, Sat., 10–4:45, Sun. 3:30–4:45, first Sat. of the month 10–3:30.*

❾ **Galleria degli Uffizi** (Uffizi Gallery). The Uffizi was built to house the administrative offices of the Medici, onetime rulers of the city. Later their fabulous art collection was arranged in a gallery on the top floor, which was opened to the public in the 17th century—making this the world's first modern public gallery. It comprises Italy's most important collection of paintings, with the emphasis on Italian art from the 13th to 16th centuries. Make sure you see the *Ognissanti Madonna* by Giotto (circa 1267–1337), and look for Botticelli's (1445–1510) *Birth of Venus* and *Primavera* in Rooms X–XIV, Michelangelo's *Holy Family* in Room XXV, and works by Raphael next door in Room XXVI. In addition to its art treasures, the gallery offers a magnificent close-up view of the Palazzo Vecchio tower from the coffee bar. Avoid long lines at the ticket booths by purchasing tickets in advance from Consorzio ITA. ✉ *Piazzale degli Uffizi 6* ☎ *055/23885* ✉ *Advance tickets, Consorzio ITA, Piazza Pitti 1, 50121* ☎ *055/294883* 🌐 *www.uffizi.firenze.it* 🎟 *€8.50, (€1.55 reservation fee)* ⏲ *Tues.–Sun. 8:15–6:50.*

Fodor'sChoice ★

❽ **Mercato Nuovo** (New Market). This open-air loggia was completed in 1551. Beyond the slew of souvenir stands, its main attraction is a copy of Pietro Tacca's bronze *Porcellino* (though it means *Little Pig*, it's actually a wild boar) on the south side, dating from around 1612 and copied from an earlier Roman work now in the Uffizi. The *Porcellino* is Florence's equivalent of the Trevi Fountain: put a coin in his mouth, and

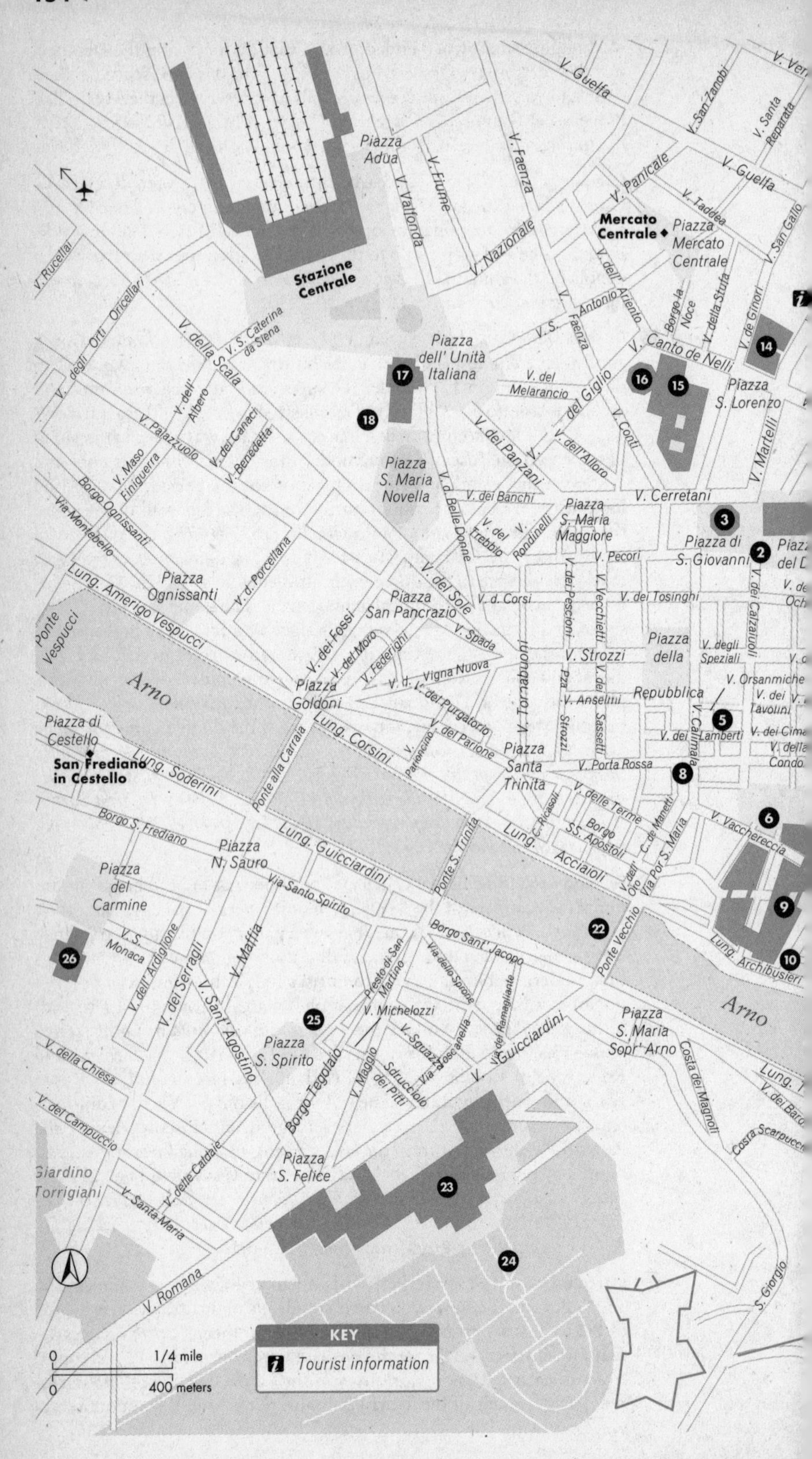

Stazione Centrale
Piazza Adua
V. Valfonda
V. Fiume
V. Faenza
V. Nazionale
V. Guelfa
V. San Zanobi
V. Santa Reparata
V. Panicale
V. Taddea
V. San Gallo
Mercato Centrale
Piazza Mercato Centrale
V. dell' Ariento
Borgo la Noce
V. della Stufa
V. de Ginori
V. S. Antonio
V. Canto de Nelli
Piazza S. Lorenzo
V. Martelli
V. Rucellai
V. Orti Oricellari
V. degli
V. S. Caterina da Siena
V. della Scala
Piazza dell' Unità Italiana
V. del Melarancio
V. del Giglio
V. Conti
V. dell' Alloro
V. dell' Albero
V. Palazzuolo
V. dei Canaci
V. Benedetta
V. Maso Finiguerra
Borgo Ognissanti
Via Montebello
V. dei Panzani
Piazza S. Maria Novella
V. d. Belle Donne
V. dei Banchi
V. Cerretani
Piazza S. Maria Maggiore
V. del Trebbio
V. Rondinelli
Piazza di S. Giovanni
V. Pecori
V. dei Pescioni
V. Vecchietti
V. dei Tosinghi
V. dei Calzaiuoli
Piazza Ognissanti
V. d. Porcellana
Lung. Amerigo Vespucci
Ponte Vespucci
V. del Sole
Piazza San Pancrazio
V. d. Corsi
V. Spada
V. dei Fossi
V. del Moro
V. Federighi
V. Vigna Nuova
V. Tornabuoni
V. Strozzi
Piazza della Repubblica
V. degli Speziali
V. Orsanmichele
V. dei Tavolini
Arno
Piazza Goldoni
V. d. Purgatorio
V. del Parione
V. Parioncino
Pza Strozzi
V. Anselmi
V. Sassetti
V. Calimala
V. dei Lamberti
V. dei Cimatori
V. della Condotta
Piazza di Cestello
San Frediano in Cestello
Lung. Soderini
Ponte alla Carraia
Lung. Corsini
Piazza Santa Trinita
V. Porta Rossa
V. delle Terme
C. Ricasoli
Borgo SS. Apostoli
C. de Manetti
V. Vacchereccia
Borgo S. Frediano
Piazza N. Sauro
Lung. Guicciardini
Ponte S. Trinita
Lung. Acciaioli
V. dell' Oro
Via Por S. Maria
Piazza del Carmine
Via Santo Spirito
V. S. Monaca
V. dell' Ardiglione
V. dei Serragli
V. Maffia
V. Sant' Agostino
Presto di San Martino
Via dello Sprone
Borgo Sant' Jacopo
Ponte Vecchio
Lung. Archibusieri
V. Michelozzi
V. Sguazza
Via Toscanella
Via del Ramagliante
Piazza S. Maria Sopr' Arno
Costa dei Magnoli
Piazza S. Spirito
Borgo Tegolaio
V. Maggio
Sdrucciolo dei Pitti
V. Guicciardini
V. della Chiesa
V. del Campuccio
V. delle Caldaie
Piazza S. Felice
Costa Scarpuccia
V. dei Bardi
Giardino Torrigiani
V. Santa Maria
V. Romana
S. Giorgio
0
1/4 mile
0
400 meters
KEY
Tourist information

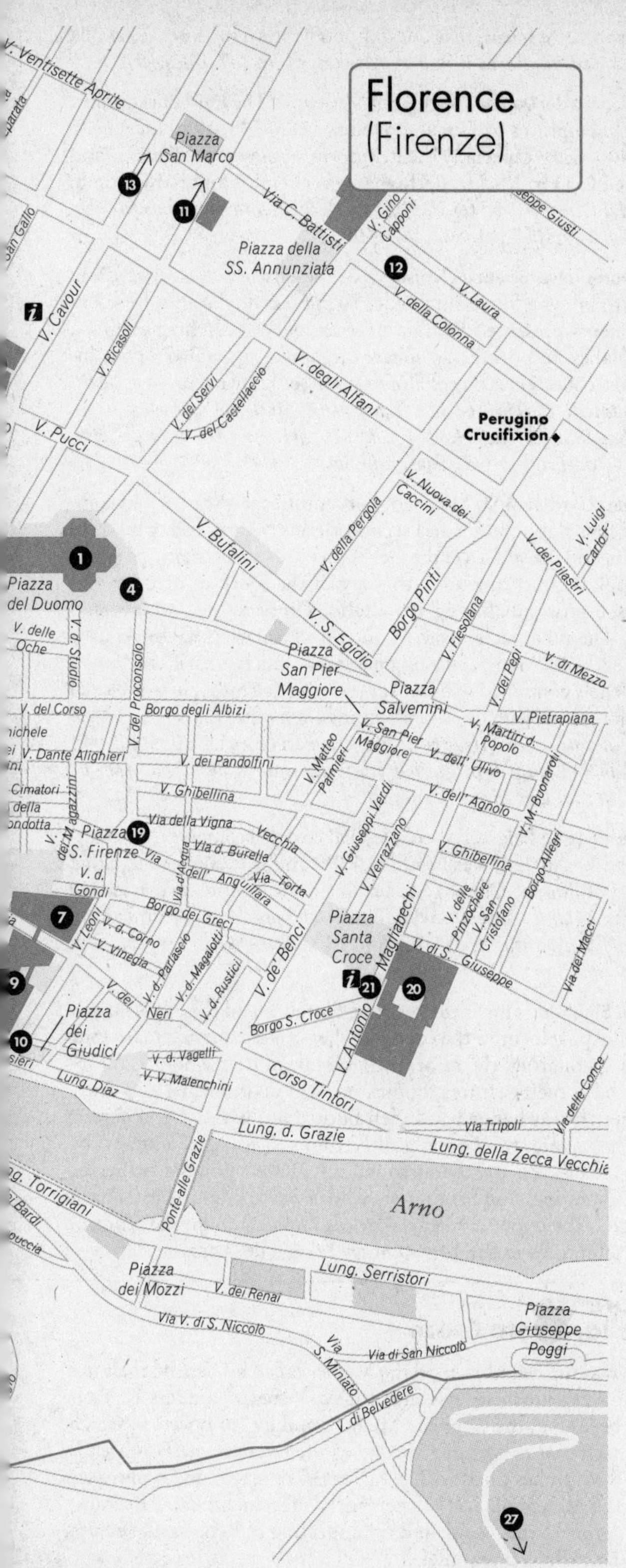

Piazza del Duomo & Piazza della Signoria

Battistero 3
Campanile 2
Duomo 1
Galleria degli Uffizi 9
Mercato Nuovo 8
Museo dell'Opera del Duomo 4
Museo di Storia della Scienza 10
Orsanmichele 5
Palazzo Vecchio 7
Piazza della Signoria 6

San Marco, San Lorenzo, Santa Maria Novella, Santa Croce

Cappelle Medicee 16
Galleria dell'Accademia 11
Museo Archeologico 12
Museo dell'Opera di Santa Croce e Cappella dei Pazzi 21
Museo di San Marco 13
Museo di Santa Maria Novella 18
Museo Nazionale del Bargello 19
Palazzo Medici-Riccardi 14
San Lorenzo 15
Santa Croce 20
Santa Maria Novella 17

The Oltrarno

Giardino di Boboli 24
Palazzo Pitti 23
Ponte Vecchio 22
San Miniato al Monte 27
Santa Maria del Carmine 26
Santo Spirito 25

if it lands properly, it means that one day you'll return to Florence. ✉ *Via Por San Maria at Via Porta Rossa* ⏲ *Market: Mon. 1–7, Tues.–Sat. 8–7.*

★ ❹ **Museo dell'Opera del Duomo** (Cathedral Museum). The museum contains some superb sculptures by Donatello (circa 1386–1466) and Luca della Robbia (1400–82)—especially their *cantorie,* or singers' galleries—and an unfinished *Pietà* by Michelangelo that was intended for his own tomb. ✉ *Piazza del Duomo 9* ☎ *055/2302885* 🌐 *www.operaduomo.firenze.it* ⏲ *Mon.–Sat. 9:30–7:30, Sun. 9–1:40.*

❿ **Museo di Storia della Scienza** (Museum of the History of Science). You don't have to know a lot about science to appreciate the antique scientific instruments presented here in informative, eye-catching exhibits. From astrolabes and armillary spheres to some of Galileo's own instruments, the collection is one of Florence's lesser-known treasures. ✉ *Piazza dei Giudici 1* ☎ *055/265311* 🌐 *www.imss.fi.it* ⏲ *Oct.–May, Mon. and Wed.–Sat. 9:30–5, Tues. 9:30–1, 2nd Sun. of month 10–1; June–Sept., Mon. and Wed.–Fri. 9:30–5, Tues. and Sat. 9:30–1.*

❺ **Orsanmichele** (Garden of St. Michael). For centuries this was an odd combination of first-floor church and second-floor granary. Today it serves as a museum, and the statues in the niches on the exterior (many of which are now copies) constitute an anthology of the work of eminent Renaissance sculptors, including Donatello, Ghiberti, and Verrocchio (1435–88). The tabernacle inside is an extraordinary piece by Andrea Orcagna (1320–68). Many of the original statues can be seen in the Museo di Orsanmichele contained within. At press time the museum was closed for restoration; check with the Tourist Information office for details. ✉ *Via dei Calzaiuoli; museum entrance at via Arte della Lana* ☎ *055/284944* ⏲ *Weekends 9–1 and 4–6; guided tours weekdays at 9, 10, and 11* ⏲ *Closed 1st and last Mon. of month.*

❼ **Palazzo Vecchio** (Old Palace). Also called Palazzo della Signoria, this massive, fortresslike city hall was begun in 1299 and was taken over, along with the rest of Florence, by the Medici. Inside, the impressive, frescoed salons and the *studiolo* (little study) of Francesco I are the main attractions. ✉ *Piazza della Signoria* ☎ *055/2768465* ⏲ *Mon.–Wed., Fri., and Sat. 9–7, Thurs. and Sun. 9–2.*

❻ **Piazza della Signoria.** This is the heart of Florence and the city's largest square. In the pavement in the center of the square a plaque marks the spot where Savonarola, the reformist Dominican friar who urged Florentines to burn their pictures, books, musical instruments, and other worldly objects, was hanged and then burned at the stake as a heretic in 1498. The square, the Fontana di Nettuno (Neptune Fountain) by Ammanati (1511–92), and the surrounding cafés are popular gathering places for Florentines and for tourists who come to admire the Palazzo della Signoria, the copy of Michelangelo's *David* standing in front of it, and the sculptures in the 14th-century Loggia dei Lanzi.

San Marco, San Lorenzo, Santa Maria Novella, Santa Croce

San Marco was the neighborhood the Medici called home, and their imprint is still very much in evidence today. Visual reminders of their power can be seen in the Cappelle Medicee and in San Lorenzo, which was the church that the Medici viewed as their very own. This area is teeming with churches filled with great works of art, and two must-see museums. The Accademia has Michelangelo's *David,* arguably the most famous sculpture in the world, and the collection of Renaissance sculpture at the Bargello is unparalleled.

★ 16 **Cappelle Medicee** (Medici Chapels). These extraordinary chapels, part of the church of San Lorenzo complex, contain the tombs of practically every member of the Medici family, which guided Florence's destiny from the 15th century to 1737. Cosimo I (1519–74), a Medici whose acumen made him the richest man in Europe, is buried in the crypt beneath the **Cappella dei Principi** (Chapel of the Princes), and Donatello's tomb is next to that of his patron, Cosimo il Vecchio (1389–1464). Upstairs is a dazzling array of colored marble panels. Michelangelo's **Sagrestia Nuova** (New Sacristy) tombs of Giuliano (1478–1534) and Lorenzo de' Medici (1492–1519) are adorned with the justly famed sculptures of *Dawn* and *Dusk, Night* and *Day.* ✉ *Piazza di Madonna degli Aldobrandini* ☎ *055/294883 reservations* 🌐 *www.sanlorenzo.com* 🕒 *Daily 8:15–5; closed 1st, 3rd, and 5th Mon. and 2nd and 4th Sun. of month.*

★ 11 **Galleria dell'Accademia** (Accademia Gallery). Michelangelo's *David* is a tour de force of artistic conception and technical ability, for he was using a piece of stone that had already been worked on by a lesser sculptor. Take time to see the forceful *Slaves,* also by Michelangelo; their roughhewn, unfinished surfaces contrast dramatically with the highly polished, meticulously carved *David.* Michelangelo left the *Slaves* "unfinished," it is often claimed, to accentuate the figures' struggle to escape the bondage of stone. Actually, he simply abandoned them because his patron changed his mind about the tomb monument for which they were planned. Try to be first in line at opening time or go shortly before closing time so you can get the full impact without having to fight your way through the crowds. ✉ *Via Ricasoli 60* ☎ *055/294 883 reservations; 055/2388609 Galleria* 🌐 *www.mega.it* 🎫 *€8.50, €1.55 reservation fee* 🕒 *Tues.–Sun. 8:15–6:50.*

12 **Museo Archeologico** (Archaeological Museum). Fine Etruscan and Roman antiquities and a pretty garden are the draw here. ✉ *Via della Colonna 38* ☎ *055/23575* 🌐 *www.mega.it* 🕒 *Mon. 2–7, Tues. and Thurs. 8:30–7, Wed. and Fri.–Sun. 8:30–2.*

21 **Museo dell'Opera di Santa Croce e Cappella dei Pazzi** (Museum of Santa Croce and Pazzi Chapel). From the cloister of the convent adjacent to Santa Croce you can visit the small museum and see what remains of the Cimbaue crucifix that was irreparably damaged by the 1966 flood, when water rose to 16 feet in parts of the church. The **Cappella dei Pazzi** in the cloister is an architectural gem by Brunelleschi. The interior is a lesson in spatial equilibrium and harmony. ✉ *Piazza Santa Croce* ☎ *055/244619* 🕒 *Mar.–Oct., Thurs.–Tues. 10–7; Nov.–Feb., Thurs.–Tues. 10–12:30 and 3–6.*

13 **Museo di San Marco.** A former Dominican convent houses this museum, which contains many works by Fra Angelico (1400–55). Within the same walls where the unfortunate Savonarola, the reformist friar, later contemplated the sins of the Florentines, Fra Angelico went humbly about his work, decorating many of the otherwise austere cells and corridors with brilliantly colored frescoes on religious subjects. Look for his masterpiece, the *Annunciation.* Together with many of his paintings arranged on the ground floor, just off the little cloister, they form a fascinating collection. ✉ *Piazza San Marco 1* ☎ *055/2388608* 🕒 *Weekdays 8:15–1:50, Sat. 8:15–6:50, Sun. 8:15–7* 🕒 *Closed 2nd and 4th Mon. of month, and 1st, 3rd, and 5th Sun. of month.*

18 **Museo di Santa Maria Novella.** Adjacent to the church, this museum is worth a visit for its serenity and the faded Paolo Uccello frescoes from Genesis, as well as the **Cappellone degli Spagnoli** (Spanish Chapel), with

frescoes by Andrea di Buonaiuto. ✉ *Piazza Santa Maria Novella 19* ☎ *055/282187.*

★ ⓳ **Museo Nazionale del Bargello.** This grim, fortresslike palace served in medieval times as the residence of Florence's chief magistrate and later as a prison. It is now filled with Italian Renaissance sculpture, including masterpieces by Donatello, Verrocchio, Michelangelo, and other major sculptors. The Bargello also has an eclectic collection of antique arms and ceramics. ✉ *Via del Proconsolo 4* ☎ *055/2388606* 🌐 *www.arca.ne* ⏲ *Daily 8:15–1:50* ⏲ *Closed 2nd and 4th Mon. of month and 1st, 3rd, and 5th Sun. of month.*

⓮ **Palazzo Medici-Riccardi.** Few tourists know about Benozzo Gozzoli's (1420–97) glorious frescoes in the tiny second-floor chapel of this palace, built in 1444 by Michelozzo for Cosimo de' Medici (Il Vecchio, 1389–1464). Glimmering with gold, they represent the journey of the Magi as a spectacular cavalcade with cameo portraits of various Medici and the artist himself. ✉ *Via Cavour 1* ☎ *055/2760340* ⏲ *Thurs.–Tues. 9–7.*

⓯ **San Lorenzo.** The facade of this church was never finished, but the Brunelleschi interior is elegantly austere. Stand in the middle of the nave at the entrance, on the line that stretches to the high altar, and you'll see what Brunelleschi achieved with the grid of inlaid marble in the pavement. Every architectural element in the church is placed to create a dramatic effect of single-point perspective. The **Sagrestia Vecchia** (Old Sacristy), decorated with stuccoes by Donatello, is attributed to Brunelleschi. ✉ *Piazza San Lorenzo* ☎ *055/290184* ⏲ *Church: Mon.–Sat. 7–noon and 3:30–5:30, Sun. 3:30–5. Old Sacristy: Mon.–Sat. 8–noon and 3:30–5:30, Sun. 3:30–5:30. Closed Dec. and Jan.*

★ ⓴ **Santa Croce.** The mighty church of Santa Croce was begun in 1294 and has become a pantheon for Florentine greats; monumental tombs of Michelangelo, Galileo (1564–1642), Machiavelli (1469–1527), and other Renaissance luminaries line the walls. Inside are two chapels frescoed by Giotto and another painted by Taddeo Gaddi (1300–66), as well as an *Annunciation* and crucifix by Donatello. But it is the scale of this grandiose church that proclaims the power and ambition of medieval Florence. ✉ *Piazza Santa Croce 16* ☎ *055/244619* ⏲ *Mar.–Oct., Mon.–Sat. 9:30–5:30, Sun. 3–5:30; Nov.–Feb., Mon.–Sat. 9:30–noon and 3–5:30, Sun. 3–5:30.*

⓱ **Santa Maria Novella.** A Tuscan interpretation of the Gothic style, this handsome church should be seen from the opposite end of Piazza Santa Maria Novella for the best view of its facade. Inside are some famous frescoes, especially Masaccio's (1401–28) *Trinity,* a Giotto crucifix in the sacristy, and Ghirlandaio's frescoes in the **Capella Maggiore** (Main Chapel). ✉ *Piazza Santa Maria Novella* ☎ *055/210113* ⏲ *Mon.–Thurs. and Sat. 9:30–5, Fri. and Sun. 1–5.*

The Oltrarno

The Oltrarno, which means "beyond the Arno," is on the south side of the Arno. It's a neighborhood filled with artisans' workshops, and in that respect, it has changed little since the Renaissance. The gargantuan Palazzo Pitti stands as a sweeping reminder of the power of the Medici family, and there are some lovely Renaissance churches, terrific restaurants, and first-rate shoe stores—all reason enough to cross over and explore.

24 **Giardino di Boboli** (Boboli Gardens). The main entrance to this park on a landscaped hillside is in the right wing of Palazzo Pitti. Laid out in 1549, the gardens were for Cosimo I's wife, Eleanora da Toledo, who made the palazzo her home. They were further developed by later Medici dukes. ✉ *Enter through Palazzo Pitti* ☎ *055/294883* ⊙ *Apr.–Oct., daily 8:15–5:30; Nov.–Mar., daily 8:15–4:30* ⊙ *Closed 1st and last Mon. of each month.*

Fodor's Choice ★

23 **Palazzo Pitti.** This enormous palace is a 16th-century extravaganza the Medici acquired from the Pitti family after the latter had gone deeply into debt to build the central portion. The Medici enlarged the building, extending its facade along the immense piazza. Solid and severe, it looks like a Roman aqueduct turned into a palace. The palace houses several museums: the **Museo degli Argenti** (Silver Museum) displays the fabulous Medici collection of objects in silver and gold; another has the collections of the **Galleria d'Arte Moderna** (Gallery of Modern Art). The most famous museum, though, is the **Galleria Palatina** (Palatine Gallery), with an extraordinary collection of paintings, many hung frame-to-frame in a clear case of artistic overkill. Some are high up in dark corners, so try to go on a bright day. ✉ *Piazza Pitti* ☎ *055/294883* 🌐 *www.thais.it* ⊙ *Museo degli Argenti: Mon.–Sun. 8:15–1:50; closed 2nd and 4th Sun. and 1st, 3rd, and 5th Mon. of month. Galleria Palatina: Nov.–Mar., Tues.–Sat. 8:15–6:50, Sun. 8:15–6:50; Apr.–Oct., Tues.–Sat. 8:15–10, Sun. 8:15–7.*

★ 22 **Ponte Vecchio** (Old Bridge). Florence's oldest bridge appears to be just another street lined with goldsmiths' shops until you get to the middle and catch a glimpse of the Arno below. Spared during World War II by the retreating Germans (who blew up every other bridge in the city), it also survived the 1966 flood. It leads into the **Oltrarno,** where fascinating artisans' workshops preserve the feel of old, working-class Florence. ✉ *East of Ponte Santa Trinita and west of Ponte alle Grazie.*

27 **San Miniato al Monte.** One of Florence's oldest churches, this charming green-and-white marble Romanesque edifice is full of artistic riches, among them the gorgeous Renaissance chapel where a Portuguese cardinal was laid to rest in 1459 under a ceiling by Luca della Robbia. ✉ *Viale Galileo Galilei, or take stairs from Piazzale Michelangelo* ☎ *055/2342731* ⊙ *Daily 8–6:30.*

26 **Santa Maria del Carmine.** The church is of little architectural interest but of immense significance in the history of Renaissance art. It contains the celebrated frescoes painted by Masaccio, Masolino, and Filippino Lippi in the **Cappella Brancacci.** The chapel was a classroom for such artistic giants as Botticelli, Leonardo da Vinci (1452–1519), Michelangelo, and Raphael, since they all came to study Masaccio's realistic use of light and perspective and his creation of space and depth. ✉ *Piazza del Carmine* ☎ *055/2382195* ⊙ *Mon. and Wed.–Sat. 10–5, Sun. 1–5.*

25 **Santo Spirito.** Its plain, unfinished facade is less than impressive, but this church is important because it is one of Brunelleschi's finest architectural creations. It contains some superb paintings, including a *Madonna* by Filippino Lippi. Santo Spirito is the hub of a colorful, trendy neighborhood of artisans and intellectuals. An outdoor market enlivens the square every morning and some Sunday afternoons, pigeons, pet owners, and pensioners take over. ✉ *Piazza Santo Spirito* ☎ *055/210030* ⊙ *Church: Thurs.–Tues. 8:30–noon and 4–6, Wed. 8:30–noon and 4–7; museum: Tues.–Sun. 10–2.*

WHERE TO EAT

Mealtimes in Florence are from 1 to 2:30 and 8 to 9 or later. Reservations are always advisable; to find a table at inexpensive places, get there early.

WHAT IT COSTS In euros				
	$$$$	**$$$**	**$$**	**$**
AT DINNER	over €22	€17–€22	€12–€17	under €12

Prices are per person for a main course.

★ **$$$$** ✕ **Cibrèo.** The food at this classic Florentine trattoria is fantastic, from the first bite of seamless, creamy *crostini di fegatini* (savory Tuscan chicken liver spread on grilled bread) to the last bite of one of the melt-in-your-mouth-good desserts. If you thought you'd never try tripe, let alone like it, this is the place to lay any doubts to rest: the cold tripe salad with parsley and garlic is an epiphany. ✉ *Via Andrea del Verrocchio 8/r* ☎ *055/2341100* ✍ *Reservations essential* ▭ *AE, DC, MC, V* ⊙ *Closed Sun. and Mon., July 25–Sept. 5, and Dec. 31–Jan. 7.*

$$$$ ✕ **Enoteca Pinchiorri.** A sumptuous Renaissance palace with high, frescoed ceilings and bouquets in silver vases is the setting for this restaurant, one of the most expensive in Italy. Some consider it one of the best, and others consider it an expensive, non-Italian rip-off: prices are high and portions are small. Fish, game, and meat dishes are always on the menu, along with pastas such as the *ignudi*—ricotta dumplings with a lobster fricassee. ✉ *Via Ghibellina 87* ☎ *055/242777* ✍ *Reservations essential* ▭ *AE, MC, V* ⊙ *Closed Sun. and Aug. No lunch Mon.*

★ **$$$$** ✕ **Taverna del Bronzino.** Would you like to have a sophisticated meal in a 16th-century Renaissance artist's studio? This restaurant, the former studio of Santi di Tito, a student of Bronzino's, has a simple formality, with white tablecloths and place settings. The classic Tuscan food, however, is superb, and the presentation is often dramatic. A wine list of solid, affordable choices rounds out the menu. The service is outstanding. Reservations are advised, especially for eating at the wine cellar's only table. ✉ *Via delle Ruote 25/r* ☎ *055/495220* ▭ *AE, DC, MC, V* ⊙ *Closed Sun. and Aug.*

★ **$$–$$$** ✕ **Beccofino.** Forget the fact that the noise levels in this place often reach the pitch of the Tower of Babel. Concentrate, instead, on the food, which might be the most creative in town. The interior has a pale-wood serpentine bar separating the ochre-walled wine bar from the green-walled restaurant. Chef Francesco Berardinelli has paid some dues in the United States, and it shows in his food, which is inventive although the results taste wholly and wonderfully Italian. The wine bar offers a shorter and less expensive menu; in the summer, you can enjoy this food on an outdoor terrace facing the Arno. ✉ *Piazza degli Scarlatti 1/r (Lungarno Guicciardini)* ☎ *055/290076* ✍ *Reservations essential* ▭ *MC, V* ⊙ *Closed Mon. Nov.–Mar.*

★ **$$–$$$** ✕ **La Giostra.** La Giostra, which means "carousel" in Italian, is owned and run by Prince Dimitri Kunz d'Asburgo Lorena. It feels like a club, with white walls and tablecloths and dim lighting accented with a few tiny blue lights twinkling on the ceiling. Try the unusually good pastas, maybe the *carbonara di tartufo,* decadently rich spaghetti with eggs and white truffles. Leave room for dessert: this might be the only show in town with a sublime tiramisu and a wonderfully gooey Sacher torte. ✉ *Borgo Pinti 12/r* ☎ *055/241341* ▭ *AE, DC, MC, V.*

★ $$–$$$ ✕ **Le Fonticine.** The area around the train station is not noted for its fine dining options, and this place provides a welcome oasis. It combines the best of two Italian cuisines: owner Silvano Bruci is from Tuscany and his wife, Gianna, is from Emilia-Romagna. Start with the mixed-vegetable antipasto plate and then move on to any of their house-made pastas. The feathery light tortelloni *nostro modo* are stuffed with fresh ricotta and served with a tomato and cream sauce, and should not be missed. The interior of the restaurant, filled with the Brucis' painting collection, provides a cheery space for this soul-satisfying food. ✉ *Via Nazionale 79/r,* ☎ *055/282106* ▭ *AE, DC, MC, V* ⊙ *Closed Sun. and Mon., Dec. and Aug.*

$–$$$ ✕ **Finisterrae.** Four large, dramatically lit rooms, with colorful walls dotted with maps detailing various Mediterranean towns, lend an aura of romance to this spot. There may not be a prettier restaurant in town. The eminently affordable menu offers a little bit from Lebanon, Spain, France, Morocco and, yes, Italy. The Spanish options are particularly fine, especially the *filetto al cabrales* (beef with Spanish blue cheese and port). The seductive bar, with its expert barmen, is dimly lit with low-slung seats; they'll even provide tobacco if you want to light up one of the hookahs. ✉ *via de' Pepi 3/5r* ☎ *055/2638675* ▭ *MC, V* ⊙ *Closed Mon. and Nov.–Mar.*

★ $–$$ ✕ **Osteria de'Benci.** Just a few minutes from Santa Croce, this charming osteria serves some of the most eclectic food in Florence. Try the spaghetti *dell'ubriacone* (literally "drunken spaghetti," cooked in red wine). The grilled meats are justifiably famous, such as the *carbonata,* a succulent piece of grilled beef served rare. When it's warm, you can dine outside with a view of the 13th-century tower belonging to the prestigious Alberti family. The English-speaking staff shouldn't scare you off: Florentines *do* eat here. ✉ *Via de'Benci 11-13/r* ☎ *055/2344923* ▭ *AE, DC, MC, V* ⊙ *Closed Sun.*

$ ✕ **La Casalinga.** "Casalinga" means "housewife," and this place has all the charm of a 1950s kitchen with Tuscan comfort food to match. Tables are set close together and the place is usually jammed, and with good reason. The menu is long, portions are plentiful, and service is prompt and friendly. If you eat ribollita anywhere in Florence, eat it here—it couldn't be more authentic. ✉ *Via Michelozzi 9/r* ☎ *055/218624* ▭ *AE, DC, MC, V* ⊙ *Closed Sun., 1 wk at Christmas, 3 wks in Aug. No lunch in July.*

WHERE TO STAY

Hotel rooms are at a premium in Florence for most of the year. Reserve well in advance. If you arrive without a reservation, the **Consorzio ITA office** (✉ Stazione Centrale di Santa Maria Novella) in the train station, open 8:20 AM–9 PM, can help you, but there may be a long line (take a number and wait). Now that much traffic is banned in the centro storico, many central hotel rooms are quieter. Local traffic and motorcycles can still be bothersome, however, so check the decibel level before you settle in. From November through March, ask for special low winter rates.

WHAT IT COSTS In euros

	$$$$	$$$	$$	$
FOR 2 PEOPLE	over €300	€225–€300	€150–€225	under €150

Hotel prices are for two people in a standard double room in high season.

★ $$$$ 🏨 **Brunelleschi.** Architects united a Byzantine tower, a medieval church, and a later building in a stunning structure in the very heart of the centro storico to make this unique hotel. Medieval stone walls and brick arches contrast pleasantly with the plush, contemporary furniture. The comfortable, soundproof rooms are done in coordinated patterns and soft colors. ✉ *Piazza Sant'Elisabetta 3/r (off Via dei Calzaiuoli), 50122* ☎ *055/27370* 📠 *055/219653* 🌐 *www.hotelbrunelleschi.it* ⇨ *96 rooms, 7 junior suites* ◊ *Restaurant, bar* ▭ *AE, DC, MC, V.*

★ **$$$$** **Excelsior.** Florentine hotels do not get much more exquisite or expensive than this. Rooms are decorated in Empire style but still feel up-to-date. High ceilings, dramatic views of the Arno, patterned rugs, and tasteful prints lend the rooms a sense of extravagant well-being. Public rooms have stained glass and acres of Oriental carpets strewn over marble floors. The opulence of 19th-century Florentine antiques is set off by charming old prints of the city and long mirrors. ✉ *Piazza Ognissanti 3, 50123* ☎ *055/264201* 📠 *055/210278* 🌐 *www.westin.com* ⇨ *155 rooms, 16 suites* ◊ *Restaurant, bar* ▭ *AE, DC, MC, V.*

$$$$ **Grand.** This Florentine classic provides all the luxuries. Rooms are furnished in either Renaissance or Empire style; the former have deep, richly hued damask brocades and canopied beds, the latter a lovely profusion of crisp prints and patterned fabric offsetting white walls. The overall effect is sumptuous, as is the view of either the Arno or a small courtyard lined with potted orange trees. Avoid the piano bar, which is high-priced karaoke. ✉ *Piazza Ognissanti 1, 50123* ☎ *055/288781* 📠 *055/217400* 🌐 *www.grandhotelflorence.com* ⇨ *107 rooms* ◊ *Restaurant, bar* ▭ *AE, DC, MC, V.*

$$$$ **Hotel Savoy.** From the outside, it looks very much like the turn-of-the-19th-century building that it is. But step inside this hotel in the heart of the centro storico and sleek minimalism prevails. Sitting rooms have a funky edge with cream-colored walls dotted with contemporary prints and photographs. Many rooms, decorated in muted colors, with clean lines and soaring ceilings, overlook Piazza Repubblica and have views of the Duomo's cupola. ✉ *Piazza della Repubblica 7, 50123* ☎ *055/27351* 📠 *055/2735888* 🌐 *www.roccofortehotels.com* ⇨ *98 rooms, 9 suites* ◊ *Restaurant, bar* ▭ *AE, DC, MC, V.*

$$$$ **Lungarno.** Rooms and suites in this hotel across the Arno from the Palazzo Vecchio and the Duomo have private terraces jutting out over the river. The chic interior approximates a breezily elegant home, with lots of crisp white fabrics trimmed in blue. Four suites in a 13th-century tower preserve exposed stone walls and old archways. More than 100 paintings and drawings—from Picassos to Cocteaus—hang in hallways and bedrooms. ✉ *Borgo San Jacopo 14, 50125* ☎ *055/27261* 📠 *055/268437* 🌐 *www.lungarnohotels.com* ⇨ *60 rooms, 13 suites* ◊ *Restaurant, bar* ▭ *AE, DC, MC, V.*

★ **$$$–$$$$** **Monna Lisa.** Housed in a 15th-century palazzo, parts of which date from the 13th century, this hotel retains some of its original coffered wood ceilings, as well as its original marble staircase. The rooms are on the small side, but they are tastefully decorated. The public rooms are decorated in a 19th-century style. ✉ *Borgo Pinti 27, 50121* ☎ *055/2479751* 📠 *055/2479755* 🌐 *www.monnalisa.it* ⇨ *45 rooms* ◊ *Bar* ▭ *AE, DC, MC, V.*

★ **$$$** **Hermitage.** This place is centrally located and, given the price, a great bargain. All rooms are hung with lively wallpaper; some have views of the Palazzo Vecchio and others of the Arno. The rooftop terrace, where you can breakfast or enjoy a cocktail, is decked with flowers. The lobby feels like a friendly living room, with warm yellow walls. ✉ *Vicolo Marzio 1 (Piazza del Pesce, Ponte Vecchio), 50122* ☎ *055/287216* 📠 *055/212208* 🌐 *www.hermitagehotel.com* ⇨ *27 rooms, 1 suite* ▭ *MC, V.*

★ **$$–$$$** **Beacci Tornabuoni.** Florentine pensioni do not come any more classic than this. In a 14th-century palazzo, it has old-fashioned style and just enough modern comfort to keep you happy. The sitting room has a large fireplace, the terrace has a tremendous view of some major Florentine monuments, and the wallpapered rooms are inviting. On Monday, Wednesday, and Friday nights from May to October, the dining room opens, serving Tuscan specialties. ✉ *Via Tornabuoni 3 50123* ☎ *055/212645* 🖷 *055/283594* 🌐 *www.bthotel.it* *28 rooms* *Restaurant, bar* 💳 *AE, DC, MC, V.*

$$ **Loggiato dei Serviti.** Occupying a 16th-century former monastery, this attractively spare Renaissance building was originally a refuge for traveling priests. Vaulted ceilings, tasteful furnishings (some antique), canopied beds, and rich fabrics give you the feel of Old Florence while you enjoy modern creature comforts. ✉ *Piazza Santissima Annunziata 3, 50122* ☎ *055/289592* 🖷 *055/289595* 🌐 *www.loggiatodeiserviti.it* *29 rooms* 💳 *AE, DC, MC, V.*

★ **$$** **Morandi alla Crocetta.** This charming and distinguished residence near Piazza Santissima Annunziata was once a monastery, and access is up a flight of stairs. It is furnished in the classic style of a Florentine home, and guests are made to feel like friends of the family. Small and exceptional, it is also a good value and must be booked well in advance. ✉ *Via Laura 50, 50121* ☎ *055/2344747* 🖷 *055/2480954* 🌐 *www.hotelmorandi.it* *10 rooms* 💳 *AE, DC, MC, V.*

$$ **Nuova Italia.** Near the main train station and within walking distance of the sights, this homey hotel in a dignified palazzo is run by a genial English-speaking family. Rooms are simply furnished, and the triple-glazed windows ensure restful nights. ✉ *Via Faenza 26, 50123* ☎ *055/268430* 🖷 *055/210941* *20 rooms* 💳 *AE, MC, V.*

$$ **Porta Faenza.** A hospitable Italian-Canadian couple owns and manages this conveniently positioned hotel near the station. Spacious rooms in Florentine style and sparkling bathrooms that, though compact, have such amenities as hair dryers make this a good value. The staff is helpful and attentive to your needs. ✉ *Via Faenza 77, 50123* ☎ *055/284119* 🖷 *055/210101* 🌐 *www.hotelportafaenza.it* *25 rooms* 💳 *AE, DC, MC, V.*

$$ **Villa Azalee.** A five-minute walk from the train station and a short distance from the Fortezza da Basso (site of the Pitti fashion shows), this 19th-century villa deftly recalls its previous incarnation as a private residence. Some rooms have private terraces, many have views of the hotel's flower-filled garden. ✉ *Viale Fratelli Rosselli 44, 50123* ☎ *055/214242* 🖷 *055/268264* 🌐 *www.villaazalee.it* *25 rooms* 💳 *AE, DC, MC, V.*

★ **$–$$** **Bellettini.** This small, central hotel occupies two floors of an old but well-kept building near San Lorenzo, in an area with many inexpensive restaurants. Rooms are large, with traditional Venetian or Tuscan furnishings, and bathrooms are modern. The management is friendly and helpful. ✉ *Via dei Conti 7, 50123* ☎ *055/213561* 🖷 *055/283551* 🌐 *www.firenze.net* *27 rooms, 4 without bath* 💳 *AE, DC, MC, V.*

$ **Albergo Losanna.** Most major sights are within walking distance of this tiny pensione just within the viale. Despite its dated feel, the property is impeccably kept. Guest rooms have high ceilings: try to get one facing away from the street—you won't have a view but you will get a quiet night's sleep. ✉ *Via V. Alfieri 9, 50121* ☎🖷 *055/245840* *8 rooms, 3 with bath* 💳 *MC, V.*

$ **Alessandra.** The location, a block from the Ponte Vecchio, and ample rooms make this a good choice for basic accommodations at reasonable rates. The English-speaking staff makes sure guests are happy. ✉ *Borgo Santi Apostoli 17, 50123* ☎ *055/283438* 🖷 *055/210619* 🌐 *www.hotelalessandra.com* *26 rooms, 18 with bath, 1 suite, 1 apartment* 💳 *AE, MC, V* ⊗ *Closed Dec. 10–26.*

NIGHTLIFE & THE ARTS

The Arts

Film

You can find movie listings in *La Nazione,* the daily Florence newspaper. On Monday and Tuesday, first-run English-language films are shown at the **Odeon** (✉ Piazza Strozzi).

Music

Most major musical events are staged at the **Teatro Comunale** (✉ Corso Italia 12 ☎ 055/211158). The box office (closed Sunday and Monday) is open from 9 to 1 and a half hour before performances. It's best to order your tickets by mail, however, as they're difficult to come by at the last minute. Amici della Musica (Friends of Music) puts on a series of concerts at the **Teatro della Pergola** (✉ Box office: Via della Pergola 10a/r ☎ 055/2479651 🌐 www.pergolafirenze.it). For information on concerts contact the **Amici della Musica** (✉ Via Alamanni 39 ☎ 055/210804) directly.

Nightlife

Bars

Negroni (✉ Via dei Renai17/r ☎ 055/243647) is exactly where you want to be at cocktail hour if you're young, or simply young at heart. **Rex** (✉ Via Fiesolana 23–25/r, Santa Croce ☎ 055/2480331) is trendy, with an artsy crowd.

Nightclubs

Central Park (✉ Via del Fosso Macinante 2 ☎ 055/353505) is a great spot if you want to put on your dancing shoes. **Maracaná** (✉ Via Faenza 4 ☎ 055/210298) is a restaurant and pizzeria serving Brazilian specialties; at 11 PM, it transforms itself into a cabaret floor show and then into a disco until 4 AM. Remember to book a table if you want to eat. Young, up-to-the-minute Florentines drink and dance 'til the wee hours at **Maramao** (✉ Via dei Macci 79/r ☎ 055/244341), which opens at 11 PM and doesn't really get going until much before 2. Those craving a night out with less raucous live music might check out **Jazz Club** (✉ Via Nuova de' Caccini 3, corner of Borgo Pinti ☎ 055/2479700). It's situated, appropriately enough, in a smoky basement. **Yab** (✉ Via Sassetti 5/r ☎ 055/215160) is one of the largest clubs, with a young clientele. Popular especially on Tuesday and Thursday nights, it packs in locals and foreigners.

SHOPPING

Markets

Don't miss the indoor, two-story **Mercato Centrale** (✉ Piazza del Mercato Centrale), near San Lorenzo, open in the morning Monday–Saturday. The **Mercato di San Lorenzo** (✉ Piazza San Lorenzo and Via dell'Ariento) is a fine place to browse for buys in leather goods and souvenirs; it's open March–December, daily 8–7; January–February, Tuesday–Saturday 8–7, June–September, Sunday 8–7.

Shopping Districts

Via Tornabuoni is the high-end shopping street. **Via della Vigna Nuova** is just as fashionable. Goldsmiths and jewelry shops can be found on and around the **Ponte Vecchio** and in the **Santa Croce** area, where there is also a high concentration of leather shops and inconspicuous shops selling gold and silver jewelry at prices much lower than those of the elegant jewelers near Ponte Vecchio. The convent of **Santa Croce** (✉ Via San Giuseppe 5/r ✉ Piazza Santa Croce 16) houses a leather-working school and showroom. Antiques dealers can be found in and around the center but are concentrated on **Via Maggio** in the Oltrarno area. **Borgo Ognissanti** has shops selling period decorative objects.

9

FLORENCE A TO Z

ADDRESSES

It is easy to find your way around in Florence: major sights can be explored on foot, as they are packed into a relatively small area. Wear comfortable shoes. The system of street addresses is unusual, with commercial addresses (those with an *r* in them, meaning *rosso*, or red) and residential addresses numbered separately (32/r might be next to or a block away from plain 32).

AIRPORTS & TRANSFERS

The airport that handles most arrivals is Aeroporto Galileo Galilei, more commonly known as Aeroporto Pisa-Galilei. Some domestic and European flights use Florence's Aeroporto Vespucci.

Aeroporto Galileo Galilei ✉ Pisa ☎ 050/500707 🌐 www.pisa-airport.com. **Aeroporto Vespucci** ✉ Peretola ☎ 055/373498 🌐 www.safnet.it.

TRANSFERS Pisa-Galilei Airport has a direct train service to the Stazione Centrale di Santa Maria Novella. There are hourly departures throughout the day, and the trip takes about 60 minutes. When departing, you can buy train tickets for the airport and check in for all flights leaving from Aeroporto Pisa-Galilei at the Florence Air Terminal at Track 5 of Santa Maria Novella. Aeroporto Vespucci is connected to downtown Florence by SITA bus.

BIKE & MOPED TRAVEL

Bike & Moped Rentals **Alinari** ✉ Via Guelfa 85/r ☎ 055/280500.

BUS TRAVEL TO & FROM FLORENCE

For excursions outside Florence, to Siena, for instance, you take SITA near the Stazione Centrale di Santa Maria Novella. The CAP bus terminal is also near the train station.

Lazzi Eurolines ✉ Via Mercadante 2, ☎ 055/363041 🌐 www.lazzi.it. **SITA** bus terminal ✉ Via Santa Caterina da Siena 17 ☎ 055/214721 🌐 www.sita-on-line.it.

BUS TRAVEL WITHIN FLORENCE

Bus maps and timetables are available for a small fee at the Azienda Transporti Autolinee Fiorentine city bus information booths. The same maps may be free at visitor information offices. ATAF city buses run from about 5:15 AM to 1 AM. Buy tickets before you board the bus; they are sold at many tobacco shops and newsstands. The cost is €1 for a ticket good for one hour, and €3.90 for four one-hour tickets, called a *multiplo*. A 24-hour tourist ticket (*turistico*) costs €4.

Azienda Transporti Autolinee Fiorentine (ATAF) ✉ near Stazione Centrale di Santa Maria Novella ✉ Piazza del Duomo 57/r ☎ 800/019794 toll-free.

CAR TRAVEL

The north–south access route to Florence is the Autostrada del Sole (A1) from Milan or Rome. The Florence–Mare autostrada (A11) links Florence with the Tyrrhenian coast, Pisa, and the A12 coastal autostrada. Parking in Florence is severely restricted.

CONSULATES

United Kingdom ✉ Lungarno Corsini 2 ☎ 055/284133.
United States ✉ Lungarno Vespucci 38 ☎ 055/2398276.

EMERGENCIES

Pharmacies are open Sunday and holidays by rotation. Signs posted outside pharmacies list those open all night and on weekends. The pharmacy at Santa Maria Novella train station is always open.

Doctors & Dentists **Tourist Medical Service** ✉ Via Lorenzo il Magnifico 59 ☎ 055/475411.

Emergency Services **Ambulance** ☎ 118. **Police** ☎ 113.

ENGLISH-LANGUAGE MEDIA

Bookstores **BM Bookshop** ✉ Borgo Ognissanti 4/r ☎ 055/294575. **Paperback Exchange** ✉ Via Fiesolana 31/r ☎ 055/2478154. **Edison** ✉ Piazza della Repubblica 27/r ☎ 055/213110.

TAXIS

Taxis wait at stands throughout the centro storico; you can also telephone them. Hailing taxis from the street is not done in Florence. Use only authorized cabs, which are white with a yellow stripe or rectangle on the door. The meter starts at €2.30, with extra charges for nights, holidays, or radio dispatch.

☎ 055/4798 or 055/4390.

TOURS

BUS TOURS A bus consortium (through hotels and travel agents) offers tours in air-conditioned buses covering the important sights in Florence with a trip to Fiesole. The cost is about €25 for a three-hour tour, including entrance fees, and bookings can be made through travel agents.

Operators offer a half-day excursion to Pisa, usually in the afternoon, costing about €25, and a full-day excursion to Siena and San Gimignano, costing about €35. Pick up a timetable at ATAF information offices near the train station or at SITA. Also inquire at the APT tourist office.

TRAIN TRAVEL

The main station is Stazione Centrale di Santa Maria Novella. Florence is on the main north–south route between Rome, Bologna, Milan, and Venice. High-speed Eurostar trains reach Rome in less than two hours and Milan in less than three.

Stazione Centrale di Santa Maria Novella ☎ 8488/88088 toll-free.

TRAVEL AGENCIES

American Express ✉ Via Dante Alighieri 22/r ☎ 055/50981. **CIT Italia** ✉ Piazza Stazione 51/r ☎ 055/284145. **Micos Travel Box** ✉ Via dell'Oriuolo 50–52/r ☎ 055/2340228.

VISITOR INFORMATION

Azienda Promozione Turistica (APT) ✉ Via Cavour 1/r, 50100 ☎ 055/290832.

Italy Basics

To research prices, get advice from other travelers, and book travel arrangements, visit www.fodors.com.

BUSINESS HOURS

Banks are open weekdays 8:30–1:30 and 2:45–3:45. Churches are usually open from early morning to noon or 12:30, when they close for about two hours or more, opening again in the afternoon until about 7 PM. National museums (*musei statali*) are usually open from about 9 AM until about 8 PM and are often closed on Monday. Private museums often have different hours, which may vary according to season. Most major archaeological sites are open every day from early morning to dusk, except some holidays. At all museums and sites, ticket offices close an hour or so before official closing time. Always check with the local tourist office for current hours and holiday closings. Shops are open, with individual variations, from 9 to 1 and from 3:30 or 4 to 7:30 or 8, although in most tourist areas, many stay open through lunchtime. They are open Monday–Saturday but close for a half day during the week; for example, in Rome most shops are closed on Monday morning, although food shops close on Thursday afternoon in fall–spring. Most shops, including food shops, close Saturday afternoon in July and August. Some tourist-oriented shops and department stores in downtown Rome, Florence, and Venice are open all day, every day.

CUSTOMS & DUTIES

For details on imports and duty-free limits in Italy, *see* Customs & Duties *in* Smart Travel Tips.

HOLIDAYS

January 1; January 6 (Epiphany); Easter Sunday and Monday; April 25 (Liberation Day); May 1 (May Day); August 15 (Assumption, known as Ferragosto); November 1 (All Saints' Day); December 8 (Immaculate Conception); December 25–26.

The feast days of patron saints are observed locally. Many businesses and shops may be closed in Florence, Genoa, and Turin on June 24 (St. John the Baptist); in Rome on June 29 (Sts. Peter and Paul); in Palermo on July 15 (Santa Rosalia); in Naples on September 19 (San Gennaro); in Bologna on October 4 (San Petronio); in Trieste on November 3 (San Giusto); and in Milan on December 7 (St. Ambrose). Venice's feast of St. Mark is April 25, the same as Liberation Day, and the city also celebrates November 21 (Madonna della Salute).

LANGUAGE

Italy is accustomed to English-speaking tourists, and in major cities you will find that many people speak at least a little English. In smaller hotels and restaurants and on public transportation, knowing a few phrases of Italian comes in handy.

MONEY MATTERS

Venice, Milan, Florence, and Rome are the more expensive Italian cities to visit. Taxes are usually included in hotel bills; there is a 20% tax on car rentals, usually included in the rates. A cup of espresso enjoyed while standing at a bar costs from €.60 to €.80, the same cup served at a table, triple that. At a bar, beer costs about €3.70, a soft drink €1.40–€2. A *tramezzino* (small sandwich) costs about €2, a more substantial one about €3. You will pay about €10 for a short taxi ride. Admission to a major museum is about €8.

CREDIT CARDS Credit cards are generally accepted in shops and hotels but may not always be welcome in restaurants. When you wish to leave a tip beyond the 15% service charge that is usually included with your bill, leave it in cash rather than adding it to the credit card slip.

CURRENCY The euro is the main unit of currency in Italy, as well as in 11 other European countries. Under the euro system, there are eight coins: 1, 2, 5, 10, 20, and 50 *centesimi* (cents), at 100 centesimi to the euro, and 1 and 2 euros. There are seven notes: 5, 10, 20, 50, 100, 200, and 500 euros. At press time, the exchange rate was about 0.94 euros to the U.S.

dollar; 0.61 euros to the Canadian dollar; 1.52 euros to the pound sterling; 0.55 euros to the Australian dollar; 0.51 euros to the New Zealand dollar; and 0.10 euros to the South African rand.

SALES TAX Foreign tourists who have spent more than €155 (before tax) in one store can obtain a refund of Italy's value-added tax (IVA). At the time of purchase, with passport or ID in hand, ask the store for an invoice describing the article or articles and the total euro amount. If your destination when you leave Italy is a non-EU country, you must have the invoice stamped at customs upon departure from Italy; if your destination is another EU country, you must obtain the customs stamp upon departure from that country. Once back home—and within 90 days of the date of purchase—you must send the stamped invoice back to the store, which should forward the IVA rebate directly to you. If the store participates in the Europe Tax-Free Shopping System (those that do display a sign to the effect), things are simpler. To calculate the price without IVA, you don't subtract 20% from the price on the label, which already includes IVA. Instead, you need to subtract roughly 16.5%. Transaction fees, which go to the companies providing the tax-free service, are 3%–4%, so in this case you should expect to get only about 13% of the purchase price back.

TELEPHONES

COUNTRY & AREA CODES The country code for Italy is 39. Do not drop the 0 in the regional code when calling Italy.

INTERNATIONAL CALLS To place an international call, insert a phone card, dial 00, then the country code, area code, and phone number. To reach an operator for collect calls, dial 170 and 172/3535 if you're having difficulty with an international call. The cheaper and easier option, however, is to use your AT&T, MCI, or Sprint calling card. You can also purchase a phone card at a tobacconist. The best card for calling North America or Europe is the Europa card, which gives you a local number to dial and a PIN. The card is sold in units of three hours (with the €5 card) or six hours (with the €10 card).

Access Codes **AT&T Direct** ☎ 800/172-444. **MCI WorldPhone** ☎ 800/172-401 or 800/172-404. **Sprint International Access** ☎ 800/172-405.

LOCAL CALLS Prepaid *carte telefoniche* (calling cards) are prevalent throughout Italy. You can buy the card (values vary) at post offices, tobacconists, most news stalls, and bars. Tear off the corner of the card and insert it in the telephone's slot. When you dial, the card's value appears in the window. After you hang up, the card is returned so you can use it until its value runs out.

LONDON

10

If London, the capital of Great Britain, contained only its famous landmarks—Buckingham Palace, Big Ben, Parliament, the Tower of London—it would still rank as one of the world's great destinations. Today it occupies 600 square miles and is home to 7 million people. A city that loves to be explored, London beckons with great museums, royal pageantry, and houses that are steeped in history. Marvel at the duke of Wellington's house, track Jack the Ripper's shadow in Whitechapel, then get Beatle-ized at Abbey Road. From the East End to the West End, you'll find London is a dickens of a place.

EXPLORING LONDON

Traditionally London has been divided between the City, to the east, where its banking and commercial interests lie, and Westminster, to the west, the seat of the royal court and of government. It is in these two areas that you will find most of the grand buildings that have played a central role in British history: the Tower of London and St. Paul's Cathedral, Westminster Abbey and the Houses of Parliament, Buckingham Palace, and the older royal palace of St. James's.

Those who restrict their sightseeing to the well-known tourist areas miss much of the best the city has to offer. Within a few minutes' walk of Buckingham Palace, for instance, lie St. James's and Mayfair, two neighboring quarters of elegant town houses built for the nobility during the 17th and early 18th centuries and now notable for the shopping opportunities they house. The same lesson applies to the City, where, tucked away in quiet corners, stand many of the churches Christopher Wren built to replace those destroyed during the Great Fire of 1666.

Other parts of London worth exploring include Covent Garden, a former fruit and flower market converted into a lively shopping and entertainment center where you can wander for hours enjoying the friendly bustle of the streets. Hyde Park and Kensington Gardens, by contrast, offer a great swath of green parkland across the city center, preserved by past kings and queens for their own hunting and relaxation. A walk across Hyde Park will bring you to the museum district of South Kensington, with three major national collections: the Natural History Museum, the Science Museum, and the Victoria & Albert Museum, which specializes in the fine and applied arts.

The south side of the River Thames has its treats as well. A short stroll across Waterloo Bridge brings you to the South Bank Arts Complex, which includes the Royal National Theatre, the Royal Festival Hall, the Hayward Gallery (with changing exhibitions of international art), and the National Film Theatre. Here also are the exciting reconstruction of Shakespeare's Globe theater and its sister museum, and Tate Modern in the massive former power station. The London Eye observation wheel gives the most stunning views—to the west are the Houses of Parliament and Big Ben; to the east the dome of St. Paul's looks smaller on London's changing modern architectural skyline. The Millennium Bridge leaps across the Thames like a so-called steel "blaze of light" joining Tate Modern to St. Paul's in the City. London, although not simple of layout, is a rewarding walking city, and this remains the best way to get to know its nooks and crannies. The infamous weather may not be on your side, but there's plenty of indoor entertainment to keep you amused if you forget the umbrella.

Westminster

Westminster is the royal backyard—the traditional center of the royal court and of government. Here, within 1 km (½ mi) or so of one another, are nearly all of London's most celebrated buildings, and there is a strong feeling of history all around you. Generations of kings and queens have lived here since the end of the 11th century—including the current monarch.

Numbers in the margin correspond to points of interest on the London map.

⓰ **Banqueting House.** On the right side of the grand processional avenue known as Whitehall—site of many important government offices—stands this famous monument of the English Renaissance period. Designed by Inigo Jones in 1625 for court entertainments, it is the only part of Whitehall Palace, the monarch's principal residence during the 16th and 17th centuries, that did not burn down in 1698. It has a magnificent ceiling by Rubens, and outside is an inscription that marks the window through which King Charles I stepped to his execution. ✉ *Whitehall, SW1* ☎ *020/7930–4179* 🌐 *www.hrp.org.uk* ⏲ *Mon.–Sat. 10–5* ⏲ *Closed bank holiday Mondays, Christmas week, and on short notice for banquets, so call first* Ⓤ *Charing Cross, Embankment, Westminster.*

❽ **Buckingham Palace.** Supreme among the symbols of London, indeed of Britain generally, and of the royal family, Buckingham Palace tops many must-see lists—although the building itself is no masterpiece and has housed the monarch only since Victoria moved here from Kensington Palace at her accession in 1837. Located at the end of the Mall, the palace is the London home of the queen and the administrative hub of the entire royal family. When the queen is in residence (normally on weekdays except in January, August, September, and part of June), the royal standard flies over the east front. Inside are dozens of ornate 19th-century-style state rooms used on formal occasions. The private apartments of Queen Elizabeth and Prince Philip are in the north wing. Parts of Buckingham Palace are open to the public during August and September; during the entire year, the **Queen's Gallery,** which shows treasures from the vast royal art collections. The ceremony of the **Changing of the Guard**

Fodor's Choice ★

takes place in front of the palace at 11:30 daily, April–July, and on alternate days during the rest of the year. Arrive early, as people are invariably stacked several deep along the railings, whatever the weather. ✉ *Buckingham Palace Rd., SW1* ☎ *020/7839–1377; 020/7799–2331 24-hr information; 020/7321–2233 credit-card reservations (50p booking charge)* 🌐 *www.royal.gov.uk* 💷 *£11.50 (prices change annually)* ⏲ *Early Aug.–early Oct. (confirm dates, which are subject to queen's mandate), daily 9:30–4:15* Ⓤ *St. James's Park, Victoria.*

10

⓬ **Cabinet War Rooms.** It was from this small maze of 17 bombproof underground rooms—in the back of the hulking Foreign Office—that Britain's World War II fortunes were directed. During air raids the Cabinet met here—the Cabinet Room is still arranged as if a meeting were about to convene. Among the rooms are the Prime Minister's Room, from which Winston Churchill made many of his inspiring wartime broadcasts, and the Transatlantic Telephone Room, from which he spoke directly to President Roosevelt in the White House. ✉ *Clive Steps, King Charles St., SW1* ☎ *020/7930–6961* 🌐 *www.iwm.org.uk* ⏲ *Apr.–Sept., daily 9:30–5:15; Oct.–Mar., daily 10–5:15* Ⓤ *Westminster.*

❻ **Carlton House Terrace.** This street, a Regency-era showpiece on the Mall, was built in 1827–32 by John Nash in imposing white stucco and with massive Corinthian columns. Number 12 is home to the Institute of Contemporary Arts. ✉ *The Mall, W1* ☎ *020/7930–3647* 🌐 *www.ica.org.uk* ⏲ *Daily noon–7:30, later for some events* Ⓤ *Charing Cross.*

⓭ **Downing Street.** Looking like an unassuming alley but barred by iron gates at both its Whitehall and Horse Guards Road approaches, this is the location of the famous **No. 10,** London's modest version of the White House, which has, at least officially, housed the prime minister since 1732. **No. 11** is traditionally the residence of the chancellor of the exchequer (secretary of the treasury), and **No. 12** is the party whips' office. Just south of Downing Street, in the middle of Whitehall, you'll see the **Cenotaph,** a stone national memorial to the dead of both world wars. At 11 AM on the Sunday closest to the 11th day of the 11th month, the queen and other dignitaries lay red poppies in tribute here. ✉ *Whitehall, SW1* Ⓤ *Westminster.*

⓱ **Horse Guards Parade.** The former tiltyard of Whitehall Palace is the site of the annual ceremony of Trooping the Colour, when the queen takes the salute in the great military parade that marks her official birthday on the second Saturday in June (her real one is on April 21). Demand for tickets is great, and tickets are available for the ceremony, as well as the queenless rehearsals on the preceding two Saturdays. There is also a daily guard-changing ceremony outside the guard house, on Whitehall, at 11 AM (10 on Sunday)—one of London's best photo ops. ✉ *Whitehall, opposite Downing St., SW1* ☎ *020/7414–2479 Trooping the Colour ticket information* Ⓤ *Westminster.*

⓮ **Houses of Parliament.** The Houses of Parliament are among the city's most famous and photogenic sights. The Clock Tower keeps watch on Parliament Square, in which stand statues of everyone from Richard the Lion-Hearted to Abraham Lincoln, and, across the way, Westminster Abbey. Also known as the **Palace of Westminster,** this was the site of the monarch's main residence from the 11th century until 1512; the court then moved to the newly built Whitehall Palace. The only parts of the original building to have survived are the **Jewel Tower,** which was built in 1365 as a treasure-house for Edward III, and **Westminster Hall,** which has a fine hammer-beam roof. The rest of the structure was destroyed in a disastrous fire in 1834 and was rebuilt in the newly pop-

Fodor's Choice ★

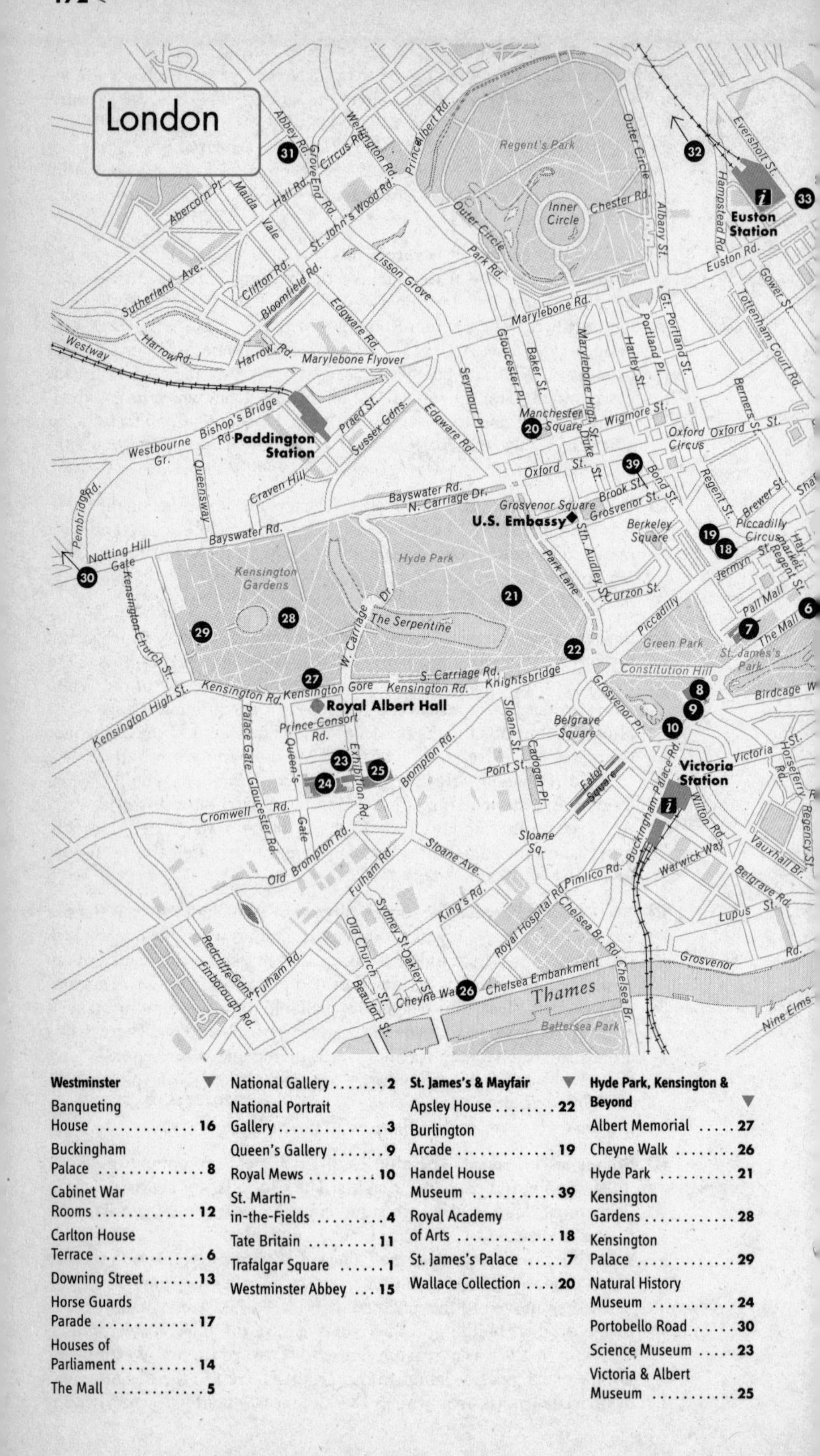

Westminster

- Banqueting House 16
- Buckingham Palace 8
- Cabinet War Rooms 12
- Carlton House Terrace 6
- Downing Street 13
- Horse Guards Parade 17
- Houses of Parliament 14
- The Mall 5
- National Gallery 2
- National Portrait Gallery 3
- Queen's Gallery 9
- Royal Mews 10
- St. Martin-in-the-Fields 4
- Tate Britain 11
- Trafalgar Square 1
- Westminster Abbey 15

St. James's & Mayfair

- Apsley House 22
- Burlington Arcade 19
- Handel House Museum 39
- Royal Academy of Arts 18
- St. James's Palace 7
- Wallace Collection 20

Hyde Park, Kensington & Beyond

- Albert Memorial 27
- Cheyne Walk 26
- Hyde Park 21
- Kensington Gardens 28
- Kensington Palace 29
- Natural History Museum 24
- Portobello Road 30
- Science Museum 23
- Victoria & Albert Museum 25

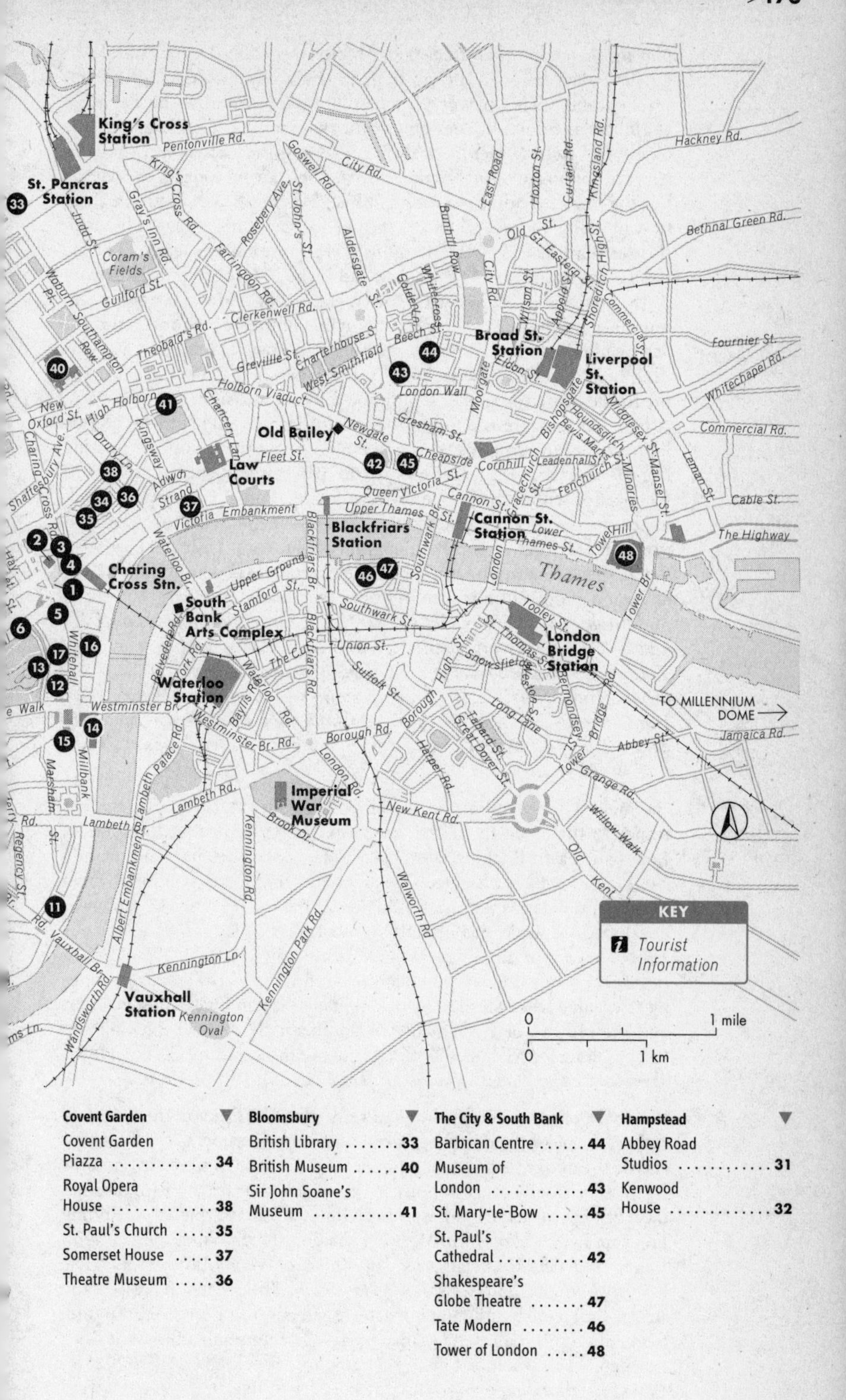

Covent Garden

Covent Garden Piazza **34**
Royal Opera House **38**
St. Paul's Church **35**
Somerset House **37**
Theatre Museum **36**

Bloomsbury

British Library **33**
British Museum **40**
Sir John Soane's Museum **41**

The City & South Bank

Barbican Centre **44**
Museum of London **43**
St. Mary-le-Bow **45**
St. Paul's Cathedral **42**
Shakespeare's Globe Theatre **47**
Tate Modern **46**
Tower of London **48**

Hampstead

Abbey Road Studios **31**
Kenwood House **32**

ular mock-medieval Gothic style. Architects Sir Charles Barry and Augustus Pugin designed the entire place, right down to the Gothic umbrella stands. This newer part of the palace contains the debating chambers and committee rooms of the two Houses of Parliament—the Commons (whose members are elected) and the Lords (whose members are appointed or inherit their seats). There are no tours of the palace, but the public is admitted to the Public Gallery of each House; expect to wait in line for several hours (the line for the Lords is generally much shorter than that for the Commons). The most famous features of the palace are its towers. At the south end is the 336-foot **Victoria Tower.** At the other end is **St. Stephen's Tower,** or the Clock Tower, better known, but inaccurately so, as **Big Ben;** that name properly belongs to the 13-ton bell in the tower on which the hours are struck. Some say Ben was "Big Ben" Caunt, heavyweight champ; others, Sir Benjamin Hall, the far-from-slim Westminster building works commissioner of the 1850s. A light shines from the top of the tower during a night sitting of Parliament. Be sure to have your name placed in advance on the waiting list for the twice-weekly tours of the private residence of the Lord Chancellor within the Palace of Westminster. You can also apply in advance for the special "line of route" tour—open only to overseas visitors—by writing to the **Parliamentary Education Unit** (⊠ House of Commons Information Office, House of Commons, London SW1A 2TT) at least a month in advance of your visit. ⊠ *St. Stephen's Entrance, St. Margaret St., SW1* ☎ *020/7219–4272 Commons information; 020/7219–3107 Lords information; 020/7222–2219 Jewel Tower; 020/7219–2184 Lord Chancellor's Residence* 🌐 *www.parliament.uk* ⊙ *Commons Mon.–Thurs. 2:30–10, Fri. 9:30–3 (although not every Fri.); Lords Mon.–Thurs. 2:30–10; Lord Chancellor's Residence Tues. and Thurs. 10:30–12:30* ⊙ *Closed Easter wk, July–Oct., and 3 wks at Christmas* Ⓤ *Westminster.*

❺ **The Mall.** The splendid and imperial **Admiralty Arch** guards the entrance to the Mall, the noted ceremonial way that leads alongside **St. James's Park** to Buckingham Palace. The Mall takes its name from a game called *palle maille,* a version of croquet that James I imported from France and Charles II popularized during the late 1600s. The park was developed by successive monarchs, most recently by George IV in the 1820s, having originally been used for hunting by Henry VIII. Join office workers relaxing with a lunchtime sandwich, or stroll here on a summer's evening when the illuminated fountains play and Westminster Abbey and the Houses of Parliament are floodlighted. Toward Buckingham Palace, along the Mall, you'll pass the foot of the imposing **Carlton House Terrace.** ⊠ *The Mall, Cockspur St., Trafalgar Sq., SW1* Ⓤ *Charing Cross.*

★ ❷ **National Gallery.** Generally ranked right after the Louvre, the National Gallery is one of the world's greatest museums. Occupying the long neoclassical building on the north side of Trafalgar Square, it contains works by virtually every famous artist and school from the 14th through the 19th centuries. Its galleries overflow with masterpieces, including Jan van Eyck's *Arnolfini Marriage,* Leonardo da Vinci's *Burlington Virgin and Child,* Velásquez's *The Toilet of Venus* (known as "The Rokeby Venus"), and Constable's *Hay Wain.* The collection is especially strong on Flemish and Dutch masters, Rubens and Rembrandt among them, and on Italian Renaissance works. The museum's Brasserie is an excellent spot for lunch. ⊠ *Trafalgar Sq., WC2* ☎ *020/7747–2885* 🌐 *www.nationalgallery.org.uk* ⊙ *Daily 10–6, Wed. until 9 (special exhibition in Sainsbury Wing, Wed. until 10); 1-hr free guided tour of whole gallery starts at Sainsbury Wing daily at 11:30 and 2:30, and 6:30 Wed.* Ⓤ *Charing Cross, Leicester Sq.*

❸ **National Portrait Gallery.** This fascinating collection contains portraits of well-known (and not-so-well-known) Britons, including monarchs, statesmen, and writers. The gallery contains a separate research center for the study of British portraiture, a bookstore, a café, and a top-floor restaurant with viewing area across to the river. Don't miss the Victorian and early-20th-century galleries. ✉ *2 St. Martin's Pl., at foot of Charing Cross Rd., WC2* ☎ *020/7312–2463 recorded information* 🌐 *www.npg.org.uk* ⏲ *Mon.–Wed. and weekends 10–6, Thurs. and Fri. 10–9* Ⓤ *Charing Cross, Leicester Sq.*

❾ **Queen's Gallery.** At the south side of Buckingham Palace, a splendid portico (designed by John Simpson) sets the scene for spacious galleries in classic theme. The main room, the Pennethorne Gallery, is dominated by the portrait of Charles I (Van Dyck), which almost overshadows the many works by other masters such as Holbein, Hals, Vermeer, and Rubens. Between and beneath the paintings are cabinets, vases, and silverwork. Other rooms display the finest porcelain from Delft and Sèvres. ✉ *Buckingham Palace, Buckingham Palace Rd., SW1* ☎ *020/7321–2233* 🌐 *www.royal.gov.uk* ⏲ *Daily 10–5:30, last admission 4:30* Ⓤ *St. James's Park, Victoria.*

❿ **Royal Mews.** Unmissable children's entertainment, this museum is the home of Her Majesty's Coronation Coach. Some of the queen's horses are stabled here, and the elaborately gilded state coaches are on view. ✉ *Buckingham Palace Rd.* ☎ *020/7839–1377* 🌐 *www.royal.gov.uk* ⏲ *Mar.–July and Oct., daily 11–4; Aug. and Sept., daily 10–5; last admission 30 mins before closing* ⏲ *Closed royal and state occasions; call ahead* Ⓤ *St. James's Park, Victoria.*

❹ **St. Martin-in-the-Fields.** Soaring above Trafalgar Square, this landmark church may seem familiar to many Americans because James Gibbs's classical-temple-with-spire design became a pattern for churches in early Colonial America. Built in about 1730, the distinctive neoclassical church is the site for regular free lunchtime music recitals and evening concerts (tickets are available from the box office in the crypt). The crypt is a hive of activity, with a café, bookshop, plus the **London Brass-Rubbing Centre,** where you can make your own souvenir knight, lady, or monarch from replica tomb brasses for about £5. ✉ *Trafalgar Sq., WC2* ☎ *020/7766–1100; 020/7839–8362 credit-card bookings for evening concerts* 🌐 *www.stmartin-in-the-fields.org* ⏲ *Church daily 8–8; crypt Mon.–Sat. 10–8, Sun. noon–6* Ⓤ *Charing Cross, Leicester Sq.*

★ ⓫ **Tate Britain.** By the river to the north of Chelsea, on traffic-laden Millbank, Tate Britain displays a vast range of modern British art. "Modern" is slightly misleading, as the gallery's collection spans from 1545 to the present, including works by Thomas Gainsborough, Sir Joshua Reynolds, and George Stubbs from the 18th century; and by John Constable, William Blake, and the Pre-Raphaelite painters from the 19th century (don't miss Millais's unforgettable *Ophelia*). Also on display is one of the highlights of the Tate's collections, the incredible Turner Bequest, consisting of the personal collection of England's greatest Romantic painter, J. M. W. Turner. The Linbury Galleries on the lower floors present changing exhibitions. Upper floors, reached by a wide, sweeping staircase, bring many works to permanent view that had previously been consigned to storage. ✉ *Millbank, SW1* ☎ *020/7887–8000; 020/7887–8008 recorded information* 🌐 *www.tate.org.uk* ⏲ *Daily 10–5:50* Ⓤ *Pimlico.*

❶ **Trafalgar Square.** This is the center of London, as noted on a plaque on the corner of the Strand and Charing Cross Road from which distances on U.K. signposts are measured. It is the home of the **National Gallery** and of one of London's most distinctive landmarks, **Nelson's Column,** a tribute to one of England's favorite heroes, Admiral Lord Horatio Nelson, who routed the French at the Battle of Trafalgar in 1805. Constantly alive with Londoners and tourists alike, the square remains London's "living room"—great events, such as New Year's, political rallies, and sporting triumphs, always see the crowds gathering in the city's most famous square. A pedestrianization design program has joined the front of the National Gallery to the rest of the square so traffic no longer roars around the north side. Even the popular pigeons have been moved on, although some still insist on making the most of the tourists. A magic time to be here is when the lights on the gigantic Christmas tree (an annual gift from Norway in thanks for harboring its Royal Family during World War II) are illuminated. ✉ *Trafalgar Sq., SW1* Ⓤ *Charing Cross.*

⓯ FodorsChoice ★ **Westminster Abbey.** It is here, in the most ancient and important of London's great churches, that Britain's monarchs are crowned. Most of the abbey dates from the 13th and 14th centuries. The main nave, which has witnessed countless splendid royal ceremonies, is packed with memories. It is also packed with crowds—so many, in fact, that there is an admission fee to the main nave (always free, of course, for participants in religious services). **Henry VII's Chapel,** an exquisite example of the heavily decorated late-Gothic style, was built in the early 1600s, and the twin towers over the west entrance are an 18th-century addition. There is much to see inside, including the tomb of the Unknown Warrior, a nameless World War I soldier buried, in memory of the war's victims, in earth brought with his corpse from France; and the famous Poets' Corner, where England's great writers—Milton, Chaucer, Shakespeare, and others—are memorialized and some are buried. Behind the high altar are the royal tombs, including those of Queen Elizabeth I and her elder sister, Mary I; her cousin, Mary, Queen of Scots; and Henry V. In the Chapel of Edward the Confessor stands the Coronation Chair.

Off the south side of the main corpus is a host of smaller abbey rooms, including the **Chapter House,** a stunning octagonal room adorned with 14th-century frescoes, where the King's Council and, after that, an early version of the Commons, met between 1257 and 1547. The **Abbey Museum** is in the undercroft and displays, among other things, a collection of macabre effigies made from the death masks and actual clothing of Charles II and Admiral Lord Nelson.

It is all too easy to forget, swamped by the crowds trying to see the abbey's sights, that this is a place of worship. Early morning is a good moment to catch something of the building's atmosphere. Better still, take time to attend a service. Photography is not permitted. ✉ *Broad Sanctuary, SW1* ☎ *020/7222–5152* 🌐 *www.westminster-abbey.org* ⏲ *Weekdays 9–4:45, Sat. 9–2:45 (last admission 1 hr before closing). Museum daily 10:30–4. Chapter House Apr.–Oct., daily 10–5:30; Nov.–Mar., daily 10–4:30* ⏲ *Abbey closed weekdays and Sun. to visitors during services* Ⓤ *Westminster.*

St. James's & Mayfair

These are two of London's most exclusive neighborhoods, where the homes are fashionable and the shopping is world class. You can start by walking west from Piccadilly Circus along Piccadilly, a busy street lined with some very English shops (including Hatchards, the booksellers; Swaine, Adeney, Brigg, the outfitters for country pursuits; and Fortnum & Mason, the department store that supplies the queen's groceries).

★ 22 **Apsley House (Wellington Museum).** Once known, quite simply, as No. 1, London, this was long celebrated as the best address in town. Built by Robert Adam in the 1770s, Apsley House was where the duke of Wellington lived from the 1820s until his death in 1852. It has been kept as the Iron Duke liked it, his uniforms and weapons, his porcelain and plate, and his extensive art collection displayed in opulent 19th-century rooms. Unmissable, in every sense, is the gigantic Canova statue of a nude (but fig-leafed) Napoléon Bonaparte, Wellington's archenemy. Special annual events include a commemoration of the Battle of Waterloo on and around June 18; call or check the Web site for details. ✉ *149 Piccadilly, SW1* ☎ *020/7499–5676* 🌐 *www.apsleyhouse.org.uk* 🕓 *Tues.–Sun. 11–4:30* Ⓤ *Hyde Park Corner.*

19 **Burlington Arcade.** This perfectly picturesque covered walkway dates from 1819. Here, shops sell cashmere sweaters, silk scarves, handmade chocolates, and leather-bound books. If not the choice shopping spot it once was, it still makes a great photo op, particularly if you can snap the uniformed beadle (he ensures that no one runs, whistles, or sings here) on duty. ✉ *Off Piccadilly, W1* Ⓤ *Piccadilly Circus.*

39 **Handel House Museum.** The former home of the composer, where he lived for more than 30 years until his death in 1759, celebrates his genius in its fine Georgian rooms. You can linger over original manuscripts (others are in the British Library) and gaze at portraits and art illustrating the times. Some of Handel's most famous pieces were created here, including *Messiah* and *Music for the Royal Fireworks.* ✉ *25 Brook St., W1* ☎ *020/7495–1685* 🌐 *www.handelhouse.org* 🕓 *Tues., Wed., Fri., and Sat. 10–6, Thurs. 10–8, Sun. noon–6* Ⓤ *Bond St.*

18 **Royal Academy of Arts.** On the north side of Piccadilly, the grand marble pile of **Burlington House** contains the offices of many learned societies and the headquarters of the Royal Academy. In addition to its permanent collection, the RA, as it is generally known, mounts a continuous program of internationally renowned loan exhibitions. Every June, the RA puts on its **Summer Exhibition,** a huge collection of sculpture and painting by Royal Academicians and a plethora of other artists working today, whose works are crammed into every nook and cranny. Craving art now? Try the shop; it's one of the best museum stores in town. ✉ *Burlington House, Piccadilly, W1* ☎ *020/7300–8000; 020/7300–5760 recorded information* 🌐 *www.royalacademy.org.uk* 🕓 *Sat.–Thurs. 10–6, Fri. 10–8:30* Ⓤ *Piccadilly Circus, Green Park.*

7 **St. James's Palace.** This historic royal palace is the current residence of the Prince of Wales. The oldest parts of the lovely brick building date from the 1530s, well before its relatively short career as the center of royal affairs—from the destruction of Whitehall Palace in 1698 until 1837, when Victoria became queen and moved the royal household down the road to Buckingham Palace. Today, the palace is closed to the public, but your viewfinder will love the picturesque exterior and regimental guard on duty. ✉ *Friary Court, Pall Mall, SW1* Ⓤ *Green Park.*

★ 20 **Wallace Collection.** A palatial town-house museum, the Wallace is important, exciting, undervisited—and free. As at the Frick Collection in New York, the setting, Hertford House itself, is part of the show—built for the duke of Manchester and now stuffed with armor, exquisite furniture, and great paintings, including Bouchers, Watteaus, Fragonard's *The Swing,* and Frans Hals's *Laughing Cavalier.* The modernized basement floor is used for educational activities, and has a Watercolour Gallery. The museum courtyard provides yet more exhibition space and an upscale restaurant. ✉ *Hertford House, Manchester Sq., W1* ☎ *020/*

7935–0687 🌐 www.the-wallace-collection.org.uk ⏲ Mon.–Sat. 10–5, Sun. noon–5 Ⓤ Bond St.

Hyde Park, Kensington & Beyond

When in need of elbow room, Londoners head for Hyde Park and Kensington Gardens. Viewed by natives as their own private backyards, they form an open swath across central London, and in and around them are some of London's most noted museums and monuments.

27 **Albert Memorial.** This gorgeously gilded 19th-century monument celebrates Queen Victoria's much-loved husband, Prince Albert, who died in 1861 at the age of 42. The monument, itself the epitome of high Victorian pomp and circumstance, commemorates the many socially uplifting projects of the prince, among them the Great Exhibition of 1851, whose catalog he is holding. The memorial is directly opposite the Royal Albert Hall. ✉ *Kensington Gore* Ⓤ *Knightsbridge.*

26 **Cheyne Walk.** The most beautiful spot in Chelsea—one of London's most arty (and expensive) residential districts—this Thamesside street is adorned with Queen Anne houses and legendary addresses. Author George Eliot died at No. 4 in 1880; Pre-Raphaelite artist Dante Gabriel Rossetti lived at No. 16. Two other resident artists were James McNeill Whistler and J. M. W. Turner. Toward the western end, outside the Church of All Saints, is a golden-face statue of the *Man for All Seasons*, Thomas More, looking beatific on a throne facing the river.

21 **Hyde Park.** Along with the smaller St. James's and Green parks to the east, Hyde Park started as Henry VIII's hunting grounds. Nowadays, it remains a tranquil oasis from urban London—-tranquil, that is, except for Sunday morning, when soapbox orators take over **Speakers' Corner,** near the northeast corner of the park (feel free to get up and holler if you fancy spreading your message to the masses). Not far away, along the south side of the park, is **Rotten Row,** which was Henry VIII's royal path to the hunt—*la route du roi*—hence the name. It's still used by the Household Cavalry, the queen's guard. You can see them leave on horseback, in full regalia, around 10:30 or await their exhausted return about noon. ✉ *Bounded by the Ring, Bayswater Rd., Park La., and Knightsbridge* ☎ *020/7298–2100* 🌐 *www.royalparks.gov.uk* ⏲ *Daily 5–midnight* Ⓤ *Hyde Park Corner, Lancaster Gate, Marble Arch, Knightsbridge.*

28 **Kensington Gardens.** More formal than neighboring Hyde Park, Kensington Gardens was first laid out as palace grounds and adjoins Kensington Palace. George Frampton's 1912 **Peter Pan,** a bronze of the boy who lived on an island in the Serpentine and never grew up, overlooks the Long Water. His creator, J. M. Barrie, lived at 100 Bayswater Road, not 500 yards from here. The **Princess Diana Memorial Playground** is designed on the theme of Barrie's Neverland. Hook's ship, crocodiles, "jungles" of foliage, and islands of sand provide a fantasy land for kids. **Round Pond** acts as a magnet for model-boat enthusiasts and duck feeders. Nearby is boating and swimming in the **Serpentine,** an S-shape lake. Refreshments can be had at the lakeside tearooms. The **Serpentine Gallery** (☎ 020/7402–6075) holds noteworthy exhibitions of modern art. ✉ *Bounded by the Broad Walk, Bayswater Rd., the Ring, and Kensington Rd.* 🌐 *www.royalparks.gov.uk* ⏲ *Daily dawn–dusk* Ⓤ *Lancaster Gate, Queensway.*

29 **Kensington Palace.** This has been a royal home since the late 17th century. From the outside it looks less like a palace than a country house,

which it was until William III bought it in 1689. Queen Victoria spent a less-than-happy childhood at Kensington Palace and Princess Diana, a less-than-happy marriage. Called the "royal ghetto," the palace is home to many Windsors (they live in a distant section cordoned off from the public). Kensington Palace's state apartments have been restored to how they appeared in Princess Victoria's day. Drop in on the Orangery here for a very elegant cup of tea. ✉ *The Broad Walk, Kensington Gardens, W8* ☎ *0870/751–5180 for advance booking and information* 🌐 *www.hrp.org.uk* 🎫 *£10.20 for tour and exhibitions* ⏲ *Daily 10–5* Ⓤ *High St. Kensington.*

24 **Natural History Museum.** The outrageously ornate French Romanesque–style terra-cotta facade of this museum belies the exciting exhibits within. The Darwin Centre displays all creatures great and small in pickling jars and vats, from a tiny Seychellian frog to the giant Komodo dragon lizard. Other highlights include the myriad arthropods in the Creepy Crawlies Gallery and the Human Biology Hall's birth-simulation chamber. Helping you circumnavigate the whole are 14 daily tours from the main information desk. ✉ *Cromwell Rd., SW7* ☎ *020/7942–5000* 🌐 *www.nhm.ac.uk* ⏲ *Mon.–Sat. 10–5:50, Sun. 11–5:50* Ⓤ *South Kensington.*

30 **Portobello Road.** Northwest of Kensington Gardens is the lively **Notting Hill** district, full of stylish restaurants and cafés where some of London's trendsetters gather. The best-known attraction in this area is Portobello Road, where a lively antiques and bric-a-brac market is held each Saturday (arrive at 6 AM for the best finds); the southern end is focused on antiques, the northern end on food, flowers, and secondhand clothes. The street is also full of regular antiques shops that are open most weekdays. Ⓤ *Notting Hill Gate, Ladbroke Grove.*

23 **Science Museum.** The leading national collection of science and technology, this museum has extensive hands-on exhibits on outer space, astronomy, and hundreds of other subjects. The dramatic Wellcome Wing, a £45 million addition to the museum, is devoted to contemporary science, medicine, and technology. It also includes a 450-seat IMAX cinema. ✉ *Exhibition Rd., SW7* ☎ *020/7942–4000* 🌐 *www.sciencemuseum.org.uk* ⏲ *Daily 10–6* Ⓤ *South Kensington.*

★ 25 **Victoria & Albert Museum.** The V&A, as it is commonly known, opened during the 19th century as a museum of the decorative arts, and today it has extensive collections of costumes, paintings, jewelry, and crafts from every part of the globe. Don't miss the sculpture court, the vintage couture collections, and the great Raphael Room with its cartoons (drawings) for tapestries. The impressive British Galleries chronicle four centuries of British history, art, and design. For an overall picture, see the museum's prized treasures on a free, one-hour daily tour, at 10:30, 11:30, 1:30, and 3:30, with a 30-minute version on Wednesday evening at 7:30. The restaurant offers lunch daily, candlelighted dinners on Wednesday nights, traditional roasts on Sunday, and occasional live music. ✉ *Cromwell Rd., SW7* ☎ *020/7942–2000* 🌐 *www.vam.ac.uk* ⏲ *Daily 10–5:45, Wed. and last Fri. of the month 10–10* Ⓤ *South Kensington.*

Covent Garden

The Covent Garden district—which lies just to the east of Soho—has gone from a down-at-the-heels area to one of the busiest, most raffishly enjoyable parts of the city. Continental-style open-air cafés create a very un-English atmosphere, with vintage fashion boutiques, art galleries, and street buskers attracting crowds.

34 **Covent Garden.** You could easily spend several hours exploring the block of streets north of the Strand known as Covent Garden. The heart of the area is a former wholesale fruit and vegetable market—made famous as one of Eliza Doolittle's haunts in *My Fair Lady*—established in 1656. The **Piazza,** the now-glass-covered Victorian market building, is a vibrant shopping center with numerous boutiques, crafts shops, and cafés. **The Apple Market** is a superior crafts market, and the more downscale **Jubilee Market** is south across the cobbles in Jubilee Hall. Housed in the old Flower Market at the southeast corner of the square, **London's Transport Museum** tells the story of mass transportation in the capital, with touch-screen interactive material and a Tube-driving simulator. Shops on Long Acre sell maps, art books and materials, and clothing; Neal Street establishments sell clothes, pottery, jewelry, tea, housewares, and stylish bags. ✉ *Bounded by the Strand, Charing Cross Rd., Long Acre, and Drury La., WC2* Ⓤ *Charing Cross, Covent Garden, Leicester Sq.*

38 **Royal Opera House.** This is the fabled home of the Royal Ballet and Britain's finest opera company. The glass-and-steel Floral Hall is the most wonderful feature, and visitors can wander in during the day and enjoy the piazza concourse and the Amphitheatre Bar, which gives a splendid panorama across the city, or listen to a free lunchtime chamber concert. ✉ *Bow St., WC2* ☎ *020/7240–1200 or 020/7304–4000* 🌐 *www.royaloperahouse.org* Ⓤ *Covent Garden.*

35 **St. Paul's Church.** A landmark of the Covent Garden market area, this 1633 church, designed by Inigo Jones, is known as the Actors' Church. Inside are numerous memorials to theater greats. Look for the open-air entertainers performing under the church's portico. ✉ *Bedford St., WC2* Ⓤ *Covent Garden.*

★ 37 **Somerset House.** An old royal palace once stood on the site, but the 18th-century building that finally replaced it was the work of Sir William Chambers during the reign of George III. It was built to house government offices, principally those of the Navy. Many of the gracious 18th-century chambers rooms are on view for free, including the Seamen's Waiting Hall, the Nelson Stair, and the Navy Commissioners' Barge. Lighting up the vaults is a museum of intricate works of silver, gold snuff boxes and Italian mosaics, **The Gilbert Collection** (☎ 020/7240–4080 🎫 £6, free after 4:30). **The Hermitage Rooms** (☎ 020/7845–4630 🎫 £5) also house objects with foreign origins; they are the permanent home for selected treasures from Russia's eponymous premier museum. The **Courtauld Institute of Art** (🎫 £5, free Mon. 10–2 except bank holidays ⏲ Mon.–Sat. 10–6, Sun. noon–6 (last admission 5:15) occupies the northern sections of the building. Here, London's finest impressionist and postimpressionist collection spans from Bonnard to van Gogh (Manet's *Bar at the Folies-Bergère* is the star), with bonus post-Renaissance works. Arts events are held in the Italianate courtyard between the Courtauld and the rest of Somerset House. Cafés and a river terrace complete the clutch of cultural delights that visitors can reach directly by walkway from Waterloo Bridge. ✉ *The Strand, WC2* ☎ *020/7845–4600* 🌐 *www.somerset-house.org.uk* ⏲ *Mon.–Sat. 10–6, Sun. noon–6 (last admission 5:15).*

36 **Theatre Museum.** A comprehensive collection of material on the history of the English theater, this museum traces the history not merely of the classic drama but also of opera, music hall, pantomime, and musical comedy. A highlight is the re-creation of a dressing room filled with memorabilia of former stars. ✉ *Russell St., WC2* ☎ *020/7836–7891* 🌐 *www.theatremuseum.org* ⏲ *Tues.–Sun. 10–6* Ⓤ *Covent Garden.*

Bloomsbury

Bloomsbury is a semiresidential district to the north of Covent Garden that contains some spacious and elegant 17th- and 18th-century squares. It could be called the intellectual center of London, as both the British Museum and the University of London are here. The area also gave its name to the Bloomsbury Group, a clique of writers and painters who thrived here in the early 20th century.

33 **British Library.** Since it opened in 1759, the British Library had always been housed in the British Museum on Gordon Square—but space ran out long ago, necessitating this grand modern edifice, a few blocks north of the British Museum. The library's treasures—the Magna Carta, a Gutenberg Bible, Jane Austen's writings, Shakespeare's First Folio, and musical manuscripts by Handel and Sir Paul McCartney—are on view to the general public in the John Ritblat Gallery. ✉ *96 Euston Rd., NW1* ☎ *020/7412–7332* 🌐 *www.bl.uk* ⏲ *Mon. and Wed.–Fri. 9:30–6, Tues. 9:30–8, Sat. 9:30–5, Sun. 11–5* Ⓤ *Euston, King's Cross.*

★ 40 **British Museum.** The focal point in this fabled collection of antiquities is the unmissable Great Court, where beneath a vast glass roof lies the museum's inner courtyard. The space also accommodates galleries, a computerized database for viewing the collection on screen, cafés, and shops. The museum's priceless collection of treasures includes Egyptian, Greek, and Roman antiquities; Renaissance jewelry; pottery; coins; glass; and drawings from virtually every European school since the 15th century. Some of the highlights are the **Elgin Marbles,** sculptures that formerly decorated the Parthenon in Athens; the **Rosetta Stone,** which helped archaeologists to interpret Egyptian hieroglyphs; and the JP Morgan Chase **North American Gallery,** which has one of the largest exhibitions of native culture outside the North American continent. The revered gold-and-blue Reading Room is open to the public and has banks of computers. It's best to pick one section that particularly interests you—to try to see everything would be an overwhelming and exhausting task. ✉ *Great Russell St., WC1* ☎ *020/7636–1555* 🌐 *www.thebritishmuseum.ac.uk* ⏲ *Museum Sat.–Wed. 10–5:30, Thurs. and Fri. 10–8:30. Great Court Sun.–Wed. 9–6, Thurs.–Sat. 9–11* Ⓤ *Tottenham Court Rd., Holborn, Russell Sq.*

★ 41 **Sir John Soane's Museum.** On the border of London's legal district, this museum is guaranteed to induce smiles with its fairground fun-house interior, complete with concealed doors, mirrors, and split-level floors. It appears, though, that Sir John—the architect of the Bank of England who bequeathed this house to the nation—was no ordinary trickster. The space is stuffed with his diverse collection of art and artifacts, including antique busts, an ancient Egyptian sarcophagus, and early-19th-century English paintings. ✉ *13 Lincoln's Inn Fields, WC2* ☎ *020/7405–2107* 🌐 *www.soane.org* ⏲ *Tues.–Sat. 10–5, also 6–9 PM 1st Tues. of every month* Ⓤ *Holborn.*

The City & South Bank

The City, the commercial center of London, was once the site of the great Roman city of Londinium. Since those days, the City has been rebuilt innumerable times, and today, ancient and modern jostle each other elbow to elbow. Several of London's most famous attractions are here, along with the adjacent area across the Thames commonly called the South Bank. Here, Shakespeare's Globe Theatre, the Tate Modern, and the British Airways London Eye—the world's largest observation wheel—draw both natives and visitors in droves.

44 **Barbican Centre.** A vast arts center, the Barbican takes its name from the watchtower that stood here during the Middle Ages. It contains a concert hall (where the London Symphony Orchestra is based), two theaters, an art gallery, a cinema, and several restaurants. The **Barbican Art Gallery** showcases modern, populist topics ranging from the Shaker movement to *Star Wars.* Also worth a look are the free displays in the Concourse Gallery. The **Barbican International Theatre Events (BITE)** calendar manages the venue's year-round dance, music, and theater performances. ☎ *020/7638–8891* ⊕ *www.barbican.org.uk* ⏲ *Barbican Centre Mon.–Sat. 9 AM–11 PM, Sun. noon–11; gallery Mon.–Sat. 10–7:30, Sun. noon–7:30* Ⓤ *Moorgate, Barbican.*

43 **Museum of London.** At **London Wall,** so called because it follows the line of the wall that surrounded the Roman settlement, the Museum of London enables you to come to grips with a great deal of the city's history. Oliver Cromwell's death mask, Queen Victoria's crinolined gowns, Selfridge's art deco elevators, and the Lord Mayor's coach are just some of the goodies here. The meticulous excavation of the Roman amphitheatre at the Guildhall is the latest and most exciting of the many archaeological finds on display. ✉ *London Wall, EC2* ☎ *020/7600–0807* ⊕ *www.museumoflondon.org.uk* ⏲ *Mon.–Sat. 10–5:50, Sun. noon–5:50* Ⓤ *Barbican.*

45 **St. Mary-le-Bow.** This landmark church has been rebuilt twice, first after the Great Fire by Christopher Wren and again after damage was sustained during World War II bombings. The peals that issue from the belfry before services are an integral part of city folklore; it is said that a Londoner must be born within the sound of Bow Bells to be a true cockney. The surrounding Cheapside district was the marketplace of medieval London (the word *ceap* is Old English for "to barter"), as the street names hereabouts indicate: Milk Street, Ironmonger Lane, and so on. ✉ *Cheapside, EC2* ☎ *020/7248–5139* ⊕ *www.stmarylebow.co.uk* ⏲ *Mon.–Thurs. 6:30–5:45, Fri. 6:30–4* Ⓤ *Mansion House.*

★ **42** **St. Paul's Cathedral.** London's symbolic heart, St. Paul's is Sir Christopher Wren's masterpiece. Its dome—the world's third largest—can be seen from many an angle in other parts of the city. The cathedral was completed in 1710 following the Great Fire. Wren was the architect who was also responsible for designing 50 parish churches in the city to replace those lost in that disaster. Fittingly, he is buried in the crypt under a simple Latin epitaph, composed by his son, which translates as: READER, IF YOU SEEK HIS MONUMENT, LOOK AROUND YOU. The remains of the duke of Wellington and Admiral Lord Nelson are also in the crypt. The cathedral has been the site of many famous state occasions, including the funeral of Winston Churchill in 1965 and the ill-fated marriage of the Prince and Princess of Wales in 1981. In the ambulatory (the area behind the high altar) is the American Chapel, a memorial to the 28,000 U.S. GIs stationed in Britain during World War II who lost their lives in active service. The greatest architectural glory of the cathedral is the dome. It consists of three distinct elements: an outer, timber-frame dome covered with lead; an interior dome built of brick and decorated with frescoes of the life of St. Paul by the 18th-century artist Sir James Thornhill; and, in between, a brick cone that supports and strengthens both. There is a good view of the church from the **Whispering Gallery,** high up in the inner dome. The gallery is so called because of its remarkable acoustics, whereby hushed words spoken on one side can be clearly heard on the other, 107 feet away. Above this gallery are two others, both external, from which there are fine views over the City and beyond. ✉ *St. Paul's Churchyard, Paternoster Sq., Ludgate Hill, EC4* ☎ *020/7236–4128*

🌐 *www.stpauls.co.uk* ⏲ *Cathedral Mon.–Sat. 8:30–4; ambulatory, crypt, and galleries Mon.–Sat. 9–5:15; shop and Crypt café also Sun. 10:30–5* Ⓤ *St. Paul's.*

★ 47 **Shakespeare's Globe Theatre.** This spectacular theater is a replica of Shakespeare's open-roof Globe Playhouse (built in 1599, incinerated in 1613), where most of the playwright's great plays premiered. It stands 200 yards from the original, overlooking the Thames. It was built with the use of authentic Elizabethan materials, including the first thatch roof in London since the Great Fire. Plays are presented in natural light (and sometimes rain) to 1,000 people on wooden benches in the "bays," plus 500 "groundlings," standing on a carpet of filbert shells and clinker, just as they did nearly four centuries ago. Although the main theater season runs from mid-May to mid-September, the Globe can be viewed year-round if you take the helpful tour offered by the **Shakespeare's Globe Exhibition Centre.** In addition, productions are now scheduled throughout the year in a second, indoor theater, built to a design by the 17th-century architect Inigo Jones. Call for performance schedule. ✉ *New Globe Walk, Bankside (South Bank)* ☎ *020/7902–1500* 🌐 *www.shakespeares-globe.org* ⏲ *Daily 10–5* Ⓤ *Blackfriars, Southwark.*

46 **Tate Modern.** Opposite St. Paul's Cathedral on the Thames in South Bank, this offspring of the Tate gallery resides in the 8½-acre Bankside Power Station, a dazzling, world-class venue for some of the Tate's more contemporary international treasures. Originally built in the 1930s, it was handsomely renovated to its present state by Swiss architects Herzog and de Meuron. The collection includes classic works by Matisse, Picasso, Dalí, Moore, Bacon, and Warhol, as well as creations of today's most-talked-about artists, such as Anish Kapoor's brilliant, mammoth installation/sculpture in the grand Turbine Hall. ✉ *25 Summer St., SE1* ☎ *020/7887–8000* 🌐 *www.tate.org.uk* ⏲ *Sun.–Thurs. 10–6, Fri. and Sat. 10–10* Ⓤ *Blackfriars, Southwark.*

★ 48 **Tower of London.** This minicity of melodramatic towers is one of London's most famous sights and one of its most crowded, too. Come as early in the day as possible (you can buy tickets in advance at any Underground stop) and head for the Crown Jewels so you can see them before the crowds arrive. The tower served the monarchs of medieval England as both fortress and palace. Every British sovereign from William the Conqueror in the 11th century to Henry VIII in the 16th lived here, and it remains a royal palace, in name at least. The **White Tower** is the oldest and also the most conspicuous building in the entire complex. Inside, the **Royal Armouries,** England's national collection of arms and armor, occupy the ground floor. On the first floor, the **Chapel of St. John** is one of the few unaltered parts of the tower, and its simple, original architecture makes it one of the most distinctive church interiors of its time in England.

The group of buildings that make up the old **Medieval Palace** is best entered by Water Lane, beside **Traitors' Gate.** There are three towers to explore: **St. Thomas's Tower,** which contains the monarch's rooms and lobby with waterside entrance (now known as Traitors' Gate); the Wakefield Tower; and Lanthorn Tower, both of which have more royal accommodations joined by a walkway along the battlements. In the furnished rooms of the **Wakefield Tower,** costumed actors describe daily life in the Medieval Palace and its evolution over the centuries. Henry VI is alleged to have been murdered in the Wakefield Tower in 1471, during England's medieval civil war, the Wars of the Roses. Among other buildings worth seeing is the **Bloody Tower.** The little princes in the tower—the uncrowned boy-king Edward V and his brother Richard, duke of York, supposedly murdered on the orders of the duke of Gloucester, later crowned Richard III—certainly lived in the Bloody Tower and may well have died here, too. It was a rare honor to be beheaded in private inside the tower on the Scaffold Site of Tower Green; most people were executed outside, on **Tower Hill**, where the crowds could get a much better view. The church of **St. Peter ad Vincula** has the burial places of the unfortunate queens and bishops who upset the Tudor monarchy and can be seen as part of a Yeoman's Tour.

The **Crown Jewels**, a breathtaking collection of regalia, precious stones, gold, and silver, used for the coronation of the present sovereign, are housed in the **Jewel House, Waterloo Barracks.** An exhibition illustrating their history precedes the gems themselves. The Royal Scepter contains the largest cut diamond in the world. The Imperial State Crown, made for the 1838 coronation of Queen Victoria, contains some 3,000 precious stones, largely diamonds and pearls. The jewels used to be housed in the **Martin Tower** (in less secure circumstances, when daring Thomas Blood made an attempt to steal them in 1671), where an exhibit—"Crowns and Diamonds"—shows the making of the royal regalia and displays some state crowns made for earlier kings and queens. Look for the ravens near the Wakefield Tower. Their presence at the Tower is traditional, and it is said that if they leave, the Tower will fall and England will lose her greatness. ✉ *H. M. Tower of London, Tower Hill, EC3N* ☎ *0870/756–7070 recorded information and advance booking* 🌐 *www.hrp.org.uk* 🎫 *£12* ⏲ *Mar.–Oct., Mon.–Sat. 9–5, Sun. 10–5; Nov.–Feb., Sun. and Mon. 10–4, Tues.–Sat. 9–4 (the Tower closes 1 hr after last admission time and all internal buildings close 30 mins after last admission)* ☞ *Yeoman Warder guides leave daily from Middle Tower, subject to weather and availability, at no charge, about every 30 mins until 3:30 in summer, 2:30 in winter* Ⓤ *Tower Hill.*

Hampstead

Hampstead is a quaint village within the city, where many famous poets and writers have lived. Today it is a fashionable residential area, with a main shopping street and some rows of elegant 18th-century houses. The heath is one of London's largest and most attractive open spaces.

㉛ **Abbey Road Studios.** Here, outside the legendary Abbey Road Studios (the facility is closed to the public), is the most famous zebra crossing in the world. Immortalized on the cover of the Beatles' *Abbey Road* album of 1969, this pedestrian crosswalk is a spot beloved to countless Beatlemaniacs and baby boomers, many of whom venture here to leave their signature on the white stucco fence that fronts the adjacent studio facility. Abbey Road is not in Hampstead but in adjacent St. John's Wood, an elegant residential area, a 10-minute ride on the Tube from central London. ✉ *3 Abbey Rd., NW8* 🌐 *www.abbeyroad.co.uk* Ⓤ *St. John's Wood.*

㉜ **Kenwood House.** On the north side of the heath is Kenwood House, built in the 17th century and remodeled by Robert Adam at the end of the 18th century. The house contains a collection of superb paintings by Rembrandt, Turner, Reynolds, Van Dyck, and Gainsborough—and *The Guitar Player,* probably the most beautiful Vermeer in England. Unfortunately, only one grand Adam interior remains: the splendid library. The house's lovely landscaped grounds provide the setting for symphony concerts in summer. ✉ *Hampstead La., NW3* ☎ *020/8348–1286* 🌐 *www.english-heritage.org.uk* ⏲ *Easter–Aug., Sat.–Tues., and Thurs. 10–5:30, Wed. and Fri. 10:30–5:30; Dec.–Easter, Sat.–Tues., and Thurs. 10–4,*

Wed. and Fri. 10:30–5; Sept.–Nov., Sat.–Tues., and Thurs. 10–4, Wed. and Fri. 10:30–4 Ⓤ *Golders Green, then Bus 210.*

Greenwich

Home to a number of historical and maritime attractions, Greenwich—situated on the Thames some 8 km (5 mi) east of central London—is an ideal destination for a day out. You can get to Greenwich by Underground, by riverboat from Westminster and Tower Bridge piers, and by Thames Line's high-speed river buses.

Cutty Sark. This romantic tea clipper was built in 1869, one of many wooden tall-masted clippers to ply the seven seas trading exotic commodities in the 19th century. The *Cutty Sark,* the last to survive, was also the fastest, sailing the China–London route in 1871 in just 107 days. The photogenic vessel lies in dry dock, a museum of one kind of seafaring life—which was anything but romantic for the 28-strong crew. ✉ *King William Walk, SE10* ☎ *020/8858–3445* 🌐 *www.cuttysark.org.uk* ⏲ *Daily 10–5, last admission 4:30* Ⓤ *DLR: Cutty Sark.*

★ **National Maritime Museum.** This grand stone building is all glass and light within, dominated by a frigate's huge revolving propeller on show in the glassed-in courtyard. Besides containing everything to do with the sea and British sea power—from seascape paintings to scientific instruments to a collection of ships from all ages—there are the compelling stories of heroes. A gallery is devoted to Admiral Nelson, including his uniform, complete with bloodstain, worn at his death at the Battle of Trafalgar. Explorers such as Captain Cook, and Robert F. Scott of the Antarctic, are celebrated. Opportunities to grapple hands-on with maritime tasks abound, especially in the All Hands Gallery, where kids and adults alike try their skills at handling ropes and docking ferries. ✉ *Romney Rd., SE10* ☎ *020/8858–4422* 🌐 *www.nmm.ac.uk* ⏲ *Apr.–Sept. daily 10–6, Oct.–Mar. daily 10–5* Ⓤ *DLR: Greenwich.*

Old Royal Observatory. Stand astride both hemispheres in the courtyard of the Old Royal Observatory, where the prime meridian—0° longitude—is set. The observatory is at the top of the hill, behind the National Maritime Museum and Royal Naval College, in the attractive **Greenwich Park,** which was originally a royal hunting ground. Founded in 1675, the observatory has original telescopes and other astronomical instruments on display. ✉ *Greenwich Park, SE10* ☎ *020/8312–6565* 🌐 *www.rog.nmm.ac.uk* ⏲ *Oct.–Mar., daily 10–5; Apr.–Sept., daily 10–6; last admission 30 mins before closing* Ⓤ *DLR: Greenwich.*

WHERE TO EAT

London has had a restaurant boom, or rather, a restaurant revolution. More than ever, the city loves its dining establishments—all 6,700 of them—from its "be-there" eateries to its tiny neighborhood joints, from pubs where young foodniks find their feet to swanky trendsetters where celebrity chefs launch their ego flights. After feasting on modern British cuisine, visit one (or two or three) of London's fabulous pubs for a nightcap.

WHAT IT COSTS In pounds sterling

	$$$$	$$$	$$	$
AT DINNER	over £22	£16–£22	£9–£15	under £9

Prices are per person for a main course.

Bloomsbury, Covent Garden & Soho

$$$–$$$$ ✕ **Asia de Cuba.** A trendy restaurant, in a trendy hotel, in a trendy city: Philippe Starck–designed, it's flashy and loud—check the dangly lightbulbs, Latino music, stacks of library books, portable TVs, and satin-clad pillars. The Pan-Asian fusion menu includes Thai beef salad with Asian greens and coconut and lobster with rum and red curry. It isn't cheap, but it's totally disco. ☒ *St. Martins Lane Hotel, 45 St. Martin's La., WC2* ☎ *020/7300–5588* ▭ *AE, DC, MC, V* Ⓤ *Leicester Sq.*

★ **$$$–$$$$** ✕ **Rules.** Come, escape from the 21st century. This is probably the single most beautiful dining salon in London; oil paintings and engravings cover the lacquered yellow walls. More than 200 years old (it opened in 1798), this gorgeous institution has welcomed everyone from Dickens to the current Prince of Wales. The menu includes fine historical dishes—try the steak-and-kidney pudding for a taste of the 18th century. For a main dish, try something from the list of daily specials, which, in season, includes game from Rules's Teesdale estate. ☒ *35 Maiden La., WC2* ☎ *020/7836–5314* ▭ *AE, DC, MC, V* Ⓤ *Covent Garden.*

★ **$$–$$$** ✕ **The Ivy.** In a wood-panel, latticed, art deco room with blinding-white tablecloths and stained glass, the theater set eat Caesar salad, kedgeree, bubble and squeak, salmon cakes, and baked Alaska. For people-watching ("Don't look now, dear, but there's Ralph Fiennes"), this is the primo spot in London. The weekend three-course lunch is a steal at £17.50. Although it's hard to get into London's favorite restaurant, try walking in off the street for a table on short notice—it's been known to work. ☒ *1 West St., WC2* ☎ *020/7836–4751* ✍ *Reservations essential* ▭ *AE, DC, MC, V* Ⓤ *Covent Garden.*

★ **$$** ✕ **Providores.** Kiwi Peter Gordon scores a perfect 10 with his Pacific Rim fusion food at Providores in ever-so-trendy Marylebone. Have a charming meal upstairs or go down to the relaxed ground-floor Tapa Rooms for the sweet potato and miso, the cassava fritters, and the roast *chioca* (a tuber similar to Jerusalem artichoke). ☒ *109 Marylebone High St., W1* ☎ *020/7935–6175* ▭ *AE, MC, V* Ⓤ *Baker St.*

$–$$ ✕ **Joe Allen.** Long hours (thespians flock here after the curtains fall in Theatreland) and a welcoming interior mean New York Joe's London branch still swings after more than two decades. The fun menu helps: roasted poblano peppers and black-bean soup are typical starters; entrées include barbecued ribs and corn muffins, or monkfish with sun-dried-tomato salsa. ☒ *13 Exeter St., WC2,* ☎ *020/7836–0651* ✍ *Reservations essential* ▭ *AE, MC, V* Ⓤ *Covent Garden.*

★ **$** ✕ **busabe eathai.** One of Londoners' favorite cheap spots in Soho, this superior Thai canteen is fitted with rattan, benches, hardwood tables, low lights, and paper lamp shades. It's no less seductive for its communal seating. The menu includes noodles, curries, and stir-fries. Try chicken with butternut squash, cuttlefish curry, or seafood vermicelli (prawns, squid, and scallops). The mantra here is *gan gin gan yuu,* which means "as you eat, so you are." ☒ *106–110 Wardour St., W1* ☎ *020/7255–8686* ✍ *Reservations not accepted* ▭ *AE, MC, V* Ⓤ *Leicester Sq.*

Chelsea, Kensington & Knightsbridge

$$$$ ✕ **The Capital.** The clublike dining room has a grown-up atmosphere with formal service. Chef Eric Chavot carries out classy French cooking, and many of his dishes astonish. These include turbot with creamed baby leeks and mushroom ravioli. Desserts follow the same exciting route. Set-price menus at lunch (£26.50) make it somewhat more affordable. ☒ *22–24 Basil St., SW3* ☎ *020/7589–5171* ✍ *Reservations essential* ▭ *AE, DC, MC, V* Ⓤ *Knightsbridge.*

★ $$$$ ✕ **Gordon Ramsay.** Ramsay whips up a storm with white beans, foie gras, scallops, and truffles. He's Britain's number one, and tables are booked months in advance. For £80, blow out on the seven-course option; for £65, wallow in three dinner courses; or grab lunch (£35 for three courses) for a less expensive check. ✉ *68–69 Royal Hospital Rd., SW3* ☎ *020/7352–4441* ✍ *Reservations essential* ▭ *AE, DC, MC, V* ⏲ *Closed weekends* Ⓤ *Sloane Sq.*

$$$–$$$$ ✕ **Bibendum.** This converted 1911 Michelin showroom, adorned with art deco prints and brilliant stained glass, remains one of London's dining showplaces. Chef Matthew Harris cooks with Euro-Brit flair. Try deep-fried calves' brains, any of the risottos, steak *au poivre,* or milk-fed lamb with garlic and mint gravy. The £25 fixed-price lunch menu is money well spent. ✉ *Michelin House, 81 Fulham Rd., SW3* ☎ *020/7581–5817* ✍ *Reservations essential* ▭ *AE, DC, MC, V* Ⓤ *South Kensington.*

$$$–$$$$ ✕ **Zafferano.** Any number of Cartier brooch–wearing Belgravians flock to Zafferano, one of London's best exponents of *cucina nuova.* The fireworks are in the kitchen, and *what* fireworks: buckwheat pasta with leek and sage, lamb cutlets with hazelnut crust and white truffle polenta. The desserts are *delizioso,* especially the poached pears and mascarpone ice cream. ✉ *15 Lowndes St., SW1* ☎ *020/7235–5800* ✍ *Reservations essential* ▭ *AE, DC, MC, V* Ⓤ *Knightsbridge.*

$$–$$$$ ✕ **Zaika.** One of London's finest Indian restaurants pushes the boundaries of Indian cuisine by mixing old flavors with modern sensibilities. You can't top the *samundri Zaika* (tandoor-smoked salmon, king prawn, and swordfish), nor can you better the scallops in coconut milk, with masala mashed potato. Sign off with chocolate samosas ("chocomosas") and Indian ice cream. ✉ *1 Kensington High St., W8* ☎ *020/7795–6533* ✍ *Reservations essential* ▭ *AE, MC, V* Ⓤ *High St. Kensington.*

$$–$$$ ✕ **Bluebird.** Sir Terence Conran presents a "gastrodome"—food market, fruit stand, butchers, kitchen shop, café, and restaurant. The place is blue and white, bright, and not in the least cozy, and the food can be fairly formulaic: veal kidneys and shallots, rabbit and spinach, then chocolate cake and espresso ice cream. Go for the people-watching and visual excitement; Conran's chefs tend to promise more than they deliver. ✉ *350 King's Rd., SW3* ☎ *020/7559–1000* ✍ *Reservations essential* ▭ *AE, DC, MC, V* Ⓤ *Sloane Sq.*

$$–$$$ ✕ **La Poule au Pot.** One of London's most charming restaurants, La Poule au Pot is superb for proposals or romantic evenings. The "Chelsea Set"—and Americans—love this candlelighted corner of France. The country cooking is fairly good, not spectacular. The *poule au pot* (stewed chicken) and *lapin à la moutarde* (rabbit with mustard) are strong and hearty, and there are fine classics, such as beef bourguignonne and French onion soup. Service comes with bonhomie. ✉ *231 Ebury St., SW1* ☎ *020/7730–7763* ✍ *Reservations essential* ▭ *AE, DC, MC, V* Ⓤ *Sloane Sq.*

$$ ✕ **The Enterprise.** Near Harrods and Brompton Cross, the Enterprise is filled with decorative types who complement the striped wallpaper, Edwardian side tables, vintage books piled up in the windows, and white linen and fresh flowers on the tables. The menu is fairly subtle—braised lamb shank with rosemary and celeriac puree—and the heartiness of the room contributes to a fun experience. ✉ *35 Walton St., SW3* ☎ *020/7584–3148* ▭ *AE, MC, V* Ⓤ *South Kensington.*

The City

★ $$–$$$$ ✕ **Club Gascon.** It's hard to find a sexier scene than this in all London, with its leather-walled interior, excellent service, and courses served on slabs of rock. Club Gascon's raison d'être is foie gras, which runs through the menu from start to finish (you can even have it for dessert, with fortified wine, gingerbread, and grapes). Bliss out on roast zander or foie gras steeped in Montilla-Moriles sherry and shot through with 10-year-old Maury wine. ✉ *57 W. Smithfield, EC1* ☎ *020/7796–0600* *Reservations essential* *AE, MC, V* *Closed Sun., no lunch Sat.* *Barbican.*

Mayfair & St. James's

$$$$ Fodor's Choice ★ ✕ **Gordon Ramsay at Claridge's.** Sit at the chef's table, a six- to eight-seat booth inside the kitchen, and watch the art and intensity. Ramsay is Britain's greatest chef, and Claridge's is booked six months in advance—Tony Blair came for his birthday. Try the eight-hour roast shoulder of lamb, braised halibut, or brill in red wine. Book months ahead and arrive early for dinner to have a drink at Claridge's art deco bar, the best cocktail lounge in London. They also do breakfast and bargain three-course lunches (£25). ✉ *Claridge's Hotel, Brook St., W1* ☎ *020/7499–0099* *Reservations essential* *Jacket and tie* *AE, MC, V* *Bond St.*

$$–$$$$ Fodor's Choice ★ ✕ **Locanda Locatelli.** Everything chef Giorgio Locatelli touches turns to gold—hence the six-week waiting list. The elegant David Collins–designed dining room at the Churchill Inter-Continental has convex mirrors, etched glass, swivel chairs, and banquettes, and the food is accomplished. Be bold: try the ravioli osso bucco or the sweetbread with Roman *agro-dolce* (sweet and sour sauce), and choose from the all–Italian wine list. ✉ *8 Seymour St., W1* ☎ *020/7935–9088* *Reservations essential* *AE, MC, V* *Closed Sun.* *Marble Arch.*

$$–$$$$ ✕ **Nobu.** Bulging with stars, this is a true destination restaurant. Nobuyuki Matsuhisa concocts new-style sashimi with a Peruvian touch—he sells 300 lb. of Alaskan black cod a day. Nobu is in the Metropolitan, a hip hotel, with staff, attitude, clientele, and prices to match. ✉ *Metropolitan Hotel, 19 Old Park La., W1* ☎ *020/7447–4747* *Reservations essential* *AE, DC, MC, V* *No lunch weekends* *Hyde Park.*

★ **$$–$$$** ✕ **Le Caprice.** Secreted behind the Ritz Hotel, Le Caprice commands deep loyalty among its patrons—including Joan Collins and David Bowie—because it gets everything right: the glossy Eva Jiricna interior; the perfect service; and the menu, halfway between Euro-peasant and fashion plate. The crispy duck and watercress salad, and San Daniele ham and figs have no business being so good. ✉ *Arlington House, Arlington St., SW1* ☎ *020/7629–2239* *Reservations essential* *AE, DC, MC, V* *Green Park.*

$–$$ ✕ **Browns.** Unpretentious, crowd-pleasing, child-friendly English feeding gets done at the former establishment of the tailors Messrs. Cooling and Wells, now converted to Edwardian style by the group behind the successful Browns eateries. The classic Browns steak-and-Guinness pie is on the menu, but king prawns, lamb shanks, roasted peppers, salads, and pastas predominate. ✉ *47 Maddox St., W1* ☎ *020/7491–4565* *AE, DC, MC, V* *Oxford Circus.*

Notting Hill

★ **$–$$$** ✕ **E&O.** If you like stars, you'll love E&O. Gwyneth, Madonna, and Nicole have all been drawn by its luxurious charm. The restaurant's name stands for Eastern and Oriental, and the Pan-Asian cuisine is an intelligent mix of Chinese, Japanese, Vietnamese, and Thai. Don't skip the Thai rare-beef salad with red *nam jhim* (bean sprouts) or the albacore sashimi, and remember to look up and then look away when the A-list star settles in at Table 5. ✉ *14 Blenheim Crescent, W11* ☎ *020/7229–5454* ✍ *Reservations essential* ▭ *AE, DC, MC, V* Ⓤ *Ladbroke Grove.*

$$ ✕ **The Cow.** Upstairs the chef whips up Anglo-French specialties for diners in this chic gastro pub, comprised of a faux-Dublin back-room bar. Salmon cakes, baked brill, and cod and mash are some of the temptations offered. Notting Hillbillies love the house special: a half-dozen Irish rock oysters with a pint of Guinness. ✉ *89 Westbourne Park Rd., W2* ☎ *020/7221–0021* ✍ *Reservations essential* ▭ *MC, V* Ⓤ *Westbourne Park.*

10

South Bank

$$$–$$$$ ✕ **OXO Tower Brasserie and Restaurant.** London has a room with a view—and *such* a view. On the eighth floor of the OXO Tower near the South Bank is this elegant space serving Euro-Asian food with the latest trendy ingredients (spinach pie with quail and pumpkin salad). The ceiling slats turn from white to blue, but who notices, with the London Eye wheel and St. Paul's Cathedral across the water? The Brasserie is slightly less expensive than the restaurant; terrace tables available in summer have the best panoramas. ✉ *Barge House St., SE1* ☎ *020/7803–3888* ▭ *AE, DC, MC, V* Ⓤ *Waterloo.*

WHERE TO STAY

Note that although British hotels have traditionally included breakfast in their nightly tariff, many of London's most expensive establishments charge extra for breakfast.

WHAT IT COSTS In pounds sterling

	$$$$	$$$	$$	$
FOR 2 PEOPLE	over £230	£160–£230	£100–£160	under £100

Prices are for a double room and include all taxes.

Bayswater

$–$$ 🏨 **Vancouver Studios.** This little hotel is run like an apartment building: rooms are actually studios with kitchens, and the front door has a security entry system. Each studio has daily maid service; some have working fireplaces; and there is a garden for guests to enjoy. ✉ *30 Prince's Sq., W2 4NJ* ☎ *020/7243–1270* 🖷 *020/7221–8678* 🌐 *www.vancouverstudios.co.uk* ⮂ *45 studios* ▭ *AE, DC, MC, V* Ⓤ *Bayswater, Queensway.*

$ 🏨 **Garden Court Hotel.** Built in 1870, the hotel consists of two 19th-century town houses in a quiet paved garden square. Each of the comfortable rooms has a character of its own, complete with some original Victorian fittings, and the owners are eager to please. Rooms with toilet and shower cost £30 extra, and family-size rooms are in the $$ category. ✉ *30–31 Kensington Gardens Sq., W2 4BL* ☎ *020/7229–2553* 🖷 *020/7727–2749* 🌐 *www.gardencourthotel.co.uk* ⮂ *32 rooms, some without bath* ▭ *MC, V* Ⓤ *Bayswater, Queensway.*

Bloomsbury

$$$ Fodor'sChoice ★ 🏨 **myhotel bloomsbury.** Before you arrive you'll be asked to fill out a preferences sheet so your room is just as you like it. If anything should go wrong, no need to call the front desk: just contact your personal assistant for help. Rooms are minimalist, with wooden floors and simple color

schemes. Superior doubles are bigger and have separate sitting rooms. From the "jinja" spa to the library stocked with CDs, books, and free beverages, myhotel's novel approach succeeds brilliantly. ✉ *11–13 Bayley St., Bedford Sq., WC1B 3HD* ☎ *020/7667–6000* 📠 *020/7667–6001* 🌐 *www.myhotels.com* *76 rooms* *Restaurant, bar* 💳 *AE, DC, MC, V* Ⓤ *Tottenham Court Rd.*

$ **Harlingford Hotel.** The Harlingford is by far the sleekest and most contemporary of the Cartwright Gardens hotels. Bold color schemes and beautifully tiled bathrooms make this family-run hotel a bargain for contemporary style. The largest rooms sleep four and are an excellent choice for traveling families. ✉ *61–63 Cartwright Gardens, WC1H 9EL* ☎ *020/7387–1551* 📠 *020/7383–4616* 🌐 *www.harlingfordhotel.com* *43 rooms* 💳 *AE, DC, MC, V* Ⓤ *Russell Sq.*

Chelsea, Kensington & Holland Park

★ $$$$ **Blakes.** Designed by owner Anouska Hempel, each room at Blakes is a fantasy packed with precious Biedermeier, Murano glass, and modern pieces collected from all over the world. Cinematic mood lighting, with recessed halogen spots, compounds the impression that you, too, are a movie star in a big-budget biopic. The foyer sets the tone with piles of cushions, Phileas Fogg valises and trunks, black walls, rattan, and bamboo. ✉ *33 Roland Gardens, SW7 3PF* ☎ *020/7370–6701* 📠 *020/7373–0442* 🌐 *www.blakeshotels.com* *38 rooms, 11 suites* *Restaurant, bar* 💳 *AE, DC, MC, V* Ⓤ *South Kensington.*

★ $$$ **Miller's Residence.** From the moment you ring the bell and are ushered up the winding staircase flanked by antiques and curios, you know you've entered another realm where history is paramount. Run by Martin Miller of famed *Miller's Antique Price Guides,* this town house serves as his home, gallery, and B&B. Sip a complimentary evening cocktail in the long, candelighted drawing room with fireplace while mixing with other guests or the convivial staff. The rooms are named for Romantic poets. ✉ *111A Westbourne Grove, W2 4UW* ☎ *020/7243–1024* 📠 *020/7243–1064* 🌐 *www.millersuk.com* *6 rooms, 2 suites* 💳 *AE, DC, MC, V* Ⓤ *Notting Hill Gate.*

$$–$$$ **Aster House.** Rooms in this delightful guest house are country casual, and the owners go out of their way to make you feel at home and answer questions. The conservatory where breakfast is served is an airy, light place, and the small garden at the back has a charming pond. Note that this is a five-story building with no elevator. ✉ *3 Sumner Pl., SW7 3EE* ☎ *020/7581–5888* 📠 *020/7584–4925* 🌐 *www.asterhouse.com* *14 rooms* 💳 *MC, V* Ⓤ *South Kensington.*

$ **Abbey House.** This pretty, white-stucco 1860 Victorian town house is in an excellent location close to trendy Notting Hill. You can spend the cash you save by staying here in the nearby antiques shops. Rooms are spacious—with four-person rooms suitable for families—and have washbasins, but every room shares a bath with another. Note that there is no elevator. ✉ *11 Vicarage Gate, W8 4AG* ☎ *020/7727–2594* 📠 *020/7727–1873* 🌐 *www.abbeyhousekensington.com* *16 rooms without bath* 💳 *No credit cards* Ⓤ *High St. Kensington.*

$ **The Vicarage.** Family-owned and set on a leafy street just off Kensington Church Street, the Vicarage occupies a large white Victorian house full of heavy and dark-stained wood furniture, patterned carpets, and brass pendant lights. All in all, it's a charmer, but it is beginning to fray around the edges. All rooms share the bathroom, but a few doubles have their own showers. ✉ *10 Vicarage Gate, W8 4AG* ☎ *020/7229–4030* 📠 *020/7792–5989* 🌐 *www.londonvicaragehotel.com* *14 rooms, 8 with bath* 💳 *No credit cards* Ⓤ *High St. Kensington.*

Knightsbridge, Belgravia & Victoria

$$$$ **The Lanesborough.** Royally proportioned public rooms distinguish this multimillion-pound, American-run conversion of St. George's Hospital. Everything undulates with richness—moiré silks and fleurs-de-lis in the colors of precious stones, magnificent antiques and oil paintings, handwoven £250-per-square-yard carpet—as if Liberace and Laura Ashley had collaborated. To check in, sign the visitor's book, then retire to your room, where you are waited on by a personal butler. ✉ *Hyde Park Corner, SW1X 7TA* ☎ *020/7259–5599; 800/999–1828 in U.S.* 📠 *020/7259–5606; 800/937–8278 in U.S.* 🌐 *www.lanesborough.com* *49 rooms, 46 suites* *2 restaurants, 2 bars* 💳 *AE, DC, MC, V* Ⓤ *Hyde Park Corner.*

$$$$ **The Rubens at the Palace.** This hotel likes to say it treats you like royalty. In fact, you're only a stone's throw from the real thing, as Buckingham Palace is just across the road. The elegant Rubens, which looks out over the Royal Mews, provides the sort of deep comfort needed to soothe away a hard day's sightseeing, with cushy armchairs crying out for you to sink into them with a cup of Earl Grey. With decent-size rooms and a location that couldn't be more central, this hotel is a favorite for many travelers. ✉ *39 Buckingham Palace Rd., SW1W 0PS* ☎ *020/7834–6600* 📠 *020/7233–6037* 🌐 *www.rubenshotel.com* *160 rooms, 13 suites* *2 restaurants, bar* 💳 *AE, DC, MC, V* Ⓤ *Victoria.*

★ $$$–$$$$ **The Pelham.** The Pelham looks like the country house to end all country houses. There's 18th-century pine paneling in the drawing room, flowers galore, quite a bit of glazed chintz and antique-lace bed linen, and the occasional four-poster bed and fireplace. The first-floor (American second-floor) suites are extra spacious, with high ceilings and chandeliers. ✉ *15 Cromwell Pl., SW7 2LA* ☎ *020/7589–8288* 📠 *020/7584–8444* 🌐 *www.firmdale.com* *51 rooms* *Restaurant, bar* 💳 *AE, MC, V* Ⓤ *South Kensington.*

$$$ **Knightsbridge Hotel.** Just off glamorous Knightsbridge in quiet Beaufort Gardens, this hotel succeeds in being cheap (relatively) and chic (enormously). The balconied suites and regular rooms benefit from CD players, writing desks, and large granite and oak bathrooms. ✉ *10 Beaufort Gardens, SW3 1PT* ☎ *020/7584–6300; 800/553–6674 in U.S.* 📠 *020/7584–6355* 🌐 *www.knightsbridgehotel.co.uk* *42 rooms, 2 suites* *Bar* 💳 *AE, MC, V* Ⓤ *Knightsbridge.*

West End

$$$$ **Brown's.** Founded in 1837 by Lord Byron's "gentleman's gentleman," James Brown, Brown's retains a cozy, oak-paneled, chintz-laden, grandfather-clock-ticking-in-the-parlor sensibility. The complex consists of 11 Georgian town houses patronized by many Anglophilic Americans—a habit established by Theodore and Franklin Delano Roosevelt. ✉ *34 Albemarle St., W1X 4BT* ☎ *020/7493–6020* 📠 *020/7493–9381* 🌐 *www.brownshotel.com* *108 rooms, 10 suites* *2 restaurants, bar* 💳 *AE, DC, MC, V* Ⓤ *Green Park.*

★ $$$$ **Claridge's.** Some of the world's classiest guests patronize this legendary hotel. The friendly, liveried staff is not in the least condescending, and the rooms are spacious and never less than luxurious. The grand staircase is magnificent, and the elevator contains a sofa to maximize comfort. Enjoy a cup of tea in the lounge, or retreat to the stylish bar for cocktails—or, better, to Gordon Ramsay's inimitable restaurant for dinner. ✉ *Brook St., W1A 2JQ* ☎ *020/7629–8860; 800/637–2869 in U.S.* 📠 *020/7499–2210* 🌐 *www.claridges.co.uk* *203 rooms* *Restaurant, bar* 💳 *AE, DC, MC, V* Ⓤ *Bond St.*

$$$$ **Covent Garden Hotel.** A former 1880s hospital in the midst of artsy,
Fodor'sChoice ★ boisterous Covent Garden, this hotel is the London home-away-from-home for a mélange of off-duty celebrities, actors, and style mavens. The public salons display painted silks, *style anglais* ottomans, and 19th-century Romantic oils, and are perfect places to decompress over sherry. Guest rooms are *World of Interiors* stylish, showcasing matching-but-mixed couture fabrics to stunning effect. ✉ *10 Monmouth St., WC2H 9HB* ☎ *020/7806–1000* 📠 *020/7806–1100* 🌐 *www.firmdale.com* *55 rooms, 3 suites* *Restaurant* ▭ *AE, MC, V* Ⓤ *Covent Garden.*

★ $$$$ **The Savoy.** This grand hotel hosted Elizabeth Taylor's first honeymoon and poured one of Europe's first dry martinis in its American Bar, a one-time haunt of Hemingway, Fitzgerald, and Gershwin. The art deco rooms are especially fabulous, but all rooms are impeccably maintained, spacious, and elegant. A room facing the Thames costs a fortune and requires an early booking, but it's worth it. ✉ *Strand, WC2R 0EU* ☎ *020/7836–4343* 📠 *020/7240–6040* 🌐 *www.savoy-group.com* *263 rooms, 19 suites* *3 restaurants, pool, 2 bars* ▭ *AE, DC, MC, V* Ⓤ *Aldwych.*

$$$–$$$$ **Hazlitt's.** One of the three early-18th-century houses on this site was the last home of essayist William Hazlitt (1778–1830). The hotel that now occupies the space is a disarmingly friendly place, full of personality but devoid of elevators. Robust antiques are everywhere, assorted prints crowd every wall, plants and stone sculptures occupy corners, and every room has a Victorian claw-foot bathtub. There are tiny sitting rooms, wooden staircases, and more restaurants within strolling distance than you could patronize in a year. ✉ *6 Frith St., W1V 5TZ* ☎ *020/7434–1771* 📠 *020/7439–1524* 🌐 *www.hazlittshotel.com* *20 rooms, 3 suites* ▭ *AE, DC, MC, V* Ⓤ *Tottenham Court Rd.*

$$ **Bryanston Court.** These three converted Georgian houses are decorated in a traditional English style, with fireplaces, leather armchairs, and oil portraits. The small bedrooms have pink furnishings, creaky floors, and tiny bathrooms, but they remain an excellent value for the hotel's location. Rooms at the back are quieter and face east toward the morning sun. ✉ *56–60 Great Cumberland Pl., W1H 8DD* ☎ *020/7262–3141* 📠 *020/7262–7248* 🌐 *www.bryanstonhotel.com* *81 rooms, 8 apartments* *Bar* ▭ *MC, V* Ⓤ *Marble Arch.*

$$ **Fielding.** On a quiet pedestrian alley just steps from the Royal Opera House, this small hotel is popular with its regular, opera-loving clientele. However, there are no amenities save for the residents' bar and the coffeemakers in each room; you can get more comfort for your money elsewhere. ✉ *4 Broad Ct., at Bow St., WC2B 5QZ* ☎ *020/7836–8305* 📠 *020/7497–0064* 🌐 *www.the-fielding-hotel.co.uk* *24 rooms* *Bar* ▭ *AE, DC, MC, V* Ⓤ *Covent Garden.*

NIGHTLIFE & THE ARTS

The Arts

The most comprehensive list of events in the London arts scene can be found in the weekly magazine *Time Out*. The *Evening Standard* also carries listings, especially in the supplement "Hot Tickets," which comes with the Thursday edition, as do the "quality" Sunday papers and the Saturday *Independent, Guardian,* and *Times*. You can pick up the free fortnightly *London Theatre Guide* leaflet from hotels and tourist information centers.

Ballet

The Royal Opera House is the traditional home of the world-famous **Royal Ballet.** As well as favorites like *The Nutcracker,* there is a spectrum of classical and innovative contemporary performances. Prices start at £3 (for ballet matinees). Bookings should be made well in advance. The **English National Ballet** (☎ 020/7632–8300) and visiting companies perform at the London Coliseum (☎ 020/7632–8300). **Sadler's Wells** (☎ 020/7863–8000) hosts regional ballet and international modern dance troupes. Prices are reasonable. A popular venue for cutting-edge modern and experimental dance is **The Place** (☎ 020/7380–1268).

Classical Music

Ticket prices for symphony orchestra concerts are still relatively moderate—between £5 and £35, although you can expect to pay more to hear big-name artists on tour. If you can't book in advance, arrive half an hour before the performance for a chance at returns.

The London Symphony Orchestra is in residence at the **Barbican Arts Centre** (☎ 020/7638–8891), although other top symphony and chamber orchestras also perform here. The **South Bank Centre** (☎ 020/7960–4242), which includes the Royal Festival Hall and the Queen Elizabeth Hall, is another major venue for choral, symphonic, and chamber concerts. For less expensive concert going, try the **Royal Albert Hall** (☎ 020/7589–8212) during the summer Promenade season (the "Proms"), when special tickets for standing room are available at the hall on the night of performance. Note, too, that the concerts are broadcast on a jumbo screen in Hyde Park, but even a seat on the grass here requires a paid ticket. The **Wigmore Hall** (☎ 020/7935–2141) is a small auditorium, ideal for recitals. Inexpensive lunchtime concerts (usually less than £5 or free) take place all over the city in smaller halls and churches, often featuring string quartets, vocalists, jazz ensembles, and gospel choirs. **St. John's, Smith Square** (☎ 020/7222–1061) offers chamber music and solo recitals. **St. Martin-in-the-Fields** (☎ 020/7839–1930) holds free lunchtime concerts.

Film

Most big West End cinemas are in the area around Leicester Square and Piccadilly Circus. Tickets average £8. Matinees and Monday evenings are often cheaper, and some theaters offer student discounts. One of the best cinemas is the **National Film Theatre** (☎ 020/7928–3232), part of the South Bank Centre. The Regus London Film Festival is based here, and throughout the year three screens show classics, foreign-language films, documentaries, cult Hollywood features, and animation.

Opera

The **Royal Opera House** (✉ Covent Garden ☎ 020/7304–4000) presents original-language productions in an extravagant theater. If you can't afford £100 for a ticket, consider showing up at 8 AM to purchase a same-day seat, of which a small number are offered for £30.

The **London Coliseum** (☎ 020/7632–8300) is the home of the English National Opera Company (ENO), whose productions are staged in English and are often innovative and exciting. Prices are lower than for the Royal Opera, ranging from £5 to £55. The ENO sells same-day seats for as little as £2.50.

Theater

Most theaters have an evening performance at 7:30 or 8 Monday–Saturday, and a matinee twice a week (Wednesday or Thursday, and Saturday). Expect to pay from £10 for a seat in the upper balcony and at least £25 for a good seat in the stalls (orchestra) or dress circle (mezzanine), and more for musicals. Tickets may be booked in person at the theater box office, over the phone by credit card, or through ticket agents. **Ticketmaster** (☎ 020/7344–0055; 800/775–2525 in U.S.) sells tickets to many theaters and productions. The **SOLT** (Society of London Theatres, "TKTS") kiosk, in Leicester Square, sells half-price tickets on the day of performance for about 25 theaters; there is a £2 service charge. It's open Monday–Saturday 2–6:30, Sunday noon–3. Beware of scalpers!

London's theater life can more or less be divided into three categories: the government-subsidized national companies; the commercial, or "West End," theaters; and the fringe. The **Royal National Theatre** (NT; ☎ 020/7452–3000 box office) shares the laurels as the top national repertory troupe with the Royal Shakespeare Company. In similar fashion to the latter troupe, the NT presents plays by writers of all nationalities, ranging from the classics of Shakespeare to specially commissioned modern works. The NT is based at the South Bank Centre. The **Royal Shakespeare Company** (RSC; ☎ 020/7638–8891 box office; 01789/403–403 general inquiries) performs at West End venues throughout the year, and you can also see the company's productions as it tours different theaters around the country. If you're visiting London in the summer, you can book tickets at the spectacular reconstruction of **Shakespeare's Globe Theatre** (☎ 020/7401–9919 box office) on the South Bank, which offers open-air, late-afternoon performances from June through September.

The **West End theaters** stage musicals, comedies, whodunits, and revivals of lighter plays of the 19th and 20th centuries, often starring TV celebrities. Occasionally there are more serious productions, including successful performances transferred from the subsidized theaters, such as those of the RSC. The two dozen or so established **fringe theaters,** scattered around central London and the immediate outskirts, frequently present some of London's most intriguing productions, if you're prepared to overlook occasional rough staging and uncomfortable seating.

Nightlife

London's nightspots are legion; here are some of the best known. For up-to-the-minute listings, buy *Time Out* magazine.

Comedy

The best comedy in town can be found in the big, bright **Comedy Store** (✉ 1A Oxendon St., near Piccadilly Circus, SW1 ☎ 020/7344–0234).

Jazz Clubs

Pizza Express (✉ 10 Dean St., W1 ☎ 020/7437–9595 or 020/7439–8722) is the capital's best-loved chain of pizza houses, but it is also one of London's principal jazz venues, with music every night except Mondays in the basement restaurant. Eight other branches also have live music. **Ronnie Scott's** (✉ 47 Frith St., W1 ☎ 020/7439–0747) is a legendary Soho jazz club where the food isn't great and service is slow, but where big-name international performers regularly take the stage.

Nightclubs

Café de Paris (✉ 3–4 Coventry St., W1V 7FL ☎ 020/7734–7700) opened in 1914 and is one of London's most glamour-puss settings. It was once the haunt of royals and stars such as Noël Coward, Marlene Dietrich, Fred Astaire, and Frank Sinatra. **Hanover Grand** (✉ 6 Hanover Sq., W1 ☎ 020/7499–7977) is a swank and opulent big West End club that attracts TV stars and others in the entertainment business for funky U.S. garage on Friday and glam disco on Saturday. The lines outside get long, so dress up to impress the bouncers. **Ministry of Sound** (✉ 103 Gaunt St., SE1 ☎ 020/7378–6528) is more of an industry than a club, with its own record label, line of apparel, and, of course, DJs. Inside, there are chill-out rooms, dance floors, Absolut shot bars—all the club kids' favorite things. If you are one, and you have time for only one night out, make it here. **Fabric** (✉ 77A Charterhouse St., EC1 ☎ 020/7336–8898) is a sprawling subterranean club with slow, reverberating bass lines and cutting-edge music from world-class DJs. Come early on weekends to avoid a lengthy wait.

Rock

The **Forum** (✉ 9–17 Highgate Rd., Kentish Town ☎ 020/7344–0044), a little out of the way, is a premier venue for medium-to-big acts. **100 Club** (✉ 100 Oxford St., W1 ☎ 020/7636–0933) is a basement dive that's always been there for R&B, rock, jazz, and beer. The **Shepherds Bush Empire** (✉ Shepherds Bush Green, W12 ☎ 020/7771–2000) is a major venue for largish acts in West London. **The Borderline** (✉ Otange Yard, off Manette St., W1V ☎ 020/7734–2095) is a small but central subterranean room with fake southwestern decor that puts on Americana, blues, and indie rock.

SHOPPING

Shopping is one of London's great pleasures. Different areas retain their traditional specialties, and it's fun to seek out the small crafts, antiques, and gift stores, designer-clothing resale outlets, and national department-store chains.

Shopping Districts

Centering on the King's Road, **Chelsea** was once synonymous with ultrafashion; it still harbors some designer boutiques, plus antiques and home furnishings stores. A something-for-everyone neighborhood, **Covent Garden** has numerous clothing chain stores, stalls selling crafts, and shops selling gifts of every type—bikes, kites, herbs, beads, hats, you name it. **Kensington**'s main drag, Kensington High Street, is a smaller, classier version of Oxford Street, with Barkers department store, and a branch of Marks & Spencer at the eastern end. Try Kensington Church Street for expensive antiques, plus a little fashion. Venture out to the W11 and W2 neighborhoods around the Holland Park–Westbourne Grove end of **Notting Hill,** and you'll find specialty shops for clothes, accessories, and home furnishings, plus lots of fashionable bistros for sustenance. Kensington's neighbor, **Knightsbridge,** has Harrods, of course, but also Harvey Nichols, the chicest clothes shop in London, and many expensive designers' boutiques along Sloane Street, Walton Street, and Beauchamp Place. Adjacent Belgravia is also a burgeoning area for posh designer stores.

Bond Street, Old and New, is the elegant lure in **Mayfair,** with the *hautest* of haute couture and jewelry outposts, plus fine art. South Molton Street offers high-price, high-style fashion—especially at Browns—and the tailors of Savile Row are of worldwide repute. Crowded and a bit past its prime, the north end of **Oxford Street** toward Tottenham Court Road has tawdry discount shops sprinkled in with upmarket fashion chains. Toward Marble Arch, Selfridges, John Lewis, and Marks & Spencer are wonderful department stores. There are interesting boutiques secreted off Oxford Street, just north of the Bond Street Tube stop, in little St. Christopher's Place and Gees Court, and south of the Tube stop for chic-est South Molton Street. Check out the cobbled streets in West Soho, behind Liberty in Regent Street, for handcrafted jewelry, designer gear, and stylish cafés. Perpendicular to Oxford Street lies **Regent Street**—famous for its curving path—with the irresistible department store Liberty's, as well as Hamley's, the capital's most comprehensive toy depot.

Shops around once-famous **Carnaby Street** stock designer youth paraphernalia and at least 57 varieties of T-shirts. The fabled English gentleman buys much of his gear at stores in **St. James's**: handmade hats, shirts, and shoes; silver shaving kits; and hip flasks. Here is also the world's best cheese shop, Paxton & Whitfield. Don't expect any bargains in this neighborhood.

Street Markets

Street markets are one aspect of London life not to be missed. Here are some of the more interesting markets:

Borough Market. This is a foodies' paradise with whole grain and organic products from Britain and a host of international flavors. ✉ *Borough High St., SE1* ⏲ *Fri. noon–6, Sat. 9–4* Ⓤ *London Bridge, Borough.*

Camden Lock. The volume and range of merchandise (and crowds) at this conglomeration of several markets is mind-blowing: vintage and new clothes, antiques and junk, jewelry and scarves. Hip teens use the area as a casual date spot. ✉ *Chalk Farm Rd., NW1* ⏲ *Shops Tues.–Sun. 9:30–5:30, stalls weekends 8–6* Ⓤ *Tube or Bus 24 or 29 to Camden Town.*

Camden Passage. The rows of little antiques stalls are a good hunting ground for silverware and jewelry. Stalls open Wednesday and Saturday, and there is also a books and prints market on Thursday. ✉ *Islington, off Upper St., N1* ⏲ *Wed. and Sat. 8:30–3* Ⓤ *Tube or Bus 19 or 38 to Angel.*

Covent Garden. Craft stalls, jewelry designers, clothes makers—particularly of knitwear—and other artisans congregate in the central Apple Market. The Jubilee Market, toward Southampton Street, has a worthwhile selection of vintage collectibles on Mondays. ✉ *The Piazza, WC2* ⏲ *Daily 9–5* Ⓤ *Covent Garden.*

Petticoat Lane. Look for budget-priced leather goods, gaudy knitwear, and fashions, plus cameras, videos, stereos, antiques, books, and bric-a-brac. ✉ *Middlesex St., E1* ⏲ *Sun. 9–2* Ⓤ *Liverpool St., Aldgate, Aldgate East.*

Portobello Market. Saturday is the best day for antiques, though Notting Hill is London's melting pot, becoming more vibrant throughout the week. Find fabulous small shops, trendy restaurants, and a Friday and Saturday flea market at the far end at Ladbroke Grove. ✉ *Portobello Rd., W11* ⏲ *Fri. 5 AM–3 PM, Sat. 6 AM–5 PM* Ⓤ *Tube or Bus 52 to Notting Hill Gate or Ladbroke Grove, or Bus 15 to Kensington Park Rd.*

LONDON A TO Z

AIR TRAVEL TO & FROM LONDON

International flights to London arrive at either Heathrow Airport, 24 km (15 mi) west of London, or Gatwick Airport, 43 km (27 mi) south of the capital. Most flights from the United States go to Heathrow, although Gatwick has grown from a European airport into one that serves 21 scheduled U.S. destinations. A third airport, Stansted, is to the east of the city. It handles mainly European and domestic traffic, although there is a scheduled service from New York.

TRANSFERS Airport Travel Line gives information and takes advance bookings on transfers to town and between airports, including National Express as listed below. The Heathrow Express train links the airport with Paddington Station in only 15 minutes. It costs £12, and service departs every 15 minutes from 5:02 AM to 11:47 PM. The Piccadilly Line serves

Heathrow (all terminals) with a direct Underground (subway) link, and the fare is £3.70. Airbus A2 costs £8 and leaves every 30 minutes 5:30 AM–9:45 PM from Terminal 4; 5:45 AM–10:08 PM from Terminal 3, to Euston and King's Cross stations, but the trip can be lengthy, as there are around 14 other stops en route. For the same price, National Express Jetlink 777 coaches leave from the Heathrow Central Bus Station every 30 minutes from 5:40 AM to 9:35 PM and run directly to Victoria Coach Station. Cars and taxis drive into London from Heathrow, often through heavy traffic, and cost £30–£40. Add a tip of 10%–15% to the basic fare.

From Gatwick the quickest way to London is the nonstop rail Gatwick Express, costing £11 one-way and taking 30 minutes to reach Victoria Station. From 5:20 AM to 6:50 AM, trains leave every 30 minutes, then every 15 minutes until 8:50 PM, and back to every 30 minutes until the last departure at 1:35 AM. National Express Jetlink bus services from North and South terminals do not go to London, but they do stop in many other major cities, such as Bristol, Cambridge, and Oxford. From Gatwick, taxi fare is at least £50, plus tip; traffic can be very heavy.

Airport Travel Line ☎ 0870/574–7777. **Gatwick Express** ☎ 0845/850–1530 🌐 www.gatwickexpress.co.uk. **Heathrow Express** ☎ 0845/600–1515 🌐 www.heathrowexpress.co.uk. **Airbus A2** ☎ 0870/574–7777. **National Express** ☎ 0870/580–8080 🌐 www.gobycoach.com.

BUS TRAVEL TO & FROM LONDON

The National Express coach service has routes to more than 1,200 major towns and cities in the United Kingdom. It's considerably cheaper than the train, although the trips usually take longer. Coaches depart every hour for Brighton (two hours) and Canterbury (one hour, 50 minutes).

National Express ✉ Victoria Coach Station, Buckingham Palace Rd., SW1 ☎ 0870/580–8080 🌐 www.nationalexpress.com.

BUS TRAVEL WITHIN LONDON

London's bus system consists of bright red London Trasport double- and single-deckers, plus other buses of various colors from different companies. Destinations are displayed on the front and back, with the bus number on the front, back, and side. Not all buses run the full length of their route at all times. Some buses are still operated with a conductor whom you pay after finding a seat, but these days you will more often find one-person buses, in which you pay the driver upon boarding. Some buses in central London (an area bounded by Paddington, Victoria, Waterloo, and Euston stations) now require prepurchased tickets. Machines at bus stops sell the tickets. For three-board "Bendy" buses, you must purchase tickets at the machines by the bus stops along these routes. Smoking is not allowed on any bus.

Buses stop only at clearly indicated stops. Main stops—at which buses should stop automatically—have a white sign with a red LT symbol on it. There are also request stops with red signs, a white symbol, and the word REQUEST added; at these you must hail the bus to make it stop. Although you can see much of the town from a bus, *don't* take one if you want to get anywhere in a hurry; traffic often slows travel to a crawl, and during peak times you may find yourself waiting at least 20 minutes for a bus and not being able to get on it once it arrives. If you intend to go by bus, ask at a Travel Information Centre for a free bus map.

All journeys within the central zone are 65p for short hops; for travel through any number of outer zones, add an extra 70p. A one-day pass through all zones is a good value at £2. Travelcards are good for Tube, bus, and National Rail trains in the Greater London zones. There are also a number of bus passes available for daily, weekly, and monthly use, and prices vary according to zones. A photograph is required for monthly bus passes.

London Transport 020/7222-1234 www.londontransport.co.uk.

CAR TRAVEL

The best advice is to avoid driving in London because of the ancient street patterns and the chronic parking restrictions. One-way streets also add to the confusion. A £5 "congestion charge" is levied on all vehicles entering central London (bounded by the Inner Ring Road and visibly displayed on street signs) on weekdays from 7 to 6:30, excluding bank holidays. Pay in advance or on that day until 10 PM if you're entering the central zone. You can pay by phone, mail, or Internet, or at indicated retail outlets. There are no tollbooths; cameras monitor the area. For current information, check www.tfl.gov.org.uk.

EMERGENCIES

Bliss Chemist is the only pharmacy in the center of London that is open around the clock. The leading chain drugstore, Boots at Piccadilly Circus, is open until 8 PM seven days, and Boots at 151 Oxford Street is open until 8 PM on Thursday. (Note: a prescription can be filled only if issued by a British registered doctor.)

Emergency Services **Police, fire brigade, or ambulance** 999.

24-Hour Pharmacies **Bliss Chemist** 5 Marble Arch, W1, 020/7723-6116.

TAXIS

London's black taxis are famous for their comfort and for the ability of their drivers to remember the city's mazelike streets. Hotels and main tourist areas have ranks (stands) where you wait your turn to take one of the taxis that drive up. You can also hail a taxi if the flag is up or the yellow FOR HIRE sign is lighted. Fares start at £1.40 and increase by units of 20p per 281 yards or 55.5 seconds until the fare exceeds £8.60. After that, it's 20p for each 188 yards or 37 seconds. Surcharges are a tricky extra, which range from 40p for additional passengers or bulky luggage to 60p for evenings 8 PM–midnight, and until 6 AM on weekends and public holidays. At Christmas, the surcharge zooms to £2, and there's 40p extra for each additional passenger. Fares are occasionally raised from year to year. Tip taxi drivers 10%–15% of the tab.

TOURS

BOAT TOURS

In summer, narrow boats and barges cruise London's two canals, the Grand Union and Regent's Canal; most vessels operate on the latter, which runs between Little Venice in the west (the nearest Tube is Warwick Avenue on the Bakerloo Line) and Camden Lock (about 200 yards north of Camden Town Tube station). Canal Cruises offers three or four cruises daily March–October on the *Jenny Wren* and all year on the cruising restaurant *My Fair Lady*. Jason's Trip operates one-way and round-trip narrow-boat cruises on this route. Trips last 1½ hours. The London Waterbus Company operates this route year-round with a stop at London Zoo: trips run daily April–October and weekends only November–March.

All year boats cruise up and down the Thames, offering a different view of the London skyline. In summer (April–October) boats run more frequently than in winter—call to check schedules and routes. Following is a selection of the main routes. For trips downriver from Charing Cross to Greenwich Pier and historic Greenwich, call Catamaran Cruisers. Westminster Passenger Service runs from Westminster Pier and onward to

Greenwich and Barrier Gardens at the Thames Barrier. Westminster Passenger Service Upriver operates through summer to Kew and Hampton Court from Westminster Pier. A Rail and River Rover ticket combines the modern wonders of Canary Wharf and Docklands development with the history of the riverside by boat. Tickets are available year-round from Westminster, Tower, and Greenwich piers, and Dockland Light Railway stations. Most launches have a public-address system and provide a running commentary on passing points of interest. Depending upon the destination, river trips may last from one to four hours.

Canal Cruises ☎ 020/7485-4433. **Catamaran Cruisers** ☎ 020/7987-1185 🌐 www.catamarancruisers.co.uk. **Jason's Trip** ☎ 020/7286-3428. **London River Services** ☎ 020/7941-2400. **London Waterbus Company** ☎ 020/7482-2660. **Rail and River Rover** ☎ 020/7363-9700. **Westminster Passenger Services** ☎ 020/7930-4097 🌐 www.wpsa.co.uk. **Westminster Passenger Service Upriver** ☎ 020/7930-2062.

BUS TOURS

There is a choice of companies, each providing daily tours, departing (8:30–9 AM) from central points, such as Haymarket (check with the individual company). You may board or alight at any of the numerous stops to view the sights, and reboard on the next bus. Tickets are bought from the driver and are good for all day, and prices vary according to the type of tour, although around £12 is the benchmark. The specialist in hop on–hop off tours is London Pride, with friendly, informative staff on easily recognizable double-decker buses. The Original London Sightseeing Tour offers frequent daily tours, departing from 8:30 AM from Baker Street (Madame Tussaud's), Marble Arch (Speakers' Corner), Piccadilly (Haymarket), or Victoria (Victoria Street) around every 12 minutes (less often out of peak summer season). The Big Bus Company runs a similar operation with Red and Blue tours. The Red Tour is a two-hour tour with 18 stops, and the Blue Tour, one hour with 13. Both start from Marble Arch, Speakers' Corner. Evan Evans offers good bus tours that also visit major sights just outside the city. Another reputable agency that operates bus tours is Frames Rickards.

The Big Bus Company ☎ 020/7233-9533 🌐 www.bigbus.co.uk. **Evan Evans** ☎ 020/7950-1777 🌐 www.evanevans.co.uk. **Frames Rickards** ☎ 020/7837-3111 🌐 www.etmtravelgroup.com. **Original London Sightseeing Tour** ☎ 020/8877-1722. **London Pride** ☎ 020/7520-2050.

EXCURSIONS

London Transport, Evan Evans, and Frames Rickards all offer day excursions (some combine bus and boat) to places of interest within easy reach of London, such as Windsor, Hampton Court, Oxford, Stratford-upon-Avon, and Bath. Prices vary and may include lunch and admission prices or admission only. Alternatively, make your own way, cheaply, to many of England's attractions on Green Line Coaches.

Green Line Coaches ☎ 020/8668-7261 or 0870/574-7777 🌐 www.greenline.co.uk.

WALKING TOURS

One of the best ways to get to know London is on foot, and there are many guided walking tours from which to choose. Original London Walks has theme tours devoted to the Beatles, Sherlock Holmes, Dickens, Jack the Ripper—you name it. For a more historical accent, check out the tours from Historical Walks. Peruse the leaflets in the Tourist Information Centre for special-interest tours.

Original London Walks ☎ 020/7624-3978 🌐 www.walks.com. **Historical Walks** ☎ 020/8668-4019. **London Walking Forum** 🌐 www.londonwalking.com.

TRAIN TRAVEL

London is served by no fewer than 15 main-line train stations, so be certain of the station for your departure or arrival. All have Underground stops either in the train station or within a few minutes' walk from it, and most are served by several bus routes. The principal routes that connect London to other major towns and cities are on a National Rail network. Seats can be reserved in person at any Rail Travel Centre, in the station from which you depart, or by phone with a credit card.

Charing Cross Station serves southeast England, including Canterbury, Margate, Dover/Folkestone, and ferry ports. Euston/St. Pancras serves East Anglia, Essex, the Northeast, the Northwest, and North Wales, including Coventry, Stratford-upon-Avon, Birmingham, Manchester, Liverpool, Windermere, Glasgow, and Inverness, northwest Scotland. King's Cross serves the east Midlands; the Northeast, including York, Leeds, and Newcastle; and north and east Scotland, including Edinburgh and Aberdeen. Liverpool Street serves Essex and East Anglia. Paddington serves the south Midlands, west and south Wales, and the west country, including Oxford. Victoria serves southern England, including Gatwick Airport, Brighton, Dover/Folkestone and ferry ports, and the south coast. Waterloo serves the southwestern United Kingdom, including Salisbury, Portsmouth, Southampton, and Isle of Wight. Waterloo International is the terminal for the Eurostar high-speed train to Paris and Brussels.

If you're combining a trip to Great Britain with stops on the Continent, you can either drive your car onto a *Le Shuttle* train through the Channel Tunnel (35 minutes from Folkestone to Calais) or book a seat from London on the Eurostar.

FARES & SCHEDULES Generally speaking, it is less expensive to buy a return (round-trip) ticket, especially for day trips not far from London, and you should always inquire at the information office about discount fares. You can hear a recorded summary of timetable and fare information to many destinations by calling the appropriate "dial and listen" numbers listed under Rail in the telephone book. The telephone information number listed below gets you through to any of the stations.
National Rail Enquiries ☎ 0845/748–4950 🌐 www.nationalrail.co.uk.

TRAVEL AGENCIES

American Express ✉ 30–31 Haymarket, SW1 ☎ 020/7484–9600 ✉ 89 Mount St., W1 ☎ 020/7659–0701. **Thomas Cook** ✉ 1 Woburn Pl., WC1 ☎ 020/7837–0393 ✉ 184 Kensington High St., W8, ☎ 020/7707–2300.

UNDERGROUND TRAVEL

Known as "the Tube," London's extensive Underground system is by far the most widely used form of city transportation. Trains run both below and aboveground to the suburbs, and all stations are clearly marked with the London Underground circular symbol. (A SUBWAY sign refers to an under-the-street pedestrian crossing.) Trains are all one class; smoking is *not* allowed on board or in the stations.

There are 10 basic lines—all named. The Central, District, Northern, Metropolitan, and Piccadilly lines all have branches, usually taking you to the outlying sections of the city, so be sure to note which branch is needed for your particular destination. Electronic platform signs tell you the final stop and route of the next train, and some signs indicate how many minutes you'll have to wait for the train to arrive. Begun in the Victorian era, the Underground is still being expanded and improved. The supermodern Jubilee line extension sweeps from Green Park to south of the river, with connections to Canary Wharf and the Docklands, and east to Stratford. The zippy Docklands Light Railway (DLR) runs through the Docklands to the *Cutty Sark* and maritime Greenwich.

FARES & SCHEDULES For both buses and Tube fares, London is divided into six concentric zones; the fare goes up the farther afield you travel. Ask at Underground ticket counters for the LT booklet "Fares and Tickets," which gives all details.

You must buy a ticket before you travel. Many types of travel cards can be bought from Pass Agents that display the sign: tobacconists, confectioners, newsdealers, and mainline overground rail stations.

For one trip between any two stations, you can buy an ordinary single (one-way ticket) for travel anytime on the day of issue; if you're coming back on the same route the same day, then an ordinary return (round-trip ticket) costs twice the single fare. Singles vary in price from £1.60 to £3.70 for a six-zone journey. A *carnet* (£10) is a convenient book of 10 single tickets to use in Central Zone 1 only.

Travelcards allow unrestricted travel on the Tube, most buses, and national rail trains in the Greater London zones. There are different options available: an unrestricted Day Travelcard costs £5.10–£10.70; off-peak (traveling after 9:30 AM) Day Travelcards are £4.10–£5.10. Weekend Travelcards, for the two days of the weekend or on any two consecutive days during public holidays, cost £6.10–£7.60. Family Travelcards are one-day tickets for one or two adults with one to four children and cost £2.70–£3.40 per adult, including one child; each extra child must pay an additional 80p fare. Visitor Travelcards are the best bet for visitors, but they must be bought before leaving home (they're available in both the United States and Canada). They are valid for periods of three, four, or seven days ($25, $32, $49, respectively) and can be used on the Tube and virtually all buses and British Rail services in London.

From Monday through Saturday, trains begin running just after 5 AM; the last services leave central London between midnight and 12:30 AM. On Sunday, trains start two hours later and finish about an hour earlier. The frequency of trains depends on the route and the time of day, but normally you should not have to wait more than 10 minutes. A pocket map of the entire Tube network is available free from most Underground ticket counters.

London Transport ☎ 020/7222-1234, 24 hours 🌐 www.londontransport.co.uk or www.thetube.com. Travelers with disabilities should call for the free leaflet **"Access to the Underground"** ☎ 020/7918-3312.

VISITOR INFORMATION

Visitorcall is the London Tourist Board's 24-hour phone service. The premium-rate recorded information line has different numbers for theater, events, museums, sports, transportation around town, and so on. Call to access the list of options, or see the separate categories in the telephone directory.

London Tourist Information Centre ✉ Victoria Station Forecourt. **Britain Visitor Centre** ✉ 1 Regent St., Piccadilly Circus, SW1Y 4NX 🕐 Weekdays 9–6:30, weekends 10–4 🌐 www.visitbritain.com. **London Tourist Board/Visitorcall** ☎ 09068/663344, calls cost 60p per minute 🌐 www.visitlondon.com.

Great Britain Basics

To research prices, get advice from other travelers, and book travel arrangements, visit www.fodors.com.

BUSINESS HOURS

Banks are open weekdays 9:30–4:30. Some have extended hours on Thursday evening, and a few are open on Saturday morning. Museum hours vary considerably from one part of the country to another. In large cities most are open Monday–Saturday 10–5; many are also open on Sunday afternoon. The majority close one day a week. Be sure to double-check the opening times of historic houses, especially if the visit involves a special trip; most stately houses in the countryside are closed November–March. Shops are open Monday–Saturday 9–5:30, and many are open Sunday. Outside the main centers most shops close at 1 PM once a week, often Wednesday or Thursday. In small villages many also close for lunch. In large cities—especially London—department stores stay open for late-night shopping (usually until 7:30 or 8) at least one day midweek. Most large shopping malls and suburban retail parks are open Sunday. London's premier shopping avenue, Oxford Street, and its main side streets are also open on Sunday.

EMBASSIES

Canadian High Commission ✉ MacDonald House, 38 Grosvenor St., London W1X 0AB ☎ 020/7258–6600 🌐 www.canada.org.uk.

United States ✉ 24 Grosvenor Sq., London W1A 1AE ☎ 020/7499–9000 🌐 www.usembassy.org.uk.

HOLIDAYS

Parliament isn't the only institution to decide which days are national holidays: some holidays are subject to royal proclamation. England and Wales: New Year's Day; Good Friday and Easter Monday; May Day (first Monday in May); Spring Bank Holiday (last Monday in May); August Bank Holiday (last Monday in August); Christmas Day and Boxing Day (day after Christmas).

MONEY MATTERS

In general, transportation in Britain is expensive in comparison with other countries. You should take advantage of the many reductions and special fares available on trains, buses, and subways. Always ask about these when buying your ticket.

London now ranks with Tokyo as one of the world's most expensive hotel capitals. Finding budget accommodations—especially during July and August—can be difficult; you should try to book well ahead if you are visiting during these months. Dining out at top-of-the-line restaurants can be prohibitively expensive, but there are new chains of French-Italian–style café-brasseries, along with a large number of pubs and ethnic restaurants that offer excellent food at reasonable prices.

The gulf between prices in the capital and outside is wide. Be prepared to pay a value-added tax (V.A.T.) of 17½% on almost everything you buy; in nearly all cases it is included in the advertised price.

Costs: in London, cup of coffee, £1–£2; pint of beer, £1.80–£2.20; glass of wine, £2–£4; soda, 80p–£1.50; 2-km (1-mi) taxi ride, £3; ham sandwich, £1.75–£3.50.

CURRENCY The British unit of currency is the pound sterling (£), divided into 100 pence (p). Bills are issued in denominations of £5, £10, £20, and £50. Coins are £2, £1, 50p, 20p, 10p, 5p, 2p, and 1p. Scottish banks issue Scottish currency, of which all coins and notes—with the exception of the £1 notes—are accepted in England. At press time (summer 2003) the pound stood at £0.63 to the U.S. dollar, £0.45 to the Canadian dollar, £0.41 to the Australian dollar, £0.36 to the New Zealand dollar, £0.08 to the South African rand, and £0.70 to the euro.

Traveler's checks are widely accepted in Britain, and many banks, hotels, and shops offer currency-exchange facilities. You will have to pay a £2 commission fee wherever you change them; banks offer the best rates, yet even these fees vary. If you are changing currency, you will have to pay (on top of commission) based on the amount you are changing. In London and other big cities, *bureaux de change* abound, but it definitely pays to shop around: they charge a flat fee, and it's often a great deal more than that at other establishments, such as banks. American Express foreign exchange desks do not charge a commission fee on AmEx traveler's checks. Credit cards are universally accepted, and the most commonly used are MasterCard and Visa.

VALUE-ADDED TAX (V.A.T.) Foreign visitors from outside Europe can avoid Britain's 17½% value-added tax (V.A.T.) by taking advantage of the following two methods. By the Direct Export method, the shopkeeper arranges the export of the goods and does not charge V.A.T. at the point of sale. This means that the purchases are sent on to your home separately. If you prefer to take your purchase with you, try the Retail Export scheme, run by most large stores: the special Form 407 (provided only by the retailer) is attached to your invoice. You must present the goods, form, and invoice to the customs officer at the last port of departure from the European Union. Allow plenty of time to do this at the airport, as there are often long lines. The form is then returned to the store and the refund forwarded to you, minus a small service charge. For inquiries call the local Customs and Excise office listed in the telephone directory.

TELEPHONES

COUNTRY & AREA CODES The United Kingdom's country code is 44. When dialing a number in Britain from abroad, drop the initial 0 from the local area code.

DIRECTORY & OPERATOR ASSISTANCE For information anywhere in Britain, dial ☎ 192. For the operator, dial ☎ 100. For assistance with international calls, dial ☎ 155.

INTERNATIONAL CALLS The cheapest way to make an overseas call is to dial it yourself. But be sure to have plenty of coins or phone cards close at hand. Newsdealers sell budget-rate international phone cards, such as First National and America First, which can be used from any phone by dialing an access number, then a personal identification number. After you have inserted the coins or card, dial 00 (the international code), then the country code—1 for the United States—followed by the area code and local number. You can also make calls through AT&T, MCI Worldphone, or Sprint Global One long-distance operators. To make a collect or other operator-assisted call, dial ☎ 155.

Access Codes **AT&T Direct** In the U.K., there are AT&T access numbers to dial the U.S. using three different phone types: ☎ 0500/890011 Cable & Wireless; 0800/890011 British Telecom; 0800/0130011 AT&T. **MCI Worldphone** ☎ 0800/890222. **Sprint International Access** ☎ 0800/890877.

LOCAL CALLS Public telephones are plentiful in British cities, especially London. British Telecom is gradually replacing the distinctive red phone booths with generic glass and steel cubicles, but the traditional boxes still remain in the countryside. There are three types of phones: those that accept (1) only coins, (2) only British Telecom (BT) phone cards, or (3) BT phone cards and credit cards.

The coin-operated phones are of the push-button variety; their workings vary, but there are usually instructions on each unit. Most take 10p, 20p, 50p, and £1 coins. Insert the coins *before* dialing (minimum charge is 20p). If you hear a repeated single tone after dialing, the line is busy; a continual tone means the number is unobtainable (or that you have dialed the wrong—or no—prefix). The indicator panel shows you how much money is left; add more whenever you like. If there is no answer, replace the receiver and your money will be returned.

All calls are charged according to the time of day. Standard rate is weekdays 8 AM–6 PM; cheaper rates are weekdays 6 PM–8 AM and all day on weekends. A local call before 6 PM costs 15p for three minutes;

this doubles to 30p for the same from a pay phone. A daytime call to the United States will cost 24p a minute on a regular phone (weekends are cheaper), 80p on a pay phone.

AREA CODES There is one area code for London—020—followed by a prefix, either 7 (for inner London) or 8 (for outer London), before the seven-digit phone number. So, for example, for a phone call to inner London, you would dial 020/7242–4444; for outer London, 020/8242–4444. Each large city or region in Britain has its own numerical prefix, which is used only when you are dialing from outside the city. In provincial areas the dialing codes for nearby towns are often posted in the booth.

MADRID

Dead center in the heart of Spain at 2,120 feet above sea level, Madrid is the highest capital in Europe and one of the continent's most exciting cities. Madrid's famous museum mile has more masterpieces per foot than anywhere else in the world. Home of Spain's royal court for the last 500 years, the city's regal palaces and gardens conceal a villagelike medieval Madrid with narrow lanes and red-tiled roofs. This is all in contrast to the rowdy Madrid one finds after midnight, when the action really begins; Madrileños are vigorous, joyful people, famous for their defiance of the need for sleep.

EXPLORING MADRID

You can see important parts of the city in one day if you stop only to visit the Prado and Royal Palace. Two days should give you time for browsing. You can begin in the Plaza Atocha (Glorieta del Emperador Carlos V), at the bottom of the Paseo del Prado.

Numbers in the margin correspond to points of interest on the Madrid map.

★ ❶ **Centro de Arte Reina Sofía** (Queen Sofía Arts Center). Spain's Queen Sofía opened this center in 1986, and it quickly became one of Europe's most dynamic venues—a Spanish rival to Paris's Pompidou Center. A converted hospital, the center houses painting and sculpture, including works by Joan Miró and Salvador Dalí as well as Picasso's *Guernica,* the painting depicting the horrific April 1937 carpet bombing of the Basque country's traditional capital by Nazi warplanes aiding Franco in the Spanish Civil War. ✉ *Main entrance, C. de Santa Isabel 52* ☎ *91/467–5062* ⏲ *Mon. and Wed.–Sat. 10–9, Sun. 10–2:30.*

❿ **Convento de las Descalzas Reales** (Convent of the Royal Barefoot Nuns). This convent, founded by Juana de Austria, daughter of Charles V, is still in use. Over the centuries, the nuns—daughters of royalty and nobility—have endowed it with an enormous wealth of jewels, religious ornaments, superb Flemish tapestries, and the works of such master painters as Titian and Rubens. A bit off the main track, it's one of Madrid's better-kept secrets. Your ticket includes admission to the nearby, but less interesting, **Convento de la Encarnación.** ✉ *Plaza de las Descalzas 3* ☎ *91/454–8809 information* ⏲ *Tues.–Thurs. and Sat. 10:30–12:45 and 4–5:45, Fri. 10:30–12:45, Sun. 11–1:45.*

❼ **Fuente de la Cibeles** (Fountain of Cybele). Cybele, the Greek goddess of fertility and unofficial emblem of Madrid, languidly rides her lion-drawn chariot here, watched over by the mighty Palacio de Comunicaciónes, a splendidly pompous, cathedral-like post office. Fans of the home football team, Real Madrid, used to celebrate major victories by splashing in the fountain, but police now blockade it during big games. The fountain stands in the center of **Plaza de la Cibeles,** one of Madrid's great landmarks. ✉ *C. de Alcalá.*

Las Ventas. Formally known as the Plaza de Toros Monumental, this is Madrid's bullring. You can buy tickets here before the fight or, for a 20% surcharge, at the agencies that line Calle Victoria, off Carrera de San Jerónimo near Puerta del Sol. During the bullfighting season corridas are held on Sunday and sometimes also on Thursday; starting times vary between 5 PM and 7 PM. The height of the taurine calendar comes with the San Isidro Festival in May, with five weeks of daily bullfights. ✉ *Alcalá 237* ☎ *91/356–2200* ⏲ *Mar.–Oct.* Ⓜ *Ventas.*

★ ❷ **Museo del Prado** (Prado Museum). On the old cobblestone section of the Paseo del Prado you'll find Madrid's number one cultural site and one of the world's most important art museums. Plan to spend at least a day here; it takes at least two days to view the museum's treasures properly. Brace yourself for crowds. The greatest treasures—the Velázquez, Murillo, Zurbarán, El Greco, and Goya galleries—are all on the upper floor. Two of the best works are Velázquez's *La Rendición de Breda* and his most famous work, *Las Meninas,* awarded a room of its own. The Goya galleries contain the artist's none-too-flattering royal portraits, his exquisitely beautiful *Marquesa de Santa Cruz,* and his famous *La Maja Desnuda* and *La Maja Vestida,* for which the 13th duchess of Alba was said to have posed. Goya's most moving works, the *Second of May* and the *Fusillade of Moncloa,* or *Third of May,* vividly depict the sufferings of Madrid patriots at the hands of Napoléon's invading troops in 1808. Before you leave, feast your eyes on Hieronymus Bosch's flights of fancy, *Garden of Earthly Delights,* and the triptych the *Hay Wagon,* both on the ground floor. The museum is adding a new wing, designed by Rafael Moneo, much of which will be occupied by long-forgotten masterpieces by Zurbarán and Pereda. ✉ *Paseo del Prado s/n* ☎ *91/330–2800* ⏲ *Tues.–Sun. 9–7.*

❹ **Museo Thyssen-Bornemisza.** This museum, in the elegant Villahermosa Palace, has plenty of airy spaces and natural light. The ambitious collection—800 paintings—traces the history of Western art through examples from each important movement, beginning with 13th-century Italy. Among the museum's gems are the *Portrait of Henry VIII,* by Hans Holbein. Two halls are devoted to the impressionists and postimpressionists, with works by Pissarro, Renoir, Monet, Degas, van Gogh, and Cézanne. The more recent paintings include some terror-filled examples of German expressionism, but these are complemented by some soothing Georgia O'Keeffes and Andrew Wyeths. ✉ *Paseo del Prado 8* ☎ *91/369–0151* ⏲ *Tues.–Sun. 10–7.*

★ ⓭ **Palacio Real** (Royal Palace). This magnificent granite-and-limestone pile was begun by Philip V, the first Bourbon king of Spain, who was always homesick for his beloved Versailles and did his best to re-create its opulence and splendor. Judging by the palace's 2,800 rooms, with their lavish rococo decorations, precious carpets, porcelain, timepieces, mirrors, and chandeliers, his efforts were successful. From 1764, when Charles

III first moved in, until the coming of the Second Republic and the abdication of Alfonso XIII in 1931, the Royal Palace proved a very stylish abode for Spanish monarchs; today, King Juan Carlos, who lives in the far less ostentatious Zarzuela Palace outside Madrid, uses it only for official state functions. ✉ *Bailén s/n* ☎ *91/454–8800* ⏲ *Apr.–Sept., Mon.–Sat. 9–6, Sun. 9–3; Oct.–Mar., Mon.–Sat. 9:30–5, Sun. 9:30–2* ⏲ *Closed during official receptions.*

★ 5 **Parque del Retiro** (Retiro Park). Once a royal retreat, Retiro is Madrid's prettiest park. Visit the beautiful rose garden, **La Rosaleda**; enjoy street musicians and magicians; row a boat around El Estanque; and wander past the park's many statues and fountains. Look particularly at the monumental **statue of Alfonso XII,** one of Spain's least notable kings (though you wouldn't think so from the statue's size), or wonder at the **Monument to the Fallen Angel**—Madrid claims the dubious honor of being the only capital to have a statue dedicated to the Devil. The **Palacio de Velázquez** and the beautiful, glass-and-steel **Palacio de Cristal,** built as a tropical plant house during the 19th century, now host occasional art exhibits. ✉ *Between C. Alfonso XII and Avda. de Menéndez Pelayo below C. de Alcalá.*

12 **Plaza de la Villa** (City Square). This plaza's notable cluster of buildings includes some of the oldest houses in Madrid. The **Casa de la Villa,** Madrid's city hall, was built in 1644 and has also served as the city prison and the mayor's home. Its sumptuous salons are occasionally open to the public; ask about guided tours, which are sometimes given in English. An archway joins the Casa de la Villa to the **Casa Cisneros,** a palace built in 1537 for the nephew of Cardinal Cisneros, primate of Spain and infamous inquisitor general. Across the square is the **Torre de Lujanes,** one of the oldest buildings in Madrid; it once imprisoned Francis I of France, archenemy of the emperor Charles V. ✉ *C. Mayor between C. Santiago and C. San Nicolás.*

★ 11 **Plaza Mayor** (Main Square). Without a doubt the capital's architectural showpiece, the Plaza Mayor was built in 1617–19 for Philip III—the figure astride the horse in the middle. The plaza has witnessed the canonization of saints, the burning of heretics, fireworks, and bullfights, and it is still one of Madrid's great gathering places. ✉ *South of C. Mayor, west of Cava San Miguel.*

6 **Puerta de Alcalá** (Alcalá Gate). Built in 1779 for Charles III, the grandiose gateway dominates the Plaza de la Independencia. A customs post once stood beside the gate, as did the old bullring until it was moved to its present site, Las Ventas, in the 1920s. At the beginning of the 20th century, the Puerta de Alcalá more or less marked the eastern edge of Madrid. ✉ *Plaza de la Independencia.*

9 **Puerta del Sol** (Gate of the Sun). The old gate disappeared long ago, but you're still at the very heart of Madrid here, and indeed at the very heart of Spain: kilometer distances for the whole nation are measured from the zero marker, a brass plaque on the south sidewalk. The square was expertly revamped in 1986 and now accommodates a copy of **La Mariblanca** (a statue that adorned a fountain here 250 years ago), a statue of Carlos III on horseback, and, at the bottom of Calle Carmen, the much-loved statue of the **bear and strawberry tree.** The Puerta del Sol is inextricably linked with the history of Madrid and of Spain; a half century ago, a generation of literati gathered in Sol's long-gone cafés to thrash out the burning issues of the day. Nearly 200 years ago, the square witnessed the patriots' uprising immortalized by Goya in his painting *The Second of May.* ✉ *Meeting of C. Mayor and C. Alcalá.*

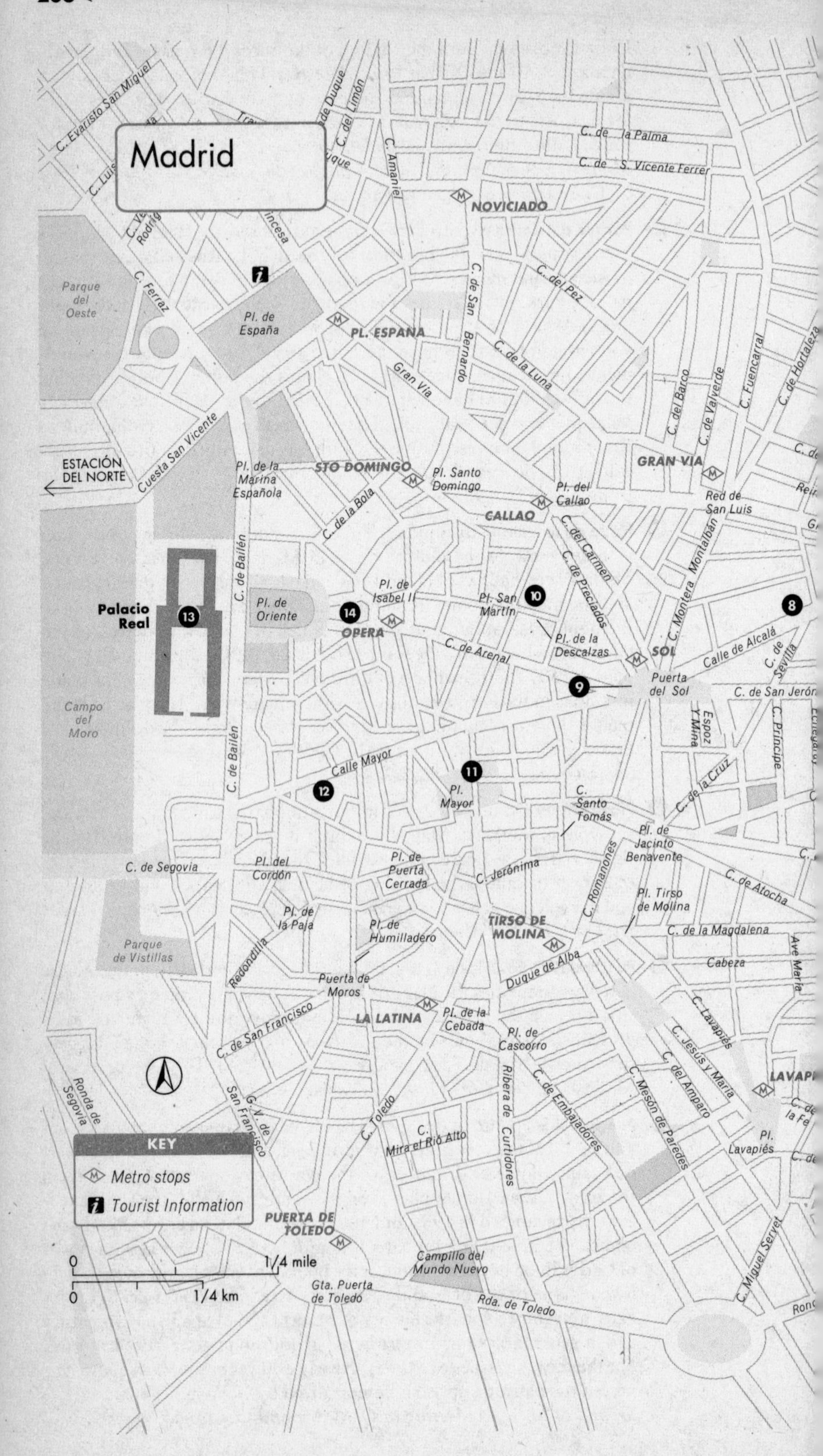

Madrid
C. Evaristo San Miguel
C. del Limón
C. Amaniel
C. de la Palma
C. de S. Vicente Ferrer
NOVICIADO
C. de San Bernardo
C. del Pez
Parque del Oeste
C. Ferraz
Pl. de España
PL. ESPAÑA
Gran Vía
C. de la Luna
C. del Barco
C. de Valverde
C. Fuencarral
C. de Hortaleza
GRAN VIA
Red de San Luis
ESTACIÓN DEL NORTE
Cuesta San Vicente
Pl. de la Marina Española
STO DOMINGO
Pl. Santo Domingo
Pl. del Callao
CALLAO
C. de la Bola
C. del Carmen
C. de Preciados
C. Montera
Montalbán
C. de Bailén
Pl. de Oriente
Pl. de Isabel II
Pl. San Martín
Palacio Real
OPERA
Pl. de la Descalzas
SOL
Calle de Alcalá
C. de Sevilla
C. de Arenal
Puerta del Sol
C. de San Jerón
Campo del Moro
Espoz Y Mina
C. Príncipe
Calle Mayor
Pl. Mayor
C. Santo Tomás
C. de la Cruz
Pl. de Jacinto Benavente
C. de Segovia
Pl. del Cordón
Pl. de Puerta Cerrada
C. Jerónima
C. Romanones
C. de Atocha
Pl. Tirso de Molina
Pl. de la Paja
Pl. de Humilladero
TIRSO DE MOLINA
C. de la Magdalena
Parque de Vistillas
Redondilla
Duque de Alba
Cabeza
Ave María
Puerta de Moros
LA LATINA
Pl. de la Cebada
C. Lavapiés
C. de San Francisco
Pl. de Cascorro
C. Jesús y María
C. del Ampàro
Ronda de Segovia
San Francisco
G. V. de
Ribera de Curtidores
C. de Embajadores
C. Mesón de Paredes
LAVAPI
Pl. Lavapiés
C. Toledo
C. Mira el Río Alto
KEY
Metro stops
Tourist Information
PUERTA DE TOLEDO
0
1/4 mile
1/4 km
Campillo del Mundo Nuevo
Gta. Puerta de Toledo
Rda. de Toledo
C. Miguel Servet

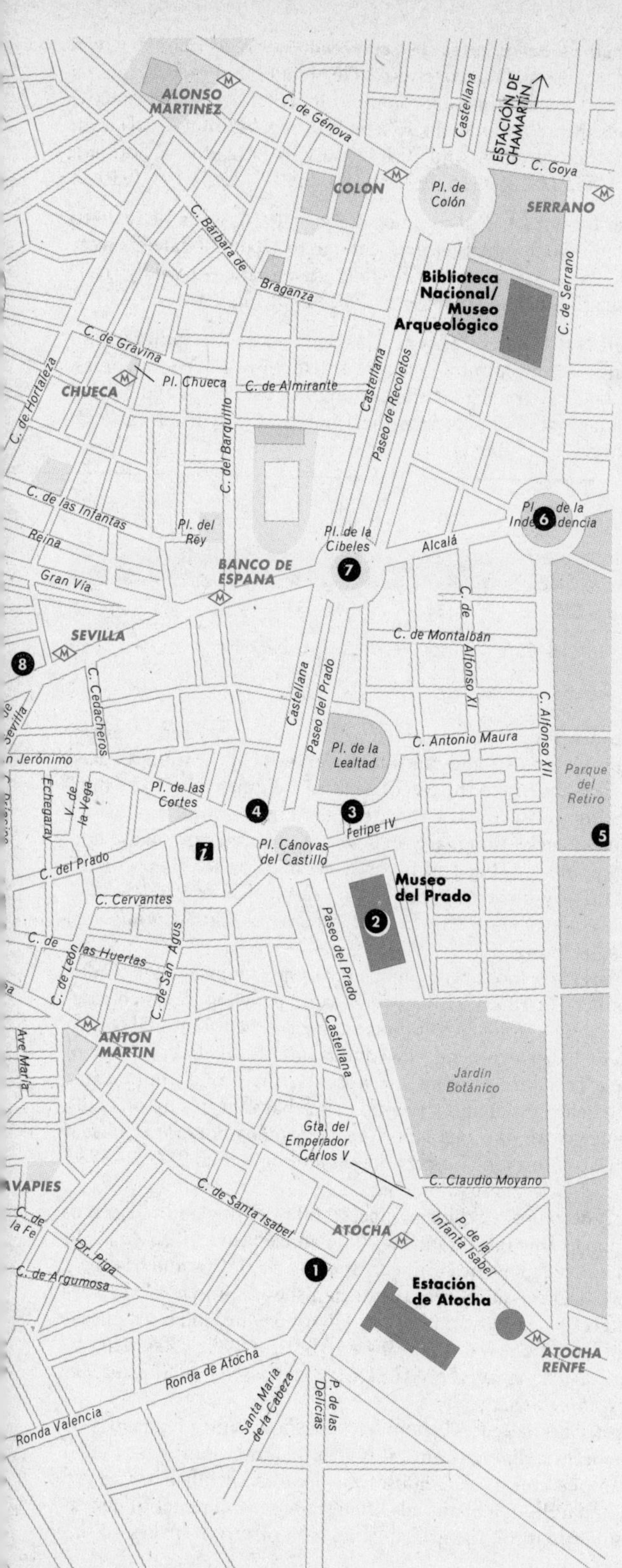

Centro de Arte Reina Sofía 1
Convento de las Descalzas Reales 10
Fuente de la Cibeles 7
Museo del Prado 2
Museo Thyssen-Bornemisza . . .4
Palacio Real 13
Parque del Retiro 5
Plaza de la Villa 12
Plaza Mayor 11
Puerta de Alcalá 6
Puerta del Sol 9
Real Academia de Bellas Artes de San Fernando 8
Ritz 3
Teatro Real 14

8 **Real Academia de Bellas Artes de San Fernando** (St. Fernando Royal Academy of Fine Arts). Often overlooked in favor of the Prado, the Reina Sofia, and the Thyssen, this surprisingly comprehensive collection covers the masters (Murillo, Zurbarán, Ribera, El Greco, Velázquez, and Goya) and also houses some 19th- and 20th-century work (Zuloaga, Sorolla). ✉ *Alcalá 13* ☎ *91/522–0046* ⏲ *Tues.–Fri. 9:30–7, Sat.–Mon. 9:30–2.*

3 **Ritz.** Alfonso II built Madrid's grande dame in 1910, when he realized that his capital had no hotels elegant enough to accommodate his wedding guests. The garden is a wonderfully aristocratic—if wildly overpriced—place to lunch in summer. ✉ *Plaza de Lealtad 5.*

14 **Teatro Real** (Royal Theater). This neoclassical theater was built in 1850 and has long been a cultural center. Replete with golden balconies, plush seats, and state-of-the-art stage equipment for operas and ballets, the theater is a modern showpiece with its vintage appeal intact. ✉ *Plaza de Isabel II* ☎ *91/516–0600.*

WHERE TO EAT

WHAT IT COSTS In Euros				
	$$$$	**$$$**	**$$**	**$**
AT DINNER	over €25	€18–€25	€12–€18	under €12

Prices are per person for a main course.

★ **$$$$** ✕ **La Broche.** Sergi Arola, who trained with celebrity chef Ferran Adriá, has added his own twists and innovations to those of the Catalan master and vaulted directly to the top of Madrid's dining charts. The minimalist dining room clears the decks for maximum taste bud protagonism—a lucky thing, as you'll want to concentrate on the hot-cold counterpoints of your codfish soup with bacon ice cream or the marinated sardine with herring roe. ✉ *Miguel Angel 29* ☎ *91/399–3437* *Reservations essential* 💳 *AE, DC, MC, V* ⏲ *Closed weekends, Easter week, and Aug.*

$$$$ ✕ **Lhardy.** This place looks pretty much the same as it must have on day one (September 16, 1839) with its dark-wood paneling, brass chandeliers, and red-velvet chairs. Most diners come for the traditional *cocido a la madrileña* (garbanzo-bean stew) and *callos a la madrileña* (tripe in spicy sauce). The dining rooms are upstairs; the ground-floor entry doubles as a delicatessen and stand-up coffee bar that fills up on chilly winter mornings with shivering souls sipping steaming-hot *caldo* (chicken broth) from silver urns. ✉ *Carrera de San Jerónimo 8* ☎ *91/521–3385* 💳 *AE, DC, MC, V* ⏲ *No dinner Sun.*

$$$$ ✕ **Zalacaín.** A deep-apricot color scheme, set off by dark wood and gleaming silver, makes this restaurant look like an exclusive villa. Zalacaín introduced nouvelle Basque cuisine to Spain in the 1970s and has since become a Madrid classic. Splurge on such dishes as prawn salad in avocado vinaigrette, scallops and leeks in Albariño wine, and roast pheasant with truffles. ✉ *Álvarez de Baena 4* ☎ *91/561–4840* *Reservations essential* *Jackets required* 💳 *AE, DC, V* ⏲ *Closed Sun., Easter wk, and Aug. No lunch Sat.*

$$$–$$$$ ✕ **La Trainera.** This place is all about fresh seafood. With a nautical style and a maze of little dining rooms, this informal restaurant has reigned as the queen of Madrid's fish houses for decades. Shellfish are served by weight, and although Spaniards often share several plates of delicacies as their entire meal, the grilled hake, sole, or turbot makes an unbeatable second course. ✉ *Lagasca 60* ☎ *91/576–8035* 💳 *AE, MC, V* ⊙ *Closed Sun. and Aug.*

$$$–$$$$ ✕ **Pedro Larumbe.** This excellent restaurant is atop the ABC shopping center. It has a lovely summer roof terrace, which is glassed in for the winter, and an Andalusian patio. Owner-chef Pedro Larumbe is famous for the presentation of his modern dishes, such as lobster salad. ✉ *Serrano 61/Castellana 34* ☎ *91/575–1112* 💳 *AE, DC, MC, V* ⊙ *Closed Sun. and 15 days in Aug. No lunch Sat.*

$$$–$$$$ ✕ **Viridiana.** This black-and-white place has the relaxed pace of a mellow bistro. Iconoclast chef Abraham García creates a new menu every two weeks, dreaming up such varied fare as red onions stuffed with *morcilla* (black pudding), soft flour tortillas wrapped around marinated fresh tuna, and filet mignon in white-truffle sauce. ✉ *Juan de Mena 14* ☎ *91/523–4478* ✍ *Reservations essential* 💳 *AE, DC, MC, V* ⊙ *Closed Sun. and Aug.*

$$–$$$ ✕ **Asador Fronton 1.** Long established in Tirso de Molina and now with two branches in northern Madrid, this popular Basque restaurant serves some of the most outstanding meat and fish in the city. The huge chunks of delicious steak, seared on a charcoal grill and then lightly sprinkled with sea salt, are for two or more. Order lettuce hearts or a vegetable to accompany. ✉ *Tirso de Molina 7 (rear, upstairs)* ☎ *91/369–1617* ✍ *Reservations essential* 💳 *AE, DC, MC, V* ⊙ *Closed Sun.*

★ $$–$$$ ✕ **Botín.** Just below Plaza Mayor, this is Madrid's oldest (1725) and most famous restaurant. The food is traditionally Castilian, as are the wood-fire ovens used for cooking. *Cochinillo asado* (roast suckling pig) and *cordero asado* (roast lamb) are the specialties. The restaurant, a Hemingway favorite featured in the final scene of *The Sun Also Rises,* is somewhat touristy, but it's still fun. ✉ *Cuchilleros 17* ☎ *91/366–4217* ✍ *Reservations essential* 💳 *AE, DC, MC, V.*

★ $$–$$$ ✕ **El Cenador del Prado.** The innovative menu has French and Asian touches, as well as exotic Spanish dishes that rarely appear in restaurants. The house specialty is *patatas a la importancia* (sliced potatoes fried in a sauce of garlic, parsley, and clams); other possibilities are shellfish consommé with ginger ravioli, veal and eggplant in béchamel, and venison with prunes. ✉ *C. del Prado 4* ☎ *91/429–1561* 💳 *AE, DC, MC, V* ⊙ *Closed Sun. and Aug. 1–15. No lunch Sat.*

★ $$–$$$ ✕ **La Gamella.** Some of the American-born former chef Dick Stephens's dishes—Caesar salad, hamburger, steak tartare—are still on the reasonably priced menu at this perennially popular dinner spot. The new selections are a fusion of Asian, Mediterranean, and American dishes. ✉ *Alfonso XII 4* ☎ *91/532–4509* 💳 *AE, DC, MC, V* ⊙ *Closed Sun. and last 2 wks in Aug. No lunch Sat.*

$–$$ ✕ **La Cava Real.** Wine connoisseurs love the intimacy of this small, elegant restaurant and bar—Madrid's first true wine bar when it opened in 1983. There are a staggering 350 wines from which to choose, including 50 by the glass. The charming, experienced maître d', Chema Gómez, can help you select. Chef Javier Collar designs good-value set menus around wines. ✉ *Espronceda 34* ☎ *91/442–5432* ✍ *Reservations essential* 💳 *AE, DC, MC, V* ⊙ *Closed Sun. and Aug.*

$–$$ ✕ **La Trucha.** This Andalusian deep-fry specialist is one of the happiest places in Madrid. The house specialty, the *trucha a la truchana* (crisped trout stuffed with ample garlic and diced jabugo ham) is a work of art. *Chopitos* (baby squid), *pollo al ajillo* (chunks of chicken in crisped garlic), and *espárragos trigueros* (wild asparagus) are among the star entrées. The Nuñez de Arce branch is usually less crowded. ✉ *Manuel Fernandez y Gonzalez 3* ☎ *91/429-3778* ✉ *Nuñez de Arce 6* ☎ *91/532–0890* 💳 *AE, MC, V* ⊙ *Nuñez de Arce branch closed Sun., Mon., and Aug.*

★ $ ✕ **Casa Mingo.** This Asturian cider tavern is built into a stone wall beneath the Norte train station. The nearby Ermita de San Antonio de la Florida with its famous Goya frescoes and Casa Mingo are a classic Madrid combination. Succulent roast chicken, sausages, and salad are the only offerings, along with *sidra* (hard cider). The long plank tables are shared with other diners, and in summer, tables are set out on the sidewalk. ✉ *Paseo de la Florida 2* ☎ *91/547–7918* ✍ *Reservations not accepted* ▭ *No credit cards.*

$ ✕ **Nabucco.** With pastel-washed walls and subtle lighting from gigantic, wrought-iron candelabras, this pizzeria and trattoria is a trendy but elegant haven in gritty Chueca. The spinach, ricotta, and walnut ravioli is heavenly, and this may be the only Italian restaurant in Madrid where you can order barbecued-chicken pizza. ✉ *Hortaleza 108* ☎ *91/310–0611* ▭ *AE, MC, V.*

WHERE TO STAY

WHAT IT COSTS In Euros				
	$$$$	$$$	$$	$
HOTELS	over € 225	€150–€ 225	€80–€150	under €80

Prices are for two people in a standard double room in high season, excluding tax and breakfast.

★ $$$$ **AC Santo Mauro.** Once the Canadian embassy, this turn-of-the-20th-century neoclassical mansion is now an intimate luxury hotel. The architecture is accented by contemporary furniture (such as suede armchairs). The best rooms are in the main building; the others are in a new annex and are split-level, with stereos and VCRs. Request a room with a terrace overlooking the gardens. ✉ *Zurbano 36, 28010* ☎ *91/319–6900* 📠 *91/308–5477* 🌐 *www.ac-hoteles.com* *50 rooms, 4 suites* *Restaurant, pool, bar* ▭ *AE, DC, MC, V.*

$$$$ **Ritz.** Alfonso XIII, about to marry Queen Victoria's granddaughter, encouraged the construction of this hotel, the most exclusive in Spain, for his royal guests. Opened in 1910 by the king himself, the Ritz is a monument to the belle epoque, its salons furnished with rare antiques, hand-embroidered linens, and handwoven carpets. Most rooms have views of the Prado. The restaurant, Goya, is famous. ✉ *Plaza Lealtad 5, 28014* ☎ *91/701–6767* 📠 *91/701–6776* 🌐 *www.ritz.es* *167 rooms* *Restaurant, bar* ▭ *AE, DC, MC, V.*

$$$$ **Villa Magna.** The concrete facade here gives way to an interior furnished with 18th-century antiques. Prices are robust, but it's hard to find flourishes such as a champagne bar and—in the largest suite in Madrid—a white baby-grand piano. All rooms have large desks, and all bathrooms have fresh flowers. One restaurant, Le Divellec, has walnut paneling and the feel of an English library, and you can dine on its garden terrace in season. The other restaurant, the Tsé-Yang, is Madrid's most exclusive for Chinese food. ✉ *Paseo de la Castellana 22, 28046* ☎ *91/431–2286* 📠 *91/575–3158* 🌐 *www.madrid.hyatt.com* *164 rooms, 18 suites* *2 restaurants, 2 bars* ▭ *AE, DC, MC, V.*

$$$$ **Villa Real.** For a medium-size hotel that combines elegance, modern amenities, friendly service, *and* a great location, look no further: the Villa Real faces Spain's parliament and is convenient to almost everything. The simulated 19th-century facade gives way to an intimate lobby with modern furnishings. Many rooms are split-level, with a small sitting area. Some suites have whirlpool baths. ✉ *Plaza de las Cortes 10, 28014* ☎ *91/*

420–3767 91/420–2547 www.derbyhotels.es 94 rooms, 20 suites *Restaurant, bar* *AE, DC, MC, V.*

★ $$$$ **Westin Palace.** Built in 1912, Madrid's most famous grand hotel is a belle epoque creation of Alfonso XIII. The guest rooms meet today's highest standards; banquet halls and lobbies have been beautified; and the facade has been finely restored. The Palace is more charming and stylish than ever—and although the glass dome over the lounge remains exquisitely original, the windows in the guest rooms are now double-glazed. *Plaza de las Cortes 7, 28014* *91/360–8000* *91/360–8100* *www.palacemadrid.com* *465 rooms, 45 suites* *2 restaurants, bar* *AE, DC, MC, V.*

$$$ **Reina Victoria.** Madrid's longtime favorite among bullfighters, this gleaming white Victorian building across the square from the Teatro Español has been transformed over the last decade into an upscale and modern establishment. The pervasive taurine theme is most concentrated in the bar. The best rooms are on the top floors, providing the most insulation from noise and great views over the rooftops and the theater. *Plaza Santa Ana 14, 28012* *91/531–4500* *91/522–0307* *195 rooms* *Bar* *AE, DC, MC, V.*

$$ **Carlos V.** If you like to be right in the center of things, hang your hat at this classic hotel on a pedestrian street: it's just a few steps away from the Puerta del Sol, Plaza Mayor, and Descalzas Reales convent. A suit of armor guards the tiny lobby, and crystal chandeliers add elegance to the second-floor lounge. All rooms are bright and carpeted, and the doubles with large terraces are a bargain. *Maestro Victoria 5, 28013* *91/531–4100* *91/531–3761* *www.carlosv.com* *67 rooms* *AE, DC, MC, V.*

$$ **El Prado.** Wedged in among the classic buildings of Old Madrid, this slim hotel is within stumbling distance of Madrid's best bars and nightclubs. Rooms are soundproof, with double-pane glass, and are surprisingly spacious. Appointments include pastel floral prints and gleaming marble baths. *Prado 11, 28014* *91/369–0234* *91/429–2829* *www.hotelgreenprado.com* *47 rooms* *AE, DC, MC, V.*

$$ **Inglés.** This hotel was once a favorite with writers and artists, including Virginia Woolf. Though dreary, the rooms are comfortable enough, and the location is key: a short walk from the Puerta del Sol in one direction, the Prado in the other. Inexpensive restaurants and distinctive bars are close at hand. *Echegaray 8, 28014* *91/429–6551* *91/420–2423* *58 rooms* *Bar* *AE, DC, MC, V.*

$$ **Liabeny.** A large, paneled lobby leads to bars, a restaurant, and a café in this 1960s hotel, centrally located near an airy plaza (and several department stores) between Gran Vía and Puerta del Sol. The large, comfortable rooms have floral fabrics and big windows; interior and top-floor rooms are the quietest. *Salud 3, 28013* *91/531–9000* *91/532–5306* *www.liabeny.es* *222 rooms* *Restaurant, 2 bars* *AE, DC, MC, V.*

$$ **Mora.** You'll find this cheery hotel, with a sparkling, faux-marble lobby and bright, carpeted hallways, across the Paseo del Prado from the Botanical Garden. Rooms are simple but large and comfortable. Those on the street have great views of the garden and Prado through soundproof, double-pane windows. For breakfast and lunch, the attached café is excellent, affordable, and popular with locals. *Paseo del Prado 32, 28014* *91/420–1569* *91/420–0564* *62 rooms* *AE, DC, MC, V.*

NIGHTLIFE & THE ARTS

The Arts

Details of all cultural events are listed in the daily newspaper *El País* and in the weekly *Guía del Ocio*. Two English-language publications, the *Broadsheet* and *In Spain*, are available free in Irish pubs and other expat hangouts and detail mainly expat activities.

Concerts & Opera

Madrid's main concert hall is the **Auditorio Nacional de Madrid** (✉ Principe de Vergara 146 ☎ 91/337–0100). Beneath the Plaza de Colón, the underground **Centro Cultural de la Villa** (✉ Plaza de Colon s/n ☎ 91/480–0300 information; 902/10–1212 tickets) hosts all kinds of performances, from gospel, spiritual, and blues festivals to Celtic dance. For opera, catch a performance at the legendary **Teatro Real** (✉ Plaza de Isabel II ☎ 91/516–0660), whose splendid facade dominates the Plaza de Oriente.

Film

Foreign films are mostly dubbed into Spanish, but movies in English are listed in *El País* or *Guía del Ocio* under "VO" (*versión original*). A dozen or so theaters now show films in English. **Alphaville** (✉ Martín de los Héros 14, off Plaza España ☎ 91/559–3836) shows films in English. **Renoir Plaza de España** (✉ Martín de los Héros 12, off Plaza España ☎ 91/559–5760) is an old favorite, and shows films in VO. The **Filmoteca Cine Doré** (✉ Santa Isabel 3 ☎ 91/369–1125) is a city-run institution showing different classic English-language films every day. Your best bet for first-run films in the original language is the **Multicines Ideal** (✉ Doctor Cortezo 6 ☎ 91/369–2518).

Theater

Most theaters have two curtain times, at 7 PM and 10:30 PM, and close on Monday. Tickets are inexpensive and often easy to come by on the night of the performance. The **Centro Cultural de la Villa** (☎ 91/575–6080), beneath the Plaza Colón, stages theater and musical events. In summer, check listings for open-air events in Retiro Park. The **Círculo de Bellas Artes** (✉ Marqués de Casa Riera 2, off Alcalá 42 ☎ 91/360–5400) houses a leading theater. **Sala Triángulo** (✉ Zurita 20 ☎ 91/530–6891) is one of the many fringe theaters in Lavapiés and is definitely worth a detour if you understand Spanish. *Zarzuela,* a combination of light opera and dance that's ideal for non–Spanish-speakers, is performed at the **Teatro Nacional Lírico de la Zarzuela** (✉ Jovellanos 4 ☎ 91/524–5400) October to July. The **Teatro Español** (✉ Príncipe 25 on Plaza Santa Ana ☎ 91/429–6297) stages Spanish classics. The **Teatro María Guerrero** (✉ Tamayo y Baus 4 ☎ 91/319–4769), the home of the Centro Dramático Nacional, stages plays from García Lorca to Els Joglars.

Nightlife

Bars & Cafés

The most traditional and colorful taverns are on Cuchilleros and Cava San Miguel, just west of Plaza Mayor, where you'll find **mesónes** with such names as Tortilla, Champiñón, and Boqueron. These are the places to start your evening out in Madrid; many serve tapas and *raciónes* and close around midnight, when crowds move on to bars and nightclubs. Wander the narrow streets between Puerta del Sol and Plaza Santa Ana in Old Madrid—most are packed with traditional tapas bars. Once lined with turn-of-the-20th-century bars playing guitar or chamber music, Calle Huertas now has more nightclubs than any other street in Madrid. Just off Alonso Martínez, Plaza Santa Bárbara is packed with fashionable bars and beer halls. Stroll along Santa Teresa, Orellana, Campoamor, or Fernando VI and take your pick. Madrid has no lack of old-fashioned cafés, with dark-wood counters, brass pumps, and marble-top tables.

The **Cervecería Alemana** (✉ Plaza Santa Ana 6 ☎ 91/429–7033) is a beer hall founded more than 100 years ago by Germans and patronized, inevitably, by Ernest Hemingway. **El Abuelo** (✉ Victoria 6 ☎ 91/532–1219), or Grandpa, serves only two tapas but does them better than anyone else: grilled shrimp and shrimp sautéed in garlic. For a more tranquil place try the lovely, old tiled bar **Viva Madrid** (✉ Fernández y González 7 ☎ 91/429–3640) early in the evening.

Casa Alberto (✉ C. Huertas 18 ☎ 91/429–9356), a quiet restaurant-tavern with brick walls, has a good selection of draft beers, and tapas. **La Fídula** (✉ C. Huertas 57 ☎ 91/429–2947) often has live classical music. For zest, try the disco **La Fontanería** (✉ Huertas 38 ☎ 91/369–4904), where the action lasts until 4 AM.

The **Cervecería Santa Bárbara** (☎ 91/319–0449), in the plaza itself, is one of the most colorful, a popular beer hall with different tapas. **Café Comercial** (✉ Glorieta de Bilbao 7 ☎ 91/521–5655) is a classic. **Café Gijón** (✉ Paseo de Recoletos 21 ☎ 91/521–5425) is a former literary hangout that offers a cheery set lunch; it's now one of many cafés with summer terraces that dot the Castellana and Paseo de Recoletos. **El Espejo** (✉ Paseo de Recoletos 31 ☎ 91/308–2347) has art nouveau furnishings and an outdoor terrace in summer.

Discos & Nightclubs

Nightlife—or *la marcha,* as the Spanish fondly call it—reaches legendary heights in Spain's capital. Smart, trendy dance clubs filled with well-heeled Madrileños are everywhere. For adventure, try the scruffy bar district in Malasaña, around the Plaza Dos de Mayo, where smoky hangouts line Calle San Vicente Ferrer. The often seedy haunts of Chueca, a popular gay area, can be exciting (watch your purse), but classy cafés and trendy live music venues occasionally break up the alleys of tattoo parlors, boutiques, techno discos, and after-hours clubs.

Amadis (✉ Covarrubias 42, under Luchana Cinema ☎ 91/446–0036) has concerts, dancing, and telephones on every table, encouraging people to call each other with invitations to dance. You must be over 25 to enter. Salsa is a fixture in Madrid; check out the most spectacular moves at **Azúcar** (✉ Paseo Reina Cristina 7 ☎ 91/501–6107). **Ave Nox** (✉ Lagasca 31 ☎ 91/576–9715) is a torrid music bar–disco in a converted chapel, complete with vaulted ceiling, choir loft, and all. **Changó** (✉ Covarrubias 42 ☎ 91/446–0036), named for the Cuban Santería Zeus, is a mega-disco with savage go-go-dancers. **El Clandestino** (✉ Barquillo 34 ☎ 91/521–5563) is a low-key bar-café with impromptu jam sessions. Madrid's hippest club for wild, all-night dancing to an international music mix is **El Sol** (✉ C. Jardines 3 ☎ 91/532–6490). **Fortuny** (✉ Fortuny 34 ☎ 91/319–0588) attracts a celebrity crowd, especially in summer, when the lush outdoor patio is open. The door is ultraselective. **Joy Eslava** (✉ Arenal 11 ☎ 91/366–3733), a downtown disco in a converted theater, is an old standby. Stop into the baroque **Palacio de Gaviria** (✉ Arenal 9 ☎ 91/526–6069), a restored 19th-century palace with a maze of rooms that have been turned into a disco, mainly for foreigners. **Pachá** (✉ Barceló 11 ☎ 91/447–0128), one of Spain's infamous chain discos, is always energetic. **Torero** (✉ Cruz 26 ☎ 91/523–1129) is for the beautiful people—a bouncer allows only those judged *gente guapa* (beautiful people) to enter.

Flamenco

Madrid has lots of flamenco shows, some good, but many aimed at the tourist trade. Dinner tends to be mediocre and overpriced, though it ensures the best seats; otherwise, opt for the show and a *consumición* (drink) only, usually starting around 11 PM and costing €20–€25.

Arco de Cuchilleros (✉ Cuchilleros 7 ☎ 91/364–0263) is one of the better and cheaper venues in the city to view flamenco. **Café de Chinitas** (✉ Torija 7 ☎ 91/559–5135) is expensive, but offers the best flamenco dancing in Madrid. **Casa Patas** (✉ Cañizares 10 ☎ 91/369–0496) is a major showplace; it offers good, if somewhat touristy, flamenco and tapas, all at reasonable prices. **Corral de la Morería** (✉ Morería 17 ☎ 91/365–8446) invites well-known flamenco stars to perform with the resident group. One of Madrid's prime flamenco showcases—and less commercial than the traditional and better known *tablaos*—**Las Carboneras** (✉ Plaza del Conde de Miranda 1 ☎ 91/542–8677) presents young artists on their way up as well as more established stars on tour. Shows are staged nightly from 10:30 PM to 2 AM.

Jazz Clubs

Seasonal citywide festivals present excellent artists; check the local press for listings and venues. The city's best-known jazz venue is **Café Central** (✉ Plaza de Angel 10 ☎ 91/369–4143). **Café del Foro** (✉ San Andrés 38 ☎ 91/445–3752) is a friendly club with live music nightly. **Clamores** (✉ Albuquerque 14 ☎ 91/445–7938) is known for its great champagne list. **Populart** (✉ Huertas 22 ☎ 91/429–8407) has blues, Brazilian music, and salsa.

SHOPPING

The main shopping area in central Madrid surrounds the pedestrian streets Preciados and Montera, off the Gran Vía between Puerta del Sol and Plaza Callao. The Salamanca district, just off the Plaza de Colón, bordered roughly by Serrano, Goya, and Conde de Peñalver, is more elegant and expensive; just west of Salamanca, the shops on and around Calle Argensola, just south of Calle Génova, are on their way upscale. Calle Mayor and the streets to the east of Plaza Mayor are lined with fascinating old-fashioned stores straight out of the 19th century.

Antiques

The main areas for antiques are the Plaza de las Cortes, Calle Prado, the Carrera San Jerónimo, and the Rastro flea market, along the Ribera de Curtidores and the courtyards just off it.

Fashion

Calle Serrano has the widest selection of smart boutiques and designer fashions—think Prada, Armani, and DKNY, as well as renowned Spanish designers, such as Josep Font-Luz Diaz. Upscale shopping centers have exclusive shops stocked with unusual clothes and gifts.

Adolfo Dóminguez (✉ Serrano 96 ☎ 91/576–7053 ✉ C. Ortega y Gasset 4 ☎ 91/576–0084), one of Spain's top designers, has several boutiques in Madrid. **Jesús del Pozo** (✉ Almirante 9 ☎ 91/531–3646) is one of Spain's premier young fashion designers, a scion of Spanish style for both men and women. **Loewe** (✉ Serrano 26 and 34 ☎ 91/577–6056 ✉ Gran Vía 8 ☎ 91/532–7024) is Spain's most prestigious leather store. **Sybilla** (✉ Jorge Juan 12 ☎ 91/578–1322) is the studio of Spain's best-known woman designer, who designs fluid dresses and hand-knit sweaters in natural colors and fabrics.

Los Jardines de Serrano (✉ C. Goya and Claudio Coello) has smart boutiques. For street-chic fashion closer to medieval Madrid, check out the **Madrid Fusion Centro de Moda** (✉ Plaza Tirso de Molina 15 ☎ 91/369–0018), where up-and-coming Spanish labels like Instinto, Kika, and Extart fill five floors with faux furs, funky jewelry, and the city's most eccentric selection of shoes. **Zara** (✉ ABC, Serrano 61 ☎ 91/575–6334 ✉ Gran Vía 34 ☎ 91/521–1283 ✉ Princesa 63 ☎ 91/543–2415) is for men, women, and children with trendy taste and slim pocketbooks.

Department Stores

Centro Comercial ABC (✉ Paseo de la Castellana 34) is a four-story mall with a large café. **El Corte Inglés** (✉ Preciados 3 ☎ 91/531–9619 ✉ Goya 76 and 87 ☎ 91/432–9300 ✉ Princesa 56 ☎ 91/454–6000 ✉ Serrano 47 ☎ 91/432–5490 ✉ Raimundo Fernández Villaverde 79 ☎ 91/418–8800 ✉ La Vaguada Mall ☎ 91/387–4000) is Spain's largest chain department store, with everything from auto parts to groceries to fashions. The British chain **Marks & Spencer** (✉ Serrano 52 ☎ 91/520–0000 ✉ La Vaguarda Mall ☎ 91/378–2234) is best known for its woolens and underwear, but most shoppers head straight for the food shop in the basement. **FNAC** (✉Preciados 28 ☎91/595–6100) is filled with books, music, and magazines from all over the world.

Food & Flea Markets

El Rastro, Madrid's most famous flea market, operates on Sunday from 9 to 2 around the Plaza de Cascorro and the Ribera de Curtidores. A **stamp and coin market** is held on Sunday morning in the Plaza Mayor. Mornings, take a look at the colorful food stalls inside the 19th-century glass-and-steel **San Miguel** market, also near the Plaza Mayor. There's a **secondhand-book market** most days on the Cuesta Claudio Moyano, near Atocha Station.

Gift Ideas

Madrid is famous for handmade leather boots, guitars, fans, and capes. **Seseña** (✉ Calle de la Cruz 23 ☎ 91/531–6840) has outfitted international celebrities in wool and velvet capes since the turn of the 20th century. **Tenorio** (✉ Plaza de la Provincia 6 ☎ No phone) is where you'll find one dedicated shoemaker who makes country boots (similar to cowboy boots) to order. The hitch is he needs five to six months to complete a pair. The boots start at €1,200.

Casa de Diego (✉Puerta del Sol 12 ☎91/522–6643), established in 1853, has fans, umbrellas, and classic Spanish walking sticks with ornamented silver handles. The British royal family buys autograph fans here—white kid-skin fans for signing on special occasions. **José Ramirez** (✉ C. La Paz 8 ☎ 91/531–4229) has provided Spain and the rest of the world with guitars since 1882, and his store includes a museum of antique instruments. Carefully selected handicrafts from all over Spain—ceramics, furniture, glassware, rugs, embroidery, and more—are sold at **Artespaña** (✉ Hermosilla 14 ☎ 91/435–0221). **Casa Julia** (✉ Almirante 1 ☎ 91/522–0270) is an artistic showcase, with two floors of tasteful antiques, paintings by up-and-coming artists, and furniture in experimental designs.

MADRID A TO Z

AIRPORTS & TRANSFERS

Barajas Airport, 16 km (10 mi) northeast of town just off the NII Barcelona Highway, receives international and domestic flights. Info-Iberia, at the airport, dispenses information on arrivals and departures.

Barajas Airport ☎ 91/305-8343 or 91/393-6000. **Info-Iberia** ☎ 91/329-5767.

TRANSFERS The fastest and most convenient way to get to and from the Madrid airport is the Line 8 metro running every few minutes daily from 6:30 AM to 1 AM between Barajas and Nuevos Ministerios. This run costs €1.10 and takes 12 minutes.

For a mere €3, there's a convenient bus to the central Plaza Colón, where you can catch a taxi to your hotel. Buses leave every 15 minutes between 4:45 AM and 2 AM (slightly less often very early or late in the day). Watch your belongings, as the underground Plaza Colón bus station is a favorite haunt of purse snatchers and con artists.

The metro is a bargain at €1.10 per ticket (or €5.20 for a 10-trip ticket that can also be used on city buses), but you have to change trains twice to get downtown, and the trip takes 45 minutes.

The most expensive route into town (and depending on traffic, not necessarily the fastest) is by taxi (about €20 plus tip in traffic). Pay the metered amount plus the €2 surcharge and €1 for each suitcase. By car take the NII (which becomes Avenida de América) into town, head straight into Calle María de Molina, then turn left on either Calle Serrano or the Castellana.

BUS TRAVEL TO & FROM MADRID

Madrid has no central bus station. Check with the tourist office for departure points for your destination. The Estación del Sur serves Toledo, La Mancha, Alicante, and Andalusia. Auto-Rés serves Extremadura, Cuenca, Salamanca, Valladolid, Valencia, and Zamora; Auto-Rés has a central ticket and information office, just off Gran Vía, near the Hotel Arosa. The Basque country and most of north-central Spain are served by Continental Auto. For Àvila, Segovia, and La Granja, use Empresa La Sepulvedana. Empresa Herranz serves El Escorial and the Valley of the Fallen. La Veloz serves Chinchón.

Auto-Rés ✉ Plaza Conde de Casal 6 ☎ 91/551-7200 Ⓜ Conde de Casal ✉ Central ticket office, Salud 19 ☎ 91/551-7200. **Continental Auto** ✉ Alenza 20 ☎ 91/530-4800 Ⓜ Ríos Rosas. **Empresa Herranz** ✉ 3 Moncloa Bus Terminal ☎ 91/890-4100 Ⓜ Moncloa. **Empresa La Sepulvedana** ✉ Paseo de la Florida 11 ☎ 91/530-4800 Ⓜ Norte. **Estación del Sur** ✉ Méndez Álvaro s/n ☎ 91/468-4200 Ⓜ Palos de la Frontera. **La Veloz** ✉ Avda. Mediterraneo 49 ☎ 91/409-7602 Ⓜ Conde de Casal.

BUS TRAVEL WITHIN MADRID

Red city buses run from about 6 AM until midnight, and cost €1.10 per ride. After midnight, buses called *buyos* (night owls) run out to the suburbs from Plaza de Cibeles for the same price. Signs at every stop list all other stops by street name, but they're hard to comprehend if you don't know the city well. Pick up a free route map from EMT kiosks on the Plaza de Cibeles or the Puerta del Sol, where you can also buy a 10-ride ticket called a Metrobus (€5.20) that's equally valid for the metro. Drivers will generally make change for anything up to a €20 note. If you've bought a 10-ride ticket, step just behind the driver and insert it in the ticket-punching machine until the mechanism rings. If you speak Spanish, call for information (☎ 91/406–8810).

CAR TRAVEL

The main roads are as follows: north–south, the Paseo de la Castellana and Paseo del Prado; east–west, Calle de Alcalá, Gran Vía, and Calle de la Princesa. The M30 circles Madrid, and the M40 is an outer ring road about 12 km (7 mi) farther out. For Burgos and France, drive north up the Castellana and follow the signs for the NI. For Barcelona and Barajas Airport, head up the Castellana to Plaza Dr. Marañón, then right onto María de Molina and the NII; for Andalusia and Toledo, head south down Paseo del Prado, and then follow the signs to the NIV and N401, respectively. For Segovia, Ávila, and El Escorial, head west along Princesa to Avenida Puerta de Hierro and onto the NVI–La Coruña.

EMERGENCIES

The general emergency number in all EU nations (akin to 911 in the United States) is 112. A list of pharmacies open 24 hours (*farmacias de guardia*) is published daily in *El País*. The Madrid Police has a special phone service in several languages for tourists. Your complaint will be sent to the nearest police station where the crime took place, and you will have two days to drop by the station and sign the report.

Emergency Services **Ambulance** ☎ 91/522–2222. **Red Cross Ambulance** ☎ 092 **Police** ☎ 091 emergencies. **Police line for tourists** ☎ 902/102112.

Hospitals **Hospital 12 de Octubre** ✉ Carretera de Andalucía, Km 5.4 ☎ 91/390–8000. **Hospital Ramon y Cajal** ✉ Carretera de Colmenar, Km 9 ☎ 91/336–8000. **La Paz Ciudad Sanitaria** ✉ Paseo de la Castellana 261 ☎ 91/358–2600.

ENGLISH-LANGUAGE MEDIA

The International Bookshop carries secondhand books only.

Bookstores **Booksellers** ✉ José Abascal 48 ☎ 91/442–8104. **Casa del Libro** ✉ Gran Vía 29 ☎ 91/521–4898. **International Bookshop** ✉ Campomanes 13 ☎ 91/541–7291.

METRO TRAVEL

The metro offers the simplest and quickest means of transport and operates from 6 AM to 1:30 AM. Metro maps are available from ticket offices, hotels, and tourist offices. The flat fare is €1.10 a ride; a 10-ride ticket costs €5.20 and is also valid for buses. Carry some change for the ticket machines, especially after 10 PM; the machines make change and allow you to skip long ticket lines.

SIGHTSEEING TOURS

Julià Tours, Pullmantur, and Trapsatur all run the same city orientation tours, conducted in Spanish and English. Reserve directly with their offices, through any travel agent, or through your hotel. Departure points are the addresses listed below, though you can often arrange to be picked up at your hotel. The Madrid Visión bus makes a one-hour tour of the city with recorded commentary in English. No reservation is necessary; catch the bus in front of the Prado every 1½ hours beginning at 10 AM daily (9:30 in summer). There are no buses on Sunday afternoon. A day pass, which allows you to get on and off at various attractions, is €13.

Julià Tours, Pullmantur, and Trapsatur also run full- or half-day trips to El Escorial, Ávila, Segovia, Toledo, and Aranjuez, and in summer to Cuenca and Salamanca. Summer weekends, the popular *Tren de la Fresa* (Strawberry Train) takes passengers from the old Delicias Station to Aranjuez (known for its production of strawberries and asparagus) on a 19th-century train. Tickets can be obtained from RENFE offices, travel agents, and the Delicias Station (Paseo de las Delicias 61). Other one- or two-day excursions by train are available on summer weekends. Contact RENFE for details.

Julià Tours ✉ Gran Vía 68 ☎ 91/559-9605. **Madrid Visión** ☎ 91/779-1888). **Pullmantur** ✉ Plaza de Oriente 8 ☎ 91/541-1807. **RENFE** ✉ Alcalá 44 ☎ 902/240202 🌐 www.renfe.es/ingles. **Trapsatur** ✉ San Bernardo 23 ☎ 91/542-6666.

WALKING TOURS The Municipal Tourist Office leads English-language tours of Madrid's Old Quarter every Saturday morning at 10. The *ayuntamiento* (city hall) has a popular selection of Spanish bus and walking tours under the name Descubre Madrid. Walking tours depart most mornings and visit many hidden corners as well as major sights; options include Madrid's Railroads, Medicine in Madrid, Goya's Madrid, and Commerce and Finance in Madrid. Schedules are listed in the "Descubre Madrid" leaflet available from the municipal tourist office. Tickets can be purchased at the Patronato de Turismo. If you want a personal tour with a local guide, contact the Asociación Profesional de Informadores.

Asociación Profesional de Informadores ✉ Ferraz 82 ☎ 91/542-1214 or 91/541-1221. **Municipal Tourist Office** ✉ Plaza Mayor 3. **Patronato de Turismo** ✉ C. Mayor 69 ☎ 91/588-2900.

TAXIS

Taxis are one of Madrid's few truly good deals. They work under three different tariff schemes. Tariff 1 is valid in the city center from 6 AM to 10 PM; meters start at €1.45 and add €.67 per kilometer (½ mi). Supplemental charges include €4 to or from the airport, and €2 from bus and train stations. Tariff 2 is from 10 PM to 6 AM in the city center (and from 6 AM to 10 PM in the suburbs) and the meter runs faster and charges more per kilometer. Tariff 3 runs at night beyond the city limits. All tariffs are listed on the taxi window.

Taxi stands are numerous, and taxis are easily hailed in the street—except when it rains, at which point they're exceedingly hard to come by. Available cabs display a LIBRE sign during the day, a green light at night. No tip is expected, but if you're inspired to give one, €.5 is about right for shorter rides; you may want to go as high as 10% for a trip to the airport. You can call a cab through Tele-Taxi, Radioteléfono Taxi, or Radio Taxi Gremial.

Radio Taxi Gremial ☎ 91/447-5180. **Radioteléfono Taxi** ☎ 91/547-8200. **Tele-Taxi** ☎ 91/371-2131.

TRAIN TRAVEL

Madrid has three railroad stations: Chamartín, Atocha, and Norte, the last primarily for commuter trains. Chamartín, in the northern suburbs beyond the Plaza de Castilla, is the main station, with trains to Portugal, France, and the north (including Barcelona, Ávila, Salamanca, Santiago, and La Coruña, San Sebastián, Burgos, León, and Oviedo). Most trains to Valencia, Alicante, and Andalusia leave from Chamartín but stop at the Atocha Station as well. Atocha sends trains to Segovia, Toledo, Extremadura, Lisbon, El Escorial, and southern and eastern cities such as Seville, Granada, Málaga, Córdoba, Valencia, and Castellón. A convenient metro stop (Atocha RENFE) connects the Atocha rail station to the city subway system. The Atocha Station, a spectacular, late-19th-century greenhouse, is Madrid's terminal for high-speed AVE service to Córdoba and Seville and service to Zaragosa and Lleida.

For all train information call or visit the RENFE offices, open weekdays 9:30–8. Ask for an English operator. You can also charge tickets to your credit card and even have them delivered to your hotel. There's another RENFE office in the international arrivals hall at Barajas Airport, or you can purchase tickets at any of the three main stations or from travel agents displaying the blue and yellow RENFE sign.

Atocha ✉ Glorieta del Emperador Carlos V, southern end of Paseo del Prado ☎ 91/ 328-9020. **Chamartín** ✉ Avda. Pío XII ☎ 91/315-9976. **RENFE** ✉ Alcalá 44 ☎ 902/ 240202 🌐 www.renfe.es/ingles.

TRANSPORTATION AROUND MADRID

Madrid is a fairly compact city, and most of the main sights can be visited on foot. If you're staying in one of the modern hotels in northern Madrid, however, off the Castellana, you may need to use the bus or subway.

TRAVEL AGENCIES

American Express ✉ Plaza de las Cortes 2 ☎ 91/743-7740. **Carlson Wagons-Lits/ Viajes Ecuador** ✉ Paseo de la Castellana 96 ☎ 91/563-1202 🌐 www.viajesecuador. net. **Carlson Wagons-Lits** ✉ Condesa de Venadito 1 ☎ 91/724-9900. **Pullmantur** ✉ Plaza de Oriente 8 ☎ 91/541-1807.

VISITOR INFORMATION

Madrid Provincial Tourist Office is the best place for comprehensive information. The municipal tourist office is centrally located, but hordes of tourists tend to deplete its stock of brochures. Other tourist offices are at the International Arrivals Hall in Barajas Airport and at Chamartín train station.

Madrid Provincial Tourist Office ✉ Duque de Medinaceli 2 ☎ 91/429-4951. **Municipal Tourist Offices** ✉ Plaza Mayor 3 ☎ 91/588-1636 ✉ International Arrivals Hall, Barajas Airport ☎ 91/305-8656 ✉ Chamartín train station ☎ 91/315-9976 🌐 www. munimadrid.es.

For Spain Basics, see Chapter 3, Barcelona.

PARIS

If there's a problem with a trip to Paris, it's the embarrassment of riches that faces you. No matter which Paris you choose—touristy, historic, fashion-conscious, pretentious-bourgeois, thrifty, or the legendary bohemian-arty Paris of undying attraction—one thing is certain: you will carve out your own Paris, one that is vivid, exciting, and ultimately unforgettable. Paris is a city of vast, noble perspectives and intimate, ramshackle streets, of formal *espaces vertes* (green open spaces) and quiet squares—and this combination of the pompous and the private is one of the secrets of its perennial pull.

EXPLORING PARIS

As world capitals go, Paris is surprisingly compact. With the exceptions of the Bois de Boulogne and Montmartre, you can easily walk from one major sight to the next. The city is divided in two by the River Seine, with two islands (Ile de la Cité and Ile St-Louis) in the middle. The Left—or South—Bank has a more intimate, bohemian flavor than the haughtier Right Bank. The east–west axis from Châtelet to the Arc de Triomphe, via the rue de Rivoli and the Champs-Élysées, is the principal thoroughfare for sightseeing and shopping on the Right Bank.

The city is divided into 20 *arrondissements* (districts). The last one or two digits of a city zip code (e.g., 75002) will tell you the arrondissement (in this case, the 2ᵉ, or 2nd). For further help, buy the *Plan de Paris* booklet, a city map and guide with a street-name index that also shows métro stations.

The **Carté Musées et Monuments** (Museums and Monuments Pass) offers unlimited access to more than 65 museums and monuments over a one-, three-, or five-consecutive-day period; the cost, respectively, is €15, €30, and €40. Because most Paris museums cost €4–€6, you have to be a serious museum goer to make this pay off, but there is one incredible plus: you get to jump to the head of the line by displaying it.

From the Eiffel Tower to Pont de l'Alma

The Eiffel Tower lords it over this southwest area of Paris. Across the way, in the Palais de Chaillot on place du Trocadéro, are a number of museums. In this area, too, is where you get the Bateaux Mouches, the boats that ply the Seine on their tours of Paris by water.

Numbers in the margin correspond to points of interest on the Paris map.

4 **Bateaux Mouches.** These popular motorboats set off on their hour-long tours of Paris waters regularly (every half hour in summer). ✉ *Pl. de l'Alma, 8e* ☎ *01–40–76–99–99* 🌐 *www.bateaux-mouches.fr* Ⓜ *Alma-Marceau.*

1 **Eiffel Tower** (Tour Eiffel). What is now the worldwide symbol of Paris nearly became 7,000 tons of scrap iron when its concession expired in 1909—now much loved, it was once widely derided by Parisians as too big and too modern. Only its potential use as a radio antenna saved the day. Architect Gustave Eiffel, whose skill as an engineer earned him renown as a builder of iron bridges, created his tower for the World Exhibition of 1889. Restoration in the 1980s didn't make the elevators any faster—long lines are inevitable unless you come in the evening (when every girder is lighted in glorious detail, with a special eye-popping display that goes off on the hour)—but decent shops and two good restaurants were added. The view from 1,000 feet up will enable you to appreciate the city's layout and proportions. ✉ *Quai Branly, 7e* ☎ *01–44–11–23–23* 🌐 *www.tour-eiffel.fr* ⏲ *July and Aug., daily 9 AM–midnight; Sept.–June, daily 9 AM–11 PM* Ⓜ *Bir-Hakeim, RER: Champ-de-Mars.*

3 **Musée d'Art Moderne de la Ville de Paris** (City of Paris Museum of Modern Art). Both temporary exhibits and a permanent collection of top-quality 20th-century art can be found at this modern art museum. It takes over, chronologically speaking, where the Musée d'Orsay leaves off. ✉ *11 av. du Président-Wilson, 16e* ☎ *01–53–67–40–00* 🌐 *www.paris.fr* ⏲ *Tues.–Fri. 10–5:30, weekends 10–6:45* Ⓜ *Iéna.*

2 **Palais de Chaillot** (Chaillot Palace). This honey-color, art deco culture center facing the Seine, perched atop tumbling gardens with sculpture and fountains, was built in the 1930s. It houses three museums: the **Musée de la Marine** (Maritime Museum), with a salty collection of seafaring paraphernalia; the **Musée de l'Homme** (Museum of Mankind), with an array of prehistoric artifacts; and the **Musée des Monuments Français,** which is undergoing renovation and will re-open in 2005, when it will share space with the Institut Français d'Architecture. ✉ *Pl. du Trocadéro, 16e* ☎ *01–44–05–72–72 Museum of Mankind; 01–53–65–69–69 Maritime Museum* 🌐 *www.mnhn.fr* ⏲ *Museum of Mankind Wed.–Mon. 9:45–5:15; Maritime Museum Wed.–Mon. 10–6* Ⓜ *Trocadéro.*

From the Louvre to the Arc de Triomphe

From the gleaming glass pyramid entrance of the Louvre, the world's greatest museum, you can see the Arc de Triomphe standing foursquare at the top of the city's most famous avenue, the Champs-Élysées. Between the Louvre and the Arc lies the city's spiritual heart—the elegant place de la Concorde.

5 **Arc de Triomphe** (Triumphal Arch). This 164-foot arch was planned by Napoléon to celebrate his military successes. Yet when Empress Marie-Louise entered Paris in 1810, it was barely off the ground. Napoléon had been dead for 15 years when the Arc de Triomphe was finished in 1836. The arch looms over place Charles-de-Gaulle, referred to by Parisians as *L'Étoile* (The Star), one of Europe's most chaotic traffic circles. Short of attempting a death-defying dash, your only way to get over

to the Arc de Triomphe is to take the pedestrian underpass. France's Unknown Soldier is buried beneath the archway; the flame is rekindled every evening at 6:30. ✉ *Pl. Charles-de-Gaulle, 8e* ☎ *01–55–37–73–77* 🌐 *www.monum.fr* ⏲ *Easter–Oct., daily 9:30 AM–11 PM; Nov.–Easter, daily 10 AM–10:30 PM* Ⓜ *Charles-de-Gaulle–Étoile.*

❻ **Champs-Élysées.** The cosmopolitan pulse of Paris beats strongest along this gracefully sloping, 2-km (1-mi) avenue, originally laid out in the 1660s by André Le Nôtre as parkland sweeping away from the Tuileries. In an attempt to reestablish this thoroughfare as one of the world's most beautiful avenues, the city has planted extra trees, broadened sidewalks, refurbished art nouveau newsstands, and clamped down on garish storefronts. Ⓜ *Franklin-D.-Roosevelt, Champs-Élysées–Clemenceau.*

❼ **Grand Palais** (Grand Palace). This so-called palace built for the World Exhibition of 1900 is closed for renovation until 2007, when it will reopen as an exhibition space for contemporary art. For the time being you can still visit the **Palais de la Découverte** (Palace of Discovery), with scientific and mechanical exhibits and a planetarium. ✉ *Av. Winston-Churchill, 8e* ☎ *01–56–43–20–21* ⏲ *Palais de la Découverte Tues.–Sat. 9:30–6, Sun. 10–7* Ⓜ *Champs-Élysées–Clemenceau.*

❽ **Jardin des Tuileries** (Tuileries Gardens). Immortalized in impressionist masterpieces by Monet and Pisarro, these enormous formal gardens are lined with trees, ponds, and statues. At the far end of the Tuileries, leading toward the Louvre, is the **Arc du Carrousel,** a dainty triumphal arch erected more quickly (1806–08) than its big brother at the far end of the Champs-Élysées. Ⓜ *Concorde, Tuileries.*

⓬ **Louvre.** Leonardo da Vinci's *Mona Lisa* and *Virgin and Saint Anne,* Van Eyck's *Madonna of Chancellor Rolin,* Giorgione's *Concert Champêtre,* and Delacroix's *Liberty Guiding the People* . . . you get the picture. Once a royal palace, now the world's largest and most famous museum, the Louvre has been given fresh purpose by more than a decade of expansion, renovation, and reorganization, symbolized by I. M. Pei's daring glass pyramid that now serves as the entrance to both the museum and an underground shopping arcade, the **Carrousel du Louvre.** Many thousands of treasures are newly cleaned and lighted, so plan on seeing it all—from the red-brocaded Napoléon III salons to the fabled Egyptian collection, from the 186-carat Regent Diamond to the rooms crowded with Botticellis, Caravaggios, Poussins, and Géricaults. After all the renovations, the Louvre is now a coherent, unified structure with a more spacious and navigable layout.

Fodor's Choice ★

The main attraction for some is a portrait of the wife of a certain Florentine millionaire, Francesco da Gioconda, better known as Leonardo da Vinci's *Mona Lisa* (in French, *La Joconde*), painted in 1503. In some of the less-crowded rooms and galleries nearby Leonardo's fellow Italians are strongly represented: Fra Angelico, Giotto, Mantegna, Raphael, Titian, and Veronese. El Greco, Murillo, and Velázquez lead the Spanish; Van Eyck, Rembrandt, Frans Hals, Brueghel, Holbein, and Rubens underline the achievements of northern European art. The English collection is highlighted by works of Lawrence, Reynolds, Gainsborough, and Turner. French front-runners include works by Delacroix, Poussin, Fragonard, Chardin, Boucher, and Watteau—together with David's *Oath of the Horatii* and Géricault's *Raft of the Medusa.* Famous statues include the soaring *Victory of Samothrace,* the celebrated *Venus de Milo,* and the realistic Egyptian *Seated Scribe.* New rooms for ancient Persian, Arab, and Greek art opened in 1997. ✉ *Palais du Louvre (it's faster to enter through the Carrousel du Louvre mall on rue de Rivoli than through the pyramid), 1er ☎ 01–40–20–51–51 🌐 www.louvre.fr 🎫 €10 ⏲ Thurs.–Sun. 9–6, Mon. and Wed. 9 AM–9:45 PM Ⓜ Palais-Royal.*

⓫ **Musée du Jeu de Paume.** This museum, at the entrance to the Tuileries Gardens, is an ultramodern, white-walled showcase for excellent temporary exhibits of bold contemporary art. The building was once the spot of *jeu de paume* games (literally, palm game—a forerunner of tennis). ✉ *1 pl. de la Concorde, 1er ☎ 01–42–60–69–69 ⏲ Tues. noon–9:30, Wed.–Fri. noon–7, weekends 10–7 Ⓜ Concorde.*

❿ **Musée de l'Orangerie** (Orangery Museum). This museum in the Tuileries Gardens contains fine early-20th-century French works by many artists, most famously Monet (on view here are his largest paintings of *Water Lilies*); it should reopen in fall 2004 after renovation. ✉ *Pl. de la Concorde, 1er ☎ 01–42–97–48–16 Ⓜ Concorde.*

❾ **Place de la Concorde.** Flanked by elegant neoclassical buildings, this huge square is often choked with traffic and perhaps at its most scenic come nightfall, when its beautiful florid fountains are illuminated. More than 1,000 people, including Louis XVI and Marie-Antoinette, were guillotined here in the early 1790s. The obelisk, a gift from the viceroy of Egypt, originally stood at Luxor and was erected here in 1833. Ⓜ *Concorde.*

The Faubourg St-Honoré

Fashions change, but the Faubourg St-Honoré—the area just north of the Champs-Élysées and the Tuileries—firmly maintains its tradition of high style. As you progress from the President's Palace, past a wealth of art galleries and the monumental Madeleine church to the stately place Vendôme, you will see that all is luxury and refinement here. On the ritzy square, famous boutiques sit side by side with famous banks—after all, elegance and finance have never been an unusual combination. Leading names in modern fashion are found farther east on place des Victoires. Sublimely Parisian are the Palais-Royal and its elegant gardens.

⓮ **Église de la Madeleine.** With its rows of uncompromising columns, this church, known simply as La Madeleine, looks more like a Greek temple. Inside, the walls are richly decorated, with plenty of gold glinting through the murk. The church was designed in 1814 but not consecrated until 1842, after futile efforts to turn the site into a train station. ✉ *Pl. de la Madeleine, 8e ⏲ Mon.–Sat. 7:30–7, Sun. 8–7 Ⓜ Madeleine.*

⓲ **Forum des Halles.** Since the city's much-lamented central glass-and-iron market halls were torn down during the late 1960s, the area has been transformed into a trendy—albeit slightly seedy—shopping complex, the Forum des Halles. A topiary garden basks in the shadow of the nearby **Bourse du Commerce** (Commercial Exchange) and bulky church of **St-Eustache.** ✉ *Main entrance on rue Pierre-Lescot, 1er Ⓜ Les Halles; RER: Châtelet–Les Halles.*

⓭ **Palais de l'Élysée** (Élysée Palace). This "palace," where the French president lives, works, and receives official visitors, was originally constructed as a private mansion in 1718 and has housed presidents only since 1873. ✉ *55 rue du Faubourg-St-Honoré, 8e ⏲ Not open to the public Ⓜ Miromesnil.*

⓰ **Palais-Royal.** This erstwhile Royal Palace, built in the 1630s and now partly occupied by the Ministry of Culture, has a beautiful garden bordered by arcades and boutiques, and an adjacent courtyard with modern, candy-stripe columns by Daniel Buren. Once home to the Bourbon kings, it is now occupied by the French Ministry of Culture and private

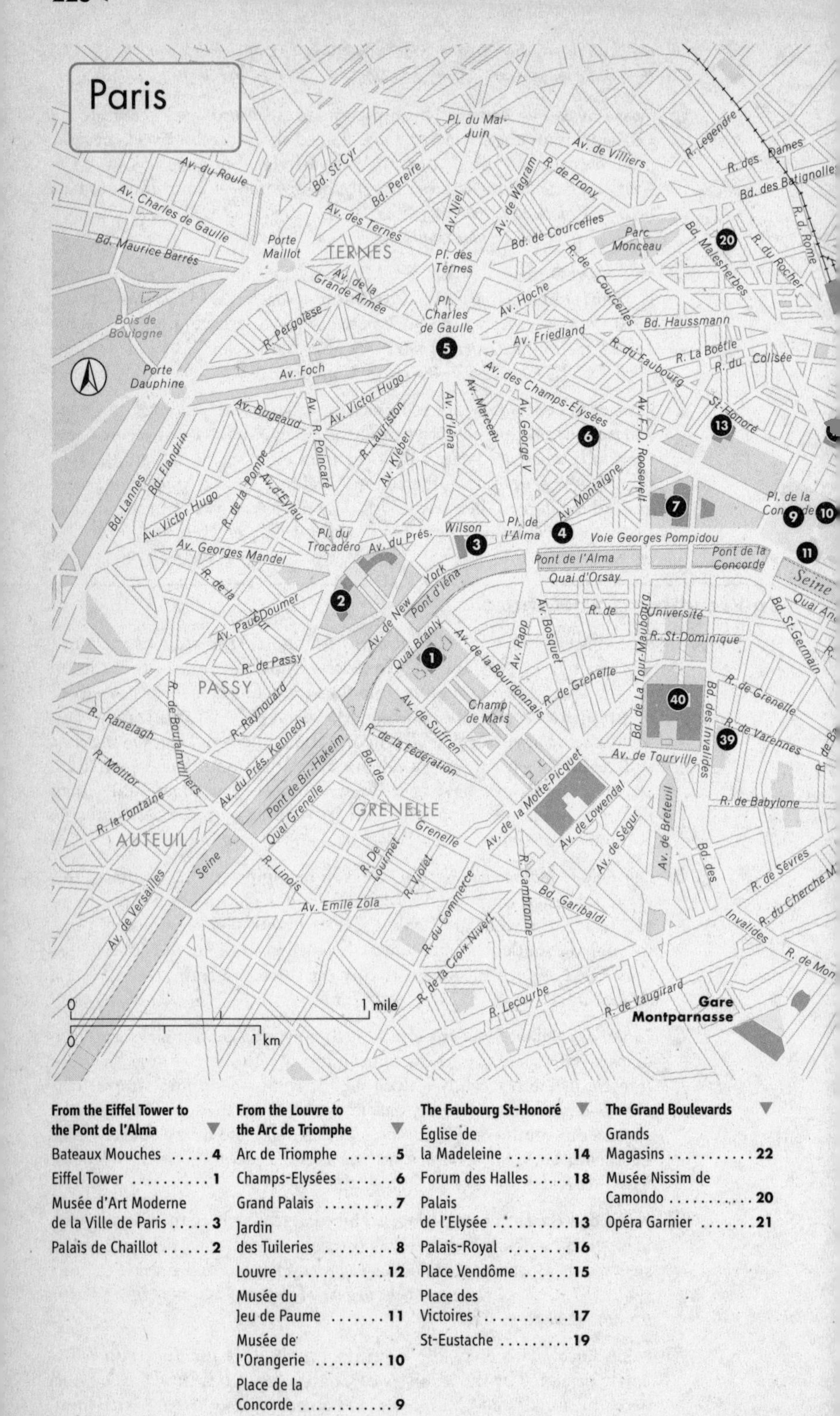

From the Eiffel Tower to the Pont de l'Alma ▼

Bateaux Mouches **4**
Eiffel Tower **1**
Musée d'Art Moderne de la Ville de Paris **3**
Palais de Chaillot **2**

From the Louvre to the Arc de Triomphe ▼

Arc de Triomphe **5**
Champs-Elysées **6**
Grand Palais **7**
Jardin des Tuileries **8**
Louvre **12**
Musée du Jeu de Paume **11**
Musée de l'Orangerie **10**
Place de la Concorde **9**

The Faubourg St-Honoré ▼

Église de la Madeleine **14**
Forum des Halles **18**
Palais de l'Elysée **13**
Palais-Royal **16**
Place Vendôme **15**
Place des Victoires **17**
St-Eustache **19**

The Grand Boulevards ▼

Grands Magasins **22**
Musée Nissim de Camondo **20**
Opéra Garnier **21**

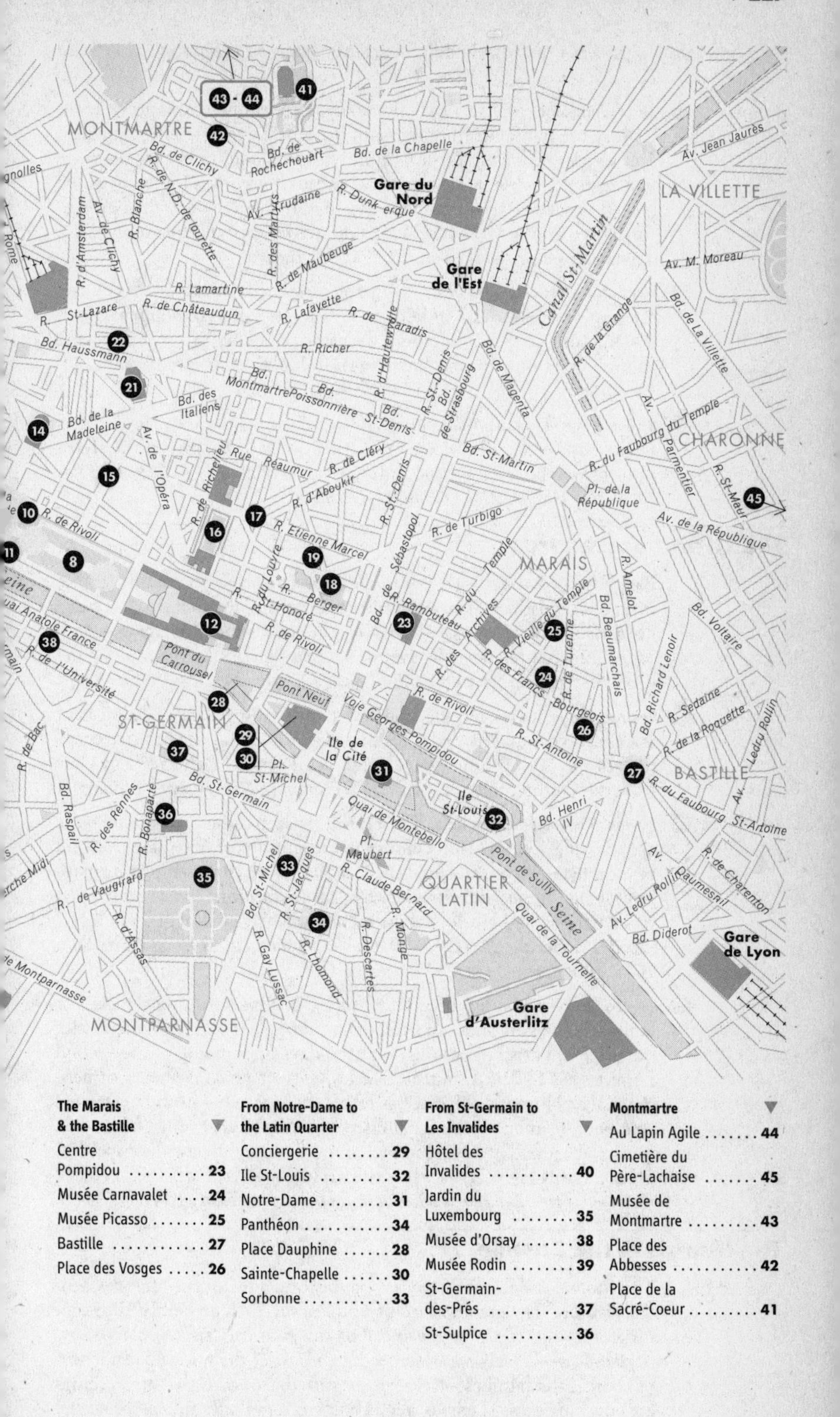

The Marais & the Bastille

Centre Pompidou 23
Musée Carnavalet 24
Musée Picasso 25
Bastille 27
Place des Vosges 26

From Notre-Dame to the Latin Quarter

Conciergerie 29
Ile St-Louis 32
Notre-Dame 31
Panthéon 34
Place Dauphine 28
Sainte-Chapelle 30
Sorbonne 33

From St-Germain to Les Invalides

Hôtel des Invalides 40
Jardin du Luxembourg 35
Musée d'Orsay 38
Musée Rodin 39
St-Germain-des-Prés 37
St-Sulpice 36

Montmartre

Au Lapin Agile 44
Cimetière du Père-Lachaise 45
Musée de Montmartre 43
Place des Abbesses 42
Place de la Sacré-Coeur 41

apartments, and its buildings are not open to the public. ✉ *Pl. du Palais-Royal, 1er* Ⓜ *Palais-Royal.*

⓯ **Place Vendôme.** Mansart's rhythmically proportioned example of 17th-century urban architecture is one of the world's most opulent squares. Top jewelers compete for attention with the limousines that draw up outside the Ritz hotel. The square's central column was forged from the melted bronze of 1,200 cannons captured by Napoléon at the Battle of Austerlitz in 1805. That's Napoléon at the top, masquerading as a Roman emperor. ✉ *Pl. Vendôme, 1er* Ⓜ *Tuileries.*

⓱ **Place des Victoires.** This circular square, now lined with many of the city's top fashion boutiques, was laid out in 1685 by Jules-Hardouin Mansart in honor of the military victories (*victoires*) of Louis XIV. The Sun King gallops along on a bronze horse in the middle. ✉ *Pl. des Victoires, 1er* Ⓜ *Sentier.*

⓳ **St-Eustache.** This colossal church, also known as the Cathedral of Les Halles, was erected between 1532 and 1637 and testifies to the stylistic transition between Gothic and classical architecture. ✉ *2 rue du Jour, 1er* Ⓜ *Les Halles; RER: Châtelet–Les Halles.*

The Grand Boulevards

Backbone of Paris's Right Bank, a wide avenue traces a continuous arc from St-Augustin, the city's grandest Second Empire church, to place de la République, whose very name symbolizes the ultimate downfall of the imperial regime. The avenue's name changes six times along the way—Parisians refer to it as the *Grands Boulevards.*

㉒ **Grands Magasins** (Department Stores). Paris's most venerable department stores can be found behind the Opéra: **Galeries Lafayette** has an elegant turn-of-the-20th-century glass dome, **Au Printemps** an excellent view from its rooftop cafeteria. ✉ *Bd. Haussmann, 8e* Ⓜ *Havre-Caumartin.*

★ ⑳ **Musée Nissim de Camondo.** The French perfected the *art de vivre*—the art of living—in the 18th century in elegant, luxurious salons. It's all beautifully preserved and on display at this *hôtel particulier* (private mansion), magnificently furnished with beautiful furniture, *boiseries* (carved wood panels), and bibelots of the rococo and neoclassical periods. ✉ *63 rue de Monceau* ☎ *01–53–89–06–40* 🌐 *www.ucad.fr* ⏲ *Wed.–Sun. 10–5* Ⓜ *Villiers.*

㉑ **Opéra Garnier.** Haunt of the *Phantom of the Opera,* setting for Degas's famous ballet paintings, and still the most opulent theater in the world, the original Paris opera house was the flagship building of the Second Empire (1851–70). Architect Charles Garnier fused elements of neoclassical architecture—like the bas-reliefs on the facade—in an exaggerated combination imbued with the subtlety of a Wagnerian cymbal crash. You can stroll around at leisure in the Grand Foyer, and view the super-opulent, Napoléon III–style auditorium. ✉ *Pl. de l'Opéra, 9e* ☎ *01–40–01–22–63* 🌐 *www.opera-de-paris.fr* ⏲ *Daily 10–5* Ⓜ *Opéra.*

Fodor's Choice ★

The Marais & the Bastille

The Marais is one of the city's most historic and sought-after residential districts. The gracious architecture of the 17th and early 18th centuries sets the tone. Today most of the Marais's spectacular *hôtels particuliers*—loosely translated as "mansions," the onetime residences of aristocratic families—have been restored, and many of the buildings are now museums. There are trendy boutiques and cafés among the kosher shops of the traditionally Jewish neighborhood around rue des Rosiers. On the eastern side of the neighborhood is place de la Bastille, site of the infamous prison stormed on July 14, 1789, an event that came to symbolize the beginning of the French Revolution. The surrounding Bastille quarter is filled with galleries, shops, theaters, cafés, restaurants, and bars.

23 **Centre Pompidou.** The futuristic, funnel-top Pompidou Center was built in the mid-1970s and named in honor of former French president Georges Pompidou. The center is most famous for its **Musée National d'Art Moderne** (Modern Art Museum), covering 20th-century art from Fauvism and Cubism to postwar abstraction and video constructions. Other highlights include the chic rooftop restaurant and the glass-tube elevator that snakes up the side of the building. On the sloping piazza below is the **Atelier Brancusi** (Brancusi's Studio), four reconstituted rooms crammed with works by Romanian-born sculptor Constantin Brancusi. ✉ *Pl. Georges-Pompidou, 4e* ☎ *01–44–78–12–33* 🌐 *www.centrepompidou.fr* ⏲ *Wed.–Mon. 11–9* Ⓜ *Rambuteau.*

★ 24 **Musée Carnavalet.** Two adjacent mansions in the heart of the Marais house this museum devoted to the decorative arts and the history of Paris. Along with riveting objects of the French kings, there are also magnificent 17th- and 18th-century period salons on view, including recreations of Marcel Proust's cork-lined bedroom and the late-19th-century Fouquet jewelry shop. ✉ *23 rue de Sévigné, 3e* ☎ *01–44–59–58–58* 🌐 *www.paris-france.org/musees* ⏲ *Tues.–Sun. 10–5:30* Ⓜ *St-Paul.*

25 **Musée Picasso.** Housed in the scuffed yet palatial 17th-century Hôtel Salé, this museum contains the paintings, sculptures, drawings, prints, ceramics, and assorted works of art given to the government by Picasso's heirs after the painter's death in 1973 in lieu of death duties. There are works from every period of Picasso's life, as well as pieces by Cézanne, Renoir, Degas, and Matisse. ✉ *5 rue de Thorigny, 3e* ☎ *01–42–71–25–21* ⏲ *Wed.–Mon. 9:30–5:30* Ⓜ *St-Sébastien.*

27 **Place de la Bastille.** Nothing remains of the prison-fortress stormed at the outbreak of the French Revolution; the soaring **Colonne de Juillet** (July Column), topped by the figure of Liberty, commemorates Parisians killed in the long-forgotten uprising of 1830. Also on the square is the **Opéra de la Bastille,** opened in 1989 in commemoration of the Revolution's bicentennial. The **Viaduc des Arts** (Arts Viaduct), a disused railway viaduct converted into boutiques below and a planted walkway on top, leads off down avenue Daumesnil. Ⓜ *Bastille.*

★ 26 **Place des Vosges.** The oldest monumental square in Paris—and probably still its most nobly proportioned—the place des Vosges was laid out by Henri IV at the start of the 17th century. Originally known as place Royale, it has kept its Renaissance beauty nearly intact, although its buildings have been softened by time, their pale pink brick crumbling slightly in the harsh Parisian air and the darker stone facings pitted with age. In the far corner is the **Maison de Victor Hugo** (Victor Hugo Museum), containing souvenirs of the great poet's life and many of his paintings and ink drawings. ✉ *Maison de Victor Hugo: 6 pl. des Vosges, 4e* ☎ *01–42–72–10–16* 🌐 *www.paris-france.org/musees* ⏲ *Tues.–Sun. 10–5:45* Ⓜ *St-Paul, Chemin-Vert.*

From Notre-Dame to the Latin Quarter

No matter how you first approach Paris—historically, geographically, emotionally—it is the river Seine that summons all, the Seine that harbors two islands, the Ile de la Cité and the Ile St-Louis, within the very center of Paris. Of them, it is the Ile de la Cité that forms the historic ground zero of the city. It was here that the earliest inhabitants of Paris, the Gaulish tribe of the Parisii, settled in about 250 BC. Here you'll find

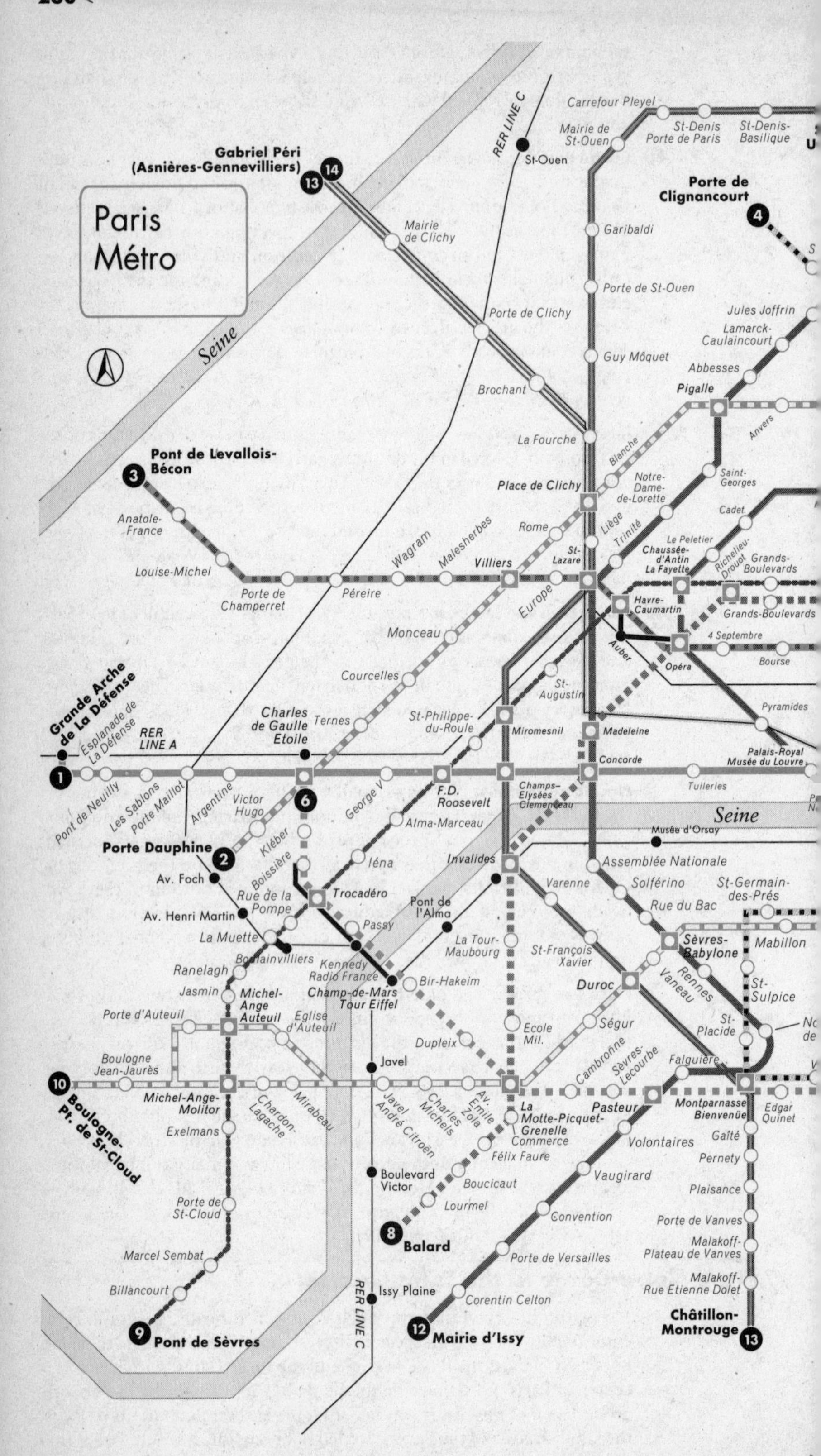
Paris Métro
Seine
RER LINE C
Gabriel Péri (Asnières-Gennevilliers)
St-Ouen
Carrefour Pleyel
Mairie de St-Ouen
St-Denis Porte de Paris
St-Denis-Basilique
Porte de Clignancourt
Mairie de Clichy
Garibaldi
Porte de St-Ouen
Porte de Clichy
Jules Joffrin
Lamarck-Caulaincourt
Guy Môquet
Abbesses
Brochant
Pigalle
Anvers
La Fourche
Blanche
Pont de Levallois-Bécon
Notre-Dame-de-Lorette
Saint-Georges
Place de Clichy
Anatole-France
Rome
Liège
Trinité
Cadet
Wagram
Malesherbes
Le Peletier
Chaussée-d'Antin La Fayette
Richelieu-Drouot
Grands-Boulevards
Louise-Michel
Villiers
St-Lazare
Porte de Champerret
Péreire
Europe
Havre-Caumartin
Grands-Boulevards
Monceau
Auber
4 Septembre
Opéra
Bourse
Courcelles
St-Augustin
Grande Arche de La Défense
Esplanade de La Défense
Charles de Gaulle Etoile
Ternes
St-Philippe-du-Roule
Miromesnil
Madeleine
Pyramides
RER LINE A
Concorde
Palais-Royal Musée du Louvre
Pont de Neuilly
Les Sablons
Porte Maillot
Argentine
Victor Hugo
George V
F.D. Roosevelt
Champs-Elysées Clemenceau
Tuileries
Alma-Marceau
Seine
Musée d'Orsay
Porte Dauphine
Kléber
Iéna
Invalides
Assemblée Nationale
Av. Foch
Boissière
Varenne
Solférino
St-Germain-des-Prés
Rue de la Pompe
Trocadéro
Pont de l'Alma
Rue du Bac
Av. Henri Martin
Passy
La Muette
La Tour-Maubourg
St-François Xavier
Sèvres-Babylone
Mabillon
Boulainvilliers
Kennedy Radio France
Ranelagh
Champ-de-Mars Tour Eiffel
Bir-Hakeim
Duroc
Vaneau
Rennes
St-Sulpice
Jasmin
Michel-Ange Auteuil
Porte d'Auteuil
Eglise d'Auteuil
Ecole Mil.
Ségur
St-Placide
Dupleix
Cambronne
Sèvres-Lecourbe
Falguière
Boulogne Jean-Jaurès
Javel
Michel-Ange-Molitor
Chardon-Lagache
Mirabeau
Javel André Citroën
Charles Michels
Av. Emile Zola
La Motte-Picquet-Grenelle
Pasteur
Montparnasse Bienvenüe
Edgar Quinet
Boulogne-Pt. de St-Cloud
Exelmans
Commerce
Volontaires
Gaîté
Félix Faure
Pernety
Boulevard Victor
Boucicaut
Vaugirard
Plaisance
Porte de St-Cloud
Lourmel
Convention
Porte de Vanves
Malakoff-Plateau de Vanves
Balard
Marcel Sembat
Porte de Versailles
Malakoff-Rue Etienne Dolet
Billancourt
Issy Plaine
Corentin Celton
Châtillon-Montrouge
Pont de Sèvres
Mairie d'Issy

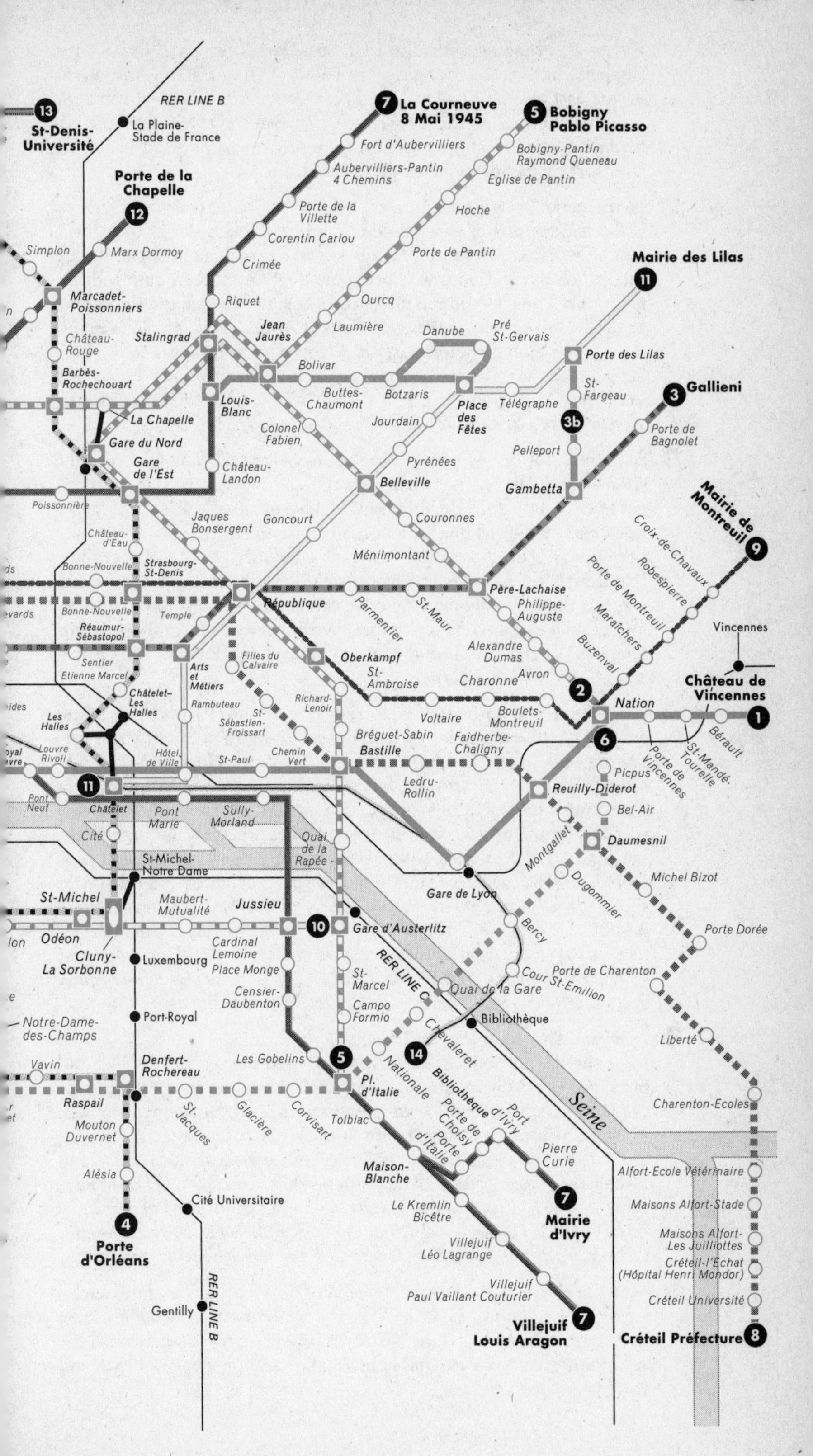
RER LINE B
La Plaine-Stade de France
13 St-Denis-Université
7 La Courneuve 8 Mai 1945
Fort d'Aubervilliers
Aubervilliers-Pantin 4 Chemins
Porte de la Villette
Corentin Cariou
Crimée
Riquet
5 Bobigny Pablo Picasso
Bobigny-Pantin Raymond Queneau
Eglise de Pantin
Hoche
Porte de Pantin
Ourcq
Laumière
Porte de la Chapelle
12
Simplon
Marx Dormoy
Marcadet-Poissonniers
Château-Rouge
Barbès-Rochechouart
La Chapelle
Gare du Nord
Gare de l'Est
Stalingrad
Jean Jaurès
Louis-Blanc
Château-Landon
Bolivar
Buttes-Chaumont
Botzaris
Danube
Pré St-Gervais
Place des Fêtes
Télégraphe
Mairie des Lilas
11
Porte des Lilas
St-Fargeau
3b
Pelleport
Gambetta
3 Gallieni
Porte de Bagnolet
Colonel Fabien
Jourdain
Pyrénées
Belleville
Couronnes
Ménilmontant
Goncourt
Jaques Bonsergent
Poissonnière
Château-d'Eau
Bonne-Nouvelle
Strasbourg-St-Denis
République
Parmentier
St-Maur
Père-Lachaise
Philippe-Auguste
Alexandre Dumas
Avron
Mairie de Montreuil
9
Croix-de-Chavaux
Robespierre
Porte de Montreuil
Maraîchers
Buzenval
Temple
Réaumur-Sébastopol
Sentier
Etienne Marcel
Arts et Métiers
Filles du Calvaire
Oberkampf
St-Ambroise
Charonne
Vincennes
Château de Vincennes
1
2
Nation
Bérault
St-Mandé-Tourelle
Porte de Vincennes
Châtelet-Les Halles
Les Halles
Rambuteau
St-Sébastien-Froissart
Richard-Lenoir
Voltaire
Boulets-Montreuil
Bréguet-Sabin
Faidherbe-Chaligny
6
Picpus
Louvre Rivoli
Hôtel de Ville
St-Paul
Chemin Vert
Bastille
Ledru-Rollin
Reuilly-Diderot
Bel-Air
Daumesnil
11
Châtelet
Pont Neuf
Pont Marie
Sully-Morland
Cité
Quai de la Rapée
Montgallet
Dugommier
Michel Bizot
Porte Dorée
St-Michel-Notre Dame
St-Michel
Gare de Lyon
Maubert-Mutualité
Jussieu
10
Gare d'Austerlitz
Bercy
Odéon
Cluny-La Sorbonne
Cardinal Lemoine
Place Monge
Luxembourg
St-Marcel
RER LINE C
Quai de la Gare
Cour St-Emilion
Porte de Charenton
Censier-Daubenton
Campo Formio
Bibliothèque
Port-Royal
Notre-Dame-des-Champs
Chevaleret
14
Liberté
Les Gobelins
5
Pl. d'Italie
Nationale
Bibliothèque
Port d'Ivry
Vavin
Denfert-Rochereau
Raspail
St-Jacques
Glacière
Corvisart
Tolbiac
Porte de Choisy
Porte d'Italie
Seine
Charenton-Ecoles
Mouton Duvernet
Pierre Curie
Maison-Blanche
Alésia
Alfort-Ecole Vétérinaire
Cité Universitaire
Le Kremlin Bicêtre
7 Mairie d'Ivry
Maisons Alfort-Stade
4 Porte d'Orléans
Villejuif Léo Lagrange
Maisons Alfort-Les Juilliottes
Créteil-l'Echat (Hôpital Henri Mondor)
Villejuif Paul Vaillant Couturier
Créteil Université
Gentilly
RER LINE B
7 Villejuif Louis Aragon
Créteil Préfecture 8

the great, brooding cathedral of Notre-Dame, the jewel-like Sainte-Chapelle, and the Conciergerie, last haunt of Queen Marie-Antoinette. To the east lies the smaller Ile St-Louis—one of Paris's most romantic nooks—while across the river on the Left Bank of the Seine is the bohemian Quartier Latin, with its warren of steep sloping streets, populated largely by Sorbonne students and academics.

29 **Conciergerie.** Bringing a tear to the eyes of Ancien Régime devotées, this is the famous prison in which dukes and duchesses, lords and ladies, and, most famously, Queen Marie-Antoinette were imprisoned during the French Revolution before being bundled off for their date with the guillotine. You can still see the queen's cell and chapel and the superb vaulted 14th-century **Salles des Gens d'Armes** (Hall of the Men-at-Arms). The **Tour de l'Horloge** (Clock Tower) near the entrance on quai de l'Horloge has a clock that has been ticking off time since 1370. ✉ *1 quai de l'Horloge, 1er* ☎ *01–53–73–78–50* 🌐 *www.monum.fr* ⏲ *Apr.–Sept., daily 9:30–6:30; Oct.–Mar., daily 10–5* Ⓜ *Cité.*

32 **Ile St-Louis.** Of the two islands in the Seine—the Ile de la Cité is to the west—it is the Ile St-Louis that best retains the loveliness of *le Paris traditionnel.* A tiny universe unto itself, shaded by trees, bordered by Seine-side quais, and overhung with ancient stone houses, the island has long been a coveted address for Parisians—Voltaire, Daumier, Cézanne, Baudelaire, Chagall, Helena Rubenstein, and the Rothschilds are just some of the lucky people who have called the St-Louis home. In summer, crowds line up for a scoop from Berthillon's ice-cream shop—savor your cone of *glace de Grande Marnier* by strolling along the isle's Seine-side streets. Ⓜ *Pont-Marie.*

★ 31 **Notre-Dame.** The cathedral of Notre-Dame remains Paris's historic and geographic heart, a place of worship for more than 2,000 years (the present building is the fourth on this site). Victor Hugo's Quasimodo sought sanctuary in its towers, kings and princes married before its great altar, and Napoléon crowned his empress here. The magnificent structure was begun in 1163, making it one of the earliest Gothic cathedrals, but wasn't finished until 1345. The interior is at its lightest and least crowded in the early morning. Window space is limited and filled with shimmering stained glass; the circular rose windows in the transept are particularly delicate. The 387-step climb up the towers is worth the effort for a perfect view of the gargoyles and Paris. ✉ *Pl. du Parvis, 4e* 🌐 *www.monum.fr* ⏲ *Cathedral daily 8–7. Towers Apr.–June, daily 9:30–7:30; July–Sept., daily 9–7:30; Oct.–Mar., daily 10–5:30* Ⓜ *Cité.*

34 **Panthéon.** This Temple to the Famous started life as a church (1758–89). Since the Revolution, the crypt has harbored the remains of such national heroes as Voltaire, Rousseau, and Zola. Its newest resident is Alexandre Dumas, whose remains were interred there in November of 2002. The austere interior is ringed with Puvis de Chavannes's late-19th-century frescoes, relating the life of Geneviève, patron saint of Paris, and contains a swinging model of the giant pendulum used here by Léon Foucault in 1851 to prove the earth's rotation. ✉ *Pl. du Panthéon, 5e* ☎ *01–44–32–18–00* 🌐 *www.monum.fr* ⏲ *Apr.–Sept., daily 9:30–6:30; Oct.–Mar., daily 10–6:15* Ⓜ *Cardinal-Lemoine; RER: Luxembourg.*

28 **Place Dauphine.** At the western tail end of the Ile de la Cité, this charming plaza was built by Henri IV. The triangular place is lined with some 17th-century houses that the writer André Maurois felt represented the very quintessence of Paris and France; take a seat on the park bench and see if you agree. Ⓜ *Cité.*

30 Fodor'sChoice ★ **Sainte-Chapelle** (Holy Chapel). Not to be missed and one of the most magical sights in European medieval art, this chapel was built by Louis IX in the 1240s to house the Crown of Thorns he had bought from Emperor Baldwin. A lower chapel leads to the dazzling upper chapel, whose walls—if you can call them that—are almost completely made of stained glass. Like an enormous magic lantern, the scenes illuminate more than a thousand figures from stories of the Bible. Try to attend a candlelighted concert here. ✉ *4 bd. du Palais, 1er* ☎ *01–53–73–78–52* 🌐 *www.monum.fr* ⏲ *Apr.–Sept., daily 9:30–6:30; Oct.–Mar., daily 10–5* Ⓜ *Cité.*

33 **Sorbonne.** Students at Paris's ancient university—one of the oldest in Europe—used to listen to lectures in Latin, which explains why the surrounding area is known as the Latin Quarter. You can visit the main courtyard and peek into the lecture halls if they're not in use. The baroque chapel is open only during exhibitions. ✉ *Rue de la Sorbonne, 5e* Ⓜ *Cluny–La Sorbonne.*

From St-Germain to Les Invalides

This area of the Left Bank extends from the lively St-Germain neighborhood (named for the oldest church in Paris) to the stately area around the Musée d'Orsay and Les Invalides. South of St-Germain is Montparnasse, which had its cultural heyday in the first part of the 20th century, when it was *the* place for painters and poets to live.

★ 40 **Hôtel des Invalides.** Soaring above expansive if hardly manicured lawns, Les Invalides was founded by Louis XIV in 1674 to house wounded war veterans. Les Invalides itself is an outstanding baroque ensemble, designed by Libéral Bruant. One of its two churches, the Église du Dôme, is graced by the city's most elegant dome and holds **Napoléon's Tomb,** where you can waft the fumes of hubris off the marble columns and onyx trim. The adjacent **Musée de l'Armée** has a collection of arms, armor, and uniforms, and the **Musée des Plans-Reliefs** contains a fascinating collection of old scale models of French towns. ✉ *Pl. des Invalides, 7e* ☎ *01–44–42–37–72* 🌐 *www.invalides.org* ⏲ *Apr.–Sept., daily 10–6; Oct.–Mar., daily 10–4:30* Ⓜ *Latour–Maubourg.*

35 **Jardin du Luxembourg** (Luxembourg Gardens). A favorite subject for 19th-century painters, Paris's most famous Left Bank park has tennis courts, flower beds, tree-lined alleys, and a large pond (with toy boats for rent alongside). The 17th-century **Palais du Luxembourg** (Luxembourg Palace) was commissioned by Queen Maria de' Medici at the beginning of the 17th century and houses the French Senate, which is not open to the public. An adjacent wing of the palace houses the Musée de Luxembourg, open only for special exhibitions. Ⓜ *Odéon; RER: Luxembourg.*

★ 38 **Musée d'Orsay.** This museum, in a spectacularly converted belle epoque train station, is one of Paris's star attractions, thanks to its imaginatively housed collections of the arts (mainly French) spanning the period 1848–1914. The chief artistic attraction is its impressionist collection, which includes some of the most celebrated paintings in the world, including Manet's *Déjeuner sur l'Herbe* (*Lunch on the Grass*) and Renoir's depiction of a famous dance hall called *Le Moulin de la Galette,* to name just two among hundreds. Other highlights include art nouveau furniture and a model of the Opéra quarter beneath a glass floor. The restaurant here is set in a dazzling 19th-century foyer. ✉ *1 rue de Bellechasse, 7e* ☎ *01–40–49–48–14* 🌐 *www.musee-orsay.fr* ⏲ *Tues., Wed., Fri., and Sat. 10–6, Thurs. 10–9:45, Sun. 9–6* Ⓜ *Solférino; RER: Musée d'Orsay.*

★ 39 **Musée Rodin.** The Faubourg St-Germain, studded with private mansions owned by the aristocracy and the rich, remains for the most part behind closed gates, but get a peek at this fabled neighborhood by visiting the 18th-century Hôtel Biron, onetime home of the sculptor Auguste Rodin and today a gracious stage for his work. In back is a pretty garden with Rodin works and hundreds of rosebushes. ✉ *77 rue de Varenne, 7e* ☎ *01–44–18–61–10* ⏲ *Easter–Oct., Tues.–Sun. 9:30–5:45; Nov.–Easter, Tues.–Sun. 9:30–4:45* Ⓜ *Varenne.*

37 **St-Germain-des-Prés.** The oldest church in Paris was first built to shelter a relic of the true cross, brought back from Spain in AD 542. The chancel was enlarged and the church consecrated by Pope Alexander III in 1163; the church tower also dates from this period. ✉ *Pl. St-Germain-des-Prés, 6e* ⏲ *Weekdays 8–7:30, weekends 8 AM–9 PM* Ⓜ *St-Germain-des-Prés.*

36 **St-Sulpice.** Dubbed the "Cathedral of the Left Bank," this enormous 17th-century church is of note for the powerful Delacroix frescoes in the first chapel on the right. The 18th-century facade was never finished, and its unequal towers add a playful touch to an otherwise sober design. ✉ *Pl. St-Sulpice, 6e* Ⓜ *St-Sulpice.*

Montmartre

On a dramatic rise above the city is Montmartre, site of the Sacré-Coeur Basilica (try to catch a sunset or sunrise over Paris from its terrace) and a once-thriving artistic community. Visiting Montmartre means negotiating a lot of steep streets and flights of steps. Some of the avenues are now totally given over to the tourist trade, but if you wander and follow your nose, you can still find quiet corners that retain the poetry that once allured Toulouse-Lautrec and other great artists.

★ 44 **Au Lapin Agile.** One of the most picturesque spots in Paris, this legendary bar-cabaret (open nights only) is a miraculous survivor from the 19th century. Founded in 1860, its adorable maison-cottage was a favorite subject of painter Maurice Utrillo, and it soon became the home-away-from-home for Braque, Modigliani, Apollinaire, Vlaminck, and most famously, Picasso. ✉ *22 rue des Saules, 18e* ☎ *01–46–06–85–87* 🌐 *www.au-lapin-agile.com* ⏲ *Tues.–Sun. 9 PM–2 AM* 🎫 *€20* ⏲ *Tues.–Sat. 9 PM–2 AM* Ⓜ *Lamarck-Caulaincourt.*

45 **Cimetière du Père-Lachaise** (Father Lachaise Cemetery). This cemetery forms a veritable necropolis with cobbled avenues and tombs competing in pomposity and originality. Leading incumbents include Frédéric Chopin, Marcel Proust, Jim Morrison, Edith Piaf, and Gertrude Stein. Get a map at the entrance and track them down. ✉ *Entrances on rue des Rondeaux, bd. de Ménilmontant, and rue de la Réunion; 18e* ⏲ *Apr.–Sept., daily 8–6; Oct.–Mar., daily 8–5* Ⓜ *Père-Lachaise, Gambetta, Philippe-Auguste.*

43 **Musée de Montmartre.** In its turn-of-the-20th-century heyday, Montmartre's historical museum quartered an illustrious group of painters, writers, and assorted cabaret artists. ✉ *12 rue Cortot, 18e* ☎ *01–46–06–61–11* ⏲ *Tues.–Sun. 11–6* Ⓜ *Lamarck-Caulaincourt.*

42 **Place des Abbesses.** This triangular square is typical of the picturesque, slightly countrified style that has made Montmartre famous. The entrance to the Abbesses métro station, a curving, sensuous mass of delicate iron, is one of Guimard's two original art nouveau entrance canopies left in Paris. The innovative brick-and-concrete art nouveau church of St-Jean de Montmartre overlooks the square. Ⓜ *Abbesses.*

41 **Sacré-Coeur.** Often compared to a "sculpted cloud" atop Montmartre, the Sacred Heart Basilica was erected as a sort of national guilt offer-

ing in expiation for the blood shed during the Paris Commune and Franco-Prussian War in 1870–71, and was largely financed by French Catholics fearful of an anticlerical backlash under the new republican regime. Stylistically, the somewhat bizarre Sacré-Coeur borrows elements from Romanesque and Byzantine models. The gloomy, cavernous interior is worth visiting for its golden mosaics; climb to the top of the dome for the view of Paris. ✉ *Pl. du Parvis-du-Sacré-Coeur, 18e* 🌐 *www.sacre-coeur-montmartre.com* Ⓜ *Anvers.*

12

WHERE TO EAT

Forget the Louvre, the Tour Eiffel, and the Bateaux Mouches—the real reason for a visit to Paris is to dine at its famous temples of gastronomy. Whether you get knee-deep in white truffles at Alain Ducasse or merely discover pistachioed sausage (the poor man's caviar) at a classic corner bistro, you'll discover that food here is an obsession, an art, a subject of endless debate. And if the lobster soufflé is delicious, the historic ambience is often more so. Just request Empress Josephine's table at Le Grand Véfour and find out.

WHAT IT COSTS In euros

	$$$$	$$$	$$	$
PER PERSON	over €38	€24–€38	€14–€23	under €14

Prices are per person for a main course. Note that when prices are quoted for a restaurant that offers only prix-fixe (set-price) meals, it is given a price category that reflects this prix-fixe price, which includes tax (19.6%) and gratuity.

Right Bank

★ $$$$ ✕ **Alain Ducasse.** You would be hard-pressed to catch the busy Alain Ducasse here these days, but it would probably be worth the wait. The rosy rococo salons have been draped with metallic organza over the chandeliers and, in a symbolic move, time stands still since all the clocks have been stopped. Overlooking the prettiest courtyard in Paris, the view is as delicious as the roast lamb garnished with "crumbs" of dried fruit or duckling roasted with fig leaves. For the price, the presentation—there are few sauce "paintings," orchid blossoms, or other visual adornments on the plate—could be enhanced. ✉ *Hotel Plaza-Athénée, 27 av. Montaigne, 8e* ☎ *01–53–67–66–65* *Reservations essential* 💳 *AE, DC, MC, V* ⏲ *Closed Sat. and Sun. No lunch Mon.–Wed.* Ⓜ *Alma-Marceau.*

★ $$$$ ✕ **Les Ambassadeurs.** Looking as if Madame de Pompadour might stroll in the door at any moment, Les Ambassadeurs offers a world of Versailles-like splendor with its marble, colored marble, even more colored marble, and gilt chandeliers. Chef Dominique Bouchet likes to mix luxe with more down-to-earth flavors: potato pancakes topped with smoked salmon, caviar-flecked scallops wrapped in bacon with tomato and basil, duck with rutabaga, turbot with cauliflower. The €62 lunch menu is well worth the splurge. ✉ *Hôtel Crillon, 10 pl. de la Concorde, 8e* ☎ *01–44–71–16–16* *Reservations essential* *Jacket and tie* 💳 *AE, DC, MC, V* Ⓜ *Concorde.*

$$$$ Fodor's Choice ★ ✕ **Le Grand Véfour.** Originally built in 1784, in the arcades of the Palais-Royal, this place is still a contender for the prize of Most Beautiful Restaurant in Paris, thanks to its 19th-century painted-glass and gilt setting. Everyone from Napoléon to Jean Cocteau has dined beneath the gilded boiseries—nearly every seat bears a plaque commemorating a famous patron. Chef Guy Martin hails from Savoie, so you'll find lake fish and

mountain cheeses on the menu alongside such luxurious dishes as foie gras–stuffed raviolis. ✉ *17 rue Beaujolais, 1er* ☎ *01–42–96–56–27* *Reservations essential* *Jacket and tie* ▭ *AE, DC, MC, V* ⊙ *Closed weekends and Aug. No dinner Fri.* Ⓜ *Palais-Royal.*

★ $$$$ ✕ **Taillevent.** Once the most traditional of all Paris luxury restaurants, this grande dame is suddenly the object of an uncharacteristic buzz, with the departure of chef Michel Del Burgo and the arrival of Alain Solivérès. Service is flawless, the 19th-century paneled salons *luxe,* the well-priced wine list probably one of the top 10 in the world—all in all, a meal here is an event. Reserve a month in advance. ✉ *15 rue Lamennais, 8e* ☎ *01–44–95–15–01* *Reservations essential* *Jacket and tie* ▭ *AE, DC, MC, V* ⊙ *Closed weekends and Aug.* Ⓜ *Charles-de-Gaulle–Étoile.*

★ $$$–$$$$ ✕ **Les Élysées du Vernet.** This may be the most perfect choice for a classique blowout in Paris today, thanks to its remarkable harmonic alignment of staff, decor, and kitchen. Chef Eric Briffard triumphs with his foie gras on toast or monkfish with ginger and lime, and the dining room is graced by a magnificently beautiful *verrière* (glass ceiling) designed by Gustave Eiffel himself. This restaurant remains relatively affordable at lunch (€45 or €60 for a set menu), the wine service is outstanding, and all departing women diners are given a rose. ✉ *Hôtel Vernet, 25 rue Vernet, 8e* ☎ *01–44–31–98–98* *Reservations essential* ▭ *AE, DC, MC, V* ⊙ *Closed weekends, Aug., and 2 wks in Dec.* Ⓜ *George-V.*

$$$–$$$$ ✕ **Spoon, Food and Wine.** Alain Ducasse's blueprint of a bistro for the 21st century has a do-it-yourself fusion-food menu that allows you to mix and match dishes diversely American, Asian, and Italian in origin. Sign of the future? There are many salads and vegetable and grain dishes on the menu. Reservations are coveted—call a month ahead—but you can always drop in for a snack at the bar. Come late for the models and movie stars. ✉ *14 rue de Marignan, 8^e^* ☎ *01–40–76–34–44* *Reservations essential* ▭ *AE, MC, V* Ⓜ *Franklin-D.-Roosevelt.*

★ $$–$$$ ✕ **L'Astrance.** *Le Point* has called L'Astrance "a miracle," and *Le Figaro* has described it as "perfect." Much of the excitement may boil down to the fact that you get the quality of haute cuisine here without the pomposity or the crushing price tag. The food—avocado-and-crab mille-feuille, a ballotine of quail and foie gras, spiced mackerel fillet on Asian-style spinach—is fantastic. ✉ *4 rue Beethoven, 16^e^* ☎ *01–40–50–84–40* *Reservations essential* ▭ *AE, DC, MC, V* ⊙ *Closed Mon., 3 wks in Aug., and Dec. 22–Jan. 3. No lunch Tues.* Ⓜ *Passy.*

$$–$$$ ✕ **Bofinger.** Settle in to one of the tables dressed in crisp white linens, under the gorgeous art nouveau glass cupola, and enjoy fine classic brasserie fare, such as oysters, grilled sole, or fillet of lamb. Note that the no-smoking section here is not only enforced but is also in the prettiest part of the restaurant. ✉ *5–7 rue de la Bastille, 4e* ☎ *01–42–72–87–82* ▭ *AE, DC, MC, V* Ⓜ *Bastille.*

$$–$$$ ✕ **La Fermette Marbeuf.** This magically beautiful belle epoque room—accidentally rediscovered during renovations in the 1970s—is a favorite haunt of French celebrities who adore the art nouveau mosaic and stained-glass mise-en-scène. The menu rolls out a solid, updated classic cuisine, such as the snails in puff pastry or the saddle of lamb with *choron* (a tomato-spiked béarnaise sauce). ✉ *5 rue Marbeuf, 8e* ☎ *01–53–23–08–00* ▭ *AE, DC, MC, V* Ⓜ *Franklin-D.-Roosevelt.*

$$–$$$ ✕ **Le Safran.** Passionate chef Caroll Sinclair works almost exclusively with organic produce—red mullet stuffed with cèpes mushrooms and *gigot de sept heures* (leg of lamb cooked for seven hours) are two of her signature dishes. The little room is pretty, intimate, and painted in sunny saffron. ✉ *29 rue d'Argenteuil, 1er* ☎ *01–42–61–25–30* ▭ *MC, V* ⊙ *Closed Sun. and 2 wks in Sept. No lunch Sat.* Ⓜ *Tuileries, Pyramides.*

★ $$ ✕ **L'Ardoise.** This minuscule white storefront, decorated with enlargements of old sepia postcards of Paris, is the model of contemporary bistros making waves in the city. Chef Pierre Jay's first-rate three-course menu (€30) includes a crab flan in a creamy parsley emulsion and fresh cod with grilled chorizo chips on a bed of mashed potatoes. With friendly service and a short but well-chosen wine list, L'Ardoise would be perfect if it weren't often crowded and noisy. ✉ *28 rue du Mont Thabor, 1er* ☎ *01–42–96–28–18* ✍ *Reservations essential* ▭ *MC, V* ⊙ *Closed Mon., Tues., and Aug.* Ⓜ *Concorde.*

$$ ✕ **La Grande Armée.** The Costes brothers tapped superstar Jacques Garcia to design this brasserie near the Arc de Triomphe. Here he's unleashed an exotic Napoléon-III bordello decor—think black lacquered tables, leopard upholstery, Bordeaux velvet—for a carefully tousled clientele picking at salads, pastas, and soothing potato puree. ✉ *3 av. de la Grande Armée, 16e* ☎ *01–45–00–24–77* ▭ *AE, DC, MC, V* Ⓜ *Charles-de-Gaulle–Étoile.*

$–$$ ✕ **Café Runtz.** Next to the noted theater of Salle Favart, this friendly bistro is still gleaming from Jacques Garcia's late 1990s Weinstube makeover. Old brass gas lamps on each table and rich woodwork create a cozy, Flaubertian atmosphere. Tasty, hearty Alsatian dishes include Gruyère salad, onion tart, choucroute, and fresh fruit tarts. ✉ *16 rue Favart, 2e* ☎ *01–42–96–69–86* ▭ *AE, MC, V* ⊙ *Closed Sun. and Aug.* Ⓜ *Richelieu-Drouot.*

$ ✕ **Chartier.** This cavernous 1896 restaurant enjoys a huge following among budget-minded students, solitary bachelors, and tourists. You may find yourself sharing a table with strangers as you study the long, old-fashioned menu of such favorites as hard-boiled eggs with mayonnaise, steak tartare, and roast chicken with fries. ✉ *7 rue du Faubourg-Montmartre, 9^e^* ☎ *01–47–70–86–29* ✍ *Reservations not accepted* ▭ *AE, DC, MC, V* Ⓜ *Montmartre.*

$ ✕ **Le Kitch.** Fighting the good fight against ennui, this fun place is a favorite in the arty Bastille neighborhood. There's more than a touch of Pee-Wee's Playhouse here, thanks to the faux-stucco walls, plastic children's furniture, and naïf paintings of cats. The food here is mainly snacky—expect pastas and sandwiches, or a bagel with *tapenade.* ✉ *10 rue Oberkampf, 11e* ☎ *01–40–21–94–14* ▭ *No credit cards* ⊙ *No lunch weekends* Ⓜ *Oberkampf.*

$ ✕ **Ladurée.** Pretty enough to bring a tear to Proust's eye, this ravishing *salon de thé* (tea salon) looks barely changed from 1862. You'll dote on the signature lemon-and-caramel macaroons (there are other outposts at 75 av. des Champs-Élysées and on the Left Bank at 21 rue Bonaparte). ✉ *16 rue Royale, 8e* ☎ *01–42–60–21–79* ▭ *AE, MC, V* Ⓜ *Madeleine.*

Left Bank

$$$–$$$$ ✕ **Hélène Darroze.** Hélène Darroze has been crowned the newest female culinary star in Paris, thanks to the creative flair she has given the tried-and-true classics of southwestern French cooking, from the lands around Albi and Toulouse. You know it's not going to be *la même chanson*—the same old song—when you spot the resolutely contemporary Tse & Tse tableware and red-and-purple color scheme. The downside? Some carp that the portions are small and the service could be much better, so you might opt for the downstairs bistro, which offers the same dishes but in even smaller, tapas-style portions. ✉ *4 rue d'Assas, 6e* ☎ *01–42–22–00–11* ▭ *AE, DC, MC, V* ⊙ *Closed Sun. and Mon.* Ⓜ *Sèvres-Babylone.*

★ $$$–$$$$ ✕ **Lapérouse.** Emile Zola, George Sand, and Victor Hugo were regulars, and the restaurant's mirrors still bear diamond scratches from the days when mistresses didn't take jewels at face value. It's hard not to fall in love with this 17th-century Seine-side town house, whose warren of intimate, boiserie-graced salons breathes history. The latest chef, Alain Hacquard, has found the right track with a daring (for Paris) spice-infused menu. ✉ *51 quai des Grands-Augustins, 5ᵉ* ☎ *01–43–26–68–04* *Reservations essential* ▭ *AE, DC, MC, V* ⊙ *Closed Sun., 3 wks in July, and 1 wk in Aug. No lunch Sat.* Ⓜ *St-Michel.*

★ $$$ ✕ **La Régalade.** As the leading priest who marries bistro and nouvelle cookery—who can resist his soup of lentils and puréed chestnuts poured over a mound of foie gras?—Yves Camdeborde has to satisfy the hordes who trek to the edge of town here in Montparnasse for three dinner sittings (and you still have to book at least two weeks ahead). The room, disappointingly, is no-frills. ✉ *49 av. Jean-Moulin, 14ᵉ* ☎ *01–45–45–68–58* *Reservations essential* ▭ *MC, V* ⊙ *Closed Sun., Mon., and Aug. No lunch Sat.* Ⓜ *Alésia.*

★ $$–$$$ ✕ **Au Bon Accueil.** To see what well-heeled Parisians eat these days, book a table here as soon as you get to town. The excellent, reasonably priced *cuisine du marché* (a daily, market-inspired menu, €25 at lunch and €29 at dinner) has made it a hit: typical of the winter fare is roast suckling pig with thyme and endives. ✉ *14 rue de Montessuy, 7ᵉ* ☎ *01–47–05–46–11* *Reservations essential* ▭ *MC, V* ⊙ *Closed weekends and 2 wks in Aug.* Ⓜ *Pont de l'Alma.*

$$–$$$ ✕ **Brasserie de l'Ile St-Louis.** On picturesque Ile St-Louis, this outpost of Alsatian cuisine turns out *coq-au-Riesling,* omelets with Muenster cheese, and onion tarts. In warm weather, the crowds move out to the terrace overlooking the Seine and Notre-Dame. ✉ *55 quai de Bourbon, 4ᵉ* ☎ *01–43–54–02–59* ▭ *MC, V* ⊙ *Closed Wed. and Aug. No lunch Thurs.* Ⓜ *Pont Marie.*

$$–$$$ ✕ **La Coupole.** This world-renowned, cavernous spot in Montparnasse practically defines the term brasserie. It might have lost its intellectual aura since restoration (the art deco murals look better than ever), but La Coupole has been popular since the days when Jean-Paul Sartre and Simone de Beauvoir were regulars and is still great fun. Expect the usual brasserie menu—including perhaps the largest shellfish platter in Paris—choucroute, and over-the-top desserts. ✉ *102 bd. du Montparnasse, 14ᵉ* ☎ *01–43–20–14–20* ▭ *AE, DC, MC, V* Ⓜ *Vavin.*

★ $$ ✕ **Ze Kitchen Galerie.** If the name isn't exactly inspired, the cooking shows unbridled creativity and a sense of fun. From a deliberately deconstructed menu featuring raw fish, soups, pastas, and "à la plancha" plates, expect dishes such as a chicken wing, broccoli, and artichoke soup with lemongrass, or pork ribs with curry jus and white beans. All in all, one of the most mouth-tickling kitchens in the city. ✉ *4 quai des Grands-Augustins, 6ᵉ* ☎ *01–44–32–00–32* ▭ *AE, DC, MC, V* ⊙ *Closed Sun. No lunch Sat.* Ⓜ *St-Michel.*

$–$$ ✕ **Le Café des Délices.** There is a lot to like about this Montparnasse bistro, from the warm Asia-meets-Africa interior, with little pots of spices on each table, to the polished service and lip-smacking food. Drop in for the bargain €14 lunch, or indulge in à la carte dishes such as sea bream on white beans cooked with anchovy, lemon, coriander, and chili pepper. ✉ *87 rue d'Assas, 6ᵉ* ☎ *01–43–54–70–00* ▭ *AE, MC, V* ⊙ *Closed Aug.* Ⓜ *Vavin.*

★ $ ✕ **Les Pipos.** The tourist-trap restaurants along romantic rue de la Montagne Ste-Genevieve are enough to make you despair—and then you stumble across this corner bistro, bursting with chatter and laughter. Slang for students of the École Polytechnique nearby, Les Pipos is everything you could ask of a Latin Quarter bistro: the space is cramped, the food substantial, and conversation flows as freely as the wine. ✉ *2 rue de*

L'Ecole-Polytechnique, 5ᵉ ☎ *01–43–54–11–40* ▭ *No credit cards* ⊙ *Closed Sun. and 2 wks. in Aug.* Ⓜ *Maubert-Mutualité.*

WHERE TO STAY

It's always a good idea to make hotel reservations in Paris as far in advance as possible, especially in late spring, summer, or fall. If you arrive without a reservation, tourist offices in major train stations and most towns may be able to find a hotel for you.

WHAT IT COSTS In euros				
	$$$$	**$$$**	**$$**	**$**
FOR 2 PEOPLE	over €250	€150–€250	€100–€150	under €100

Prices are for standard double rooms in high season and include tax (19.6%) and service charges.

Right Bank

$$$$ **Costes.** Baron de Rothschild hasn't invited you this time? No matter—just stay here at Jean-Louis and Gilbert Costes's sumptuous hotel and you won't know the difference. The darling of the fashion and media set, the place conjures up the palaces of Napoléon III, with stunning rooms swathed in rich garnet and bronze tones and luxurious fabrics. ✉ *239 rue St-Honoré, 75001* ☎ *01–42–44–50–50* 🖷 *01–42–44–50–01* 🌐 *www.hotelcostes.com* *77 rooms, 5 suites* *Restaurant, pool, bar* ▭ *AE, DC, MC, V* Ⓜ *Tuileries.*

★ **$$$$** **Crillon.** The Crillon began life as a regal palace designed for Louis XV in 1758 by Jacques-Ange Gabriel to preside over the north side of the fabled place de la Concorde. In 1909 it became a hostelry and since then has played host to generations of diplomats, celebrities, and refined travelers. Most rooms are lavishly decorated with rococo and Directoire antiques, crystal-and-gilt wall sconces, and gilt fittings. The sheer quantity of marble downstairs—especially in highly praised Les Ambassadeurs restaurant—is staggering. ✉ *10 pl. de la Concorde, 75008* ☎ *01–44–71–15–00; 800/888–4747 in the U.S.* 🖷 *01–44–71–15–02* 🌐 *www.crillon.com* *90 rooms, 57 suites* *2 restaurants, 2 bars* ▭ *AE, DC, MC, V* Ⓜ *Concorde.*

★ **$$$$** **Meurice.** One of the finest hotels in the world is now even finer, thanks to the multimillion-dollar face-lift funded by the Sultan of Brunei. Few salons are as splendorous as the famous dining room here—all gilt boiseries, pink roses, and Edwardian crystal—and guest rooms, furnished with Persian carpets, marble mantelpieces, and ormolu clocks, are now more soigné than ever. ✉ *228 rue de Rivoli, 75001* ☎ *01–44–58–10–10* 🖷 *01–44–58–10–15* 🌐 *www.meuricehotel.com* *160 rooms, 36 suites* *2 restaurants, bar* ▭ *AE, DC, MC, V* Ⓜ *Tuileries, Concorde.*

★ **$$$$** **Pavillon de la Reine.** This magnificent hotel, filled with Louis XIII–style fireplaces and antiques, is in a mansion reconstructed from original 17th-century plans. Ask for a duplex with French windows overlooking the first of two flower-filled courtyards behind the historic Queen's Pavilion. ✉ *28 pl. des Vosges, 75003* ☎ *01–40–29–19–19; 800/447–7462 in the U.S.* 🖷 *01–40–29–19–20* 🌐 *www.pavillon-de-la-reine.com* *30 rooms, 25 suites* *Bar* ▭ *AE, DC, MC, V* Ⓜ *Bastille, St-Paul.*

$$$ **Axial Beaubourg.** A solid bet in the Marais, this hotel in a 16th-century building has beamed ceilings in the lobby and in the six first-floor rooms. A top-to-bottom reworking has resulted in a sleeker, hipper interior, with higher prices to match the fancy brown fabrics and added amenities. The Centre Pompidou and the Picasso Museum are five minutes away. ✉ *11 rue du Temple, 75004* ☎ *01–42–72–72–22* 🖷 *01–42–72–03–53* 🌐 *www.axialbeaubourg.com* *39 rooms* 💳 *AE, DC, MC, V* Ⓜ *Hôtel-de-Ville.*

★ $$–$$$ **Caron de Beaumarchais.** The theme of this intimate jewel is the work of Caron de Beaumarchais, who wrote *The Marriage of Figaro* in 1778. Rooms are faithfully decorated to reflect the taste of 18th-century French nobility. The second- and fifth-floor rooms with balconies are the largest; those on the sixth floor have views across Right Bank rooftops. ✉ *12 rue Vieille-du-Temple, 75004* ☎ *01–42–72–34–12* 🖷 *01–42–72–34–63* 🌐 *www.carondebeaumarchais.com* *19 rooms* 💳 *AE, DC, MC, V* Ⓜ *Hôtel-de-Ville.*

$$–$$$ **Deux-Iles.** A tiny Ile St-Louis hotel, the best asset of the Deux-Iles is its lovely neighborhood setting. With red-and-gold floral fabrics and contemporary art on the walls, the rooms unsuccessfully try to mix modern and 17th-century fashions. Ask for one overlooking the little garden courtyard. In winter a roaring fire warms the basement lounge. ✉ *59 rue St-Louis-en-l'Ile, 75004* ☎ *01–43–26–13–35* 🖷 *01–43–29–60–25* 🌐 *www.hotel-ile-saintlouis.com* *17 rooms* 💳 *AE, MC, V* Ⓜ *Pont-Marie.*

★ $$–$$$ **Étoile-Péreire.** Behind a quiet, leafy courtyard in the chic residential district of Parc Monceau is this unique, intimate hotel, consisting of two parts: a fin-de-siècle building on the street and a 1920s annex overlooking an interior courtyard. All of the rooms have individually decorated period or cultural themes. The copious breakfast is legendary, featuring 40 assorted jams and jellies. ✉ *146 bd. Péreire, 75017* ☎ *01–42–67–60–00* 🖷 *01–42–67–02–90* 🌐 *www.etoileper.com* *21 rooms, 5 suites* *Bar* 💳 *AE, DC, MC, V* Ⓜ *Péreire.*

$$ **Bretonnerie.** This small hotel is in a 17th-century *hôtel particulier* (town house) on a tiny street in the Marais. Rooms are done in Louis XIII style, complete with upholstered walls, but vary considerably in size from spacious to cramped. ✉ *22 rue Ste-Croix-de-la-Bretonnerie, 75004* ☎ *01–48–87–77–63* 🖷 *01–42–77–26–78* 🌐 *www.labretonnerie.com* *22 rooms, 7 suites* 💳 *MC, V* Ⓜ *Hôtel-de-Ville.*

$$ **Place des Vosges.** A loyal, eclectic clientele swears by this small, historic Marais hotel on a delightful street just off place des Vosges. The Louis XIII–style reception area and rooms with oak-beamed ceilings, rough-hewn stone, and a mix of rustic finds from secondhand shops evoke the old Marais. ✉ *12 rue de Birague, 75004* ☎ *01–42–72–60–46* 🖷 *01–42–72–02–64* *16 rooms* 💳 *AE, DC, MC, V* Ⓜ *Bastille.*

★ $–$$ **Queen's Hôtel.** One of a handful of hotels in the tony residential district near the Bois de Boulogne, Queen's is a small, comfortable, old-fashioned hotel with a high standard of service. Each room focuses on a different 20th-century French artist. ✉ *4 rue Bastien-Lepage, 75016* ☎ *01–42–88–89–85* 🖷 *01–40–50–67–52* 🌐 *www.queens-hotel.fr* *21 rooms, 1 suite* 💳 *AE, DC, MC, V* Ⓜ *Michel-Ange Auteuil.*

$ **Louvre Forum.** This friendly hotel is a find: smack in the center of town, it has clean, comfortable, well-equipped rooms at extremely reasonable prices. ✉ *25 rue du Bouloi, 75001* ☎ *01–42–36–54–19* 🖷 *01–42–33–66–31* 🌐 *www.hotellouvreforum.com* *27 rooms, 16 with shower* *Bar* 💳 *AE, DC, MC, V* Ⓜ *Louvre.*

$ **Tiquetonne.** Just off marché Montorgueil and a short hoof from Les Halles, this is one of the least expensive hotels in the city center. The rooms aren't much to look at, but they're always clean. Book a room facing the quiet, pedestrian rue Tiquetonne, not the loud rue Turbigo. ✉ *6 rue Tiquetonne, 75002* ☎ *01–42–36–94–58* 🖷 *01–42–36–02–94* *45 rooms* 💳 *AE, MC, V* Ⓜ *Etienne Marcel or Châtelet.*

Left Bank

$$$$ **Pont Royal.** Once a favorite watering hole of T. S. Eliot and Gabriel Garcia Marquez, this sumptuously refurbished hotel now attracts more businessmen than writers. You can't find a more comfortable hotel, however, or a better location—a quiet street just off boulevard St-Germain. The views from the top floors are magnificent. The library-themed bar resembles a British reading room, and the Atelier Joël Robuchon restaurant is a popular luncheon spot among well-heeled locals. ✉ *7 rue de Montalembert, 75007* ☎ *01–42–84–70–00* 📠 *01–42–84–71–00* 🌐 *www.hotel-pont-royal.com/hpr* *65 rooms, 10 suites* *Restaurant, bar* 💳 *AE, DC, MC, V* Ⓜ *Rue de Bac.*

★ $$$–$$$$ **Hôtel d'Aubusson.** This 17th-century mansion, once setting to Paris's first literary salon, is now one of the finest *petites hôtels de luxe* in the city, with original Aubusson tapestries, Versailles-style parquet floors, and a chiseled stone fireplace. Even the small rooms are good size by Paris standards, and all are decked out in rich burgundies, greens, or blues. The 10 best rooms have canopied beds and ceiling beams. In summer, you can have your breakfast or predinner drink in the paved courtyard. ✉ *33 rue Dauphine, 75006* ☎ *01–43–29–43–43* 📠 *01–43–29–12–62* 🌐 *www.hoteldaubusson.com* *49 rooms* *Bar* 💳 *AE, MC, V* Ⓜ *Odéon.*

★ $$$–$$$$ **Relais St-Germain.** With a gracious staff and all the countrified flowers, beams, and flea-market finds you could dream of, the Relais St-Germain oozes with traditional 17th-century flavor. The rooms, done in bright yellow-and-red printed fabrics and paints, are at least twice the size of what you find at other hotels for the same price. Breakfast is included. ✉ *9 carrefour de l'Odéon, 75006* ☎ *01–43–29–12–05* 📠 *01–46–33–45–30* 🌐 *www.hotel-rsg.com* *21 rooms, 1 suite* *Bar* 💳 *AE, DC, MC, V* Ⓜ *Odéon.*

$$$ **Grands Hommes.** The "Great Men" this hotel has in mind are resting in peace in the Panthéon, which the Grands Hommes overlooks. The hotel's look is neo-Greek and Roman, combining plaster busts, urns, and laurel-wreath motifs with plush beige, eggplant, and burgundy fabrics. Top-floor rooms have balconies and fantastic north-facing views of the cityscape. ✉ *17 pl. du Panthéon, 75005* ☎ *01–46–34–19–60* 📠 *01–43–26–67–32* 🌐 *www.hoteldesgrandshommes.com* *31 rooms* 💳 *AE, DC, MC, V* Ⓜ *RER: Luxembourg.*

$$$ **Latour Maubourg.** In the residential heart of the 7e arrondissement, this homey and unpretentious town house accents intimacy and personalized service. Its simply furnished rooms have antique armoires, marble fireplaces, and high ceilings. ✉ *150 rue de Grenelle, 75007* ☎ *01–47–05–16–16* 📠 *01–47–05–16–14* 🌐 *www.latour-maubourg.fr* *9 rooms, 1 suite* 💳 *MC, V* Ⓜ *La Tour–Maubourg.*

★ $$$ **Relais Saint-Sulpice.** A savvy clientele frequents this fashionable little hotel sandwiched between place St-Sulpice and the Luxembourg Gardens. Eclectic art objects and furnishings, some with an Asian theme, somehow pull off a unified look. The rooms, set around an ivy-clad courtyard, are understated, with simple colors and comfortable furnishings. There's a sauna downstairs, right off the breakfast salon. ✉ *3 rue Garancière, 75006* ☎ *01–46–33–99–00* 📠 *01–46–33–00–10* *26 rooms* 💳 *AE, DC, MC, V* Ⓜ *St-Germain-des-Prés, St-Sulpice.*

$$ **Bonaparte.** The congeniality of the staff only makes a stay in this intimate place more of a treat. Old-fashioned upholsteries, 19th-century furnishings, and paintings create a quaint feel in the relatively spacious rooms. And a night in the heart of St-Germain is incomparable. ✉ *61 rue Bonaparte, 75006* ☎ *01–43–26–97–37* 📠 *01–46–33–57–67* *29 rooms* 💳 *MC, V* Ⓜ *St-Germain-des-Prés.*

$$ Grandes Écoles. Distributed among a trio of three-story buildings, the baby-blue-and-white rooms and their flowery Louis-Philippe furnishings create a grandmotherly vibe, which may not be to everyone's taste. But the verdant interior courtyard can be your second living room or a perfect breakfast spot. *✉ 75 rue du Cardinal-Lemoine, 75005 ☎ 01-43-26-79-23 🖷 01-43-25-28-15 🌐 www.hotel-grandes-ecoles.com 51 rooms ▭ MC, V Ⓜ Cardinal-Lemoine.*

$$ Hôtel du Lys. Just climb the convoluted stairway to your room (there's no elevator) in this former 17th-century royal residence, one of the city's oldest. Well maintained by Madame Steffen, the hotel's rooms reveal unique quirks and nooks, weathered antiques and exposed beams throughout. *✉ 23 rue Serpente 75006 ☎ 01-43-26-97-57 🖷 01-44-07-34-90 🌐 www.hoteldulys.com 22 rooms ▭ MC, V Ⓜ St-Michel, Odéon.*

$$ Jardin du Luxembourg. Blessed with a charming staff and a stylish look, this hotel is one of the most sought-after in the Latin Quarter. Rooms are a bit small (common for this neighborhood) but intelligently furnished for optimal space, and warmly decorated *à la Provençal.* Ask for one with a balcony overlooking the street. *✉ 5 impasse Royer-Collard, 75005 ☎ 01-40-46-08-88 🖷 01-40-46-02-28 27 rooms ▭ AE, DC, MC, V Ⓜ Luxembourg.*

★ $$ Le Tourville. Here is a rare find: an intimate, upscale hotel at affordable prices. Each room has crisp, virgin-white damask upholstery set against pastel or ocher walls, a smattering of antiques, original artwork, and fabulous old mirrors. *✉ 16 av. de Tourville, 75007 ☎ 01-47-05-62-62; 800/528-3549 in the U.S. 🖷 01-47-05-43-90 🌐 www.hoteltourville.com 27 rooms, 3 suites Bar ▭ AE, DC, MC, V Ⓜ École Militaire.*

$-$$ Familia. The hospitable Gaucheron family bends over backward for you. The rooms are snazzed up with murals of typical city scenes, and bathrooms have modern fixtures and tilework. Book a month ahead for one with a walk-out balcony on the second or fifth floor. *✉ 11 rue des Écoles, 75005 ☎ 01-43-54-55-27 🖷 01-43-29-61-77 🌐 www.hotel-paris-familia.com 30 rooms ▭ AE, MC, V Ⓜ Cardinal-Lemoine.*

$ Hotel du Parc Montsouris. This modest hotel in a 1930s villa is on a quiet residential street next to the lovely Parc Montsouris on the southern edge of the city. Attractive oak pieces and high-quality French fabrics embellish the small but clean rooms. *✉ 4 rue du Parc-Montsouris, 75014 ☎ 01-45-89-09-72 🖷 01-45-80-92-72 🌐 www.hotel-parc-montsouris.com 28 rooms, 7 suites ▭ AE, MC, V Ⓜ Montparnasse-Bienvenue.*

NIGHTLIFE & THE ARTS

For detailed entertainment listings, look for the weekly magazines *Pariscope, L'Officiel des Spectacles, Zurban,* and *Figaroscope.* The **Paris Tourist Office** (☎ 08-92-68-31-12 for 24-hr English-language hot line 🌐 www.parisbienvenu.com) is a good source of information about weekly events.

Tickets can be purchased at the place of performance (beware of scalpers: counterfeit tickets have been sold); otherwise, try your hotel or a travel agency such as **Opéra Théâtre** (✉ 7 rue de Clichy, 9e ☎ 01-40-06-01-00 Ⓜ Trinité). For most concerts, tickets can be bought at the music store **FNAC** (✉ 1-5 rue Pierre-Lescot, Forum des Halles, 1er ☎ 01-49-87-50-50 Ⓜ Châtelet–Les Halles). **Virgin Megastore** (✉ 52 av. des Champs-Élysées, 8e ☎ 08-03-02-30-24 Ⓜ Franklin-D.-Roosevelt) has a particularly convenient ticket booth. Half-price tickets for same-day theater performances are available at the **Kiosques Théâtre** (✉ across from 15 pl.

de la Madeleine Ⓜ Madeleine ✉ in front of the Gare Montparnasse, pl. Raoul Dautry, 14e Ⓜ Montparnasse-Bienvenüe). Both are open Tuesday–Saturday 12:30–8, Sunday 12:30–4. Expect to pay a €3 commission per ticket and to wait in line.

The Arts

Classical Music & Opera

Inexpensive organ or chamber music concerts take place in many churches throughout the city. Following are other venues for opera, orchestral concerts, and recitals. Classical- and world-music concerts are held at the **Cité de la Musique** (✉ 221 av. Jean-Jaurès, Parc de La Villette, 19e ☎ 01–44–84–44–84 Ⓜ Porte de Pantin). **Opéra de la Bastille** (✉ pl. de la Bastille, 12e ☎ 08–92–69–78–68 🌐 www.opera-de-paris.fr Ⓜ Bastille) is the main venue for opera; however, grand opera deserves a grand house (not the modern Bastille one), so you might plan your trip around dates when the troupe presents an opera at the historic Opéra Garnier, about twice a year. The Orchestre de Paris and other leading international orchestras play regularly at the **Salle Pleyel** (✉ 252 rue du Faubourg-St-Honoré, 8e ☎ 08–25–00–02–52 Ⓜ Ternes). **Théâtre des Champs-Élysées** (✉ 15 av. Montaigne, 8e ☎ 01–49–52–50–50 Ⓜ Alma-Marceau), an art deco temple, hosts concerts and ballet.

Dance

Opéra Garnier (✉ pl. de l'Opéra, 9e ☎ 08–92–69–78–68 🌐 www.opera-de-paris.fr Ⓜ Opéra), the "old Opéra," now concentrates on dance. In addition to being the home of the well-reputed Paris Ballet, it also bills a number of major foreign troupes. The **Théâtre de la Ville** (✉ 2 pl. du Châtelet, 4e Ⓜ Châtelet ✉ 31 rue des Abbesses, 18e Ⓜ Abbesses ☎ 01–42–74–22–77 for both 🌐 www.chatelet-theatre.com) is the place for contemporary dance.

Film

Paris has hundreds of cinemas. Admission is generally €7–€9, with reduced rates at some theaters on Monday. In principal tourist areas such as the Champs-Élysées and Les Halles, and on the boulevard des Italiens near the Opéra, theaters show English films marked *"version originale"* (v.o., i.e., not dubbed). Classics and independent films often play in Latin Quarter theaters. **Cinémathèque Française** (✉ 42 bd. de Bonne-Nouvelle, 10e ☎ 01–56–26–01–01 Ⓜ Bonne-Nouvelle ✉ Palais de Chaillot, 7 av. Albert-de-Mun, 16e ☎ 01–56–26–01–01 Ⓜ Trocadéro) shows classic French and international films Wednesday–Sunday.

Theater

A number of theaters line the Grand Boulevards between Opéra and République, but there is no Paris equivalent of Broadway or the West End. Shows are mostly in French. The **Comédie Française** (✉ pl. Colette, 1er ☎ 01–44–58–15–15 Ⓜ Palais-Royal) performs distinguished classical drama by the likes of Racine, Molière, and Corneille. The **Théâtre de la Huchette** (✉ 23 rue de la Huchette, 5e ☎ 01–43–26–38–99 Ⓜ St-Michel) is a tiny venue where Ionesco's short plays make a deliberately ridiculous mess of the French language. The **Odéon Théâtre de l'Europe** (✉ 8 bd. Berthier, 17e ☎ 01–44–85–40–40 Ⓜ Porte de Clichy) is undergoing extensive renovations at the moment and has moved to this Clichy address until 2005.

Nightlife

Bars & Clubs

The hottest area at the moment is around Ménilmontant and Parmentier, and the nightlife is still hopping in and around the Bastille. The Left Bank tends to be more subdued. The Champs-Élysées is making a strong comeback, though the crowd remains predominantly foreign. Gay and lesbian bars are mostly concentrated in the Marais (especially around rue Ste-Croix-de-la-Bretonnerie) and include some of the most happening addresses in the city.

If you want to dance the night away, some of the best clubs are the following: **Les Bains** (⊠ 7 rue du Bourg-l'Abbé, 3e ☎ 01–48–87–01–80 Ⓜ Étienne-Marcel) opened in 1978 and back in the disco era was often featured in French *Vogue*—believe it or not, this is still a hot ticket and difficult to get past the velvet rope. **Le Nouveau Casino** (⊠ 109 rue Oberkampf, 11e ☎ 01–43–57–57–40 Ⓜ St-Maur, Parmentier) will have you dancing until dawn in this electro-baroque atmosphere complete with Murano chandeliers. **Queen** (⊠ 102 av. des Champs-Élysées, 8e ☎ 01–53–89–08–90 Ⓜ George-V) is one of the hottest nightspots in Paris: although it's predominantly gay, everyone else lines up to get in, too.

Paris has many bars; following is a sampling. The famous brasserie **Alcazar** (⊠ 62 rue Mazarine, 6e ☎ 01–53–10–19–99 Ⓜ Odéon) comes complete with a stylish bar on the first floor, where you can sip a glass of wine under the huge glass roof. From Wednesday to Saturday a DJ spins either lounge or Latin music. Pop into the **Barrio Latino** (⊠ 46–48 rue du Faubourg-St-Antoine, 12e ☎ 01–55–78–84–75 Ⓜ Bastille) for Franco-Latino opulence—red velvet couches, wide, airy atrium, warm, sexy colors—in this three-story club. **Batofar** (⊠ 11 quai François-Mauriac, 11e ☎ 01–45–83–33–06 Ⓜ Quai-de-la-Gare) is an old lighthouse tug refitted to include a bar, a club, and a concert venue. **Café Charbon** (⊠ 109 rue Oberkampf, 11e ☎ 01–43–57–55–13 Ⓜ St-Maur/Parmentier) is in a beautifully restored 19th-century café. **Le Fumoir** (⊠ 6 rue Amiral-de-Coligny, 1er ☎ 01–42–92–00–24 Ⓜ Louvre) is a fashionable spot for cocktails, with comfy leather sofas and a library. **Polo Room** (⊠ 3 rue Lord-Byron, 8e ☎ 01–40–74–07–78 Ⓜ George-V) is the very first martini bar in Paris; there are polo photos on the walls, regular live jazz concerts, and DJs every Friday and Saturday night. **Wax** (⊠ 15 rue Daval, 11e ☎ 01–40–21–16–16 Ⓜ Bastille) is worth a visit simply for its decor—check out the orange-and-pink walls and the molded plastic banquettes by the window; DJs spin techno and house every evening.

Cabarets

Paris's cabarets are household names, shunned by Parisians and beloved of foreign tourists, who flock to the shows. Prices range from €40 (simple admission plus one drink) to more than €125 (dinner plus show). **Crazy Horse** (⊠ 12 av. George-V, 8e ☎ 01–47–23–32–32 Ⓜ Alma-Marceau) shows more bare skin than anyone else. **Lido** (⊠ 116 bis av. des Champs-Élysées, 8e ☎ 01–40–76–56–10 Ⓜ George-V) shows are oceans of feathers and sequins. **Moulin Rouge** (⊠ 82 bd. de Clichy, 18e ☎ 01–53–09–82–82 Ⓜ Blanche) has come a long way since the days of the cancan.

Jazz Clubs

Paris is one of the great jazz cities of the world. For nightly schedules consult the magazines *Jazz Hot, Jazzman,* or *Jazz Magazine.* Nothing gets going until 10 or 11 PM, and entry prices vary widely from about €10 to €25. **New Morning** (⊠ 7 rue des Petites-Écuries, 10e ☎ 01–45–23–51–41 Ⓜ Château-d'Eau) is a premier spot for serious fans of avant-garde jazz, folk, and world music. The greatest names in French and international jazz play at **Le Petit Journal** (✉ 71 bd. St-Michel, 5e ☎ 01–43–26–28–59 Ⓜ Luxembourg); it's closed Sunday.

Rock Clubs

Lists of upcoming concerts are posted on boards in the FNAC stores. Following are the best places to catch big French and international stars: **L'Élysée Montmartre** (✉ 72 bd. Rochechouart, 18e ☎ 01–55–07–06–00 Ⓜ Anvers) is one of the prime venues for emerging French and international rock groups. **L'Olympia** (✉ 28 bd. des Capucines, 9e ☎ 01–47–42–25–49 Ⓜ Opéra) once hosted legendary concerts by Jacques Brel and Edith Piaf, but the theater has since been completely rebuilt. **Palais Omnisports de Paris-Bercy** (✉ 8 bd. de Bercy, 12e ☎ 08–25–03–00–31 Ⓜ Bercy) is the largest venue in Paris and is where top international stars perform. **Zenith** (✉ Parc de la Villette, 19e ☎ 01–42–08–60–00 Ⓜ Porte-de-Pantin) stages large rock shows.

SHOPPING

Boutiques

Although the born and bred French designer is a rarity these days, Paris still remains the capital of European chic. The top designer shops are found on **avenue Montaigne, rue du Faubourg-St-Honoré,** and **place des Victoires.** The area around **St-Germain-des-Prés** on the Left Bank is full of small specialty shops and boutiques, and has recently seen an influx of the elite names in haute couture. The top names in jewelry are grouped around the **place Vendôme,** and scores of trendy boutiques can be found around **Les Halles.** Between the pre-Revolution mansions and tiny kosher food stores that characterize the **Marais** are numerous gift shops and clothing stores. Search for bargains on the streets around the foot of Montmartre, or in the designer discount shops (Cacharel, Rykiel, Chevignon) along **rue d'Alésia** in Montparnasse.

Department Stores

Au Bon Marché (✉ 24 rue de Sèvres, 7e Ⓜ Sèvres-Babylone). **Au Printemps** (✉ 64 bd. Haussmann, 9e Ⓜ Havre-Caumartin). **Galeries Lafayette** (✉ 40 bd. Haussmann, 9e Ⓜ Chaussée-d'Antin). **La Samaritaine** (✉ 19 rue de la Monnaie, 1er Ⓜ Pont-Neuf).

Food & Flea Markets

Every *quartier* (neighborhood) has at least one open-air food market. Some of the best are on rue de Buci, rue Mouffetard, rue Montorgueil, rue Mouffetard, and rue Lepic. Sunday morning until 1 PM is usually a good time to go; they are likely to be closed Monday.

The **Marché aux Puces de St-Ouen** (Ⓜ Porte de Clignancourt), just north of Paris, is one of Europe's largest flea markets; it's open Saturday through Monday. Best bargains are to be had early in the morning. Smaller flea markets also take place at **Porte de Vanves** and **Porte de Montreuil** (weekends only).

Gifts

Old prints are sold by *bouquinistes* (secondhand booksellers) in stalls along the banks of the Seine. **Fauchon** (✉ 30 pl. de la Madeleine, 8e Ⓜ Madeleine) is perhaps the world's most famous gourmet food shop. **Guerlain** (✉ 47 rue Bonaparte, 6e Ⓜ Mabillon) carries legendary French perfumes. **Lavinia** (✉ 3–5 bd. de la Madeleine, 8e ☎ 01–42–97–20–20 Ⓜ St-Augustin) has the largest selection of wine of any store in Europe—more than 6,000 wines and spirits from all over the world ranging from the simple to the sublime. **Les Salons du Palais-Royal Shiseido** (✉ Jardins du Palais-Royal, 142 Galerie de Valois, 25 rue de Valois, 1er ☎ 01–49–27–09–09 Ⓜ Palais-Royal) is a magical boutique where each year Shiseido's creative genius Serge Lutens dreams up two new scents, which are then sold exclusively here. The **Musée des Arts Décoratifs** (✉ 107 rue de Rivoli, 1er Ⓜ Palais-Royal) has superchic home decorations. **Sentou Galerie** (✉ 24 rue du Pont Louis-Philippe, 4e ☎ 01–42–71–00–01 Ⓜ St-Paul) is the place to find the original gift; look for the oblong suspended crystal vases that would look great hanging above the dinner table or in front of a mirror.

PARIS A TO Z

AIRPORTS & TRANSFERS

International flights arrive at either Charles de Gaulle Airport (known as Roissy to the French), 24 km (15 mi) northeast of Paris, or at Orly Airport, 16 km (10 mi) south of the city. Both airports have two terminals.

TRANSFERS Both airports have train stations from which you can take the RER, the local commuter train, to Paris. The advantages of this are speed, price (€8 to Paris from Roissy, €9 from Orly via the shuttle-train Orlyval with a change to the RER at Antony), and the RER's direct link with the métro system. The disadvantage is having to lug your bags around. Taxi fares between the airports and Paris are about €25 (Orly) and €35 (Roissy), with a €1 surcharge per bag. The Paris Airports Service and PariShuttle run eight-passenger vans to any destination in Paris from Roissy (€19 for one person, €13 per person for two or more) and Orly (€17 for one, €13 per person for two or more). You need to book at least two days in advance; there are English-speaking operators.

From Roissy, Air France Buses (open to all) leave every 15 minutes from 5:40 AM to 11 PM. The fare is €10 and the trip takes from 40 minutes to 1½ hours during rush hour. You arrive at the Arc de Triomphe or Porte Maillot, on the Right Bank by the Hôtel Concorde-Lafayette. From Orly, buses operated by Air France leave every 12 minutes from 6 AM to 11 PM and arrive at the Air France terminal near Les Invalides on the Left Bank. The fare is €8, and the trip takes 30–60 minutes, depending on traffic. Alternatively, the Roissybus, operated by Paris Transport Authority (RATP), runs directly to and from rue Scribe, by the Opéra, every 15 minutes and costs €8. RATP also runs the Orlybus to and from Denfert-Rochereau and Orly every 15 minutes for €6; the trip takes around 35 minutes.

ℹ Taxis & Shuttles **Paris Airports Service** ☎ 01–55–98–10–80 📠 01–55–98–10–89 🌐 www.parisairportservice.com. **PariShuttle** ☎ 01–43–90–91–91 📠 01–43–90–91–10 🌐 www.parishuttle.com.

BUS TRAVEL WITHIN PARIS

Most buses run from around 6 AM to 8:30 PM; some continue until midnight. Routes are posted on the sides of buses. *Noctambus* (night buses) operate from 1 AM to 6 AM between Châtelet and nearby suburbs. They can be stopped by hailing them at any point on their route. You can use a métro ticket on the bus, or you can buy a one-ride ticket on board. You need to show weekly/monthly/special tickets to the driver; if you have individual tickets, punch one in the red and gray machines on board the bus.

CAR TRAVEL

Expressways converge on the capital from every direction: A1 from the north (225 km [140 mi] to Lille); A13 from Normandy (225 km [140 mi] to Caen); A4 from the east (500 km [310 mi] to Strasbourg); A10 from the southwest (580 km [360 mi] to Bordeaux); and A7 from the Alps and Côte d'Azur (465 km [290 mi] to Lyon). Each connects with the *périphérique*, the beltway, around Paris. Exits are named by *porte* (gateway), not numbered. The "Périphe" can be fast, but gets very busy; try to avoid it between 7:30 and 10 AM and between 4:30 and 7:30 PM. Car travel within Paris is best avoided because finding parking is difficult and there is heavy traffic for much of the day.

EMERGENCIES

Automatic phone booths can be found at various main crossroads for use in police emergencies (Police-Secours) or for medical help (Services Médicaux).

Doctors & Dentists **Dentist** ☎ 01-43-37-51-00. **Doctor** ☎ 01-43-07-77-77.

Emergency Services **Ambulance** ☎ 15 or 01-45-67-50-50. **Police** ☎ 17.

Hospitals **American Hospital** ✉ 63 bd. Victor-Hugo, Neuilly ☎ 01-46-41-25-25. **British Hospital** ✉ 3 rue Barbès, Levallois-Perret ☎ 01-47-58-13-12.

24-hour Pharmacies **Pharmacie Dérhy** ✉ 84 av. des Champs-Élysées, 8e ☎ 01-45-62-02-41, open 24 hrs. **Pharmacie Européenne** ✉ 6 pl. de Clichy, 9e ☎ 01-48-74-65-18 Ⓜ Place de Clichy.

ENGLISH-LANGUAGE MEDIA

Most newsstands in central Paris sell *Time, Newsweek,* and the *International Herald Tribune,* as well as the English dailies. Some English-language bookstores include the ones listed below.

Bookstores **Brentano's** ✉ 37 av. de l'Opéra. **Galignani** ✉ 224 rue de Rivoli. **Shakespeare & Co.** ✉ 37 rue de la Bûcherie. **W. H. Smith** ✉ 248 rue de Rivoli.

MÉTRO TRAVEL

Fourteen métro lines crisscross Paris and the nearby suburbs, and you are seldom more than a five-minute walk from the nearest station. It's essential to know the name of the last station on the line you take, since this name appears on all signs within the system. A connection (you can make as many as you please on one ticket) is called a *correspondance.* At junction stations illuminated orange signs bearing the names of each line terminus appear over the corridors that lead to the various correspondances.

The métro connects at several points in Paris with RER trains that race across Paris from suburb to suburb: RER trains are a sort of supersonic métro and can be great time-savers. All métro tickets and passes are valid for RER and bus travel within Paris.

Some lines and stations in the seedier parts of Paris are a bit risky at night—in particular, Line 2 (Porte-Dauphine–Nation) and the northern section of Line 13 from St-Lazare to St-Denis/Asnières. The long, bleak corridors at Jaurès and Stalingrad are a haven for pickpockets and purse snatchers. But the Paris métro is relatively safe, as long as you don't walk around with your wallet in your back pocket or travel alone (especially women) late at night.

Access to métro and RER platforms is through an automatic ticket barrier. Slide your ticket in flat and pick it up as it pops up farther along. Keep your ticket; you'll need it again to leave the RER system. Sometimes green-clad métro authorities will ask to see it when you enter or leave the station: be prepared—they aren't very friendly, and they will impose a large fine if you can't produce your ticket.

FARES & SCHEDULES The métro runs from 5:30 AM to 1:15 AM. Métro tickets cost €1.30 each, though a *carnet* (10 tickets for €9.70) is a far better value. If you're staying for a week or more, the best deal is the *coupon jaune* (weekly) or *carte orange* (monthly) ticket, sold according to zone. Zones 1 and 2 cover the entire métro network (€13 per week or €45 per month). If you plan to take a suburban train to visit monuments in the Ile-de-France, you should consider a four-zone ticket (Versailles, St-Germain-en-Laye; €22 per week) or a six-zone ticket (Rambouillet, Fontainebleau; €30 per week). For these weekly or monthly tickets, you need a pass (available from train and major métro stations), and you must provide a passport-size photograph.

Alternatively, there are one-day (*Mobilis*) and two-, three-, and five-day (*Paris Visite*) unlimited travel tickets for the métro, bus, and RER. Unlike the coupon jaune, which is good from Monday morning to Sunday evening, the latter are valid starting any day of the week and give you admission discounts to a number of museums and tourist attractions. Prices are €8.50, €14, €18.50, and €27 for Paris only; €15, €27, €38, and €46 for the suburbs, including Versailles, St-Germain-en-Laye, and Disneyland Paris.

TAXIS

Taxi rates are based on location and time. Daytime rates, A (7 AM–7 PM), within Paris are €0.55 per kilometer (½ mi), and nighttime rates, B, are around €0.90 per kilometer. Suburban zones and airports, C, are €1.10 per kilometer. There is a basic hire charge of €2 for all rides, a €0.90 supplement per piece of luggage, and a €0.75 supplement if you're picked up at an SNCF station. Waiting time is charged at €19.85 per hour. The easiest way to get a taxi is to ask your hotel or restaurant to call a taxi for you, or go to the nearest taxi stand (there's one every couple of blocks); cabs with their signs lighted can be hailed but are difficult to spot; they are not all a single, uniform color. There is an average supplement of €2.30 for a fourth passenger. It is customary to tip the driver about 10%.

TOURS

BICYCLE TOURS There are a number of companies that rent bikes for the day and organize interesting cycling tours around the city. Paris à Vélo, C'est Sympa rents bikes for €13 per day and also organizes three-hour excursions of both the heart of Paris and lesser-known sites. Mike's Bike Tours organizes guided tours of Paris daily from March to November.

Fees & Schedules **Paris à Vélo, C'est Sympa** ✉ 37 bd. Bourdon, 4e ☎ 01-48-87-60-01 🌐 www.parisvelosympa.com. **Mike's Bike Tours** ✉ 24 rue Edgar-Faure, 15e ☎ 01-56-58-10-54 🌐 www.mikesbiketoursparis.com.

BOAT TOURS Boats depart in season every half hour from 10:30 to 5 (less frequently in winter) and cost €6–€15. Lunch or dinner tours average about €46–€90. The *Bateaux Mouches* leave from the Pont de l'Alma, at the bottom of avenue George-V. The *Bateaux Parisiens* leave from the Pont d'Iéna, by the Eiffel Tower. The *Vedettes du Pont-Neuf* set off from beneath square du Vert-Galant on the western edge of the Ile de la Cité.

BUS TOURS Bus tours of Paris provide a good introduction to the city. Tours usually start from the tour company's office and are generally given in double-decker buses with either a live guide or tape-recorded commentary. They last two to three hours and cost about €23. Tour operators also have theme tours (historic Paris, modern Paris, Paris by night) that last from 2½ hours to all day and cost up to €60, as well as excursions to Chartres, Versailles, Fontainebleau, the Loire Valley, and Mont-St-Michel (for a cost of €50–€150). Cityrama is one of the largest bus operators in Paris;

it also runs minibus excursions that pick you up and drop you off at your hotel. Paris Vision is another large bus tour operator.

Fees & Schedules **Cityrama** ✉ 4 pl. des Pyramides, 1er ☎ 01-44-55-60-00. **Paris Vision** ✉ 214 rue de Rivoli, 1er ☎ 08-00-03-02-14.

PRIVATE GUIDES Tours of Paris or the surrounding areas by limousine or minibus for up to seven passengers for a minimum of three hours can be organized. The cost starts at about €50 per hour. Contact Paris Major Limousines, Paris Bus, or Cityscope.

Cityscope ✉ 11 bis bd. Haussmann, 9e ☎ 01-53-34-11-91. **Paris Bus** ✉ 22 rue de la Prévoyance, Vincennes ☎ 01-43-65-55-55. **Paris Major Limousines** ✉ 14 rue Atlas, 19e ☎ 01-44-52-50-00.

12

WALKING TOURS Numerous special-interest tours concentrate on historical or architectural topics. Most are in French and cost between €6 and €10. Details are published in the weekly magazines *Pariscope* and *L'Officiel des Spectacles* under the heading "Conférences."

TRAIN TRAVEL

Paris has five international stations: Gare du Nord (for northern France, northern Europe, and England via Calais or the Channel Tunnel); Gare de l'Est (for Strasbourg, Luxembourg, Basel, and central Europe); Gare de Lyon (for Lyon, Marseille, the Côte d'Azur, Geneva, and Italy); Gare d'Austerlitz (for southwest France and Spain); and Gare St-Lazare (for Normandy and England via Dieppe). The Gare Montparnasse serves western France (Nantes, Rennes, and Brittany) and is the terminal for the TGV Atlantic service from Paris to Tours, Poitiers, and Bordeaux. Call SNCF for information. You can reserve tickets at any Paris station regardless of the destination. Go to the Grandes Lignes counter for travel within France or to the Billets Internationaux desk if you're heading out of France.

SNCF ☎ 08-36-35-35-35 🌐 www.sncf.com.

TRAVEL AGENCIES

Contacts **American Express** ✉ 11 rue Scribe, 9e ☎ 01-47-77-77-07. **Wagons-Lit** ✉ 32 rue du Quatre-Septembre, 2e ☎ 01-42-66-15-80.

VISITOR INFORMATION

The Paris Tourist Office is open Monday–Saturday 9–8 and Sunday 11–8.

Paris Tourist Office ✉ 127 av. des Champs-Élysées ☎ 08-92-68-31-12 for recorded information in English 🌐 www.parisbienvenu.com.

France Basics

To research prices, get advice from other travelers, and book travel arrangements, visit www.fodors.com.

BUSINESS HOURS

BANKS & OFFICES Banks are open weekdays 9:30–5, with variations; most close for at least an hour at lunch.

MUSEUMS & SIGHTS The usual opening times for museums and other sights are from 9:30 to 5 or 6. Many close for lunch (noon–2). Most are closed one day a week (generally Monday or Tuesday) and on national holidays. National museums are free to the public the first Sunday of every month.

SHOPS Shops in big towns are open from 9 or 9:30 to 7 or 8 without a lunch break; though it's still rare, an increasing number are now open on Sunday. Smaller shops often open earlier and close later but take a lengthy lunch break (12:30–3 or 4). This siesta-type schedule is more typical in the south of France. Corner grocery stores frequently stay open until around 10 PM.

EMBASSIES

Australia ⊠ 4 rue Jean-Rey, 15e, Paris ☎ 01-40-59-33-00.

Canada ⊠ 35 av. Montaigne, 8e, Paris ☎ 01-44-43-29-00.

New Zealand ⊠ 7 ter rue Léonardo-da-Vinci, 16e, Paris ☎ 01-45-00-24-11.

United Kingdom ⊠ 35 rue du Faubourg-St-Honoré, 8e, Paris ☎ 01-44-51-31-00.

United States ⊠ 2 av. Gabriel, 8e, Paris ☎ 01-43-12-22-22; 01-43-12-23-47 in emergencies.

HOLIDAYS

New Year's Day; Easter Monday; Labor Day (May 1); VE Day (May 8); Ascension (usually early May); Pentecost Monday (usually mid-May); Bastille Day (July 14); Assumption (August 15); All Saints' Day (November 1); Armistice (November 11); Christmas.

LANGUAGE

The French study English for a minimum of four years at school and, although few are fluent, their English is probably better than the French of most Americans. English is widely understood in major tourist areas, and in most hotels there is likely to be at least one person who can converse with you. Even if your own French is rusty, try to master a few words: people will greatly appreciate your efforts.

It's always a good idea to make hotel reservations in Paris as far in advance as possible, especially in late spring, summer, or fall. If you arrive without a reservation, tourist offices in major train stations and most towns may be able to find a hotel for you.

MONEY MATTERS

There's no way around it: France is expensive. But many travel basics—hotels, restaurants, plane, and train tickets—can be made more affordable by planning ahead, taking advantage of prix-fixe menus, and staying in smaller, family-run places. Prices are highest in Paris and on the Côte d'Azur, though even in these areas you can find reasonable accommodations and food.

Prices vary greatly depending on the region, proximity to tourist sights, and—believe it or not—whether you're sitting down (and where—inside or on the terrace) or standing up in a café. Here are a few samples: cup of coffee, €1–€3; glass of beer, €1.50–€4; soft drink, €1.50–€3; ham sandwich, €2.50–€5; 1½-km (1-mi) taxi ride, €5.

CURRENCY France has adopted the euro (€) as its sole currency, one of the 12 European Union countries to do so. At press time (summer 2003), the exchange rate for the euro was €0.89 to the U.S. dollar, €0.64 to the Canadian dollar, €1.42 to the pound sterling, €0.58 to the Australian dollar, €0.52 to the New Zealand dollar, and €0.11 to the South African rand.

TAXES All taxes must be included in posted prices in France. The initials TTC (*toutes taxes comprises,* which means taxes included) are sometimes included on price lists, but they are superfluous. Restaurant and hotel prices must *by law* include taxes and service charges: if they are tacked onto your bill as additional items, you should complain.

A number of shops offer VAT refunds to foreign shoppers. You are entitled to an export refund of the 19.6% tax, depending on the item purchased, but it is often applicable only if your purchases in any given store reach a minimum of €430 (for U.K. and EU residents) or €184 (for others, including U.S. and Canadian residents). In most instances, you must fill out a form at the point of purchase, which must then be tendered to a customs official at your last port of departure. Remember to ask for the refund and note that VAT refunds can't be processed after you arrive back home.

TELEPHONES

French phone numbers have 10 digits. All phone numbers have a two-digit prefix determined by zone: Paris and the Ile-de-France, 01; the northwest, 02; the northeast, 03; the southeast, 04; and the southwest, 05.

COUNTRY & AREA CODES The country code for France is 33 and for Monaco 377. To call France from the United States, dial 011 (for all international calls), then dial 33 (the country code), and the number in France, minus any initial 0. To dial France from the United Kingdom, dial 00–33, then the number in France, minus any initial 0.

INTERNATIONAL CALLS To call a foreign country from France, dial 00 and wait for the tone, then dial the country code, area code, and number. You can also contact your long-distance carrier directly and charge your call to your calling card or make a collect call.

Access Codes **AT&T** ☎ 08-00-99-00-11. **MCI** ☎ 08-00-99-00-19. **Sprint** ☎ 08-00-99-00-87.

LOCAL CALLS To make calls within a region or to another region in France, simply dial the full, 10-digit number. A local call in France costs €.034 cents per minute. Cheaper rates apply between 10 PM and 8 AM and between noon Saturday and 8 AM Monday. Dial ☎ 12 for local operators.

PUBLIC PHONES The rare French person who doesn't have a mobile phone uses *télécartes* (phone cards), which you can buy just about anywhere, from post offices, tabacs, métro stations, magazine kiosks, small grocery stores, or any France Telecom office. The international rates these phone cards offer have been negotiated and are the best you will find. There are two télécartes available; *une pétite* that costs €8 for 50 units or *une grande* that costs €15 for 120 units. Scratch the card to uncover your personal PIN, dial the toll-free number and the number you wish to reach (be it local or international) and the operator will tell you the time available for your call. Note that it is virtually impossible to find a phone that will take coins.

PRAGUE

Poets, philosophers, and residents alike have long sung the praises of Praha (Prague), also referred to as the Golden City of a Hundred Spires. Like Rome, Prague is built on seven hills, which slope gently or tilt precipitously down to the Vltava (Moldau) River. The riverside location, enhanced by a series of graceful bridges, makes a great setting for two of the city's most notable features: its extravagant, fairy-tale architecture and its memorable music. Mozart claimed that no one understood him better than the citizens of Prague, and he was only one of several great masters who lived or lingered here.

It was under Karel IV (Charles IV), in the 14th century, that Prague first became the seat of the Holy Roman Empire—virtually the capital of Western Europe—and acquired its distinctive Gothic imprint. The medieval inheritance is still here under the overlays of graceful Renaissance and exuberant baroque. Prague escaped serious wartime damage, but it didn't escape neglect. During the 1990s, however, artisans and their workers have restored dozens of the city's historic buildings with care and sensitivity.

EXPLORING PRAGUE

Shades of the five medieval towns that combined to form Prague linger in the divisions of its historic districts. On the flat eastern shore of the Vltava River are three areas arranged like nesting boxes: **Josefov** (the old Jewish Quarter) within **Staré Město** (Old Town) bordered by **Nové Město** (New Town). **Malá Strana** (Lesser Quarter) and **Hradčany** (Castle District) perch along the river's hillier west bank. Spanning the Vltava is **Karlův most** (Charles Bridge), which links the Old Town to the Lesser Quarter; everything within the historic center can be reached on foot in a half hour or less from here.

Nové Město & Staré Město (New Town & Old Town)

New Town is more than 500 years old, and only new when compared with Old Town, which dates from the 12th century. Both neighborhoods have a mix of Renaissance, baroque, and modern architecture. Old Town has the slight advantage in historic sites, with its world-famous Astronomical Clock Tower and Old Town Square. New Town, with its store-packed Wenceslas Square and multiple department stores, has the lead in shopping. Almost every street in this area has a building or monument worth checking out.

Numbers in the margin correspond to points of interest on the Prague map.

11 **Betlémská kaple** (Bethlehem Chapel). The martyr and national hero Jan Hus thundered his reform teachings from the chapel pulpit during the early 15th century. The structure was rebuilt in the 1950s, but the little door through which Hus came to the pulpit is original, as are some of the inscriptions on the wall. ✉ *Betlémské nám 5* 30 Kč *Apr.–Sept., daily 9–6; Oct.–Mar., daily 9–5.*

3 **Celetná ulice.** Medieval kings took this street on their way to their coronation at Prague Castle. The **Royal Route** continues past the Gothic spires of the Týn Church in Old Town Square; it then crosses Charles Bridge and goes up to the castle. Along the route stands every variety of Romanesque, Gothic, Renaissance, and baroque architecture.

10 **Clam-Gallas palác** (Clam-Gallas Palace). Squatting on a constricted site in the heart of the Old Town, this pompous baroque palace was designed by the great Viennese architect J. B. Fischer von Erlach. All the sculptures, including the titans that struggle to support the two doorways, are the work of one of the great Bohemian baroque artists, Matthias Braun. An exhibition hall on the first floor is open daily from 10 to 6, which is one way to peek inside the building. Another is to attend an evening concert in the large hall. ✉ *Husova 20* *www.ahmp.cz.*

4 **Dům U černé Matky Boží** (House of the Black Madonna). This Cubist building adds a jolt to the architectural styles along Celetná ulice. In the second decade of the 20th century, several leading Czech architects boldly applied Cubism's radical reworking of visual space to structures. The Black Madonna, designed by Josef Gočár, is unflinchingly modern yet topped with an almost baroque tile roof. The building has become part of the National Gallery, with a permanent exhibit of Cubist art. ✉ *Celetná ul. (at Ovocný trh)* *www.ngprague.cz* *Tues.–Sun. 10–6.*

6 **Expozice Franze Kafky** (Franz Kafka's Birthplace). A museum in the house displays photos, editions of Kafka's books, and other memorabilia from the author's life. (Kafka's grave lies in the New Jewish Cemetery at the Želivského Metro stop.) ✉ *Nám. Franze Kafky 5* *Tues.–Fri. 10–6, Sat. 10–5.*

2 **Na Příkopě.** Once part of the moat surrounding the Old Town, this street is now an elegant (in places) pedestrian mall. It leads from the bottom of Wenceslas Square to the **Obecní dům** (Municipal House), Prague's most lavish art nouveau building. Tours are sometimes available; otherwise, it is difficult to see the upper floors. Evening concerts are held in the Great Hall. A bridge links it to the **Prašná brána** (Powder Tower), a 19th-century neo-Gothic restoration of the medieval original. ✉ *Nám. Republiky* ☎ 222/002101 *www.obecnidum.cz.*

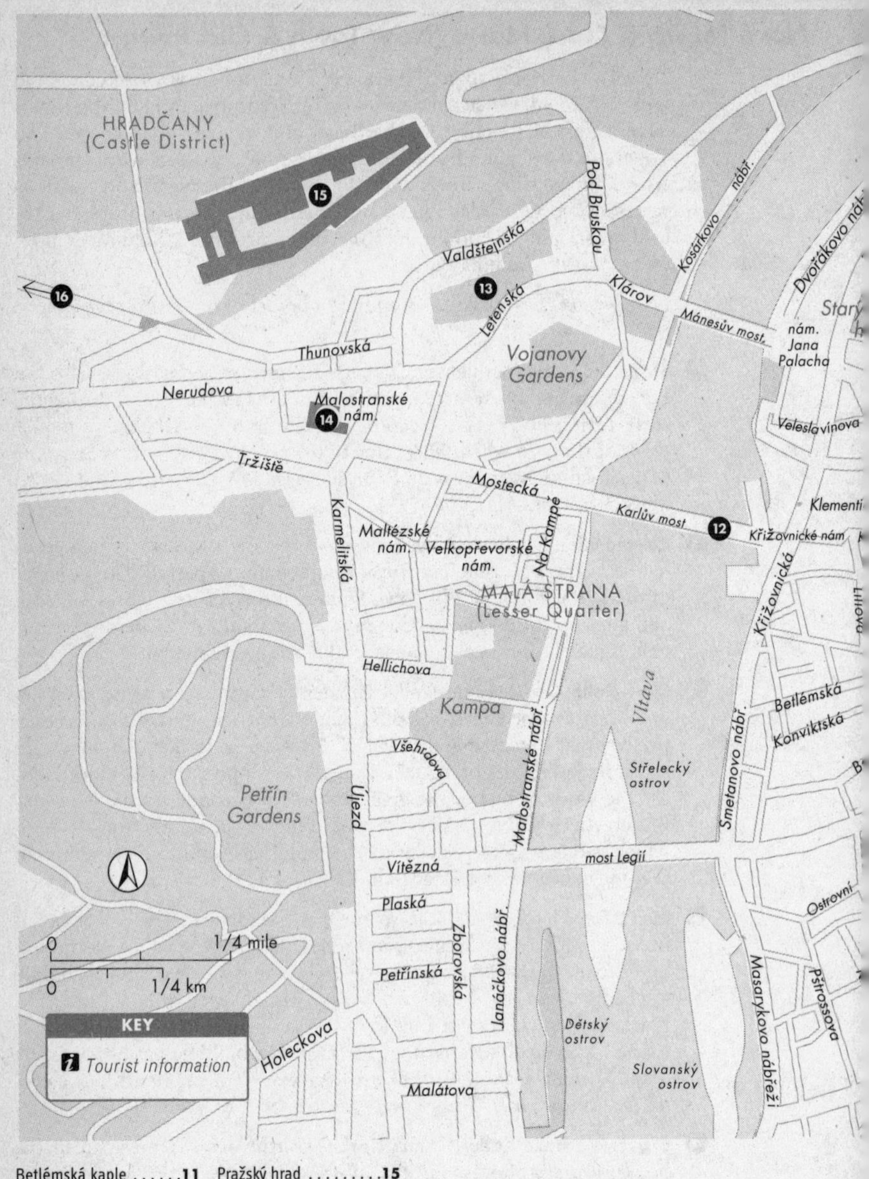

Betlémská kaple 11
Celetná ulice 3
Chrám svatého Mikuláše 14
Clam-Gallas palác 10
Dům U černé Matky Boží 4
Expozice Franze Kafky 6
Karlův most 12
Loreta 16
Na Příkopě 2
Pražský hrad 15
Staroměstské náměstí 5
Staronová synagóga 8
Starý židovský hřbitov 9
Václavské náměstí 1
Valdtejnská zahrada 13
Židovské muzeum 7

Prague
(Praha)
Vilava River
nábř. Ludvíka Svobody
Na Františku
U milosrdných
JOSEFOV
(Jewish
Quarter)
Revoluční
Klimentská
17. listopadu
Bílkova
Haštalská
Soukenická
Pařížská
Široká
Dlouhá
Stift
Göttweig
Masná
Rybná
Truhlářská
Zlatnická
Florenc Bus Station
Na Poříčí
STARÉ MĚSTO
(Old Town)
Maiselova
Kaprova
Jakubská
Havlíčkova
Na Florenci
Staroměstské
nám.
nám.
Republiky
Masaryk Station
Platnéřská
Husova
U Radnice
Clock
Tower
Celetná
Hybernská
Malé
nám.
Karlova
Melantrichova
Havelská
Havířská
Na Příkopě
Nekázanka
Senovážné nám.
Liliová
Jilská
Panská
Betlémské
nám.
Rytířská
Růžová
Main Train Station
(Hlavní Nádraží)
Bartolomějská
Na Perštýně
Václavské náměstí
Jindřišská
Politických vězňů
Opletalova
Jungmannovo
nám.
Frantiskánská
zahrada
třída
Národní
Washingtonova
Wilsonova
(Wenceslas Sq.)
Vodičkova
Vladislavova
Jungmannova
Spálená
Španělská
Italská
Národní
Muzeum
Lazarská
Křemencova
Černá
NOVÉ MĚSTO
(New Town)
Štěpánská
Ve Smečkách
Krakovská
Školská
Mánesova
Vinohradská
Myslíkova
Žitná
Rimska

5 Fodor's Choice ★ **Staroměstské náměstí** (Old Town Square). The commercial center of the Old Town is now a remarkably harmonious hub—architecturally beautiful and relatively car-free and quiet. Looming over the center, the twin towers of **Kostel Panny Marie před Týnem** (Church of the Virgin Mary before Týn) look forbidding despite Disneyesque lighting. The large **sculptural group** in the square's center commemorates the martyr Jan Hus, whose followers completed the Týn Church during the 15th century. The white baroque **Kostel svatého Mikuláše** (Church of St. Nicholas) is tucked into the square's northwest angle. It was built by Kilian Ignatz Dientzenhofer, co-architect also of the Lesser Quarter's church of the same name. Every hour, mobs converge on the Astronomical Clock Tower of the **Staroměstská radnice** (Old Town Hall) as the clock's 15th-century mechanism activates a procession that includes the 12 Apostles. A skeleton figure of Death tolls the bell. ✉ *Pařížská, Dlouhá, Celetná, Železná, Melantrichova, and Kaprova.*

8 **Staronová synagóga** (Old-New Synagogue). A small congregation still attends the little Gothic Old-New Synagogue, one of Europe's oldest surviving houses of Jewish prayer. Men are required to cover their heads upon entering; skullcaps are sold for a small fee at the door. ✉ *Červená 3 at Pařížská* ☎ *222/317191* 🌐 *www.jewishmuseum.cz* 🕒 *Sun.–Thurs. 9–5, Fri. 9–2.*

★ 9 **Starý židovský hřbitov** (Old Jewish Cemetery). The crowded cemetery is part of **Josefov,** the former Jewish Quarter, and is one of Europe's most unforgettable sights. Here, ancient tombstones lean into one another; below them, piled layer upon layer, are thousands of graves. Many gravestones—they date from the mid-14th to the late 18th centuries—are carved with symbols indicating the name, profession, and attributes of the deceased. If you visit the tomb of the 16th-century scholar Rabbi Löw, you may see scraps of paper covered with prayers or requests stuffed into the cracks. In legend, the rabbi protected Prague's Jews with the help of a *golem,* or artificial man; today he still receives appeals for assistance. The same admission fee gives you access to four other sites that are all part of the Jewish Museum. ✉ *Entrance at Pinkas Synagogue, Široká 3* ☎ *222/317191* 🌐 *www.jewishmuseum.cz* 🕒 *Sun.–Thurs. 9–5, Fri. 9–2.*

1 **Václavské náměstí** (Wenceslas Square). In the Times Square of Prague hundreds of thousands voiced their disgust for the Communist regime in November 1989 at the outset of the Velvet Revolution. The "square" is actually a broad boulevard that slopes down from the **Národní muzeum** (National Museum) and the equestrian **statue of St. Václav** (Wenceslas). ✉ *Between Wilsonova and jct. Na příkopě and 26 Října.*

7 **Židovské muzeum** (Jewish Museum). The rich exhibits in Josefov's Pinkas Synagogue, Maisel Synagogue, Klaus Synagogue, Ceremonial Hall, and the newly renovated Spanish Synagogue, along with the Old Jewish Cemetery, make up the museum. Jews, forced to fulfill Adolf Hitler's plan to document the lives of the people he was trying to exterminate, gathered the collections. They include ceremonial objects, textiles, and displays covering the history of Bohemia's and Moravia's Jews. The interior of the Pinkas Synagogue is especially poignant, as it is painted with the names of 77,297 Jewish Czechs killed during World War II. Pinkas Synagogue also contains a permanent exhibition of drawings by children who were interned at the Terezín (Theresienstadt) concentration camp from 1942 to 1944. *Museum ticket offices* ✉ *U starého hřbitova 3a* ✉ *Široká 3* 🕒 *Apr.–Oct., Sun.–Fri. 9–6; Nov.–Mar., Sun.–Fri. 9–4:30; closed Sat. and Jewish holidays. Old-New Synagogue closes 2–3 hrs early on Fri.*

Karlův Most & Malá Strana (Charles Bridge & the Lesser Quarter)

Many of the houses in the charmingly quaint Lesser Quarter have large signs above the door with symbols such as animals or religious figures. These date to the time before houses were numbered, when each house was referred to by name. Aristocrats built palaces here during the 17th century to be close to Prague Castle. Many of their private gardens have evolved into pleasant public parks with strutting peacocks. Some of the former palaces have become embassies, but increased security makes it hard to have more than a quick glance at the exterior.

⓮ **Chrám svatého Mikuláše** (Church of St. Nicholas). Designed by the late-17th-century Dientzenhofer architects, father and son, this is among the most beautiful examples of the Bohemian baroque, an architectural style that flowered in Prague after the Counter-Reformation. On clear days you can enjoy great views from the tower. ✉ *Malostranské nám.* ⏲ *Sept.–May, daily 9–4; June–Aug., daily 9–6.*

Fodor's Choice ★

⓬ **Karlův most** (Charles Bridge). As you stand on this statue-lined stone bridge, unsurpassed in grace and setting, you see views of Prague that would be familiar to its 14th-century builder Peter Parler and to the artists who started adding the 30 sculptures in the 17th century. Today, nearly all the sculptures on the bridge are skillful copies of the originals, which have been taken indoors to be protected from the polluted air. The 12th on the left (starting from the Old Town side of the bridge) depicts St. Luitgarde (Matthias Braun sculpted the original, circa 1710). In the 14th on the left, a Turk guards suffering saints. (F. M. Brokoff sculpted the original, circa 1714.) The bridge itself is a gift to Prague from the Holy Roman emperor Charles IV. ✉ *Between Mostecká ul. on Malá Strana side and Karlova ul. on Old Town side.*

off the beaten path

VILLA BERTRAMKA – While in Prague, Mozart liked to stay at the secluded estate of his friends the Dušeks. The house is now a small museum packed with Mozart memorabilia. From Karmelitská ulice in Malá Strana, take Tram 12 south to the Anděl metro station; walk down Plzeňská ulice a few hundred yards, and take a left at Mozartova ulice. In the summer, there are occasional garden concerts. ✉ *Mozartova ul. 169, Smíchov* ☎ *257/318461* 🌐 *www.bertramka.cz* ⏲ *Daily 9:30–6.*

⓭ **Valdštejnská zahrada** (Wallenstein Gardens). This is one of the most elegant of the many sumptuous Lesser Quarter gardens. In the 1620s the Habsburgs' victorious commander, Czech nobleman Albrecht of Wallenstein, demolished a wide swath of existing structures to build his oversize palace with its charming walled garden. A covered outdoor stage of late-Renaissance style dominates the western end. ✉ *Entrance, Letenská 10* ⏲ *May–Sept., daily 9–7.*

Pražsky Hrad & Hradčany (Prague Castle & the Castle District)

No feature dominates the city more than Prague Castle, which, because of its hilltop location, can be seen from most of the city. The neighborhood in front of the castle once housed astronomers, alchemists, counts, and clergy hoping to obtain royal favors. Some of the palaces near the castle have become museums, others are used by government ministries. A large number of churches can be found here as well. Some offer tours, others can be viewed only after early-morning religious services.

⑯ **Loreta.** This baroque church and shrine are named for the Italian town to which angels supposedly transported the Virgin Mary's house from Nazareth to save it from the infidels. The glory of its fabulous treasury is the *Sun of Prague,* a monstrance (a vessel that contains the consecrated Host and has an opening through which it can be viewed) decorated with 6,222 diamonds. Arrive on the hour to hear the 27-bell carillon. ✉ *Loretánské nám. 7* ⊙ *Tues.–Sun. 9–12:15 and 1–4:30.*

★ ⑮ **Pražský hrad** (Prague Castle). From its narrow hilltop, the monumental castle complex has witnessed the changing fortunes of the city for more than 1,000 years. The castle's physical and spiritual core, **Chrám svatého Víta** (St. Vitus Cathedral), took from 1344 to 1929 to build, so you can trace in its lines architectural styles from high Gothic to art nouveau. The eastern end, mostly the work of Peter Parler, builder of the Charles Bridge, is a triumph of Bohemian Gothic. "Good King" Wenceslas (in reality a mere prince, later canonized) has his own chapel in the south transept, dimly lit and decorated with fine medieval wall paintings. Note the fine 17th-century carved wooden panels on either side of the chancel. The left-hand panel shows a view of the castle and town in November 1620 as the defeated Czech Protestants flee into exile. The three easternmost chapels house tombs of Czech princes and kings of the 11th to the 13th centuries, although Charles IV and Rudolf II lie in the crypt, the former in a bizarre modern sarcophagus. On the southern facade of the cathedral, the 14th-century glass and quartz mosaic of the Last Judgment, long clouded over, has been restored to its original, brightly colored appearance.

Behind St. Vitus's, don't miss the miniature houses of **Zlatá ulička** (Golden Lane). Its name, and the apocryphal tale of how Holy Roman emperor Rudolf II used to lock up alchemists here until they transmuted lead into gold, may come from the gold-beaters who once lived here. Knightly tournaments often accompanied coronation ceremonies in the **Královský palác** (Royal Palace), next to the cathedral, hence the broad Riders' Staircase leading up to the grandiose Vladislavský sál (Vladislav Hall), with its splendid late-Gothic vaulting and Renaissance windows. Oldest of all the castle's buildings, though much restored, is the complex of **Bazilika svatého Jiří** (St. George's Basilica and Convent). The basilica's cool Romanesque lines hide behind a glowing salmon-color baroque facade. The former convent houses a superb collection of Bohemian art from medieval religious sculptures to baroque paintings. The castle **ramparts** afford glorious vistas of Prague's fabled 100 spires rising above the rooftops. ✉ *Approach via Nerudova, Staré zámecké schody, or Keplerova. Main castle ticket office in Second Courtyard* ☎ *224/373368* 🌐 *www.hrad.cz* ⊙ *Castle: Nov.–Mar., daily 9–4; Apr.–Oct., daily 9–5. Castle gardens: Apr.–Oct., daily 9–5.*

WHERE TO EAT

Dining options include restaurants; the *vinárna* (wine cellar), which covers anything from inexpensive wine bars to swank restaurants; the more down-to-earth *pivnice* or *hospody* (beer taverns); cafeterias; and coffee shops and snack bars. Be wary of food bought from street vendors, as sanitary conditions may not be ideal.

Prague ham is a favorite first course. The most typical main dish is roast pork (or duck or goose) with sauerkraut. Also try the outstanding trout, carp, and other freshwater fish. Crepes, here called *palačinky,* are ubiquitous and come with savory or sweet fillings. Dumplings in various forms, generally with a rich gravy, accompany many dishes. A typical Czech breakfast is cold cuts and spreadable cheese or jam with rolls, washed down with coffee. Privatization has brought more culinary variety, especially in Prague.

WHAT IT COSTS In Czech Republic Koruny				
	$$$$	$$$	$$	$
AT DINNER	over 350	240–350	130–240	under 130

Prices are per person for a main course.

13

$$$$ ✕ **Peklo.** This subterranean chamber (*peklo* is the Czech word for "hell") beneath a former monastery was once a favorite drinking spot of King Wenceslas IV. The old wine cellar has been replaced by a restaurant that offers a good selection of Czech and French wines. ✉ *Strahovské nádvoří 1/132* ☎ *220/516652* ▭ *AE, MC, V.*

$$$–$$$$ Fodor'sChoice ★ ✕ **Circle Line Brasserie.** Elegant yet decidedly unstuffy, this dining spot tucked into a restored baroque palace in Malá Strana offers delicious nouvelle cuisine specialties. Appetizers and main courses may include hare terrine with sun-dried plums and apricots, roasted lamb sweetbreads with truffle sauce, and grilled veal ribs with mustard-seed sauce. A pianist plays unobtrusively each evening; and service is gracious and discreet. Smaller degustation portions of most entrees are available. ✉ *Malostranské nám. 12* ☎ *257/530022* 🌐 *www.zatisigroup.cz* ✍ *Reservations essential* ▭ *AE, DC, MC, V.*

$$$–$$$$ ✕ **Palffy palác.** The faded charm of an old-world palace makes this a lovely, romantic spot for a meal. Very good Continental cuisine is served with elegance that befits the surroundings. Try the potatoes au gratin or chicken stuffed with goat cheese. In summer, ask to dine on the terrace. Brunches here are not worth the price. ✉ *Valdštejnská 14* ☎ *257/530522* ▭ *MC, V.*

★ $$$–$$$$ ✕ **U Modré Kachničky.** The exuberant, eclectic decor is as attractive as the Czech and international dishes, which include steaks, duck, and game in autumn, and Bohemian trout and carp. ✉ *Nebovidská 6* ☎ *257/320308* 🌐 *www.umodrekachnicky.cz* ✍ *Reservations essential* ▭ *AE, MC, V.*

★ $$$–$$$$ ✕ **Vinárna V Zatiší.** Continental cuisine is exquisitely prepared and presented here—fish and game specialties are outstanding, and set menus including wine are available. The wine list is extensive, with special emphasis on French vintages. Most meals are available in smaller sample portions. ✉ *Liliová 1* ☎ *222/221155* ✍ *Reservations essential* ▭ *AE, MC, V.*

$$–$$$$ ✕ **U Zlaté Hrušky.** Careful restoration has returned this restaurant to its original 18th-century style. It specializes in Moravian wines, which are well matched with fillet steaks and goose liver. Dining is also available at the garden across the street in the warmer weather. ✉ *Nový Svět 3* ☎ *220/514778* 🌐 *www.zlatahruska.cz* ✍ *Reservations essential* ▭ *AE, V.*

$$–$$$ ✕ **Dynamo.** With a consistent clientele of beautiful people, this little green diner is one of the trendiest spots on what is fast becoming a veritable restaurant row. Dynamo's quirky menu offers tasty variations on Continental themes, such as liver and apples on toast, and succulent eggplant filled with grilled vegetables. They also have a wide range of single malt scotches to help end the evening. ✉ *Pštrossova 221/29* ☎ *224/932020* ▭ *AE, MC, V.*

$$–$$$ ✕ **U Mecenáše.** This restaurant manages to be elegant despite the presence of medieval swords and battle axes. Try to get a table in the back room. The chef specializes in thick, juicy steaks served with a variety of sauces. ✉ *Malostranské nám. 10* ☎ *257/531631* ✍ *Reservations essential* ▭ *AE, MC, V.*

$$ ✕ **Chez Marcel.** This authentic French bistro on a quiet, picturesque street offers a little taste of Paris in the center of Prague's Old Town. French owned and operated, Chez Marcel has an extensive menu suitable for lingering over a three-course meal (French cheeses, salads, pâtés, rabbit, and some of the best steaks in Prague) or just a quick espresso. ✉ *Haštalská 12* ☎ *222/315676* ▭ *No credit cards.*

$–$$$ ✕ **Novoměstský pivovar.** Always packed with out-of-towners and locals alike, this microbrewery-restaurant is a maze of rooms, some painted in mock-medieval style, others decorated with murals of Prague street scenes. Pork knee (*vepřové koleno*) is a favorite dish. The beer is the cloudy, fruity, fermented style exclusive to this venue. ✉ *Vodičkova 20* ☎ *222/232448* 🌐 *www.npivovar.cz* ▭ *AE, MC, V.*

$–$$ ✕ **Bohemia Bagel.** This casual, American-owned and child-friendly bagel shop serves a good assortment of fresh bagels with all kinds of spreads and toppings. The thick soups are among the best in Prague for the price, and the bottomless cups of coffee (from gourmet blends) are a further draw. There are now two locations. ✉ *Újezd 16* ☎ *257/310694* 🌐 *www.bohemiabagel.cz* ✉ *Masná 2* ☎ *224/812560* ▭ *No credit cards.*

$–$$ ✕ **Česká hospoda v Krakovské.** Right off Wenceslas Square, this clean pub noted for its excellent traditional fare is the place to try Bohemian duck. Pair it with cold Krušovice beer. ✉ *Krakovská 20* ☎ *222/210204* ▭ *No credit cards.*

$–$$ ✕ **Kavárna Slavia.** This legendary hangout for the best and brightest of the Czech arts world—from composer Bedřich Smetana and poet Jaroslav Seifert to then-dissident Václav Havel—offers a spectacular view both inside and out. Its art deco decor is a perfect backdrop for people-watching, and the vistas (the river and Prague Castle or the National Theater) are a compelling reason to linger over an espresso. Meals are available, but most people just come for the coffee and the view. ✉ *Smetanovo nábřeží 1012/2* ☎ *224/218493* ▭ *No credit cards.*

Fodor'sChoice ★

★ $–$$ ✕ **Pivovarský dům.** Beer made on the premises is the main attraction here. They make not only traditional Pilsner-style but also a rotating choice of coffee, cherry, or even eucalyptus beer. The menu offers well-made traditional pub fare such as *guláš* with dumplings. Peek at the vats behind the glass to see beer fermenting. ✉ *Lipová 20* ☎ *296/216666* ▭ *No credit cards.*

$–$$ ✕ **U Sedmi Švábů.** A medieval theme accents the truly old-fashioned Bohemian fare that includes millet pudding and mead. The less adventuresome can opt for the roast meat and poultry dishes. A special knight's feast requires 24 hours' advance notice. At the bottom of the stairs you can find a dungeon. ✉ *Janský vršek 14* ☎ *257/531455* 🌐 *www.viacarolina.cz.*

$–$$ ✕ **U Zlatého Tygra.** This crowded hangout is the last of a breed of authentic Czech pivnice. The smoke and stares preclude a long stay, but it's worth a visit for such pub staples as ham and cheese plates or fried pork steak. The service is surly, but the beer is good. ✉ *Husova 17* ☎ *222/221111* ✍ *Reservations not accepted* ▭ *No credit cards.*

$ ✕ **Country Life.** A godsend for Praguers and travelers, this health-food cafeteria offers a bounteous (and fresh) salad bar and daily rotating meat-free specials. The dining area has that rare Prague luxury for a low-end eating establishment: no blaring techno music. There's table service evenings after 6:30. It's off the courtyard connecting Melantrichova and Michalská streets. ✉ *Melantrichova 15* ☎ *224/213366* ▭ *No credit cards* ⏲ *Closed Sat.*

$ ✕ **U Bakaláře.** Hidden just inside a university-owned building on one of the main streets leading to Old Town Square, "at the bachelor of arts" offers some Czech standards such as meat-stuffed dumplings with sauerkraut. This is a perfect place for a quick bite while checking out the major attractions. Be aware that there is no table service. ✉ *Celetna 13* ☎ *224/817769* ✍ *Reservations not accepted* ▭ *No credit cards.*

WHERE TO STAY

Many of Prague's older hotels have been renovated, and more hotels are opening in old buildings in the Old Town and Lesser Quarter, making finding a decent room much easier than it used to be. Very few hotel rooms in the more desirable districts go for less than $120 per double room in high season; most less-expensive hotels are far from the center of Prague. Private rooms and pensions remain the best budget deal.

WHAT IT COSTS In Czech Republic Koruny				
	$$$$	**$$$**	**$$**	**$**
FOR 2 PEOPLE	over 5,300	2,800–5,300	1,700–2,800	under 1,700

Hotel prices are for a standard double room in high season.

$$$$ **Diplomat.** One of the first places to open after the Velvet Revolution, the Diplomat fuses style with Western efficiency. It's convenient to the airport: the Old Town is a 10-minute taxi or subway ride away. The hotel is modern and tasteful, with a huge, sunny lobby and comfortable rooms. ✉ *Evropská 15, 160 00 Prague 6* ☎ *296/559111* 📠 *296/559215* 🌐 *www.diplomat-hotel.cz* *369 rooms, 13 suites* *2 restaurants, bar* ▭ *AE, DC, MC, V.*

$$$$ ★ **Dům U Červeného Lva.** In Malá Strana, a five-minute walk from Prague Castle's front gates, the Baroque House at the Red Lion is an intimate, immaculately kept hotel. The spare but comfortable guest rooms have parquet floors, 17th-century painted-beam ceilings, superb antiques, and all-white bathrooms with brass fixtures. The two top-floor rooms can double as a suite. There is no elevator, and stairs are steep. ✉ *Nerudova 41, 118 00 Prague 1* ☎ *257/533832* 📠 *257/532746* 🌐 *www.hotelredlion.com* *5 rooms, 3 suites,* *2 restaurants* ▭ *AE, DC, MC, V.*

$$$$ Fodor'sChoice ★ **Hoffmeister.** On a picturesque (if a bit busy) corner near the Malostranská metro station, this is one of the most stylish small hotels in the city. Rooms have finely crafted wood built-ins and luxuriously appointed bathrooms. Museum-quality prints by the proprietor's father hang throughout the hotel. ✉ *Pod Bruskou 7, 118 00 Prague 1* ☎ *251/017111* 📠 *251/017120* 🌐 *www.hoffmeister.cz* *38 rooms* *Restaurant, bar* ▭ *AE, DC, MC, V.*

$$$$ **Kampa.** An early baroque armory turned hotel, the Kampa is tucked away in a residential corner of the Lesser Quarter. The rooms are clean, if spare, but the bucolic setting one block from the river as well as a lovely park compensate for its relative remoteness. ✉ *Všehrdova 16, 118 00 Prague 1* ☎ *257/320508 or 257/320404* 📠 *257/320262* 🌐 *www.bestwestern.com* *85 rooms* *Restaurant* ▭ *AE, DC, MC, V.*

$$$$ Fodor'sChoice ★ **Palace Praha.** The art nouveau–style palace is Prague's most elegant and luxurious hotel, though it now faces competition from other luxury hotels. Rooms have high ceilings, marble baths with phones, and minibars. Its central location just off Wenceslas Square offers more convenience than local character. ✉ *Panská 12, 110 00 Prague 1* ☎ *224/093111* 📠 *224/221240* 🌐 *www.palacehotel.cz* *114 rooms, 10 suites* *2 restaurants* ▭ *AE, DC, MC, V.*

$$$ **Hotel U staré paní.** The Old Lady is a delightfully cozy hotel only a five-minute walk from Old Town Square, in a renovated building on one of Prague's most atmospheric Old Town lanes. Comfortable rooms are decorated in soft tones with simple Scandinavian-style furnishings.

One of Prague's best jazz clubs has concerts nightly here in the basement. (Yes, it is soundproofed.) ✉ *Michalská 9, 110 00 Prague 1* ☎ *224/228090 or 224/226659* 🖷 *224/212172* 🌐 *www.ustarepani.cz* *18 rooms* *Restaurant* 💳 *AE, MC, V.*

$$$ **Opera.** Once the lodging of choice for divas performing at the nearby State Theater, the Opera greatly declined under the Communists. The mid-1990s saw the grand fin-de-siècle facade rejuvenated with a perky pink-and-white paint job and the installation of bathrooms and TVs in all rooms. Comfy wing chairs add to the rooms, which are decorated in tan and white. ✉ *Těšnov 13, 110 00 Prague 1* ☎ *222/315609* 🖷 *222/311477* 🌐 *www.hotel-opera.cz* *65 rooms, 2 suites* *Restaurant, bar* 💳 *AE, DC, MC, V.*

$$$ **Central.** Quite conveniently, this hotel lives up to its name, with a site near Celetná ulice and Náměstí Republiky. Rooms are sparely furnished, but all have baths. The baroque glories of the Old Town are steps away. ✉ *Rybná 8, 110 00 Prague 1* ☎ *222/321919* 🖷 *222/323100* 🌐 *www.orfea.cz* *68 rooms* *Restaurant, bar* 💳 *AE, MC, V.*

$$ **Balkán.** The hotel is a spiffy yellow building on an otherwise drab street not far from the Lesser Quarter. Rooms are small, simple, and clean, with white spreads and walls, tan paneling, and lacy curtains. Request a room at the back, as the hotel is on a major street, one block from the tram stop and a large shopping and entertainment area. ✉ *Svornosti 28, 150 00 Prague 5* ☎🖷 *257/327180* *24 rooms* *Restaurant* 💳 *AE.*

$ **Hostel Estec.** A prefabricated, but renovated, dormitory next to the world's largest stadium and right above a large park offers fairly basic accommodation, just a 15-minute walk from Prague Castle. Bathrooms are shared; breakfast is available in a nearby restaurant for a small additional fee. ✉ *Vaníčkova 5, 160 00 Prague 6* ☎ *257/210410* *200 rooms with shared bath* *Bar* 💳 *AE, MC, V.*

$ **Pension Unitas.** Operated by the Christian charity Unitas in an Old Town convent, this well-run establishment has sparely furnished rooms. Part of the facility once served as a prison, and rooms with bunk beds are available in the former cells. Reserve well in advance, even in the off-season. ✉ *Bartolomějská 9, 110 00 Prague 1* ☎ *224/221802* 🖷 *224/217555* 🌐 *www.unitas.cz* *43 rooms with shared bath* *Restaurant* 💳 *No credit cards.*

$ **Penzion Sprint.** Basic, clean, no-frills rooms, most of which have their own tiny bathrooms, make the Sprint a fine budget choice. The rustic-looking pension is on a quiet residential street in the outskirts of Prague, about 20 minutes from the airport; Tram 18 rumbles directly to Old Town. ✉ *Cukrovarnická 64, 160 00 Prague 6* ☎ *233/343338* 🖷 *233/344871* 🌐 *web.telecom.cz* *21 rooms* *Restaurant* 💳 *AE, MC, V.*

$ **Travellers' Hostel.** Single and double rooms are available for a reasonable price, but it costs even less to stay in the dormitory. The hostel is in the same building as a popular nightclub, Roxy, which is quite an asset if you like to stay up late. Old Town's sights are just a few feet from the door. Apartments, also a good deal, have kitchens, bathrooms, and remarkable views of the city. Breakfast and linen is included. ✉ *Dlouha 33, 110 00 Prague 1* ☎ *224/826662* 🖷 *224/826665* 🌐 *www.travellers.cz* *5 apartments, 50 rooms with shared bath* *Bar* 💳 *MC, V.*

NIGHTLIFE & THE ARTS

The Arts

Prague's cultural life is one of its top attractions—and its citizens like to dress up and participate; performances can be booked far ahead. Monthly programs of events are available at the PIS, Čedok, or hotels.

The English-language newspaper *Prague Post* carries detailed entertainment listings. The main ticket agency for classical music is **Bohemia Ticket International** (✉ Na Příkopě 16 ☎ 224/227832). **Ticketpro** (✉ Salvátorská 10 ☎ 296/329999 📠 224/814021) sells tickets for most rock and jazz events, as well as theatrical performances and some tours. Tickets for some concerts, events, and tours are available from **Ticketstream** (✉ Koubkova 8, ☎ 224/263049). For some events, including opera, it's much cheaper to buy tickets at the box office.

13

Concerts

Performances are held in many palaces and churches. Too often, programs lack originality (how many different ensembles can play the *Four Seasons* at once?), but the settings are lovely, and the acoustics can be superb. Concerts at the churches of St. Nicholas in both the Old Town Square and the Lesser Quarter are especially enjoyable. At **St. James's Church** on Malá Štupartská (Old Town) cantatas are performed amid a flourish of baroque statuary.

The excellent Czech Philharmonic plays in the intimate, lavish Dvořák Hall in the **Rudolfinum** (✉ Nám. Jana Palacha ☎ 224/893111). The lush home of the Prague Symphony, **Smetana Hall** (✉ Nám. Republiky 5 ☎ 222/002100), has been beautifully restored along with the rest of the Obecní dům Building, and is a suitably ornate venue for a classical concert.

Opera & Ballet

Opera is of an especially high standard in the Czech Republic. One of the main venues in the grand style of the 19th century is the beautifully restored **Národní divadlo** (National Theater; ✉ Národní třída 2 ☎ 224/901448). The **Statni opera Praha** (State Opera of Prague; ✉ Wilsonova 4 ☎ 224/227266), formerly the Smetana Theater, is another historic site for opera lovers. The **Stavovské divadlo** (Estates Theater; ✉ Ovocný trh 1 ☎ 224/901448) hosts opera, ballet, and theater performances by the National Theater ensembles. Mozart conducted the premiere of *Don Giovanni* here.

Puppet Shows

This traditional form of Czech entertainment, generally adaptations of operas performed to recorded music, has been given new life at the **Národní divadlo marionet** (National Marionette Theater; ✉ Žatecká 1 ☎ 224/819322).

Theater

A dozen or so professional companies play in Prague to packed houses. Nonverbal theater abounds as well, notably "black theater," a melding of live acting, mime, video, and stage trickery that, despite signs of fatigue, continues to draw crowds. The popular **Archa Theater** (✉ Na Poříčí 26 ☎ 221/716333) offers avant-garde and experimental theater, music, and dance and hosts world-class visiting ensembles, including the Royal Shakespeare Company. The theater was very badly damaged in the floods of 2002, and the performances have been moved to other locations until repairs can be made. **Laterna Magika** (Magic Lantern; ✉ Národní třída 4 ☎ 224/914129) is one of the more established producers of black-theater extravaganzas.

Nightlife

Discos & Cabaret

Discos catering to a young crowd blast sound onto lower Wenceslas Square. The newest dance music plays at the ever-popular **Radost FX** (✉ Bělehradská 120, Prague 2 ☎ 224/254776).

Four clubs in one can be found at **Karlový lázně** (✉ Novotného lávka) in a renovated spa building near the Charles Bridge. Several live acts or DJs perform nightly and a café with Internet access is open during the day.

Jazz & Rock Clubs

Jazz clubs are a Prague institution, although foreign customers keep them in business. Excellent Czech groups play the tiny **AghaRTA** (✉ Krakovská 5 ☎ 222/211275 🌐 www.arta.cz); arrive well before the 9 PM show time to get a good seat. Top jazz groups (and the odd world-music touring ensemble) play **Jazz Club U staré paní** (✉ Michalská 9 ☎ 224/228090 🌐 www.ustarepani.cz) in Old Town. **Malostranské Beseda** (✉ Malostranské nám. 21 ☎ 257/532092 🌐 mb.muzikus.cz) is a funky hall for rock, jazz, and folk. At **Palác Akropolis** (✉ Kubelíkova 27 ☎ 296/330913 🌐 www.palacakropolis.cz) you can hear world music, well-known folk, rock, and jazz acts, plus DJs. **Reduta** (✉ Národní třída 20 ☎ 224/933487), the city's best-known jazz club for three decades, stars mostly local talent. Hip locals congregate at **Roxy** (✉ Dlouhá 33 ☎ 224/826296 🌐 www.roxy.cz) for everything from punk to funk to New Age tunes.

SHOPPING

Many of the main shops are in and around Old Town Square and Na Příkopě, as well as along Celetná ulice and Pařížská. On the Lesser Quarter side, Nerudova has the densest concentration of shops.

Department Stores

The two adjacent modern steel-and-glass shopping complexes, **Anděl** and **Nový Smíchov** (✉ intersection of Plzeňská and Nádražní), include a Carrefour supermarket and many other stores and restaurants. **Bílá Labuť** (✉ Na Poříčí 23) is a good-value option. The biggest downtown department store is **Kotva** (✉ Nám. Republiky 8), which grows flashier and more expensive every year. The basement supermarket at **Tesco** (✉ Národní třída 26) is the best and biggest in the center of the city.

Specialty Shops

Shops specializing in Bohemian crystal, porcelain, ceramics, and antiques abound in Old Town and Malá Strana and on Golden Lane at Prague Castle. Look for the name **Dílo** (✉ Staroměstské nám. 15 ✉ U Lužického semináře 14) for glass and ceramic sculptures, prints, and paintings by local artists. **Lidová Řemesla** (✉ Jilská 22 ✉ Mostecká 17) shops stock wooden toys, elegant blue-and-white textiles, and charming Christmas ornaments made from straw or pastry. **Moser** (✉ Na Příkopě 12 ☎ 224/211293 🌐 www.moser.cz) is the source for handmade glass.

PRAGUE A TO Z

AIRPORTS & TRANSFERS

All international flights arrive at Prague's Ruzyně Airport, about 20 km (12 mi) from downtown.

Ruzyně Airport ☎ 220/113314 or 221/113321 🌐 www.csa.cz or www.prague-airport.cz.

TRANSFERS The private Cedaz minibus shuttle links the airport and Náměstí Republiky. Shuttles run every 30–60 minutes between 5:30 AM and 9 PM daily. The trip costs 90 Kč one-way and takes about 30 minutes. On regular Bus 119 the cost is 12 Kč, but you'll need to change to the metro station at the Dejvická Station to reach the center. Bus 100 also goes between the airport and the Metro Zličín stop. By taxi, expect to pay

600 Kč to the center. Only one city-authorized firm, Belinda, is permitted to have taxis waiting at the airport. (You may take any taxi *to* the airport, however, or call a taxi.)

BUS TRAVEL TO & FROM PRAGUE

The Czech bus network (ČSAD) operates from a station near Prague's main train station. Take Metro B or C to the Florenc stop.

ČSAD Křižíkova 4 222/630851 www.jizdnirady.cz.

BUS & TRAM TRAVEL WITHIN PRAGUE

Trams are often more convenient than the metro for short hops. Most bus lines connect outlying suburbs with the nearest metro station. Trams 50–59 and buses numbered 500 and above run all night—at, however, intervals of up to an hour—after the metro stops.

CAR TRAVEL

In the center of the city, meters with green stripes let you park up to six hours; an orange stripe indicates a two-hour limit. Blue-marked spaces are reserved for local residents. (Parking boots may be attached to offending vehicles.) There is an underground parking lot near Old Town Square.

EMERGENCIES

Be prepared to pay in cash for medical treatment, whether you are insured or not. The Lékárna U Andělais 24-hour pharmacy is near the Anděl metro station, and the Lékárna Palackého 24-hour pharmacy is located downtown.

Emergency Services **Ambulance** 155. **Police** 112.

Hospitals **American Medical Center** Janovského 48 220/807756. **Foreigners' Department of Na Homolce Hospital** Roentgenova 2 257/272144 or 257/272146.

24-hour Pharmacies **Lékárna U Anděla** Štefánikova 6 257/320918. **Lékárna Palackého** Palackého 5 224/946982.

ENGLISH-LANGUAGE MEDIA

The Knihkupectví U černé Matky Boží is good for hiking maps and atlases; go downstairs.

Bookstores **Anagram Bookshop** Týn 4, Prague 1. **Big Ben Bookshop** Malá Štupartská 5, Prague 1. **Globe Bookstore and Coffeehouse** Pštrossova 6, Prague 1. **Knihkupectví U černé Matky Boží** Celetná ul. 34 at Ovocný trh, Prague 1. **U Knihomola** Mánesova 79, Prague 2.

SUBWAY TRAVEL

Prague's three modern metro lines are easy to use and relatively safe. They provide the simplest and fastest means of transportation, and most maps of Prague mark the routes. The metro runs from 5 AM to midnight, seven days a week.

TAXIS

Regulations have set taxi rates at 22 Kč per kilometer plus 4 Kč per minute of waiting time, with an initial fee of 30 Kč. Drivers must also display a small license, although this has not stopped fare-related problems. It is still advisable to order a taxi in advance by telephone. Try AAA for quick, reliable service. Profitaxi is also fast and efficient. Some larger hotels have their own fleets, which are a little more expensive.

Do not pick up cabs waiting at taxi stands in the tourist areas: many of these drivers have doctored their meters and have other tricks to rip you off.

Taxi Companies **AAA** 14014. **Profitaxi** 14035.

TOURS

BUS TOURS Čedok offers a daily three-hour tour of the city, starting at 10 AM from two offices. Martin-Tour offers a tour departing from Náměstí Republiky and three other Old Town points four times daily. PIS arranges guided tours at its Na Příkopě and Old Town Square locations.

Čedok's one-day tours out of Prague include excursions to the lovely medieval town of Kutná Hora, the unusual sandstone formations of the Bohemian Paradise region, famous spa towns and castles, wineries, and the Terezín Ghetto.

Fees & Schedules **Čedok** Na Příkopě 18 224/197121 or 224/197306 Pařížská 6 224/197618. **Martin-Tour** 224/212473. **PIS** 221/714130.

PRIVATE GUIDES Contact Čedok or PIS to arrange a personal walking tour of the city. Prices start at around 500 Kč per hour.

SPECIAL-INTEREST TOURS For cultural tours call Čedok. These include visits to the Jewish quarter, performances of folk troupes, Laterna Magika, opera, and concerts.

TRAIN TRAVEL

The main station is Hlavní Nádraží, not far from Wenceslas Square. Some international trains use Nádraží Holešovice, on the same metro line (C) as the main station.

Domestic and international schedules for both stations 221/111122 www.idos.cz. **Hlavní Nádraží** Wilsonova ul. **Nádraží Holešovice** Vrbenského ul.

TRANSPORTATION AROUND PRAGUE

Public transportation is a bargain. *Jízdenky* (tickets) can be bought at hotels, newsstands, and dispensing machines in metro stations. Transport passes for unlimited use of the system for 1 day (70 Kč) up to 15 days (280 Kč) are sold at some newsstands and at the windows marked DP or JÍZDENKY in the main metro stations. Be sure to validate your pass by signing it where indicated. A basic 12 Kč ticket allows one hour's travel, with unlimited transfers (90 minutes on weekends and between 8 PM and 5 AM weekdays) on the metro, tram, and bus network within the city limits. Cheaper 8 Kč tickets are good for a tram or bus ride up to 15 minutes without transferring, or 30 minutes on the metro including transfers between lines; on the metro, though, you cannot travel more than four stops from your starting point. For the metro punch the ticket in the station before getting onto the escalators; for buses and trams punch the ticket inside the vehicle. (Enter the tram or bus through any door and stick the tickets horizontally—and gently—into the little yellow machines, which should stamp them with the date and time; it's an acquired trick of hand-eye coordination; ask for help from another passenger if your machine is not cooperating, which is often the case.) If you fail to validate your ticket, you may be fined 800 Kč by a ticket inspector, which is reduced to 400 Kč for on-the-spot payment.

Note: Prague has quite a pickpocketing racket, to which the police apparently turn a blind eye. Be very wary of raucous groups of people making a commotion as they get on and off trams and metros; generally they are working the passengers. Keep close watch on your belongings and purses on crowded streets and in crowded sites.

TRAVEL AGENCIES

Local Agent Referrals **American Express** Václavské nám. 56 224/818205 222-211-131. **Thomas Cook** Karlova 3 221/221055.

VISITOR INFORMATION

The English-language weekly *Prague Post* lists current events and entertainment programs.

Čedok main office ✉ Na Příkopě 18, near Wenceslas Sq. ☎ 224/197121 or 224/197306 ✉ Rytířská 16 ✉ Pařížská 6 🌐 www.cedok.cz. **Prague Information Service** (PIS) ✉ Na Příkopě 20 ✉ Staroměstské nám. 22 ☎ 12444 or 221/714130.

Tourist Bureaus Outside Prague **Český Krumlov** Infocentrum ✉ Nám. Svornosti 2 ☎ 380/704622 🌐 www.ckrumlov.cz. **Karlovy Vary** ✉ Vřídelní kolonáda ☎ 353/244097 🌐 www.karlovyvary.cz. **Mariánské Lázně** Infocentrum ✉ Hlavní 47 ☎ 353/622474 🌐 www.marianskelazne.cz. **Mikulov** ✉ Regional Tourist Center, Nám. 1 ☎ 519/510855 🌐 www.mikulov.cz. **Olomouc** ✉ Horní nám. ☎ 585/513385 🌐 www.olomoucko.cz. **Tábor** ✉ Žižkovo nám. 2 ☎ 381/486230 🌐 www.tabor.cz. **Telč** ✉ Town hall, Nám. Zachariáše z Hradce 10 ☎ 567/234145 🌐 www.telc-etc.cz.

Czech Republic Basics

To research prices, get advice from other travelers, and book travel arrangements, visit www.fodors.com.

BUSINESS HOURS

Banks are open weekdays 8–5. Museums are usually open Tuesday–Sunday 10–5. Shops are generally open weekdays 9–6; some close for lunch between noon and 2. Many stores, especially larger ones in the downtown area, are now open weekends.

CUSTOMS & DUTIES

You may import duty-free 200 cigarettes, 50 cigars, 1 liter of spirits, 2 liters of wine, and gifts with a total value of 1,000 Kč. Goods worth up to 3,000 Kč (approximately US$90) are not liable for duty upon arrival. Declare items of greater value (jewelry, computers, and so on) on arrival to avoid problems with customs officials on departure. You may export only antiques that are certified as not having historical value; reputable dealers will advise. Play it safe, and hang on to your receipts.

EMBASSIES

Australia **The Honorary Consulate and Trade Commission of Australia** ✉ Klimentská 10 ☎ 251-018-352.

Canada ✉ Mickiewiczova 6, Hradčany ☎ 272-101-800 🌐 www.canada.cz.

Ireland ✉ Tržiště 13 ☎ 257/530061.

New Zealand consulate ✉ Dykova 19 ☎ 257/530061.

South Africa ✉ Ruska 65, Vršovice ☎ 267/311114.

United Kingdom ✉ Thunovská 14, Malá Strana ☎ 257/402111 🌐 www.britain.cz.

United States ✉ Tržiště 15, Malá Strana ☎ 257/530663 🌐 www.usis.cz.

HOLIDAYS

January 1; Easter Sunday and Monday; May 1 (Labor Day); May 8 (Liberation Day); July 5 (Sts. Cyril and Methodius); July 6 (Jan Hus); September 28 (Day of Czech Statehood); October 28 (Czechoslovak Proclamation Day); November 17 (Uprising of Students for Freedom and Democracy); December 24–26.

LANGUAGE

Czech, which belongs to the Slavic family of languages along with Russian, Polish, and Slovak, uses the Latin alphabet like English but adds special diacritical marks to make certain sounds: č is written for the "ch" sound, for instance. Unlike words in many other languages, Czech words are spelled phonetically, and the emphasis is almost always on the first syllable. You'll find a growing number of English-speakers, especially among young people and in the tourist industry. German is generally understood throughout the country.

MONEY MATTERS

Costs are highest in Prague and only slightly lower in the main Bohemian resorts and spas, though even in these places you can now find inexpensive accommodations in private homes. The least expensive area is southern Moravia. Note that many public venues in Prague and the Czech Republic continue the practice of adhering to a separate pricing system for Czechs and for foreigners. (Foreigners may be charged double or more on museum admission, for example.) This practice should end after the Czech Republic joins the European Union in 2004.

Costs: cup of coffee, 30 Kč; beer (½ liter), 19 Kč–40 Kč; Coca-Cola, 30 Kč; ham sandwich, 40 Kč; 1½-km (1-mi) taxi ride, 50 Kč–70 Kč; museum and castle admission, 20 Kč–300 Kč.

CURRENCY The unit of currency in the Czech Republic is the crown, or koruna (plural koruny), written as Kč, and divided into 100 haléřů (hellers). There are bills of 50, 100, 200, 500, 1,000, and 5,000 koruny and coins of 50 hellers and 1, 2, 5, 10, 20, and 50 koruny. Coins of 10 and 20 hellers were phased out in 2003.

At press time, the rate of exchange was 29.50 Kč to the U.S. dollar, 19.80 Kč to the Canadian dollar, 55.19 Kč to the pound sterling, 17.85 Kč to the Australian dollar, 16.54 Kč to the New Zealand dollar, 3.62 Kč to the South African rand, and 31.80 Kč to the euro. Banks and ATMs give the best rates. Banks and private exchange outlets, which litter Prague's tourist routes, charge either a set fee or a percentage of the transaction or both. It's wise to compare. Ask exactly how much you will get back before converting your money. Signs promising no commission are often misleading. The koruna is fully convertible and can be purchased outside the country and changed into other currencies, but you should keep your receipts and convert your koruny before you leave the country just to be sure.

TELEPHONES

Most people use mobile phones, so cards for working pay phones are becoming hard to find. To use a public phone, buy a phone card at a newsstand or tobacconist in the downtown area. Cards cost 175 Kč for 50 units or 320 Kč for 100 units (local calls cost one unit each). To place a call, lift the receiver, insert the card, and dial. Another option is Karta X, which comes in denominations of 300 Kč to 1,000 Kč and can be used for discount long-distance calling on any phone by entering a 14-digit number. It's available at exchange booths and newsstands.

COUNTRY & AREA CODES The Czech Republic's country code is 420. The country dropped regional codes and adopted a nationwide nine-digit standard in late 2002.

INTERNATIONAL CALLS Some special international pay-phone booths in central Prague will take 5 Kč coins or accept phone cards that allow automatic dialing. You will also find coin and card booths at the main post office (Jindřišská 14, near Václavské náměstí [Wenceslas Square]); the entrance for telephone service is in this building but around the corner on Politických vězňů. The international dialing code is 00. Dial 1181 for international inquiries to the United States, Canada, or the United Kingdom. Calls can be placed using AT&T USA Direct, MCI, and Sprint international operators. International rates vary according to destination.

Access Codes **AT&T USA Direct** ☎ 0042-000101. **MCI** ☎ 0042-000112. **Sprint** ☎ 0042-087187.

ROME

14

For 2,500 years, emperors, popes, and the citizens of the ages have left their mark on Rome, and the result is like nothing so much as a hustling, bustling open-air museum. Most of the city's major sights are in the *centro storico* (historic center), which lies between the long, straight Via del Corso and the Tevere (Tiber River), and the adjacent area of *Roma antica* (ancient Rome), site of the Foro Romano (Roman Forum) and Colosseo (Colosseum). The best way to discover the city is to wander, taking time to notice the layers of history that make Rome unique. On your way between monuments and museums note the changing architectural landscape: the soft curves of medieval Rome, which covered the horn of land that pushes the Tiber toward the Vatican and extended across the river into Trastevere, and the formal elegance of Renaissance Rome, which was erected upon medieval foundations and extended as far as the Vatican, with showcase villas created in what were then the outskirts of the city.

EXPLORING ROME

The layout of the centro storico is irregular, but several landmarks serve as orientation points to identify the areas that most visitors come to see: the Colosseo, Pantheon, Piazza Navona, St. Peter's Basilica, the Spanish Steps, and the Baths of Caracalla. You'll need a good map to find your way around; newsstands offer a wide choice. Much of your sightseeing in the historic center can, and should, be done on foot, since most automobile traffic is barred during the day. To move between the center and sites that are farther afield, take taxis, buses, or the metro. If you are in Rome during a hot spell, do as the Romans do: start out early in the morning, have a light lunch and a long siesta during the hottest hours, then resume sightseeing in the late afternoon and end your evening with a leisurely meal outdoors, refreshed by cold Frascati wine and the *ponentino,* the cool evening breeze.

Ancient Rome

The geographic center of the city is at Piazza Venezia, site of the late-19th-century monument to the first king of a united Italy, Vittorio Emanuele II. The most evocative ruins of the ancient city extend from the Campidoglio across the Foro Romano to the Colosseo and the Terme di Caracalla and include the Palatino and Circo Massimo. This is one of the world's most striking and significant concentrations of historic remains; stand at the back of the Campidoglio overlooking the Roman Forum and take in 2,500 years of history at a glance.

Numbers in the margin correspond to points of interest on the Rome map.

❽ **Arco di Costantino** (Arch of Constantine). The best preserved of Rome's triumphal arches, this 4th-century monument commemorates Constantine's victory over Maxentius at the Milvian Bridge. Just before this battle in AD 312, Constantine had a vision of a cross in the heavens and heard the words: "In this sign thou shalt conquer." The victory led not only to the construction of this majestic marble arch but also to a turning point in the history of Christianity: soon afterward a grateful—and converted—Constantine decreed that it was a lawful religion and should be tolerated throughout the empire. His newfound faith didn't seem to cure his imperial sticky fingers, however; the arch's decorations were pilfered from monuments to earlier emperors. ✉ *Piazza del Colosseo.*

❷ **Campidoglio** (Capitoline Hill). The majestic ramp and beautifully proportioned piazza are the handiwork of Michelangelo (1475–1564), who also designed the facades of the three palaces that face this square on Capitoline Hill. Palazzo Senatorio, at the center, is still the ceremonial seat of Rome's City Hall; it was built over the Tabularium, where ancient Rome's state archives were kept. The statue at the center of the square is a copy of an ancient Roman bronze of Marcus Aurelius (AD 120–180). The Capitoline Museums, the two palaces flanking the Senatorio, house the original. ✉ *Piazza del Campidoglio.*

★ ❻ **Colosseo** (Colosseum). Massive and majestic, this ruin is ancient Rome's hallmark monument, inaugurated in AD 80 with a program of games and shows that lasted 100 days. Before the imperial box, gladiators would salute the emperor and cry, "*Ave, imperator, morituri te salutant*" ("Hail, emperor, men soon to die salute thee"); it is said that when one day they heard the emperor Claudius respond, "Or maybe not," they became so offended that they called a strike. The Colosseum could hold more than 50,000 spectators; it was faced with marble, decorated with stuccos, and had an ingenious system of awnings to provide shade. It was built in just eight years. The Colosseum takes its name from a colossal, 118-foot statue of Nero that once stood nearby. ✉ *Piazza del Colosseo,* ☎ *06/39967700* 🌐 *www.archeorm.arti.beniculturali.it* ⏲ *Tues.–Sun. 9–4:30.*

❼ **Domus Aurea.** Nero's "Golden House" is a sprawling example of the excesses of Imperial Rome. After fire destroyed much of the city in AD 64, Nero took advantage of the resultant open space to construct a palace so large that contemporary accounts complained his house was bigger than the rest of the city. One wing of the building was given over to public functions, and the other served as the emperor's private residence. More than 150 rooms have been excavated (although only a few are open to the public), revealing a subterranean trove of ancient Roman architecture and some well-preserved Roman paintings decorating the walls. ✉ *Via della Domus Aurea,* ☎ *06/39967700 reservations* 🌐 *www.archeorm.arti.beniculturali.it* ⏲ *Wed.–Mon. 9–7:45.*

5 **Foro Romano** (Roman Forum). Rome's foundations as a world capital and crossroads of culture are to be found here—literally. Excavations have shown that this site was in use as a burial ground as far back as the 10th century BC, hundreds of years before Rome's legendary founding by Romulus. But the Forum gained importance (and the name in use today) during Roman and Imperial times, when this marshy hollow was the political, commercial, and social center of Rome, and by extension, of the ancient world. The majestic ruins of temples and palaces visible today are fragments of the massive complex of markets, civic buildings, and houses of worship that dominated the city in its heyday. Wander down the **Via Sacra,** which runs the length of the Roman Forum, and take in the timeless view; then climb the **Colle Palatino** (Palatine Hill), where the emperors had their palaces and where 16th-century cardinals strolled in elaborate Renaissance gardens. From the *belvedere* (overlook) you have a good view of the **Circo Massimo** (Circus Maximus). Audio guides are available at the bookshop–ticket office at the Via dei Fori Imperiali entrance. ✉ *Entrances at Via dei Fori Imperiali and Piazza del Colosseo,* ☎ *06/39967700* 🌐 *www.pierreci.it* ⏲ *Daily 9–4:30.*

3 **Musei Capitolini** (Capitoline Museums). The **Museo Capitolino** and **Palazzo dei Conservatori,** the palaces flanking Palazzo Senatorio on the Campidoglio, form a single museum holding some fine classical sculptures, including the gilded bronze equestrian statue of Marcus Aurelius that once stood on the pedestal in the piazza, as well as the *Dying Gaul,* the *Capitoline Venus,* and a series of portrait busts of ancient philosophers and emperors. In the courtyard of Palazzo dei Conservatori on the right of the piazza are mammoth fragments of a colossal statue of the emperor Constantine (circa 280–336). Inside are splendidly frescoed salons still used for municipal ceremonies, as well as sculptures and paintings. Don't miss the superb baroque painting collection in the Pinacoteca, which holds masterpieces by Caravaggio and Rubens, among other stars. ✉ *Piazza del Campidoglio,* ☎ *06/39967800* 🌐 *www.pierreci.it* ⏲ *Tues.–Sun. 9–8.*

Fodor'sChoice ★

1 **Piazza Venezia.** Considered the geographical heart of the city, the square is dominated by the **Monumento a Vittorio Emanuele II,** or Altare della Patria (Victor Emmanuel Monument, or Altar of the Nation), the enormous marble monument (1911) honoring the first king of unified Italy, Vittorio Emanuele II (1820–78). Climb to the top of the "Vittoriano" for a stunning panorama over Rome. The piazza takes its name from the smaller but more historically important Palazzo Venezia, once Mussolini's headquarters. His most famous speeches were delivered from its balcony to the roaring crowds below. ✉ *Square at intersection of Via del Corso, Via del Plebiscito, and Via del Fori Imperiali,* ⏲ *Tues.–Sun. 10:30–1 hr before sunset.*

4 **Santa Maria d'Aracoeli.** The 13th-century church on the Campidoglio can be reached by a long flight of steep stairs or, more easily, by way of the stairs on the far side of the Museo Capitolino. Stop in to see the medieval pavement, the Renaissance gilded ceiling that commemorates the victory of Lepanto, and the Pinturicchio (1454–1513) frescoes. ✉ *Piazza Aracoeli,* ☎ *06/6798155* ⏲ *Oct.–May, daily 7–noon and 4–6; June–Sept., daily 7–noon and 4–6:30.*

9 **Terme di Caracalla** (Baths of Caracalla). The scale of the towering ruins of ancient Rome's most beautiful and luxurious public baths hint at their past splendor. Inaugurated by Caracalla in AD 217, the baths were used until the 6th century. An ancient version of a swank athletic club, the baths were open to all, though men and women used them separately; citizens could bathe, socialize, and exercise in huge pools and richly dec-

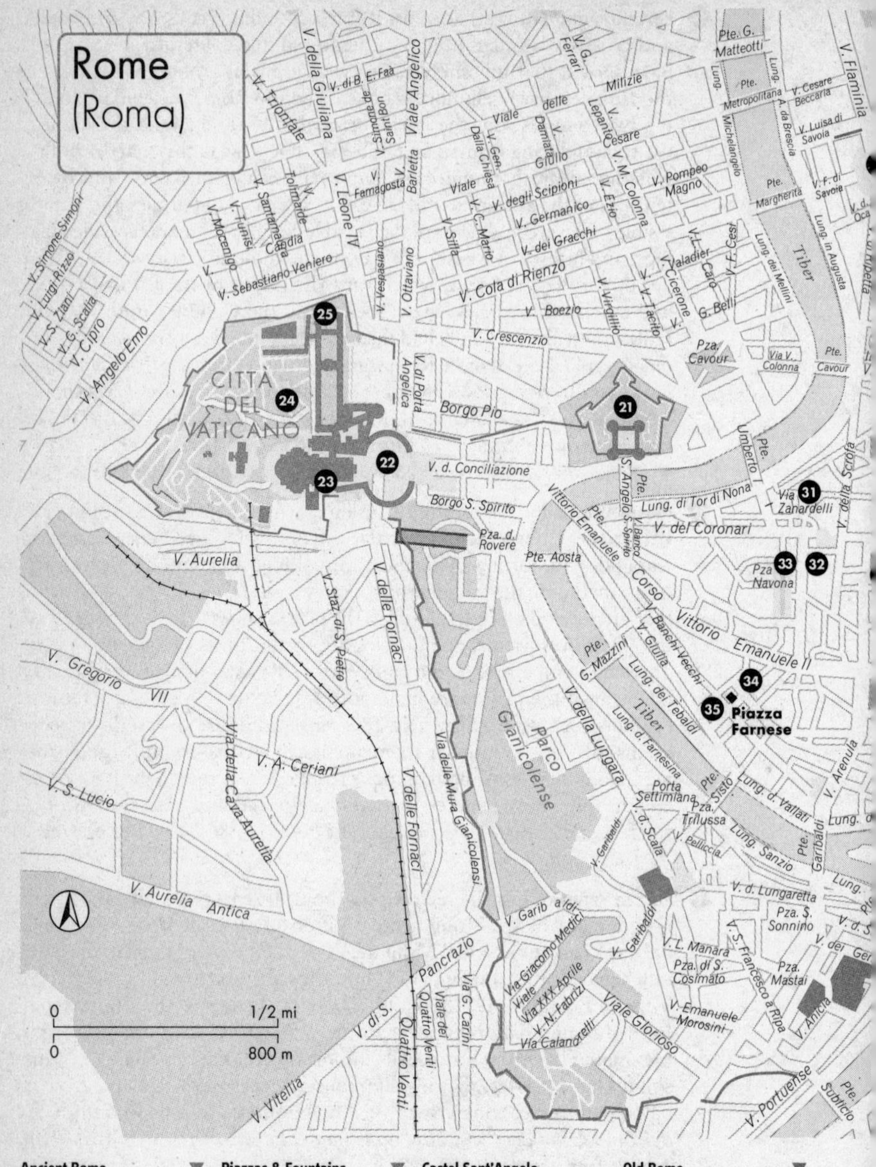

Ancient Rome

Arco di Costantino 8
Campidoglio 2
Colosseo 6
Domus Aurea 7
Foro Romano 5
Musei Capitolini 3
Piazza Venezia 1
Santa Maria d'Aracoeli 4
Terme di Caracalla 9

Piazzas & Fountains

Fontana di Trevi 16
Galleria Borghese 20
Keats-Shelley Memorial House 15
Museo Etrusco di Villa Giulia 12
Palazzo Barberini 18
Piazza Barberini 17
Piazza del Popolo 10
Piazza di Spagna 13
Santa Maria della Concezione 19
Santa Maria del Popolo .11
Scalinata di Trinitá dei Monti 14

Castel Sant'Angelo & the Vatican

Castel Sant'Angelo 21
Giardini Vaticani 24
Musei Vaticani 25
Piazza San Pietro 22
St. Peter's Basilica 23

Old Rome

Campo de' Fiori 34
Chiesa del Gesù 27
Fontana delle Tartarughe 26
Galleria Doria Pamphili 28
Isola Tiberina 36
Palazzo Altemps 31
Palazzo Farnese 35
Pantheon 30
Piazza Navona 33
San Luigi dei Francesi 32
Santa Maria sopra Minerva 29

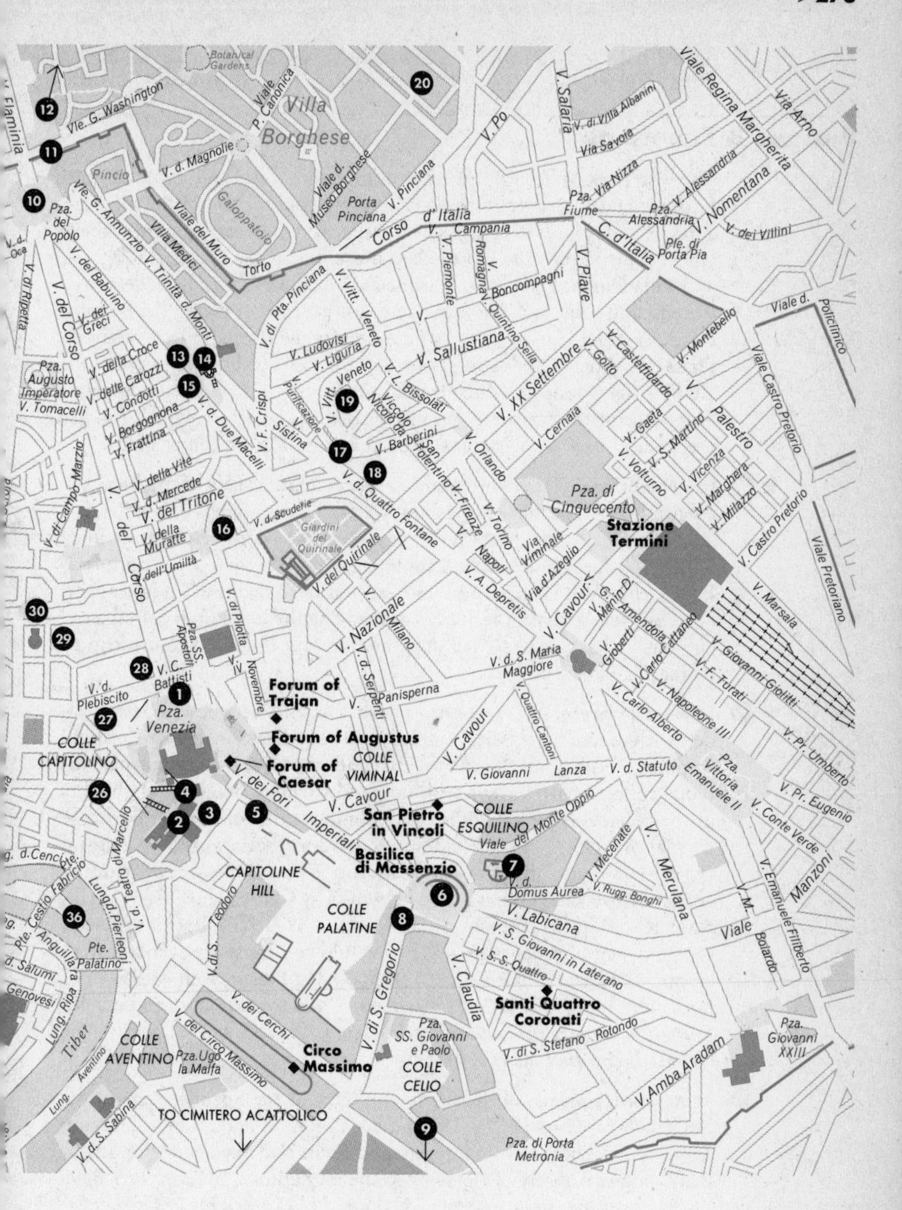
Villa Borghese
Pincio
Pza. del Popolo
Stazione Termini
Pza. di Cinquecento
Giardini del Quirinale
Forum of Trajan
Forum of Augustus
Forum of Caesar
COLLE VIMINALE
COLLE CAPITOLINO
San Pietro in Vincoli
COLLE ESQUILINO
Basilica di Massenzio
CAPITOLINE HILL
COLLE PALATINE
Santi Quattro Coronati
Circo Massimo
COLLE CELIO
COLLE AVENTINO
Pza. Venezia
Tiber
TO CIMITERO ACATTOLICO
Corso d' Italia
V. del Corso
V. Nazionale
V. Cavour
V. dei Fori Imperiali
V. XX Settembre
V. Vitt. Veneto
Via Merulana
V. Labicana
Pza. di Porta Metronia
Pza. Giovanni XXIII

orated halls and libraries. ✉ *Via delle Terme di Caracalla 52* ☎ *06/39967700* 🌐 *www.pierreci.it* 🕓 *Mon. 9–2, Tues.–Sun. 9–4.*

Piazzas & Fountains

The lush park of Villa Borghese is dotted with pines and fountains and faux neoclassical-style ruins. It is a happy conjunction of the pleasure gardens and palaces of Renaissance prelates on the site of ancient Roman villas. It also holds the world-class museums of the Galleria Borghese and Villa Giulia. The Pincio, the ancient Pincian Hill, is a belvedere over the city and a vantage point over elegant pedestrian Piazza del Popolo, below. Via del Corso, with its many midrange shops, runs straight to Piazza di Venezia and is intersected with upscale shopping streets, including Via Condotti, which lead to the bustle of the Piazza di Spagna. The scene at the nearby Fontana di Trevi is equally crowded, forcing the wishful to toss their coins into the fountain from center field.

★ ⓰ **Fontana di Trevi** (Trevi Fountain). A spectacular fantasy of mythical sea creatures and cascades of splashing water, this fountain is one of Rome's baroque greats. The fountain as you see it was completed in the mid-1700s, but there had been a drinking fountain on the site for centuries. Pope Urban VIII (1568–1644) almost sparked a revolt when he slapped a tax on wine to cover the expenses of having the fountain repaired. Legend has it that a coin tossed into the fountain ensures a return trip to Rome. ✉ *Piazza di Trevi.*

★ ⑳ **Galleria Borghese.** At the southeast corner of Villa Borghese, a park studded with pines and classical statuary, is this gallery created by Cardinal Scipione Borghese in the early 17th century as a showcase for his fabulous collection of ancient sculpture and baroque painting. Highlights of the collection are the seductive reclining statue of Pauline Borghese by Canova (1757–1822) and some extraordinary works by Bernini (1598–1680), including the virtuoso *Apollo and Daphne*. The painting collection is no less impressive, with works by Caravaggio (1573–1610), Raphael (1483–1520), and Titian (circa 1488–1576), but the palace's restored magnificence is such that it would be a must-see even if it were empty. ✉ *Piazza Scipione Borghese 5, off Via Pinciana* ☎ *06/8548577 information; 06/328102 reservations* 🌐 *www.galleriaborghese.it information or www.beniculturali.it ticketing* 🕓 *Tues.–Sun. 9–7; reservations required, entrance every 2 hrs.*

⓯ **Keats–Shelley Memorial House.** To the right of the Spanish Steps is the house where Keats (1795–1821) died; the building is now a museum dedicated to English Romanticism and Keats and Shelley memorabilia. It also houses a library of works by Romantic authors. ✉ *Piazza di Spagna 26, next to the Spanish Steps* ☎ *06/6784235* 🌐 *www.keats-shelley-house.org* 🕓 *Weekdays 9–1 and 3–6, Sat. 11–2 and 3–6.*

⓬ **Museo Etrusco di Villa Giulia** (Etruscan Museum of Villa Giulia). Pope Julius III (1487–1555) built this gracious Renaissance villa as a summer retreat. It's been turned into a fine museum dedicated to the Etruscans, central Italy's pre-Roman inhabitants. The collection, a well-explained cross section of Etruscan statuary and sculpture, provides an introduction to this complex and ancient culture that is an interesting counterpoint to the city's usual emphasis on Imperial and Papal Rome. ✉ *Piazzale di Villa Giulia 9* ☎ *06/32810* 🌐 *www.beniculturali.it* 🕓 *Tues.–Sun. 8:30–7:30.*

⓲ **Palazzo Barberini** (Barberini Palace). Rome's most splendid 17th-century palace houses the **Galleria Nazionale di Arte Antica.** Its gems include Raphael's *La Fornarina* and many other fine paintings, some lavishly frescoed ceilings, and a suite of rooms decorated in 1782 on the occasion of the marriage of a Barberini heiress. ✉ *Via Barberini 18* ☎ *06/32810* 🌐 *www.galleriaborghese.it* ⏲ *Tues.–Sun. 9–7.*

⓱ **Piazza Barberini.** This busy crossroads is marked by two Bernini fountains: the saucy **Fontana del Tritone** (Triton Fountain) in the middle of the square and the **Fontana delle Api** (Fountain of the Bees) at the corner of Via Veneto. Decorated with the heraldic Barberini bees, the shell-shape fountain bears an inscription that was immediately seen as an unlucky omen by the superstitious Romans: it proclaimed that the fountain had been erected in the 22nd year of the reign of Pope Urban VIII, who commissioned it, whereas in fact the 21st anniversary of his election was still some weeks away. The incorrect numeral was hurriedly erased, but to no avail: Urban died eight days before the beginning of his 22nd year as pontiff. ✉ *Square at intersection of Via del Tritone, Via Vittorio Veneto, and Via Barberini.*

⓾ **Piazza del Popolo.** Designed by neoclassical architect Giuseppe Valadier in the early 1800s, this circular square is one of the largest and airiest in Rome. It's a pleasant spot for an afternoon stroll. The 3,000-year-old obelisk in the middle of the square, brought to Rome from Egypt by the emperor Augustus, once stood in the Circus Maximus. ✉ *Southern end of Via Flaminia and northern end of Via del Corso.*

⓭ **Piazza di Spagna.** The square is the heart of Rome's chic shopping district and a popular rendezvous spot, especially for the young people who throng the **Spanish Steps** on evenings and weekend afternoons. In the center of the elongated square, at the foot of the Spanish Steps, is the **Fontana della Barcaccia** (Old Boat Fountain) by Pietro Bernini (Gian Lorenzo's father). ✉ *Southern end of Via del Babuino and northern end of Via Due Macelli.*

⓳ **Santa Maria della Concezione.** In the crypt under the main Capuchin church, skeletons and scattered bones of some 4,000 Capuchin monks are arranged in odd decorative designs, intended as a macabre reminder of the impermanence of earthly life. ✉ *Via Veneto 27* ☎ *06/4871185* ⏲ *Fri.–Wed. 9–noon and 3–6.*

⓫ **Santa Maria del Popolo.** This medieval church rebuilt by Gian Lorenzo Bernini in baroque style is rich in art; the pièces de résistance are two stunning Caravaggios in the chapel to the left of the main altar. ✉ *Piazza del Popolo,* ☎ *06/3610836* ⏲ *Mon.–Sat. 7–7, Sun. 8–2 and 4:30–7:30.*

★ ⓮ **Scalinata di Trinitá dei Monti** (Spanish Steps). The 200-year-old stairway got its nickname from the nearby Spanish Embassy to the Holy See (the Vatican), though it was built with French funds in 1723 as the approach to the French church of **Trinità dei Monti** at the top of the steps. Rome's classic picture-postcard view is even more lovely when the steps are banked with blooming azaleas, from mid-April to mid-May. ✉ *Piazza di Spagna and Piazza Trinità dei Monti.*

Castel Sant'Angelo & the Vatican

Given that the Vatican has many of Rome's (and the world's) greatest art treasures, as well as being the spiritual home of a billion Catholics, this area of the city is full of tourists and pilgrims almost year-round. Between the Vatican and the once-moated bulk of Castel Sant'Angelo, the pope's covered passageway flanks an enclave of workers and craftspeople, the old Borgo neighborhood, whose workaday charm is beginning to succumb to gentrification.

21 **Castel Sant'Angelo** (Sant'Angelo Castle). Transformed into a formidable fortress, this castle was originally built as the tomb of Emperor Hadrian (AD 76–138) in the 2nd century AD. In its early days it looked much like the Augusteo (Tomb of Augustus), which still stands in more or less its original form across the river. Hadrian's Tomb was incorporated into the city's walls and served as a military stronghold during the barbarian invasions. According to legend it got its present name in the 6th century, when Pope Gregory the Great, passing by in a religious procession, saw an angel with a sword appear above the ramparts to signal the end of the plague that was raging. Enlarged and fortified, the castle became a refuge for the popes, who fled to it along the Passetto, an arcaded passageway that links it with the Vatican.

Inside the castle are ancient corridors, medieval cells, and Renaissance salons, a museum of antique weapons, courtyards piled with stone cannonballs, and terraces with great views of the city. The highest terrace of all, under the bronze statue of the legendary angel, is the one from which Puccini's heroine Tosca threw herself to her death. **Ponte Sant'Angelo,** the ancient bridge spanning the Tiber in front of the castle, is decorated with lovely baroque angels designed by Bernini. ✉ *Lungotevere Castello 50* ☎ *06/39967700* 🌐 *www.pierreci.it* ⏲ *Tues.–Sun. 9–8.*

24 **Giardini Vaticani** (Vatican Gardens). The attractively landscaped gardens can be seen in a two-hour tour that shows you a few historical monuments, fountains, and the lovely 16th-century house of Pius IV (1499–1565), designed by Pirro Ligorio (1500–83), as well as the Vatican's mosaic school. Vistas from within the gardens give you a different perspective on the basilica itself. Reserve two or three days in advance. ✉ *Centro Servizi, south side of Piazza San Pietro* ☎ *06/69884466* 📠 *06/69885100* 🌐 *www.vatican.va* 🎫 *€9 for the Gardens tour; €19 for Gardens and Sistine Chapel* ⏲ *Mon.–Sat.*

25 **Musei Vaticani** (Vatican Museums). One of the world's greatest collections of Western art, the holdings of the Vatican Museum are an embarrassment of riches that include Ancient Egyptian sarcophagi, Greek and Roman statuary, paintings by Giotto, Leonardo, and Raphael, and Michelangelo's magnificent frescoes in the Sistine Chapel. The nearly 8 km (5 mi) of displays are said to represent only a small part of the Vatican's holdings. The museums are almost unavoidably overwhelming and include the famed **Cappella Sistina** (Sistine Chapel). In 1508 Pope Julius II (1443–1513) commissioned Michelangelo to paint the more than 10,000 square feet of the chapel's ceiling. For four years Michelangelo dedicated himself to painting in the fresco technique, over wet plaster, and the result is one of the Renaissance's masterworks. Cleaning has removed centuries of soot and revealed the original and surprisingly brilliant colors of the ceiling and the *Last Judgment.* The chapel is almost always unpleasantly crowded—try to avoid the tour groups by going early or late. A pair of binoculars and an illustrated or audio guide will contribute greatly to understanding and appreciating the work.

Fodor's Choice ★

A complete list of the great works on display would go on for pages; don't-miss highlights, however, certainly include the Egyptian collection, the Roman mosaics and wall paintings, and the great classical- and Hellenistic-style statuary in the Belvedere Courtyard, including the *Laocoön,* the *Belvedere Torso* (which inspired Michelangelo), and the *Apollo Belvedere.* The **Stanze di Raffaello** (Raphael Rooms) are decorated with masterful frescoes, and there are more of Raphael's works in the **Pinacoteca** (Picture Gallery). Bored children may perk up in the whimsical **Sala degli Animali,** a seemingly forgotten room full of animal statuary. ✉ *Viale Vaticano* ☎ *06/69884947* 🌐 *www.vatican.va* ⏲ *Easter week* *and mid-Mar.–Oct., weekdays 8:45–4:45 (no admission after 3:45), Sat. and last Sun. of month 8:45–1:45 (no admission after 12:30); Nov.–mid-Mar. (except Easter week), Mon.–Sat. and last Sun. of month 8:45–1:45 (no admission after 12:30). Note: Ushers at the entrance of St. Peter's Basilica and the Vatican Museums will not allow entry to persons with inappropriate clothing (no bare knees, shoulders, or low-cut shirts).*

22 **Piazza San Pietro** (St. Peter's Square). Gian Lorenzo Bernini designed this vast, circular piazza in the 17th century with an eye to the dramatic contrast between the dark, narrow medieval streets of the area and the wide open space of the piazza, presided over by the magnificence of St. Peter's Basilica. Unfortunately for art history, Mussolini had his own ideas about dramatic effect, which led him to raze much of the medieval neighborhood around the square to create Via della Conciliazione, the broad avenue that leads to the square today. Other aspects of Bernini's vision of architectural harmony remain, however: look for the stone disks in the pavement halfway between the fountains and the obelisk. From these points the colonnades seem to be formed of a single row of columns all the way around. The square was designed to accommodate crowds, and it has held up to 400,000 people at one time. At noon on Sunday when he is in Rome, the pope appears at his third-floor study window in the **Palazzo Vaticano,** to the right of the basilica, to bless the crowd in the square, and in warm months he blesses visitors from a podium on the basilica steps on Wednesday mornings. ⊠ *End of Via Conciliazione.*

Since the Lateran Treaty of 1929, Vatican City has been an independent and sovereign state, which covers about 108 acres and is surrounded by thick, high walls. Its gates are watched over by the Swiss Guards, who still wear the colorful dress uniforms based on a Michelangelo design. Sovereign of this little state is the pope of the Roman Catholic Church. For many visitors a **papal audience** is the highlight of a trip to Rome. Mass audiences take place on Wednesday morning in the square or in a modern audience hall (capacity 7,000) off the left-hand colonnade. Tickets are necessary. For audience tickets write or fax well in advance indicating the date you prefer, language you speak, and hotel in which you will stay. Or, apply for tickets in person on the Monday or Tuesday before the Wednesday audience. ⊠ *Tickets: Prefettura della Casa Pontificia, 00120 Vatican City* ☎ *06/69883273* 📠 *06/69885863* ⏲ *Mon.–Sat. 9–1.*

★ 23 **St. Peter's Basilica** (Basilica di San Pietro). In its staggering grandeur and magnificence, St. Peter's Basilica is best appreciated as the lustrous background for ecclesiastical ceremonies thronged with the faithful. The original basilica was built in the early 4th century AD by the emperor Constantine, above an earlier shrine that supposedly marked the burial place of St. Peter. After more than 1,000 years, the decrepit old basilica had to be torn down. The task of building a new, much larger one took almost 200 years and employed the genius of many of the Renaissance's greatest architects, including Alberti (1404–72), Bramante (1444–1514), Raphael, Peruzzi (1481–1536), Antonio Sangallo the Younger (1483–1546), and Michelangelo, who died before the dome he had planned could be completed. The structure was finally finished in 1626.

The most famous work of art inside is Michelangelo's *Pietà* (1498), in the first chapel on the right as you enter the basilica. Michelangelo carved four statues of the Pietà, or Mary cradling her dead son; this one is the earliest and best known, two others are in Florence, and the fourth, the *Rondanini Pietà,* is in Milan. At the end of the central aisle is the bronze statue of St. Peter, its foot worn by centuries of reverent kisses. The bronze throne above the altar in the apse was created by Bernini to contain a simple wood-and-ivory chair believed to have once belonged to St. Peter. Bernini's baldachin over the papal altar was made with bronze stripped from the dome of the Pantheon at the order of Pope Urban VIII, one of the powerful Roman Barberini family. His practice of plundering ancient monuments for material with which to carry out his grandiose decorating schemes inspired the famous quip "*Quod non fecerunt barbari, fecerunt Barberini*" ("What the barbarians didn't do, the Barberinis did").

As you stroll up and down the aisles and transepts, notice the fine mosaic copies of famous paintings above the altars, the monumental tombs and statues, and the fine stuccowork. Stop at the **Museo Storico** (Historical Museum), which contains some priceless liturgical objects. ⏲ *Apr.–Sept., daily 9–6; Oct.–Mar., daily 9–5.*

The entrance to **Le Sacre Grotte Vaticane** (Tombs of the Popes) is in one of the huge piers under the dome, next to the central altar. It's best to leave this visit for last, as the crypt's only exit takes you outside the church. It occupies the area of the original basilica, over the necropolis (left beyond Arco delle Campane entrance to Vatican), the ancient burial ground where evidence of what may be St. Peter's burial place has been found. ⏲ *Apr.–Sept., daily 7–6; Oct.–Mar., daily 7–5.*

To see the **roof and dome** of the basilica, take the elevator or climb the stairs in the courtyard near the exit from the Vatican Grottoes. From the roof you can climb a short interior staircase to the base of the dome for an overhead view of the basilica's interior. Then, and only if you are in good shape, you should attempt the very long, strenuous, and claustrophobic climb up the narrow stairs to the balcony of the lantern atop the dome, where you can look down on the Giardini Vaticani (Vatican Gardens) and out across all of Rome. ✉ *Entrance in courtyard to the left as you leave the basilica* ⏲ *Daily 8–5. Closed during ceremonies in the piazza.*

Free 60-minute tours of St. Peter's Basilica are offered in English daily (Monday–Saturday usually starting about 10 AM and 3 PM, Sunday at 2:30 PM) by volunteer guides. They start at the information desk under the basilica portico. At the Ufficio Scavi you can book special tours of the necropolis. Note that entry to St. Peter's, the Musei Vaticani, and the Gardens is barred to those wearing shorts, miniskirts, sleeveless T-shirts, and otherwise revealing clothing. Women can cover bare shoulders and upper arms with scarves; men should wear full-length pants or jeans. ✉ *Piazza San Pietro* ☎ *06/69884466; 06/69885318 necropolis* 🌐 *www.vatican.va* ⏲ *Apr.–Sept., daily 7–7; Oct.–Mar., daily 7–6. Closed during ceremonies in the piazza. Apply for a special tour a few days in advance to Ufficio Scavi, or try in morning for the same day. Office: Mon.–Sat. 9–5.*

Old Rome

The land between the Corso and the Tiber bend is packed with churches, patrician palaces, baroque piazzas, and picturesque courtyards, with Piazza Navona as a magnificent central point. In between are narrow streets and intriguing little shops, interspersed with eating places and cafés that are a focus of Rome's easygoing, itinerant nightlife.

Fodor's Choice ★

34 **Campo de' Fiori** (Field of Flowers). This wide square is the site of Rome's best-loved morning market, a crowded and colorful circus of fruits, flowers, and fish, raucously peddled daily 9–2. If you'd rather watch than

participate in the genial chaos, sit at one of the casual cafés that line the square. The hooded bronze figure brooding over the piazza is philosopher Giordano Bruno (1548–1600), who was burned at the stake for heresy here in 1600. ✉ *Piazza Campo dei Fiori.*

27 **Chiesa del Gesù.** This huge 16th-century church is a paragon of the baroque style and the tangible symbol of the power of the Jesuits, who were a major force in the Counter-Reformation in Europe. Its interior gleams with gold and precious marbles, and it has a fantastically painted ceiling that flows down over the pillars, merging with painted stucco figures to complete the three-dimensional illusion. ✉ *Piazza del Gesù* ☎ *06/697001* ⏲ *Daily 7–noon and 4–7.*

26 **Fontana delle Tartarughe** (Turtle Fountain). The winsome turtles that are this 16th-century fountain's hallmark are thought to have been added around 1658 by Bernini as a low-budget way to bring the Renaissance fountain into the baroque. Visit it on a stroll through Rome's former Jewish Ghetto, an atmospheric old neighborhood with medieval inscriptions and friezes on the buildings on Via Portico d'Ottavia, and the remains of the Teatro di Marcello (Theater of Marcello), a theater built by Julius Caesar to hold 20,000 spectators. ✉ *Piazza Mattei.*

28 **Galleria Doria Pamphili.** You can visit this formidable palazzo, still the residence of a princely family, to view the gallery housing the family's art collection, which includes works by Velázquez and Bernini. ✉ *Piazza del Collegio Romano 2* ☎ *06/6797323* 🌐 *www.doriapamphilj.it* ⏲ *Fri.–Wed. 10–5.*

36 **Isola Tiberina.** Built in 62 BC, Rome's oldest bridge, the **Ponte Fabricio,** links the Ghetto neighborhood on the Tiber's left bank to this little island, with a hospital and the church of San Bartolomeo. The island has been dedicated to healing ever since a temple to Aesculapius was erected here in 291 BC. **Ponte Cestio** links the island with the Trastevere neighborhood on the right bank.

off the beaten path

OSTIA ANTICA (Ancient Ostia) – The well-preserved Roman port city of Ostia Antica, near the sea, is now a vast archaeological park just outside Rome, a lovely day trip into the ancient past. Wander through ancient markets and ruined houses, or bring a picnic and enjoy the sea breeze. There's regular train service from the Ostiense Station (Piramide Metro B stop). ✉ *Via dei Romagnoli, Ostia Antica, not far from Fiumicino Airport* ☎ *06/56358099* 🌐 *www.itnw.roma.it* ⏲ *Tues.–Sun. 8:30–5.*

31 **Palazzo Altemps.** A 15th-century patrician dwelling, the palace is a showcase for the sculpture collection of the **Museo Nazionale Romano** (National Museum of Rome). Informative labels in English make it easy to appreciate such famous sculptures as the intricate carved reliefs on the *Ludovisi Sarcophagus* and the *Galata*, representing the heroic death of a barbarian warrior. ✉ *Piazza Sant'Apollinare 46* ☎ *06/39967700* 🌐 *www.archeorm.arti.beniculturali.it* ⏲ *Tues.–Sun. 9–7:45.*

35 **Palazzo Farnese.** Now the French Embassy, one of the most beautiful of Rome's many Renaissance palaces dominates Piazza Farnese, where Egyptian marble basins from the Terme di Caracalla have been transformed into fountains. Note the unique brickwork patterns on the palace's facade. ✉ *Piazza Farnese.*

★ 30 **Pantheon.** Lauded for millennia for its architectural harmony, the Pantheon is no less impressive in the 21st century. Built in 27 BC by Augustus's general Agrippa and totally rebuilt by Hadrian in the 2nd century AD, this unique temple (consecrated as a church in the Middle Ages) is a must-see. Notice the equal proportions of the height of the dome and the circular interior—unlike most angular buildings, the Pantheon is designed after a globe. The oculus, or opening in the ceiling, is meant to symbolize the all-seeing eye of heaven; in practice, it illuminates the building and lightens the heavy stone ceiling. In earlier times the dome was covered in bronze, which was later pilfered to construct the baldachin over the altar in St. Peter's. ✉ *Piazza della Rotonda* ☎ *06/68300230* ⏲ *Mon.–Sat. 8:30–7:30, Sun. 9–6, holidays 9–1.*

★ 33 **Piazza Navona.** This elongated 17th-century piazza traces the oval form of the underlying Circus of Diocletian. At the center, Bernini's lively **Fontana dei Quattro Fiumi** (Four Rivers Fountain) is a showpiece. The four statues represent rivers in the four corners of the world: the Nile, with its face covered in allusion to its then-unknown source; the Ganges; the Danube; and the Rio de la Plata, with its hand raised. You may hear the legend that this was Bernini's mischievous dig at Borromini's design of the facade of the church of **Sant'Agnese in Agone,** from which the statue seems to be shrinking in horror. In point of fact, the fountain was created in 1651; work on the church's facade began a year or two later. ✉ *North of Corso Vittorio Emanuele and west of Corso Rinascimento.*

32 **San Luigi dei Francesi.** The clergy of San Luigi considered Caravaggio's roistering and unruly lifestyle scandalous enough, but his realistic treatment of sacred subjects—seen in three paintings here—was just too much for them. They rejected his first version of the altarpiece and weren't particularly happy with the other two works either. Thanks to the intercession of Caravaggio's patron, an influential cardinal, they were persuaded to keep them—a lucky thing, since they are now recognized to be among the artist's finest paintings. Have some coins handy for the light machine. ✉ *Piazza San Luigi dei Francesi* ☎ *06/688271* ⏲ *Fri.–Wed. 8:30–12:30 and 3:30–5, Thurs. 8:30–12:30.*

29 **Santa Maria sopra Minerva.** Rome's only major Gothic church takes its name from the temple of Minerva over which it was built. Inside are some beautiful frescoes by Filippino Lippi (circa 1457–1504); outside in the square is a charming elephant by Bernini carrying an obelisk on its back. ✉ *Piazza della Minerva* ☎ *06/6793926* ⏲ *Daily 7:30–7.*

WHERE TO EAT

Rome has no shortage of restaurants, and what the city lacks in variety of fare is made up for by overall quality. Don't make the mistake of assuming that expensive restaurants serve better or more authentic food; in Rome, you may pay top dollar for nothing more than a flourish of linen and silver. Some of Rome's prime restaurants are worth the expense, but you'll often do better at a more unassuming trattoria or osteria. Romans eat out a lot, and there's Italian fast food that caters to workers on lunch breaks. These places serve anything from a fruit salad and fresh spinach to lasagna and deep-fried cod fillets. Unfortunately, non-Italian cuisines haven't really caught on in Rome, although there are a few excellent Eritrean and Ethiopian places near Termini and some less appealing Chinese restaurants throughout the center. That old Roman standby, the paper-thin, crispy wood-oven pizza, is a low-budget favorite among locals and travelers alike, as is its to-go cousin, the heartier *pizza al taglio*. During August and over Christmas many restaurants close for vacation.

WHAT IT COSTS In euros				
	$$$$	$$$	$$	$
AT DINNER	over €22	€17–€22	€12–€17	under €12

Prices are per person for a main course.

★ $$$$ ✕ **La Pergola.** High atop Monte Mario, the Cavalieri Hilton's rooftop restaurant has a commanding view of the city below. Trompe-l'oeil ceilings and handsome wood paneling combine with low lighting to create a feeling of intimacy. Celebrated wunder-chef Heinz Beck brings Rome its finest example of Mediterranean *alta cucina* (haute cuisine); dishes are balanced and light, and presentation is striking. For a window table, reserve a month in advance; otherwise, two weeks. ✉ *Cavalieri Hilton, Via Cadlolo 101* ☎ *06/3509221* *Reservations essential* *Jacket and tie* ▭ *AE, DC, MC, V* ⊙ *Closed Sun. and Mon. and 2 wks in Dec. No lunch.*

$$$–$$$$ ✕ **Papà Baccus.** Italo Cipriani, owner of Rome's best Tuscan restaurant, takes his meat as seriously as any Tuscan, using real Chianina beef for the house special, *bistecca alla fiorentina* (grilled, thick bone-in steak). If you're avoiding beef, you can sample such dishes as Tuscan bean soup and the sweet and delicate prosciutto from Pratomagno. The welcome here is warm, the service excellent, and the interior elegant. ✉ *Via Toscana 36* ☎ *06/42742808* ▭ *AE, DC, MC, V* *Reservations essential.*

$$$–$$$$ ✕ **Il Simposio di Costantini.** At the classiest wine bar in town—done out in wrought-iron vines, wood paneling, and velvet—choose from about 30 wines in *degustazione* (available by the glass) or order a bottle from a list of more than 1,000 Italian and foreign labels sold in the shop next door. Food is appropriately fancy: marinated and smoked fish, designer salads, fine cured meats, terrines and pâtés, and stellar cheeses. ✉ *Piazza Cavour 16* ☎ *06/3211502* ▭ *AE, DC, MC, V* ⊙ *Closed Sun. and last 2 wks of Aug. No lunch Sat.*

★ $$–$$$ ✕ **Antico Arco.** Antico Arco has won the hearts of foodies from Rome and beyond. The menu changes with the season, but you may find such delights as *flan di taleggio con salsa di funghi* (taleggio flan with mushrooms), or a *carré d'agnello* (rack of lamb) with foie gras sauce and pears in port wine. Don't miss dessert, especially the chocolate soufflé with melted chocolate center. ✉ *Piazzale Aurelio 7* ☎ *06/5815274* *Reservations essential* ▭ *AE, DC, MC, V* ⊙ *No lunch. Closed Sun. and 2 wks in Aug.*

$$–$$$ ✕ **Checchino dal 1887.** Carved out of a hillside made of potsherds from Roman times, Checchino serves the most traditional Roman cuisine—carefully prepared and served without fanfare—in a clean and sober environment. You can try the different meats that make up the soul of Roman cooking, including *trippa* (tripe) and *coratella* (sweetbreads). There's also plenty to choose from for those uninterested in innards. ✉ *Via di Monte Testaccio 30* ☎ *06/5746318* ▭ *AE, DC, MC, V* ⊙ *Closed Mon., Aug., and during Christmas. No dinner Sun.*

★ $$–$$$ ✕ **Sangallo.** Small and intimate, this is an old-fashioned restaurant where the owner buys the fish himself and where dinner is meant to last all night. The traditional menu leans heavily toward the gourmet, with dishes like oysters tartare, snapper with foie gras, Texas steaks, and a fixed-price menu based on truffles. There are few tables in the tiny dining room, so make sure to book ahead. ✉ *Vicolo della Vaccarella 11/A* ☎ *06/6865549* ▭ *AE, DC, MC, V* ⊙ *Closed Sun., 1 wk in Jan., and 2 wks in Aug. No lunch Mon.*

$–$$$ ✕ **Myosotis.** Myosotis does things the old-fashioned way: with hand-rolled pastas, fresh-baked bread, and olive oil brought direct from the owner's farm in Umbria. The vast menu is a selection of updated takes on classic ingredients, as in the *vellutata di ceci e funghi porcini* (chickpea and porcini mushrooms soup), or a time-honored *spigola* (sea bass) filleted and served *in crosta di patate* (in a potato crust). ✉ *Via della Vaccarella 3/5* ☎ *06/6865554* ▭ *AE, DC, MC, V* ⊙ *Closed Sun., no lunch Mon.*

$$ ✕ **Dal Bolognese.** This classic restaurant is a trendy choice for a leisurely lunch between sightseeing and shopping. Contemporary paintings decorate the dining room, but the real attraction is the lovely piazza—prime people-watching real estate. As the name of the restaurant promises, the cooking here adheres to the hearty tradition of Bologna, with delicious homemade *tortellini in brodo* (tortellini in broth), fresh pastas in creamy sauces, and *bollito misto* (steaming trays of boiled meats). ✉ *Piazza del Popolo 1* ☎ *06/3611426* ▭ *AE, D, MC, V* ⊙ *Closed 3 wks in Aug. No lunch Mon. or Tues.*

$–$$ ✕ **Dal Toscano.** The hallmarks of this great family-run Tuscan trattoria near the Vatican are friendly and speedy service, an open wood-fired grill, and such classic dishes as *ribollita* (a dense bread and vegetable soup) and the prized bistecca alla fiorentina. Wash it all down with a strong Chianti. All desserts are homemade and delicious. ✉ *Via Germanico 58* ☎ *06/39725717* ▭ *DC, MC, V* ⊙ *Closed Mon., Aug., and 2 wks in Dec.*

$ ✕ **Alfredo e Ada.** There's no place like home, and you'll feel like you're back there from the moment you squeeze into a table at this hole in the wall just across the river from Castel Sant'Angelo. There's no menu, just plate after plate of whatever Ada thinks you should try, from hearty, classic pastas to *involtini di vitello* (savory veal rolls with tomato) and homemade sausage. Sit back and enjoy—it's all good. ✉ *Via dei Banchi Nuovi 14* ☎ *06/6878842* ▭ *No credit cards* ⊙ *Closed weekends.*

$ ✕ **Arancia Blu.** Owner and chef Fabio Passan has a mission: to prove that "vegetarian cuisine" isn't an oxymoron. Start with a leek-and-almond quiche or lemon-ricotta ravioli with squash and sage, and move on to *polpettine vegetali* (meatless meatballs) with a tomato–coriander seed sauce. Gourmet palates will be tickled by the selections of coffee and olive oil, and by the chocolate tasting—14 varieties in all. Vegan and wheat-free dishes are available on request. ✉ *Via dei Latini 65* ☎ *06/4454105* ▭ *No credit cards* ⊙ *No lunch.*

$ ✕ **Perilli.** A bastion of authentic Roman cooking and trattoria charm since 1911 (the interior has changed very little), this is the place to go to try rigatoni *con pajata* (with veal intestines)—if you're into that sort of thing. Otherwise the carbonara and *all'amatriciana* (spicy tomato sauce with pancetta) are classics. The house wine is a golden nectar from the Castelli Romani. ✉ *Via Marmorata 39* ☎ *06/5742415* ▭ *AE, DC, MC, V* ⊙ *Closed Wed.*

WHERE TO STAY

Hotels listed are within walking distance of at least some sights and handy to public transportation. Those in the $$ and $ categories do not have restaurants but serve Continental breakfast. Rooms facing the street may get traffic noise throughout the night, and few hotels in the lower price categories have double-glazed windows. Ask for a quiet room—or bring earplugs. Always make reservations, even if only a few days in advance. Always inquire about discounts. Should you find yourself in Rome without a hotel booking, contact **HR** (✉ Termini Station; Aeroporto Fiumicino ☎ 06/6991000), a reservation service. **EPT** (✉ Via Parigi 5 ☎ 06/48899253 📠 06/4819316 ✉ Near Piazza della

Repubblica ✉ Aeroporto Fiumicino ☎ 06/65956074 ✉ Stazione Termini ☎ 06/4871270), the local tourist office, may be able to help with hotel reservations.

WHAT IT COSTS In euros				
	$$$$	$$$	$$	$
FOR 2 PEOPLE	over €300	€225–€300	€150–€225	under €150

Hotel prices are for two people in a standard double room in high season.

14

★ $$$$ **Eden.** The historic Eden, a haunt of Hemingway, Ingrid Bergman, and Fellini, merits superlatives for dashing elegance and stunning vistas of Rome from the rooftop restaurant and bar (also from some of the most expensive rooms). Precious but discreet antique furnishings, fine linen sheets, and marble baths whisper understated opulence. ✉ *Via Ludovisi 49, 00187* ☎ *06/478121* 🖷 *06/4821584* 🌐 *www.hotel-eden.it* *112 rooms, 14 suites* *Restaurant, bar* 💳 *AE, DC, MC, V* 🍽 *EP.*

$$$–$$$$ **Scalinata di Spagna.** An old-fashioned pensione loved by generations of romantics, this tiny hotel is booked solid for months ahead. Its location at the top of the Spanish Steps, inconspicuous little entrance, quaint hodgepodge of old furniture, and view from the terrace where you breakfast make it seem like your own special, exclusive inn. ✉ *Piazza Trinità dei Monti 17 00187* ☎ *06/6793006* 🖷 *06/69940598* 🌐 *www.hotelscalinata.com* *16 rooms* 💳 *AE, D, MC, V.*

★ $$$ **Farnese.** An early-20th-century mansion, the Farnese is in a quiet but central residential district. Art deco–style furniture is mixed with enchanting fresco decorations amid its compact rooms, plenty of lounge space, and a roof garden. ✉ *Via Alessandro Farnese 30 00192* ☎ *06/3212553* 🖷 *06/3215129* *23 rooms* *Bar* 💳 *AE, DC, MC, V* 🍽 *EP.*

★ $$–$$$ **Britannia.** A quiet locale off Via Nazionale is only one of the attractions of this small, special hotel, where you will be coddled with luxurious touches such as English-language dailies and local weather reports delivered to your room each morning. The well-furnished rooms (two with a rooftop terrace), frescoed halls, and lounge (where a rich breakfast buffet is served) attest to the fact that the management really cares about superior service and value. ✉ *Via Napoli 64, 00184* ☎ *06/4883153* 🖷 *06/4882343* 🌐 *www.hotelbritannia.it* *32 rooms, 1 suite* *Bar* 💳 *AE, DC, MC, V.*

$$–$$$ **Residenza Paolo VI.** Located inside the Vatican walls, the Paolo VI (pronounced Paolo Sesto, Italian for Pope Paul VI) is a convenient base for seeing St. Peter's and the Vatican sights. Rooms in this former monastery have plain furniture and marble floors, but their simplicity is balanced out by the wonderful roof terrace with a view of the basilica. Breakfast is an American-style buffet. ✉ *Via Paolo VI 29, 00193* ☎ *06/68134108* 🖷 *06/6867428* 🌐 *www.residenzapaolovi.com* *29 rooms* *Bar* 💳 *AE, D, MC, V.*

$$ **Amalia.** Handy to St. Peter's, the Vatican, and the Cola di Rienzo shopping district, this small hotel is owned and operated by the Consoli family—Amalia and her brothers. On several floors of a 19th-century building, it has large rooms with functional furnishings, TVs, minibars, pictures of angels on the walls, and gleaming marble bathrooms (hair dryers included). The Ottaviano stop of Metro A is a block away. ✉ *Via Germanico 66 00192* ☎ *06/39723356* 🖷 *06/39723365* 🌐 *www.hotelamalia.com* *30 rooms, 25 with bath or shower* 💳 *AE, MC, V.*

$$ **La Residenza.** A converted town house near Via Veneto, this hotel offers good value and first-class comfort at reasonable rates. Public areas are spacious, and guest rooms are comfortable and have large closets

and TVs. The hotel's clientele is mainly from the United States. Rates include a generous buffet breakfast. ✉ *Via Emilia 22 00187* ☎ *06/4880789* 📠 *06/485721* 🌐 *www.thegiannettihotelsgroup.com* 28 *rooms* *Bar* ▭ *AE, MC, V.*

$$ **Romae.** Near Termini Station, this midsize hotel has clean, spacious rooms with light-wood furniture and small but bright bathrooms. The congenial, helpful management offers special winter rates and welcomes families. Low rates that include breakfast and free Internet access make this a good deal. ✉ *Via Palestro 49, 00185* ☎ *06/4463554* 📠 *06/4463914* 🌐 *www.hotelromae.com* *32 rooms* ▭ *AE, MC, V.*

★ **$** **Margutta.** This small hotel near the Spanish Steps and Piazza del Popolo has an unassuming lobby but bright, attractive bedrooms with wrought-iron bedsteads and modern baths. ✉ *Via Laurina 34 00187* ☎ *06/3223674* 📠 *06/3200395* *24 rooms* ▭ *AE, DC, MC, V.*

$ **Panda.** This is one of the best deals in the neighborhood—particularly remarkable given that the neighborhood is Via della Croce, one of the chic shopping streets around the Spanish Steps. Guest rooms are outfitted in terra-cotta and wrought iron; they're smallish, but quiet, thanks to double-glazed windows. Pay even less by sharing a bath, and in low season, you may have it to yourself. ✉ *Via della Croce 35, 00187Piazza di Spagna* ☎ *06/6780179* 📠 *69942151* *20 rooms, 14 with bath* ▭ *MC, V.*

NIGHTLIFE & THE ARTS

You will find information on scheduled events and shows at the main APT office and other tourist booths. The monthly booklet *Un Ospite a Roma,* free from concierges at some hotels, is another source of information, as is *Wanted in Rome,* published every other Wednesday and available at newsstands. There are listings in English in the back of the weekly *roma c'è* booklet, with handy price and opening hours information for each listing; it is published on Wednesdays and sold at newsstands. If you want to go to the opera, the ballet, or a concert, it's best to ask your concierge to get tickets for you. You can buy some online or at box offices a few days before performances.

The Arts

Concerts

The main year-round classical concert series in Rome is organized by the **Accademia di Santa Cecilia** (✉ Via della Conciliazione 4 ☎ 06/68801044 🌐 www.santacecilia.it) near the Vatican. With the 2002 opening of the **Auditorium-Parco della Musica** (✉ Via de Coubertin 15 ☎ 06/80693444; 06/68801044 for information and tickets 🌐 www.musicaperroma.it), Rome has three concert halls, with state-of-the-art acoustics, that host the symphonic music season of the Accademia di Santa Cecila and other important classical, jazz, rock, and pop concerts.

Film

There is one entirely original-language movie theater in Rome, the **Pasquino** (✉ Piazza Sant'Egidio 10, near Piazza Santa Maria in Trastevere ☎ 06/5815208). Otherwise both the **Metropolitan** (✉ Via del Corso 7, off Piazza del Popolo ☎ 06/32600500) and the **Warner Village Moderno** (✉ Piazza della Repubblica 45-46 near the station, ☎ 06/47779202) have one screen dedicated to English-language films from September to June. Programs are listed in Rome's daily newspapers and *roma c'è*. Several other movie theaters now show at least one film in English from time to time; look for *versione originale* (original version) in the listings.

Opera

The opera season runs from November or December through May, and performances are staged in the **Teatro dell'Opera** (✉ Piazza Beniamino Gigli 8, ☎ 06/481601; 06/48160255 for tickets). From May through August performances are held in various outdoor venues, such as the Stadio Olimpico. Smaller opera companies put up their own low-budget, high-quality productions in various venues. Look for posters advertising performances.

Nightlife

Rome's "in" nightspots change frequently, and many fade into oblivion after a brief moment of glory. The best places to find an up-to-date list are the weekly entertainment guide "Trovaroma," published each Thursday in the Italian daily *La Repubblica,* and *roma c'è,* the weekly guide sold at newsstands.

Bars

Chic wine bars are drawing more and more trendy Romans all the time. Try the area between the Tiber and Campo de' Fiori or the area west of Piazza Navona for a bit of bar-hopping. One of the grandest places for a drink in well-dressed company is **Le Grand Bar** (✉ Via Vittorio Emanuele Orlando 3 ☎ 06/47091) in the St. Regis Grand Hotel. **Jazz Café** (✉ Via Zanardelli 12 ☎ 06/68210119), near Piazza Navona, is an upscale watering hole with good live music downstairs. A classic choice for a cocktail or evening drink is **Bar della Pace** (✉ Via della Pace 5 ☎ 06/6861216) in the ultra-happening area of town west of Piazza Navona. In summer the atmospheric leafy piazza is excellent for both stargazing and people-watching. **Trinity College** (✉ Via del Collegio Romano 6, near Piazza Venezia ☎ 06/6786472) has two floors of Irish pub trappings, with happy chatter and background music until 3 AM.

Discos & Nightclubs

A good area for nightclubs is Testaccio (across the river from Trastevere) and its winding Via di Monte Testaccio, which is literally lined with discos and live music clubs that cater to all tastes. **Suite** (✉ Via degli Orti di Trastevere 1 ☎ 06/5861888) is a hip nightclub in Trastevere with a sleek, futuristic interior. You might spot an American celeb at **Gilda** (✉ Via Mario de' Fiori 97 ☎ 06/6784838), with a disco, piano bar, and live music. It's closed Monday and jackets are required. Just as exclusive is **Bella Blu** (✉ Via Luciani 21 ☎ 06/3230490), a club in Parioli that caters to Rome's elite.

Music Clubs

For the latest jazz, independent, and ethnic sounds try the **La Palma Club** (✉ Via Giuseppe Mirri 35, ☎ 06/43599029), which, despite its off-the-beaten-track location in the Tiburtino district, has become synonymous with quality and an uncanny ability to woo the best names on the international music scene. Live performances of jazz, soul, and funk by leading musicians draw celebrities to **Alexanderplatz** (✉ Via Ostia 9, in the Vatican area ☎ 06/39742171). The music starts about 10 PM, and you can have supper while you wait.

SHOPPING

Via Condotti, directly across from the Spanish Steps, and the streets running parallel to Via Condotti, as well as its cross streets, form the most elegant and expensive shopping area for clothes and accessories in Rome—head here first for top Italian and European designer shops. Lower-price fashions are on display at shops on **Via Frattina** and **Via del Corso.** Romans in the know do much of their shopping along **Via Cola di Rienzo** and **Via Nazionale.** For prints, browse among the stalls at **Piazza Fontanella Borghese** or stop in at the shops in the Pantheon area. For minor antiques, **Via dei Coronari** and other streets around Piazza Navona and Campo de' Fiori are good. High-end antiques dealers are situated in **Via del Babuino** and its environs. The open-air markets in **Campo de' Fiori** and in other neighborhoods throughout the city provide an eyeful of typically Roman color. For local artisans making and selling their wares, try the area northwest of Campo de' Fiori and the winding medieval streets of **Trastevere.**

ROME A TO Z

AIRPORTS & TRANSFERS

Rome's principal airport is Aeroporto Leonardo da Vinci, usually known as Fiumicino. The smaller Ciampino, on the edge of Rome, is used as an alternative by international and domestic lines, especially for charter flights.

Aeroporto Leonardo da Vinci ✉ 29 km/18 mi southeast of Rome at Fiumicino ☎ 06/65951 🌐 www.adr.it. **Ciampino** ☎ 06/794941 flight information 🌐 www.adr.it.

TRANSFERS Two trains link downtown Rome with Fiumicino: inquire at the airport (EPT tourist information counter in the International Arrivals hall or train information counter near the tracks) to determine which takes you closest to your destination in Rome. The 30-minute nonstop Airport–Termini express goes directly to Track 22 at Termini Station, Rome's main train station, well served by taxis and hub of metro and bus lines. Departures from the airport begin at 8 AM and run hourly, with the final departure at 8 PM. Trains from Termini Station to the airport run every half hour, from 6:37 AM until 11:37 PM. Tickets cost €8.80. The other airport train, FM1, leaves from the same tracks and runs from the airport to Rome and beyond, serving commuters as well as air travelers. The main stops in Rome are at Trastevere (35 minutes), Ostiense (40 minutes), and Tiburtina (50 minutes); at each you can find taxis and bus and/or metro connections to other parts of Rome. The FM1 trains run from Fiumicino between 6:28 AM and 1:28 AM, with departures every 20 minutes, a little less frequently in off-hours; the schedule is similar going to the airport. Tickets cost €2.27. For either train, buy your ticket at a vending machine or at ticket counters at the airport and at some stations (Termini Track 22, Trastevere, Tiburtina). At the airport, stamp the ticket at the gate. Remember when using the train at other stations to stamp your ticket in the little yellow or red machine near the track before you board. During the night, take COTRAL buses from the airport to Tiburtina Station in Rome (45 minutes); they depart from in front of the International Arrivals hall at 1:15, 2:15, 3:30, and 5 AM. Buses leave Tiburtina Station for the airport at 12:30, 1:15, 2:30, 3:45, and 5 AM. Tickets either way cost €3.60.

A taxi to or from Fiumicino costs about €50, including extra charges for baggage and off-hours. At a booth inside the terminal you can hire a four- or five-passenger car with driver for a little more. If you decide to take a taxi, use only the yellow or the newer white cabs, in line at the official stand outside the terminal; make sure the meter is running. Gypsy cab drivers solicit your business as you come out of customs; they're not reliable, and their rates are usually much higher. Ciampino is connected with the Anagnina Station of the Metro A by bus (runs every half hour). A taxi between Ciampino and downtown Rome costs about €30.

BIKE & MOPED TRAVEL

Pedaling through Villa Borghese, along the Tiber, out on the Via Appia Antica, and through the city center when traffic is light is a pleasant way to see the sights, but remember: Rome is hilly. Rental concessions are at the Piazza di Spagna and Piazza del Popolo metro stops, and at Piazza San Silvestro and Largo Argentina. You will also find rentals at Viale della Pineta and Viale del Bambino on the Pincio, inside Villa Borghese. Collalti, just off Campo de' Fiori, leases and repairs bikes. St. Peter's Motor Rent carries bikes and mopeds. You can also rent a moped or scooter and mandatory helmet at Scoot-a-Long.

Bike & Moped Rentals **Colatti** ✉ Via del Pellegrino 82 ☎ 06/68801084. **Scoot-a-Long** ✉ Via Cavour 302 ☎ 06/6780206. **St. Peter Moto** ✉ Via di Porta Castello 43 ☎ 06/6875714 or 06/4885485 ✉ Via Fosse di Castello 7 ☎ 06/6874909.

14

BUS & TRAM TRAVEL WITHIN ROME

Orange ATAC city buses (and a few streetcar lines) run from 5:30 AM to midnight, with night buses (indicated N) on some lines. Bus lines 116, 117, and 119, with compact electric vehicles, make a circuit of limited but scenic routes in downtown Rome. They can save you from a lot of walking, and you can get on and off as you please.

ATAC urban buses ☎ 800/431784.

CAR TRAVEL

If you come by car, put it in a parking space (and note that parking in central Rome is generally either metered or prohibited) or a garage, and use public transportation. If you must park in a metered (blue-outlined) space, buy credits at the blue machines near parking areas, scratch off the time you've paid for, and display them on your dashboard. If you plan to drive into or out of the city, take time to study your route, especially on the GRA (Grande Raccordo Anulare, a beltway that encircles Rome and funnels traffic into the city, not always successfully). The main access routes to Rome from the north are the A1 autostrada from Florence and Milan, and the Aurelia highway (SS 1) from Genoa. The principal route to or from points south, such as Naples, is the A2 autostrada.

EMBASSIES

Canada ✉ Via G. B. de Rossi 27, Rome ☎ 06/445981.
United Kingdom ✉ Via XX (pronounced "Venti") Settembre 80a ☎ 06/4825441.
United States ✉ Via Veneto 121 ☎ 06/46741.

EMERGENCIES

Pharmacies are open 8:30–1 and 4–8. Some stay open all night, and all open Sunday on a rotation system; a listing of the neighborhood pharmacies open all night is posted at each pharmacy. The number below gives an automated list of three open pharmacies closest to the telephone from which you call. When calling for ambulance service, say *Pronto Soccorso* ("emergency room") and be prepared to give your address.

Emergencies **Ambulance** ☎ 118. **General Emergencies** ☎ 113. **Police** ☎ 112.
Hospitals **Rome American Hospital** ✉ Via Emilio Longoni 69, Tor Sapienza ☎ 06/22551 🌐 www.rah.it. **Salvator Mundi Hospital** ✉ Viale delle Mura Gianicolensi 66, Monte Verdi Vecchio ☎ 06/588961 🌐 www.smih.pcn.net.
24-hour Pharmacies **Farmacia della Stazione** ✉ Piazza Cinquecento 51 ☎ 06/4880019. **Internazionale** ✉ Piazza Barberini 49 ☎ 06/4825456.

ENGLISH-LANGUAGE MEDIA

Bookstores **Anglo-American Bookstore** ✉ Via della Vite 102 ☎ 06/6795222 🌐 www.aab.it. **Corner Bookstore** ✉ Via del Moro 45, Trastevere ☎ 06/5836942. **Economy Book and Video Center** ✉ Via Torino 136 ☎ 06/4746877 🌐 www.booksitaly.

com. **Feltrinelli International** ✉ Via Emanuele Orlando 78/81 ☎ 06/4870171. **Open Door Bookshop** secondhand books ✉ Via Lungaretta 23 ☎ 06/5896478.

METRO TRAVEL

The metro (subway) is a fast and easy way to get around, but it doesn't serve many of the areas you'll probably want to visit, particularly Old Rome. It opens at 5:30 AM, and the last train leaves each terminal at 11:30 PM. Metro A runs from the eastern part of the city to Termini Station and past Piazza di Spagna and Piazzale Flaminio to Ottaviano-S. Pietro, near St. Peter's and the Vatican museums. Metro B serves Termini, the Colosseum, and Tiburtina Station (where the FM1 Fiumicino Airport train stops).

TAXIS

Taxis wait at stands and, for a small extra charge, can also be called by telephone. They're very difficult to hail, but you can try to flag down taxis whose roof lights are illuminated. The meter starts at €2.33 during the day, €4.91 after 10 PM, and €3.36 on Sundays and holidays. There's a supplement of €1.04 for each piece of baggage. Note that these charges do not appear on the meter. If you take a taxi at night and/or on a Sunday, or if you have baggage or have had the cab called by phone, the fare will legitimately be more than the figure shown on the meter.

ℹ ☎ 06/3570, 06/5551, 06/4994, or 06/6645.

TOURS

Most operators offer half-day excursions to Tivoli to see the Villa d'Este's fountains and gardens; Appian Line and CIT run half-day tours to Tivoli that also include Hadrian's Villa and its impressive ancient ruins. Operators also offer all-day excursions to Assisi, to Pompeii and/or Capri, and to Florence. For do-it-yourself excursions to Ostia Antica and other destinations, pick up information at the APT information offices. American Express, Appian Line, ATAC, and CIT all offer orientation tours of Rome.

ℹ **American Express** ☎ 06/67641. **Appian Line** ☎ 06/487861. **Carrani** ☎ 06/4880510. **CIT** ☎ 06/4620311.

WALKING TOURS Enjoy Rome offers walking and bicycling tours in English, including a nighttime tour of Old Rome. All About Rome, Scala Reale, Through Eternity, and Walks of Rome all offer a range of English-language tours.

ℹ **All About Rome** ☎ 06/7100823. **Enjoy Rome** ☎ 06/4451843. **Scala Reale** ☎ 06/4745673 or 800/732-2863 Ext. 4052 🌐 www.scalareale.org. **Through Eternity** ☎ 06/7009336 🌐 www.througheternity.com. **Walks of Rome** ☎ 06/484853.

TRAIN TRAVEL

Termini Station is Rome's main train terminal, although the Tiburtina, Ostiense, and Trastevere stations serve some long-distance trains, many commuter trains, and the FM1 line to Fiumicino Airport. For train information call the toll-free number below, or try the English-speaking personnel at the information office in Termini, or at any travel agency. Tickets and seats can be reserved and purchased at travel agencies bearing the FS (Ferrovie dello Stato) emblem. Tickets are sold up to two months in advance. Short-distance tickets are also sold at tobacconists and ticket machines in the stations.

ℹ **Trenitalia** ☎ 166/105050 🌐 www.trenitalia.it.

TRANSPORTATION AROUND ROME

Rome's transportation system includes buses and trams (ATAC), metro and suburban trains and buses (COTRAL), and some other suburban trains (Trenitalia) run by the state railways. A ticket valid for 75 minutes on any combination of buses and trams and one admission to the metro costs €.75 (time-stamp your ticket when boarding the first vehicle; you're supposed to stamp it again if you board another vehicle just before the ticket runs out, but few do). Tickets are sold at tobacconists, newsstands, some coffee bars, automated ticket machines in metro stations, some bus stops, and at ATAC and COTRAL ticket booths. A BIG tourist ticket, valid for one day on all public transport, costs €3.10. A weekly ticket (Settimanale, also known as CIS) costs €12.40 and can be purchased only at ATAC and metro booths.

TRAVEL AGENCIES

American Express Piazza di Spagna 38 06/67641. **CIT** Piazza della Repubblica 64 06/4620311 www.citonline.it. **CTS** Via Genova 16 06/4620431 www.cts.it for youth and budget travel and discount fares.

VISITOR INFORMATION

APT Rome Provincial Tourist Agency, main office Via Parigi 5, 00185 06/36004399 Termini Station 06/47301 Leonardo da Vinci (Fiumicino) Airport 06/65951. **City tourist information booths** Largo Goldoni, corner of Via Condotti Via del Corso in the Spanish Steps area Via dei Fori Imperiali, opposite the entrance to the Roman Forum Via Nazionale, at Palazzo delle Esposizioni Piazza Cinque Lune, off the north end of Piazza Navona; Piazza Sonnino, in Trastevere www.romaturismo.it.

For Italy Basics, see chapter 9, Florence.

VENICE

It was called La Serenissima Repubblica, the majestic city that for centuries was the unrivaled mistress of trade between Europe and the Far East, and the staunch bulwark of Christendom against the tides of Turkish expansion. Venice is a labyrinth of narrow streets and waterways, and though many of its magnificent palazzi could use a face-lift, shabby here is magically transformed into beauty and charm. Romance is everywhere is Venice, especially at night when starlight dances on the water and streetlights all but revive those gargoyles glaring down from centuries-old facades. Venice's glory days as a wealthy city-state may be only a memory, but art and fantasy live on, and with a courtesan's guile, they'll seduce your eye and your very soul.

EXPLORING VENICE

To enjoy the city you will have to come to terms with the crowds of day-trippers, who take over the center around San Marco from May through September and during Carnevale. Venice is cooler and more welcoming in early spring and late fall. Romantics like the winter, when streets are often deserted and a haunting melancholy descends with the sea mist on *campi* (squares) and canals. Piazza San Marco is the pulse of Venice, but after elbowing the crowd to visit the Basilica di San Marco and the Doge's Palace, strike out on your own—let your feet and your eyes pick a direction. You won't be disappointed.

Piazza San Marco & the San Polo Neighborhood

Piazza San Marco put Venice on the world voyagers' grand tour circuit centuries before mass tourism crammed the square with more than 100,000 people in a single day (during Carnevale). San Marco is a great place to begin exploring monuments and streets packed with boutiques and expensive shops, but whatever you do, don't stop here; the less crowded, more affordable San Polo district, with its lively backstreets, can be even more fun to explore on foot.

Numbers in the margin correspond to points of interest on the Venice map.

★ ❸ **Basilica di San Marco** (St. Mark's Basilica). When the Doge's agents returned from Egypt in the 9th century with the stolen corpse of St. Mark the Evangelist, a church was built. That building burned to the ground, but the relics of the city's patron saint survived. Today they rest in an 11th-century structure, a blend of Byzantine, Gothic, and Renaissance architectural elements, beneath a ceiling adorned with 43,055 square feet of golden mosaics. Don't miss the **Pala d'Oro,** a dazzling gilded screen with 1,927 precious gems. Riding atop the richly decorated facade are copies of four famous bronze horses; you'll find the originals up a steep staircase in **Museo Marciano.** ✉ *Piazza San Marco* ☎ *041/5225205* ⏲ *May–Oct., Mon.–Sat. 9:45–5, Sun. 2–5; Nov.–Apr., Mon.–Sat. 9:45–4, Sun. 2–4; last entry 30 min before closing; tours June–Aug., Mon.–Sat* Ⓥ *Vallaresso/San Zaccaria.*

★ ❺ **Campanile.** Venice's original brick bell tower (325 feet tall, plus the angel) had been standing nearly 1,000 years when in 1902, practically without warning, it collapsed. The new tower, rebuilt on the old plan, reopened in 1912. During the 15th century, clerics guilty of immoral behavior were suspended in wooden cages from the tower, some forced to subsist on bread and water for as long as a year, others left to starve. The stunning view from the tower includes the Lido, the lagoon, and the mainland as far as the Alps, but, strangely enough, none of the myriad canals that snake through the city. ✉ *Piazza San Marco* ☎ *041/5224064* ⏲ *June–Sept., daily 9–sunset or 9 PM; Oct.–May, 9–4; last entry 30 min before closing.*

❷ **Museo Correr.** Exhibits in this museum of Venetian art and history range from the absurdly high-soled shoes worn by 16th-century Venetian ladies (who walked with the aid of a servant) to Jacopo de' Barbari's (circa 1440–1515) huge *Grande Pianta Prospettica,* detailing in carved wood every inch of 16th-century Venice. Through Correr, you can access the **Museo Archeologico** and the **Biblioteca Marciana.** ✉ *Piazza San Marco, Ala Napoleonica* ☎ *041/5225625* ⏲ *Apr.–Oct., daily 9–7; Nov.–Mar., 9–5; last tickets sold 1½ hrs before closing.*

★ ❹ **Palazzo Ducale** (Doge's Palace). During the Republic's heyday, this was combination White House, Senate, torture chamber, and prison rolled into one. The facade is a Gothic-Renaissance fantasia of pink-and-white marble, and the interior is filled with frescoes, paintings, and sculptings by some of the greatest artists of the times. Don't miss the balcony view over the piazza and across the water to the island church of San Giorgio Maggiore. ✉ *Piazzetta San Marco* ☎ *041/5224951* 🎟 *Piazza San Marco museums: €9.50. Musei Civici: €15.50* ⏲ *Apr.–Oct., daily 9–7; Nov.–Mar., 9–5; last tickets sold 1½ hrs before closing. Guided tours in English: Tues.–Thurs. and Sat. 11:30* Ⓥ *Vallaresso/San Zaccaria.*

★ ❶ **Piazza San Marco.**This is Venice's only *piazza*—all the other squares are called *campi* (fields)—and it's so popular that pedestrians and pigeons seem to be competing for space. The side opposite the basilica is known as the **Ala Napoleonica,** a wing built by Napoléon to enclose the square, or what he called "the most beautiful drawing room in all of Europe."

❻ **Santa Maria Gloriosa dei Frari.** The soaring Gothic basilica, known as I Frari, contains Titian's *Assumption of the Virgin* (main altar) and *Madonna di Ca' Pesaro* (left nave), both loved from the day they were unveiled. So beloved was the artist himself, that he was exhumed from a communal grave for plague victims to be buried here. ✉ *Campo dei*

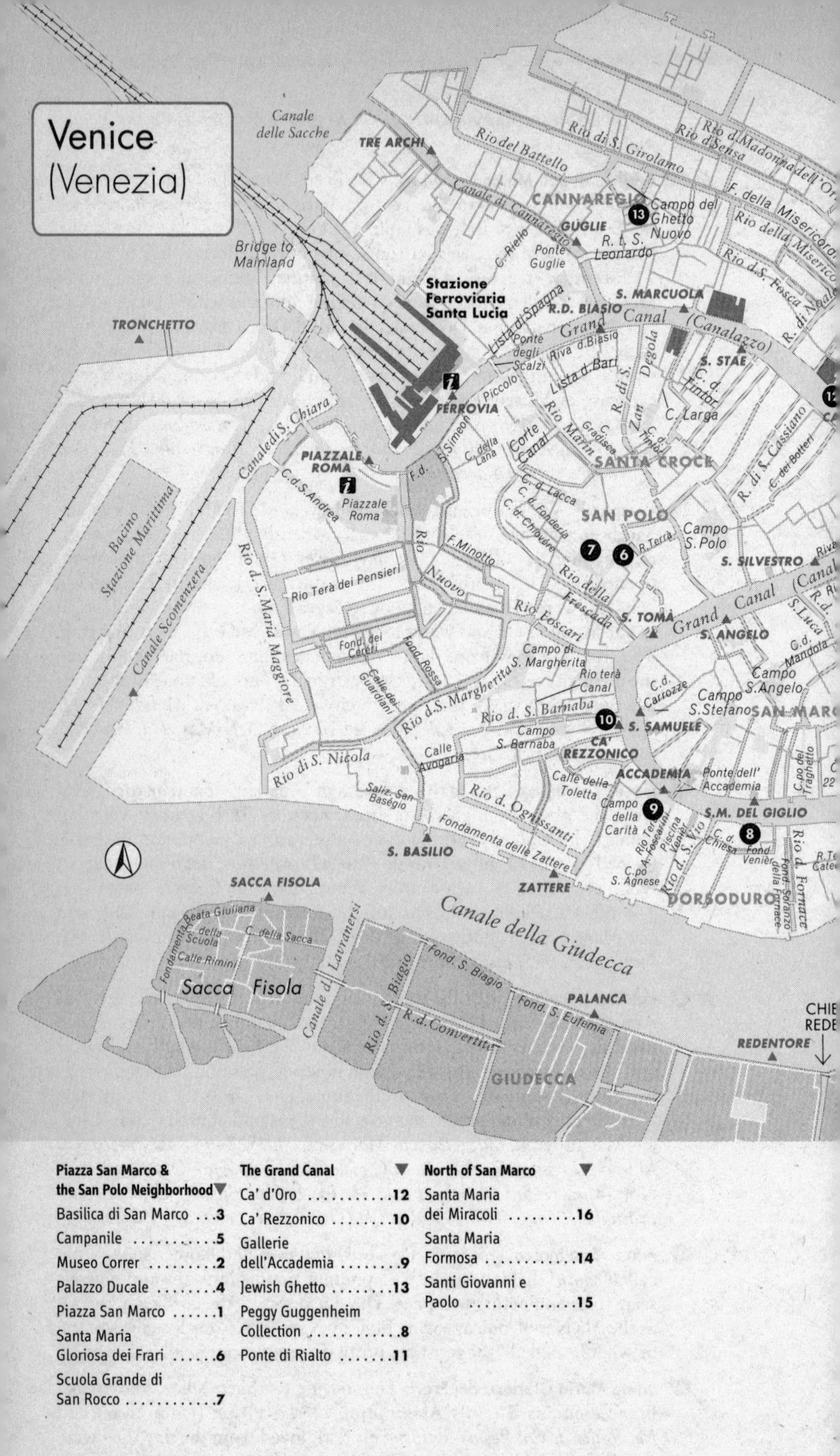
Venice
(Venezia)
Canale delle Sacche
TRE ARCHI
Rio del Battello
Rio di S. Girolamo
Rio d'Sensa
Rio d. Madonna dell'Orto
F. della Misericordia
Rio della Misericordia
Canale di Cannaregio
CANNAREGIO
Campo del Ghetto Nuovo
GUGLIE
R. t. S. Leonardo
Ponte Guglie
C. Riello
Rio d. S. Fosca
Bridge to Mainland
Stazione Ferroviaria Santa Lucia
S. MARCUOLA
R.D. BIASIO
Grand Canal (Canalazzo)
TRONCHETTO
Lista di Spagna
Ponte degli Scalzi
Riva d. Biasio
Lista d. Bari
Degola
S. STAE
C. d. Tintor
C. Larga
FERROVIA
Piccolo
Rio Marin
Canal d. S. Chiara
PIAZZALE ROMA
Piazzale Roma
C. d. S. Andrea
S. Simeon
C. della Lana
Corte Canal
C. Gradisca
SANTA CROCE
Rio d. S. Cassiano
C. dei Botteri
Bacino Stazione Marittima
Canale Scomenzera
Rio d. S. Maria Maggiore
Rio
Nuovo
F. Minotto
C. d. Lacca
C. d. Fonderia
C. d. Chiovere
SAN POLO
Campo S. Polo
R. Terà
S. SILVESTRO
Rio Terà dei Pensieri
Rio della Frescada
Rio Foscari
S. TOMÀ
Grand Canal
S. ANGELO
Fond. dei Cereri
Fond. Rossa
Calle dei Guardiani
Campo di S. Margherita
Rio d. S. Margherita
Rio terà Canal
C. d. Mandola
Campo S. Angelo
C. d. Carrozze
Campo S. Stefano
SAN MARCO
Rio d. S. Barnaba
Campo S. Barnaba
S. SAMUELE
CA' REZZONICO
Calle Avogaria
Rio di S. Nicola
Calle della Toletta
ACCADEMIA
Ponte dell' Accademia
Saliz. San Basègio
Rio d. Ognissanti
Campo della Carità
S.M. DEL GIGLIO
C. d. Chiesa
Fond. Venièr
Rio d. Fornace
Fondamenta delle Zattere
S. BASILIO
ZATTERE
C.po S. Agnese
DORSODURO
SACCA FISOLA
Beata Giuliana
C. della Sacca
C. della Scuola
Calle Rimini
Fondamenta
Sacca Fisola
Canale della Giudecca
Canale d. Lavranersi
Rio d. S. Biagio
Fond. S. Biagio
R. d. Convertite
Fond. S. Eufemia
PALANCA
GIUDECCA
REDENTORE
Piazza San Marco & the San Polo Neighborhood
Basilica di San Marco . . . 3
Campanile 5
Museo Correr 2
Palazzo Ducale 4
Piazza San Marco 1
Santa Maria Gloriosa dei Frari 6
Scuola Grande di San Rocco 7
The Grand Canal
Ca' d'Oro 12
Ca' Rezzonico 10
Gallerie dell'Accademia 9
Jewish Ghetto 13
Peggy Guggenheim Collection 8
Ponte di Rialto 11
North of San Marco
Santa Maria dei Miracoli 16
Santa Maria Formosa 14
Santi Giovanni e Paolo 15

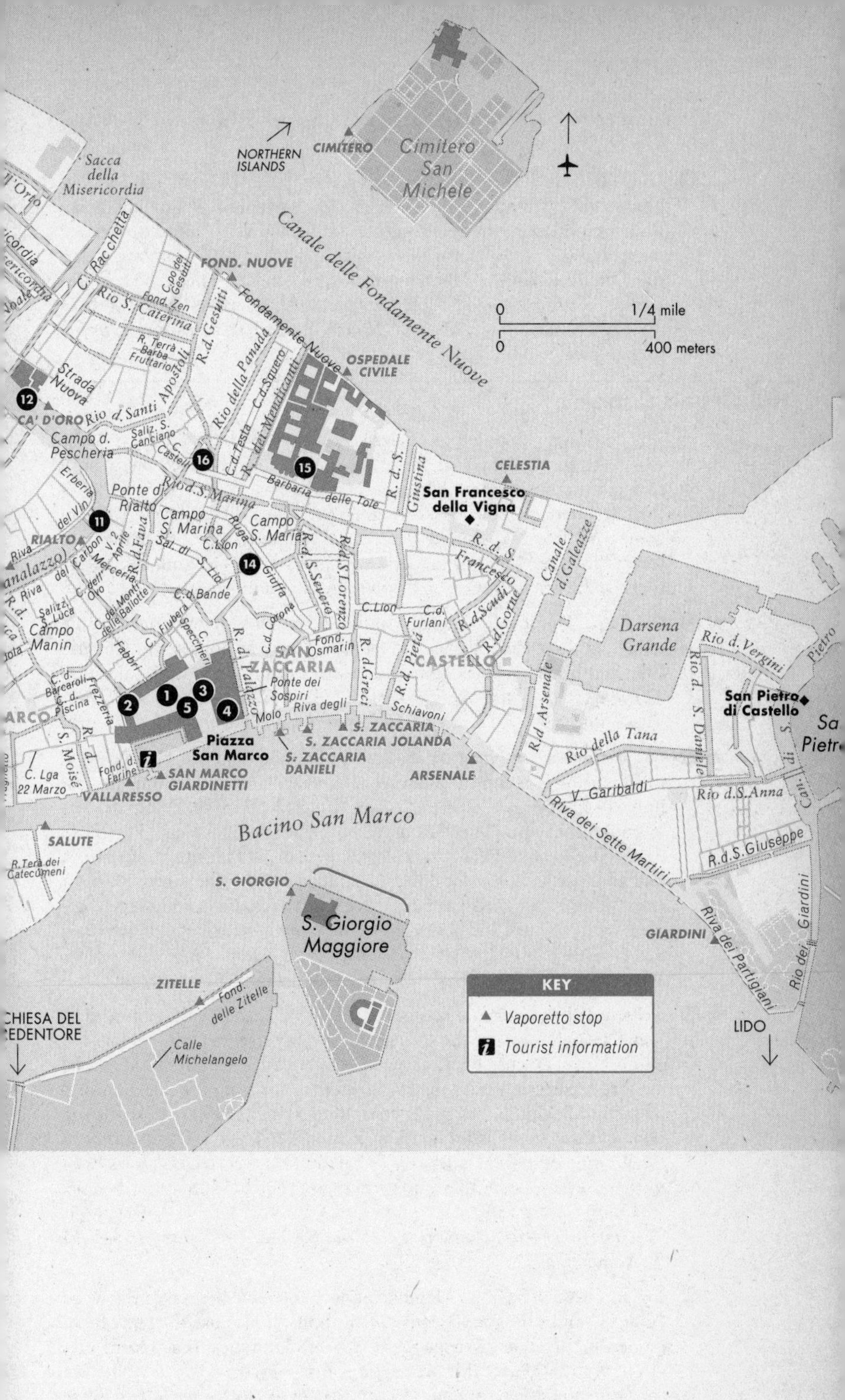

NORTHERN ISLANDS
CIMITERO
Cimitero San Michele
Sacca della Misericordia
Canale delle Fondamente Nuove
FOND. NUOVE
Fondamente Nuove
OSPEDALE CIVILE
0
1/4 mile
0
400 meters
C. Racchetta
Rio S. Caterina
Fond. Zen
C.po dei Gesuiti
R.d. Gesuiti
R. Terrà Barba Fruttarioli
Strada Nuova
Apostoli
Rio della Panada
C.d.Squero
R. dei Mendicanti
CA' D'ORO
Rio d. Santi Apostoli
Campo d. Pescheria
Saliz. S. Canciano
C.d.Testa
CELESTIA
Erberia
Ponte di Rialto
Riod.S.Marina
Barbaria delle Tole
R. d. S. Giustina
San Francesco della Vigna
RIALTO
Campo S. Marina
Campo S. Maria
C.Lion
R.d. S. Severo
R.d.S.Lorenzo
R. d. S. Francesco
Canale d.Galeazze
Merceria
C.d.Bande
C.d. Corona
C.Lion
C.d. Furlani
R.d.Scudi
R.d.Gorne
Darsena Grande
Rio d. Vergini
Campo Manin
Fabbri
Specchieri
R. di Palazzo
SAN ZACCARIA
Fond. Osmarin
R. d.Greci
R.d. Pietà
CASTELLO
R.d. Arsenale
Rio d. S. Daniele
San Pietro di Castello
Ponte dei Sospiri
Riva degli Schiavoni
Frezzeria
Molo
S. ZACCARIA
S. ZACCARIA JOLANDA
Piazza San Marco
S. ZACCARIA DANIELI
ARSENALE
Rio della Tana
V. Garibaldi
Rio d.S.Anna
C. Lga 22 Marzo
SAN MARCO GIARDINETTI
VALLARESSO
Riva dei Sette Martiri
Bacino San Marco
SALUTE
R.Terà dei Catecumeni
S. GIORGIO
R.d.S.Giuseppe
S. Giorgio Maggiore
GIARDINI
Riva dei Partigiani
Rio dei Giardini
ZITELLE
Fond. delle Zitelle
CHIESA DEL REDENTORE
Calle Michelangelo
KEY
Vaporetto stop
Tourist information
LIDO

Frari ☎ *041/2728618; 041/2750462 Chorus.* ⏲ *Mon.–Sat. 9–6, Sun. 1–6* Ⓥ *San Tomà.*

❼ **Scuola Grande di San Rocco.** Venice's *scuole* (plural) weren't schools, but benevolent fraternities that helped society's neediest. Following in San Rocco's footsteps, this wealthy group helped the sick. Tintoretto painted more than 60 canvases for the scuola during the 1500s, among which the *Crucifixion* in the Albergo (off the great hall) is said to be his masterpiece. ✉ *Campo San Rocco, San Polo 3052,* ☎ *041/5234864* ⏲ *Nov. 3–Mar. 27, daily 10–4; Mar. 28–Nov. 2, 9–5:30; last entrance ½ hr before closing* Ⓥ *San Tomà.*

The Grand Canal

The canal may be called Canalazzo by Venetians, but to the rest of the world, it's the Grand Canal. Here 200 opulent and fantastic palazzi, born of a culture obsessed with opulence and fantasy, appear by day in all their architectural splendor. By night, they appear like a voyeur's dream come true. Take a 45-minute ride aboard vaporetto Line 1 from the train station to San Marco (4 km or 2½ mi) and do try to grab one of the seats in the prow, from which you'll have an unobstructed view.

★ ⓬ **Ca' d'Oro.** This lovely Venetian Gothic palace got its name from the pure gold that once embellished its facade. Today it houses the **Galleria Franchetti,** a fine collection of tapestries, sculptures, and paintings. ✉ *Calle Ca' d'Oro, Cannaregio 3933,* ☎ *041/5222349* ⏲ *Mon. 8:15–2, Tues.–Sun. 8:15–7:15; last entry 30 min before closing* Ⓥ *Ca' d'Oro.*

★ ❿ **Ca' Rezzonico.** Designed by Baldassare Longhena in the 17th century, this mansion was completed nearly 100 years later and became the last home of English poet Robert Browning (1812–89). The **Museo del Settecento Veneziano** (Museum of Venice in the 1700s) feels like you've dropped into an old Venetian palazzo, with period furniture, tapestries, and gilded salons. Recent donations added nearly 300 paintings, most from Venetian schools of artists. There's also a restored apothecary, complete with powders and potions. ✉ *Fondamenta Rezzonico, Dorsoduro 3136* ☎ *041/2410100.* ⏲ *Apr.–Oct., Wed.–Mon. 10–6; Nov.–Mar., Wed.–Mon. 10–5; last entry 1 hr before closing* Ⓥ *Ca' Rezzonico.*

★ ❾ **Gallerie dell'Accademia.** (Accademia Gallery). Trace the development of Venetian painting and the changes in the city itself as you explore the world's most extensive collection of Venetian art. From Byzantine roots, explore the art of Venice through the centuries. On view are paintings by Jacopo Bellini, father of Venetian Renaissance (1400–1471), his son Giovanni (1430–1516); Giorgione's *Tempest*; Titian's *Presentation of the Virgin,* and several works by Tintoretto (1518–94). Don't miss *Feast in the House of Levi* that got Veronese branded (1528–88) a heretic. ✉ *Campo della Carità* ☎ *041/5222247; 041/5200345 reservations* 🌐 *www.gallerieaccademia.org* ⏲ *Mon. 8:15–2, Tues.–Sun. 8:15–7:15* Ⓥ *Accademia.*

⓭ **Jewish Ghetto.** The quiet island neighborhood gave the world the word "ghetto" and still houses Jewish institutions. It also has Europe's highest density of ancient synagogues, each one a unique cross-cultural creation. At the **Museo Ebraico,** you'll discover the history of Jewish culture within the Republic. ✉ *Campo del Ghetto Nuovo, Cannaregio 2902/B,* ☎ *041/715359* 🌐 *www.museoebraico.it* ⏲ *Oct.–May, Sun.–Fri. 10–5:45; June–Sept., Sun.–Fri. 10–6:45. Last hourly tour at 5:30 in summer (at 4:30 in winter) on Fri. at sunset* Ⓥ *San Marcuola or Guglie.*

❽ **Peggy Guggenheim Collection.** Peggy Guggenheim was one of the 20th century's greatest art collectors. At Palazzo Venier, her former Grand

Canal home, you'll see works by Picasso, Kandinsky, Magritte, Motherwell, Pollock, and Ernst (at one time her husband). ✉ *Calle San Cristoforo, Dorsoduro 701* ☎ *041/2405411* 🌐 *www.guggenheim-venice.it* ⏲ *Nov.–Mar., Wed.–Mon. 10–6; Apr.–Oct., Wed.–Fri., Sun., and Mon. 10–6, Sat. 10–10* Ⓥ *Accademia.*

★ ⓫ **Ponte di Rialto** (Rialto Bridge). The late-16th-century competition to design a stone bridge across the Grand Canal (replacing earlier wooden versions) attracted the best architects of the period, including Michelangelo, Palladio, and Sansovino, but the job went to the appropriately named Antonio da Ponte. His pragmatic design included 90 feet of shop space and was high enough for galleys to pass beneath; it also kept decoration and cost to a minimum at a time when the Republic's coffers were suffering from wars with the Turks and loss of its Eastern trading monopoly. The bridge offers one of the city's most famous views: the Grand Canal alive with gondola and motorboat traffic. Don't miss the Rialto's fruit and vegetable market and its *pescheria,* where fish have been bartered for 1,000 years. Ⓥ *Rialto/San Silvestro.*

North of San Marco

Put away your map and let yourself get lost in the picturesque neighborhoods north of San Marco. Here, where low-key shops, bakeries, and tiny watering holes haven't yet been replaced by tourist stops, wooden boats still line jade-green canals and residents of less palatial homes still hang their laundry to dry in the breeze.

⓰ **Santa Maria dei Miracoli.** Tiny, yet perfectly proportioned, this Renaissance jewelbox is sheathed in marble outside and decorated inside with exquisite marble reliefs. Architect and illusionist Pietro Lombardo varied color on the exterior to create the effect of greater distance, and used extra pilasters so the building's canal side looks longer than it is. ✉ *Campo Santa Maria Nova* ☎ *041/2750462 Chorus* ⏲ *Mon.–Sat. 10–5, Sun. 1–5* Ⓥ *Rialto.*

⓮ **Santa Maria Formosa.** Mauro Coducci built this 15th-century marble church atop 11th-century foundations. Visit Bartolomeo Vivarini's *Our Lady of Mercy* and Jacopo Palma il Vecchio's *Santa Barbara,* then enjoy the cafés and produce market in the bustling square. ✉ *Campo Santa Maria Formosa* ☎ *041/5234645* ⏲ *Mon.–Sat. 10–5, Sun. 1–5* Ⓥ *Rialto.*

⓯ **Santi Giovanni e Paolo.** While Franciscan friars were laboring away on their church in San Polo, the Dominicans were similarly busy in Castello. *San Zanipolo,* as Venetians call it, contains a wealth of artwork and the tombs of 25 doges. In the campo rides **Bartolomeo Colleoni** (1400–75), Venice's most famous mercenary, immortalized on horseback. ✉ *Campo dei Santi Giovanni e Paolo* ☎ *041/5235913* ⏲ *Mon.–Sat. 7:30–12:30 and 3:30–6, Sun. 3–6* Ⓥ *Fondamente Nuove /Rialto.*

Venetian Lagoon

The perfect vacation from your Venetian vacation is an escape to the lagoon islands. Let a vaporetto whisk you away from busy streets and into the world of Murano's glassworks, Burano's wonderland houses painted a riot of colors, and Torcello, dreamily romantic and lushly green.

Burano. Centuries ago, lace-making rescued the economy of this former fishing village. At the **Museo del Merletto** (Museum of Lace), you can watch women carrying on the lace-making tradition. They sometimes have pieces for sale, but don't expect bargains—handmade Burano lace costs $1,000 to $2,000 for a 10-inch doily. ✉ *Piazza Galuppi 187* ☎ *041/730034* ⏲ *Apr.–Oct., Wed.–Mon. 10–5; Nov.–Mar., Wed.–Mon. 10–4.*

★ **Murano.** During the 13th century, the Republic, concerned about fires, moved its **glassworks** to Murano. Factories that you can visit line the **Fondamenta dei Vetrai,** the canalside walkway leading from the Colonna vaporetto landing. The glass collection at **Museo Vetrario** ranges from priceless antiques to equally expensive modern pieces. ✉ *Fondamenta Giustinian 8* ☎ *041/739586* ⏲ *Apr.–Oct., Thurs.–Tues. 10–5; Nov.–Mar., Thurs.–Tues. 10–4.*

Basilica dei Santi Maria e Donato has an elaborate mosaic floor that dates from 1140 and a wooden ship's keel roof. ✉ *Fondamenta Giustinian,* ☎ *041/739056* ⏲ *Daily 8–noon and 4–7.*

Torcello. This is where some of the first Venetians landed in their flight from the barbarians, 1,500 years ago. During the 16th century the island had 10 churches and 20,000 inhabitants; today you'll be lucky to see one of the island's 16 residents. The 11th-century **Santa Maria Assunta** testifies to Torcello's former wealth. The Byzantine mosaic *Last Judgment* shows sinners writhing, and the Madonna looks down from her field of gold. Do climb the **Campanile** for an incomparable view of the lagoon wetlands. ☎ *041/730119* ⏲ *Apr.–Oct., daily 10:30–6; Nov.–Mar., 10–5.*

WHERE TO EAT

Venetians love seafood, and it figures prominently on most restaurant menus, sometimes to the exclusion of meat dishes. Fish is generally expensive, and you should remember when ordering that the price given on menus for fish as a main course is often per 100 grams, not the total cost of what you are served, which could be two or three times that amount. *Sarde in saor* (fried sardines marinated with onions, vinegar, pine nuts, and raisins) is a tasty traditional dish that can cost as little as a pizza. City specialties also include *pasta e fagioli* (pasta and bean soup), risotto, and the delicious *fegato alla veneziana* (calves' liver with onions) served with grilled polenta.

WHAT IT COSTS In euros

	$$$$	$$$	$$	$
AT DINNER	over €22	€17–€22	€12–€17	under €12

Prices are per person for a main course.

$$$$ ✕ **Osteria Da Fiore.** Long a favorite with Venetians, Da Fiore has been discovered by tourists, so reservations are imperative. It's known for its excellent seafood, which might include such specialties as *pasticcio di pesce* (fish pie) and *seppioline* (little cuttlefish). Not easy to find, it's just off Campo San Polo. ✉ *Calle dello Scaleter, 2202/A San Polo* ☎ *041/721308* ✍ *Reservations essential* 💳 *AE, DC, MC, V* ⏲ *Closed Sun. and Mon., Aug. 10–early Sept., and Dec. 25–Jan. 15.*

$$$–$$$$ ✕ **Da Arturo.** This tiny eatery on the Calle degli Assassini has the distinction in Venice of *not* serving seafood. On offer are tasty, tender, meat courses in generous portions, such as the subtly pungent *braciola alla veneziana* (pork chop schnitzel with vinegar), and an authentic creamy homemade tiramisu to finish. Vegetarian Venetians and visitors make their way here as well, as the antipasti and *primi* offerings are more than hospitable. ✉ *Calle degli Assassini, 3656 San Marco* ☎ *041/5286974*

Reservations essential ▭ No credit cards ⊙ Closed Sun., 10 days after Carnevale, and 4 wks in Aug.

★ $$$–$$$$ ✕ **Alle Testiere.** A strong local following can make it tough to get one of the five tables at this tiny trattoria near Campo Santa Maria Formosa. Chef Bruno Gavagnin's dishes stand out for lightness and balance: try the *gnocchetti con moscardini* (little gnocchi with tender baby octopus), the linguine with *coda di rospo* (monkfish), or the carpaccio special of the day. The well-assembled wine list is particularly strong on local whites. ✉ *Calle del Mondo Novo, 5801 Castello* ☎ *041/5227220* *Reservations essential* ▭ *MC, V* ⊙ *Closed Sun. and Mon.*

15

$$–$$$$ ✕ **Fiaschetteria Toscana.** Contrary to what the name suggests, there's nothing Tuscan about this restaurant's menu. It was formerly a storehouse for Tuscan wine and oil, and it's worth a trip for its cheerful and courteous service, fine *cucina* (cooking), and noteworthy cellar. Gastronomic highlights include a light *tagliolini neri al ragù di astice* (thin spaghetti served with squid ink and mixed with a delicate lobster sauce), and *zabaione* (zabaglione). ✉ *Campo San Giovanni Crisostomo, 5719 Cannaregio* ☎ *041/5285281* ▭ *AE, DC, MC, V* ⊙ *Closed Tues. and 4 wks in July and Aug. No lunch Mon.*

★ $$ ✕ **L'Incontro.** A faithful clientele, attracted by flavorful Sardinian food, flocks to this place. Starters include Sardinian sausages, but you might sample the delicious traditional primi like *culingiones* (large ravioli filled with pecorino, saffron, and orange peel). Don't miss the herb-crusted meat dishes such as *coniglio al mirto* (rabbit baked on a bed of myrtle sprigs) and the *costine d'agnello con rosmarino e mentuccia* (baby lamb's ribs with rosemary and wild mint). ✉ *Rio Terrà Canal, 3062/A Dorsoduro* ☎ *041/5222404* ▭ *AE, DC, MC, V* ⊙ *Closed Mon., Jan., and 2 wks in Aug. No lunch Tues.*

★ $–$$ ✕ **Vini da Gigio.** A quaint, friendly, family-run trattoria on the quay side of a canal just off the Strada Nuova, da Gigio is very popular with Venetians and other visiting Italians, who appreciate the affable service; the well-prepared homemade pasta, fish, and meat dishes; the imaginative and varied cellar; and the high-quality draft wine. It's good for a simple lunch at tables in the barroom. ✉ *Fondamenta de la Chiesa, 3628/A Cannaregio* ☎ *041/5285140* ▭ *AE, DC, MC, V* ⊙ *Closed Mon., 3 wks in Jan. and Feb., 1 wk in June, and 3 wks in Aug. and Sept.*

$ ✕ **Alla Madonna.** At times it seems there are more foreigners eating here than locals, but this osteria is hard to beat for quality and price. In short, it's a rare Venetian bargain. The *granseola* (spider crab) is a real winner; make sure to ask for some extra virgin olive oil. And try to save room for the tiramisu. ✉ *Calle della Madonna, 594 San Polo* ☎ *041/5223824* ▭ *AE, MC, V* ⊙ *Closed Wed. and Aug.*

★ $ ✕ **Bancogiro.** Here's a place to consider if you're tired of typical Venetian food. Yes, fish is on the menu—the *mousse di gamberoni con salsa di avocado* (shrimp mousse with an avocado sauce) provides a tasty diversion. But you can also sample offbeat offerings such as the Sicilian-style *sarde incinte* (stuffed, or "pregnant," sardines). Set in the heart of the Rialto market in a 15th-century loggia, the restaurant's tables are upstairs in a carefully restored no-smoking room with a partial view of the Grand Canal. ✉ *Campo San Giacometto 122 (under the porch), Santa Croce* ☎ *041/5232061* ▭ *No credit cards* ⊙ *Closed Mon. No dinner Sun.*

WHERE TO STAY

Space in the time-worn but renovated palaces-cum-hotels is at a premium in this city, and even in the best hotel, rooms can be small and offer little natural light. Preservation restrictions on buildings often preclude the installation of such things as elevators and air-conditioning. On the other hand, Venice's luxury hotels can offer rooms of fabulous opulence and elegance, and even in the more modest hotels you can find comfortable rooms of great charm and character, sometimes with stunning views. Venice attracts visitors year-round, although the winter months, with the exception of Carnevale time, are generally much quieter, and most hotels offer lower rates during this period. It is always worth booking in advance, but if you haven't, AVA (Venetian Hoteliers Association) booths will help you find a room after your arrival in the city.

WHAT IT COSTS In euros				
	$$$$	$$$	$$	$
FOR 2 PEOPLE	over €300	€225–€300	€150–€225	under €150

Hotel prices are for two people in a standard double room in high season.

$$$$ **Danieli.** Parts of this rather large hotel are built around a 15th-century palazzo bathed in sumptuous Venetian colors. The downside is that the Danieli also has several modern annexes that some find bland and impersonal, and the lower-price rooms can be exceedingly drab. Still, celebrities and English-speaking patrons crowd its sumptuous four-story-high lobby, chic salons, and dining terrace with a fantastic view of St. Mark's Basin. *Riva degli Schiavoni, 4196 Castello, 30122 041/5226480 041/5200208 www.luxurycollection.com 221 rooms, 12 suites Restaurant, bar AE, DC, MC, V.*

$$$$ **Gritti Palace.** This haven of pampering luxury is like an aristocratic private home, with fresh flowers, fine antiques, lavish appointments, and attentive service. The dining terrace overlooking the Grand Canal is best in the evening when boat traffic dies down. *Campo Santa Maria del Giglio, 2467 San Marco, 30124 041/794611 041/5200942 www.luxurycollection.com 87 rooms, 6 suites Restaurant, bar AE, DC, MC, V.*

$$$$ **Hotel Londra Palace.** The hotel's 100 windows overlook the lagoon and the island of San Giorgio, which imparts a hearty dash of sunlight to many of its finely decorated rooms. The view must have been pleasing to Tchaikovsky, who wrote his 4th Symphony here in 1877. Neoclassical-style public rooms, with splashes of blue and green glass suggesting the sea, play nicely off guest rooms, with their fine fabric, damask drapes, Biedermeier furniture, and Venetian glass. *Riva degli Schiavoni, 4171 Castello, 30122 041/5200533 041/5225032 www.hotelondra.it 36 rooms, 17 suites Restaurant, bar AE, DC, MC, V.*

★ $$$$ **Il Palazzo at the Bauer.** A $38 million restoration has turned il Palazzo into the ultimate word in luxury. Bevilacqua and Rubelli fabrics cover the walls, and no two rooms are decorated the same. Il Palazzo is separate from the Bauer Hotel, but both have rooms with high ceilings, Murano glass, marbled bathrooms, and damask drapes. The outdoor hot tub on the 7th floor offers wonderful views of La Serennissima. *Campo San Moisè, 1459 San Marco, 30124 041/5207022 041/5207557 www.bauervenezia.it 35 rooms, 40 suites Restaurant, bar AE, DC, MC, V.*

★ $$$$ **Metropole.** Guests can step from their water taxi or gondola into the lobby of this small, well-run hotel, rich in precious antiques and just five minutes from Piazza San Marco. Many rooms have a view of the lagoon and others overlook the garden at the back. *Riva degli Schiavoni, 4149 Castello, 30122 041/5205044 041/5223679 www.hotelmetropole.com 43 rooms, 26 suites Restaurant, bar AE, DC, MC, V.*

$$$ **American.** At first sight, it's hard to pick out this quiet, family-run hotel from the houses along the fondamenta: there are no lights, flags, or big signs on the hotel's yellow stucco facade. Rooms vary in size and shape, but sage green and delicate pink fabrics and lacquered Venetian-style furniture are found throughout. *San Vio, 628 Dorsoduro, 30123 041/5204733 041/5204048 www.hotelamerican.com 28 rooms, 2 suites AE, DC, MC, V.*

$$$ **Hotel Pausania.** From the moment you ascend the grand staircase rising above the fountain of this 14th-century palazzo, you sense the combination of good taste and modern comforts that characterize this hotel. Light-shaded rooms are spacious, with comfortable furniture and carpets with rugs thrown over them. Some rooms face the small canal (which can become a bit noisy early in the morning) in front of the hotel, and others look out over the large garden courtyard. *Fondamenta Gherardini, 2824 Dorsoduro, 30123 041/5222083 041/5222989 www.hotelpausania.it 26 rooms Bar AE, MC, V.*

$$ **Hotel Antico Doge.** If you're looking for a small, intimate hotel in a quiet, central location, look no further. This delightful palazzo once belonged to Doge Marino Falier; since then, it's been modernized with lovely results: some rooms have canopy beds or baldacchini; all have fabric walls and hardwood floors. On a small canal, only minutes away from San Marco and the Rialto Bridge, this is an oasis of tranquillity. An ample buffet breakfast is served in a room with a frescoed ceiling and Murano chandelier. *Campo SS. Apostoli, Cannaregio 5643, 30131 041/241 1570 041/244 3660 www.anticodoge.com 13 rooms, 2 suites Bar AE, DC, MC, V.*

$$ **Paganelli.** The lagoon views here so impressed Henry James that he described the Paganelli in the preface to his *Portrait of a Lady.* This enchanting small hotel on the waterfront near Piazza San Marco is tastefully decorated in the Venetian style. The quieter annex in Campo San Zaccaria is a former convent, and some rooms preserve the original coffered ceilings. *Riva degli Schiavoni, 4687 Castello, 30122 041/5224324 041/5239267 22 rooms Bar AE, MC, V.*

$$ **Wildner.** Right between the superdeluxe Danieli and Londra Palace hotels, this pleasant, unpretentious, family-run pensione enjoys the same views. The rooms are spread over four floors (no elevator), half with a view of San Giorgio and half looking out onto the quiet Campo San Zaccaria. The no-nonsense interior has parquet floors, solid, dark furniture, and brown leather headboards. White curtains and creamy bedspreads enhance the Wildner's simplicity. *Riva degli Schiavoni, 4161 Castello, 30122 041/5227463 041/2414640 www.veneziahotels.com 16 rooms AE, DC, MC, V.*

$–$$ **Agli Alboretti.** The Alboretti is one of the many hotels clustered at the foot of the Ponte dell'Accademia. Its unpretentious, rather small rooms are blessed with plenty of light. Some steep climbing might be part of your stay, as there are four floors and no elevator. In warm weather, breakfast is served in an inner courtyard under a rose bower; a small terrace with potted plants is open during the warmer months. *Rio Terrà Foscarini, 884 Dorsoduro, 30123 041/5230058 041/5210158 www.aglialboretti.com 20 rooms Restaurant, bar AE, DC, MC, V.*

$–$$ Fodor's Choice ★ **La Calcina.** The Calcina sits in an enviable position along the sunny Zattere, with views across the wide Giudecca Canal. A stone staircase (no elevator) leads to the rooms upstairs, with shiny wooden floors, original art deco furniture and lamps, and firm beds. Some rooms suffer from a lack of storage space, and anyone staying in a single room should note that a few of the rooms have a shared bath. *Zattere 780 Dorsoduro, 30123 041/5206466 041/5227045 www.lacalcina.com 29 rooms, 26 with bath; 5 suites Restaurant AE, DC, MC, V.*

★ $ **Dalla Mora.** On a quiet lane beyond the main flow of traffic, this hotel occupies two simple, well-maintained houses, both with a view. The tiny, cheerful entrance hall leads upstairs to a terrace lined with potted geraniums—a perfect place to catch the breeze on summer evenings. Rooms are spacious, with basic wooden furniture and tile floors. The annex across the street has rooms without private bathrooms and others with only showers and sinks. The excellent price and good views make this an especially attractive place to stay if you're on a budget. ✉ *Off Salizzada San Pantalon, 42 Santa Croce, 30135* ☎ *041/710703* 📠 *041/723006* *14 rooms, 6 with bath* ▭ *MC, V.*

NIGHTLIFE & THE ARTS

To find out what's going on, pick up a *Guest in Venice* booklet, free at hotels, or *Venezia News,* which is sold at newsstands. Both have information in English (and Italian) concerning concerts, opera, ballet, theater, exhibitions, movies, sports, and clubs. They also print schedules for the busiest vaporetto and bus lines, and the main trains and flights from Venice.

The Arts

Venice is a stop for major traveling exhibits, from ancient Mayan to contemporary art. In odd-numbered years, from mid-June to early November, the **Biennale dell'Arte** attracts several hundred contemporary artists from around the world. Biennale also holds the Venice International Film Festival each August as well as numerous music and dance events throughout the year. ✉ *Ca' Giustinian* ☎ *041/5218711* 📠 *041/5227539* 🌐 *www.labiennale.org.*

Concerts

Biennale Musica spotlights contemporary music, and clubs around town occasionally have jazz and Italian pop, but the vast majority of music played in Venice is classical, with Vivaldi (Venice's star composer) usually featured. You'll find posters and costumed youth pitching concerts, but especially worth seeking out are **L'Offerta Musicale** (☎ 041/5241143 call for information) and **Gruppo Accademia di San Rocco,** which performs at Scuola di San Rocco (☎ 041/5234864 or 041/962999). Travel agency **Kele e Teo** (✉ Ponte dei Bareteri, between San Marco and Rialto ☎ 041/5208722) handles tickets for a number of orchestras. A great source of information is **Vivaldi** (✉ Fontego dei Tedeschi 5537, opposite Rialto Post Office ☎📠 041/5221343), which sells CDs by local groups and often has tickets available.

Opera

Teatro La Fenice, one of Italy's oldest opera houses, has witnessed memorable premieres, including Verdi's 1853 first-night flop of *La Traviata.* It has also endured its share of disasters, like the fire of January 1996, which badly damaged it. Until La Fenice rises again, as its name (*The Phoenix*) promises, opera, symphony, and ballet events alternate between the **Teatro Malibran** (✉ Campo San Giovanni Crisostomo) and the tent-like **Palafenice** (✉ Tronchetto parking area). Visit (🌐 www.teatrolafenice.it) for a calender of performances or to buy tickets for either venue. Tickets are available at the theater one hour before show time. Information and tickets are also available through **Vela** (✉ Piazzale Roma or Calle dei Fuseri ☎ 899/909090).

Nightlife

Hybrid **Caffè Blue** (✉ San Pantalon ☎ 041/710227) reserves one bar for whiskey drinkers and also serves afternoon tea from a samovar. It's open noon 'til 2 AM and has live music on Friday. Lido's summery **Discoteca Acropolis** (✉ Lungomare 22 ☎ 041/5260466) beach disco has a terrace bar and occasional live music. Near Accademia Gallery, **Piccolo Mondo** (✉ Dorsoduro 1056/A ☎ 041/5200371) has a tiny dance floor open until 4 AM. **Martini Scala Club** (✉ Campo San Fantin ☎ 041/5224121), attached to the elegant restaurant of the same name, serves full meals until 2 AM and has live music until 3:30 AM.

SHOPPING

At **Gilberto Penzo** (✉ Calle Seconda dei Saoneri, 2681 San Polo ☎ 041/719372 🌐 www.veniceboats.com) you'll find small-scale models of gondolas and their graceful oarlocks known as *forcole*. **Norelene** (✉ Calle della Chiesa, 727 Dorsoduro, near the Peggy Guggenheim Collection ☎ 041/5237605) has hand-painted fabrics that make wonderful wall hangings or elegant jackets and chic scarves. In San Marco, **Venetia Studium** (✉ Calle Larga XXII Marzo ☎ 041/5229281 🌐 www.venetiastudium.com) is famous for Fortuny-inspired lamps and elegant scarves.

Glass

There's a lot of cheap, low-quality Venetian glass for sale around town; if you want something better, try **l'Isola** (✉ Campo San Moisè, 1468 San Marco ☎ 041/5231973), where Carlo Moretti's contemporary designs are on display. **Domus** (✉ Fondamenta dei Vetrai, Murano ☎ 041/739215), on Murano, has a good selection of glass objects.

Shopping Districts

Le Mercerie, the **Frezzeria,** and **Calle dei Fabbri** are some of Venice's busiest shopping streets and lead off of Piazza San Marco.

VENICE A TO Z

AIRPORTS & TRANSFERS

Aeroporto Marco Polo ✉ 10 km (6 mi) north of Venice on the mainland ☎ 041/2609260 flight information.

TRANSFERS The cheapest, most direct airport transfer to historic Venice is Alilaguna. The company's free airport shuttle bus takes you to the dock, where for €10 per person, including bags, you board one of the boats that leave hourly (until midnight). The trip to Piazza San Marco takes an hour, and you will stop at the Lido on the way. Blue ATVO buses run nonstop to Piazzale Roma in 25 minutes and cost €2.70. Yellow ACTV local buses (Line 5) cost €.77, but you must buy tickets before boarding, and large bags can be awkward during rush hour. From Piazzale Roma you can catch a vaporetto to your hotel. Private water taxis, called *motoscafi,* should carry four persons and four bags to a single stop for €78, but agree on the price before boarding. Land taxis cost about €30.

Alilaguna ☎ 041/5235775. **Radio Taxi** ☎ 041/936222 **Motoscafo** ☎ 041/5415084 airport transfers.

BOAT & FERRY TRAVEL

BY GONDOLA If you can't leave Venice without a gondola ride, take it in the evening, when traffic has died down and palace windows are illuminated. Let the gondolier know that you want to see the *rii,* or smaller canals, as well as the Grand Canal. The fixed minimum is €62 for 50 minutes with a nighttime supplement of €15.50, but agree on prices before getting into the boat.

BY TRAGHETTO Few tourists know about the two-man gondola ferries that cross the Grand Canal at various fixed points. At €.40, they're the cheapest and shortest gondola ride in Venice, but they can save a lot of walking. Look for TRAGHETTO signs and hand your fare to the gondolier when you board.

BY VAPORETTO ACTV water buses serve several routes daily and after 11 PM provide limited night service. Some cover the Grand Canal, and others circle the city or connect Venice with lagoon islands. One ride costs €3.10, but tourist tickets are a better deal: buy a 24-hour ticket for €9.30, three days for €18.08, and seven days for €30.99. Remember to validate your ticket in the yellow box before boarding, and if you board without a ticket, buy one immediately. Line information is posted at landings, and complete timetables are sold at ticket booths for €.50. Landings are marked with name and line number, but check before boarding, particularly with lines 1 and 82, to make sure the boat is going in your direction.

Line 1, the Grand Canal local, calls at every stop between Piazzale Roma and San Marco (about 45 minutes), then continues to the Lido. Lines 41 (counterclockwise) and 42 (clockwise) circle the island and connect San Zaccaria with Murano. Lines 51 and 52 are express boats between the train station and the Lido. In one direction, Line 82 is the Grand Canal express; in the other direction, it stops at Tronchetto parking, Zattere, and Giudecca before arriving at San Zaccaria. Line N runs from midnight to 6 AM, stopping at the Lido, Vallaresso, Accademia, Rialto, the train station, Piazzale Roma, Giudecca, and San Zaccaria, then making the return trip in reverse order.

BY WATER TAXI Motoscafi, or water taxis aren't cheap; you'll spend about €48 for a short trip in town, €60 to the Lido, and €75 per hour for an island visit. Luggage handling, waiting time, early or late hours, and even ordering a taxi from your hotel can add expense so always agree on price first.

ACTV ☎ 041/5287886 🌐 www.actv.it. **Motoscafo** ☎ 041/5224281 or 041/5222303. **Vela Information and Tickets** ☎ 041/2714747 or 899/909090 €.40/min 🌐 www.velaspa.com.

CAR TRAVEL

PARKING If you bring a car to Venice, you will have to pay for a garage or parking space. Ignore anyone trying to flag you down with offers of parking and hotels. Drive directly to one of the parking garages.

Parking at Autorimessa Comunale costs €18.59 for 24 hours. The private Garage San Marco costs €19 for up to 12 hours, and €26 for 12–24 hours. To reach Tronchetto parking (€18 for 1–24 hours), watch for signs as you cross the bridge from the mainland; you'll have to turn right before you get to Piazzale Roma. Many hotels have discounts with garages; get a voucher when you check in and present it when you pay the garage. Line 82 connects Tronchetto with Piazzale Roma and Piazza San Marco, but if there's thick fog or extreme tides, a bus will take you to Piazzale Roma. Garage San Marco and Autorimessa Comunale accept reservations.

Autorimessa Comunale ✉ Piazzale Roma, end of S11 road, ☎ 041/2727301, 🌐 www.asmvenezia.it. **Garage San Marco** ✉ Piazzale Roma 467/F, turn right into bus park, ☎ 041/5232213 🌐 www.garagesanmarco.it. **Tronchetto** ☎ 041/5207555.

CONSULATES

United Kingdom ✉ Campo della Carità, near Gallerie dell'Accademia ☎ 041/5227207.

EMERGENCIES

The U.K. Consulate or your hotel can recommend doctors and dentists. Venice's pharmacies are open 9–12:30 and 3:30–7:30, and they take turns staying open lunches, nights, weekends, and holidays.

Emergency Services **Ambulance** ☎ 118. **Carabinieri** ☎ 112. **General emergencies** ☎ 113.

TOURS

BOAT TOURS

Boat tours to Murano, Burano, and Torcello islands leave various docks around San Marco daily. These 3- to 3½-hour trips cost €15–€17 and can be annoying, often pressuring you to buy at showroom prices even higher than normal. From April to October trips depart at 9:30 and 2:30, and from November to March they leave at 2.

More than a dozen major travel agents have grouped together to form the Consorzio San Marco, which provides frequent, quality tours of the city. Serenaded gondola trips, with or without dinner (€68/31), can be purchased at any of their offices or at American Express. Tours leave at 7:30 PM and 8:30 PM May–September; at 7:30 PM in April and October; and at 3:30 PM November–March.

American Express ✉ Salizada San Moisè, San Marco 1471 ☎ 041/5200844 🖷 041/5229937. **Consorzio San Marco** ☎ 041/2406712.

WALKING TOURS

The Consorzio San Marco offers a two-hour walking tour of the San Marco area (€24), which ends with a glassblowing demonstration (no Sunday tour in winter). From April to October, there's also an afternoon walking tour that ends with a gondola ride (€29). Venicescapes, an Italo-American cultural association, focuses itineraries on history and culture as well as tourist sights. Venice à la Carte customizes tours specifically to clients' needs. Both cater only to small groups (two to eight people), and reservations are recommended during busy seasons.

Albatravel ✉ Calle dei Fabbri, San Marco 4538 ☎ 041/5210123 🖷 041/5200781. **Consorzio San Marco** ☎ 041/2406712. **Venice à la Carte** ☎ 349/1447818 🖷 240/208-7273 in U.S. 🌐 www.tourvenice.org. **Venicescapes** ☎🖷 041/5206361 🌐 www.venicescapes.org.

TOURS OF THE SURROUNDING REGION

American Express and other agencies offer excursions in the Veneto region. Tuesday, Thursday, and Saturday from March to October you can take a boat trip to Padua along the Brenta River, stopping at three Palladian villas and returning to Venice by bus for €62 per person (€86 with lunch). Wednesday's Palladio Tour by eight-person minibus includes villas and Vicenza (€108 per person).

The Hills of the Veneto minibus tour visits Marostica, Bassano del Grappa, and Asolo, with a vineyard stop along Strada del Prosecco for wine tasting (Tuesday, Thursday, and weekends; €104 per person; lunch €13). Monday and Friday you can cool off with the scenic Dolomite Mountains Tour. You'll see Titian's birthplace—Pieve di Cadore—and Cortina d'Ampezzo (€113 includes a packed lunch). Reservations for all tours are suggested during high season.

American Express ✉ Salizada San Moisè, San Marco 1471, ☎ 041/5200844 🖷 041/5229937.

PRIVATE GUIDES

Pick up a list of more than 100 licensed guides from the tourist information office or the guides' association. Two-hour tours with an English-speaking guide for up to 30 people start at €113. Agree on a total price before you begin, as there are some hidden extras. Guides are of variable quality.

Guides' Association ✉ San Marco 750, near San Zulian ☎ 041/5209038 🖷 041/5210762.

TRAIN TRAVEL

Venice has rail connections with every major city in Italy and Europe. Some continental trains do not enter historic Venice but stop at the mainland Mestre Station. All trains traveling to and from Venice Santa Lucia stop at Mestre, so it's not difficult to hop on the next passing train, but if you upgrade from regional train to Intercity or Eurostar, don't forget to buy a *supplemento* or you can be fined. You'll also be fined if you forget to purchase and validate train tickets in the yellow machines found on or near platforms. Venice Station is well equipped with tourist information, a baggage depot, and free hotel booking. Just outside, nearly every vaporetto line has a landing to take you to your hotel's neighborhood. Be prepared with advance directions from the hotel and a good map.

APT ☎ 041/5298727. **Trenitalia** ☎ 892021 local call in Italy 🌐 www.trenitalia.it.

TRANSPORTATION AROUND VENICE

Venice has more than 100 islands, in excess of 400 bridges, and few straight lines. The city's house-numbering seems nonsensical, and the *sestieri* (six districts) of San Marco, Cannaregio, Castello, Dorsoduro, Santa Croce, and San Polo all copy each other's street names. Traveling by vaporetto can be bewildering, and often you're forced to walk, whether you want to or not. Yellow signs, posted on many corners, point toward major landmarks—San Marco, Rialto, Accademia—but you won't find them deep in residential neighborhoods. Three ways to enjoy yourself more are to wear comfortable shoes, buy a good map at a newsstand, and accept the fact that you will get lost.

TRAVEL AGENCIES

Gran Canal ✉ Ponte del Ovo, San Marco 4759 near Rialto Bridge ☎ 041/2712111 📠 041/5223380. **Kele e Teo** ✉ Ponte dei Bareteri, San Marco 4930 between San Marco and Rialto ☎ 041/5208722 📠 041/5208913 also handles train tickets.

VISITOR INFORMATION

The train station branch of the Venice Tourist Office is open daily 8–6:30; other branches generally open at 9:30. Vela's Hello Venezia Center is open 8 AM–8 PM.

Venice Tourist Offices 🌐 www.turismovenezia.it ✉ Train Station ☎ 041/5298727 ✉ Procuratie Nuove San Marco 71/F, near Museo Correr ☎ 041/5298740 ✉ Venice Pavilion, near Giardini Reali ☎ 041/5225150 ✉ Garage Comunale ☎ 041/2411499 ✉ Summer only: S. Maria Elisabetta 6/A ☎ 041/5265721. **Vela** ☎ 041/2714747 or 899/909090 €.40/min.

Associazione Veneziana Albergatori, an association of hotel keepers, operates a booking service by phone, fax, and at booths around Venice. There's a kiosk inside Santa Lucia train station (open 8 AM–9 PM), one at Marco Polo Airport (open 8 AM–10 PM), and one kiosk in each of the two Piazzale Roma parking garages (open 9 AM–10 PM). This service is free, but you'll pay a deposit (€11–€47 per person; V and MC accepted), which will be deducted from your hotel bill. Another service, **Venezia Sì,** makes free reservations by phone Monday–Saturday 9–7.

Reserving a Room **AVA Booths** ✉ Piazzale Roma ☎ 041/5231397 and 041/5228640 ✉ Train station ☎ 041/715288 and 041/715016 ✉ Marco Polo Airport ☎ 041/5415133. **Venezia Sì** ☎ 800/843006 in Italy (toll-free, Mon.–Sat. 9 AM–7 PM); 0039/0415222264 from abroad 📠 0039/0415221242.

For Italy Basics, see chapter 9, Florence.

VIENNA

16

Vienna has been characterized as an "old dowager of a town"—an Austro-Hungarian empress widowed in 1918 by the Great War. It's not just the aristocratic and courtly atmosphere, with monumental doorways and facades of former palaces at every turn. Nor is it just that Vienna (Wien in German) has a higher proportion of middle-aged and older citizens than any other city in Europe, with a concomitant air of stability, quiet, and respectability. Rather, it's these factors—combined with a love of music; a discreet weakness for rich food (especially cakes); an adherence to old-fashioned and formal forms of address; a high regard for the arts; and a gentle mourning for lost glories—that preserve the city's enchanting elegance and dignity.

EXPLORING VIENNA

Most main sights are in the inner zone, the oldest part of the city, encircled by the Ringstrasse (Ring Road), once the course of the city walls and today a broad, tree-lined boulevard. As you wander around, train yourself to look upward; some of the most memorable architectural delights are found on upper stories and along rooflines. Note that addresses throughout the chapter ending with "-strasse" or "-gasse" (both meaning "street") are abbreviated "str." or "g." respectively (Augustinerstrasse will be "Augustinerstr."; Dorotheergasse will be "Dorotheerg").

Vienna addresses include a roman numeral that designates in which of the city's 23 districts the address is located. The First District (I, the inner city) is bounded by the Ringstrasse and the Danube Canal. The 2nd through 9th (II–IX) districts surround the inner city, starting with the 2nd district across the Danube Canal and running clockwise; the 10th through the 23rd (X–XXIII) districts form a second concentric ring of suburbs.

The Heart of Vienna

The Inner Stadt (Inner City), or First District, comprised the entire city in medieval times, and for more than eight centuries the enormous bulk of the Stephansdom (St. Stephen's Cathedral) remained the nucleus around which the city grew. Beginning in the 1870s, when Vienna reached the zenith of its imperial prosperity, the medieval walls were replaced by the Ringstrasse, along which a series of magnificent buildings were erected: the Staatsoper (opera house), the Hofburg Palace, the Kunsthistorisches Museum, the Parliament building, and the Rathaus (city hall). The pedestrian zone around the Stephansdom is lined with designer boutiques, cafés, and upscale restaurants.

Numbers in the margin correspond to points of interest on the Vienna map.

❶ **Albertina.** After years of renovation, this museum has reopened and once again exhibits one of the world's largest collections of drawings, sketches, engravings, and etchings. Originally a 17th-century palace, the original structure has been expanded to include halls for temporary exhibitions and a vast study area. The permanent collection contains some of the greatest old master drawings, including Dürer's *Praying Hands.* Other highlights include works by Rembrandt, Michelangelo, and Correggio. ✉ *Augustinerstr. 1* ☎ *01/53483–544* 🌐 *www.albertina.at* 🕓 *Thurs.–Tues. 10–6, Wed. 10–9* Ⓤ *U3/Herreng.*

❸ **Augustinerkirche** (St. Augustine's Church). The interior of this 14th-century church has undergone restoration. Much of the earlier baroque ornamentation was removed in the 1780s, but the gilt organ decoration and main altar remain as visual sensations. This was the court church; the Habsburg rulers' hearts are preserved in a chamber here. On Sunday, the 11 AM mass is sung in Latin. ✉ *Josefspl.* Ⓤ *U3/Herreng.*

㉓ **Figarohaus** (Mozart Memorial Rooms). A commemorative museum occupies the small apartment in the house on a narrow street just east of St. Stephen's Cathedral where Mozart lived from 1784 to 1787. It was here that the composer wrote *The Marriage of Figaro* (hence the nickname Figaro House) and, some claim, spent the happiest years of his life. Fascinating Mozart memorabilia are on view, unfortunately displayed in an inappropriately modern fashion. ✉ *Domg. 5* ☎ *01/513–6294* 🕓 *Tues.–Sun. 9–6* Ⓤ *U1 or U3/Stephanspl.*

㉕ **Freud Apartment.** The original famous couch is gone (there's a replica), but the apartment in which Sigmund Freud treated his first patients is otherwise generally intact. Other rooms include a reference library. ✉ *Bergg. 19* ☎ *01/319–1596* 🕓 *Daily 9–5* Ⓤ *U2/Schottentor.*

⑱ **Haus der Musik** (House of Music). It would be easy to spend an entire day at this new, ultra high-tech museum housed on several floors of an early-19th-century palace near Schwarzenbergplatz. There are special rooms dedicated to each of the great Viennese composers—Haydn, Mozart, Beethoven, Strauss, and Mahler—complete with music samples and manuscripts. There are also dozens of interactive computer games. You can even record your own CD with a variety of everyday sounds. ✉ *Seilerstätte 30* ☎ *01/51648–51* 🌐 *www.hdm.at* 🕓 *Daily 10–10* Ⓤ *U1, U2, or U4/Karlsplatz, then Streetcar D to Schwarzenbergpl.*

㉜ **Heeresgeschichtliches Museum** (Museum of Military History). Designed by Theophil Hansen, this impressive neo-Gothic building houses war artifacts ranging from armor and Turkish tents confiscated from the Turks during the 16th-century siege of Vienna to fighter planes and tanks. Also on display is the bullet-riddled car that Archduke Franz Ferdinand and his wife were riding in when they were assassinated in Sarajevo in 1914. ✉ *Arsenal 3, Bldg. 18* ☎ *01/795–610* 🌐 *www.bmlv.gv.at* 🕓 *Sat.–Thurs. 9–5* Ⓤ *Tram 18/Ghegastr., near the Belvedere.*

★ 7 **Hofburg** (Imperial Palace). This centerpiece of Imperial Vienna is actually a vast complex comprising numerous buildings, courtyards, and other must-sees. Start with the magnificent domed entry—Michaelertor (St. Michael's Gate), the principal gateway to the Hofburg—and go through the courtyards to the vast, grassy Heldenplatz (Hero's Square), on the front. The palace complex, with sections dating from the 13th through 18th centuries, includes the **Augustinerkirche** (Augustianian Church), the **Nationalbibliothek**—its central room is one of the most spectacular baroque showpieces anywhere—and the **Hofburgkapelle,** home to the Vienna Boys Choir. Here, too, are the famous **Spanische Reitschule**—where the Lipizzaners go through their paces—and three fascinating museums: the **Silberkammer,** the **Schauräume in der Hofburg,** and the **Schatzkammer,** as well as the **Schmetterlinghaus** (Butterfly House), alive with unusual butterflies. ✉ *Hofburg: main streets circling complex—Opernring, Augustinerstr., Schauflerg., and Dr. Karl Renner-Ring;* ✉ *Schmetterlinghaus: entrance in Burggarten* ☎ *01/533–7570* 🌐 *www.hofburg-wien.at* ⏲ *Daily 9–5; Schmetterlinghaus: Nov.–Mar., daily 10–3:45; Apr.–Oct., weekdays 10–4:45, weekends 10–6:15* Ⓤ *U3/Herreng.*

10 **Hofburgkapelle** (Court Chapel). Home of the renowned Vienna Boys Choir, this Gothic chapel dates from 1449. You'll need tickets to hear the angelic boys sing mass (only 10 side balcony seats afford views) at 9:15 AM on Sunday, mid-September through June; tickets are available from travel agencies at a substantial markup, at the chapel itself (open daily 11–1 and 3–5), or by writing two months in advance to the **Hofmusikkapelle** (📫 Hofburg, Schweizerhof, A-1010, Vienna). General seating costs €5; prime seats in the front of the church, €29. The City Tourist Office can sometimes help with ticket applications. Limited standing room is available for free; get to the chapel by at least 8:30 AM on Sunday for a shot at a spot. ✉ *Hofburg, Schweizer Hof* ☎ *01/533–9927* Ⓤ *U3/Herreng.*

20 **Judenplatz Museum.** In what was once the old Jewish ghetto, construction workers discovered the remains of a 13th-century synagogue while digging for a new parking garage. Simon Wiesenthal (a Vienna resident) helped to turn it into a museum dedicated to the Austrian Jews who died in World War II. Marking the outside is a rectangular concrete cube resembling library shelves, signifying Jewish love of learning, designed by Rachel Whiteread. Downstairs are three exhibition rooms on medieval Jewish life and the synagogue excavations. ✉ *Judenpl. 8* ☎ *01/535–0431* ⏲ *Sun.–Thurs. 10–6, Fri. 10–2* Ⓤ *U1 or U4/Schwedenpl.*

19 **Jüdisches Museum der Stadt Wien** (Jewish Museum). Housed in the former Eskeles town palace, the city's Jewish Museum offers exhibits that portray the richness of the Jewish culture and heritage that contributed so much to Vienna and Austria. On the top floor is a staggering collection of Judaica. ✉ *Dorotheerg. 11* ☎ *01/535–0431* 🌐 *www.jmw.at* ⏲ *Sun.–Wed. and Fri. 10–6, Thurs. 10–8* Ⓤ *U1 or U3/Stephanspl.*

17 **Kapuzinerkirche** (Capuchin Church). The ground-level church is nothing unusual, but the basement crypt holds the imperial vault, the Kaisergruft, a final resting place for many sarcophagi of long-dead Habsburgs. The oldest tomb is that of Ferdinand II; it dates from 1633. The most recent one is that of Empress Zita, widow of the last of the Kaisers, who died in 1989. ✉ *Neuer Markt 1* ☎ *01/512–6853–12* ⏲ *Daily 9:30–4* Ⓤ *U1 or U3/Stephanspl., or U1 or U4/Karlspl.*

★ 34 **Karlskirche** (St. Charles's Church). The classical baroque facade and dome flanked by vast twin columns instantly identify the Karlskirche, one of the city's best-known landmarks. The church was built around 1715 by

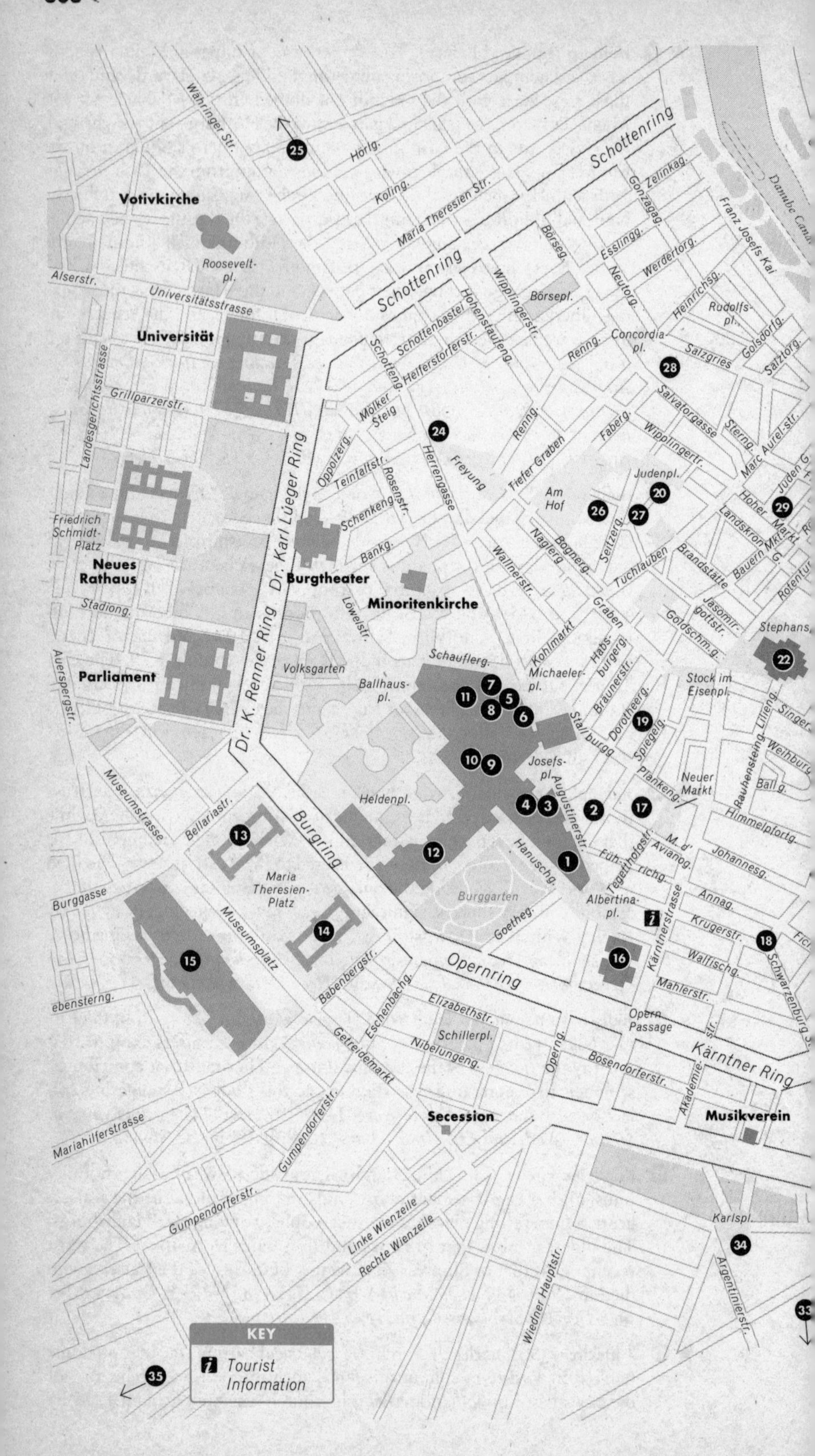

Währinger Str.
Hörlg.
Koling.
Maria Theresien Str.
Schottenring
Zelinkag.
Gonzagag.
Danube Canal
Franz Josefs Kai
Votivkirche
Roosevelt-pl.
Alserstr.
Universitätsstrasse
Börseg.
Esslingg.
Werdertorg.
Börsepl.
Neutorg.
Heinrichsg.
Rudolfs-pl.
Schottenbastei
Hohenstaufeng.
Wipplingerstr.
Universität
Landesgerichtsstrasse
Schotteng.
Helferstorferstr.
Renng.
Concordia-pl.
Salzgries
Golsdorfg.
Salztorg.
Grillparzerstr.
Mölker Steig
Salvatorgasse
Dr. Karl Lueger Ring
Oppolzerg.
Herrengasse
Freyung
Renng.
Faberg.
Wipplingerstr.
Sterng.
Marc Aurel-str.
Teinfaltstr.
Rosenstr.
Tiefer Graben
Judenpl.
Am Hof
Hoher Markt
Friedrich Schmidt-Platz
Schenkeng.
Landskrong.
Bankg.
Wallnerstr.
Naglerg.
Bognerg.
Seitzerg.
Tuchlauben
Brandstätte
Bauernmkt.
Neues Rathaus
Burgtheater
Minoritenkirche
Stadiong.
Löwelstr.
Graben
Jasomirgottstr.
Goldschm.g.
Kohlmarkt
Stephans
Auerspergstr.
Parliament
Volksgarten
Schauflerg.
Habsburgerg.
Michaeler-pl.
Ballhaus-pl.
Braunerstr.
Stock im Eisenpl.
Dr. K. Renner Ring
Stallburgg.
Dorotheerg.
Spiegelg.
Lilieng.
Singerstr.
Weihburg
Josefs-pl.
Plankeng.
Neuer Markt
Ballg.
Raubensteing.
Museumstrasse
Heldenpl.
Augustinerstr.
Himmelpfortg.
Bellariastr.
Burgring
M. d' Avianog.
Hanuschg.
Führichg.
Johannesg.
Tegetthofstr.
Maria Theresien-Platz
Burggarten
Albertina-pl.
Annag.
Burggasse
Museumsplatz
Goetheg.
Kärntnerstrasse
Krugerstr.
Walfischg.
Schwarzenburg
Opernring
Mahlerstr.
Babenbergstr.
Eschenbachg.
Elizabethstr.
Oper Passage
Schillerpl.
Nibelungeng.
Operng.
Bosendorferstr.
Kärntner Ring
Akademiestr.
Getreidemarkt
Secession
Musikverein
Mariahilferstrasse
Gumpendorferstr.
Gumpendorferstr.
Linke Wienzeile
Rechte Wienzeile
Karlspl.
Argentinierstr.
Wiedner Hauptstr.
KEY
Tourist Information

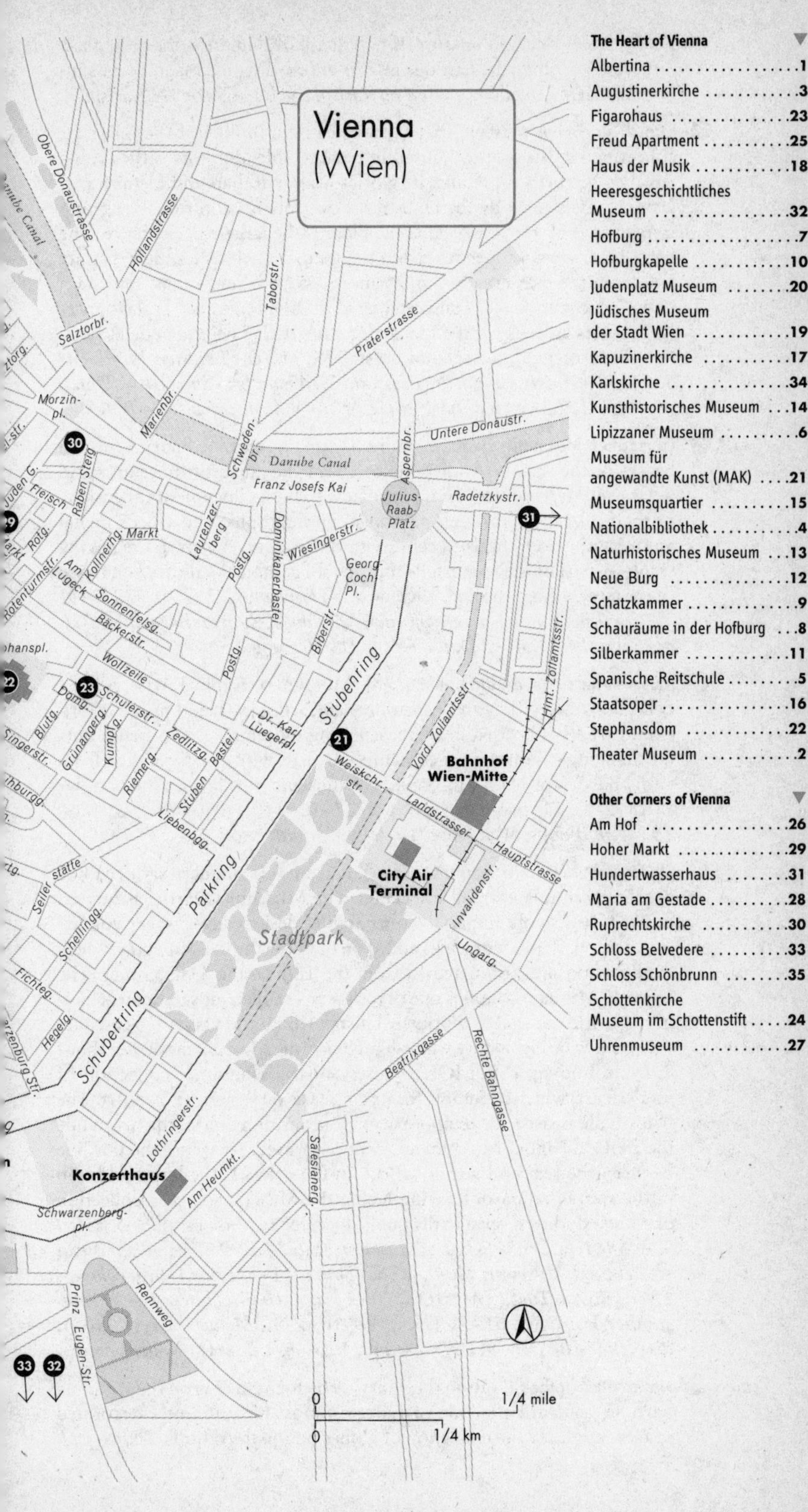
Vienna
(Wien)
The Heart of Vienna
Albertina 1
Augustinerkirche 3
Figarohaus 23
Freud Apartment 25
Haus der Musik 18
Heeresgeschichtliches
Museum 32
Hofburg 7
Hofburgkapelle 10
Judenplatz Museum 20
Jüdisches Museum
der Stadt Wien 19
Kapuzinerkirche 17
Karlskirche 34
Kunsthistorisches Museum . . .14
Lipizzaner Museum 6
Museum für
angewandte Kunst (MAK) 21
Museumsquartier 15
Nationalbibliothek 4
Naturhistorisches Museum . . .13
Neue Burg 12
Schatzkammer 9
Schauräume in der Hofburg . . .8
Silberkammer 11
Spanische Reitschule 5
Staatsoper 16
Stephansdom 22
Theater Museum 2
Other Corners of Vienna
Am Hof 26
Hoher Markt 29
Hundertwasserhaus 31
Maria am Gestade 28
Ruprechtskirche 30
Schloss Belvedere 33
Schloss Schönbrunn 35
Schottenkirche
Museum im Schottenstift 24
Uhrenmuseum 27
Obere Donaustrasse
Danube Canal
Hollandstrasse
Taborstr.
Praterstrasse
Salztorbr.
Morzinpl.
Marienbr.
Schwedenbr.
Aspernbr.
Untere Donaustr.
Franz Josefs Kai
Julius-Raab-Platz
Radetzkystr.
Raben Steig
Fleisch Markt
Laurenzerberg
Dominikanerbastei
Wiesingerstr.
Georg-Coch-Pl.
Postg.
Rotg.
Kollnerhg.
Am Lugeck
Sonnenfelsg.
Bäckerstr.
Biberstr.
Wollzeile
Stubenring
Schulerstr.
Dr. Karl Luegerpl.
Zedlitzg.
Stubenbastei
Grunangerg.
Kumpfg.
Riemerg.
Blutg.
Singerstr.
Weiskchr.-str.
Vord. Zollamtsstr.
Hint. Zollamtsstr.
Bahnhof Wien-Mitte
Landstrasser Hauptstrasse
Liebenbgg.
City Air Terminal
Invalidenstr.
Seilerstätte
Parkring
Stadtpark
Schellingg.
Ungarg.
Fichteg.
Hegelg.
Schubertring
Beatrixgasse
Rechte Bahngasse
Lothringerstr.
Salesianerg.
Konzerthaus
Am Heumkt.
Schwarzenbergpl.
Rennweg
Prinz Eugen-Str.
0
1/4 mile
0
1/4 km

Fischer von Erlach. In the surprisingly small oval interior, the ceiling has airy frescoes, while the baroque altar is adorned with a magnificent sunburstlike array of gilded shafts. ✉ *Karlspl.* Ⓤ *U1, U2, or U4/Karlspl.*

⓮ **Kunsthistorisches Museum** (Art History Museum). One of the finest art collections in the world, housed in palatial splendor, this is the crown jewel of Vienna's museums. Its glories are the Italian and Flemish collections, assembled by the Habsburgs over many centuries. The group of paintings by Pieter Brueghel the Elder is the largest in existence. The large-scale works concentrated in the main galleries shouldn't distract you from the masterworks in the more intimate side wings. One level down is the remarkable Kunstkammer (Art Cabinet), which displays priceless objects created for the Habsburg emperors. These include curiosities made of gold, silver, and crystal. ✉ *Maria-Theresien-Pl.* ☎ *01/525–240* 🌐 *www.khm.at* ⏲ *Tues. and Wed. and Fri.–Sun. 10–6, Thurs. 10–9* Ⓤ *U2/MuseumsQuartier, U2 or U3/Volkstheater.*

Fodor's Choice ★

❻ **Lipizzaner Museum.** To learn more about the extraordinary Lipizzan horses of the Spanish Riding School, visit the adjacent museum set in what used to be the imperial pharmacy. Exhibits document the history of the Lipizzaners through paintings, photographs, and videos giving an overview from the 16th century to the present. A visit to the nearby stables—part of the Spanish Riding School complex—allows you to see the horses up close through a window. ✉ *Reitschulg. 2* ☎ *01/533–7811* *Combination ticket with morning training session at the Spanish Riding School €14.50* ⏲ *Daily 9–6* Ⓤ *U3/Herreng.*

㉑ **Museum für angewandte Kunst (MAK)** (Museum of Applied Arts). A large collection of Austrian furniture, porcelain, art objects, and priceless Oriental carpets is housed in this fascinating museum. The museum puts on changing exhibitions of contemporary art, with artists ranging from Chris Burden to Nam June Paik. The museum also houses the popular MAK Café. ✉ *Stubenring 5* ☎ *01/711–36–0* 🌐 *www.mak.at* ⏲ *Tues. 10 AM–midnight; Wed.–Sun. 10–6* Ⓤ *U3/Stubentor.*

⓯ **Museumsquartier** (Museum Quarter). Baroque and modern styles collide dazzlingly in this vast culture center. The MuseumsQuartier is housed in the 250-year-old Imperial Court Stables designed by Fischer von Erlach, with sleek modern wings added on to house the five museums, which exhibit thousands of artworks from the 18th to the 21st century. The **Leopold Museum** contains one of the greatest collections of Egon Schiele in the world, as well as works by Gustav Klimt and Oskar Kokoschka. Adjacent, in an eight-story whale-like edifice, the **Museum moderner Kunst Stiftung Ludwig (MUMOK)** houses Austria's national collection of modern art, which is notable for its emphasis on American Pop Art. The **Kunsthalle** is used for temporary exhibitions of avant-garde art, while the **ZOOM Kinder Museum** lets children 7 and up explore the fine line between the real and virtual world. In **Quartier21**, the latest addition in the sprawling baroque wing facing the Museumsplatz, a collection of artists' studios is open to the public for free. ✉ *Museumspl. 1–5* ☎ *01/523–5881; ZOOM Kinder Museum: 01/524–7908* 🌐 *www.mqw.at* ⏲ *Leopold Museum: Mon., Wed., Thurs. 11–7, Fri. 11–9, weekends 10–7, closed Tues.; MUMOK: Tues.–Sun. 10–6, Thurs. 10–9; Kunsthalle: Fri.–Wed. 10–7, Thurs. 10–10; ZOOM: weekdays 8:30–5, weekends 10–5:30* Ⓤ *U2/MuseumsQuartier, U2 or U3/Volkstheater.*

❹ **Nationalbibliothek** (National Library). The focus here is on the stunning baroque central hall—one of Europe's most magnificently decorated spaces. Look for the collection of globes on the third floor. ✉ *Josefspl.*

1 ☎ 01/534–10 or 01/534–10–297 ⏲ May–Oct., Fri.–Wed. 10–4, Thurs. 10–7; Nov.–Apr., Fri.–Wed. 10–2, Thurs. 10–7 Ⓤ U3/Herreng.

⓭ **Naturhistorisches Museum** (Natural History Museum). The twin building opposite the art-filled Kunsthistorisches Museum houses ranks of showcases filled with preserved animals, but such special collections as butterflies are better presented. Here, too, is the Venus of Willendorf, a 25,000-year-old statuette discovered in Lower Austria. ✉ *Maria-Theresien-Pl.* ☎ *01/521–77–0* 🌐 *www.khm.at* ⏲ *Thurs.–Mon. 9–6:30, Wed. 9–9* Ⓤ *U2 or U3/Volkstheater.*

16

⓬ **Neue Burg** (New Wing of the Imperial Palace). This 19th-century edifice—Hitler announced the annexation of Austria from its balcony in 1938—now houses a series of museums whose exhibits range from musical instruments (Beethoven's piano) to weapons (tons of armor) to the collections of the Völkerkunde (Ethnological) and Ephesus (Classical Antiquity) museums. ✉ *Heldenpl. 1* ☎ *01/525–240* 🌐 *www.khm.at* ⏲ *Wed.–Mon. 10–6* Ⓤ *U2/MuseumsQuartier.*

❾ **Schatzkammer** (Imperial Treasury). An almost overpowering display includes the magnificent crown jewels, the imperial crowns, the treasure of the Order of the Golden Fleece, regal robes, and other secular and ecclesiastical treasures. The imperial crown of the Holy Roman Empire is more than 1,000 years old. ✉ *Hofburg, Schweizer Hof* ☎ *01/52524–0* ⏲ *Wed.–Mon. 10–6* Ⓤ *U3/Herreng.*

❽ **Schauräume in der Hofburg** (Imperial Apartments). The long, repetitive suite of conventionally luxurious rooms is decorated (19th-century imitation of 18th-century rococo) to look regal but ends up looking merely official. Among the few signs of genuine life are Emperor Franz Josef's spartan, iron field bed, and Empress Elizabeth's wooden gymnastics equipment. Obsessed with her looks, she suffered from anorexia and was fanatically devoted to exercise. ✉ *Michaelerpl. 1; entrance under Michaelertor dome* ☎ *01/533–7570* 🌐 *www.hofburg-wien.at* ⏲ *Daily 9–4:30* Ⓤ *U3/Herreng.*

⓫ **Silberkammer** (Court Silver and Tableware Museum). See how royalty dined in this brilliant showcase of imperial table settings. Little wonder Marie-Antoinette—who, as a child of Maria Theresa, grew up in Schloss Schönbrunn—had a taste for extreme luxury. A combination ticket includes the imperial apartments around the corner. ✉ *Burghof inner court, Michaelertrakt* ☎ *01/533–7570* ⏲ *Daily 9–4:30* Ⓤ *U3/Herreng.*

★ ❺ **Spanische Reitschule** (Spanish Riding School). Probably the most famous interior in Vienna, the riding arena of the Spanish Riding School—wedding-cake white and crystal-chandeliered—is where the beloved white Lipizzaner horses train and perform dressage when they are not stabled in stalls across the Reitschulgasse to the east side of the school. For performance schedules and tickets, write to the Spanische Reitschule *at least* three months in advance. The AmEx office sometimes has a few last-minute tickets, but expect a 22% service charge. Performances are usually March–December, with the school on vacation in July and August. Generally, the full 80-minute show takes place Sunday at 11 AM plus selected Fridays at 6 PM. Morning training sessions with music are held Tuesday–Saturday from 10 to noon, and tickets can be bought *only* at the Josefplatz entrance, between 9:40 and 12:30. ✉ *Michaelerpl. 1, Hofburg, A-1010, Vienna* ☎ *01/533–9031–0* 🖷 *01/535–0186* 🌐 *www.srs.at* 🎫 *€35–€105, standing room €24–€28; morning training sessions €11.50; Sat. classical dressage final rehearsal, €20* ⏲ *Mar.–June and late Aug.–mid-Dec.; closed tour wks* Ⓤ *U3/Herreng.*

⓰ **Staatsoper** (State Opera House). Considered one of the best opera houses in the world, the Staatsoper is a focus of Viennese social life as well. Almost totally destroyed in the last days of World War II (only the walls and front foyers were saved), it was rebuilt in its present, simpler elegance and reopened in 1955. Tickets for seats can be expensive and scarce, but among the very best bargains in Vienna are the Staatsoper standing-room tickets, available for each performance at delightfully affordable prices—as low as €3.50. Backstage tours are also available. ✉ *Opernring 2* ☎ *01/514–4426–13* 🌐 *www.wiener-staatsoper.at* Ⓤ *U1, U2, or U4/Karlspl.*

★ ㉒ **Stephansdom** (St. Stephen's Cathedral). The towering Gothic spires and gaudy 19th-century tile roof of the city's central landmark dominate the skyline. The oldest parts of the structure are the 13th-century entrance, the soaring Riesentor (Great Entry), and the Heidentürme (Heathens' Towers). Inside, the church is mysteriously shadowy, filled with monuments, tombs, sculptures, paintings, and pulpits. Despite numerous baroque additions—and extensive wartime damage—the cathedral seems authentically medieval. Climb the 343 steps of the south tower—der alte Steffl (Old Stephen) as the Viennese call it—for a stupendous view over the city. If you take a 30-minute tour of the crypt, you can see the copper jars in which the entrails of the Habsburgs are carefully preserved. ✉ *Stephanspl.* ☎ *01/515–5237–67* ⏲ *Daily 6 AM–10 PM. Guided tour in English daily, Apr.–Oct. at 3:45; catacombs tour (minimum 5 people) Mon.–Sat. every half hr 10–11:30 and 1:30–4:30, Sun. every half hr 1:30–4:30; North Tower elevator to Pummerin bell, Apr.–Oct., daily 9–6; July and Aug., daily 9–6:30; Nov.–Mar., daily 8:30–5* Ⓤ *U1 or U3/Stephanspl.*

❷ **Theater Museum.** Housed in the noted 18th-century Palais Lobkowitz—Beethoven was a regular visitor here—this museum covers the history of Austrian theater. A children's museum in the basement is reached, appropriately, by a slide. The facility is short-staffed, so have your hotel or the tourist office check first to see if it's open. Personnel speak only German. ✉ *Lobkowitzpl. 2* ☎ *01/512–8800–610* 🌐 *www.theatermuseum.at* ⏲ *Tues.–Sun. 10–5, Wed. 10–8; Kindermuseum Tues.–Sun. 10–10:30 and 2–2:30* Ⓤ *U3/Herreng.*

Other Corners of Vienna

City planning in the late 1800s and early 1900s was essential to manage the growth of the burgeoning imperial capital. Within a short walk of Stephansdom are other sights that give a sense of the history of old Vienna, with colorful cobblestone squares, statues, and baroque churches. A little farther out, the glories of imperial Austria are nowhere shown off more than in Shönnbrunn Palace, the summer residence of the court, and Belvedere Palace. Both palaces and their extensive gardens are in what was once the countryside, but the land is now incorporated into the city proper.

㉖ **Am Hof.** The name of this remarkable square translates simply as "at court." On the east side of Am Hof is the massive **Kirche am Hof** (also known as the Church of the Nine Choirs of Angels); most of the building's baroque overlay both inside and out dates from the 1600s. In style, the somewhat dreary interior is reminiscent of those of many Dutch churches. In the northeast corner of the square check out what is possibly the most ornate fire station in the world. You'll find an open-air antiques market in the square on Thursday and Friday in summer and frequent seasonal markets at other times. ✉ *Bounded by Tiefer Graben on west, Naglerg. on south, and Seitzerg. on east* Ⓤ *U3/Herreng.*

29 **Hoher Markt.** This ancient cobblestone square with its imposing central monument celebrating the betrothal of Mary and Joseph sits atop **Roman ruins** (✉ Hoher Markt 3 ☎ 01/535–5606), remains of the 2nd-century Roman legion encampment. On the north side of Hoher Markt is the amusing **Anker-Uhr,** a clock that marks the hour with a parade of moving figures. The figures are identified on a plaque at the lower left of the clock. ✉ *Judeng. and Fisch-hof Str.* Ⓤ *U1 or U4/Schwedenpl.*

31 **Hundertwasserhaus** (Hundertwasser House). This structure is an eccentric modern masterpiece envisioned by the late Austrian avant-garde artist Friedensreich Hundertwasser—an astonishing apartment complex marked by turrets, towers, unusual windows, and uneven floors. The nearby **KunstHaus Wien** (Vienna House of Art; ✉ Untere Weissgerberstr. 13 ☎ 01/712–0491 🌐 www.kunsthauswien.com) is an art museum designed by the artist; it offers a floor of his work plus changing exhibits of other modern art. ✉ *Kegelg. and Löweng.* 🌐 *www.hundertwasserhaus.at* ⏲ *Daily 10–7* Ⓤ *U1 or U4/Schwedenpl., then Tram N or O to Radetzkypl.*

28 **Maria am Gestade** (St. Mary's on the Bank). When built around 1400, this was a church for fishermen from the nearby canal, hence the name. Note the arched stone doorway and the ornate carved-stone-latticework "folded hands" spire. ✉ *Salvatorg. and Passauer Pl.* Ⓤ *U1 or U3/Stephanspl.*

30 **Ruprechtskirche** (St. Rupert's Church). Vienna's oldest church, dating from the 11th century, is usually closed but sometimes opens for local art shows and summer evening classical concerts. ✉ *Ruprechtspl.* Ⓤ *U1 or U4/Schwedenpl.*

33 **Schloss Belvedere** (Belvedere Palace). On a rise overlooking the city, this baroque palace is one of the showpieces of Vienna. It was commissioned by Prince Eugene of Savoy and built by Johann Lukas von Hildebrandt in 1721–22. The palace consists of two separate buildings, one at the foot of the hill and the other at the top. The Upper Belvedere houses a gallery of 19th- and 20th-century Viennese art, with works by Klimt (including his world-famous painting *The Kiss*), Schiele, Waldmüller, and Makart; the Lower Belvedere has a baroque museum together with exhibits of Austrian art of the Middle Ages. ✉ *Prinz-Eugen-Str. 27* ☎ *01/79557–100* 🌐 *www.belvedere.at* ⏲ *Tues.–Sun. 10–6* Ⓤ *U1, U2, or U4/Karlspl., then Tram D/Schloss Belvedere.*

35 **Schloss Schönbrunn** (Schönbrunn Palace). The Versailles of Vienna, this magnificent baroque residence with grandly formal gardens was built for the Habsburgs between 1696 and 1713. The complex was also a summer residence for Maria Theresa and Napoléon. Kaiser Franz Josef I was born and died here. His "office" (kept as he left it in 1916) is a touching reminder of his spartan life. In contrast, other rooms are filled with spectacular imperial elegance. The ornate reception areas are still used for state occasions. A guided tour leading through more than 40 of the palace's 1,441 rooms is the best way to see inside the palace (the most dazzling salons start at No. 21). Ask to see the Berglzimmer, ornately decorated ground-floor rooms generally not included in tours. ✉ *Schönbrunner Schloss-Str.* ☎ *01/81113–239* 🌐 *www.schoenbrunn.at* 🎫 *€12.30 with guided tour (40 rooms)* ⏲ *Apr.–June and Sept. and Oct., daily 8:30–5; July and Aug., daily 8:30–7; Nov.–Mar., daily 8:30–4:30* Ⓤ *U4/Schönbrunn.*

Fodor'sChoice ★

On the grounds of the Schönbrunn Palace is the **Tiergarten** (zoo), Europe's oldest menagerie, established in 1752 to amuse and educate the court. It houses an extensive assortment of animals; the original baroque enclosures now serve as viewing pavilions, with the animals housed in effective, modern settings. ☎ *01/877–9294–0* 🌐 *www.zoovienna.at* ⏲ *Nov.–Jan., daily 9–4:30; Feb., daily 9–5; Mar. and Oct., daily 9–5:30; Apr., daily 9–6; May–Sept., daily 9–6:30.*

Pathways lead up through the formal gardens to the **Gloriette,** an 18th-century baroque folly on the rise behind Schloss Schönbrunn built to afford superb views of the city. A café is inside. ⏲ *Apr.–June and Sept., daily 9–6; July and Aug., daily 9–7; Oct., daily 9–5.*

The **Wagenburg** (Imperial Coach Collection), near the entrance to the palace grounds, displays splendid examples of bygone conveyances, from ornate children's sleighs to the grand carriages built to carry the coffins of deceased emperors in state funerals. ☎ *01/877–3244* ⏲ *Nov.–Mar., daily 10–4; Apr.–Oct., daily 9–6.*

Wander the grounds to discover the **Schöner Brunnen** (Beautiful Fountain) for which the Schönbrunn Palace is named; the re-created but convincing massive **Römische Ruinen** (Roman Ruins); and the great glass **Palmenhaus** (Palm House), with its orchids and exotic plants. ✉ *Palm House: nearest entrance Hietzing* ☎ *01/877–5087* 🌐 *www.federal-gardens.at* ⏲ *May–Sept., daily 9:30–6.*

24 **Schottenkirche, Museum im Schottenstift** (Scottish Church and Museum). Despite its name, this church was founded in 1177 by monks who were Irish, not Scots. The present imposing building dates from the mid-1600s. In contrast to the plain exterior, the interior bubbles with cherubs and angels. The Benedictines have set up a small but worthwhile museum of mainly religious art, including a late-Gothic winged altarpiece removed from the church when the interior was given a baroque overlay. The museum entrance is in the courtyard. ✉ *Freyung 6* ☎ *01/534–98–600* 🌐 *www.schottenstift.at* ⏲ *Mon.–Sat. 10–5, Sun. 2–5* Ⓤ *U2/Schottentor.*

27 **Uhrenmuseum** (Clock Museum). Tucked away on several floors of a lovely Renaissance structure is an amazing collection of clocks and watches. Try to be here when the hundreds of clocks strike the noon hour. ✉ *Schulhof 2* ☎ *01/533–2265* ⏲ *Tues.–Sun. 9–4:30* Ⓤ *U3/Herreng.*

Vienna Environs

Wienerwald (Vienna Woods). You can reach a small corner of the historic Vienna Woods by streetcar and bus: take a streetcar or the U2 subway line to Schottentor/University and, from there, Streetcar 38 (Grinzing) to the end of the line. To get into the woods, change in Grinzing to Bus 38A. This will take you to the Kahlenberg, which provides a superb view out over the Danube and the city. You can take the bus or hike to the Leopoldsberg, the promontory over the Danube from which Turkish invading forces were repulsed during the 16th and 17th centuries. Grinzing itself is a village out of a picture book. Unfortunately, it also attracts its fair share of tour buses. For less touristy wine villages, try Sievering (Bus 39A), Neustift am Walde (U4, U6 subway to Spittelau, then Bus 35A), or the suburb of Nussdorf (Streetcar D).

WHERE TO EAT

In the mid-1990s Vienna, once a culinary backwater, produced a new generation of chefs willing to slaughter sacred cows and create a *Neue Küche,* a new Vienna cuisine. This trend relies on lighter versions of the old standbys and combinations of such traditional ingredients as *Kürbiskernöl* (pumpkin-seed oil) and fruit sauces instead of butter and cream.

In a first-class restaurant you will pay as much as in most other Western European capitals. But you can still find good food at refreshingly low prices in the simpler neighborhood Gasthäuser (rustic inns). If you eat your main meal at noon (as the Viennese do), you can take advantage of the luncheon specials available at most restaurants.

WHAT IT COSTS In euros				
	$$$$	$$$	$$	$
PER PERSON	over €22	€16–€22	€10–€15	under €10

Prices are for a main course.

$$$$ Fodor'sChoice ★ ✕ **Steirereck.** Plans are under way for the new Steirereck am Stadtpark to be housed in the former Milk Drinking Hall, which was built in 1901 and stands next to a pretty pond in Vienna's city park. The haute cuisine Steirereck is known for will remain the same, such as delicate smoked catfish, turbot in an avocado crust, or tender lamb with crepes. At the end of the meal, be sure to sample the outstanding selection of cheeses from the cheese cellar. ✉ *Stadtpark* ☎ *01/713–3168* ✍ *Reservations essential* 👔 *Jacket and tie* ▭ *AE, DC, MC, V* ⏲ *Closed weekends* Ⓤ *U3/Stubentor or Tram 1 or 2.*

$$$–$$$$ ✕ **Fabio's.** Though not much on decor, this minimalist, super-trendy, always crowded hot spot just off the Graben offers plenty in the way of people-watching. In summer it's especially agreeable with floor-to-ceiling windows opening onto a charming, narrow street. Start with an appetizer of marinated octopus, calamari, and mussels, then try the buttery risotto with grilled shrimp or lasagna stuffed with tender strips of steak and vegetables. Don't forget to order the luscious crème caramel for dessert. Service is pleasant, though it can be uneven. ✉ *Tuchlauben 6* ☎ *01/532–2222* ▭ *AE, DC, MC, V* ⏲ *Closed Sun.* Ⓤ *U1, U3/Stephanspl.*

★ $$–$$$ ✕ **Artner.** This sleek restaurant with discreet lighting has one of the most innovative menus in the city, and it showcases exceptional wines from its own 350-year-old winery in the Carnuntum region east of Vienna. Delicious appetizers include a salad of field greens and grilled goat cheese (another house specialty), and recommended main courses are crispy pike perch with black-olive risotto or wild boar schnitzel with a potato-and-greens salad. You can choose to sit at the bar and have a glass of wine and the Artner sandwich—crusty grilled bread stuffed with melted goat cheese and grilled steak strips. ✉ *Florag. 6 (entrance on Neumanng.)* ☎ *01/503–5033* ▭ *AE, DC, MC, V* ⏲ *No lunch weekends* Ⓤ *U1/Taubstummeng.*

$$–$$$ ✕ **Barbaro's.** The downstairs bistro with an open kitchen is *the* place to go in the city for superb pizzas and pastas. Settle into comfortable red leather chairs and wait for the wood-fired oven to turn out foccaccia and thin-crust pizzas topped with arugula and shaved Parmesan or ham and buffalo mozzarella. ✉ *Neuer Markt 8* ☎ *01/955–2525* ▭ *AE, DC, MC, V* Ⓤ *U1 or U4/Karlspl.*

$$ ✕ **Palmenhaus.** Twenty-foot-high palm trees and exotic plants decorate this large, contemporary restaurant in the Hofburg Palace conservatory, at the back of the Burggarten and next to the Schmetterlinghaus. Seafood is the focus here, and it's temptingly featured in soups and risottos or simply grilled with lemon. A blackboard lists daily fish specials, and several vegetarian dishes are offered, such as pumpkin gnocchi. In fine weather, tables are set outside on the terrace overlooking the park. Service can be slow. ✉ *Burggarten (or through Goetheg. gate after 8 PM)* ☎ *01/533–1033* ✍ *Reservations essential* ▭ *DC, MC, V* Ⓤ *U2/MuseumsQuartier or Trams 1, 2, and D/Burgring.*

$–$$ ✕ **Brezl Gwölb.** Housed in a medieval pretzel factory between Am Hof and Judenplatz, this snug restaurant fills up fast at night. Try the scrumptious *Tyroler G'röstl,* home-fried potatoes with slivered ham and onions served in a blackened skillet. Best tables are downstairs in the authentic medieval cellar, which looks like a set from *Phantom of the Opera.* ✉ *Ledererhof 9* ☎ *01/533–8811* 💳 *AE, DC, MC, V* Ⓤ *U2/Schottentor.*

$–$$ ✕ **Figlmüller.** Known for its gargantuan Wiener schnitzel—so large it usually overflows the plate—Figlmüller is always packed with diners sharing benches and long tables. Food choices are limited, and everything is à la carte. Try to get a table in the greenhouse passageway area. ✉ *Wollzeile 5 (passageway from Stephansdom)* ☎ *01/512–6177* 💳 *No credit cards* ⏲ *Closed Aug.* Ⓤ *U1/Stephanspl.*

$–$$ ✕ **Frank's.** A cavernous cellar-like restaurant with aged brick walls, arches, and candlelight is not exactly what you'd expect to find inside the ultramodern central post office building. People come to Frank's for fun, and to choose from the vast selection of pizzas, burgers (both chicken and beef), salads, and pastas. There are also plenty of vegetarian and fresh-fish items. From October to April, Frank's offers a popular Sunday brunch with, among other American-style staples, bagels and Bloody Marys. ✉ *Laurenzerberg 2 (entrance Postpassage Schwedenpl.)* ☎ *01/533–7805* ✍ *Reservations essential* 💳 *D, MC, V* ⏲ *No lunch Sat., no dinner Sun.* Ⓤ *U1, U4/Schwedenpl.*

$–$$ ✕ **Hansen.** Housed downstairs in the Börse (Vienna Stock Exchange), this unique restaurant is also an exotic, upscale flower market. The decor is elegant, with close-set tables covered in white linen. The menu highlights Mediterranean-inspired dishes such as scampi risotto or spaghettini with oven-dried tomatoes in a black-olive cream sauce. There are also Austrian dishes done with a fresh, light slant. Lunch is the main event here, though you can also come for breakfast or a pretheater dinner. ✉ *Wipplingerstr. 34* ☎ *01/532–0542* ✍ *Reservations essential* 💳 *AE, DC, MC, V* ⏲ *Closed Sun. and after 8 PM* Ⓤ *Tram 2 or D/Börse.*

$–$$ ✕ **Lebenbauer.** Vienna's premier vegetarian restaurant has a no-smoking room, rare in this part of Europe. Specialties include soy and fennel in a curry sauce with ginger, pineapple, and wild rice, and spinach tortellini in a Gorgonzola sauce. ✉ *Teinfaltstr. 3, near Freyung* ☎ *01/533–5556–0* 💳 *AE, DC, MC, V* ⏲ *Closed weekends and first 2 wks in Aug.* Ⓤ *U2/Schottentor.*

$ ✕ **Beim Czaak.** Pronounced "bime chalk," this simple spot with friendly service is a favorite with locals. It's long and narrow, with forest-green walls, framed caricatures of a few well-known Viennese on the walls, and limited seating outdoors. Choose a glass of Austrian wine to go along with Waldviertler pork stuffed with bacon, onions, and mushrooms, or spinach dumplings drizzled with Parmesan and browned butter. ✉ *Postg. 15, corner of Fleischmarkt* ☎ *01/513–7215* 💳 *No credit cards* ⏲ *Closed Sun.* Ⓤ *U1 or U4/Schwedenpl.*

$ ✕ **Salzgries.** A typical old Viennese *Beisl,* which is a cross between a café and a pub, the Salzgries has an unpretentious, rather worn look. It's known for having good schnitzels, and you can get pork, milk-fed veal, or chicken breast, all fried to a golden crispness, with potato salad on the side. The *Vanillerostbraten* (garlicky rump steak) is also worth trying, and the *Moor im Hemd,* warm chocolate cake with whipped cream, is scrumptious. ✉ *Marc-Aurel-Str. 6* ☎ *01/968–9645* 💳 *No credit cards* Ⓤ *U1 or U4/Schwedenpl.*

Cafés

A quintessential Viennese institution, the coffeehouse, or café, is club, pub, and bistro all rolled into one. To savor the atmosphere of the coffeehouses you must take your time: set aside an afternoon, a morning, or at least a couple of hours, and settle down in one of your choice. There is no need to worry about overstaying your welcome, even over a single small cup of Mokka—although in some of the more opulent coffeehouses this cup of coffee and a pastry can cost as much as a meal.

Alte Backstube (✉ Langeg. 34 ☎ 01/406–1101), in a gorgeous baroque house—with a café in front and restaurant in back—was once a bakery and is now a museum as well. **Café Central** (✉ Herreng. 14, in Palais Ferstel ☎ 01/533–3763–26) is where Trotsky played chess; in the Palais Ferstel, it's one of Vienna's most beautiful cafés. **Cafe Landtmann** (✉ Dr. Karl Leuger Str. 4 ☎ 01/532–0621), next to the dignified Burgtheater, with front-row views of the Ringstrasse, was reputedly Freud's favorite café. A 200-year-old institution, **Demel** (✉ Kohlmarkt 14 ☎ 01/535–1717–0) is the grande dame of Viennese cafés. The elegant front rooms have more atmosphere than the airy modern atrium, while the first room is reserved for nonsmokers. Order the famous coffee and compare the Sacher torte with the one served up at the Sacher—for more than 100 years there has been an ongoing feud over who owns the original recipe. **Gerstner** (✉ Kärtnerstr. 11–15 ☎ 01/512–496377) is in the heart of the bustling Kärntnerstrasse and is one of the more modern Viennese cafés, though it has been going strong since the mid-18th century. **Museum** (✉ Friedrichstr. 6 ☎ 01/586–5202), with its original interior by the architect Adolf Loos, draws a mixed crowd and has an ample supply of newspapers. The **Sacher** (✉ Philharmonikerstr. 4 ☎ 01/514560) is hardly a typical Vienna café; more a shrine to plush gilt and marzipan, it's both a must-see and a must-eat, despite the crowds of tourists here to order the world's ultimate chocolate cake.

WHERE TO STAY

Vienna's first district (A-1010) is the best base for visitors because it's so close to most of the major sights, restaurants, and shops. This accessibility translates, of course, into higher prices. Try bargaining for discounts at the larger international chain hotels during the off-season.

WHAT IT COSTS In euros

	$$$$	$$$	$$	$
FOR 2 PEOPLE	over €250	€175–€250	€100–€175	under €100

Prices are for a standard double room in high season, including local taxes (usually 10%), service (15%), and breakfast (except in the most expensive hotels).

$$$$ **Bristol.** This venerable landmark, dating from 1892, has one of the finest locations in the city, on the Ring next to the Opera House. The accent here is on tradition, and guest rooms are sumptuously furnished in Biedermeier style with decorative fireplaces, thick carpets, wing chairs, crystal chandeliers, and lace curtains. Penthouse rooms have terraces with staggering views of the Opera. The Bristol also houses the acclaimed Korso restaurant, the convivial Café Sirk, and a music salon complete with a pianist lulling the after-theater crowd with tunes on a time-burnished Boesendorfer. ✉ *Kärntner Ring 1 A-1010* ☎ *01/515–16–0* 🖷 *01/515–16–550* 🌐 *www.westin.com* *141 rooms* *2 restaurants* 💳 *AE, DC, MC, V.*

$$$$ Fodor's Choice ★ **Imperial.** The hotel is as much a palace today as when it was formally opened in 1873 by Emperor Franz Josef. The emphasis is on Old Vienna elegance and privacy; the guest list is littered with famous names, from heads of state to Michael Jackson. The beautiful rooms are furnished in antique style, though only the first three floors are part of the original house and have high ceilings; subsequent floors were added in the late 1930s. Suites include your own personal butler. ✉ *Kärntner Ring 16, A-1010* ☎ *01/501–10–0* 📠 *01/501–10–410* 🌐 *www.luxurycollection.com* ⇆ *138 rooms* ⓘ *Restaurant* 💳 *AE, DC, MC, V.*

$$$$ **Palais Schwarzenberg.** Set against a vast formal park, the palace, built in the early 1700s, seems like a country estate though it's just a few minutes' walk from the heart of the city. The public salons are grand and glorious, while each guest room is individual and luxuriously appointed, with original artwork adorning the walls. A renovated wing has ultramodern suites by Italian designer Paolo Piva. You don't have to be a guest here to come for a drink, coffee, or light lunch, served outside on the terrace in summer or beside a roaring fireplace in the main sitting room in winter. ✉ *Schwarzenbergpl. 9 A-1030* ☎ *01/798–4515–0* 📠 *01/798–4714* 🌐 *www.palais-schwarzenberg.com* ⇆ *44 rooms* ⓘ *Restaurant, pool, bar* 💳 *AE, DC, MC, V.*

★ $$$$ **Sacher.** The grand old Sacher dates from 1876, and it has retained its sense of history over the years while providing luxurious, modern-day comfort. The corridors are a veritable art gallery, and the exquisitely furnished bedrooms also contain original artwork. The location directly behind the Opera House could hardly be more central, and the ratio of staff to guests is more than two to one. Meals in the Red Room or Anna Sacher Room are first-rate; the Café Sacher, of course, is legendary. ✉ *Philharmonikerstr. 4, A-1010* ☎ *01/514–56–0* 📠 *01/514–57–810* 🌐 *www.sacher.com* ⇆ *113 rooms* ⓘ *Restaurant, bar* 💳 *AE, DC, MC, V.*

$$$ **König von Ungarn.** In a dormered, 16th-century house in the shadow of St. Stephen's Cathedral, this hotel began catering to court nobility in 1815. The hotel radiates charm—rooms (some with Styrian wood-paneled walls) are furnished with country antiques and have walk-in closets and double sinks in the sparkling bathrooms. The eight suites are two-storied, and two have balconies with rooftop views. The inviting atrium bar, bedecked with marble columns, ferns, and hunting trophies, beckons you in to sit and have a drink. Insist on written confirmation of bookings. ✉ *Schulerstr. 10, A-1010* ☎ *01/515–84–0* 📠 *01/515–848* 🌐 *www.kvu.at* ⇆ *33 rooms* ⓘ *Restaurant* 💳 *DC, MC, V.*

$$–$$$ **Regina.** This dignified old hotel with grand reception rooms sits regally on the edge of the Altstadt, commanding a view of Sigmund Freud Park. It's near the Votivkirche, and about a 10-minute walk from the center. The high-ceiling rooms are quiet, spacious, and attractively decorated with contemporary furniture, and most have charming sitting areas. Freud, who lived nearby, used to eat breakfast in the hotel's café every morning. Buffet breakfast is included. ✉ *Rooseveltpl. 15, A-1090* ☎ *01/404–460* 📠 *01/408–8392* 🌐 *www.hotelregina.at* ⇆ *125 rooms* ⓘ *Restaurant* 💳 *AE, DC, MC, V.*

★ $$ **Altstadt.** A cognoscenti favorite, this small hotel set in one of Vienna's most pampered neighborhoods was once a patrician home. Close to the shops of Spittelberg and one streetcar stop from the main museums, this place is known for its personable and helpful management. Palm trees, a Secession-style wrought-iron staircase, modernist fabrics, and halogen lighting make for a design-style interior. Rooms are large with all the modern comforts, and upper floors have views of the city roofline. The English-style lounge has a fireplace and plump floral sofas. ✉ *Kircheng. 41, A-1070* ☎ *01/526–3399–0* 📠 *01/523–4901* 🌐 *www.altstadt.at* ⇆ *25 rooms* 💳 *AE, DC, MC, V.*

$$ **Austria.** Tucked away on a tiny cul-de-sac, this older house offers the ultimate in quiet only five minutes' walk from the heart of the city. The high-ceiling rooms are pleasing in their combination of dark wood and lighter walls, and Oriental carpets cover many floors. The courtyard ter-

race is a perfect place to sip coffee. ✉ *Wolfeng. 3/Fleischmarkt 20, A-1010* ☎ *01/515–23–0* 🖷 *01/515–23–506* 🌐 *www.hotelaustria-wien.at* ⇆ *46 rooms* ▭ *AE, DC, MC, V.*

$$ **Museum.** In a beautiful belle epoque mansion just a five-minute walk from the Art History and Natural History museums, this elegant pension offers large, comfortable rooms with TV. There is also a sunny sitting room with deep, stuffed sofas and wing chairs, perfect for curling up in with a good book. This is a popular place, so book ahead. ✉ *Museumstr. 3 A-1070* ☎ *01/523–44–260* 🖷 *01/523–44–2630* ⇆ *15 rooms* ▭ *AE, DC, MC, V.*

$$ **Zur Wiener Staatsoper.** A great deal of loving care has gone into this family-owned hotel near the State Opera, reputed to be one of the Viennese settings in John Irving's *Hotel New Hampshire*. Rooms are small but have high ceilings and are charmingly decorated with pretty fabrics. ✉ *Krugerstr. 11, A-1010* ☎ *01/513–1274* 🖷 *01/513–1274–15* 🌐 *www.zurwienerstaatsoper.at* ⇆ *22 rooms* ▭ *AE, MC, V.*

$ **Pension Riedl.** Across the square from the Postsparkasse—the famous 19th-century postal savings bank designed by Otto Wagner—this small establishment offers pleasant rooms with cable TV. Breakfast is delivered to your room. Friendly owner Maria Felser is happy to arrange concert tickets and tours. ✉ *Georg-Coch-Pl. 3/4/10 (near Julius-Raab Pl.), A-1010* ☎ *01/512–7919* 🖷 *01/512–7919–8* ⇆ *8 rooms* ▭ *DC, MC, V* ⊗ *Closed last wk in Jan. and first 2 wks in Feb.*

$ **Reimer.** The cheery, comfortable Reimer is in a prime location just off the Mariahilferstrasse. Rooms have high ceilings and large windows. Breakfast is included. ✉ *Kircheng. 18, A-1070* ☎ *01/523–6162* 🖷 *01/524–3782* ⇆ *14 rooms* ▭ *MC, V.*

NIGHTLIFE & THE ARTS

The Arts

Music

Classical concerts are held in the **Konzerthaus** (✉ Lothringerstr. 20 ☎ 01/242002 🌐 www.konzerthaus.at), featuring the Vienna Symphonic Orchestra, which also occasionally plays modern and jazz pieces. The **Musikverein** (✉ Bösendorferstr. 12 ☎ 01/505–8190–0 🌐 www.musikverein.at) is the home of the acclaimed Vienna Philharmonic Orchestra. Tickets can be bought at their box offices or ordered by phone. Tickets to various musical events are sold through the **Vienna Ticket Service** (☎ 01/534–130).

Theater & Opera

Check the monthly program published by the city; posters also show opera and theater schedules. The **Staatsoper,** one of the world's great opera houses, presents major stars in its almost-nightly original-language performances. The **Volksoper** offers operas, operettas, and musicals, also in original-language performances. Performances at the **Akadamietheater** and **Burgtheater** are in German. Tickets for the Staatsoper, the Volksoper, and the Burg and Akademie theaters are available at the **central ticket office** (✉ Bundestheaterkassen, Hanuschg. 3 ☎ 01/514–440 or 01/513–1513 🖷 Staatsoper and Volkstheater 01/51444–3669; Akadamietheater and Burgtheater 01/514444–4147), or you can go in person to the office at the left rear of the Opera, open weekdays 8–6, Saturday 9–2, Sunday and holidays 9–noon. Tickets go on sale a month before performances. Unsold tickets can be obtained at the evening box office. Tickets can be ordered three weeks or more in advance in writing, by fax, or a month in advance by phone. Standing-room tickets for the Staatsoper are a great bargain.

Theater is offered in English at **Vienna's English Theater** (✉ Josefsg. 12 ☎ 01/402–1260–0). The **International Theater** (✉ Porzellang. 8 ☎ 01/319–6272) is also a popular choice for seeing plays in English.

Nightlife

The central district for nightlife in Vienna is nicknamed the **Bermuda-Dreieck** (Bermuda Triangle). Centered on Judengasse/Seitenstettengasse, next to St. Ruprecht's, a small Romanesque church, the area is jammed with everything from good bistros to jazz clubs.

Cabarets

Cabaret has a long tradition in Vienna. To get much from any of it, you'll need good German with a smattering of Viennese vernacular as well, plus some knowledge of local affairs. A popular cabaret-nightclub is **Moulin Rouge** (✉ Walfischg. 11 ☎ 01/512–2130), where there are floor shows and some striptease. **Simpl** (✉ Wollzeile 36 ☎ 01/512–4742) continues earning its reputation for barbed political wit.

Discos

Atrium (✉ Schwarzenbergpl. 10, A-1040 ☎ 01/505–3594) offers everything from hip-hop and rap to pop-rock. **Eden Bar** (✉ Lilieng. 2 ☎ 01/512–7450) is the leading spot for the well-heeled, mature crowd with a live band playing most nights. **Havana** (✉ Mahlerstr. 11 ☎ 01/513–2075) is great for salsa and dancing and draws the young adult crowd. The **U-4** (✉ Schönbrunnerstr. 222 ☎ 01/815–8307) has a different theme every night, including gay night on Thursday.

Nightclubs

A former 1950s cinema just off the Kärtnerstrasse, **Kruger** (✉ Krugerstr. 5 ☎ 01/512–2455) now draws crowds with its deep leather sofas and English gentleman's club atmosphere. Near the Vienna Stock Exchange is the **Planter's Club** (✉ Zelinkag. 4 ☎ 01/533–3393–16), offering a nice selection of rums in a tropical colonial atmosphere. An outdoor glass elevator whisks you up to the **Skybar** (✉ Kärtnerstr. 19 ☎ 01/513–1712) at the top of the Steffl department store, where dramatic views and piano music set the mood.

Wine Taverns

Some of the city's atmospheric *Heurige,* or wine taverns, date from the 12th century. Open at lunchtime as well as evenings, the **Augustinerkeller** (✉ Augustinerstr. 1 ☎ 01/533–1026), in the Albertina Building, is a cheery wine tavern with live, schmaltzy music after 6 PM. The **Esterházykeller** (✉ Haarhof 1 ☎ 01/533–3482), in a particularly mazelike network of rooms, has good wines. The **Zwölf Apostelkeller** (✉ Sonnenfelsg. 3 ☎ 01/512–6777), near St. Stephen's, has rooms that are down, down, down underground.

SHOPPING

Boutiques

Famous names line the **Kohlmarkt** and **Graben** and their respective side streets, as well as the side streets off **Kärntnerstrasse.**

Folk Costumes

The main resource for exquisite Austrian *Trachten* (native dress) is **Loden-Plankl** (✉ Michaelerpl. 6 ☎ 01/533–8032).

Food & Flea Markets

The **Naschmarkt** (foodstuffs market; ✉ between Rechte and Linke Wienzeile) is a sensational open-air market offering specialties from around the world. The fascinating **Flohmarkt** (flea market; Ⓤ U-4 to Kettenbrückeng.), open Saturday 8–4, operates year-round beyond the Naschmarkt. An **Arts and Antiques Market** (✣ beside Danube Canal near Salztorbrücke) has a mixed selection, including some high-quality offerings. It's open May–September, weekends 10–6. Check Am Hof Square for antiques and collectibles on Thursday and Friday from late spring to early fall. Also try the seasonal markets in Freyung Square.

16

Shopping Districts

Kärntnerstrasse is lined with luxury boutiques and large emporiums. The Viennese do much of their in-town shopping in the many department and specialty stores of **Mariahilferstrasse.**

VIENNA A TO Z

AIRPORTS & TRANSFERS

All flights use Schwechat Airport, about 16 km (10 mi) southwest of Vienna.

Schwechat Airport ☎ 01/7007-0.

TRANSFERS A new super-fast double-decker train runs from Vienna's Schwechat Airport to Wien-Mitte in the center of the city. The ride takes only 15 minutes and operates every 30 minutes between 5:30 AM and midnight. The price of a one-way ticket is €9. Otherwise, the cheapest way into town is the S7 train (called the *Schnellbahn*), which shuttles every half hour between the airport and the Landstrasse/Wien-Mitte (city center) and Wien-Nord (north Vienna) stations; the fare is about €3, and the trip takes 35 minutes. Follow the picture signs of a train to the basement of the airport. Your ticket is also good for an immediate transfer to your destination within the city on the streetcar, bus, or U-Bahn.

Buses from the airport go to the City Air Terminal at the Hilton every 20 minutes between 6:30 AM and 11 PM, and every 30 minutes after that; traveling time is 20 minutes. Another line goes to the South and West train stations (Südbahnhof and Westbahnhof) in 20 and 35 minutes, respectively. Departure times are every 30 minutes from 8:10 AM to 7:10 PM, hourly thereafter, and not at all 12:10–3:30 AM. Fare is €5.80 one-way, €10.90 for a round-trip. A taxi from the airport to downtown Vienna costs about €30–€40; agree on a price in advance. The cheapest cab service to the airport is C+K Airport Service, charging a set price of €23 (don't forget to tip, usually a couple of euros). C+K will also meet your plane at no extra charge if you let them know your flight information in advance.

C+K Airport Service ☎ 01/44444. **City Air Terminal** ✉ Am Stadtpark ☎ 05/1717.

BIKE TRAVEL

Vienna has hundreds of miles of marked bike routes, including reserved routes through the center of the city. Paved routes parallel the Danube. For details, get the city brochure on biking. Bicycles can be rented at a number of locations and can be taken on the Vienna subway year-round all day Sunday and holidays from 9 to 3, after 6:30 on weekdays, and, from May through September, after 9 AM Saturday. You'll need a half-fare ticket for the bike.

BUS TRAVEL WITHIN VIENNA

Inner-city buses are numbered 1A through 3A and operate weekdays until about 8 PM, Saturday until 7 PM. Reduced fares are available for these routes (buy a *Kurzstreckenkarte*; it allows you four trips for €3) as well as designated shorter stretches (roughly two to four stops) on all other bus and streetcar lines. Streetcars and buses are numbered or lettered according to route, and they run until midnight. Night buses marked "N" follow 22 special routes every half hour between 12:30 AM and 4:30 AM. Get a route plan from the public transport or VORVERKAUF offices. The fare is the same as for a regular daytime ticket, €1.50. The central terminus is Schwedenplatz. Streetcars 1 and 2 run the circular route around the Ring clockwise and counterclockwise, respectively.

CAR TRAVEL

The main access routes are the expressways to the west and south (Westautobahn A1, Südautobahn A2). Routes leading to the downtown area are marked ZENTRUM.

Unless you know your way around the city, a car is more of a nuisance than a help. The center of the city is a pedestrian zone, and city on-street parking is a problem. Observe signs; tow-away is expensive. In winter, overnight parking is forbidden on city streets with streetcar lines. Overnight street parking in Districts I, VI, VII, VIII, and IX is restricted to residents with stickers; check before you leave a car on the street, even for a brief period. You can park in the inner city for free on weekends and holidays and at night from 7 PM until midnight, but check street signs first.

CONSULATES

United Kingdom ✉ Jauresg. 10, near Schloss Belvedere ☎ 01/71613-5151.
United States ✉ Gartenbaupromenade, Parkring 12A, in Marriott building ☎ 01/313-39.

EMERGENCIES

If you need a doctor, ask your hotel, or in an emergency, phone your embassy or consulate. In each neighborhood, one pharmacy (*Apotheke*) in rotation is open all night and weekends; the address is posted on each area pharmacy.

Emergency Services **Ambulance** ☎ 144. **Police** ☎ 133.

ENGLISH-LANGUAGE MEDIA

Bookstores **British Bookshop** ✉ Weihburgg. 24–26 ☎ 01/512–1945–0 ✉ Mariahilferstr. 4 ☎ 01/522–6730. **Shakespeare & Co.** ✉ Sterng. 2 ☎ 01/535–5053.

SUBWAY TRAVEL

Subway (U-bahn) lines—stations are marked with a huge blue "U"—are designated U-1, U-2, U-3, U-4, and U-6, and are clearly marked and color-coded. Trains run daily until about 12:30 AM. Additional services are provided by fast suburban trains, the S-bahn, indicated by a stylized blue "S" symbol. Both are tied into the general city fare system.

TAXIS

Cabs can be flagged on the street if the FREI (free) sign is lit. You can also dial ☎ 60160, 31300, or 40100 to request one. All rides around town are metered. The initial fare is €2, but expect to pay €5–€9 for an average city ride. There are additional charges for luggage, and a surcharge of €1 is added at night, on Sunday, and for telephone orders. Tip the driver by rounding up the fare.

TOURS

BUS TOURS Tours will take you to cultural events and nightclubs, and there are daytime bus trips to the Danube Valley, Salzburg, and Budapest, among other spots. Check with the City Tourist Office or your hotel.

The following are city orientation tours. Prices are similar, but find out whether you will visit or just drive past Schönbrunn and Belvedere palaces and whether admission fees are included. Cityrama provides city tours with hotel pickup. Vienna Sightseeing Tours offers a short highlights tour or a lengthier one to the Vienna Woods, Mayerling, and other sights near Vienna. Tours start in front of or beside the Staatsoper on the Operngasse.

Cityrama ☎ 01/534-130. **Vienna Sightseeing Tours** ☎ 01/712-4683-0.

WALKING TOURS Guided walking tours in English are available almost daily and include such topics as "Jewish Vienna." Check with the City Tourist Office or your hotel.

TRAIN TRAVEL

Vienna has four train stations. The Westbahnhof is for trains to and from Linz, Salzburg, and Innsbruck and to and from Germany, France, and Switzerland. The Südbahnhof is for trains to and from Graz, Klagenfurt, Villach, and Italy. The Franz-Josefs-Bahnhof, or Nordbahnhof, is for trains to and from Prague, Berlin, and Warsaw. Go to the Wien-Mitte/Landstrasse Hauptstrasse station for local trains to and from the north of the city. Budapest trains use both the Westbahnhof and Südbahnhof, and Bratislava trains both Wien-Mitte and the Südbahnhof, so check.

TRANSPORTATION AROUND VIENNA

Vienna is fairly easy to explore on foot; much of the heart of the city—the area within the Ringstrasse—is a pedestrian zone. Public transportation is comfortable, convenient, and frequent, though not cheap. Tickets for buses, subways, and streetcars are available in subway stations and from dispensers on buses and streetcars. Tickets in multiples of five are sold at cigarette shops—look for the sign TABAK-TRAFIK—or at the window marked VORVERKAUF at such central stations as Karlsplatz or Stephansplatz. A block of five tickets costs €7.50, a single ticket €1.50, a 24-hour ticket €5, a three-day tourist ticket €12, and an eight-day ticket €24. Maps and information in English are available at the Stephansplatz, Karlsplatz, and Praterstern U-Bahn stations.

The Vienna Card, available for €15.25 at tourist offices and most hotels, combines 72 hours' use of public transportation with discounts at certain museums and shops throughout the city.

TRAVEL AGENCIES

American Express ✉ Kärntnerstr. 21–23 ☎ 01/515–40–0. **Ökista** ✉ Garnisong. 7, A-1090 ☎ 01/401–480. **Österreichisches Verkehrsbüro** (Austrian Travel Agency) ✉ Friedrichstr. 7, A-1010 ☎ 01/588–000 📠 01/58800–280.

VISITOR INFORMATION

City Tourist Office ✉ Am Albertinapl. 1, A-1010 ☎ 01/24555 📠 01/216–84–92 🌐 www.info.wien.at.

Austria Basics

To research prices, get advice from other travelers, and book travel arrangements, visit www.fodors.com.

BUSINESS HOURS

BANKS & OFFICES Banks are open weekdays 8–noon or 12:30 and 1:30–3; until 5 on Thursday; closed Saturday. Hours vary from one city to another. Principal offices in cities stay open during lunch.

MUSEUMS & SIGHTS Museum opening days and times vary considerably from one city to another and depend on the season and other factors. Monday is often a closing day. Your hotel or the local tourist office will have current details.

SHOPS Shops are open weekdays from 8 or 9 until 6, in shopping centers until 7:30, and Saturday until 5, although some may still close at noon or 1. Many smaller shops close for one or two hours at midday. Larger food markets are open weekdays from 7:30 to 7:30, Saturday to 5.

CUSTOMS & DUTIES

Austria's duty-free allowances are as follows: 200 cigarettes or 50 cigars or 250 grams of tobacco; 2 liters of wine and 1 liter of spirits; 1 bottle of toilet water (about 250-milliliter size); and 50 milliliters of perfume for those age 17 and over arriving from non–European Union countries. Tourists also do not have to pay duty on personal articles brought into Austria temporarily for their own use.

EMBASSIES

For consulates, *see* Vienna Essentials.

Canada ✉ Laurenzerberg 2, 3rd floor of Hauptpost building complex, Vienna ☎ 01/53138-3000.

United Kingdom ✉ Jauresg. 12, near Schloss Belvedere, Vienna ☎ 01/71613-5151.

United States ✉ Boltzmanng. 16, Vienna ☎ 01/313-39.

HOLIDAYS

All banks and shops are closed on national holidays: New Year's Day; Epiphany (January 6); Easter Sunday and Monday; May Day (May 1); Ascension Day (mid-May); Pentecost Sunday and Monday (late May); Corpus Christi; Assumption (August 15); National Day (October 26); All Saints' Day (November 1); Immaculate Conception (December 8); December 25–26. On the December 8 holiday, banks and offices are closed but most shops are open.

LANGUAGE

German is the official national language. In larger cities and most resort areas you will have no problem finding English speakers; hotel and restaurant employees, in particular, speak English reasonably well. Most younger Austrians speak at least passable English.

MONEY MATTERS

Austria has become expensive, but as inflation is relatively low, the currency has remained fairly stable. Vienna and Salzburg are the most expensive cities, along with fashionable resorts at Kitzbühel, Seefeld, Badgastein, Velden, Zell am See, Pörtschach, St. Anton, Zürs, and Lech. Many smaller towns near these resorts offer virtually identical facilities at half the price. Drinks in bars and clubs cost considerably more than in cafés or restaurants. Austrian prices include service and tax.

Sample prices include a cup of coffee in a café or restaurant, €3–€4; half a liter of draft beer, €3–€4; small glass of wine, €4–€8; Coca-Cola, €3; open-face sandwich, €3.50; midrange theater ticket, €20; concert ticket, €30–€50; opera ticket, €40 and up; 2-km (1.6-mi) taxi ride, €6.

CREDIT CARDS Credit cards are not as widely used in Austria as they are in other European countries, and not all establishments that accept plastic take all cards. Some may require a minimum purchase if payment is to be made by card. Many restaurants take cash only. American Express has money machines in Vienna at its main office and at the airport. Many of the Bankomat money dispensers will also accept Visa cards if you have an encoded, international personal identification number.

American Express (main office) ✉ Kärntnerstr. 21–23.

CURRENCY As it is a member of the European Union (EU), Austria's unit of currency is the euro.

Exchange traveler's checks at banks, post offices, or American Express offices to get the best rate. All charge a small commission; some smaller banks or "change" offices may give a poorer rate *and* charge a higher fee. All change offices at airports and at main train stations in major cities cash traveler's checks. In Vienna, bank-operated change offices with extended hours are found on Stephansplatz and at the main rail stations. Bank Austria machines on Stephansplatz, at Kärntnerstrasse 51 (to the right of the Opera), and at the Raiffeisenbank on Kohlmarkt (at Michaelerplatz) change bills from other currencies into euros, but rates are poor and the commission hefty.

VALUE-ADDED TAX (VAT) A value-added tax (VAT) of 20% is charged on all sales and is automatically included in prices. If you purchase goods worth €75 or more and are not a citizen of an EU country, you can claim a refund of the tax either as you leave or after you've returned home. Ask the store clerk to fill out the necessary papers. Get them stamped at the airport or border crossing by customs officials (who may ask to see the goods). You can get an immediate refund of the VAT, less a service charge, at international airports or at main border crossings, or you can return the papers by mail to the shop(s). The VAT refund can be credited to your credit card account or remitted by check.

TELEPHONES

COUNTRY & AREA CODES The country code for Austria is 43. When dialing an Austrian number from abroad, drop the initial 0 from the local area code.

INTERNATIONAL CALLS It costs considerably more to telephone *from* Austria than it does *to* Austria. Calls from post offices are least expensive. To avoid hotel charges, call overseas and ask to be called back; use an international credit card, available from AT&T and MCI. Use the AT&T access code to reach an operator. Another option for long-distance access is MCI WorldPhone. To make a collect call—you can't do this from pay phones—dial the operator and ask for an *R*-Gespräch (pronounced "air-ga-*shprayk*"). For international information dial 118200 for numbers in Germany, 118202 for numbers in other European countries, and 118202 for overseas numbers. Most operators speak English; if yours doesn't, you'll be passed along to one who does.

Access Codes **AT&T** ☎ 0800-200-288. **MCI WorldPhone** ☎ 0800-200-235.

LOCAL CALLS Pay telephones take €1, €0.50, €0.20, and €0.10 coins. Emergency calls are free. Instructions are in English in most booths. The initial connection for a local call costs €0.20. Insert €0.10 or more to continue the connection when you hear the tone warning that your time is up. Phone cards, available at post offices, work in all phones marked WERTKARTENTELEFON. The cost of the call will be deducted from the card automatically. Phone numbers throughout Austria are currently being changed. A sharp tone indicates either no connection or that the number has been changed. Dial 118200 for numbers in Austria.

ZÜRICH

Stroll around on a fine spring day and you'll ask yourself if this city, with its glistening lake, swans on the river, sidewalk cafés, and hushed old squares of medieval guild houses, can really be one of the great business centers of the world. There's not a gnome—a mocking nickname for a Swiss banker—in sight. For all its economic importance, this is a place where people enjoy life.

Zürich started in 15 BC as a Roman customs post on the Lindenhof overlooking the Limmat River, but its growth really began around the 10th century AD. It became a free imperial city in 1336, a center of the Reformation in 1519, and gradually assumed commercial importance during the 1800s. Today the Zürich stock exchange is the fourth largest in the world, and the city's extraordinary museums and galleries and luxurious shops along the Bahnhofstrasse, Zürich's 5th Avenue, attest to its position as Switzerland's cultural—if not political—capital.

EXPLORING ZÜRICH

Although Zürich is Switzerland's largest city, it has a population of only 360,000 and is small enough to be explored on foot. The Limmat River, crisscrossed with lovely low bridges, bisects the city. On the left bank are the Altstadt (Old Town), the polished section of the old medieval center; the Hauptbahnhof, the main train station; and the Bahnhofplatz, a major urban crossroads and the beginning of the world-famous luxury shopping street, Bahnhofstrasse. The right bank, divided into the Oberdorf (Upper Village), toward Bellevueplatz, and the Niederdorf (Lower Village), around the Central, is young and lively and buzzes on weekends. The latest addition to the city's profile is Zürich West, an industrial neighborhood that's quickly being reinvented. Amid the cluster of cranes, former factories are being turned into spaces for restaurants, bars, art galleries, and dance clubs. Construction and restoration will most likely be ongoing well into 2006.

Numbers in the margin correspond to points of interest on the Zürich map.

9 **Altstadt.** Zürich's medieval core is a maze of well-preserved streets and buildings easily explored on foot in a few hours. The area stretches from Bahnhofplatz to Bürkliplatz on the left bank. On the right bank of the city's historic center is a livelier section known as the **Niederdorf,** which reaches from Central to Bellevueplatz.

2 **Bahnhofstrasse.** Zürich's principal boulevard offers concentrated luxury shopping, while much shifting and hoarding of the world's wealth takes place discreetly behind the upstairs windows of the banking institutions. ✉ *Runs north–south, west of Limmat.*

★ 5 **Fraumünster.** Of the church spires that are Zürich's signature, the Fraumünster's is the most delicate, a graceful sweep to a narrow spire. The Romanesque, or pre-Gothic, choir has stained-glass windows by Chagall. ✉ *Stadthausquai* ⏲ *May–Sept., Mon.–Sat. 9–6; Mar.–Apr. and Oct., Mon.–Sat. 10–5; Nov.–Feb., Mon.–Sat. 10–4.*

12 **Graphische Sammlung** (Graphic Collection). This impressive collection of the Federal Institute of Technology displays portions of its vast holdings of woodcuts, etchings, and engravings by European masters such as Dürer, Rembrandt, Goya, and Picasso. ✉ *Rämistr. 101* ☎ *01/6324046* ⏲ *Mon.–Tues. and Thurs.–Fri. 10–5, Wed. 10–7.*

★ 10 **Grossmünster** (Great Church). In the 3rd century AD, St. Felix and his sister Regula were martyred nearby by the Romans. Legend maintains that having been beheaded, they then walked up the hill carrying their heads and collapsed on the spot where the Grossmünster now stands. On the south tower of this 11th-century structure you can see a statue of Charlemagne (768–814), who is said to have founded the church when his horse stumbled on the same site. In the 16th century, the Zürich reformer Huldrych Zwingli preached sermons here that were so threatening in their promise of fire and brimstone that Martin Luther himself was frightened. ✉ *Zwinglipl.* ☎ *01/2513860* ⏲ *Mid-Mar.–Oct., daily 9–6; Nov.–mid-Mar., daily 10–5.*

★ 11 **Kunsthaus.** With a varied, high-quality permanent collection of paintings—medieval, Dutch and Italian baroque, and impressionist—the Kunsthaus is Zürich's best art museum. There's a rich collection of works by Swiss artists, though some could be an acquired taste. Besides those of Ferdinand Hodler (1853–1918), there are darkly ethereal paintings by Johann Heinrich Füssli and a terrifying *Walpurgisnacht* by Albert Welti. Other European artists, including Picasso, Klee, Degas, Matisse, Kandinsky, Chagall, and Munch, are satisfyingly represented. ✉ *Heimpl. 1* ☎ *01/2538484* 🌐 *www.kunsthaus.ch* ⏲ *Tues.–Thurs. 10–9, Fri.–Sun. 10–5.*

3 **Lindenhof.** A Roman customhouse and fortress and a Carolingian palace once stood on the site of this quiet square overlooking both sides of the river. A fountain commemorates the day in 1292 when Zürich's women saved the city from the Habsburgs. As the story goes, the town was on the brink of defeat when its women donned armor and marched to the Lindenhof. On seeing them, the enemy thought they were faced with another army and promptly beat a strategic retreat. ✉ *Bordered by Fortunag. to west and intersected by Lindenhofstr.*

8 **Rathaus** (Town Hall). Zürich's 17th-century town hall is strikingly baroque, with its interior as well preserved as its facade. There's a richly decorated stucco ceiling in the Banquet Hall and a fine ceramic stove in the government council room. ✉ *Limmatquai 55* ⏲ *Tues., Thurs., and Fri. 10–11:30 AM.*

Altstadt 9
Bahnhof-strasse 2
Fraumünster . . 5
Graphische Sammlung . . . 12
Gross-münster 10
Kunsthaus . . . 11
Lindenhof 3
Rathaus 8
St. Peters Kirche 4
Schweizerisches Landes-museum 1
Wasserkirche . . 7
Zunfthaus zur Meisen 6

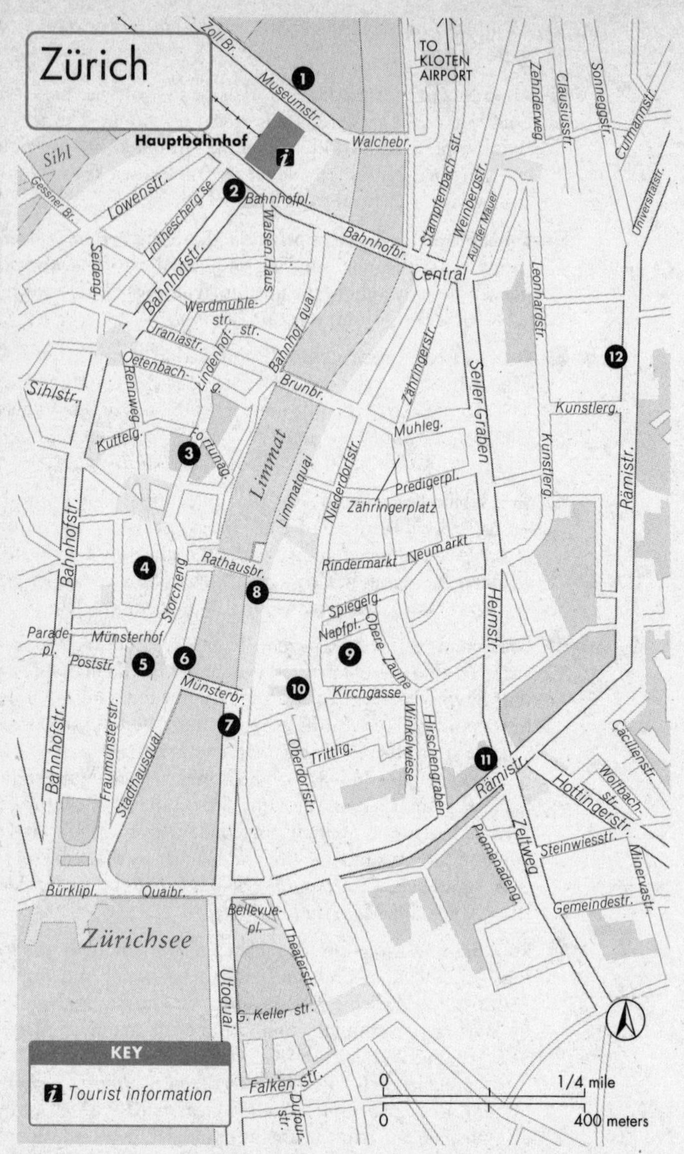

❹ **St. Peters Kirche** (St. Peter's Church). Zürich's oldest parish church, dating from the early 13th century, has the largest clock face in Europe. ✉ *St. Peterhofstatt* ⏲ *Weekdays 8–6, Sat. 8–4.*

★ ❶ **Schweizerisches Landesmuseum** (Swiss National Museum). In a gargantuan neo-Gothic building, this museum possesses an enormous collection of objects dating from the Stone Age to modern times, including costumes, furniture, early watches, and a great deal of military history, including thousands of toy soldiers reenacting battles. ✉ *Museumstr. 2* ☎ *01/2186511* 🌐 *www.musee-suisse.ch* ⏲ *Tues.–Sun. 10:30–5.*

❼ **Wasserkirche** (Water Church). This is one of Switzerland's most delicate late-Gothic structures; its stained glass is by Augusto Giacometti. ✉ *Limmatquai 31* ⏲ *Tues. and Wed. 2–5.*

6 **Zunfthaus zur Meisen.** Erected for the city's wine merchants during the 18th century, this baroque guildhall today houses the Landesmuseum's exquisite ceramics collection. ✉ *Münsterhof 20* ☎ *01/2212807* 🌐 *www.musee-suisse.ch* ⏲ *Tues.–Sun. 10:30–5.*

WHERE TO EAT

Since the mid-1990s, new restaurants, both Swiss and international, have been sprouting up all over town. The newcomers tend to favor lighter cuisine and bright rooms, frequently open to the street. Prices are often steep; for savings, watch for posted Tagesteller lunches.

WHAT IT COSTS in Swiss francs				
	$$$$	$$$	$$	$
PER PERSON	over 50	30–50	20–30	under 20

Prices are per person for a main course at dinner.

$$$$ Fodor'sChoice ★ ✕ **Petermann's Kunststuben.** This is one of Switzerland's culinary destinations, and although it's south of the city center—in Küssnacht on the lake's eastern shore—it's more than worth the 8-km (5-mi) pilgrimage. The ever-evolving menu may include lobster with artichoke and almond oil or Tuscan dove with pine nuts and herbs. Come here for serious, world-class food—and prices to match. ✉ *Seestr. 160, Küssnacht* ☎ *01/9100715* ✍ *Reservations essential* 💳 *AE, DC, MC, V* ⏲ *Closed Sun. and Mon., 2 wks in Feb., and 3 wks in late summer.*

★ $$$–$$$$ ✕ **Kronenhalle.** From Stravinsky, Brecht, and Joyce to Nureyev, Deneuve, and Saint-Laurent, this beloved landmark has always drawn a stellar crowd for its genial, formal but relaxed atmosphere; hearty cooking; and astonishing collection of 20th-century art. Try the roast chicken with garlic and rosemary, or lobster thermidore with *Spätzli* (tiny dumplings). Have a cocktail in the adjoining bar: anyone who's anyone in Zürich drinks here. ✉ *Rämistr. 4* ☎ *01/2516669* ✍ *Reservations essential* 💳 *AE, DC, MC, V.*

$$$–$$$$ ✕ **Veltliner Keller.** Though its rich, carved-wood decor borrows from Graubündner Alpine culture, this ancient dining spot is no tourist-trap transplant: the house, built in 1325, has functioned as a restaurant since 1551. There is a definite emphasis on the heavy and the meaty, but the kitchen is flexible and reasonably deft with more modern favorites as well: sole in creamed pepper sauce, osso buco with saffron rice, and dessert mousses. ✉ *Schlüsselg. 8* ☎ *01/2254040* 💳 *AE, DC, MC, V* ⏲ *Closed weekends.*

$$–$$$ ✕ **La Salle.** This is a favorite of theatergoers heading for the Schiffbauhalle Theater, as it conveniently shares the same building. The glass, steel and concrete interior mixes well with the brick elements left from the original building. Elegantly dressed patrons enjoy delicate dishes such as breaded lamb fillet or sole in coconut-vanilla sauce, beneath an enormous Murano glass chandelier. A smaller version of the menu is available at the bar. ✉ *Schiffbaustr. 4* ☎ *01/2587071* 💳 *AE, DC, MC, V.*

★ $$–$$$ ✕ **Oepfelchammer.** This was once the haunt of Zürich's beloved writer Gottfried Keller, and it still draws unpretentious literati. The bar is dark and riddled with graffiti, with sagging timbers and slanting floors; the welcoming little dining rooms have carved oak paneling, coffered ceilings, and damask linens. The traditional meats—calves' liver, veal, tripe in white wine sauce—come in generous portions; salads are fresh and seasonal. It's always packed and service can be slow. ✉ *Rindermarkt 12* ☎ *01/2512336* 💳 *MC, V* ⏲ *Closed Sun. and Mon.*

★ $$–$$$ ✕ **Zunfthaus zur Zimmerleuten/Küferstube.** While the pricier Zunfthaus upstairs is often overwhelmed with conference crowds, at basement level a cozy, candlelighted haven dubbed "Coopers' Pub" serves meals in a dark-beamed, Old Zürich setting. Standard dishes have enough novelty to stand apart: strawberry risotto with asparagus, roasted duck breast in mango sauce, and homemade cinnamon ice cream with wine-poached pears. ✉ *Limmatquai 40* ☎ *01/2505363* ▭ *AE, DC, MC, V.*

$–$$ ✕ **Adler's Swiss Chuchi.** Right on the Niederdorf's busy main square, Hirschenplatz, this squeaky-clean, Swiss-kitsch restaurant has an airy, modern decor, with carved fir, Alpine-rustic chairs. The fondue stands out among the good home-cooked national specialties. Excellent lunch menus are rock-bottom cheap and served double-quick. ✉ *Roseng. 10* ☎ *01/2669666* ▭ *AE, DC, MC, V.*

★ $–$$ ✕ **Bierhalle Kropf.** Under the mounted boar's head and restored century-old murals, businesspeople, workers, and shoppers share crowded tables to feast on generous portions of traditional Alamannic cuisine, in which no part of an animal is ever wasted. Whether pig's knuckles or ribs, liver dumplings or one of the huge selection of sausages—add potatoes on the side and wash it down with a foamy local lager. ✉ *In Gassen 16* ☎ *01/2211805* ▭ *AE, DC, MC, V* ⊗ *Closed Sun.*

$–$$ ✕ **Reithalle.** In a downtown theater complex behind the Bahnhofstrasse, this old military horse barn is now a noisy and popular restaurant, with candles perched on the mangers and beams and heat ducts exposed. Young locals share long tables arranged mess-hall style to sample French and Italian specialties, many vegetarian, and an excellent, international blackboard list of wines. ✉ *Gessnerallee 8* ☎ *01/2120766* ▭ *AE, MC, V.*

★ $–$$ ✕ **Zeughauskeller.** Built as an arsenal in 1487, this enormous stone-and-beam hall offers truly affordable *Zurigschnätzlets* (sliced veal in mushroom sauce) and a variety of beers and wines amid comfortable, friendly chaos. The waitstaff is harried and brisk, especially at lunchtime, when the crowd is thick with locals—don't worry, just roll up your sleeves and dig in. ✉ *Bahnhofstr. 28, at Paradepl.* ☎ *01/2112690* ▭ *AE, DC, MC, V.*

$ ✕ **Les Halles.** This old warehouse space in Zürich West is enhanced with an eclectic mix of antiques and '50s collectibles. The fare is health conscious, made from organic ingredients sold in the attached health food store; try the couscous with vegetables or the chicken with peppers, tomatoes, and eggplant. ✉ *Pfingstweidstr. 6* ☎ *01/2731125* ▭ *AE, DC, MC, V.*

WHERE TO STAY

Zürich has an enormous range of hotels, from chic and prestigious to modest. Deluxe hotels—the five-star landmarks—average between 500 SF and 800 SF per night for a double, and you'll be lucky to get a shower and toilet in your room for less than 160 SF. The Dolder Grand, one of the country's landmark hotels, will be closed for a major renovation beginning in summer 2004; for updates see their Web site, www.doldergrand.ch.

WHAT IT COSTS In Swiss francs

	$$$$	$$$	$$	$
HOTELS	over 350	250–350	150–250	under 150

Prices are for two people in a double room with bath or shower, including taxes, service charges, and Continental breakfast.

★ $$$$ **Baur au Lac.** This is the highbrow patrician of Swiss hotels, with luxurious but low-key facilities—like the Rolls-Royce limousine service. Its broad back is turned to the commercial center, whereas its front rooms overlook the lake, canal, and manicured lawns of the hotel's private park. The decor is posh, discreet, and firmly fixed in the Age of Reason. ✉ *Talstr. 1, CH-8022* ☎ *01/2205020* 📠 *01/2205044* 🌐 *www.bauraulac.ch* *108 rooms, 17 suites* *2 restaurants, bar* 💳 *AE, DC, MC, V.*

★ $$$$ **Florhof.** In a quiet residential area by the Kunstmuseum, this is an anti-urban hotel—a gentle antidote to the bustle of downtown commerce. This Romantik property pampers guests with its polished wood, blue-willow fabrics, and wisteria-sheltered garden. ✉ *Florhofsg. 4, CH-8001* ☎ *01/2614470* 📠 *01/2614611* 🌐 *www.florhof.ch* *33 rooms, 2 suites* *Restaurant* 💳 *AE, DC, MC, V.*

$$$$ **Splügenschloss.** Befitting its age (built in 1897 in the art nouveau style), this Relais & Châteaux property maintains its ornate, antiques-filled decor. One room is completely paneled in Alpine-style pine; others are decorated in fussy florals. Its location (a 10-minute walk from Paradeplatz) may be a little out of the way for sightseeing, but those who appreciate atmosphere will find it worth the effort. ✉ *Splügenstr. 2, CH-8002* ☎ *01/2899999* 📠 *01/2899998* 🌐 *www.splugenschloss.ch* *50 rooms, 2 suites* *Restaurant, bar* 💳 *AE, DC, MC, V.*

$$$$ Fodor's Choice ★ **Widder.** One of the city's most captivating hotels, the Widder revels in the present while preserving the past. Ten adjacent medieval houses were gutted and combined to create it. Behind every door is a fascinating mix of old and new—a guest room could pair restored 17th-century frescoes with a leather bedspread and private fax. ✉ *Rennweg. 7, CH-8001* ☎ *01/2242526* 📠 *01/2242424* 🌐 *www.widderhotel.ch* *42 rooms, 7 suites* *2 restaurants, bar* 💳 *AE, DC, MC, V.*

★ $$$$ **Zum Storchen.** In a stunning central location, tucked between Fraumünster and St. Peters Kirche, this 600-year-old structure has become an impeccable modern hotel. It has warmly appointed rooms, some with French windows opening over the Limmat, and a lovely restaurant with riverfront terrace seating. ✉ *Weinpl. 2, CH-8001* ☎ *01/2272727* 📠 *01/2272700* 🌐 *www.storchen.ch* *73 rooms* *Restaurant, bar* 💳 *AE, DC, MC, V.*

$$$–$$$$ **Haus zum Kindli.** This charming little bijou hotel could pass for a model Laura Ashley home, with every cushion and bibelot as artfully styled as a magazine ad. The result is welcoming, intimate, and a sight less contrived than most cookie-cutter hotels. At the Opus restaurant downstairs, guests get 10% off menu prices, though you may have to vie with locals for a table. ✉ *Pfalzg. 1, CH-8001* ☎ *01/2115917* 📠 *01/2116528* *21 rooms* *Restaurant* 💳 *AE, DC, MC, V.*

$$–$$$ **Rössli.** This ultrasmall but friendly hotel is in the heart of Oberdorf. The chic white-on-white decor mixes stone and wood textures with bold textiles and mosaic bathrooms. Extras include safes and bathrobes—unusual in this price range. Some singles are tiny, but all have double beds. The top-floor suite has its own roof terrace. ✉ *Rösslig. 7, CH-8001* ☎ *01/2567050* 📠 *01/2567051* 🌐 *www.hotelroessli.ch* *16 rooms, 1 suite* *Bar* 💳 *AE, DC, MC, V.*

$–$$ **Leoneck.** From the cowhide-covered front desk to the edelweiss-print curtains, this budget hotel wallows in its Swiss roots but balances this with no-nonsense conveniences: tile baths (with cow-print shower curtains) and built-in pine furniture. It's one stop from the Central tram stop, two from the Hauptbahnhof. ✉ *Leonhardst. 1, CH-8001* ☎ *01/2542222* 📠 *01/2542200* 🌐 *www.leoneck.ch* *65 rooms* *Restaurant* 💳 *AE, DC, MC, V.*

$ **Limmathof.** This spare but welcoming city hotel inhabits a handsome historic shell and is ideally placed on the Limmatquai, minutes from the

Hauptbahnhof. Rooms have tile bathrooms and plump down quilts. There's an old-fashioned *Weinstube* (wine bar), as well as a vegetarian restaurant that doubles as the breakfast room. ✉ *Limmatquai 142, CH-8023* ☎ *01/2676040* 📠 *01/2620217* *62 rooms* *Restaurant* *AE, DC, MC, V.*

NIGHTLIFE & THE ARTS

Zürich's nightlife scene is largely centered in the Niederdorf area on the right bank of the Limmat. The small city supports a top-ranked orchestra, an opera company, and a theater. For information on goings-on, check *Zürich News,* published weekly in English and German. Also check "Züri-tipp," a German-language supplement to the Friday edition of the daily newspaper *Tages Anzeiger.* Tickets to opera, concert, and theater events can also be bought from the tourist office. **Ticketcorner** (☎ 0848/800800) allows you to purchase advance tickets by phone for almost any event. **Musik Hug** (✉ Limmatquai 28–30 ☎ 01/2694100) can make reservations for selected events. **Jecklin** (✉ Rämistr. 30 ☎ 01/2537676) sells tickets for all major concert events, plus its own productions, which showcase small classical concerts and independent artists.

The Arts

During July or August, the **Theaterspektakel** takes place, with circus tents housing avant-garde theater and experimental performances on the lawns by the lake at Mythenquai. The Zürich Tonhalle Orchestra, named for its concert hall **Tonhalle** (✉ Claridenstr. 7 ☎ 01/2063434), was inaugurated by Brahms in 1895 and enjoys international acclaim. Tickets sell out quickly, so book directly through the Tonhalle. The music event of the year is the **Züricher Festspiele,** hosted by the Tonhalle. From late June to mid-July, orchestras and soloists from all over the world perform and plays and exhibitions are staged. Book well ahead. Details are available from the Tonhalle ticket office or on-line (🌐 www.zuercher-festspiele.ch).

Nightlife

Bars & Lounges

Not just for intellectuals, **I.Q.** (✉ Hardstr. 316 ☎ 01/4407440) has a good selection of whiskies. The **Jules Verne Panorama Bar** (✉ Uraniastr. 9 ☎ 01/2111155) shakes up cocktails with a wraparound downtown view. The narrow bar at the **Kronenhalle** (✉ Rämistr. 4 ☎ 01/2511597) draws mobs of well-heeled locals and internationals. Serving a young, arty set until 4 AM, **Odéon** (✉ Am Bellevue ☎ 01/2511650) is a cultural and historic landmark (Mata Hari danced here and James Joyce scrounged drinks).

Dancing

The medieval-theme **Adagio** (✉ Gotthardstr. 5 ☎ 01/2063666) offers classic rock, jazz, and tango to well-dressed thirtysomethings. **Kaufleuten** (✉ Pelikanstr. 18 ☎ 01/2253333) is a landmark dance club that draws a well-dressed, upwardly mobile crowd. **Mascotte** (✉ Theaterstr. 10 ☎ 01/2524481) draws all ages on weeknights, and a young crowd on weekends, for funk and soul.

Jazz Clubs

Moods (✉ Schiffbaustr. 6 ☎ 01/2768000) hosts international and local acts in the hip new Zürich West district. The **Widder Bar** (✉ Widderg. 6 ☎ 01/2242411), in the Hotel Widder, attracts local celebrities with its 800-count "library of spirits" and international jazz groups.

SHOPPING

One of the broadest assortments of watches in all price ranges is available at **Bucherer** (✉ Bahnhofstr. 50 ☎ 01/2112635). ★ **Heimatwerk** (✉ Rudolf-Brun Brücke, Rennweg 14 and Bahnhofstr. 2 ☎ 01/2178317) specializes in Swiss handicrafts, all of excellent quality. **Jelmoli** (✉ Seideng. 1 ☎ 01/2204411), Switzerland's largest department store, carries a wide range of tasteful Swiss goods. You can snag some of last season's fashions at deep discounts at **Check Out** (✉ Tödistr. 44 ☎ 01/2027226), which jumbles chichi brands on thrift shop–style racks. If you have a sweet tooth, stock up on truffles at **Sprüngli** (✉ Paradepl. ☎ 01/2244711). The renowned chocolatier **Teuscher** (✉ Storcheng. 9 ☎ 01/2115153) concocts a killer champagne truffle. For the latest couture, go to one of a dozen **Trois Pommes** (✉ Weggengasse 1 ☎ 01/2124710) boutiques featuring top-name designers such as Versace and Armani.

ZÜRICH A TO Z

AIRPORTS & TRANSFERS

Unique Zürich Airport (ZRH), 11 km (7 mi) north of Zürich is Switzerland's most important airport. Several airlines fly directly to Zürich from major cities in the United States, Canada, and the United Kingdom.

Unique Zürich Airport ☎ 0900/300313.

TRANSFERS You can take a Swiss Federal Railways feeder train directly from the airport to Zürich's Hauptbanhof (main train station). Tickets cost 5.40 SF one-way, and trains run every 10–15 minutes, arriving in 10 minutes. The Airport Shuttle costs about 22 SF per person for a one-way trip and runs roughly every half hour to a series of downtown hotels.

Airport Shuttle ☎ 01/3001410.

BUS TRAVEL TO & FROM ZÜRICH

All bus services to Zürich will drop you at the Hauptbahnhof (main train station), which is between Museumstrasse and Bahnhofplatz.

BUS TRAVEL WITHIN ZÜRICH

ZVV (Zürich Public Transport) buses and trams run daily from 5:30 AM to midnight. On Friday and Saturday nights buses run every two hours until morning to major towns within the canton of Zürich. Before you board, you must buy your ticket from one of the vending machines found at every stop. An all-day pass is a good buy at 7.20 SF. Free route plans are available from ZVV offices and larger kiosks. The tourist office sells the ZürichCARD, which allows unlimited travel for 24 hours (15 SF) or 72 hours (30 SF), including free admission to 43 museums and discounts at restaurants and nightclubs.

CAR TRAVEL

Highways link Zürich to France, Germany, and Italy. The quickest approach is from Germany; the A5 autobahn reaches from Germany to Basel, and the A2 expressway leads from Basel to Zürich. The A3 expressway feeds into the city from the southeast.

CONSULATES

United Kingdom ✉ Minervastr. 117, Zürich ☎ 01/3836560.

EMERGENCIES

Doctors & Dentists **Doctor/Dentist Referral** ☎ 144.
Emergency Services **Ambulance** ☎ 144. **Police** ☎ 117.
24-hour Pharmacies **Bellevue** ✉ Theaterstr. 14 ☎ 01/2525600.

ENGLISH-LANGUAGE MEDIA

Bookstores The Bookshop ✉ Bahnhofstr. 70 ☎ 01/2110444. **Payot** ✉ Bahnhofstr. 9 ☎ 01/2115452.

TAXIS

Taxis are very expensive, with an 8 SF minimum.

TOURS

BUS TOURS The daily "Trolley Zürich" tour (32 SF) gives a good general tour of the city in two hours. "Zürich's Surroundings" covers more ground and includes an aerial cableway trip to Felsenegg; it takes three hours and costs 45 SF for adults. The daily "Cityrama" tour hits the main sights, then visits Rapperswil, a nearby lakeside town; it costs 45 SF. All tours start from the Hauptbahnhof. Contact the tourist office for reservations. This tourist office service also offers day trips by coach to Luzern; up the Rigi, Titlis, or Pilatus mountains; and the Jungfrau.

WALKING TOURS Two-hour walking tours (20 SF) organized by the tourist office start at the train station. Times for groups with English-language commentary vary, so call ahead.

TRAIN TRAVEL

Zürich is the northern crossroads of Switzerland, with swift and punctual trains arriving from Basel, Geneva, Bern, and Lugano. All routes lead to the Hauptbahnhof (main train station).

Hauptbahnhof ✉ Between Museumstr. and Bahnhofpl. ☎ 0900/300300.

TRAVEL AGENCIES

Imholz Reisen ✉ Central 2 ☎ 01/2675050. **Kuoni Travel** ✉ Bahnhofpl. 7 ☎ 01/2243333.

VISITOR INFORMATION

Zürich Tourist Information ✉ Hauptbahnhof ☎ 01/2154000 🌐 www.zuerich.com. **Hotel reservations** ☎ 01/2154040 📠 01/2154044.

Switzerland Basics

To research prices, get advice from other travelers, and book travel arrangements, visit www.fodors.com.

BUSINESS HOURS

Banks are open weekdays 8:30–4:30 or 5 but are often closed at lunch. Many museums close on Monday—check locally. Shops are generally open 8–noon and 1:30–6:30, though some are open weekday evenings until 8. Some close Monday morning and at 4 or 5 on Saturday. In cities, many large stores do not close for lunch. All shops are closed on Sundays except those in resort areas during high season and in the Geneva and Zürich airports and train stations.

CUSTOMS & DUTIES

For details on imports and duty-free limits, *see* Customs & Duties *in* Smart Travel Tips.

EMBASSIES

Australia ✉ Chemin des Fins 2, Geneva ☎ 022/7999100.
Canada ✉ Kirchenfeldstr. 88, Bern ☎ 031/3573200.
Ireland ✉ Kirchenfeldstr. 68, Bern ☎ 031/3521442.
South Africa ✉ Alpenstr. 29, Bern ☎ 031/3501313.
United Kingdom ✉ Thunstr. 50, Bern ☎ 031/3597700.
United States ✉ Jubiläumsstr. 93, Bern ☎ 031/3577011.

HOLIDAYS

New Year's (January 1–2); Good Friday; Easter Sunday and Monday; Ascension; Whitsunday, Pentecost; National Day (August 1); Christmas (December 25–26). Note that May 1 (Labor Day) is celebrated in most cantons, but not all.

LANGUAGE

French is spoken in the southwest, around Lake Geneva (Lac Léman), and in the cantons of Fribourg, Neuchâtel, Jura, Vaud, and the western portion of Valais; Italian is spoken in the Ticino; and German is spoken everywhere else—in more than 70% of the country, in fact. (Keep in mind that the Swiss versions of these languages can sound very different from those spoken in France, Italy, and Germany.) The Romance language called Romansh has regained a firm foothold throughout the Upper and Lower Engadine regions of the canton Graubünden, where it expresses itself in five different dialects. English is spoken widely. Many signs are in English as well as in the regional language, and all hotels, restaurants, tourist offices, train stations, banks, and shops have at least a few English-speaking employees.

MONEY MATTERS

You'll pay more for luxury here than in almost any other European country, and Switzerland's exorbitant cost of living makes travel noticeably expensive. You'll find plenty of reasonably priced digs and eats, however, if you look for them.

Zürich and Geneva are Switzerland's priciest cities, followed by Basel, Bern, and Lugano. Price tags at resorts—especially the better-known Alpine ski centers—rival those in the cities. Off the beaten track and in the northeast, prices drop considerably.

Some sample prices include cup of coffee, 3 SF; bottle of beer, 3.50 SF; soft drink, 3.50 SF; sausage and Rösti, 16 SF; 2-km (1-mi) taxi ride, 12 SF (more in Geneva, Lugano, Zürich).

CREDIT CARDS Most major credit cards are generally, though not universally, accepted at hotels, restaurants, and shops. Traveler's checks are almost never accepted outside banks and railroad station change counters.

CURRENCY The unit of currency is the Swiss franc (SF), divided into 100 centimes (in Suisse Romande) or rappen (in German Switzerland). There are coins of 5, 10, 20, and 50 rappen/centimes and of 1, 2, and 5 francs. Bills come in denominations of 10, 20, 50, 100, 200, and 1,000 francs. Many stores in the major cities accept payment in euros; change is given in Swiss francs. At press time (summer 2003) the Swiss franc stood at 1.38 SF to the U.S. dollar, 0.93 SF to the Canadian dollar, 1.48 SF to the euro, 0.83 SF to the Australian dollar, 0.75 SF to the New Zealand dollar, and 0.17 SF to the South African rand.

TAXES

A 7.6% value-added tax (V.A.T.) is included in the price of all goods. Nonresidents spending at least 400 SF (including V.A.T.) at one time at a particular store may get a V.A.T. refund. To obtain a refund, pay by credit card; at the time of purchase, the store clerk should fill out and give you a red form and keep a record of your credit card number. When leaving Switzerland, you must hand deliver the red form to a customs officer—at the customs office at the airport or, if leaving by car or train, at the border. Customs will process the form and return it to the store, which will refund the tax by crediting your card.

TELEPHONES

COUNTRY & AREA CODES

The country code for Switzerland is 41, for Liechtenstein 423. When dialing Switzerland from outside the country, drop the initial zero from the area code.

INTERNATIONAL CALLS

To dial international numbers directly from Switzerland, dial 00 before the country's code. If a number cannot be reached directly, dial 1141 for a connection. Dial 1159 for international numbers and information. International access codes will put you directly in touch with an operator who will place your call. Calls to the United States and Canada cost 0.12 SF per minute; calls to the United Kingdom, Australia, and New Zealand cost 0.25 SF per minute. International telephone rates are lower on weekends.

Access Codes **AT&T** ☎ 0800/890011. **MCI WorldCom** ☎ 0800/890222. **Sprint** ☎ 0800/899777.

PUBLIC PHONES

Since the cell phone boom, the number of public phone booths in Switzerland has been drastically reduced, but they can still be found at train stations, town centers, and in shopping districts. Calls from booths are far cheaper than those made from hotels. A phone card, available in 5 SF, 10 SF, and 20 SF units at the post office, kiosk, or train station, allows you to call from any public phone. Note that very few public phones accept coins.

INDEX

A

Abbey Road Studios, *184*
Abbey Theatre, *139*
AC Santo Mauro 🏨, *212*
Accademia Gallery (Florence), *157*
Accademia Gallery (Venice), *294*
Acropolis, *22–23*
Acropolis Museum, *22*
Admiralty Arch, *174*
Africa Museum, *86*
Agios Eleftherios, *22*
Agora 🏨, *13*
Ägyptisches Museum, *64–65*
Air travel, *F10–F14*
Amsterdam, 17
Athens, 36
Barcelona, 58
Berlin, 76
Brussels, 92–93
Budapest, 110–111
Copenhagen, 128
Dublin, 147
Florence, 165
London, 196–197
Madrid, 218
Paris, 246
Prague, 264–265
Rome, 286
Venice, 301
Vienna, 321
Zürich, 333
Airports, *F14*
Akropolis, *22–23*
Alain Ducasse ✕, *235*
Albert Memorial, *178*
Albertina, *306*
Alcalá Gate, *207*
Alle Testiere ✕, *297*
Altes Museum, *70*
Altstadt 🏨, *318*
Am Hof, *312*
Amalienborg, *116*
Amalienborg Museum, *116*
Amigo 🏨, *89*
Amstel Inter-Continental 🏨, *11–12*
Amsterdam Historisch Museum, *6*
Amusement parks, *122*
Anafiotika, *27*
Ancient Agora, *23*
Andromeda Athens Hotel 🏨, *31*
Animal Park (Berlin), *69*
Anker-Uhr, *313*
Anne Frankhuis, *2*
Antico Arco ✕, *281*
Apsley House, *177*
Apterou Nikis, *22*
Aquincum, *103*
Aquincum Museum, *103*
Arc de Triomphe, *223–224*
Arc du Carrousel, *224*
Archaeological Museum (Florence), *157*
Archaia Agora, *23*
Arco di Costantino, *270*
Areios Pagos, *23*
Ariel Guest House 🏨, *144*
Aristera-Dexia ✕, *29*
Art galleries and museums
Amsterdam, 8–9
Athens, 23, 27
Barcelona, 45, 48, 49, 50, 51
Berlin 65, 68, 70
Brussels, 84, 85, 86
Budapest, 98, 103
Copenhagen, 120, 121, 122
Dublin, 136–137, 139
Florence, 153, 156–157, 158, 159
London, 174, 175, 177–178, 180, 181, 183, 184
Madrid, 205, 206, 210
Paris, 223, 224–225, 229, 233, 234
Rome, 271, 274, 276–277, 279
Venice, 294–295
Vienna, 306, 310, 313
Zürich, 327, 329
Art History Museum, *310*
Artner ✕, *315*
Atelier Brancusi, *229*
Atomium, *86*
Au Bon Accueil ✕, *238*
Au Lapin Agile, *234*
Augustinerkirche, *306, 307*

B

Ballet
Amsterdam, 14
Barcelona, 55
Berlin, 75
Budapest, 108
London, 192–193
Paris, 243
Prague, 263
Bancogiro ✕, *297*
Bank of Ireland, *133*
Banqueting House, *170*
Baptistery, *152–153*
Baraka ✕, *105*
Barberini Palace, *274–275*
Barbican Centre, *182*
Bars
Amsterdam, 14–15
Athens, 34
Barcelona, 55–56
Berlin, 75
Brussels, 91
Budapest, 109
Dublin, 146
Florence, 164
Madrid, 214–215
Paris, 244
Rome, 285
Vienna, 320
Zürich, 332
Basilica dei Santi Maria e Donato, *296*
Basilica di San Marco, *291*
Basilica di San Pietro, *277–278*
Bastille Opera, *229*
Bateaux Mouches (motorboats), *223*
Baths of Caracalla, *271, 274*
Battistero, *152–153*
Baur au Lac 🏨, *330*
Bazilika svatého Jiří, *258*
Beacci Tornabuoni 🏨, *162–163*
Beccofino ✕, *160*
Begijnhof (Beguine Court), *6*
Belgian Comic-Strip Center, *84*
Bellettini 🏨, *163*
Belvárosi plébánia templom, *99*
Belvedere Palace, *313*
Benaki Museum, *23*
Berggruen Collection, *68*
Berlage's Stock Exchange, *2*
Berlin Wall Memorial Site, *70*
Berliner Dom (Cathedral), *69*
Berliner Fernsehturm, *69–70*
Betlémská kaple (Bethlehem Chapel), *253*
Beurs van Berlage, *2*
Big Ben clock tower, *174*
Bike travel, *F14, 17, 111, 128, 165, 287, 321*
Bildungs- und Gedenkstätte Haus der Wansee-Konferenz (Educational and Memorial Site House of the Wannsee Conference), *65*
Blakes 🏨, *190*
Bloemenmarkt, *6*
Bloody Tower, *183–184*
Boat and ferry travel, *F14–F15*
Amsterdam, 17
Athens, 37
Barcelona, 58
Brussels, 93
Dublin, 148
Venice, 301–302
Boboli Gardens, *159*
Borchardt ✕, *71*
Borghese Gallery, *274*
Børsen, *117*
Botafumeiro ✕, *52*
Botanical Garden (Copenhagen), *117*
Botanisk Have, *117*
Botin ✕, *211*
Bouzoukia clubs, *34*
Brancusi's Studio, *229*
Brandenburger Tor, *65*
Breweries and distilleries
Copenhagen, 117
Dublin, 140, 141

Brewery Museum, *84*
Britannia, *283*
British Library, *181*
British Museum, *181*
Brunelleschi, *161–162*
Buckingham Palace, *170–171*
Buda Castle, *98*
Budapesti Történeti Múzeum, *98*
Burano, *295–296*
Burlington House, *177*
Bus travel, *F15–F16*
Amsterdam, 18–19
Athens, 37
Barcelona, 58–59
Berlin, 77
Brussels, 93
Budapest, 111
Copenhagen, 128
Dublin, 148
Florence, 165
London, 197–198
Madrid, 218
Paris, 246
Prague, 265
Rome, 287
Vienna, 322
Zürich, 333
busabe eathai ✕, *186*
Butterfly House, *307*
Byzantine Museum, *28*

C

Ca' d'Oro, *294*
Ca' Rezzonico, *294*
Cabarets
Barcelona, 56
Dublin, 145
Paris, 244
Prague, 263–264
Vienna, 320
Cabinet War Rooms, *171*
Cable car, *60–61*
Café Kör ✕, *105*
Cafés
Amsterdam, 14–15
Barcelona, 56
Dublin, 143
Madrid, 214–215
Vienna, 316–317
Cameras & photography, *F16*
Campanile (Florence), *153*
Campanile di San Marco, *291*
Can Gaig ✕, *51*
Can Majó ✕, *52*
Capella de Santa Àata, *48*
Capitoline Museums, *271*
Cappella dei Pazzi, *157*
Cappella dei Principi, *157*
Cappella Sistina, *276*
Cappelle Medicee, *157*
Capuchin Church, *307*
Car rental, *F16–F17*
Car travel, *F17–F18*
Amsterdam, 17
Athens, 37
Berlin, 77
Brussels, 93
Budapest, 111
Copenhagen, 128–129
Dublin, 148
Florence, 165
London, 198
Madrid, 219
Paris, 247
Prague, 265
Rome, 287
Venice, 302
Vienna, 322
Zürich, 333
Carlsberg Bryggeri, *117*
Carlton House Terrace, *171, 174*
Caron de Beaumarchais, *240*
Casa Amatller, *49*
Casa Batlló, *49*
Casa Cisneros, *207*
Casa Lleó Morera, *49*
Casa Milà, *49*
Casa Mingo ✕, *212*
Casa Montaner i Simó-Fundació Tàpies, *49*
Casinos
Amsterdam, 15
Budapest, 109
Castel Sant'Angelo, *276*
Castles. ⇨ *See* Palaces and castles
Catalan Music Palace, *48*
Catedral de la Seu, *45*
Cathedral Museum, *156*
Cathédrale des Sts-Michel-et-Gudule, *81, 84*
Cattedrale di santa Maria del Fiore, *153*
Caixaforum, *50*
Cenotaph, *171*
Centraal Station, *2*
Centre Belge de la Bande Dessinée, *84*
Centre de Cultura Contemporània (CCCB), *45*
Centre Pompidou, *229*
Centro de Arte Reina Sofía, *205*
Chaillot Palace, *223*
Chain Bridge (Budapest), *102*
Changing of the Guard, *170–171*
Channel Tunnel, *F18*
Chapel of St. Agatha, *48*
Charles Bridge, *257*
Charlottenburger Hof, *73*
Chester Beatty Library, *136*
Chiesa del Gesù, *279*
Children, traveling with, *F18–F19*
Chrám svatého Mikuláše, *257*
Chrám svatého Víta, *258*
Christ Church Cathedral, *133*
Christiania, *117*
Christiansborg Slot, *117*
Church of Our Lady, *122*
Church of St. Mary, *71*
Church of St. Nicholas, *257*
Church of the Virgin Mary before Týn, *256*
Churches
Amsterdam, 3, 6
Athens, 22, 26
Barcelona, 45, 48, 49–50
Berlin, 68, 69, 70, 71
Brussels, 81, 84, 85
Budapest, 98–99, 102
Copenhagen, 120, 121, 122
Dublin, 133, 137–138
Florence, 152–153, 157, 158, 159
London, 175, 176, 180, 182–183
Paris, 225, 228, 232, 233, 234
Prague, 253, 256, 257, 258
Rome, 271, 275, 277–278, 280
Venice, 291, 294, 295, 296
Vienna, 306, 307, 310, 312, 313, 314
Zürich, 327, 328
Churchillparken, *120*
Cibréo ✕, *160*
Cimetière du Père-Lachaise, *234*
Circle Line Brasserie ✕, *258*
Citadel (Copenhagen), *120*
City Hall (Dublin), *133*
City Hall (Madrid), *207*
City History Museum (Barcelona), *48*
City Museum (Brussels), *84*
City of Paris Museum of Modern Art, *223*
Clam-Gallas palác, *253*
Claridge's, *191*
Claris, *53*
Classical music. ⇨ *See* Concerts
Clock Museum, *314*
Club Gascon ✕, *187–188*
Colón, *54*
Colosseum (Colosseo), *270*
Columbus Monument, *45*
Comedy clubs, *194*
Comerç 24 ✕, *51–52*
Comme Chez Soi ✕, *87*
Concertgebouw (Concert Hall), *8*
Concerts
Amsterdam, 14
Athens, 33
Barcelona, 55
Berlin, 74
Brussels, 90–91
Budapest, 108
Copenhagen, 126
Dublin, 145
Florence, 164
London, 193
Madrid, 214
Paris, 243
Prague, 263
Rome, 284
Venice, 300
Vienna, 319
Zürich, 332

Conciergerie, *232*
Condes de Barcelona, *53*
Consulates. ⇨ *See* Embassies and consulates
Consumer protection, *F19*
Convento de las Descalzas Reales, *205–206*
Copenhagen Synagogue, *120*
Court Chapel, *307*
Court Silver and Tableware Museum, *307, 311*
Courtauld Institute of Art, *180*
Covent Garden, *180*
Covent Garden Hotel, *192*
Credit cards, *F6, F27*
Crillon, *239*
Crown Jewels, *184*
Cruise travel, *F19*
Cultural Forum, *68*
Custom House (Dublin), *139*
Customs and duties, *F19–F21*
Cutty Sark (ship), *185*
Cybele's Fountain, *206*

D

Dahlemer Museen, *65*
Dalla Mora, *300*
Dam Square, *2*
Dance. ⇨ *Also* Ballet
Athens,33
Barcelona, 55
Brussels, 91
Budapest, 108
Copenhagen, 126–127
Paris, 243
Dance clubs. ⇨ *See* Nightclubs and discos
D'Angleterre, *125*
Danubius Hotel Gellért, *107*
De Silveren Spiegel ✕, *10*
De Waag, *2*
Deutscher Dom (German cathedral), *70*
Deutsches Historisches Museum, *69*
Dining, *F21–F22*
Disabilities and accessibility, *F22*
Discos. ⇨ *See* Nightclubs and discos
Discounts and deals, *F23–F24*
Divani Apollon Palace, *31*
Doge's Palace, *291*
Domus Aurea, *270*
Dublin Castle, *133, 136*
Dublin Civic Museum, *136*
"Dublin Experience" audiovisual presentation, *139*
Dublin Writers Museum, *139*
Dům U Červeného Lva, *261*
Dům U černé Matky Boží, *253*
Duomo, *153*

E

E&O ✕, *188–189*
Eden ✕, *283*
Église de la Madeleine, *225*
Egyptian Museum, *64–65*
Eiffel Tower, *223*
El Cenador del Prado ✕, *211*
Electricity, *F24*
Élysée Palace, *225*
Embassies and consulates
Amsterdam, 17, 19
Athens, 38, 42
Barcelona, 59
Berlin, 79
Brussels, 95
Budapest, 114
Copenhagen, 130
Dublin, 149
Florence, 166
London, 202
Paris, 250
Prague, 267
Rome, 287
Venice, 302
Vienna, 322, 324
Zürich, 333, 334
Emergencies
Amsterdam, 17
Athens, 38
Barcelona, 59
Berlin, 77
Brussels, 93
Budapest, 111
Copenhagen, 129
Dublin, 148
Florence, 166
London, 198
Madrid, 219
Paris, 247
Prague, 265
Rome, 297
Venice, 303
Vienna, 322
Zürich, 333
Engelse Kerk (English Church), *6*
Erasmus House, *86*
Erechtheion, *22*
Espai Gaudí, *49*
Ethniko Archaiologiko Museo (National Archeological Museum), *23*
Ethniko Kipos, *27–28*
Ethnographic Museum (Berlin), *65*
Étoile-Péreire, *240*
Etruscan Museum of Villa Giulia, *274*
European Parliament, *86*
European Union Institutions, *86*
Excelsior ✕, *9–10*
Excelsior, *162*
Expiatory Church of the Holy Family, *49–50*
Expozice Franze Kafky, *253*

F

Farnese, *283*
Father Lachaise Cemetery, *235*
Ferry travel. ⇨ *See* Boat and ferry travel
Figarohaus, *306*
Film
Amsterdam, 13–14
Athens, 33
Barcelona, 55
Brussels, 90
Florence, 164
London, 193
Madrid, 214
Paris, 243
Rome, 284
Filmmuseum Berlin, *68*
Fine Arts Museum (Brussels), *85*
Fine Arts Museum (Budapest), *103*
First Floor ✕, *71*
Flamenco clubs
Barcelona, 56
Madrid, 216
Florhof, *331*
Fontana dei Quattro Fiumi, *280*
Fontana del Tritone, *275*
Fontana della Barcaccia, *275*
Fontana delle Api, *275*
Fontana delle Tartarughe, *279*
Fontana di Trevi, *274*
Foro Romano, *271*
Four Courts, *140*
Four Seasons Hotel Berlin, *72–73*
Frank, Anne, *2*
Franz Kafka's birthplace, *253*
Französischer Dom (French cathedral), *70*
Fraumünster, *327*
French Monuments Museum, *223*
Freud Museum, *306*
Frihedsmuseet, *117, 120*
Fuente de la Cibeles, *206*
Fundació Miró, *50*

G

Galleria Borghese, *274*
Galleria d'Arte Moderna, *159*
Galleria degli Uffizi, *153*
Galleria dell'Accademia (Florence), *157*
Galleria dell'Accademia (Venice), *294*
Galleria Doria Pamphili, *279*
Galleria Franchetti, *294*
Galleria Nazionale de Arte Antica, *274–275*
Galleria Palatina, *159*
Gardens
Athens, 27–28
Barcelona, 51
Copenhagen, 116, 117
Florence, 156, 159
London, 178
Madrid, 207
Paris, 224, 233
Prague, 257
Rome, 276
Gate of the Sun, *207*
Gaudí, Antonio, *48*

Gay and lesbian travel, F24, 15
Gedenkstätte Berliner Mauer, 69
Gemäldegalerie, 68
General Post Office (Dublin), 139–140
German Historical Museum, 69
German Parliament, 68
Giardini Vaticani, 276
Giardino Boboli, 159
Gordon Ramsay ×, 187
Gordon Ramsay at Claridge's ×, 188
Gouden Bocht (Golden Bend), 6–7
Goulandri Museo Kikladikis ke Archaias Technis, 23, 27
Gran Teatre del Liceu, 45
Grand Amsterdam 🏨, 12
Grand Hyatt Berlin 🏨, 73
Grand Palais, 224
Grande Bretagne 🏨, 31
Graphische Sammlung, 327
Great Church, 327
Great Synagogue (Budapest), 102
Green Forest, 65
Greenwich Park, 185
Gresham Palota, 102
Grossbeerenkeller ×, 72
Grossmünster, 327
Grotte Vaticane, 278
Grunewald, 65
Guinness Brewery, 140
Gundel ×, 104

H

Hackesche Höfe (Hackesche Warehouses), 70
Hadrian's Arch, 26–27
Hadtörténeti Múzeum, 98
Hamburger Bahnhof, 65
Handel House Museum, 177
Ha'penny Bridge, 140
Haus am Checkpoint Charlie, 65
Haus der Musik, 306
Heeresgeschichtliches Museum, 306
Hephaisteion, 23
Heraldic Museum, 136
Hermitage 🏨, 162
Het Koninklijk Paleis te Amsterdam, 2
Hirschprungske Samling, 120
Hofburg, 307
Hofburgkapelle, 307
Hoffmeister 🏨, 261
Hoher Markt, 313
Holocaust Mahnmal, 65
Holy Chapel (Paris), 233
Horse Guards Parade, 171
Horta Museum, 86
Hotel Adlon Berlin 🏨, 73
Hôtel d'Aubusson 🏨, 241
Hôtel de L'Europe 🏨, 12
Hôtel de Ville (Brussels), 84
Hôtel des Invalides, 233
Hotel Inter-Continental Budapest 🏨, 106
House of Music, 306
House of the Black Madonna, 253
Houses of Parliament (London), 171, 174
Hugo, Victor, 229
Hundertwasserhaus, 313
Hungarian Academy of Sciences, 102
Hungarian National Gallery, 98
Hungarian National Museum, 99
Hungarian State Opera House, 99
Hyde Park, 178

I

Ida Davidsen ×, 123–124
Il Palazzo at the Bauer 🏨, 298
Ile St-Louis, 232
Imperial ×, 317–318
Imperial Apartments, 307, 311
Imperial Coach Collection, 314
Imperial Palace, 307
Imperial Treasury, 307, 311
Inner-City Parish Church, 99
Insurance, F24
Irish Museum of Modern Art, 141
Irodion, 26
Isola Tiberina, 279
Ivy, The ×, 186

J

Jánoshegy, 104
Jardi 🏨, 54
Jardin des Tuileries, 224
Jardin du Luxembourg, 233
Jazz clubs
Amsterdam, 15
Athens, 34
Barcelona, 57
Brussels, 91
Budapest, 109
Copenhagen, 127
London, 194
Madrid, 216
Paris, 244–245
Prague, 264
Rome, 285
Zürich, 332
Jewel Tower, 171
Jewish Museum (Prague), 256
Jodenbreestraat, 7
Joods Historisch Museum (Jewish Historical Museum–Amsterdam), 7
Judenplatz Museum, 307
Jüdisches Museum (Jewish Museum–Berlin), 65, 68
Jüdisches Museum der Stadt Wien (Jewish Museum–Vienna), 307

K

Kafka, Franz, 253
Kaiser-Wilhelm-Gedächtniskirche, 68
Kapuzinerkirche, 307
Karlskirche, 307, 310
Karlův most, 257
Kastellet, 120
Kavárna Slavia ×, 260
Keats-Shelley Memorial House, 274
Kensington Gardens, 178
Kensington Palace, 178–179
Kenwood House, 184–185
Kilmainham Gaol, 141
King's House (Brussels), 84
Királyi Palota, 98
Kirche am Hof, 312
Københavns Synagoge, 120
Kommandanten ×, 123
Kong Hans Kælder ×, 123
Kongelig Teater, 122
Kongelige Bibliotek, 120
Koninklijke Museum voor Midden-Afrika, 86
Kostel Panny Marie před Tynem, 256
Kostel svatého Mikuláše, 256
Královský palác, 258
Kronenhalle ×, 329
Kulturforum, 68
Kunstgewerbemuseum, 68
Kunsthalle, 310
Kunsthaus, 327
KunstHaus Wien, 313
Kunsthistorisches Museum, 310
Kunstindustrimuseet, 120

L

La Broche ×, 210
La Calcina 🏨, 299
La Gamella ×, 211
La Giostra ×, 160
La Pedrera, 49
La Pergola ×, 281
La Régalade ×, 238
La Rive ×, 10
La Stampa ×, 142
La Truffe Noire ×, 87
Language, F24
L'Ardoise ×, 237
Lapérouse ×, 237–238
L'Astrance ×, 236
Le Caprice ×, 188
Le Fonticine ×, 161
Le Grand Véfour ×, 235–236
Le Méridien (Brussels) 🏨, 89
Le Méridien Budapest 🏨, 106
Le Tourville 🏨, 242
Leinster House, 136
Leopold Museum, 310
Les Ambassadeurs ×, 235
Les Éysées du Vernet ×, 236
Les Pipos ×, 238–239
Les Salons de Wittamer ×, 88
Liberty Museum, 117, 120

Libraries
Copenhagen, 120
Dublin, 136, 137, 138
London, 181
Vienna, 307, 310–311
Lieutenant's Palace, 48
Likavitos, 26
Lille Havfrue statue, 117
L'Incontro ✕, 297
L'Indochine ✕, 10
Lipizzaner Museum, 310
Locanda Locatelli ✕, 188
Lodging, F25–F26
Amsterdam, 11–13
Athens, 30–33
Barcelona, 53–54
Berlin, 72–74
Brussels, 88–90
Budapest, 105–107
Copenhagen, 124–126
Dublin, 143–145
Florence, 161–163
London, 189–192
Madrid, 212–213
Paris, 239–242
Prague, 261–262
Rome, 282–284
Venice, 297–300
Vienna, 317–319
Zürich, 330–332
L'Ogenblik ✕, 87
Long Pura ✕, 10
Loreta church, 258
Louvre, 224–225
Ludwig Múzeum, 98
Lurblæserne, 120
Luxembourg Gardens, 233
Luxembourg Palace, 233

M

Magyar Állami Operaház, 99
Magyar Nemzeti Galéria, 98
Magyar Nemzeti Múzeum, 99
Magyar Tudományos Akadémia, 102
Maison de Victor Hugo, 229
Maison d'Erasme, 86
Maison du Roi, 84
Majestic 🏨, 53
Manneken Pis fountain, 84
Mansion House, 137
Marble Church, 120
Marè, Frederic, 45
Margutta 🏨, 284
Maria am Gestade church, 313
Maritime Museum (Barcelona), 45
Maritime Museum (Paris), 223
Marmorkirken, 120
Marsh's Library, 136
Mátyás templom (Matthias Church), 98–99
Medici Chapels, 157
Meal plans, F7
Memorial Site Berlin Wall, 69
Merrion 🏨, 144
Metropole 🏨, 298
Meurice 🏨, 239
Mies van der Rohe Pavilion, 50
Millenniumi Emlékmü, 103
Miller's Residence 🏨, 190
Mini-Europe model attraction, 86
Miró Foundation, 50
Mnimeio Agnostou Stratiotou, 27
Mnimeio Lysikratous, 27
Modern Art Museum (Paris), 229
Molnár Panzió 🏨, 107
Monasteries and convents
Barcelona, 51
Madrid, 205–206
Prague, 258
Monestir de Pedralbes, 51
Money matters, F26–F27
Monna Lisa 🏨, 162
Montmartre Museum, 234
Monument a Colom, 45
Monument of Lysikrates, 27
Morandi alla Crocetta 🏨, 163
Mt. Lycabettus, 26
Mozart, W. A., 257, 306
Mücsarnok, 103
Municipal House (Prague), 253
Munttoren (Mint Tower), 7
Murano, 296
Musée Carnavalet, 229
Musée d'Art Ancien, 85
Musée d'Art Moderne, 85
Musée d'Art Moderne de la Ville de Paris, 223
Musée de la Marine, 223
Musée de la Ville de Bruxelles, 84
Musée de l'Armée, 233
Musée de l'Homme, 223
Musée de l'Orangerie, 225
Musée de Montmartre, 234
Musée des Monuments Français, 223
Musée des Plans-Reliefs, 233
Musée d'Orsay, 233
Musée du Jeu de Paume, 225
Musée Horta, 86
Musée Instrumental, 85
Musée National d'Art Moderne, 229
Musée Nissim de Camondo, 228
Musée Picasso, 229
Musée Rodin, 234
Musei Capitolini, 271
Musei Vaticani, 276–277
Museo Akropoleos, 26
Museo Archeologico (Florence), 157
Museo Archeologico (Venice), 291
Museo Correr, 291
Museo degli Argenti, 159
Museo del Merletto, 295–296
Museo del Prado, 206
Museo del Settecento Veneziano, 294
Museo dell'Opera del Duomo, 156
Museo dell'Opera di Santa Croce e Cappella dei Pazzi, 157
Museo di San Marco, 157
Museo di Santa Maria Novella, 157–158
Museo di Storia della Scienza, 156
Museo Ebraico, 294
Museo Ellinikis Laikis Technis, 27
Museo Ellinikon Laikon Musikon Organon, 27
Museo Etrusco di Villa Giulia, 274
Museo Marciano, 291
Museo Nazionale del Bargello, 158
Museo Nazionale Romano, 279
Museo Storico (Rome), 278
Museo Thyssen-Bornemisza, 206
Museo tis Agoras, 23
Museo Vetrario, 296
Museu d'Art Contemporani de Barcelona (MACBA), 45
Museu d'Història de la Ciutat, 48
Museu Frederic Marès, 45
Museu Marítim, 45
Museu Nacional d'Art de Catalunya, 50
Museu Picasso, 45, 48
Museum Amstelkring, 2–3
Museum für angewandte Kunst (MAK), 310
Museum het Rembrandthuis, 7–8
Museum im Schottenstift, 314
Museum Island, 70
Museum moderner Kunst Stiftung Ludwig, 310
Museum of Applied Arts, 310
Museum of Decorative Art (Copenhagen), 120
Museum of Decorative Arts (Berlin), 68
Museum of 18th-century Venice, 294
Museum of Ethnography, 102
Museum of Lace, 295–296
Museum of London, 182
Museum of Mankind (Paris), 223
Museum of Military History (Budapest), 98
Museum of Military History (Vienna), 306
Museum of Modern Art (Amsterdam), 8–9
Museum of Modern Art (Brussels), 85

Museum of Music History, *99*
Museum of Popular Greek Musical Instruments, *27*
Museum Willet-Holthuysen, *7*
Museums. ⇨ *Also* Art galleries and museums
Acropolis, 22
African culture, 86
in Amsterdam, 2–3, 6, 7–8, 9
archaeology, 23, 103, 157, 223, 291
in Athens, 22, 23, 26, 27, 28
in Barcelona, 45, 48, 50
in Berlin, 64–65, 68, 69, 70
brewing, 84
in Brussels, 84, 85, 86
in Budapest, 98, 99, 102, 103
Byzantine culture, 28
children, 310
clocks and watches, 314
comic strips, 84
in Copenhagen, 116, 117, 120, 121, 122
Cycladic civilization, 23, 27
in Dublin, 136, 137, 139, 141
Egyptian civilization, 64–65
Erasmus, 86
ethnography, 65, 102
Etruscan civilization, 274
film, 68
in Florence, 153, 156, 157–158, 159
Freud, 306
Gaudí, 49
heraldry, 136
history, 6, 7, 23, 48, 65, 68, 70, 98, 121, 137, 177, 181, 182, 229, 234, 256, 294, 306, 307, 328
Jewish culture, 7, 65, 68, 256, 294, 307
Kafka, 253
Keats and Shelley, 274
lace, 295–296
Lipizzaner horses, 310
literary history, 139
in London, 174, 175, 176, 177–178, 179, 180, 181, 182, 183, 184, 185
in Madrid, 205, 206, 210
maritime history, 3, 45, 185, 223
military history, 98, 233, 306
Mozart, 257, 306
music history, 99, 177, 306
musical instruments, 27, 85
natural history, 179, 311
in Paris, 223, 224–225, 228, 229, 233, 234
photography, 120
Picasso, 45, 48, 229
in Prague, 253, 256
religious history, 2–3, 7
Rembrandt, 7–8
Rodin, 234
in Rome, 271, 274, 276–277, 279
royalty, 116, 117, 121, 175, 307, 311
science, 3, 156, 179
Shakespeare, 183
silver and gold, 159
theater, 180, 312
Van Gogh, 9
in Venice, 291, 294, 295–296
Victor Hugo, 229
in Vienna, 306, 307, 310, 311, 312, 313, 314
World War II resistance movements, 117, 120
in Zürich, 327, 329
Museumsinsel, *70*
Museumsquartier, *310*
Musical Instruments Museum, *85*
Muziektheater/Stadhuis, *8*
myhotel bloomsbury 🏨, *189–190*

N

Nagy Zsinagóga, *102*
Náncsi Néni ✕, *105*
Naos Athenas Nikis, *22*
Napoléon's Tomb, *233*
National Archaeological Museum (Athens), *23*
National Art Gallery (Copenhagen), *122*
National Gallery (London), *174*
National Gallery of Ireland, *136–137*
National Garden (Athens), *27–28*
National Library (Dublin), *137*
National Library (Vienna), *310–311*
National Maritime Museum (London), *185*
National Museum (Copenhagen), *121*
National Museum (Dublin), *137*
National Museum (Prague), *256*
National Museum of Catalan Art, *50*
National Museum of Photography, *120*
National Museum of Rome, *279*
National Portrait Gallery (London), *175*
Nationalbibliothek, *307, 310–311*
Nationalgalerie, *68, 70*
Natural History Museum (London), *179*
Naturhistorisches Museum, *311*
Nederlands Scheepvaartmuseum, *3*
Nelson's Column, *176*
Nemo Science & Technology Center, *3*
Neo Museo Akropoleos, *26*
Néprajzi Múzeum, *102*
Netherlands Maritime Museum, *3*
New Carlsberg Sculpture Museum, *121*
New Church (Amsterdam), *3*
New National Gallery (Berlin), *68*
New Synagogue (Berlin), *70–71*
New Wing of the Imperial Palace, *311*
Nieuwe Kerk, *3*
Nightclubs and discos
Amsterdam, 14–15
Athens, 33–34
Barcelona, 56
Berlin, 75
Brussels, 91
Budapest, 109
Copenhagen, 127
Dublin, 146
Florence, 164
London, 194–195
Madrid, 215
Paris, 244–245
Prague, 263–264
Rome, 285
Venice, 300–301
Vienna, 320
Zürich, 332
Nikolaikirche, *71*
Nikolaj Kirken, *121*
Notre-Dame Cathedral, *232*
Notre Dame de la Chappelle, *85*
Notre Dame du Sablon, *85*
Number 31 🏨, *144*
Ny Carlsberg Glyptotek, *121*

O

O Platanos ✕, *30*
Obecní dům, *253*
Observatories. ⇨ *See* Planetariums and observatories
O'Connell Bridge, *137*
Odeon of Herod Atticus, *26*
Oepfelchammer ✕, *329*
Old Bridge (Florence), *159*
Old Church (Amsterdam), *3*
Old Jameson Distillery, *141*
Old Jewish Cemetery (Prague), *256*
Old Museum (Berlin), *70*
Old-New Synagogue (Prague), *256*
Old Palace (Florence), *156*
Old Royal Observatory (London), *185*
Old Town Hall (Prague), *256*
Olympic Games (Athens), *38–39*
Opera
Amsterdam, 14
Berlin, 74
Brussels, 91
Budapest, 108

Copehagen, 126–127
London, 193
Madrid, 214
Paris, 243
Prague, 263
Rome, 285
Venice, 300
Vienna, 319–320
Opéra de la Bastille, *229*
Opéra Garnier, *228*
Opera houses
Barcelona, 45
Budapest, 99, 108
London, 180
Paris, 228, 229
Vienna, 312, 319
Orangery Museum, *225*
Orsanmichele (Garden of St. Michael), *156*
Orsay Museum, *233*
Országház, *102*
Osteria de'Benci ✕, *161*
Ostia Antica, *279*
Oude Kerk, *3*
Our Savior's Church, *122*

P

Packing, *F27–F28*
Padellàs Palace, *48*
Painting Gallery, *68*
Palace of Discovery, *224*
Palace of Exhibitions, *103*
Palace of Westminster, *171*
Palace Praha 🏨, *261*
Palaces and castles
Amsterdam, 2
Barcelona, 48, 49, 50
Berlin, 69
Brussels, 84, 85
Budapest, 98, 102, 103
Copenhagen, 116, 117, 121
Dublin, 133, 138
Florence, 156, 158, 159
London, 170–171, 177, 178–179
Madrid, 206–207
Paris, 223, 224, 225, 228, 233
Prague, 253, 258
Rome, 270, 274–275, 276, 279
Venice, 292, 294
Vienna, 307, 311, 312, 313–314
Palacio Real, *206–207*
Palais de Chaillot, *223*
Palais de la Découverte, *224*
Palais de l'Élysée, *225*
Palais du Luxembourg, *233*
Palais Royal (Brussels), *85*
Palais-Royal (Paris), *225, 228*
Palau de la Generalitat, *49*
Palau de la Música Catalana (Music Palace), *48*
Palau de la Virreina, *48*
Palau del Lloctinent, *48*
Palau Güell, *48*
Palau Padellàs, *48*
Palazzo Altemps, *279*
Palazzo Barberini, *274–275*
Palazzo dei Conservatori, *271*
Palazzo Ducale, *291*
Palazzo Farnese, *279*
Palazzo Medici-Riccardi, *158*
Palazzo Pitti, *159*
Palazzo Vecchio, *156*
Panathinaiko Stadio, *26*
Panthéon (Paris), *232*
Pantheon (Rome), *279–280*
Papal audience, *277*
Parc Güell, *51*
Parliament (Athens), *27*
Parliament (Budapest), *102*
Parque del Retiro, *207*
Parthenonas (Parthenon), *22–23*
Passports and visas, *F28–F29*
Patrick Guilbaud ✕, *141*
Pavillon de la Reine 🏨, *239*
Peggy Guggenheim Collection, *294–295*
Pelham, The 🏨, *191*
Pergamonmuseum, *70*
Petermann's Kunststuben ✕, *329*
Phoenix Park, *141*
Picasso, Pablo, *45, 48, 229*
Pier 10 ✕, *11*
Pili tou Adrianou, *26–27*
Pivovarský dům ✕, *260*
Plaka, *27*
Plane travel. ⇨ *See* Air travel
Planetariums and observatories
London, 185
Paris, 224
Pompidou Center, *229*
Ponte Cestio, *279*
Ponte Fabricio, *279*
Ponte Rialto, *295*
Ponte Sant'Angelo, *276*
Ponte Vecchio, *159*
Portugese Israelitische Synagoge, *8*
Prado Museum, *206*
Pražsky hrad (Prague Castle), *258*
Price categories
Amsterdam, 9, 11
Athens, 28, 30
Barcelona, 51, 53
Berlin, 71, 72
Brussels, 87, 89
Budapest, 104, 106
Copenhagen, 123, 125
Dublin, 141, 143
Florence, 160, 161
London, 185, 189
Madrid, 210, 212
Paris, 235, 239
Prague, 259, 261
Rome, 281, 283
Venice, 296, 298
Vienna, 315, 317
Zürich, 329, 330
Princess Diana Memorial Playground, *178*
Propylaia, *22*
Providores ✕, *186*
Psirri, *27*
Pubs, *142–143, 146*
Puerta de Alcalá, *207*
Puerta del Sol, *207*
Pulitzer 🏨, *12*
Puppet shows, *263*
Puyck ✕, *11*

Q

Queen Sofía Arts Center, *205*
Queen's Gallery, *175*
Queen's Hôtel 🏨, *240*

R

Rathaus (Zürich), *327*
Real Academia de San Fernando, *210*
Record Tower, *133*
Reichstag, *68*
Reinwalds ✕, *124*
Relais St-Germain 🏨, *241*
Relais Saint-Sulpice 🏨, *241*
Rembetika clubs, *34*
Rembrandt's House, *7–8*
Restaurants
Amsterdam, 9–11
Athens, 28–30
Barcelona, 51–52
Berlin, 71–72
Brussels, 86–88
Budapest, 104–105
Copenhagen, 123–124
Dublin, 141–143
Florence, 160–161
London, 185–189
Madrid, 210–212
Paris, 235–239
Prague, 258–261
Rome, 280–282
Venice, 296–297
Vienna, 314–317
Zürich, 329–330
Rey Juan Carlos I-Conrad International 🏨, *54*
Rialto Bridge, *295*
Ribbeckhaus, *71*
Rijksmuseum, *8*
Ritz, *210*
Ritz 🏨, *54*
Rock clubs, *195, 245*
Rodin Museum, *234*
Roman Forum *271*
Roman ruins, *313, 314*
Rosenborg Slot, *117, 121*
Rosse Buurt (Red-Light District), *3*
Rotunda Hospital, *140*
Round Tower, *121–122*
Royal Academy of Arts, *177*
Royal Armouries, *183*
Royal Hospital Kilmainham, *141*
Royal Irish Academy, *137*
Royal Library, *120*
Royal Mews, *175*
Royal Opera House, *180*

Royal Palace (Brussels), *86*
Royal Palace (Budapest), *98*
Royal Palace (Madrid), *206–207*
Royal Palace (Paris), *225, 228*
Royal Palace (Prague), *258*
Royal Palace in Amsterdam, *2*
Royal Theater (Copenhagen), *122*
Royal Theater (Madrid), *210*
Rules ✕, *186*
Rundetårn, *121–122*
Ruprechtskirche, *313*

S

Sacher 🏨, *318*
Sacré-Coeur basilica, *234–235*
Safety, *F29–F30*
St. Alban's church, *120*
St. Augustine's Church, *306, 307*
Sainte-Chapelle, *233*
St. Charles' Church, *307, 310*
St. Eleftherios, *22*
St-Eustache church, *228*
St. Fernando Royal Academy of Fine Arts, *210*
St. George's Basilica and Convent, *258*
St-Germain-des-Prés church, *234*
St. James's Palace, *177*
St. James's Park, *174*
St. Marienkirche, *71*
St. Mark's Basilica, *291*
St. Martin-in-the-Fields church, *175*
St. Mary-le-Bow church, *182*
St. Mary of the Sea church, *49*
St. Mary's on the Bank church, *313*
St. Nicholas Church (Copenhagen), *121*
St. Nicholas's Church (Berlin), *71*
St. Patrick's Cathedral, *137–138*
St. Paul's Cathedral, *182–183*
St. Paul's Church, *180*
St. Peter's Basilica, *277–278*
St. Peter's Church (Zürich), *328*
St. Peter's Square, *277*
St. Rupert's Church, *313*
St. Stephen's Basilica, *102*
St. Stephen's Cathedral, *312*
St. Stephen's Tower, *174*
St-Sulpice church, *234*
St. Vitus Cathedral, *258*
Saló de Cent, *48–49*
Saló de Tinell, *48*
Sammlung Berggruen, *68*
San Lorenzo church, *158*
San Luigi dei Francesi church, *280*
San Miniato al Monte church, *159*
Sangallo ✕, *281*
Santa Croce church, *158*
Santa Maria Assunta Cathedral, *296*
Santa Maria d'Aracoeli, *271*
Santa Maria dei Miracoli church, *295*
Santa Maria del Carmine church, *159*
Santa Maria del Mar church, *49*
Santa Maria del Popolo church, *275*
Santa Maria della Concezione church, *275*
Santa Maria Formosa church, *295*
Santa Maria Gloriosa dei Frari church, *291, 294*
Santa Maria Novella church, *158*
Santa Maria sopra Minerva church, *280*
Sant'Agnese in Agone, *280*
Sant'Angelo Castle, *276*
Santi Giovanni e Paolo church, *295*
Santo Spirito church, *159*
Savoy, The 🏨, *192*
Scalinata di Trinitá dei Monti, *275*
Schatzkammer, *307, 311*
Schauräume in der Hofburg, *307, 311*
Schauspielhaus, *70*
Scheepvaartshuis, *3*
Schloss Belvedere, *313*
Schloss Charlottenburg, *69*
Schloss Schönbrunn, *313*
Schmetterlinghaus, *307*
School of St. Rocco, *294*
Schottenkirche, Museum im Schottenstift, *314*
Schreierstoren, *3, 6*
Schweizerisches Landesmuseum, *328*
Science Museum (London), *179*
Scottish Church and Museum, *314*
Scuola Grande di San Rocco, *294*
Sea Grill ✕, *87*
Senior citizen travel, *F30*
Shakespeare's Globe Theatre, *183*
Shelbourne Méridien Hotel 🏨, *144*
Shelley, Percy, *274*
Shipping Offices, *3*
Siegessäule, *69*
Silberkammer, *307, 311*
Sir John Soane's Museum, *181*
Sistine Chapel, *276*
Somerset House, *180*
Sorbonne, *233*
Spanische Reitschule (Spanish Riding School) *307, 311*
Spanish Steps, *275*
Spire, *140*
Spui (Sluice), *7*
Staatsoper, *312*
Staroměstská radnice, *256*
Staronová synagóga, *256*
Starý židovský hřbitov, *256*
State Museum (Amsterdam), *8*
State Opera House (Vienna), *312*
Statens Museum for Kunst, *122*
Stathmo Syntagma, *27*
Stedelijk Museum (Museum of Modern Art), *8–9*
Steirereck ✕, *315*
Stephansdom *312*
Stiles Olymbiou Dios, *27*
Stock exchanges
Amsterdam, 2
Copenhagen, 117
Story of Berlin, *69*
Student travel, *F30*
Swiss National Museum, *328*
Swissôtel Berlin 🏨, *73*
Symbols, *F7*
Synagogues
Amsterdam, 8
Berlin, 70–71
Budapest, 102
Copenhagen, 120
Prague, 256
Syntagma, *27–28*
Széchenyi lánchíd, *102*
Szent István Bazilika, *102*
Szépmüvészeti Múzeum, *103*

T

Taillevent ✕, *236*
Tate Britain, *175*
Tate Modern, *183*
Taverna del Bronzino ✕, *160*
Taverne Falstaff ✕, *88*
Taxes, *F30*
Taxis
Amsterdam, 18
Athens, 43
Barcelona, 59
Berlin, 77
Brussels, 94
Budapest, 111
Copenhagen, 129
Dublin, 148
Florence, 166
London, 198
Madrid, 220
Paris, 248
Prague, 265
Rome, 288
Vienna, 322
Zürich, 334
Teatro Real, *210*
Telephones, *F30–F31*
Temple Expiatori de la Sagrada Família, *49–50*
Temple of Olympian Zeus, *27*
Ten Downing Street, *171*
Terme di Caracalla, *271, 274*

Theater
Amsterdam, 8, 14
Barcelona, 55
Brussels, 91
Copenhagen, 126–127
Dublin, 146
London, 193–194
Madrid, 214
Paris, 243
Prague, 263
Vienna, 319–320
Zürich, 332
Theater buildings
Athens, 27
Copenhagen, 122
Dublin, 139
London, 183
Madrid, 210
Paris
Theater Museum (Vienna), *312*
Theatre Museum (London), *180*
Theatro Dionyssou, *28*
Theatrum Anatomicum, *2*
Thornton's ✕, *142*
Thorvaldsen Museum, *122*
Tiergarten, *69, 313–314*
Time, *F31*
Tivoli amusement park, *122*
To Varoulko ✕, *29*
Tomb of the Unknown Soldier (Athens), *27*
Topographie des Terrors, *69*
Torcello, *296*
Torre de Lujanes, *207*
Tour Eiffel, *223*
Tours and packages, *F31*
Tower Hill, *184*
Tower of London, *183–184*
Town Hall (Brussels), *84*
Town Hall (Copenhagen), *121*
Town Hall (Zürich), *327*
Train travel, *F32–F34*
Amsterdam, 18
Athens, 40
Barcelona, 60
Berlin, 78
Brussels, 94
Budapest, 112
Copenhagen, 130
Dublin, 149
Florence, 166
London, 199–200
Madrid, 220–221
Paris, 249
Prague, 266
Rome, 288
Venice, 304
Vienna, 323
Zürich, 334
Tram-Tram ✕, *52*
Transportation
Amsterdam, 18–19
Athens, 36–37, 39–41
Barcelona, 61
Berlin, 78
Brussels, 92–93
Budapest, 112
Copenhagen, 130
London, 200–201
Madrid, 221
Paris, 247
Prague, 266
Rome, 288–289
Venice, 304
Vienna, 323
Travel agencies, *F34*
Trevi Fountain, *274*
Trinità dei Monti church, *275*
Trinity College, *138–139*
Triumphal Arch, *223–224*
Tuileries Garden, *224*

U

U Mondré Kachničky ✕, *259*
Uffizi Gallery, *153*
Uhrenmuseum, *314*

V

Vajdahunyad Vár, *103*
Valdštejnská zahrada, *257*
Van Gogh, Vincent, *9*
Variety shows (Berlin), *74*
Vatican Gardens, *276*
Vatican Grottoes, *278*
Vatican Museums, *276–277*
VAU ✕, *71*
Victor Hugo House, *229*
Victoria & Albert Museum, *179*
Victoria Tower, *174*
Victory Column, *69*
Vienna House of Art, *313*
Vienna Woods, *314*
Vigadó (Concert Hall), *103*
Villa Bertramka, *257*
Vinárna V Zatíši ✕, *259*
Vini da Gigio ✕, *297*
Visitor information, *F34–F36*
Amsterdam, 19
Athens, 41
Barcelona, 61
Berlin, 78
Brussels, 94
Budapest, 112–113
Dublin, 149
Florence, 166
London, 201
Madrid, 221
Paris, 249
Prague, 267
Rome, 289
Venice, 304
Vienna, 323
Zürich, 334
Vismet, *85*
Vizantino Museo, *28*
Vlassis ✕, *30*
Vondelpark, *9*
Vor Frelsers Kirken, *122*
Vor Frue Kirken, *122*
Vörös és Fehér ✕, *105*
Vouli, *27*

W

Wagenburg, *314*
Wakefield Tower, *183*
Wallace Collection, *177–178*
Wallenstein Gardens, *257*
Wasserkirche (Water Church), *328*
Web sites, *F36–F37*
Weighhouse, *2*
Welcome Hotel 🏨, *90*
Westerkerk (West Church), *6*
Westin Palace 🏨, *213*
Westminster Abbey, *176*
Westminster Hall, *171, 174*
When to go, *F37*
White Tower, *183*
Widder 🏨, *331*
Wienerwald, *314*
Wingless Victory statue, *22*

Z

Ze Kitchen Galerie ✕, *238*
Zenetörténeti Múzeum, *99*
Zeughauskeller ✕, *330*
Židovské muzeum, *256*
Zoologischer Garten, *69*
ZOOM Kinder Museum, *310*
Zoos
Berlin, 69
Budapest, 103
Vienna, 313–314
Zum Storchen 🏨, *331*
Zunfthaus zur Meisen, *329*
Zunfthaus zur Zimmerleuten/ Küferstube ✕, *330*

FODOR'S KEY TO THE GUIDES

America's guidebook leader publishes guides for every kind of traveler. Check out our many series and find your perfect match.

FODOR'S GOLD GUIDES
America's favorite travel-guide series offers the most detailed insider reviews of hotels, restaurants, and attractions in all price ranges, plus great background information, smart tips, and useful maps.

COMPASS AMERICAN GUIDES
Stunning guides from top local writers and photographers, with gorgeous photos, literary excerpts, and colorful anecdotes. A must-have for culture mavens, history buffs, and new residents.

FODOR'S CITYPACKS
Concise city coverage in a guide plus a foldout map. The right choice for urban travelers who want everything under one cover.

FODOR'S EXPLORING GUIDES
Hundreds of color photos bring your destination to life. Lively stories lend insight into the culture, history, and people.

FODOR'S TRAVEL HISTORIC AMERICA
For travelers who want to experience history firsthand, this series gives in-depth coverage of historic sights, plus nearby restaurants and hotels. Themes include the Thirteen Colonies, the Old West, and the Lewis and Clark Trail.

FODOR'S POCKET GUIDES
For travelers who need only the essentials. The best of Fodor's in pocket-size packages for just $9.95.

FODOR'S FLASHMAPS
Every resident's map guide, with dozens of easy-to-follow maps of public transit, restaurants, shopping, museums, and more.

FODOR'S CITYGUIDES
Sourcebooks for living in the city: thousands of in-the-know listings for restaurants, shops, sports, nightlife, and other city resources.

FODOR'S AROUND THE CITY WITH KIDS
Up to 68 great ideas for family days, recommended by resident parents. Perfect for exploring in your own backyard or on the road.

FODOR'S HOW TO GUIDES
Get tips from the pros on planning the perfect trip. Learn how to pack, fly hassle-free, plan a honeymoon or cruise, stay healthy on the road, and travel with your baby.

FODOR'S LANGUAGES FOR TRAVELERS
Practice the local language before you hit the road. Available in phrase books, cassette sets, and CD sets.

KAREN BROWN'S GUIDES
Engaging guides—many with easy-to-follow inn-to-inn itineraries—to the most charming inns and B&Bs in the U.S.A. and Europe.

BAEDEKER'S GUIDES
Comprehensive guides, trusted since 1829, packed with A–Z reviews and star ratings.

OTHER GREAT TITLES FROM FODOR'S
Baseball Vacations, The Complete Guide to the National Parks, Family Vacations, Golf Digest's Places to Play, Great American Drives of the East, Great American Drives of the West, Great American Vacations, Healthy Escapes, National Parks of the West, Skiing USA.

At bookstores everywhere. www.fodors.com/books